Best of Baseball Prospectus 1996-2011 Volume 1

THE ESSENTIAL SYNOPSIS OF THE WORLD'S GREATEST SPORTS WEBSITE
Featuring the Best of Over 15,000 Carefully Tended Features and Articles

Featuring never-before-published material by
Mike Fast · Steven Goldman · Jay Jaffe · Christina Kahrl · Geoff Young

Ben Lindbergh, Editor
Christina Kahrl, Consulting Editor
Dave Pease, Editor at Large

Foreword by King Kaufman
Cover by Amanda Bonner
Layout by Dave Pease

Copyright 2011 Prospectus Entertainment Ventures, LLC
ISBN 1466472790
All Rights reserved

Without limiting the rights under copyright reserved above, no part of this publication may be reproduced, stored in or introduced into a retrieval system, or transmitted, in any form, or by any means (electronic, mechanical, photocopying, recording, or otherwise), without the prior written permission of both the copyright owner and the above publisher of this book.

This book is dedicated to the memory of

Doug Pappas
1962-2004

Always our brother, always our friend

http://bbp.cx/a/6256

Thank You

Thank you to our beautiful and talented interns Charles Dahan, Clark Goble, and Daniel Rathman for fighting through the hazing and helping us produce this book. Thank you to Jay Jaffe, Tommy Bennett, everyone at Baseball Prospectus, and all the contributors to this book for your patience and assistance.

Thank you to Gary Huckabay, Clay Davenport, Christina Kahrl, Rany Jazayerli, and Joe Sheehan, both for getting the Prospectus ball rolling and for providing the structure and the backbone for the Best of book.

Thank you to our Baseball Prospectus Premium subscribers.
None of this would have been possible without your support.

Thank you for reading this.

Table of Contents

Foreword
by King Kaufman..................................iv

Preface
by Ben Lindbergh...............................vi

PART 1 : OFFENSE

Introduction by Jay Jaffe.......................1

Measuring Offense
by Dayn Perry..6

About EqA
by Clay Davenport.............................10

Just Another Out?
by Ryan Wilkins..................................14

Everything You Wanted to Know About Run Estimation But Were Afraid to Ask, Part 1
by Colin Wyers....................................17

Top Sluggers and Their Home Run Breakdowns
by Jay Jaffe...21

Running Afoul
by Jay Jaffe...27

No Asterisks Necessary
by Will Carroll and Clay Davenport.......32

Staff Takes on a Landmark
by Baseball Prospectus.......................36

Adrian Gonzalez
by Marc Normandin............................46

Nomar Garciaparra
by Marc Normandin............................49

Playing With the Lineup
by James Click....................................54

Getting Shifty
by Dan Fox...60

Stolen Bases and How to Use Them
by Joe Sheehan..................................69

The Running Man
by Dan Fox...73

The Whole, the Sum, and the Parts
by Dan Fox...81

PART 2 : PITCHING

Introduction by Mike Fast....................89

How Much Control Do Hurlers Have?
by Vörös McCracken............................95

Another Look at Pitchers Preventing Hits
by Keith Woolner...............................102

Does Vörös' Theory Work on the Farm?
by Clay Davenport............................108

Any Such Thing?
by Nate Silver...................................113

The Origins of the Closer
by Nate Silver...................................120

The Support-Neutral Stats
by Michael Wolverton........................124

Thirty Years of Fixing Pitchers
by Thomas Gorman............................127

How We Measure Pitch Usage
by Rany Jazayerli..............................132

Discussing Jonathan Papelbon's Worth
by Marc Normandin and Tommy Bennett.136
Cliff Lee
by Marc Normandin, Eric Seidman, and Kevin Goldstein..141
Adventures in Consulting
by Gary Huckabay..151
Adventures in Consulting, Part Two
by Gary Huckabay..154
Adventures in Consulting, Part Three
by Gary Huckabay..157
C.J. Wilson
by David Laurila..160
Craig Breslow
by David Laurila..166
Brian Bannister
by David Laurila..171
Jim Palmer
by David Laurila..178
Why the "Earned" Run Needs To Go
by Michael Wolverton..185
The Real Strike Zone
by Mike Fast..189

PART 3 : FIELDING

Introduction by Christina Kahrl............201

Evaluating Defense
by James Click..206
Simple Fielding Runs Version 1.0
by Dan Fox..209
Reminiscing with SFR
by Dan Fox..220
Improving on Defensive Efficiency
by James Click..231
Park Effects on Team Defense
by James Click..235

What Would Bacon Do?
by Dan Fox..239
Adventures in Team Fielding
by Ben Lindbergh..244
What Do We Really Know About Defense?
by Colin Wyers..251
Looking Farther Afield
by Colin Wyers..255
How Do You Solve a Problem Like Derek Jeter?
by Colin Wyers..261

PART 4 : HISTORY

Introduction by Steven Goldman..........267

Interleague Numerology
by Jay Jaffe..271
Consider the K
by Jay Jaffe..274
The Myth of the Golden Age
by Dan Fox..279
Tilting the Playing Field
by Dan Fox..288
The Burgess Shale and Other Weighty Matters
by Dan Fox..302
Age Before Beauty
by Dan Fox..310
Prestige, D, and Derek Jeter
by Christina Kahrl..323
Penning a New Recipe
by Jay Jaffe..326
Oh Rickey, You're So Fine
by Jay Jaffe..332
Throwing Rice
by Jay Jaffe..339
Gamesmanship, Dammit
by Steven Goldman..345

Infinite Edition #4
    by Steven Goldman.....................350

Position Changes
    by Steven Goldman.....................356

Judge Landis on Steroids Edition
    by Steven Goldman.....................360

Why Babe Phelps and I Weren't in St. Louis Last Week
    by Steven Goldman.....................364

Enhanced?
    by Steven Goldman.....................369

The Statheads vs. Blondy Ryan
    by Steven Goldman.....................375

Dusty Baker and the Johnny Oates Affair
    by Steven Goldman.....................381

Odds and Ends
    by Christina Kahrl.....................386

A Peach of a Deal
    by Christina Kahrl.....................393

The New Guys
    by Christina Kahrl.....................399

Harden-ed
    by Christina Kahrl.....................406

Teixeira Two-Step
    by Christina Kahrl.....................412

Is Moneyball Dead?
    by Derek Jacques.....................417

Cardinals' Special Era Reaches a Crossroads
    by Bradford Doolittle.....................421

BONUS BASEBALL

Caught in the Camera Eye: The Story of Max Bishop
    by Geoff Young.....................431

Contributor Biographies.....................439

Foreword
by King Kaufman

I don't know where I'd be today without Baseball Prospectus.

I know where I might be: Wrestling with the vexing question of whether the batting champion or the RBI leader should win the MVP. Complaining that giving the Cy Young award to a 13-game winner is a joke when there are guys with 20 wins in the same season. Howling about how my home team doesn't bunt, hit and run, or steal bases, the little things that win games. Admiring intangibles. Campaigning for Jack Morris's induction into the Hall of Fame.

Well, maybe not. I'd like to think that by now I'd have been swept up in the sabermetric revolution one way or another if I hadn't become a dedicated BP reader. But in the universe of things that actually happened, which is where I try to spend at least some of my time, becoming a dedicated BP reader is what did the trick.

Bill James didn't get me to question the baseball wisdom I'd grown up with. I knew who he was and had even paged through his annual Baseball Abstracts in bookstores, but somehow I'd never gotten hooked. Which is odd and disappointing to me, because I fancy myself a question-conventional-wisdom kind of person.

But at some point I stumbled upon Baseball Prospectus and the Baseball Primer message board at about the same time, and—well, I don't think there were scales on my eyes, exactly, but I learned a lot in a hurry, and it changed the way I viewed my favorite sport.

What's that old saying? There's no obnoxious putz like a convert?

That was me.

I don't remember when I started reading Prospectus. I remember starting to come around, beginning to see things in new ways, starting to feel a little superior to my friends, who were still happily grubbing around in the century-old sandbox of batting average, pitcher wins, and the ol' hit-and-run. The savages.

But I do remember my "Holy crap! I don't know anything!" moment. That's a great moment, if you can accept it, that moment when you realize how little you know, how much you have to learn. It's a moment rich with possibilities. So much ahead of you.

That moment for me was reading Vörös McCracken's famous piece about balls in play, "How Much Control Do Hurlers Have?", which you'll find in the following pages. It's hard to convey now, only a decade later, what a shocker this sentence was: "There is little if any difference among major-league pitchers in their ability to prevent hits on balls hit in the field of play." It sounded "insane," which is what McCracken wrote was the usual reaction to his saying it.

It sounded insane to me, but McCracken's argument was convincing. That argument didn't convince me that everything I knew about baseball was wrong. But it did teach me that everything I knew beyond the basic inarguable facts—you get three outs, you run to first base and turn left, that sort of thing—might be wrong. Everything was up for reconsideration.

There's a life lesson in here somewhere too as long as we're at it. If I ever get tired of thinking about baseball I'll try to figure out what it is.

Much of that suddenly necessary reconsideration, much of my sabermetric baseball education, appears in the pages of this book and its companion volume. Maybe you'll find here the piece that led you to an epiphany similar to the one I had. Better yet, maybe you haven't had that epiphany and you'll find a piece here that will lead you to it.

If so, lucky you.

King Kaufman is a writer and editor who lives in San Francisco. He is the manager of the Writer Program at Bleacher Report. He previously wrote and edited for Salon and the San Francisco Examiner, among other publications.

Preface
by Ben Lindbergh

In August of 2011, the rock band Breaking Benjamin (or the rock band Breaking Benjamin's label) deemed it necessary to release a collection called *Shallow Bay: The Best of Breaking Benjamin*, the title of which was taken from one of the group's songs but could have just as easily have referred to its back catalog's conspicuous lack of depth. At the time, Breaking Benjamin had been a going concern for less than a decade, with all of four albums and 50 tracks to its name. A dedicated Breaking Benjamin fan (a creature whose existence I can't confirm, having been blissfully ignorant of BB's oeuvre before beginning this preface) could have run through the entirety of the band's studio output in just over three hours. It seems unlikely that such a fan would have needed a reminder of the group's "early" work so, well, early, or that those four albums contained both enough great material for a successful retrospective *and* enough filler to make segregating those standout tracks on a single disc a worthwhile pursuit. Nonetheless, *The Best of Breaking Benjamin* (also available in a two-disc, 24-track "deluxe" edition) was born. No sooner had it appeared on a torrent site near you than it was revealed that two of the group's four members had been fired: Breaking Benjamin was broken. With the band on indefinite hiatus and locked in the sort of legal battles that often accompany the dissolution of productive partnerships, it's possible that *The Best of Breaking Benjamin* will serve as the coda to the group's relatively brief career.

The arrival of a "Best Of" retrospective usually suggests that the artist it features has produced something worth reissuing and experiencing anew (Creed's *Greatest Hits* notwithstanding). However, the very act of preserving its "best" output in a crystallized package also seems to signal that whatever comes next—if anything does—won't be as good as what went before. Indeed, a decade and a half after turning pro, were Baseball Prospectus a player, we'd have left our peak long behind. Most of our founding members have moved on to other endeavors, and those who remain contribute only infrequently. In that sense, we're a bit like Breaking Benjamin. Fortunately, baseball think tanks aren't bound by the same unforgiving aging curves that cut the careers of athletes and musicians short. Unlike a band on indefinite hiatus, we're more active than ever, and the work we produce—despite some new bylines—remains recognizable as that of Baseball Prospectus. As Steven Goldman wrote in his preface to *Baseball Prospectus 2011*:

> True institutions do not survive due to the efforts of any one or two people, but because a collective of believers holds true to their animating principle, thus forming an unbroken chain from founders to inheritors. In our case, we continue

to focus on cutting through baseball's homilies—stomping the dead, whenever possible, along the way—in favor of realism and hard truths.

A year later, with a few more roster additions and subtractions behind us, Steven's observation holds true (though he might perhaps have mentioned the sense of humor with which we do some of that stomping). Two more book projects loom large on BP's horizon, including the 17th edition of our best-selling annual, which, as usual, we expect to be our best yet. Our web site features new content daily, some of which could form the foundation of a future retrospective. This collection contains more material from our most recent year than from our first few years combined, and not just because it's fresh in our minds. We've also held ourselves to a higher standard than we did in the early days, which has led to even more of the groundbreaking insight, astute analysis, and witty commentary that you'll find in the following pages.

Perhaps you've been burned by a "Best Of" before. Maybe you bought *Clapton Chronicles: The Best of Eric Clapton* expecting to hear some Cream and Derek and the Dominoes only to find that what you'd actually brought home from the store was an unplugged version of "Layla" and some soft rock unrecognizable as the work of a guitar god. Maybe you enjoy the Eagles and—like many millions before you—bought *Their Greatest Hits (1971-1975)* only to discover that *Hotel California* came out in 1976 and your collection was still incomplete. Maybe you bought *The Best of the Knack*, *Very Best of the Knack*, and *Best of the Knack* only to discover that you'd been suckered into purchasing three separate CDs that started with "My Sharona" and went downhill from there. While we crammed everything we could into *The Best of Baseball Prospectus*, I expect (and welcome) a chorus of complaints and kind-hearted suggestions from readers who wish we'd chosen a particular article that didn't make the final cut. We know how you feel—whichever article it is, we wish we'd included it, too. With an article archive that has grown well into the five figures, we could have doubled or tripled the size of this book without any significant reduction in the quality of the work. Unfortunately, we couldn't have doubled or tripled its size and produced something you could carry and still read without a magnifying glass.

I wish I could say I learned about baseball at Nate Silver's knee, but for someone who went on to work for Baseball Prospectus, I came late to objective analysis. The Yankees of my youth spared me some of the embarrassing beliefs that most BP writers and readers can recall holding during the days before they saw the sabermetric light; the teams I grew up watching were so good that there weren't a lot of empty batting averages, RBI mirages, or deceptive win totals around to mislead me. Still, once I finally rallied to BP's banner, I found I had quite an education in store. While I enjoyed creating my own curriculum, I would've preferred to have *The Best of Baseball Prospectus* as a syllabus.

At its, well, best, the "Best Of" album, book, or Blu-Ray offers a career-spanning collection that simultaneously functions as a fitting introduction for someone who's new to the material and a welcome refresher for someone who's heard, read, or seen it before. We believe this book (and its companion volume) fulfills both purposes. If you've been with us from the start, we hope you'll enjoy reminiscing about how we got here while perusing the previously unreleased material. If you're just joining us, our past work will keep while you catch up. Meanwhile, we'll be back in the studio, working on our next big hit.

Ben Lindbergh
Editor
New York, November 27, 2011

Part 1
OFFENSE
Introduction by Jay Jaffe

Maybe it began with a baseball card. "A chart of numbers that would put an actuary to sleep can be made to dance if you put it on one side of a card and Bombo Rivera's picture on the other," wrote Bill James in 1982. Maybe it was a box score in the morning paper, or the cryptic numbers on the screen beneath the muscular slugger's name when he came to bat.

Chances are, if you got hooked on baseball statistics at a young age, you got hooked on batting statistics. Batting average was the gateway drug, a bit of simple math magically imbued with the means to measure skill. You learned that stars hit .300, and that once upon a time, sepia-toned legends hit .400. Home run totals measured a player's strength, with the best of those numbers providing a window into baseball history, numbers like 60 and 61, 714 and 755, numbers that told stories of unprecedented dominance and persistence, numbers that people admired as though they were works of art. Runs batted in measured a player's ability to help his team by driving in other baserunners, and if not his moral fiber, then at least his grace under pressure, his clutchness, his ability to add another 100 runs to his team's ledger.

If you arrived in the mid-nineties still clinging to those standards, boy, were you in for a bumpy ride. While nobody hit .400, scoring levels shot up, aided by expansion into better hitting environments such as high-altitude Colorado. In 1996, teams scored just over five runs per game, the first time they'd reached that level since 1936. Balls flew out of the yard at record paces, and hulking sluggers boldly lit out for the summit of Roger Maris' single-season home run record. The 1994 players' strike froze two of them, Matt Williams and Ken Griffey Jr., in their tracks roughly two-thirds of the way there, but it wasn't long before Griffey mounted another assault, this time accompanied by Mark McGwire. Griffey's 56 homers led the American League in 1997, but it was the 58 that McGwire compiled in a season split between Oakland and St. Louis—the most any player had hit since Maris in 1961—that hinted at what would come next.

The following year McGwire and another hulking slugger, Sammy Sosa, would both blow past Maris' record while maintaining a friendly rivalry that captivated the nation, seemingly healing the wounds caused by the strike. When the dust settled, McGwire had 70 home runs, Sosa 66, and history was in the rear view mirror. A mysteriously muscular Barry Bonds would top both of those totals with 73 in 2001. He never reached those heights again thanks to pitchers' fear of his surgically precise swing, but by the end of 2004, he had not only topped his own godfather, Willie Mays, but reached the 700 plateau previously occupied by only Babe Ruth and Hank Aaron.

Of course, by that time, Bonds had been implicated as having used performance-enhancing drugs via the Bay Area Laboratory Co-operative scandal. Numerous other sluggers, McGwire and Sosa among them, would be outed as performance-enhancing drug (PED) users, and Major League Baseball would soon be pressured by Congress into introducing mandatory testing, a step that many inside the game and out saw as long overdue. Public outrage at the institutional failure of the players' union, the owners, the commissioner's office, and the media sucked the joy out of Bonds' assault on Aaron's record of 755 home runs, which he finally reached and then passed in 2007. A bumpy ride indeed.

It is only a slight oversimplification to say that Baseball Prospectus came into being armed with a toolkit built to grasp this new era. Students of the work of Bill James and Pete Palmer, we appreciated first and foremost that those oft-cited triple crown stats and their benchmark plateaus—a .300 batting average, 30 home runs, 100 RBI—weren't even all that good at telling the most basic story. As Dayn Perry explains in the first article of this chapter, **"Measuring Offense,"** counting stats such as home runs and RBI aren't very informative because they're highly context-dependent; the former owes much to a player's era and his ballpark, while the latter owes something to the ability of his teammates to get on base ahead of him. Neither accounts for how many outs—how much of baseball's clock, so to speak—a player is using. On-base percentage (the frequency with which a player doesn't make an out) and slugging percentage (the rate of total bases per at bat) are more demonstrative of a player's skill, and not subject to the influence of his teammates or his lineup slot.

Yet even those raw rate stats carry distortions. With offensive levels climbing to heights unseen for six or seven decades, the value of each individual run diminished slightly, and while hitters compiled eye-popping stats, their effect was diluted amid the inflated offensive levels. Enter Equivalent Average, a complex metric created by Clay Davenport that expresses runs created per plate appearance on the familiar and easy-to-understand scale of batting average (.300 is very good). In **"About EqA,"** Clay shows that not only does his creation correlate better with scoring than any of the aforementioned rate stats, it works better than most other advanced attempts, from a quick-and-dirty metric such as OPS (on-base plus slugging) to more complicated ones with their basis in linear weights. Furthermore, EqA is built to normalize production across different park and league scoring environments, such that a .260 EqA is the definition of league average, and a .300 mark is as valuable in 1936 (when major-league teams averaged 5.19 runs per game and hit a collective .284/.349/.404) as it is in 1968 (when teams averaged 3.42 runs per game on .237/.299/.340 hitting) or 2000 (when teams averaged 5.14 runs per game with .270/.345/.437 rates), regardless of the ebb and flow of offense.

THE LINEUP

Measuring Offense
by Dayn Perry..6

About EqA
by Clay Davenport...10

Just Another Out?
by Ryan Wilkins..14

Everything You Wanted to Know About Run Estimation But Were Afraid to Ask, Part 1
by Colin Wyers...17

Top Sluggers and Their Home Run Breakdowns
by Jay Jaffe..21

Running Afoul
by Jay Jaffe..27

No Asterisks Necessary
by Will Carroll and Clay Davenport................32

Staff Takes on a Landmark
by Baseball Prospectus...................................36

Adrian Gonzalez
by Marc Normandin..46

Nomar Garciaparra
by Marc Normandin..49

Playing With the Lineup
by James Click..54

Getting Shifty
by Dan Fox..60

Stolen Bases and How to Use Them
by Joe Sheehan...69

The Running Man
by Dan Fox..73

The Whole, the Sum, and the Parts
by Dan Fox..81

With balls flying out of the yard at unprecedented paces, strikeout rates reached unprecedented levels as well, and they're still climbing even after home run rates have tapered off. Some of that may have to do with the popularization of newer pitches such as the split-fingered fastball and the cut fastball, and some may owe to the shift to more frequent bullpen usage, with fresher pitchers throwing harder for shorter stints. Some may owe to a renewed understanding brought about by sabermetrics. For pitchers, strikeouts are a key indicator of success and potential longevity, but for batters they're "**Just Another Out**," as Ryan Wilkins writes. While strikeout rates correlate negatively with batting average and on base percentage, they correlate positively to an even greater extent with slugging percentage and walk rates.

Along with PEDs, an extended construction boom that brought 23 new ballparks into the majors from 1990 through 2010 was viewed by many as a reason for the rise in home runs, though as it turned out, the conventional wisdom wasn't entirely correct. The replacement of large multi-use facilities with more intimate baseball-only parks reduced seating capacities by about 10 percent, with luxury boxes taking over a greater share of real estate. As I documented in "**Running Afoul**," fence distances actually increased by a foot or two from 1990 through 2007, such that a smaller percentage of home runs went to left field or left center field, the "pull" field for the majority of hitters.

The changing pool of ballparks didn't mean that some of the game's top sluggers didn't benefit greatly from their home parks—they did. Bonds was not one of them, however; he wound up hitting 379 home runs at home and 383 on the road, a ratio which falls several rungs below the man he replaced atop the all-time home run list, as I wrote in "**Hank Aaron's Home Cooking**"—a list I would update again in 2007 when Bonds tied Aaron.

One way or another, the all-time list would remain an article of fascination for BP's staff. In "**No Asterisk Necessary**," Will Carroll pointed out that Davenport's translations, which effectively adjust for inflation, still held Ruth atop the charts by a wide margin, though Bonds was light years ahead of his contemporaries given the degree of difficulty of hitting home runs in Pac Bell/AT&T/Insert Phone Network Here park. In "**Staff Takes on a Landmark**," the Prospectus crew offered its in-the-moment views on Bonds finally topping Aaron, a set of responses that offered more relief and regret than admiration and elation.

Speaking of home parks and translated statistics, Marc Normandin's profile of Adrian Gonzalez uses Davenport's translations to examine the performance of a slugger stuck—at least circa 2009—in Petco Park, the majors' most pitcher-friendly venue. While hardly unimpressive even under such run-suppressing circumstances, his numbers look much different when translated to Coors Field, the majors' most hitter-friendly environment, or the then-brand-new Yankee Stadium. Elsewhere in this section, Normandin turns his profiling talents towards one-time Fenway favorite Nomar Garciaparra on the occasion of his spring 2010 retirement.

While home runs were emblematic of the era, the BP staff dug more than just the long ball and wasn't shy about turning its collective attention to less well-understood facets of offense. In "**Stolen Bases and How to Use Them**," Joe Sheehan highlighted the reasons for turning to the running game and showed that high stolen base totals hardly provide the means to turn a bad offense into a good one; rather, they are just so much strategic wheel-spinning. In "**The Running Man**" and "**The Whole, the Sum, and the Parts**," Dan Fox went even further, creating a run expectancy-based methodology to quantify all baserunning—advancements on groundouts, air outs, and hits as well as on stolen bases—in the form of our Equivalent Baserunning Runs (EqBRR) suite of stats. In doing so, he showed that individual players rarely added more than a few runs a year via all of these areas put together. Hell, he showed that whole teams rarely added more than a full win (roughly 10 runs) to their ledger via the basepaths over the course of a season, though far more teams found ways to subtract a win or two that way, particularly by stealing bases at rates well below the break-even point (around 70 percent). As offensive levels increased, many a team struggled to recognize that the steal had become a higher-risk/lower-reward endeavor.

In "**Getting Shifty**," Fox turned his attention to the extreme shifts used to counter left-handed pull hitters. The tactic was popularized in 1946, when the Indians employed a shift against Ted Williams, but it actually dates back to the 19th century. The move has been frequently used against several lefty sluggers of recent vintage such as Adam Dunn, Jason Giambi, David Ortiz, and

Jim Thome, but Fox points out that—theoretically, at least—there exist pull-heavy right-handed hitters against whom such a shift might be successfully employed as well.

Fox did such high-quality work in his short time at BP that he soon left for a job in the front office of the Pittsburgh Pirates, and he wasn't alone in making such a leap. James Click eventually departed for the Tampa Bay Devil Rays' front office, where he would participate in one of the great franchise turnarounds of the era, but not before he left behind some impressive work at BP. In **"Playing with the Lineup,"** Click examined various theories of lineup construction using a simulator to model the effects of a team grouping its best hitters, spreading them out as much as possible, or ordering by ascending or descending batting average, on-base percentage, or slugging percentage. Where others would go on to show in more specific terms that the difference between various iterations of a lineup only amounted to a small handful of runs over the course of a year, Click's simulations remind us that the wide distribution of possibilities for a single set of hitters makes identifying an optimal solution very difficult.

Speaking of models, in **"Everything You Wanted to Know About Run Estimation But Were Afraid to Ask, Part 1,"** Colin Wyers discusses the ways one can model run-scoring in sabermetric terms. He elegantly lays out the differences between linear models (with no interaction between basic terms) such as Equivalent Runs, dynamic models (with interaction between the terms, generally in the form of on-base and advancement terms) such as Runs Created, and algorithms such as Monte Carlo simulations and Markov Chains. He reminds us that each has its advantages depending upon what question one is trying to answer.

In the end, that's why Baseball Prospectus' sabermetric toolkit exists: to answer some of the day's burning questions in a way that helps us make sense not only of how the game has played today, but how it has changed over time. A .300 batting average, a stolen base, and a dollar may not be worth what they once were, but by understanding what those values were based upon, we can better appreciate not only what happened a century ago, but what is happening today.

BASEBALL PROSPECTUS BASICS
Measuring Offense
Dayn Perry

Batting average, runs, and RBI are the stats you saw on the back of the baseball cards you collected as a kid, but there's more to evaluating offense than those traditional numbers, which provide only an incomplete picture of a player's performance. Baseball Prospectus has long sought to present a complete picture of a player's production with a single advanced statistic (like VORP or TAv), but it's both possible to form a better understanding with the aid of some even less intimidating acronyms, and important to understand why you should.

Before delving into those harrowing inhabitants of the Baseball Prospectus statistics page like VORP, RARP, EqA, or any other acronym that sounds like a débutante sneezing or something uttered on Castle Wolfenstein circa 1986, it's worth asking: What's wrong with those comfy traditional offensive measures like RBI, batting average, and runs scored?

This Baseball Prospectus Basics column is going to address that question and, ideally, demonstrate why the traditional cabal of offensive baseball statistics tells only a piece of the story. Later, someone smarter (but shockingly less handsome) than I will take you on a tour of the more advanced and instructive metrics like the aforementioned VORP, RARP, and EqA. For now, though, we'll keep our focus on why we need those things in the first place.

Many of the stats you encounter in mainstream baseball circles are what we call "counting stats." That is, they count things: 23 homers, 107 RBI, six triples, etc. This may sound painfully obvious, but the more a hitter plays in a given season, the higher his counting stats are likely to be. Some counting stats, like RBI and runs scored, are highly team- and batting-order-dependent. A cleanup hitter logging 600 plate appearances in a potent lineup must work very hard not to rack up at least 100 RBI, whereas a leadoff hitter on an otherwise weak offensive team won't crack the 100-RBI mark no matter how effective he is. If a superior player is surrounded by weak hitters, it's entirely possible that he'll cash in on a much greater percentage of his RBI opportunities and still have a lower RBI total than a lesser player in a stronger lineup.

The thing to understand about counting stats is that, absent supporting information, they're really only useful at the margins. That's to say, it's hard to rack up 140 RBI and somehow stink.

Conversely, it's difficult to log a season's worth of plate appearances, total 40 RBI, and somehow be any good.

The flip side of this is that it's entirely possible, especially in eras conducive to run scoring, to break the vaunted 100-RBI barrier and still be an ineffective player. It's debatable what the worst 100-RBI season is, but Ruben Sierra in 1993 may be hard to beat. More later on why he was a lousy player that season.

So, highly context-dependent counting stats like RBI and runs scored can be inflated or deflated by a panoply of factors that have nothing to do with that hitter's true abilities. One of the prevailing missions of sabermetrics is to evaluate the player in a vacuum: What is he doing independent of his teammates and environment? Using only RBI or runs scored to judge a player or to frame an argument at the tavern is a fool's errand.

Home runs, since they have almost nothing to do with a hitter's teammates, are more reliable than RBI, but they're still not an ideal metric. It's fully possible for a player with fewer home runs than another to be a far superior player. How's that? Again, it's context. Home runs (and singles, doubles, triples, etc.) aren't lineup- and teammate-dependent like RBI and runs scored, but, like any other unadjusted statistic, they are dependent upon the ballpark and, when comparing players across history, the era (more on park and league effects later in this series).

Another factor to consider when comparing hitters is the notion of positional scarcity. This is the idea that it's easier to find good hitters at the less demanding defensive positions than it is at those positions that require a great deal of skill with the glove. The less demanding positions are the corner slots: left field, right field, third base, and first base. The more exacting positions are those up the middle: catcher, shortstop, second base, and center field. Up-the-middle defenders handle more balls and cover more ground than corner players, or, in the case of the catcher, they have defensive duties distinct from those who man other positions.

So if a first baseman and a shortstop have identical offensive statistics and equal defensive abilities relative to their positions, who's the better player? The shortstop, because the offensive-productivity bar for shortstops is notably lower than it is for first baseman, since it's far easier to find a good-hitting first baseman than it is a good-hitting shortstop. Generally, from highest level of positional scarcity to least, the positions go shortstop, catcher, second baseman, center fielder, third baseman, right fielder, left fielder, and first baseman. Those can vary from year to year, but most seasons up-the-middle defenders who can hit will always be rarer beasts than corner players who can hit. This is why Alex Rodriguez is such a special player: he hits like an All-Star first baseman, yet he plays the most challenging defensive position on the diamond and does it well to boot. Again, many stats you'll find on this site are already adjusted to reflect the demands of the position.

And what of batting average? Well, it's a percentage stat and not a counting stat, so it has a somewhat different set of concerns and caveats. First, it's subject to sample-size errors. To provide an extreme example, a hitter who goes one-for-three on Opening Day and one who plays the entire season going 200-for-600 will both be hitting .333 when you check the box scores; however, it's the latter hitter whose .333 average is more legit. Why? Because it's been borne out over time, whereas the former hitter may be a banjo-hitting fringe player who had a lucky day. (As an aside, counting stats are also prone to a different kind of sample-size error. It's the dreaded "on pace to" statistical distraction. When some unlikely player is, say, leading the league in RBI after the first two weeks of the season, we'll hear how he's "on pace" to put up 380 RBI on the season or some such nonsense.) Basically, if a hitter is doing something that's completely out of step with the rest of his career, you should be skeptical and demand a larger sample before you buy into those reports that his stroke has been tweaked or that he's seeing the ball better since he started drinking liver smoothies. Sample size is a major principle to grasp, and you'll never look foolish by being roundly unmoved by what a player does in the first few weeks of the season.

That's not all that's wrong with batting average. As much as the .300 hitter is a lionized, what does that really tell us about a player? It tells us he got a hit of some kind in 30 percent of his at-bats. We have no idea what kinds of hits he got, and we have no idea how he fared in terms of reaching base by other means. We don't even know how many times he came to the plate.

When dealing with percentage statistics, having at least a rough idea of the number of plate appearances is essential. And as far as batting average goes, you can tell much more about a player if his average (AVG) is presented along with his on-base percentage (OBP) and slugging percentage (SLG).

OBP is how often a player reached base via hit, walk or hit by pitch; among traditional offensive statistics, it's the most important. The higher a player's OBP, the less often he's costing his team an out at the plate. Viewed another way, 1-OBP = out percentage. In other words, OBP subtracted from the number 1 will yield the percentage of how often a hitter comes up to bat and uses up one of his team's 27 outs for that game. A player can play all season, rack up impressive counting stats, and still be using up far too many outs.

SLG measures a player's power, albeit not perfectly. It places more value on extra-base hits than it does on singles, and what you're looking at when you see a hitter's SLG is the total bases he averages per at-bat. For example, a player with a .500 SLG averages one-half of a total base per at-bat.

You'll often see AVG, OBP and SLG presented in the following format: .300/.400/.500, where .300 is the player's AVG, .400 is the player's OBP, and .500 is the player's SLG. Another statistic you can glean from this "holy trinity" is Isolated SLG, which is the player's SLG minus his AVG. This expresses how much "raw" power he's producing by focusing solely on his extra-base hits. Of the trinity, AVG, which by far the most popular and heavily relied upon, really provides you with the least important information. It's good info in the presence of OBP and SLG, but by itself it's almost as useless as RBI.

What's a good OBP and SLG? Well, as we've already mentioned, offensive statistical standards depend greatly upon a player's era, home ballpark, and defensive position. Generally speaking, if a player today puts up a .360 OBP and .500 SLG, he's doing his job. If he's a shortstop in Dodger Stadium with these numbers (and with an ample number of plate appearances, of course), he's an MVP candidate; if he's a first baseman in Denver with these numbers, he's nothing special. Again, context is where the rubber hits the road. (We discuss OPS, the stat that adds OBP + SLG, later in this series.)

Remember our pal Ruben Sierra and his 101 RBI from 1993? Let's go back and look at him, knowing what we know now. Yeah, there are his 101 RBI. But that season his trinity numbers were .233/.288/.390. Those are ugly, and they get even uglier when you recall that he split his time between DH and the outfield corners. That means he had little defensive value, and, hence, his offensive standard was higher than that of most players. A .288 OBP and .390 SLG are patently unacceptable for a corner defender, no matter how many RBI he racks up.

So, in summary:

- Counting stats (RBI, HR, runs scored) aren't very informative because they're highly context-dependent and don't account for how many outs a player is using up.
- Percentage stats are far better than counting stats, but only in the presence of a sizeable data sample (i.e., plate appearances).
- Percentage stats are only negligibly influenced by teammates and lineup slotting, but, like all traditional statistics, they are influenced by ballpark and historical era.
- Players at the corner positions generally produce better offensive numbers than those players at the more vital up-the-middle positions.
- AVG isn't really useful unless viewed in tandem with OBP, SLG, and plate appearances.
- The greatest of these is OBP because it can also tell you how often a player creates outs at the plate.

And that's that. Like I said, there's a whole other world of statistics out there besides the ones that have been foisted upon you since you bought your first set of Topps. Now that you know what's wrong with traditional offensive statistics, you're ready to arm yourselves with the tools of state-of-the-art baseball analysis.

FEBRUARY 24, 2004

http://bbp.cx/a/2596

BASEBALL PROSPECTUS BASICS
About EqA
Clay Davenport

Using one number as a snapshot of offensive performance makes things easier, but it matters which number you use. Clay Davenport invented Equivalent Average, or EqA, to serve as an accurate, unbiased measure of a player's performance at the plate, oriented on the same scale as batting average to make it more accessible to fans who grew up looking at other numbers. EqA has since been refined even further and renamed "True Average," or TAv, but the original spirit of the stat persists.

Dayn Perry explained why various statistics—like batting average (AVG) and runs batted in (RBI)—were not as reliable as you've always been told, and why we at Baseball Prospectus don't use them in our analysis terribly often. Today, we're going to look into one of the statistics we do use: Equivalent Average, or EqA.

In its rawest state, EqA is a simple combination of batting numbers, not very different from OPS:

$$EqA = \frac{H + TB + 1.5*(BB + HBP) + SB}{AB + BB + HBP + CS + SB/3}$$

Compared to OPS, it counts walks and HBP a little higher (at 1.5 instead of 1), it has stolen bases, and hits and extra bases are counted a little less (since they are divided by plate appearances, not just walks). What, then, makes EqA different from the other statistics? Simply put, it's more accurate, it's unbiased, and it models the scale of batting average, so it's easy for a new fan to understand.

Let us start with accuracy. Accuracy is traditionally measured in one of two ways—by correlation and Root Mean Square Error (RMSE) against runs scored. Correlation is a statistical tool that measures how closely one set of numbers tracks a second set. It is measured from negative-one (-1) to positive-one (1); negative scores mean that when one number goes down, the other number tends to go up; positive scores mean that both sets rise and fall together. The closer you get to either end, the more perfect the relationship is, while a score close to zero means that knowing the first number tells you squat about the second number. You'll sometimes see people use r-squared instead, but that is essentially the same thing (mathematicians use "r" to stand for correlation). RMSE is just a fancy way to say how much you missed by, on average—it's a form of standard deviation. Statistics that have better correlation (closer to +1 or -1) usually have lower RMSEs as well.

Consider the following table of fairly traditional statistics.

Metric	Correl	RMSE
Batting Average	.828	39.52
On-base Percentage	.866	34.16
Slugging Percentage	.890	31.56

This shows how well the statistics have done for every team in history, from 1871 to 2003. In each case, I have compared the statistic relative to the league (team batting average divided by league batting average, for instance) to the relative run rate (team runs per plate appearance, divided by the league RPPA). Batting average has, truthfully, a very good correlation... it is just that on-base percentage is even better, and slugging percentage is better still. Combine the last two elements into OPS, and the results get better still:

Metric	Correl	RMSE
On-base plus slugging	.922	25.54

This is pretty much it for advanced methods, since they all represent only a rather small improvement over what OPS provides. Still, the mindset that some improvement is better than none has spawned a variety of stats that have been called "best" by one person or another, stats such as:

Metric	Correl	RMSE
Equivalent Average	.928	24.13
BaseRuns	.930	24.38
eXtrapolated Runs (per PA)	.920	24.83
Runs Created (per PA)	.928	24.96
Total Average	.926	25.33

Here you see a big reason why we use EqA: because its ability to estimate runs scored from team and league data is unsurpassed. What the chart does not show is how these errors change over time. If you looked only at the years from 1971 to 2003, eXtrapolated Runs would have a virtually identical RMSE to EqA (20.98 for EqA, 21.06 for XR), while BaseRuns actually does a little better (20.77). However, if you look at the 30 years from 1871 to 1900, the same XR and BsR equations get more than 60 percent worse—their RMSEs shoot up to 34.16 and 33.41, respectively. EqA, in contrast, loses "only" about 50 percent, scoring a 31.69. EqA is less sensitive to the conditions of the times than many of the other metrics which have been "tuned" to fit recent performances, so it's especially good for historical performances.

(*Aside for the technically interested*: In all of the above, the formulas are limited to the same set of input statistics: at-bats, hits, doubles, triples, home runs, walks and hit-by-pitch, steals and caught-stealing. These are the basic forms; most of them, including EqA, have more advanced versions that count things like sacrifices and intentional walks, and these can generally squeeze another run or so out of the RMSE. The RMSEs have been calculated using a best-fit relationship of estimated runs equals team plate appearances times league runs per plate appearance times (A times relative statistic plus B).)

All of this is intrinsic to the equation. The rest of what goes into EqA is what we, the users, force onto it. The first thing we can do—something nobody does for OPS, for instance—is establish how to move between the rate statistic and the number of runs that come from it. Equivalent Runs is simply the number of runs that you get from a given EqA and plate appearances, and it goes up twice as fast as the EqA does. In formula form:

$$EqR = (2 * EqA/LgEqA - 1) * PA * (LgR / LgPA)$$

Equivalent Runs is tied to the league average runs for two reasons. One, it serves to reinforce the idea that everything is relative—that you cannot say for certain whether any statistic is good or bad, unless you know the average value. Secondly, there is always information in the league total that is not part of the normal statistical line—things like reaching on errors, balks, wild pitches, and... well, you get the idea. All of the statistics in the chart above drew upon the same data, and none of them was able to put that information to use as well as EqA.

The second thing we force onto the EqA/EqR figures ties into the second point I made, way back at the beginning: biases. The two primary biases are the league offensive level and the home park. When league offense is high, players can put up astronomical totals—but since everything is relative, the numbers don't lead to as many wins as you might think. It is the same with home parks: a hitter-friendly park, like any park in Colorado, lifts both sides up, so that once again you don't get the kind of winning results you would probably expect from the production.

Since winning and losing are what the game is all about, we have to adjust for this if we want to have a good, unbiased statistic. We already know how many EqR a player has; think of that as runs scored. We can easily calculate how many runs an average player would have produced, if he played in the same league, with the same home park, and made just as many outs as the player did. If you think of that as runs allowed, then you can use some form of the Pythagorean formula to estimate a winning percentage for that player.

The nice thing here is that, no matter what the batting conditions in the league may be, the winning percentage of the whole (and of an average player) will always be .500. We could rate the player's performance entirely by this number, except that virtually nobody has any comprehension of how good a .600 winning percentage is in player terms. Sure, it is better than average, but is it league-leading material? Top 10? For that reason, we re-map the winning percentage onto a familiar scale: batting average. For all its faults, anybody who is even a casual fan has a good feel for what is good, bad, or ordinary in a batting average. The final adjustment is entirely to make it easy to tell how good it is:

$$\text{EQA (adjusted)} = [\,(\text{winpct})/(1 - \text{winpct})\,]\,\wedge\,0.2\,*.26$$

By this formula, an average player will have a .260 Equivalent Average—always. Compare that to the all-time major-league batting average of .262. A .300 EqA (.672 WPCT) is almost exactly as common, historically, as a .300 batting average; a .400 EqA (.896 WPCT) represents the top-14 seasons in history. The .600 winning percentage I mentioned above would be reported as a .282 EqA—good, but not overly impressive. Ease of understanding—the third stump in EqA's wicket.

FEBRUARY 29, 2004

http://bbp.cx/a/2617

BASEBALL PROSPECTUS BASICS
Just Another Out?
Ryan Wilkins

The strikeout has long been stigmatized as a form of failure, but does it truly deserve its bad rap? As Ryan Wilkins explains, simply putting the ball in play isn't all it's cracked up to be.

As we've stated on a number of different occasions throughout the Baseball Prospectus Basics series, one of the goals of performance analysis is to separate perception from reality. Sometimes that means interpreting numbers, and sometimes that means interpreting events with our eyes. Either way, it's about collecting information and getting a little bit closer to the truth.

Evaluating the importance of strikeouts, especially for hitters, is something that has traditionally fallen into the second category. It's easy to understand why: baseball is a game that centers around the ongoing conflict between batter and pitcher, and there are few outcomes that capture the drama of that conflict better than a mighty whiff, followed by a long walk back to the bench. On the surface, at least, a strikeout appears to be the ultimate failure for a hitter, infinitely worse than a Texas Leaguer or a flyout to center.

From a quantitative perspective, however, there is little evidence to suggest that a strikeout is "worse" than a groundout, popout, or any other means of making an out, with respect to generating runs. Sure, it might look bad to be unable to put the ball into play, but the fact is that error rates, in this era of improved equipment, are as low as they've ever been. Granted, putting the ball in play, whether in the air or on the ground, can sometimes enable a hitter to advance a runner, but it also increases the chance of hitting into a double play, a far more effective rally-killer than a strikeout.

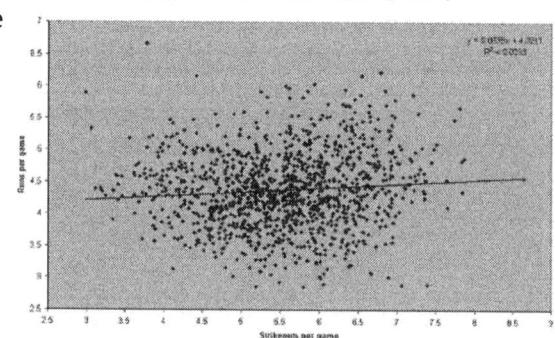

As a result of all that, the value of "just putting the ball in play" is as low as it's ever been. This graph illustrates the correlation—or lack thereof—between team strikeouts and team run-scoring from 1950-2002.

As you can see by the round, lifeless blob in the middle of the graph, there is virtually no positive correlation between a team's strikeout totals and its runs-scored totals. When it comes to offense, an out is an out is an out.

On an individual level, the evidence against strikeouts as the scourge of the earth gets only more damning. Check out the correlation between Ks and the various elements of offensive production:

Correlation of SO/PA with other offensive statistics (all players 1950-2002, 300+ PA)

Metric	Correl
ISO	.388
SLG	.198
BB/PA	.125
OBP	-.100
AVG	-.290
OPS	.106
MLVr	.005

While it might not be overwhelming, there is a distinct, positive correlation between an individual's strikeout rate and a number of useful attributes: hitting for power, as represented in this case by isolated power (ISO, or slugging percentage minus batting average) and slugging percentage (SLG), as well as drawing walks, as represented by walk rate (BB/PA). Of course, causation is a sticky subject, so try not to misinterpret the above data as "proof" that increased strikeouts cause an improvement in a player's secondary skills. It's just that where one group shows up, often so does the other.

Notice, also, the virtually non-existent (albeit positive) correlation between strikeout rate and "complete" measures of offensive performance like on-base plus slugging (OPS) and Marginal Lineup Value Rate (MLVr). No matter how you slice it, it just doesn't appear that strikeouts have much of an effect on a team's—or an individual's—ability to produce runs.

That holds true for hitters, but pitchers are a completely different story. Where the value of "just putting the ball in play" has often been overstated for hitters, the opposite has long been the case for pitchers. In their case, a strikeout is most definitely not "just another out." In fact, the ability to create outs for one's self is among the most important skills a pitcher can possess.

Why? There are a number of reasons, but mainly it's because more strikeouts mean fewer balls in play. Fewer balls in play mean (on average) fewer hits surrendered. And with fewer hits surrendered come fewer runs allowed. The steps aren't perfect, mind you, but on a macro level they hold up. This graph illustrates the correlation between individual strikeout rate and ERA from 1993-2002.

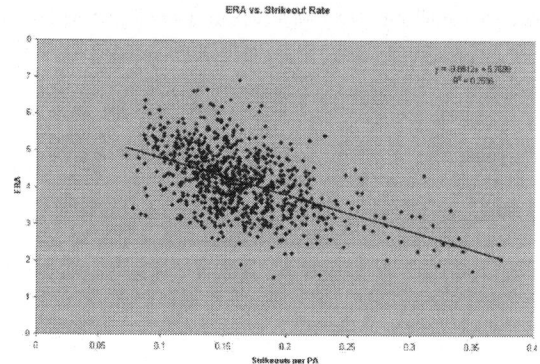

Or, to perhaps give this conclusion some real-world resonance, look at the disparity in ERA between those pitchers with the highest strikeout rates in the league in 2003 and those at the bottom of the barrel:

Pitcher	SO/9	ERA
Kerry Wood	11.35	3.20
Mark Prior	10.43	2.43
Curt Schilling	10.39	2.95
Pedro Martinez	9.93	2.22
Javier Vazquez	9.40	3.24

Pitcher	SO/9	ERA
Joe Mays	3.46	6.30
Danny Graves	3.20	5.33
Aaron Cook	3.12	6.02
Kirk Rueter	2.51	4.53
Nate Cornejo	2.13	4.67

The difference isn't accidental. In a nine-inning complete game, Kerry Wood is roughly 30 percent less reliant upon his defense to convert batted balls into outs than someone like Kirk Rueter or Nate Cornejo would be. That's not just a huge difference, that's a Marlon-Brando-pulling-up-a-chair-to-the-buffet difference.

Strikeout rate also has predictive value. According to a study conducted by Keith Woolner, pitchers with high strikeout rates age better than comparable pitchers (i.e., pitchers who posted similar park-adjusted ERAs at the same age) with low strikeout rates. Bill James also gave this subject some treatment in his most recent edition of the *Historical Baseball Abstract* when discussing Mark Fidrych, and he came to a similar—if slightly hyperbolic, as Tommy John can attest—conclusion: "There is simply no such thing as a starting pitcher who has a long career with a low strikeout rate."

The prominence of the strikeout in Major League Baseball has been increasing steadily over the past 130 years, and it may continue to grow as teams begin to let go of their macho attachment to "just putting the ball in play" on offense, while further valuing pitchers who are self-sufficient on the mound. Like many other developments in baseball, this will be a sign of evolution, and a better game overall will be the result.

Don't fear the strikeout. In many ways it is a harbinger of better things to come.

MANUFACTURED RUNS
Everything You Wanted to Know About Run Estimation But Were Afraid to Ask, Part 1

Colin Wyers

What are the fundamental objectives of a player at the plate, and how can we measure how well he succeeds in pursuing them? Colin Wyers tackled that question and summarized the strengths and weaknesses of the various approaches to estimating run-scoring from component performance.

We spend a lot of time analyzing baseball, studying it, trying to learn about it, and simply enjoying it. But what if I were to tell you that there was a secret to understanding baseball, a shortcut to knowing (almost) everything you would ever need to know?

Well, there is. And it's hiding in plain sight—it's the second line of the official rules of baseball: "The objective of each team is to win by scoring more runs than the opponent."

Yes, it seems obvious... OK, it seems obvious because it is obvious. But if you free yourself from the obviousness of that statement and let yourself ruminate on it, it's a pretty bold statement of some pretty powerful truths:

- Baseball is a team sport. What matters is not how well an individual plays in the abstract, but how well he is able to contribute to his team.
- The point is winning. When we measure something in baseball, we should always be asking ourselves, "How does this contribute to wins and losses?"
- You win by scoring more runs than the other team. Runs are the building blocks of wins. In order to understand how teams win games, we have to understand how they score—and prevent—runs.

The rub is in the "almost." We know that the key to understanding baseball is knowing how teams score runs. That still leaves a lot of work for us to do, though.

So let's break down—piece by piece—how run-scoring works and how we can model the process. In this article, we'll look at some of the fundamental principles of how teams score runs. Next, we'll look at the history of run estimation. And to wrap it up, we'll do a mathematical autopsy of sorts on some selected run estimators, to see how they work.

Start the clock
Baseball is somewhat unusual among modern team sports in that it does not feature, as such, a clock. The length of a game is—hypothetically, at least—infinite.

Instead of keeping time, we keep track of outs. You get 27 of them (ignoring, for a moment, that the bottom of the ninth ends when the home team is leading—so in a win by the home team, it can be as little as 24 outs). Once you've made all of your outs, you're done batting.

But so long as you have outs available, you can keep batting. And so long as you can keep batting, you can score more runs. That's why outs are the lifeblood of an offense—it's as important as clock management in other sports.

The other interesting thing to note about the lineup is that it's cyclical—like a conveyor belt, it keeps looping over and over, until all the outs are used. That's another unusual feature of baseball—everybody takes their turn batting in order. In basketball, your big scorer can take most of your team's shots. In football, you can throw to your best wide receiver as much as you want to. (Yes, obviously there are reasons why you may not want to, but nothing prevents you from doing it.)

But in baseball, everyone takes their turn in the batting order, regardless of situation. You can't try to get your best hitter to take most of your at-bats. You can't even try to get him most of your key at-bats. Once you've turned the lineup, you can't move hitters around.

What this means is that, on offense, there is precious little "specialization" possible. Yes, certain lineup spots may entail more of a "table-setting" role, and some more of a "run-producing" role, but only as a matter of degree. Every spot of the lineup can—and hopefully, does—contribute in all facets of run-scoring.

The hitter's role
So what are the facets of run scoring? There are three jobs for the hitter at the plate:

1. Avoid making outs. Again, outs are the clock in baseball. On offense, you want to keep as much time on the clock as possible to give your team the most chances to score runs.

2. Provide a baserunner. You want to get on base to give other hitters a chance to drive you in. (The home run is a special case, where you in essence get on base to drive yourself in.)

3. Advance the other runners. It'd be great to advance them all the way to home, but not necessary—any base advancement you can provide puts your team in a better position to score runs.

If you want to truly measure a hitter's contribution to the offense, you need to measure all of these in the right proportion. All of them are important to team run-scoring—and again, due to the cyclical nature of the lineup, no hitter can "specialize" in one to the exclusion of others without negative effects.

Counting bases

The counterpart to counting outs is counting bases—you want to accumulate as many bases as possible. After all, it takes four bases to score one run, right?

Now, ask yourself this—how many bases is a walk worth?

The answer is one, of course—if there is no runner on first. The batter advances one base on a walk. But if there's a runner on first, he gets to advance a base. If the bases are loaded, a walk is worth four total bases, as many as a solo home run. (And it drives in the same number of runs for the team, as well.)

We're used to talking about bases in terms of the batter alone—it's how we count bases for the misleadingly named total bases and its rate counterpart, slugging average. Of course it's wrong, and of course we know it's wrong—who would say that a walk and a single were equally valuable? And we know it's for that very reason that they aren't. We understand this, but we often neglect to put this knowledge into practice.

You see, there are limits to how many bases a runner can advance. Only the hitter, for instance, can advance four bases. So for all other baserunners, a home run and a triple are indistinguishable. And for a runner on third, a home run and a single are equally as valuable. So by paying attention only to the batter's rate of base advancement, we tend to overrate extra-base hits relative to hits in general.

Explicit knowledge

That's the most important thing to remember about modeling run scoring—any assumptions you don't make will end up being made by something else, be it historical accident, peer pressure, minimization of least square errors in collinear data sets, etc.Or to put it another way—if you don't explicitly think about it, you are going to end up with whatever implicit assumptions are in the underlying material. Many smart, talented people have been led astray by looking at data without first trying to grasp the fundamental principles at hand. It's like trying to sail a boat without a chart—you wind up adrift at sea, with no landmarks to guide you.

Three types of models

There are, broadly speaking, three ways to model run scoring. Before we proceed with discussing them, let's briefly ask, why might we want to model run scoring?

There are several reasons, probably too many to list. But I'll go over the obvious ones. Building a model helps you examine the run-scoring process and forces you to think critically about it. It lets you apply understanding of the run-scoring process in a uniform way to make comparisons between players and teams. And, frankly, some of us enjoy the process of making and perfecting models.

Now, on to the three basic models of run scoring (or run estimators, if you prefer):

- A linear model is a formula for estimating runs with no interaction between the basic terms—an additive model, if you will. It will sometimes feature multiplication (say, weighting a single at half of a walk) but it will never multiply two component inputs. Examples: Batting Runs, Estimated Runs Produced, Equivalent Runs, OPS.

- A dynamic model is a formula that does feature interaction between the basic terms. Most dynamic models feature, at the very least, a "baserunners" term and an "advancement" term. Examples: Runs Created, Base Runs.

- More complicated models are not formulas at all, but algorithms, or a series of instructions used to model run scoring. (Each of the instructions can be—and typically is—a formula in its own right.) Think of algorithms like computer programs (and in fact, computer programs are a type of algorithm). There are typically two kinds of algorithms used to model run scoring: a Monte Carlo simulation or a Markov Chain.

Inherently, none of those approaches is superior to the others; each has advantages and disadvantages. The question one is trying to answer usually determines which of them is the "correct" approach at the time.

Speaking broadly, when dealing with questions about individual hitters, who have little control over the run environment as a whole, linear approaches work best. For entities that do have control over the run environment—like pitchers and whole teams—dynamic estimators work better. An algorithmic approach offers more fine-grained control over particular elements, but at the expense of much greater complexity.

Next time, we'll look at the history of run estimation and review a few of the key advancements of our understanding of run estimation. Until then, take care, and estimate your runs responsibly.

HANK AARON'S HOME COOKING
Top Sluggers and Their Home Run Breakdowns
Jay Jaffe

One of the qualities that makes baseball unique is its embrace of non-standard playing surfaces. Football fields and basketball courts are always the same length, but no two outfields are created equal. As Jay Jaffe explains via a look at Barry Bonds and the all-time home run leaderboard, a player's home park can have a significant effect on how often he goes yard.

It's been a couple of weeks since the 30th anniversary of Hank Aaron's historic 715th home run and the accompanying tributes, but Barry Bonds' exploits tend to keep the top of the all-time chart in the news. With homers in seven straight games and counting at this writing, Bonds has blown past Willie Mays at number three like the Say Hey Kid was standing still, which—congratulatory road trip aside—he has been, come to think of it.

Baseball Prospectus' Dayn Perry penned an affectionate tribute to Aaron last week. In reviewing Hammerin' Hank's history, he notes that Aaron's superficially declining stats in 1968 (the Year of the Pitcher, not coincidentally) led him to consider retirement, but that historian Lee Allen reminded him of the milestones which lay ahead. Two years later, Aaron became the first black player to cross the 3,000 hit threshold, two months ahead of Mays. By then he was chasing 600 homers and climbing into some rarefied air among the top power hitters of all time.

Aaron produced plenty of late-career homer heroics after 1968. From ages 35 (1969) through 39, he smacked 203 dingers, and he added another 42 in his 40s, meaning that nearly a third of his homers (32.4 percent) came after age 35. The only batters other than Aaron to top 200 homers after 35 are Bonds and Rafael Palmeiro.

As amazing as that late kick is, one thing neither Perry, nor any of the other writers whose Aaron tributes I came across, mentioned is the influence his ballpark may have played on those totals. When examining the effect of parks on any player's career, one should bear in mind the sheer contrast between the comforts of home and the drudgery of travel, as well as the venue's specifications and the sample sizes which may affect a single season. Playing at home means getting to sleep in your own bed, and who among us doesn't prefer that to living out of a suitcase?

Nonetheless, the pattern for Aaron is rather convincing. The Braves moved from Milwaukee to Atlanta in 1966. According to Ballparks.com, Milwaukee County Stadium's fences at the time they left were (left to right) 320'-362'-402'-362'-315', ranging from 8'4" to 10' tall. Atlanta-Fulton County Stadium's fences were further back to begin with (325'-385'-402'-385'-325') but they stood only 6' tall. The park underwent some rejiggering in the team's first few years and stood at 330'-375'-400'-375'-330' by 1969. While those dimensions made the field larger than Milwaukee's, the Atlanta stadium's altitude of 1,000 feet above sea level placed it as the highest park in the majors until the Colorado Rockies came along, and its impact on homer totals gave it the nickname "The Launching Pad."

In his nine years in Atlanta, Aaron hit 192 homers at home versus 145 on the road. But besides the home runs, the park wasn't especially a hitter's park, at least until a few new NL ballparks came into play midway through that string. Here are Aaron's home-road breakdowns, as taken from the *Bill James Historical Abstract* (the 1987 version), along with the Batters' Park Factors from Baseball-Reference.com. Remember that the BPFs are for runs and not homers, an important distinction which Perry recently discussed in the context of Dodger Stadium. I've split Aaron's Atlanta period into two eras, one in which his park played as essentially neutral on scoring and the other when it became a hitter's park; the average Park Factors for those eras are weighted by Aaron's plate appearances:

Year	PF	HHR	RHR	PA	PA/HR	Notes
1966	102	21	23	688	15.6	fences 325-385-402-385-325
1967	99	23	16	669	17.2	
1968	100	17	12	676	23.3	
1969	100	23	23	639	13.9	fences 330-375-400-375-330; add Jarry (MON), Murphy (SD)
TOT	100.3	84	74	2672	16.9	

Year	PF	HHR	RHR	PA	PA/HR	Notes
1970	106	23	15	598	15.7	add Three Rivers (Pit), Riverfront (Cin)
1971	106	31	16	573	12.2	add Veterans (Phi)
1972	109	19	15	544	16.0	
1973	108	24	16	465	11.6	fences 330-375-402-375-330
1974	104	11	9	382	19.1	fences 330-385-402-385-330
TOT	106.7	108	71	2562	14.3	

Aaron's increased homer frequency did coincide with the 1969 change in dimensions; he went from one every 18.2 PA in his first three years in Atlanta to one every 14.2 afterwards. Judging from the BPFs, the stadium's impact on runs was due more to the retirement of Crosley Field (an extreme hitter's park) in favor of Riverfront (a pitcher's park), and the addition of pitcher-friendly Jack Murphy Stadium, the expansion San Diego Padres' park, than to the changed dimensions. A quick scan of various park factors around the league confirms this. Throwing out 1970 because both new stadiums were added mid-season, we see the following Batter Park Factors among the stadiums listed above (weighted to account for the two expansion franchises' late entry):

Years	PIT	CIN	PHI	MON	SD	AVG	ATL
1966-69	99.5	107.8	99.5	100.0	96.0	101.6	**100.3**
1971-74	97.8	96.5	102.5	103.0	93.5	98.7	**106.8**

So Aaron's stadium favored offense. How much did it aid homers? Retrosheet's team splits for the era go back only to 1969, but the data quite clearly shows the "Launching Pad" tag was deserved. From 1969-1974, the Braves and their opponents hit 1.35 homers in Atlanta for every one on the road:

Year	AFCS	Road	Notes
1969	161	124	
1970	206	134	
1971	186	119	
1972	154	125	
1973	205	145	Aaron, Evans & Johnson top 40 HR
1974	109	108	league HR rate dropped 21%
TOT	1021	755	
AVG	170	126	

Aaron's rate for that interval was 1.39 home HR for every road HR, slightly above the Braves and their opponents. But among the great home run hitters, how big a deal is all of this? Using the aforementioned *Historical Abstract*, Retrosheet, and BigLeaguers.com, I compiled the home-road breakdowns of the top 20 home run hitters of all time. Asterisks denote active players, totals are through April 20, and yes, Barry has caused me to update this a few times.

Rank	Player	HR	HHR	RHR
1	Hank Aaron	755	385	370
2	Babe Ruth	714	347	367
3	**Barry Bonds***	**667**	**327**	**340**
4	Willie Mays	660	335	325
5	Frank Robinson	586	321	265
6	Mark McGwire	583	285	298
7	Harmon Killebrew	573	291	282
8	Reggie Jackson	563	280	283
9	Mike Schmidt	548	265	283
10	**Sammy Sosa***	**543**	**292**	**251**
11	Mickey Mantle	536	266	270
12	Jimmie Foxx	534	299	235
13	**Rafael Palmeiro***	**529**	**288**	**241**
t14	Willie McCovey	521	264	257
t14	Ted Williams	521	248	273
t16	Ernie Banks	512	290	222
t16	Eddie Mathews	512	237	275
18	Mel Ott	511	323	188
19	Eddie Murray	504	248	256
20	Lou Gehrig	493	251	242

As a whole, these men were aided slightly by their parks, hitting 51.4 percent of their homers at home, an average advantage of 16 homers (292 to 276). Aaron's decisive Atlanta advantage is mostly mitigated by his Milwaukee years, and while he ranks towards the top in his ratio of home HR to road HR, he's still below the group average:

Player	H/R Ratio
Ott	1.718
Banks	1.306
Foxx	1.272
Robinson	1.211
Palmeiro*	1.195
Sosa*	1.163
Aaron	1.041
Gehrig	1.037
Killebrew	1.032
Mays	1.031
McCovey	1.027
Jackson	0.989
Mantle	0.985
Murray	0.969
Bonds*	0.962
McGwire	0.956
Ruth	0.946
Schmidt	0.936
Williams	0.908
Mathews	0.862
AVG	1.058

Mel Ott took advantage of the Polo Grounds' short foul lines to an almost absurd extreme, while Ernie Banks, Jimmie Foxx, and Frank Robinson also benefited greatly from their home parks. Interestingly enough, lefty-hitting Eddie Mathews, a teammate of Aaron's from 1954-1966, was hurt the most of any of these players; he played only one season in Atlanta and so didn't gain the late-career advantage that Aaron did. One of the bigger surprises on this list was Babe Ruth's home/road breakdown: Despite the "House That Ruth Built" tag applied to Yankee Stadium, he actually had more homers on the road than at home. Here's a quick breakdown of the Bambino's career by phase:

Years	Park	HHR	RHR
1914-19	Fenway	11	38
1920-22	Polo	75	73
1923-34	Yankee	259	252
1935	Braves	2	4
TOT		347	367

At the outset, I would have wagered that the extreme split in Fenway had more to do with his career on the mound, with the Sox pitching their sensation at home whenever possible to boost attendance and letting him play outfield on the road. But the data to be gleaned from Retrosheet (which doesn't have splits for that era) doesn't support this. Ruth played the outfield for the Sox only in 1918 and 1919, a time during which his homer split, according to James, was nine in Fenway and 31 on the road. At that point his pitching career was on the wane; he made only 34 starts in those two years, compared to 79 in the previous two. Of those 34 starts, only 19 came at Fenway, a minimal advantage. It's more likely that Fenway's righty-favoring dimensions (initially 321'-388'-488'-550' (deepest right center)-402'-314', according to *Take Me Out to the Ballpark*) really did have an impact on his totals.

In any event, the home/road splits of the top home run hitters make for interesting data. One quick-and-dirty way of looking at this, or rather two ways, is to double the home totals and the road totals to get numbers approaching their true totals, then comparing them to the current list (whose numbers many of us substitute for sheep in our insomnia-addled hours). The former gives us a number which the hitter might have achieved had he enjoyed all of the advantages of home, while the latter gives us an idea of how he would have fared in more neutral surroundings. Leaving their overall rankings alongside their names to emphasize the shifts, we get:

Rank	Player	2x HHR	Rank	Player	2x RHR
1	Aaron	770	1	Aaron	740
2	Ruth	694	2	Ruth	734
4	Mays	670	3	Bonds*	680
3	Bonds*	654	4	Mays	650
18	Ott	646	6	McGwire	596
5	Robinson	642	8	Jackson	566
12	Foxx	598	9	Schmidt	566
10	Sosa*	584	7	Killebrew	564
7	Killebrew	582	t16	Mathews	550
t16	Banks	580	t14	Williams	546
13	Palmeiro*	576	11	Mantle	540
6	McGwire	570	5	Robinson	530
8	Jackson	560	t14	McCovey	514
11	Mantle	532	19	Murray	512
9	Schmidt	530	10	Sosa*	502
t14	McCovey	528	20	Gehrig	484
20	Gehrig	502	13	Palmeiro*	482
t14	Williams	496	12	Foxx	470
19	Murray	496	t16	Banks	444
t16	Mathews	474	18	Ott	376

The "home-doubled" list makes for a few dramatic changes. Aaron's advantage on Ruth is increased, but more notably, Ott zooms into the top five from the lower reaches of the chart, Frank Robinson crosses the 600 threshold, and Jimmie Foxx reclaims the top-10 status he held a quarter-century ago. Two Chicago Cubs, Sammy Sosa and Ernie Banks, move up considerably in their totals, but then so does the majority of this list. In all, three members of the true top 10 fall out of that elite. The "road doubled" list is much more similar to the actual one in the rankings. Aaron holds only a bare six-homer advantage on Ruth, and Bonds vaults way past his godfather Mays. Only two of the true top 10 fall out, and the jockeying at the top of the list is very minor, with Mathews and Ted Williams both joining its lower reaches. At the bottom of the list, the changes are more dramatic; four members of the 500 HR club fall below that mark with their road-doubled totals, with Ott undercutting 400.

The take-home message of all of this is that while Hank Aaron's homer totals, particularly his late-career surge, were helped by his home park, in the context of the game's top home run hitters, the effect was not all that pronounced. For many of the hitters, switching teams or moving into new ballparks tended to balance out their favorable and unfavorable conditions. Taking advantage of one's playing environment isn't a crime, and before we dish out an asterisk for Aaron's tremendous achievement, we ought to consider also that he racked up a good amount of his homer totals in the pitcher-friendly 1960s. Baseball history is full of such fluctuations, and while it's important to consider a player's accomplishments in the context of the terrain, that shouldn't diminish our admiration for Aaron's feat.

That goes for Bonds as well. One fact that's been lost in his homer surge of the past few years is that the Giants' new stadium, SBC Park (formerly Pac Bell) is a terrible home run environment for EBB (Everybody But Barry). Comparing Bonds' home and road HR totals to those of the Giants and their opponents in games at SBC/Pac Bell and elsewhere:

Year	BBH	BBR	SF	RD
2000	25	24	171	206
2001	37	36	146	234
2002	19	27	114	200
2003	23	22	143	173
TOT	104	109	574	813

In the park's first four years, Bonds hit 0.954 homers at home for every one on the road. Think about that—as amazing as his feats have been, *his numbers may still be limited by his home park*. The Giants and their opponents have suffered even more, hitting only 0.706 homers there for every homer elsewhere. Some might point to darker explanations for Barry's ability to overcome his park, but his achievements deserve some appreciation as well. If he eventually passes Aaron for the top spot, it won't be because of his environment, it will be in spite of it.

Best of Baseball Prospectus: 1996-2011   Part 1: Offense

MARCH 13, 2008   http://bbp.cx/a/7227

PROSPECTUS HIT AND RUN
Running Afoul
Jay Jaffe

The impact of a ballpark's construction on offense isn't all about fence distance. Jay Jaffe looked into the effects caused by an often overlooked factor—the amount of foul territory—to determine how much of the so-called "Steroid Era's" home run boom was attributable to smaller parks.

Last time around, after discussing how the baseball itself may have changed in a manner that helped to boost home run rates over the past two decades, I took a look at the myth of the shrinking ballpark. To recap, the notion that the stadium construction boom that's taken place over the past 20 years has left us with a game full of bandboxes is actually a false one, at least when it comes to fence distances:

MLB	1990	2007	Change
LF	329.6	332.0	2.4
LCF	375.5	376.6	1.2
CF	404.9	404.9	-0.1
RCF	376.0	377.6	1.6
RF	329.1	329.3	0.2

With the exception of straightaway center field, those distances have increased by a hair through the 21 new ballparks that have come into play since 1990. However, it's true that park capacities have dropped about 10 percent in this time, a trend that will continue as the Yankees, Mets, Athletics, and Twins move into new parks able to seat fewer paying customers in the next several years.

These findings drew a considerable amount of responses from our readers, who made a couple of good points that are worth exploring. The first one relates to the 1995 introduction of Coors Field, which has deeper fences to help offset the extra distance the ball carries at high altitude. A couple of

Position	2007	Coors	2007'	90-07	90-07'
LF	332.0	347.0	331.4	2.4	1.9
LCF	376.6	390.0	376.2	1.2	0.7
CF	404.9	415.0	404.9	-0.1	-0.4
RCF	377.6	375.0	377.7	1.6	1.7
RF	329.1	350.0	328.6	0.2	-0.5

readers worried that the addition of Coors distorts the average fence distance changes too much, so I've recomputed the averages to show its impact.

The 2007' numbers are the averages sans Coors, and the 90-07' figure is the change from 1990 to 2007 excluding Coors. Note that its removal swings right field from a slight gain to a slight decrease, and that four out of the five measurements decrease by at least some fraction. (Also note that there are some rounded decimals in there which make the deltas look less straightforward.)

The take-home point here is that the balance is still in favor of increased fence distances, particularly on the left side (LF and LCF). That's important, because about half of all homers are hit to those two areas, thanks to the lefty/righty distribution of hitters (58.8 percent of all plate appearances were from the right side in 2007) and the natural tendency to pull the ball. In fact, a quick-and-dirty look using the Baseball-Reference.com Play Index shows that the increased distances may have an impact on home run distribution. In 1990, 54.4 percent of homers were hit to left field and left-center field. Last year it was 50.8 percent. The intermediate data is a little squirrely, likely as a result of being integrated from multiple sources:

- In the years immediately prior to 1991, the locations of more than 100 home runs per year are unaccounted for in the Retrosheet logs, but from 1991 on, that drops down to about 10-15 homers per year.
- The 2006 data at B-R doesn't distinguish left-center field or right-center field; I corrected this by using harder-to-obtain data from BP's internal database instead.
- The 1999 data from B-R shows 1,024 homers to center field; that's up from 571 the previous year, and well above the 683 scored to dead center the following year. BP's data is of no help here, lacking the left-center and right-center distinctions for that year.

As imperfect as the data may be, the trend is apparent. The percentage of left-side homers hasn't topped 51.0 percent since Coors opened in 1995. Ladies and gentlemen, my first-ever graph for a Baseball Prospectus article, and it's ugly enough to put this graphic designer to shame; we'll spruce things up next time. Anyway, the trend meshes with the finding that fence distances have in fact increased over the past two decades.

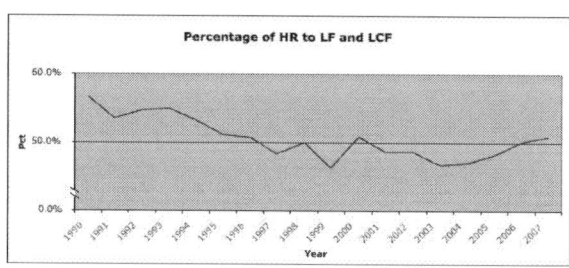

The second major point made by my readers is that the new ballparks may feature less foul territory, which could be helping to drive up offensive levels, including home run rates, by creating more opportunities for balls to be hit into fair territory. Alas, this isn't an easy avenue to explore, nor is it an exciting one, far closer to a methodical trudge through the cardboard box factory than a debauchery-laden weekend in Las Vegas. But metaphorically speaking, if we chase down some foul balls, we may catch a thing or two.

Start with the problem that foul territory measurements aren't systematically reported; at best, the distance from home plate to the backstop can sometimes be found. Even the most definitive source of ballpark data available on the web, the KJOK Park Database, has major gaps in its data; the most recent season available, 2004, contains backstop distances for only 20 out of 30 teams, while for 1990 it's just 12 out of 26 teams—virtually useless for our purposes.

Luckily, some time spent drilling in Google helped me find Clem's Baseball page, which contains all kinds of information on stadia, including backstop distance figures or estimates for 66 current or former ballparks. With the caveat that there are significant differences between the existing KJOK data and Clem's estimates, if we use the latter we find that backstop distances have indeed decreased over the years. Back in 1985 (a year I chose so as to encompass all of the modern stadium changes as well as the 1987 home run spike), the average backstop distance was 60.6 feet. In 2007, it was 56.3 feet.

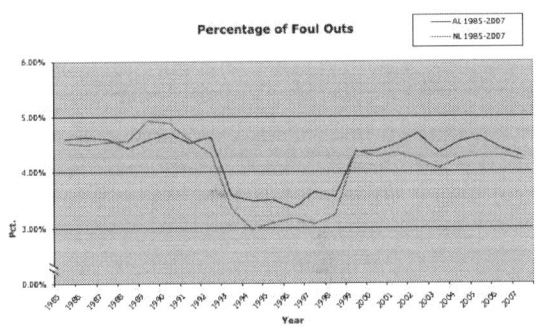

Even if that means an overall decrease in foul territory—and no, I don't know of anyone who's bothered to systematically quantify that particular area—is that really having an effect on the matter in question by resulting in fewer foul outs and thus more balls in fair territory? To answer this, I looked at play-by-play data to see whether the wave of new stadia has changed the frequency of foul-ball outs. Because strikeout rates have gradually risen over the time frame in question—from 5.37 per nine innings in 1985 to 6.67 last year, or from 14.0 percent of all plate appearances in 1985 to 17.1 percent last year—I used foul outs per contact out. When I did, I found something odd.

Foul-out rates have fallen slightly in the grand scheme, from 4.57 percent of all contact outs in 1985 to 4.25 percent last year. That supports the notion that foul territory has decreased in recent years, thus creating more opportunities for home runs. But there's a major dip in the data as seen in both leagues from 1993 to 1998. It's unclear whether this is simply another squirrel running amok in our database, a result of the union of differing sources of play-by-play data, or a legitimate—if curious—trend. It's worth noting that there is considerable stability over the three neatly-divided time periods of this data.

Period	PctFoul	StDev
1985-1992	4.60	0.10
1993-1998	3.34	0.08
1999-2007	4.36	0.08
TOTAL	4.19	0.51
Non-DIP	4.47	0.15

To review, 1993 saw the introduction of Coors Field's precursor, Mile High Stadium (no backstop distance recorded), as well as Your Ad Here Stadium in Miami (Joe Robbie until 1996, Pro Player from 1996 to 2005, Dolphin Safe Tuna more or less since then). Cleveland's Jacobs Field and the Rangers' Ballpark in Arlington came along in 1994, Coors in 1995, Atlanta's Turner Field in 1997, Arizona's Bank One Ballpark and the then-Devil Rays' Tropicana Field in 1998, and Seattle's Safeco Field in 1999. That's a fair bit of turnover, and the trend has continued in recent years, but I'm not sure it explains the temporary dip. Nor, I'll wager, do the truncated 1994 and 1995 seasons. Looking at the data on a more granular level—every team, every year since 1985—doesn't offer much greater clarity. Consider the following:

- Of the 47 times foul-out rates dipped more than 1.0 percent in the same ballpark from one year to the next, 15 come in 1993, the year rates systematically fell. Similarly, of the 43 times foul-out rates jumped more than 1.0 percent, 15 of them come in 1999, the year rates rose again.
- Within a sample size of 601 contiguous park-seasons from 1985-2006, we find a moderate amount of year-over-year correlation ($r = .61$) in foul-out rates. That correlation, for some reason, suffers considerably if we excise the 1992-1999 data (the questionable 1993-1998 period, plus the contiguous year on each side), dropping to $r = .41$.
- Within the much smaller sample size of 17 instances where an existing team (not an expansion one) changed park from one year to the next, the correlation between foul-out rates is higher than in the other two samples, $r = .68$. This opens up the possibility that foul-out frequency may be more a product of personnel—pitchers, hitters, and/or fielders who are more or less prone to produce such events—than of environment.
- There is actually very little correlation between the estimated backstop distances and foul-out rates, and what correlation there is is negative. Using raw percentages for the 1985-2007 data, $r = -0.1$. Indexing the data in a manner similar to ERA+ (where 100 is league average, every increment away from 100 is the percentage above or below average; we'll call the result FO+), the correlation is a bit stronger, $r = -.15$.

Even if raw backstop distance has nothing to do with the foul-out frequency, it's quite reasonable to assume that the frequency is something that requires multiple years of data to show anything meaningful, particularly given that such events happen roughly one or two times per game. We can start to get a hint of the effect of the building boom on foul ball rates once we classify the parks into four groups:

Group 1: Ballparks of existing teams that have been constant from 1985-2007
Teams: ANA, BOS, CHN, KCA, LAN, MIN, NYA, NYN, OAK

Group 2: Ballparks of expansion teams
Teams: ARI, COL (two parks), FLO, TBA

Group 3: Ballparks that have been replaced during the time in question
Teams: ATL, BAL, CHA, CIN, CLE, DET, HOU, MIL, MON, PHI, PIT, SDN, SEA, SFN, SLN, TEX, TOR

Group 4: Ballparks that have replaced other parks during that time
Teams: ATL, BAL, CHA, CIN, CLE, DET, HOU, MIL, PHI, PIT, SDN, SEA, SFN, SLN, TEX, TOR, WAS (was MON)

Here's the breakdown. Reading across, we have the group (Grp), the backstop distance (Bkstp), the foul-out percentage (Pct), the percentage relative to the league (FO+), and the group's relative share of our sample size (Share). Foul outs in the old-guard stadia, the ones unchanged since 1985, occur at a frequency that is nearly two percent lower than the league average despite relatively short backstop distances, a counterintuitive finding. The expansion stadia, on the other hand, yield foul outs at a rate 3.7 percent above the league average, this despite the fact that this relatively small share of the sample includes a pair of home run havens in Arizona and Denver, another counterintuitive finding. Meanwhile, the new parks that have replaced older ones have resulted in a slight increase in terms of foul-out frequency, despite the fact that the changes have been as extreme as a 9.8 percent increase in Texas and a 16.3 percent decrease in Atlanta.

Grp	Bkstp	Pct	FO+	Share
1	56.6	4.15	98.2	32.3
2	55.0	4.16	103.7	7.5
3	62.8	4.17	100.0	36.3
4	56.8	4.27	101.3	23.9

Further grouping these to illustrate the impact of the newer parks:

Grp	Pct	FO+	Share
Old (1+3)	4.16	99.2	68.6
New (2+4)	4.21	101.9	31.4

We close with the exciting conclusion that ~~a field trip to the box factory is pretty lame~~ foul outs in general have decreased slightly in frequency since 1985, but the newer stadia aren't to blame for this. On the contrary, they've produced relatively higher foul-out frequencies. Even if we've identified a way in which ballparks have shrunk over the years, the decrease in foul territory—or at least a perceived decrease, since there's no systematic measurement of foul territories—doesn't appear to have contributed to the rise in home runs over the past two decades by providing more opportunities for balls to be hit into fair territory. Coupled with the chapter I wrote in Will Carroll's *The Juice*, which showed that the impact of the newer parks on rising home run rates was minimal at best, this data tells us that it's time to retire the complaint that newer, smaller parks have driven the boom.

JULY 15, 2007 — http://bbp.cx/a/6454

THE ANSWER
No Asterisks Necessary
Will Carroll and Clay Davenport

One of the happy byproducts of baseball's long history is the comparisons it permits between men who played it decades apart, but the sport's different eras have produced markedly different conditions. With some statistical heavy lifting behind the scenes, Baseball Prospectus can put players of all eras on a level playing field, enabling more accurate comparisons. Take a look at what a "neutralized" setting does to the all-time home run leaderboard.

You're going to have to pick your poison here, old-timers. You can either hate Barry Bonds, or you can hate statheads, but when it comes to solving the "problem" of the all-time home run title, you can't have it both ways. Those who want to place an asterisk on Bonds' achievements have always focused on the question of whether or not he's been cheating, something that remains unproven in the legal if not literal sense. In that argument, you can never win, not until Bonds pumps out a positive steroid test, something that seems pretty unlikely at this late stage of his career. Instead, if you really want to make your point sans the Frickian asterisk, you're going to have to rely on that other thing that baseball purists hate: math.

Over and over, people insist that we can't compare Babe Ruth or Hank Aaron to Barry Bonds. To that, we say "nuts," because we most certainly can. There's some question as to how physical skills might translate, but it's easy enough to translate statistics to adjust for park, league, and era. In fact, it's one of the bedrocks of Baseball Prospectus. Since before BP's founding, Clay has been making translations available. Translations of player performance aren't that complex on the surface and are easily read, just like a normal stat line. It's behind the scenes where things gets complex, but despite that complexity, Davenport Translations have never been seriously contested. Unlike attempts at the "One True Stat" like VORP, Runs Created, WARP, and Win Shares, all with their various degrees of success or failure, translations seldom raise any significant argument among serious statheads, and no one has developed a competing system.

What goes into a translation? According to the BP Glossary, a single-season translation involves adjustments "made to account for the home park and for the offensive level of the league as a whole. Hitters have an adjustment for not having to face their own team's pitchers; pitchers have a similar adjustment for not having to face their own hitters. Hitters in the AL since 1973 have a disadvantage in these statistics, since the league average is artificially inflated by the use of the DH and no adjustment is made for that." This is of no concern, since Ruth and Aaron played before the DH era and Bonds spent his career in the National League. (We know, we're not mentioning those few occasions that he DH'd in interleague play. The statheads are already riled up.)

To get to an all-time translation, you have to go a bit further. "Statistics that have been adjusted for all-time have all of the adjustments for a single season, plus two more. One adjustment normalizes the average fielding numbers over time. Historically, the fielding share of total defense has diminished with time, since more walks, more strikeouts, and more home runs mean less work for fielders. In the single-season adjustments, fielders from before WWII have a lot more value (to their teams) than fielders do today; the all-time adjustments have attempted to remove that temporal trend. The second adjustment is for league difficulty. League quality has generally increased with time. Each league has been rated for difficulty and compared to a trend line defined by the post-integration National League. In addition to the adjustments for season, an adjustment is made for league difficulty."

Once the heavy lifting is done, we're left with statistics that are on a level playing field. It's as if all the players that ever played the game did it at the same time in the same stadium against the same competition. Where is that stadium, you ask? The most neutral stadium in the year used, 2000, happens to be Montreal's Stade Olympique, so in some small way, baseball in that fine city lives on. It's the ultimate simulation, calculated in a manner similar to the method economists use to calculate inflation with 1973 dollars. What does this mean for those of you asteriskers? First, it means we can abandon the number "755" as some sort of ultimate achievement. That number is only good enough for ninth place on the Davenport Translation All-Time Home Run list, and it's Mike Schmidt who hits that number exactly in the translations.

Player	Adjusted HR
Babe Ruth	1070
Hank Aaron	971
Barry Bonds	**931**
Mel Ott	861
Willie Mays	856
Lou Gehrig	792
Jimmie Foxx	765
Reggie Jackson	757
Mike Schmidt	755
Ted Williams	752

That makes for a pretty nice list. It passes the "looks right test," in that most of the all-time greats are here, with Ruth and Aaron atop it and with Mays and Gehrig in historically significant positions. It removes Sammy Sosa and Mark McGwire from the list while inserting Ted Williams. Mel Ott makes for a nice conversation-starter. Reggie Jackson and his connections to Curtis Wentzlaff aside, it acknowledges Barry Bonds on the list without giving him any sort of primacy.

All in all, it's a good asterisk-free list that should appeal to all. Even Bonds' most ardent defenders can't argue that he's not being rewarded with a number of homers lost to cavernous AT&T Park and the winds of Candlestick—just not enough to put him above Ruth or Aaron. At least not yet; Bonds would need roughly 30 more home runs, most of them at home, to pass Aaron on the translated list.

If you're wondering about other major leagues, Sadaharu Oh is not your man. The level of play in the Japanese league is translatable too, but down, due to its level, which is somewhere between the major leagues and Triple-A. That leaves him with a rough estimate of 505 career translated homers for the purposes of this exercise.

Is there anyone else currently in the game who has a chance to edge onto the list? Let's contribute to the current lovefest for Ken Griffey Jr. Here is the current active list:

Player	Adjusted HR
Barry Bonds	931
Ken Griffey Jr.	719
Sammy Sosa	684
Frank Thomas	628
Alex Rodriguez	576
Gary Sheffield	576
Manny Ramirez	565
Jim Thome	559
Carlos Delgado	501
Mike Piazza	469

Griffey is almost certain to edge onto the top ten all-time list, depending on how long the Indian summer of his career lasts. Going as high as sixth is quite possible, especially if we take for his own the career of his father, a player who kept value into his forties. Alex Rodriguez, to be sure, is noticeable on this list, coming up to almost 600 translated home runs at the same time that he's pushing the 500 mark in reality; at 32, Rodriguez should bash his way into the translated career top ten in the next two years and then will begin to creep up the list. It's notable that A-Rod leaving Yankee Stadium for his home games might actually hurt his chances at the translated career title. That's because park effects are a big part of translating performance and help the numbers of those players who have to hit in pitcher's parks. Once again, this is a list that looks good. It should be no surprise to see any of these names, and it matches up well with what most fans would expect.

So if we've solved the 755 problem, what then of the 73 issue? The easy answer might be Alex Rodriguez, currently on pace for a translated 70. Bonds' 2001 translates to 72; all the math essentially cancels itself out for Bonds' 2001 and actually costs him one home run. I hear the asteriskers cheering. But who's in the translated 70 home run club? Here is that list.

Player	Year	Adj HR
Babe Ruth	1927	75
Babe Ruth	1920	74
Babe Ruth	1921	73
Babe Ruth	1924	73
Babe Ruth	1928	73
Barry Bonds	**2001**	**72**
Mark McGwire	1998	72
Jimmie Foxx	1932	70
Babe Ruth	1923	70
Babe Ruth	1926	70
Alex Rodriguez	2007	70

Once again, we get a list that passes the "looks right" test. Ruth has seven—seven!—seasons of 70 or more, while Bonds and McGwire's so-called tainted seasons fall in the middle. Jimmie Foxx gets to be the guy we all shrug our shoulders on, a forgotten great to most fans, while Alex Rodriguez makes the list with his "on pace for" number this season. Rodriguez will have to keep up the same pace to stay on the list, but we added it here for entertainment purposes.

We're not finished yet. There is one player with two seasons we've purposefully left off the list of the Seventies Club. That player is one who might surprise you, not for having two of the great slugging seasons of all time, but for having the single greatest slugging season of all time. That's right, it's not Ruth at the top of the list. The translated 70 home run club has another member, its king.

Player	Year	Adj HR
Lou Gehrig	1927	76
Lou Gehrig	1934	71

There are no asterisks flitting around Gehrig's career, but that amazing 1927 season is pretty surprising and caused me (Will) to ask me (Clay) to check the math. Remember, Ruth hit 60 real home runs to Gehrig's real 47. Dutiful double-checking confirms that while Ruth had a 60-47 edge on Gehrig in real life, Gehrig had an 18-8 lead in triples and a 52-29 lead in doubles, and when you translate from before World War II to the modern era, a lot of doubles and triples get turned into home runs, enough for the Iron Horse to pass the Babe in this case. Gehrig got those hits because he had power, not speed, and in today's game that power would translate over the fence.

So there you have it, the problem is solved. We've wiped Barry Bonds off the top of both the all-time and single-season home run lists, restoring balance to the universe and aligning the stars in a neutral fashion. Any taint of the steroid era is shifted down (as many argue it should be), though only through the context of the era rather than any unproven allegations and guesses about what PEDs do to player performance. Perhaps that's just as well. Performance-enhancing drugs may have been in the game of baseball and its Hall of Fame since the Age of Spalding, from Pud Galvin's elixir of bull testicles—a primitive testosterone that may have led to his death—on down to Willie Mays, Henry Aaron, and Mike Schmidt's use of stimulants, and who wants to get into that? Instead, it's time to take the translations into account and play the game on the most even of fields. Purists of the world, no thanks are necessary.

JULY 15, 2007 http://bbp.cx/a/6454

BONDS RESPONSES
Staff Takes on a Landmark
Baseball Prospectus

When Barry Bonds passed Hank Aaron to claim the top spot on the all-time home run leaderboard, he prompted some strong reactions from observers across the country, many of whom felt that his alleged steroid use had tainted the record. Several members of BP's staff weighed in on how they felt about the new home run king's achievement.

Maury Brown: There ought to be one word that comes to mind when taking in Bonds' place as the all-time home run king. Maybe that word is 'confused.' Or cloudy, muddy, murky... take your pick. In the history of sports, I don't think anyone has ever faced the dilemma of asking whether or not a record was legitimately set or not. Barry Bonds has forced us to look at that issue with arguably the most revered and sacred of records in baseball. After all, the record has been achieved, and controversy be damned, he hasn't failed a drug test, nor has he been indicted by the Feds, nor has some mountain of evidence landed in George Mitchell's lap that makes one think that Bonds is going to be the focus of his soon-to-be published report.

Yet, I couldn't sit there and watch the historic event without asking, how do one's head and feet grow when they are in their 40s? HGH? Adding to the confusion was the reaction by Commissioner Selig, which at best seemed clumsy and at worst looked petty. He appeared to be a man who either caved in to pressure to witness some of Bonds' games leading up to 756, or who decided that, by not being there for the record-breaker yet making it to some of the games, he'd appear as if he'd tried. Nice try, but what Selig actually accomplished was something that all the spin doctors in the world might not have been able to do—make Barry Bonds into a sympathetic figure.

The future is loaded with unknowns. What will happen when he appears on the ballot for the Hall of Fame? What if he is indicted? Suffice it to say that the record-setting home run is unsettling to fans, and with that, the breaking of the record is tarnished and something that simply did not reach its full potential. My sense is that we were all somehow robbed of one of the greatest moments in Major League Baseball history.

Will Carroll: I'm considered an apologist for Bonds in large part because I've kept an open mind. I'm okay with that; I've been called worse. For me, it was a great baseball moment. I'll remember the deep drive he hit to center, the look on his face as he rounded first, and the look on his son's face as his father crossed home plate.

As I get older, the father-son relationships are what I've noticed more and more about baseball. If you look at Nikolai Bonds, you'll see the same look we saw from Matt McGwire back in 1998. I remember the kiss that Shawon Dunston gave his son after hitting a home run in the World Series. Heck, I'll remember the look of relief on Dusty Baker's face as he pulled his son to him after the tyke was almost being crushed by J.T. Snow. (Snow's miracle save is, to me, perhaps as great a play as I've ever seen on a field.)

Every time I go to a game, I see a family or a father and son sitting in the stands. We all learned our love of baseball somewhere; I learned mine on dusty fields where we'd play in the hot sun for hours but also from watching the deep green grass of Wrigley Field from a thousand miles away on cable. I never met Harry Caray, but on many a spring and summer day, I felt as if that man was teaching me to love baseball. I may have learned more about the game from Steve Stone, but it was the passion that I learned from Harry. I'm not sure what Harry would have to say about Bonds' situation, but I do know that Bonds spelled backwards is Sdnob.

As Bonds goes into the record book, he'll have his detractors, but he'll always have that moment, a moment in time when for just a little while there were no shadows, there was no pending investigation, there was no frowning Bud Selig, and there was nothing else but a bat, a ball, and forty thousand screaming fans. Plus me, watching on Tivo, clapping alone in my living room.

John Erhardt: I have a memory storage problem—I tend to be a bit sketchy on what really matters, but not so much on the unimportant details. Those details that I retain, I remember in agonizing detail. The only real memory I have of a friend's wedding in Maine is that I bought a pair of brown clogs at the Bass outlet in Kittery on the drive home. I was in Maine for three days, and that's all I've got.

Home run #756 doesn't feel like one of those memories. It feels like something I'll have a good, accurate mental video of—in its entirety—long after we've all grown tired of complaining about whomever replaces Bud Selig as Commissioner. Steroids or no steroids, I'm OK with that, because most of my mental videos come sans commentary, silent-movie style (though without the Scott Joplin soundtrack). I was at the game in 2002 when Bonds hit home run #599, and while I don't remember whom he hit it off of (I've outsourced that job to Retrosheet), I will always remember the goosebumps, and how the hair on my arm stood up every time he walked to the plate. Five years later, I still own every second of that.

As for the steroid issue, I'm pretty apathetic about the whole thing. I'm not exactly proud of that, nor am I looking for recruits, but it's true. Did Bonds break the rules and use something to enhance his performance? Probably, but I just don't care. It might be that I won't buy the media attacks on Bonds until someone argues as forcefully to put an asterisk next to Carlos Almanzar's 13 career wins for consistency's sake. It also might be that I once formulated a philosophy of life that covered this stuff with great conviction but have long since forgotten the major components of it, instead being left with the memory that I might have written it all down in a red notebook using a pen I accidentally took from a Jiffy Lube in Wauseon, Ohio.

I can't say I'm the type to get too worked up over pointless superlatives, and this, to me, is one of them. If the home run record is nothing more than a counting exercise, then the title of "Home Run King" is pretty easy to bestow, and it can be a crown made from any material you choose. If you want to discuss the "Best Home Run Hitter Ever," and you want to bring honesty or integrity into the discussion, I'll have to excuse myself, because I don't know anything about any baseball figure that hasn't already been filtered through some kind of media lens.

Ultimately, I guess I just refuse to be shocked at the potential for yet another absence of chemical, moral, or behaviorist purity in the world. Perhaps this marks my official move from casual cynic to full-fledged Randian, but I don't see the point in carefully crafting rhetoric to condemn him because he may have taken mysterious substances to maybe enhance his ability to hit a ball a few feet farther than other people. I'm going to wake up tomorrow, have breakfast with my wife, take a Prilosec, and go to work. Who knows? The possibility always exists that in 30 years, the only thing I can remember about Bonds' record-breaking home run is that he hit it off a guy named Mike, and that I was wearing brown shoes when he did it.

Steven Goldman: I've stayed out of the Bonds debate and avoided forming an opinion because I don't find myself overly attracted to or committed to the discussion. You can argue about whether this is a dereliction of duty for someone in our line, but the degree of scrutiny to which colleagues like Joe Sheehan and Will Carroll have subjected this issue renders me the merest dilettante. I'm a Bonds agnostic.

On one hand, I accept that there is a large amount of superficial evidence that suggests that he did at the very least dabble in chemistry. Yes, some of that superficial evidence is sketchy, but I remember Bill James writing, long, elaborate, eloquent pieces in defense of Pete Rose; eloquent, and 200 percent wrong. Sometimes, where there is smoke, fire inevitably follows.

At the same time, I'm impressed by arguments made by Will and others that you can't easily separate the athlete from the juice. We don't know exactly how these things help a ballplayer, and there will never be a medical study that shows what they do with real specificity. Everything is and will remain anecdotal. I'm pretty sure the East German government showed that they could pervert the heck out of the body chemistry of female athletes, but beyond that, we don't know.

If I can pull out yet a third hand, Bonds hit 73 home runs at age 36, and we know that hitters just don't do that (not so much the 73 part, although that's obviously unusual, but the part about peaking at 36). And on a fourth hand, I'm not impressed by the absence of a failed drug test. My understanding is that testing procedures are not exactly rigorous. Fifth? While we've seen a lot of chicanery at the Justice Department lately, you'd have to have some Attorney Ahab with a real obsession to argue that this was all a witch hunt.

So there's a lot of stuff to sort out, and as I'm not a religious believer in the sanctity of the record book, I can't get exercised enough to take the time to work through it. I suspect I'll have to once Jose Canseco throws A-Rod under the bus, but until then I'm content to watch others more invested fight this battle and pick and choose from among their arguments. Ruth and Aaron had various outside influences and conditions that they benefited from. In our own time, it seems pretty obvious that as baseball emerged from the labor struggles of 1994-1995, the ball got jazzier, the current strike zone is to the old one as Liechtenstein is to Russia, batters are allowed to stand with one foot on the plate, and pitchers are effectively forbidden from brushing them back. Compared to that, the advantages provided by juicing, if any, have got to be infinitesimal. The home run record has been cheapened, yes, but with the connivance of Baseball, and perhaps a cascading series of unintended consequences.

Again, I offer no warranties on this series of disconnected, conflicting thoughts. I assume the evidence will emerge eventually and we'll be able to come to a conclusion without so much guesswork. Heck, we even found out who Deep Throat was, so nothing stays buried forever. For now, I wait, neither cheering nor booing.

Kevin Goldstein: I actually got lucky and tuned into the Giants/Nationals game just in time, maybe 10 seconds before Barry Bonds stepped up to the plate and made history. Here is what went through my mind:

"Who would have thought that in August I'd be watching a game between two last-place teams that I have no rooting interest in."
"That really is Mike Bacsik. I remember when he came over to the Mets in the Roberto Alomar trade. What was the last big-league team he pitched for?" (Answer: Texas, in 2004.)
"There's that brace Will talked to the guy about; I've never really looked at it before, but it actually looks like a pretty complicated device."
"Other than the pitcher, I think Barry Bonds is the only first-round pick in the lineup for the Giants. I think the Nationals have four."
"Wow."
"That's really cool."
"Wow."
"Awesome."
"Wow."

The most interesting thing to note here is that despite all the hullabaloo, from the time I turned on the television, including Bonds stepping to the plate, hitting the home run, and the post-event celebratory spectacle, I didn't think about steroids, or congressional hearings, or suspensions, or what he looked like 20 years ago, or cream, or clear, or anything like that. I just thought about baseball.

Derek Jacques: It's a strange, post-756 world we're living in. After four months of rabid editorializing from every person with a soapbox to stand on, it feels like, for a moment, the world has run out of venom for Barry Lamar Bonds. Part of this is human nature—the public has always been less interested in the steroids story than the media has been, and there is a natural feeling of getting carried away in a spectacle at times like these. I wasn't surprised to hear people cheer homer 755 in San Diego, and although I think San Francisco's fans deserved to see the tiebreaker live as a reward for their support of Bonds over the years, I don't believe that fans anywhere would have greeted homer number 756 with boos, for the same reason that people generally don't greet a no-hitter against the home team with boos.

Everyone should enjoy these calm, post-756 waters while they can. As the Commissioner's press releases during the final stages of the record chase constantly reminded us, with their intonations of "every American is innocent until proven guilty," another shoe is likely to drop in this matter, soon, whether it comes from former Senator George Mitchell or from a federal grand jury. So enjoy the moment while it lasts.

Jay Jaffe: I'm not happy to see Bonds break the record, but I'm elated to see the circus leave town. I watched #755 and #756 once or twice and then turned away in disinterest and disgust. Good riddance.

The record is what it is, something to be taken in context. Even absent a positive test, the mountain of evidence that Bonds used performance enhancing drugs is enough to convince me that his accomplishment is tainted. We'll never know the extent to which Bonds was aided, but the fact that his historically unprecedented late-career surge matches up with the well-documented timeline of his alleged usage is enough for me. Bonds isn't alone among players in having take PEDs, and culpability for the whole sordid scene is shared by Bud Selig, the owners, and a complicit media. I'm not advocating an asterisk in the record books or the expungement of any statistics; if the fabric of baseball history can withstand the variable impacts of the spitballers, scuffers, bat-corkers, sign-stealers, and greenie-poppers, to say nothing of the Black Sox and Pete Rose, it can withstand this. But that doesn't mean we have to worship the record or the man who achieved it.

I hope that the all-time list finds a new man atop it—Alex Rodriguez, Albert Pujols, Miguel Cabrera, Jason Tyner—by the time that I need to explain this record to my children, and that the next chase is more fun for all of us.

Christina Kahrl: I've been an unapologetic fan of Barry's work going back a couple of years now, but that's simply on the basis of what we know versus what's been implied, inferred, or wishcasted by a number of people who really just want to see Bonds go down in flames—bitter exes, equally bitter old men, sanctimonious non-players, and petty fourth-estate types with well-nursed grievances.

In September of 2005, when Bonds came back from his then-most-recent knee injury, I wrote on this subject at some length, but the basic sentiment was that I don't know Barry Bonds, and not many of us—anybody, inside the game or out—do. I'm willing to give the benefit of the doubt to anyone I haven't met, virtually or in the flesh. As I expected at the time, when talk drifts to how baseball celebrates records, I could not then and cannot now help but think how Rickey Henderson was treated for setting the stolen base record while not saying anything particularly offensive afterwards, or how his setting the runs record was effectively overlooked. These things bring me to the conclusion that, however sad it may be to acknowledge, race still matters. We don't need to throw Bonds a pity party over it, but PEDs make up only a small part of what was already going to be an unfortunate and perhaps ugly narrative.

As I said then, for me, steroids are like cocaine was in the early '80s. It's a spectacular issue, which is to say, it is a spectacle. I don't think we can say with absolute confidence what either substance (or amphetamines) does to player performance. I don't think we can prove that any of these things perverted the game, or that they reflect anything more than that the game is played by our fellow men, prone to the same temptations, the same errors of judgment, and the same mistakes. Perhaps my view is overly broad, but if the game had a problem, however large or small, it has long since been identified and fixed. Would that all social ills were so readily addressed, however belatedly, tentatively, or imperfectly.

Bonds was then and is now caught in a bind: he'll never overcome reasonable doubt, so instead of being presumed innocent, he will always be condemned by a large number of people, for reasons as varied as reasonable doubt to conditioned dislike to overt racism, to name a few of what might be an unlimited range of possible responses to his setting the record. My problem is that I will never escape this doubt: the extent to which Barry Bonds was condemned from the start, and how too-ready the media was to go for a rope, and ratings.

If Bonds is guilty—if—then he joins a long list of tainted men in the game's pantheon. If he's guilty, he's a great player and a reflection of his time. And lest we make too much of contemporary wrongs relative to someone like, say, Cap Anson, he would be merely guilty of a stupid little thing, the full measure of which we'll never know, and not something fundamentally evil (the full measure of which we'll also never know). But that's me: beyond a certain curiosity for trivia, I couldn't care less about the record book. It is already a product of an injustice, one from before your birth or mine.

What we know is that Bonds is as spartan as they come, a man as devoted to the craft of hitting as any chestnut about Tony Gwynn or Ted Williams reveals they were about their work habits, a man as fundamentally gifted at hammering his pitch as legend claims the Babe must have been, or that facts reflect Mickey Mantle or Hank Aaron were, and that present reality tells us that Alex Rodriguez or Ken Griffey Jr. are. Bonds was, is, and remains great, and his greatness is a reflection of his ability. His place in history ranks not as an insult to anyone's legacy, but as a testament to his talent.

The shame is that we're left with the crack of Barry's batting potentially getting drowned out by the crankily croaked judgments of a generation of men old enough to be on a first-name basis with their urologists, men devoted to condemning their younger charges to their own cupped lot, men cynically and belatedly listening to Jiminy Cricket now that the money has been made and their actions in 1994 have been papered over by the players' achievements of 1998. As going concerns go, this should not be theirs to judge.

Congratulations, Barry, and take it as far as you can by creating as many souvenirs as possible till the very end, whenever you're ready. The fun for us as fans and as analysts in the future will be to see whether A-Rod can climb a new Everest, and that will be every bit as brilliant as your own accomplishment.

David Laurila: In following Barry Bonds' pursuit of the home run record, I found myself rooting not for or against the individual—no man is more important than the game itself—but rather for or against what Bonds stands for. Love him or hate him, there is no question that Bonds has come to symbolize the steroid era and cheating in baseball.

While it is conceivable that Bonds has never used an illegal performance-enhancing substance, reports seem to indicate otherwise. Reports also indicate that others have done the same, with pitchers who have given up home runs to Bonds surely among them. They are equally guilty, as are the multitude of non-players whose complicity has helped to compromise the integrity of the game.

While recognizing that he is one of the greatest players that baseball has seen, I have long disliked Barry Bonds because of his well-chronicled history of arrogant surliness. However, when home run number 756 sailed into the history books, I did not look at it as being hit by an individual. I saw it as being hit by a symbol of something that is terribly wrong with the game I have loved for decades. Barry Bonds isn't responsible for baseball's steroid era, but he is the poster child for it. I did not cheer when that symbol surpassed Henry Aaron.

Ben Murphy: I grew up a fan of Barry Bonds, I've always respected him for his talent on the field, and I've kind of admired the way that he's dealt with the adversity that has come with a lot of the steroids circus.

As far as the statistical aspects of the record go, I think way too many people that should appreciate the concept of statistical context fail to realize the percentage of pitchers that may have been using steroids or other PEDs and are too quick to scrutinize the hitters for their alleged usage. We've seen that many more pitchers have failed tests than hitters, so it seems only reasonable to assume that at least as many pitchers are or were using PEDs as hitters. Whether you believe Bonds used or not, if you combine that balance in usage between hitters and pitchers with facts like the recent information about the size of Bonds' arms not changing, and the fact that most of the drugs in question would do little to improve coordination and pitch recognition (two areas where Bonds excels), it stands to reason that Bonds achieved all of his greatness by surpassing his peers.

In that sense, his performance is every bit as valid as Ruth's or Aaron's, so his record should stand unadulterated, untarnished, and unmodified in the record books.

Marc Normandin: It may be that it's easier for me to cheer for Barry Bonds given that I wasn't around when Hank Aaron passed Ruth and eventually retired at 755 homers. I have been in awe of Bonds since my early days of fandom, and his performance this century has only enhanced that, regardless of the controversial and confusing means that may have inched him towards the finish line. The truth is, we don't know as much as we pretend to about what Bonds did or didn't do, and as fans of the game we should cheer the moment, even if you don't want to celebrate the man. I have chosen to do both, Bud Selig has chosen to celebrate neither; I hope that many of you at the least lean towards the middle.

Congratulations Barry, and enjoy your reign as baseball's home run king.

John Perrotto: I had the privilege of covering Barry Bonds' first major-league game with the Pirates back on May 30, 1986, two years before I became a full-time baseball writer, and have had the opportunity to get to know baseball's new all-time home run leader over the course of his 21-year career. Thus, a lot of people have asked me in the last few days how I feel about Bonds breaking Hank Aaron's record. I certainly realize I'm in the minority on this, but I actually kind of like Bonds.

I realize he rubs many people the wrong way with his bouts of churlishness and self-absorption, but I've also learned that Bonds' bark is a lot worse than his bite. If you let him understand you are not going to be bullied during an interview, he can be delightfully charming, incredibly candid, and extremely insightful. Let's put it this way—talking to Bonds is 100 times more interesting than hearing the same filtered stuff that the majority of executives, managers, and players in the major leagues have to say on a daily basis.

The best interview of my 20 years covering baseball came late in the 1990 season when Barry spoke for the first time on the record about his father Bobby, the former star outfielder, and explained why their relationship had been strained for many years. Bonds' willingness to admit he resented his father as a child for being away from home so much because of his job, and then spending too much time at the bar when he was at home, was simply extraordinary. His willingness to stand behind every word once the rather controversial story was printed, instead of hiding behind the usual "I was misquoted/taken out of context" defense, forever won my admiration.

On the other hand, it's hard to overlook the overwhelming evidence that points to Bonds using steroids to aid the latter stages of his career. *Game of Shadows*, last year's best-selling book, makes it pretty clear that Bonds had the help of chemistry to perform like no other player ever has in his late 30s and early 40s.

I'm not necessarily the world's most religious person, but I truly believe people should not lead their lives in illegal, immoral, or unethical ways. Sadly, it appears Bonds has. Thus, the whole thing has left me conflicted and, for one of the very few times in my life, without a clear-cut opinion on a matter. Part of me is happy for Bonds, who has worked as hard as any player I've ever been around, but part of me is also sad that he now sits atop the home run list under such a cloud.

David Pinto: Since Ken Griffey, Jr. appeared on the scene in the late 1980s, I've kept my eye on players' progress toward breaking Aaron's record. First Griffey, then Alex Rodriguez kept putting distance between themselves and Hank at the same age; they would need that distance to survive the falloff in their 30s. I looked forward to the record falling, but the controversy surrounding the players who emerged as most likely to break it in the late 1990s spoiled the moment somewhat. I'm glad it was Bonds and not Mark McGwire or Sammy Sosa, since Bonds is a much more complete hitter than either of those two. But I wonder if Barry had done this organically, and taken the training and nutrition route as Ruth did before his 1926 season, how many homers he'd have hit. He had the batting eye and the sweet swing. If he just concentrated on hitting home runs, given his extremely competitive nature, might he have made it anyway?

Bryan Smith: More than anything, I have felt for Barry Bonds in the last two months as he's come closer to eclipsing this vaunted record. Bonds is the subject of one of the worst displays of journalism the mainstream media has ever committed, and the widespread hatred against him is a result. Most of the media has too much interest in denouncing superstars rather than uncovering facts, like, for example, how many home runs Bonds hit off of chemically-aided pitchers. It was a disgrace for those of us in the profession of journalism, so I rooted for Barry Bonds in spite of the writers aligned against him. Perhaps, with the acceptance that the record is broken, the media will return to do its job and upturn the stones in this scandal. I certainly hope so.

Bonds is not the greatest player I've ever seen, and I'm not old enough to have seen Willie Mays or Hank Aaron. This contradicts most of what I've heard this week, as even those that dislike him seem to be calling him the best they've seen. Personally, I'd watch the 1990s Griffey or the shortstop version of Alex Rodriguez ahead of Bonds any day. But his ability to withstand this onslaught while achieving an elite accomplishment for career longevity makes him history's home run king. And, amazingly, it will put the public behind Alex Rodriguez when he attempts to break the record in about eight years. I'll be rooting for the record to fall then, too.

Best of Baseball Prospectus: 1996-2011   **Part 1: Offense**

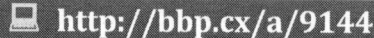 JUNE 30, 2009   http://bbp.cx/a/9144

BP FANTASY BEAT
Adrian Gonzalez
Marc Normandin

In-depth player profiles and analyses are of interest to fans, front office members, and fantasy players alike, and we've devoted an awful lot of ink, both virtual and otherwise, to producing them. Here's a prime example by Marc Normandin, which reveals how digging deeper into the numbers can illuminate a player's hidden value.

You don't hear much said about how good a hitter Adrian Gonzalez actually is. The main problem is his home park, Petco. Even though Gonzalez consistently performs better there than his teammates, the pitcher-friendly setting still drags down his overall line. That's why he has hit "just" .288/.357/.504 from 2006-2008 in spite of a very impressive .306/.367/.560 road line. The split is even more extreme this year, in Gonzalez' age-27 season: hitting .254/.428/.492 is great for someone stuck in Petco (the league is hitting a very ugly .222/.308/.351 there), but his performance on the road towers above that, as he's hitting .288/.401/.674.

Adjusting for context shows that Gonzalez is a beast at the plate, and one of the best hitters in the National League. You can't see it in his traditional numbers, however, which raises a few questions. How would Gonzalez do if he didn't have to deal with Petco for 81 games a year, and if he had a chance to check out that greener grass on the other side of the fence? There are a few ways to look at this, but what BP statistician Clay Davenport has done is give you Gonzalez' 2009 season to date, translated into a few other parks. Below we have his actual numbers, followed by what he would have done if his home park had been Coors Field rather than Petco:

Home Park	AB	H	HR	BB	SO	R	RBI	AVG	OBP	SLG	EqA
Petco	254	69	24	61	52	48	47	.272	.415	.587	.351
Coors	254	77	30	61	52	55	57	.303	.440	.701	.351

The bump in batting average is expected, given how many hits Petco takes away. The extra home runs, on the other hand, are something else. Petco is in San Diego, where the temperature is close to what Hit Tracker considers to be an average game temperature. This means that the ball does not move more easily through the air than it does in a neutral park—warm air is less dense than cold air, so the ball can move through it more easily and therefore travel a greater distance. Put him in Coors, a mile above sea level where there is less air resistance or drag on the ball, and his batted balls would fly further. Balls that didn't get any extra love from the air in San Diego would reach the bleachers in Colorado. Coors also has a higher BABIP than other parks due to the ball traveling farther, which is another reason that A-Gonz's average and slugging would shoot up.

Next we can see how Gonzalez would do not only out of Petco but in a different league. The new Yankee Stadium has been hitter-friendly during its initial months of existence, though it has punished pitchers less of late; that doesn't stop Gonzalez from hypothetically tearing up the American League:

Home Park	AB	H	HR	BB	SO	R	RBI	AVG	OBP	SLG	EqA
YS III	257	77	30	58	53	56	58	.300	.430	.696	.342

Gonzalez loses some Equivalent Average due to the relative difficulty involved in changing leagues—the American League is still superior to the senior circuit—but those raw numbers are still a sight. They're on par with what Albert Pujols has done this year, in what may be his best season yet. He doesn't have the boost from the lack of air resistance, but he's still well ahead of what your average hitter is doing in the Bronx these days (.267/.351/.466). By year's end, Yankee Stadium may have a different park factor, so if we were to run these same numbers in October, his line might not be this positive. Then again, his translation for a neutral park yields a line of .299/.437/.646, so it's not as if he needs much help, other than for someone to get him out of Petco.

It should be noted that these translations are an estimate of sorts, and that different parks work in different ways depending on what kind of hitter you're dealing with. If you have a guy who is going to go deep no matter where he hits, there are very few places where he can go to receive a major boost in production. For hitters who often end up hitting balls to the warning track, though, moving to a place like Coors is a great way to show superficial improvement. Gonzalez fits into both camps, as he's a serious power hitter who is hampered significantly by the dimensions of his home park. Sure, he hits better at Petco than most—check those league numbers again for reference—but as you can see by his translated numbers or even his road stats, not being at Petco would be best for his production.

The other issue Gonzalez is facing is the league itself. It's obvious at this point that opposing pitchers are scared of the havoc he can wreak, partially because he's just that good, and also because the rest of the Friars' lineup isn't very intimidating. He has drawn 10 intentional passes this year, which isn't too far off of last year's pace that gave him first base for free 18 times; if he finished with 700 plate appearances again, he would have four more IBB. Unintentional intentional walks are where it's at for A-Gonz, though, as his walk rate has nearly doubled, from 10.7 percent in 2008 (a career high) to 19.4 percent this year. He had 74 unintentional walks all of last season and already has accumulated 61 in 2009. This has also helped him cut down on strikeouts; he's on pace for 115 in 700 plate appearances, rather than 2008's 142.

Since the opposition has been loathe to pitch directly to him, he has cut down on his swings outside the zone, from 28 percent or more the previous two years down to 22 percent this year. He's seeing fewer first-pitch strikes and has swung at fewer pitches in the zone, as well, as he's either willing to get on base via the inevitable walk or waiting for a pitch that he can jack. Whether it intends to or not, the rest of the league may be making Gonzalez even more dangerous, as he can focus and wait for the pitch he wants. When a guy with his power is allowed to sit on his pitch, bad things are sure to follow when that pitch is thrown.

Gonzalez is under contract through 2011, assuming that the Padres pick up his club option for that year, so he's stuck in Petco where he can't do the damage he is capable of, which is a sad thing for those who are not fans of the Padres. If he were to be traded, even to a neutral park, you can be sure that you would see something special, without having to adjust for anything. For now, though, we can only hypothesize and dream about his performance in a more hitter-friendly park, which is fun in its own way.

PLAYER PROFILE
Nomar Garciaparra
Marc Normandin

Player profiles aren't just about the numbers: they also draw upon personal connections and history to provide a picture of how a player evolved from rookie year to retirement. After seeing much of Nomar Garciaparra's career first-hand, Marc Normandin encapsulated his career in the following piece.

As sports fans, we sometimes experience moments where time freezes: you remember where you were, whom you were with, and what happened with such clarity that it seems that it happened yesterday. It's a concept that may seem silly to those who have never invested themselves fully in a team or sport, but given where you are reading this, chances are good that you're aware of the phenomenon. For any of you who are Red Sox fans—especially younger ones—July 31, 2004 may have yielded one of those moments.

Nomar Garciaparra, still at that point one of the faces of the franchise, if not the face, was traded to the Chicago Cubs in a four-team, eight-player deal that brought Orlando Cabrera to Boston as his replacement at shortstop. To put it kindly, this was a bad breakup for the organization and Garciaparra, and it came out of nowhere to shock even the most attentive fans. Sure, his name had come up in trade discussions a year earlier, but that was when Alex Rodriguez, the highest-paid player in baseball, was reportedly coming to Boston. At least that rumor was on a level everyone could understand, with one star departing in a deal and another star coming back. The Red Sox traded away a player who had been an important part of their batting order since 1997 in exchange for a guy whose first failing was that he wasn't Nomar. Factor in the offensive comparison, and it's little wonder why so many fans turned on Theo Epstein and company without waiting to see how things shook out.

This trade was about defense, though, and Nomar was slowing down in that regard. The Red Sox felt Cabrera more than made up for the offensive differential with his glove, and that they could not compete at a high level without that upgrade. Contract discussions with Garciaparra were not progressing: the Red Sox made the mistake of letting Nomar know whom his comps were, salary-wise, one of whom was Miguel Tejada, a player Boston valued less than Nomar. When Tejada received a six-year, $72-million contract from the Orioles as a free agent the previous winter that was unexpectedly more than the amount Boston had in mind for him, the Red Sox knew

Garciaparra would require more money than they were willing to pay. This led to no deal at all and was one of the factors that prompted them to trade Garciaparra.

I was torn. As a long-time supporter of Garciaparra (his is one of the few jerseys I have ever owned), I was sad to see him go, but as someone who had an interest in the statistical side of things (and knew how highly Boston's front office valued statistical analysis), I couldn't shake the feeling that there was something to it, especially given the trouble negotiating his extension. Nomar wanted to be in Boston, and the Red Sox wanted him, but maybe neither of them wanted each other for the same reason. Nomar wanted to extend his legacy with the organization, as he was easily one of the most popular and productive players in franchise history. The Sox were a tougher call. Did they actually want Nomar back, or were they just trying to save face with their fan base? That may seem like a pointless or accusatory question, but let's remember how the last stars to leave Boston were treated—constant media rumors and whispers and dismissal by trade or half-hearted extension offer, always done in a way that put someone besides the Sox at the center of the issue. That's not meant to be a negative, by the way. Boston has it tough with the media in town and the team's demanding fans, and both parties want answers when a popular and productive player like Nomar, Manny Ramirez, Pedro Martinez, or Jason Bay moves on. So, it's understandable if the Red Sox occasionally do their best to make it seem like their machinations had more to do with the player than their own desires.

Whether or not trading Garciaparra was the right move, it was a bold one that put more pressure on the other hitters in the lineup to succeed on a daily basis but also set Boston's pitching staff up for more success in October. In a way, it relates to how the 2010 Red Sox are being built, and the doomsday cries coming from parts of both the fan base and the media bring me back to '04 as well.

When the trade occurred, I was hanging out where my friends and I normally did, at Planet Syrinx, a LAN gaming place in my hometown. We had just graduated high school a few months prior and were wasting away our last summer before college with rounds of Battlefield 1942 and Counterstrike. Sure, we could have been outside in the sunlight, but then I couldn't have followed the trade deadline. This was pre-Twitter and before smart phones seemed to outnumber regular ones, so I had to actually log out of games to check up on how the day's transactions were going—tortuous even consider, I know, but that's how things worked all the way back in 2004. When the news of Nomar's trade hit, everyone in the room stopped what they were doing to see and hear the details.

I remember calling my dad, who was also torn on the subject, but given that the 2003 Red Sox had been so close to the World Series, partially thanks to the same front office, he was also willing to be patient. My dad had always been a pitching-and-defense kind of guy, so when he saw Cabrera was coming to town to replace Nomar's errant throws and botched grounders, he was relieved in a way. He always felt that Nomar made some amazing plays but then booted or plain missed balls that were hit right at him. Whether or not his defensive shortcomings were overstated, it's hard to argue with the ultimate result of the trade, as the the Red Sox won their first World Series championship in 86 years by sweeping the Cardinals.

Nomar was a hero in Boston thanks to a strong career prior to 2004. While considered a good prospect who would become a quality big-league shortstop, Garciaparra turned it on in Triple-A in 1996, overshadowing his previous years in the minors, as well as his Olympic and college career. While Red Sox fans were a bit upset at first that he displaced John Valentin at shortstop, Garciaparra's production from the high minors carried over to the majors, and he won American League Rookie of the Year honors in 1997. He set major-league records for most homers by a rookie shortstop and most RBI by a leadoff hitter with 30 and 98 respectively, which easily earned him unanimous RoY honors. He was an All-Star, as well, and had a top-10 finish in the MVP race. Thanks to his name and the magic of the Boston accent, it was easy for fans to identify with "Nomah."

He would get better from there. In 1998, he was Boston's top offensive player and finished second in the MVP voting thanks to 35 homers and a line of .323/.362/.584. He was part of the "Holy Trinity" of shortstops that included Rodriguez and the Yankees' Derek Jeter, but that was just the start for Nomar. While Pedro Martinez was on the mound tossing some of the best-pitched games in Boston history, Garciaparra was in the lineup putting his previous campaigns to shame: in 1999, he was the focal point of the offense, putting together a .357/.418/.603 season. Nomar was so on that year that he was intentionally walked twice in Game Five of the American League Division Series against Cleveland—once with a man on base, and another time to load the bases. Both trips resulted in homers for the man behind him, Troy O'Leary, but chances are good that if you asked then-Indians manager Mike Hargrove today, he wouldn't change a thing about his strategy, despite the outcome.

If Hargrove would stick with his decision, it would be with good reason, as Nomar hit .372/.434/.599 in 2000, showing that 1999 was no fluke. Things started to go downhill from there, though. Nomar was hit on the wrist late in the 1999 season by a pitch from the Orioles' Al Reyes. While the wrist didn't affect his performance much at first (see: .372 batting average in 2000), it eventually became a problem. The wrist swelled during spring training of 2001, and when rest didn't allow it to heal, his production and playing time suffered, as he played in just 21 games and hit .282/.352/.470. The 2001 season would see Garciaparra rebound to record a .310 batting average.

Even as a younger fan, I could see what was causing part of the problem. Nomar's wrists had always been incredibly fast and were the main reason for his apparent ability to make the kind of contact he wanted whenever he wanted. When he hurt his wrist, his approach did not change. He still swung at everything he could put his bat on. However, without the same quickness in his wrist, there were a lot more fouls and pop-ups. Garciaparra's 2003 was similar to his 2002, but he struggled in the playoffs: zero homers and a .241/.290/.310 line from one of your star hitters against the Yankees sticks out when your teams loses in seven games in the American League Championship Series, especially when that star also strikes out eight times following a poor September.

That offseason brought the trade talks, which effectively ended any chance of Nomar and the Red Sox working on an extension. Despite a strong start on offense (.321/.367/.500, though in just 38 games) No. 5 was shipped off to the Cubs, where he was forced to be No. 8 until Michael Barrett gave up No. 5. It was a shock. Even when the Red Sox were celebrating their victory over the Cards, one of the things I wondered was whether Nomar would be sent a championship ring for his contributions to the franchise. Thankfully, his former organization decided that he should receive one.

The Red Sox were more convincingly vindicated as time went by, even beyond winning the World Series. Nomar tore his groin in early 2005 with the Cubs (tore and groin are two words that should never be in the same sentence, let alone one after the other), which was another injury that caused him to miss significant time. When he returned, it was as a third baseman to fill in for the injured Aramis Ramirez, though Nomar had volunteered to make the shift.

Nomar signed with the Dodgers for 2006 to form what was basically Red Sox West: Bill Mueller, Derek Lowe, and former Sox manager Grady Little were all in Los Angeles. Nomar was converted into a first baseman by the Dodgers because of his shaky health situation and declining glove. However, his bat was revitalized: Nomar hit .303/.367/.505 and made the All-Star team for the first time since 2003. Additionally, he had two walk-off homers while the Dodgers were fighting for a playoff spot that helped them secure October baseball in Chavez Ravine. On September 18, the Dodgers hit four consecutive homers in the ninth inning against the Padres to send the game into extras. The Padres went ahead in the top of the 10th, but Nomar hit a two-run homer in the bottom half of the inning to end the game. On September 24, he hit a grand slam to end a game against the Diamondbacks. For his efforts, he won the NL Comeback Player of the Year award.

That would be his final full and productive season, though, as 2007 saw him playing, but not particularly well, and he was pushed off first base by prospect James Loney. He missed most of 2008 due to various injuries: he had microfracture surgery on his hand after being struck by a pitch in spring training, strained a left calf muscle in April not long after his return, then was placed on the disabled list on Aug. 1 with a sprained knee to make room on the active roster for Ramirez, now a Dodger after being acquired from the Red Sox in a trade. Following the season, Nomar had a hard time finding suitors, but the Athletics signed him as a free agent in the middle of spring training.

Garciaparra wore No. 1 on the A's because Matt Holliday had laid claim to No. 5, though he eventually got it back when Holliday was traded to the Cardinals in late July. On July 6, Garciaparra returned to Fenway Park for the first time since he was dealt, nearly five years prior. The fans cheered before his first at-bat and even when he picked up the game's first RBI for the A's. This was one of the only highlights for Nomar in a season full of lows, as he appeared in just 65 games and had one of his poorest seasons at the plate. In a surprise move, the Red Sox signed Nomar to a minor-league contract last year so he could retire as a member of the organization. As a fan of both Nomar and the Sox, it was nice to see the healing process in action and watch one of my childhood favorites come back to the organization for whom he was a star.

He may not have been able to finish his career with the numbers of a Hall of Famer, but I prefer to remember all of the times in Boston when he hit like one. I was oddly jealous to see him succeed with the Dodgers, even for one year and despite the Red Sox's success without him. All in all, though, I'm glad that the rift has been repaired, and that Nomar ended his career where he started it, even if it didn't end quite like I thought it would at the start.

CROOKED NUMBERS
Playing With the Lineup
James Click

Fans love to debate the merits of a manager's lineup, but how much difference does the order in which the players appear make? James Click ran the numbers and came to some interesting conclusions.

On the radio in Boston yesterday, the hosts of a talk show asked me if I thought that Edgar Renteria would be a good fit for the second spot in the Red Sox lineup. My response was that yes, Renteria would make for a good candidate for the two spot because he has a good OBP; their theory was that he would make a good #2 hitter because he hits for contact. We briefly discussed the idea that the batter in the two hole should be a contact hitter, able to get the leadoff hitter into scoring position for the big bats behind, and the general theories that higher-OBP players should bat higher in the lineup to get them more plate appearances.

The more I think about it, though, I'm not sure that we know how much difference the lineup makes most of the time, or whether some of those conventional theories about lineup structure make sense. There has been work on lineup theory out there, from Keith Woolner's efforts to more advanced research using Markov Models.

The lineup is the part of the game over which the manager has the most control. Like the recent trends in bullpen management, however, it's so ruled by convention that managers really can't do anything that contradicts mainstream thinking without drawing the ire and consternation of fans and writers alike. When Tony La Russa starting batting his pitcher eighth instead of ninth to get more guys on base in front of Mark McGwire, he was lambasted. When the A's put Jeremy Giambi —who was as good at stealing as *The Shawshank Redemption*'s Tommy Williams—in the leadoff spot, the outcry from the media was even greater. Writers stacked soapboxes on top of soapboxes to scream about the essential skills that a leadoff hitter must have, conclusions drawn from years of experience watching and playing baseball.

A lineup's construction has two ramifications: how many times each player bats, and how those plate appearances interact with each other (for the time being, I'm going to disregard tactical matters such as alternating left-handed and right-handed hitters to mitigate platoon issues). The first effect is quite simple and can easily be estimated by average team performance and lineup position. If Barry Bonds bats first, he's going to get significantly more plate appearances over the course of the season than if he bats lower. Usually, that's a good thing, but the reason that Bonds doesn't bat first is the second ramification. Conventional wisdom teaches that the value of those extra plate appearances will be nullified by the fact that Bonds will frequently come to the plate with no one on base by virtue of batting leadoff or, later in the game, after the weaker hitters at the bottom of the lineup. His ability to advance baserunners with long hits is wasted.

In order to start to tackle the problem of lineup optimization from a more theoretical and mathematical standpoint, I've written a program that simulates games from a probabilistic perspective. This program is quite similar to something like Strat-O-Matic; it is given a large set of probabilities for game situations and it "plays" out the games, going through each batter and determining the outcome based on the given probabilities. A basic example would be the following:

- Single: .232 (23.2 percent)
- Double: .035
- Triple: .012
- Home Run: .002
- Walk/HBP: .069

The sum of these (.350) would be a player's on-base percentage (OBP). For a plate appearance by this player, the program will generate a random number between 0 and 1. If that number is less than .350, the player reaches base. If the number is between 0 and .232 (the player's probability of a single), the player is credited with a single. Similarly, if the number is between .233 and .267 (the sum of the probability of a single and a double), the player is credited with a double, and so on. The program then adjusts the game situation accordingly and moves on to the next batter.

By providing the program with a full lineup of player probabilities and then running the program for a full 162 games, we can approximate the number of runs a given lineup would score. It would be prudent to note at this point that there are a number of assumptions built into the program. First off, there are no stolen bases. Secondly, while there are several situations in baseball where multiple situations can result from the same inputs—e.g., if there is a man on second base when a single is hit, that runner can remain at second, advance to third, score, or be thrown out on the bases—because no speed component of any kind has been employed yet, the major-league average probability is assigned to each of these events.

With all of that stated, we can now begin to test various theories about lineup construction using the program. For each lineup, the program will run 1,000 seasons, producing a minimum runs scored, a maximum runs scored, and a mean. To establish a baseline, we'll use the major-league average for each probability for all nine players in the lineup, essentially seeking to determine what an average major-league lineup would generate in the program.

(Keep in mind that this result is not exactly intended to be identical to major-league run-scoring averages for several reasons. First, and most obviously, stolen bases, double plays, sacrifices, and other more specific game events have yet to be considered. Second, these simulated games will never go into extra innings. Third, park and opposing pitching effects are not calculated).

For each batter in the lineup, we will use the following probabilities:

- Single: .155 (15.5 percent)
- Double: .047
- Triple: .005
- Home Run: .028
- Walk/HBP: .095

Running through 1,000 iterations yields the results to the right, with minimum runs 657, mean runs 785, and maximum runs 923.

Here are the results for each player by position in the batting order. (The standard deviation of runs per season is about 77, a rather large number. More on this later.)

Thus, the program baseline for an average major-league lineup given the absence of auxiliary game factors is 785 runs. Of course, that says absolutely nothing practical. There's no such thing as a major-league average lineup, much less any team with nine identical hitters. However, it does provide a baseline for the program.

Batting Order	PA	AVG	OBP	SLG
Player 1	799	.260	.331	.415
Player 2	780	.259	.330	.415
Player 3	761	.260	.330	.416
Player 4	743	.260	.330	.415
Player 5	725	.261	.331	.417
Player 6	707	.260	.331	.416
Player 7	690	.260	.331	.417
Player 8	673	.259	.330	.414
Player 9	655	.260	.330	.415

To start addressing some more practical problems, changes to the players in the lineup must be made. In order to minimize the difference between the new players' output and the old, the new lineup will attempt to sum up closely to the old. In essence, home-run power removed from one hitter will be added to another. I'll also generate a group of players comprising a typical major-league lineup, not quite the Red Sox, yet not the Diamondbacks, either.

Players 1 and 2 are the higher on-base percentage players with little power; Player 3 is the big slugger; Players 4 and 5 are the more typical middle-of-the-lineup power hitters; Player 6 is a slightly less powerful hitter with a slightly higher average; Players 7 and 8 are the bottom fillers with little power but respectable OBPs; and Player 9 is a pitcher (we'll play NL for now, though it should be noted that using the DH in finding the average ML player does make this a slightly more robust NL lineup). Again, this team's total probability of each batting outcome is the same as that of the major-league average team above, just disbursed more normally among the players.

Batting Order	AVG	OBP	SLG
Player 1	.305	.361	.346
Player 2	.305	.361	.346
Player 3	.318	.398	.511
Player 4	.274	.350	.463
Player 5	.274	.350	.463
Player 6	.276	.334	.437
Player 7	.241	.325	.321
Player 8	.241	.325	.321
Player 9	.106	.166	.176

Running through 1,000 iterations yields the results to the right, with minimum runs 665, mean runs 801, and maximum runs 934.

From these results, we can see that this lineup does slightly better than the previous version, to the tune of 16 runs on average. Thus, conventional lineup structure, at least so far, seems to improve upon theoretical lineup structure slightly.

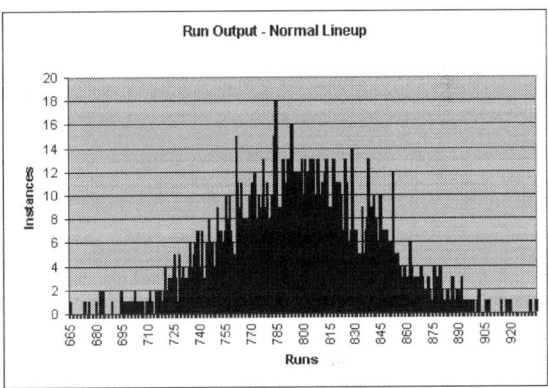

Now it's time to start mixing things up and having a little fun. In an effort to generate an optimal lineup structure, the first step is to verify some of the basic underlying principles. First, the idea that players with higher AVG, OBP, or SLG should be higher in the lineup can easily be tested. To avoid tainting the results, each player will have the same stats except for the stat being tested. For example, when testing AVG, each player will have the same OBP and SLG. The program will be given six different lineups, two for each of three "teams." Each of the three teams will have one statistic in which they all differ, and the other two will remain the same. These three teams will be analyzed twice, one with the variant statistic in descending order and once in ascending order. Further, the range of the difference in the variant statistic will be closely mapped to actual major-league distribution. So despite the occasional Bonds, the program won't have anyone with a .605 OBP.

After running each lineup, the program produced the following results. Below are the minimum number of runs, the mean, the maximum, and the 25th and 75th quartiles. From the numbers, a fair idea of the curve of each lineup can be gathered.

Lineup	Min	Quartile	Mean	Quartile	Max
AVG Desc	672	752	780	806	923
AVG Asc	662	755	782	808	919
OBP Desc	705	790	818	846	947
OBP Asc	660	762	792	821	926
SLG Desc	676	762	790	816	912
SLG Asc	656	747	777	805	926

To maintain the continuity of the two control statistics, the three different "teams" were not equal, so it's important not to compare across statistics. However, comparing the same teams with the different lineups is revealing. The two lineups with variant AVG produced nearly identical results, indicating that a player's batting average has little impact on lineup performance. However, stacking a lineup with respect to SLG and, to a greater extent, OBP, does seem to result in an increased chance of run-scoring.

Another tenet of lineup structure is grouping or bunching better players together. Generating lineups to test this is very simple: a team is created with only two different kinds of players, six average players and three superstars. The first iteration will have the superstars batting second, fifth, and eighth. The second will have them batting third, fifth, and seventh. The third will have them fourth, fifth, and sixth. By keeping them balanced around the middle of the lineup, the effects of having better players higher in the order should be reduced.
The following results came back:

Lineup	Min	Quartile	Mean	Quartile	Max
Not bunched (2,5,8)	792	952	985	1017	1154
Somewhat bunched (3,5,7)	857	953	986	1019	1136
Very bunched (4,5,6)	824	962	994	1026	1173

Looking at the quartiles and the mean, it's clear that bunching doesn't make much effect until the players are actually batting sequentially. Even then, however, the effect at the mean is fewer than 10 runs.
Getting back to that average lineup that scored 801 runs (with a minimum of 665 and a max of 934), we can quickly test some more theories about lineup construction.

First, let's look at Tony La Russa's infamous shift of the pitcher to the eighth spot in the lineup:

Lineup	Min	Mean	Max
LaRussa's Gambit	673	803	947

Not much difference to speak of; though the difference is slight, all three metrics adjust slightly upward. Next, let's try the idea that players with high OBP should be moved to the top of the lineup, regardless of their power numbers, to give them the most plate appearances while expending fewer outs:

Lineup	Min	Mean	Max
The Bonds Opening	670	797	934

While the difference is again slight, this measure seems to have decreased the potency of the lineup, though it should be noted that the hypothetical lineup doesn't have a standout OBP player to the degree of Bonds, and its initial structure was already quite close to a descending OBP strategy.

It would be interesting to add things like double plays, stolen bases, and baserunning skills to the program, but I'll save that for a follow-up. At this point, the most interesting conclusion to me is just how wide the runs-scored results set is for identical lineups. For the initial average lineup, the standard deviation was 77 runs; the distribution for other lineups were much closer to 40. The implication of this is that even if a general manager knows exactly what each player is going to hit in a given season, the 95 percent confidence range (typically two standard deviations) is about 160 runs. This is something that we don't talk about too much, but think about that: you know *exactly* how each player is going to hit this year and your team could win 84 games or they could win 100. That's just statistics for you. Yes, 65 percent of the time they're going to win between 88 and 96, but keep that in mind when you review preseason predictions at the end of the year.

With regard to lineup structure, this was far from exhaustive research on the subject, but it appears that bunching better players together and sorting by descending OBP yields the best results for run-scoring with similar lineups. However, the differences between those lineups and the traditional lineup structure are minimal. It's entirely possible that adding factors such as steals, extra bases, and left-right alternation may make enough of a difference to counteract losses in OBP towards the top of the lineup or bunching of the better hitters.

Back to the Boston question: will Renteria be a good #2 hitter in Boston this year? Renteria will be a good hitter. If he bats second, then he'll be a good #2 hitter, but it doesn't seem to make too much difference where he bats.

SCHRODINGER'S BAT
Getting Shifty
Dan Fox

Unorthodox defensive alignments have been a part of the game since its beginning, but before the advent of batted-ball data, it was hard to know when and against whom it made sense. Drawing upon those new sources of information, Dan Fox evaluated the efficacy of the infield shift and identified the batters against whom it would do the most good.

> "You know, they used to shift to right field for me too. But I could cross them up, choke my bat and poke shots to left. Ted never will hit to left until he learns a new stance and swing. The way he's swinging now he pulls too much to right."
> —Babe Ruth, on the "Williams Shift," September 1946

When asked what he did in the winter when there was no baseball, Rogers Hornsby famously replied that he would "stare out the window and wait for spring." Fortunately, these days fans of the game have plenty to keep them occupied in the cold winter months. Not least among the off-season events is looking forward to the baseball-oriented Christmas loot that keeps us busy until spring. While I can't claim the massive haul of our Jay Jaffe, I'll keep warm with a new Cubs fleece from my lovely wife and keep occupied with Lee Lowenfish's hefty biography of Branch Rickey, *Branch Rickey: Baseball's Ferocious Gentleman*, and Cait Murphy's romp through the 1908 season, *Crazy '08: How a Cast of Cranks, Rogues, Boneheads, and Magnates Created the Greatest Year in Baseball History* (both additions to my library coming courtesy of my in-laws).

But besides the holiday reading material given to me by my family, I treated myself to a copy of THT's latest book and spent several enjoyable hours poring over it. As you might imagine, I'm partial to the "Analysis" section, and although I wasn't particularly impressed with one of the essays, it was a section of the essay "Of Home Runs and Free Agents" by Greg Rybarczyk of Hit Tracker fame that partially inspired today's column. In that essay, Greg has a section titled "'Did Anyone Order a Center fielder?' Case Study: All Batted Balls by Torii Hunter and Andruw Jones," in which, as the title implies, he takes an in-depth look at the balls in play for these two players and in doing so mentions the idea of employing an infield shift against Jones.

The idea of other players who, like Jones, might be candidates for the shift, plus a question about the defensive skills of Ryan Zimmerman, and finally the concept of shifts in general, form the basis of the trio of related topics (which we'll take in reverse order) discussed in today's column.

Shifts and The Splinter

Like the invention of platooning which is often attributed to Casey Stengel and sometimes even to Earl Weaver, the history of repositioning defenders to deal with specific hitters goes back farther than most people imagine. On July 14, 1946, Lou Boudreau applied his famous shift against Ted Williams in the second game of a double header after The Splinter had hit three home runs in the opener and a double down the right-field line in his first at-bat of the second game. For many fans that event marked the introduction of this strategy. But in fact, as documented by Peter Morris in Volume I of *A Game of Inches*, not only had teams been shifting against Williams as far back as 1941, shifts are known from as early as May of 1877. It was then that a Louisville paper reported that the manager of the Hartford club, Bob Ferguson, would adjust his fielders by placing his second baseman on the left side of the infield for some right-handed pull hitters. He further refined the shift by incorporating a version of it for lefties, as reported in May of 1879, with others following suit from time to time over the next twenty years.

In describing one such shift in the first decade of the twentieth century, F.C. Lane, editor of *Baseball Magazine*, quoted Cubs pitcher Ed Reulbach regarding Phillies outfielder Roy Thomas in his compilation on offense titled *Batting*:

> He not only hit almost all the time to left field, but he was a short field hitter as well. This tendency handicapped him tremendously. When Thomas was at bat, the left fielder moved close to the foul line and came well in. The center fielder shifted away over toward left and at the same time advanced close up behind short and second. The third baseman moved over nearly to the foul line, and the shortstop followed him to a point at least fifteen feet beyond his natural position. At the same time he fell back and played a rather deep field.

He goes on to describe how pitchers like his teammate Mordecai "Three Finger" Brown would work Thomas (who surely was a "short field hitter," as only 160 of his 1,011 career hits went for extra bases):

> With this combination against him, Thomas was like clay in the hands of the pitcher. Mordecai Brown was a pitcher with excellent control and he doted on just such a situation. He would shoot over a fast ball on the outside of the plate and away from Thomas, who was a left-handed hitter. In nine cases out of ten Thomas was literally forced to hit the ball to left field. There were four fielders waiting for him instead of one, or at the most two. Thomas naturally realized the force of the conspiracy against him. But if he

tried to pull the ball to the other field, the nearest he could come to that aim would be perhaps to loop it over the pitcher's box.

Lane then goes on to point out that one effective way to battle the shift is to "hit hard," citing the case of Frank "Home Run" Baker who, as a lefty, was a dead pull hitter with considerably more power than Thomas. As Roger Peckinpaugh said of his own tendency to pull the ball:

> I admit I did not succeed in overcoming my natural preference for hitting to left field. On the other hand, I practiced hitting to that field, getting my full strength behind the ball. As a result I hit hard, and I don't believe my batting average suffered.

Another player who was regularly shifted against and who also refused to alter his style was lefty slugger Fred "Cy" Williams, a mainstay of the Phillies teams in the 1920s. As former opposing manager Bill McKechnie tells it, Phils manager Arthur Fletcher "would even order Cy to bunt toward third" but that "Cy would listen to Fletcher's pleadings and orders and then just go to bat and take his usual swing and slam the ball to right."

Although oft-derided by old-timers like Ruth, Ted Williams wasn't quite so proud and would occasionally attempt to hit through the vacated left side, as he did to end an 0-for-17 slump against Washington in 1954. Further, there is evidence that in his later years Williams perhaps wasn't the prodigious pull hitter he was when Boudreau and company first implemented the shift. Using Retrosheet data from 1956 through 1960 we find that Williams put 1,498 balls in play for which Retrosheet records a fielder or position to which the ball was hit (including home runs). The breakdown of his final five seasons is shown in the table below, where **CPP** stands for Center Pull Percentage, defined as the percentage of balls fielded up the middle (catcher, pitcher, center fielder) or to the pull side (third, short, and left for right-handed hitters, and second, first, and right for lefties). Also provided is an accompanying chart that shows the aggregate percentages.

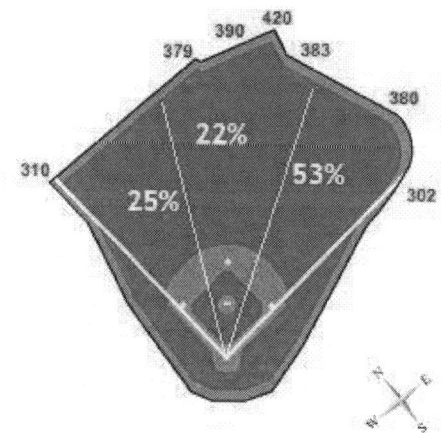

Figure 1: Ted Williams' Balls in Play Distribution, 1956-1960

Year	BIP	L	M	R	CPP
1956	341	28%	22%	50%	72%
1957	343	23%	24%	54%	77%
1958	332	27%	22%	52%	73%
1959	222	23%	24%	52%	77%
1960	260	23%	21%	56%	77%

So in his final five seasons, Williams hit the ball to the center or right side of the diamond three-quarters of the time, which turns out not to be all that different from the rest of those who swung from the left side during those five seasons shown in Figure 2. The biggest left-handed pull hitter during that time period was actually Roger Maris, who hit the ball to center or right 82 percent of the time and against whom I've not heard it said that teams shifted. From the right side, Harmon Killebrew was the most extreme pull hitter, doing so 85.6 percent of the time.

Figure 2: All Left-Handed Batters' Balls in Play Distribution, 1956-1960

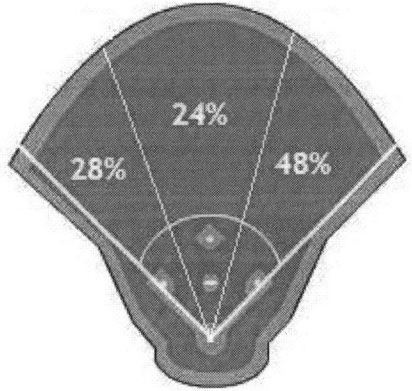

The similarities between Williams and the rest of the league's left-handed hitters in terms of balls in play distribution likely indicate that later in his career, either strategically or out of necessity as he aged, Williams did indeed look to spray the ball a bit more. Anecdotal evidence to support this notion can be found in this snippet from an article by *Boston Globe* writer Hy Hurwitz after Opening Day, on April 17, 1956:

> With his two doubles going into the left field area, and his single to center field, Ted hinted after the game he might go more to left this year to break-up the so-called Williams Shift.

The attention that the Williams Shift garnered ensured that variants of it would be tried on other hitters such as Joe DiMaggio and Mickey Mantle. It also made sure that the strategy would remain in almost continuous use for 130 years.

Let's Turn Two
From the perspective of the defense, the shift is utilized to raise the probability that a fielder will find himself in the path of the ball. What is less often remembered, however, is that this also has the side effect of forcing some fielders into unfamiliar positions.

This point was brought home recently when on our internal email list Christina Kahrl noted that Nats third sacker Ryan Zimmerman had been the pivot man on seven double plays in 2007. That factoid in service of larger points forms the basis for Zimmerman's player comment in the soon-to-be-released *Baseball Prospectus 2008*:

> Of the 33 DPs turned (but not started) by all major-league third basemen last year, Zim turned seven, the most in a single season of any third baseman in our database (going back to 1959). That was a reflection of Acta's aggressiveness in every phase of the game, as the skipper played the shift on lefty pull hitters more than any manager of recent memory, a gambit which paid off in part because of Zimmerman's shortstop-level athleticism. Six were 4-5-3s (three hit by Ryan Howard, two by Carlos Delgado, and one by Adam Dunn), and the last was a 6-5-3 hit into by Barry Bonds. Zim isn't perfect—he could do better charging bunts—but he's already among the best gloves at third in the game today, and he has the gifts to become one of the game's historic greats with the leather. ...

Those seven double plays represent an amazing 5.2 percent of all ground-ball double plays turned by the Nats when Zimmerman was on the field. To put that in perspective, since 2000 only 94 times has a third baseman made the turn at second on a double play (19 times in 2007, including Zimmerman's seven) representing just 0.3 percent, or one of every 330 ground-ball double plays. It should then come as no surprise that Zimmerman leads all third baseman in turning DPs on the shift with nine since 2000, while Eric Chavez (eight), Troy Glaus (five), Aramis Ramirez (five), David Wright (four) and Chipper Jones(four) are next in line.

While a double plays turned by a third baseman is a clear indication that a shift was put on for a left-handed hitter, we have no such clue in the play-by-play data for right-handed hitters. So although Vladimir Guerrero is the target of shifts from time to time, as he was when hitting against the Rangers in 2007, in almost all cases the scoring of double plays is not affected, and the shift is invisible in the play-by-play record. It should be noted, though, that shifts aren't employed as much against right-handers because the first baseman of necessity needs to remain within hailing distance of the bag. Looking at the other side of the coin, we'll find ten sluggers, all lefties, who are primary objects of the shift based on the number of shift double plays they hit into.

Player	Bats	DPs
Barry Bonds	L	12
David Ortiz	L	12
Jim Thome	L	11
Jason Giambi	L	11
Carlos Delgado	L	9
Ken Griffey Jr.	L	8
Ryan Howard	L	5
Adam Dunn	L	2
Mo Vaughn	L	2
Rafael Palmeiro	L	2

Because the sample size is very small and further complicated by managerial changes and unbalanced schedules, the play-by-play data won't tell us which managers used the shift most often. But for what it's worth, Washington does lead all of baseball in shift double plays turned since 2000 at nine, with the Blue Jays (eight), Mets (eight), and A's (eight) on their heels.

Bring on the Shift

As mentioned in the introduction, Rybarczyk dissects the 2007 balls in play for both Andruw Jones and Torii Hunter in his essay using his Hit Tracker analytical engine. Those familiar with his excellent site will know that his engine uses an aerodynamic model to recreate the trajectory of baseballs in flight in order to estimate the actual and standardized (taking out the effects of wind, temperature, and elevation) distance, the speed off the bat, the angle and direction the ball took, the apex, and the impacts due to wind, temperature, and altitude. Using this model, we can learn that Aramis Ramirez hit the longest home run in 2007 in terms of actual distance at 495 feet on September 21st, but the very next day Chris Young hit the longest homer in terms of standard distance at 476 feet.

In the essay Rybarczyk adds to his repertoire a model for ground balls based on dynamic friction and timing the ball from the time it leaves the bat until it is fielded, which he does in order to estimate speed off the bat in addition to direction for grounders. He then plots all of the grounders for both Jones and Hunter, noting their outcomes. After calling attention to the plots, he has this to say:

> The first thing that jumps off these plots is the distinct lack of hard-hit ground balls to the right side of the infield by Jones. John Dewan's "Stat of the Week" at ACTA Sports for April 27, 2007 [*actually it was April 24, 2007*] described Andruw Jones as a candidate for an infield shift, and this plot certainly supports that. . .

He goes on to note that of the 178 ground balls Jones hit in 2007, only three would have required normal positioning by a second baseman, and then argues that by moving the second baseman just to the shortstop side of second, *as many as 15* of Jones' hits could have been eliminated. While tools like my BIP Chart software (the 2007 ground ball plot for Jones is shown below, and you'll notice that he got eight hits up the middle in 2007) and the list that Dewan provides in his stat are evidence enough that teams should at least consider employing a shift against the likes of Jones, adding the granularity of the speed off the bat and more precise direction in terms of angle can either make the case air-tight or tilt the decision the other way.

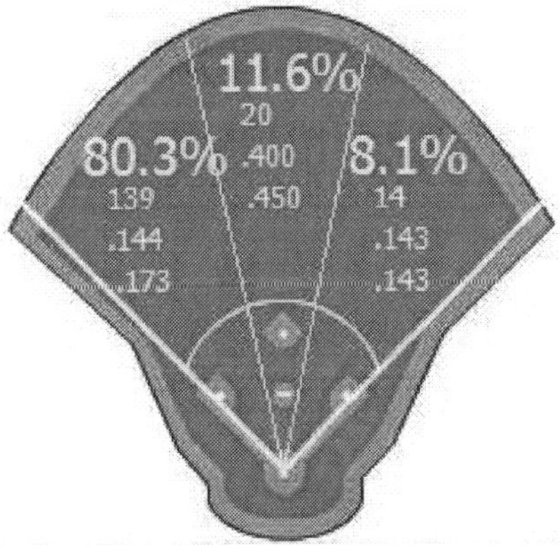

Figure 3: Andruw Jones' Groundball Distribution, 2007

We don't yet have such detailed data to pore through, but be that as it may, we'll finish up with a short list of candidates for an infield shift using the same data the BIP Chart software uses.

The first table below lists the top 20 players who hit more than 20 grounders (excluding bunts) and includes ground ball percentage (G%) ordered by Center-Pull Percentage (CPP). Keep in mind that CPP is not the same as a strict pull percentage, since a ball fielded by the center fielder may in fact pass through the infield on either side of second base.

Player	Bats	Year	GB	G%	CPP
Brad Eldred	R	2005	35	.190	1.000
Alejandro Freire	R	2005	25	.250	1.000
Jose Cruz Jr.	L	2006	49	.433	.980
Nick Swisher	R	2005	35	.167	.971
David Dellucci	L	2007	61	.214	.967
Mike Mahoney	R	2005	28	.400	.964
Doug Mirabelli	R	2007	27	.304	.963
Mark Bellhorn	R	2005	25	.261	.960
Chris Young	R	2006	25	.294	.960
Eli Marrero	R	2006	24	.211	.958
Franklin Gutierrez	R	2006	47	.417	.957
Chris Heintz	R	2007	23	.571	.957
Aaron Guiel	L	2006	41	.313	.951
Eli Marrero	R	2005	40	.320	.950
Carlos Beltran	R	2005	38	.425	.947
Morgan Ensberg	R	2007	75	.246	.947
Craig Wilson	R	2005	56	.269	.946
Kelly Stinnett	R	2005	35	.344	.943
Russell Branyan	L	2005	35	.176	.943
Jose Cruz Jr.	L	2005	86	.299	.942

There are three interesting things about this list.

- The dead pull hitters do not include Andruw Jones.
- The percentages are higher than I had expected; Brad Eldred and the little-remembered Alejandro Freire managed to "center pull" every ground ball in 2005, and Jose Cruz Jr. managed to do so in 49 of 50 tries when batting left-handed
- Two-thirds of the 20 hitters are right-handed

The first two observations can be explained by the fact that all of these players were either part-timers or switch-hitters, so if we restrict our list to players who hit 150 or more grounders in a season, as shown in the table below, we find that Jones makes the list in each of the three seasons but also that that Jason Bay and Mike Cameron become prime candidates for an infield shift. As previously noted, with right-handed hitters teams will naturally be more wary to use an extreme shift, since the first baseman cannot afford to move too far toward second base.

Player	Bats	Year	GB	G%	CPP
Jason Bay	R	2006	175	.288	.931
Mike Cameron	R	2007	154	.279	.929
Morgan Ensberg	R	2005	154	.282	.929
Andruw Jones	R	2007	173	.236	.919
Andruw Jones	R	2006	180	.259	.917
Khalil Greene	R	2007	177	.206	.915
Jimmy Rollins	L	2006	193	.305	.907
Chris Young	R	2007	157	.292	.904
Melvin Mora	R	2005	166	.308	.904
Adam LaRoche	L	2007	164	.257	.902
Jason Bay	R	2005	171	.240	.901
Craig Monroe	R	2006	160	.277	.900
Jason Bay	R	2007	154	.263	.896
Mike Lowell	R	2006	200	.255	.895
Curtis Granderson	L	2006	168	.316	.893
Alex Rodriguez	R	2005	213	.381	.892
Mike Cameron	R	2006	157	.331	.892
Garrett Atkins	R	2007	166	.253	.892
Andruw Jones	R	2005	201	.227	.891
Alex Rodriguez	R	2007	199	.290	.889

As far as the third observation goes, it should be remembered that right-handed hitters naturally pull grounders more frequently. From 2003-07 they center-pulled 79.1 percent of ground balls, whereas left-handed hitters did so only 76 percent of the time. When coupled with the greater percentage of right-handed hitters in the league as a whole, you get a predominance of right-handers in the sample above (59 percent). The next lefty who makes the list, at spots 25 and 31, is Grady Sizemore at 88.4 percent in 2006 and then 88 percent in 2007.

Finally, let's take a peek at the aggregated 2005-through-2007 CPP leaders among players who hit 250 or more ground balls:

Player	Bats	GB	G%	CPP
Morgan Ensberg	R	342	.272	.930
Eric Hinske	L	285	.266	.912
Jason Bay	R	500	.263	.910
Andruw Jones	R	554	.241	.908
Khalil Greene	R	410	.245	.907
David Dellucci	L	269	.263	.903
Nick Swisher	L	300	.238	.890
Alex Rodriguez	R	603	.333	.889
Moises Alou	R	418	.326	.888
Mike Cameron	R	405	.321	.886
Mike Piazza	R	386	.279	.886
Craig Monroe	R	499	.298	.886
Jimmy Rollins	L	532	.298	.876
Pedro Feliz	R	618	.286	.874
Adam LaRoche	L	467	.221	.872
Corey Hart	R	252	.352	.869
Curtis Granderson	L	390	.289	.864
Jeff Kent	R	439	.264	.861
Troy Glaus	R	387	.259	.860
Edwin Encarnacion	R	357	.301	.860

Morgan Ensberg takes the top spot at 93 percent, while lefty Eric Hinske (91.2 percent) takes second. As Dewan mentions, Jimmy Rollins has a tendency to roll over on the ball when batting left-handed, although it turns out that when batting right-handed he center-pulls 90 percent of the time. (He had just 227 grounders and consequently didn't make the cutoff). Here we also see new White Sox outfielder Nick Swisher when he's batting from the left side, as well as everyday lefties Curtis Granderson (86.4 percent) and Adam LaRoche (87.2 percent)

Come on Baby, Let's Do the Shift

Given the relatively high percentages shown here and the ever-increasing ability to accurately track hit balls along several axes (as illustrated in Rybarczyk's essay), you would expect that defenses would in fact become more specialized in their fielder placement in the future. This is analogous to the promise of more targeted pitch selection as technologies like PITCHf/x become available. Fortunately for us lucky fans, all of these strategic innovations will continue to increase the level at which the game is played.

Acknowledgements: The short but wonderful thread titled "The Ted Williams Shift" on Baseball Fever.com included scans of several of the articles mentioned here.

BASEBALL PROSPECTUS BASICS
Stolen Bases and How to Use Them
Joe Sheehan

The stolen base is one of the most exciting plays in baseball, and it's also one of the ways that a manager can make his impact felt. However, as Joe Sheehan observed, stolen bases can do more harm than good if they're not employed with some understanding of the risks and probabilities involved.

Think of stealing bases as a bit like one of those commercials for breakfast cereal. You know, the ones where they say it takes 14 bowls of Cereal X to equal what you get from one bowl of Cereal Y. In this case, it takes three stolen bases to equal one walk of shame back to the dugout. If you're stealing at less than a 75 percent success rate, you're better off never going at all.

Consider the run-expectation table from 2003. A runner on first with no one out is worth .9116 runs. A successful steal of second base with no one out would bump that to 1.1811 runs, a gain of .2695 expected runs. If that runner is caught, however, the expectation —now with one out and no one on base—drops to .2783, a loss of .6333 expected runs. That loss is about 2.3 times the potential gain.

Men on	0 out	1 out	2 out
none	0.5219	0.2783	0.1083
1st	0.9116	0.5348	0.2349
2nd	1.1811	0.7125	0.3407
1st 2nd	1.5384	0.9092	0.4430
3rd	1.3734	1.0303	0.3848
1st 3rd	1.8807	1.2043	0.5223
2nd 3rd	2.0356	1.4105	0.5515
1st 2nd 3rd	2.4366	1.5250	0.7932

Not all steals come with a runner on first and no one out, of course, and there's a lot of math that goes into the 75 percent conclusion. The main point is that in considering stealing bases, you have to consider both the benefit and the cost. In all but the most specific situations, outs are more valuable than bases, which is why the break-even point for successful base-stealing is so high.

Much of the frustration "statheads" have with base-stealing isn't that it's happening but with how teams misuse the tactic. You want to steal bases when:

- The value of one run is of great importance. In general, one-run strategies—steals, bunts, the hit-and-run—are overused early in games. Especially in today's game, teams aren't willing enough to give themselves a chance at a big inning, and they cut off a rally with a caught stealing where no attempt would have been the best choice.

- The batter at the plate is a double-play threat. Stealing makes more sense with a right-handed batter up than a left-handed one, and with a groundball hitter up rather than a strikeout or flyball hitter.

- The batter at the plate is much more likely to score the runner from second than he is from first. Teams will often use their best base stealers at the top of the lineup, even players with low on-base percentages, in front of their most powerful batters. In fact, they should be using those players lower in the lineup, in front of their least powerful hitters. Risking an out to advance from first base to second base is much more important when the guy at the plate can't get the runner home from first base.

The vaunted secondary effects of stealing bases—distracting the pitcher, putting pressure on the defense—do not appear to exist. In fact, most secondary effects argue in favor of keeping the runner on first base. A runner on first is more disruptive to a defense, with the first baseman holding and the second baseman cheating toward second for a double play, than a runner on second. Additionally, studies show that stolen-base attempts negatively impact the performance of the batter at the plate, presumably due to hitters getting themselves into negative counts by taking pitches or swinging at bad balls to protect the runner.

While you can use stealing bases to assist in run scoring, you can't run your way into a good offense. The core elements of offense are getting on base and advancing runners on hits. Teams—more often managers—that announce plans to create more runs by stealing bases are usually saying, "we can't hit, and we hope that if we move around a lot, no one will notice." It won't work.

Here are the top basestealing teams since the 1993 expansion:

Rank	Year	Team	Steals	Runs	Lg Rank
1	1993	Expos	228	732	7
2	1996	Rockies	201	961	1
3	1996	Royals	195	746	14
4	1997	Reds	190	651	14
4	1995	Reds	190	747	2
6	1998	Blue Jays	184	816	8
7	1996	Astros	180	753	8
8	2002	Marlins	177	699	12
9	1995	Astros	176	747	3
10	1999	Padres	174	710	15
10	2001	Mariners	174	927	1
12	1996	Reds	171	778	2
12	1997	Astros	171	777	5
14	1993	Blue Jays	170	847	2
15	1993	Angels	169	684	13
16	2000	Marlins	168	731	14
17	1999	Dodgers	167	793	11
18	1999	Astros	166	823	8
19	1999	Reds	164	865	4
19	1997	Cardinals	164	689	11

Stealing a lot of bases doesn't have anything to do with having a good offense. Here's the flip side:

Rank	Year	Team	Runs	Steals	Lg Rank
1	1999	Indians	1009	147	1
2	1996	Mariners	993	90	9
3	2000	White Sox	978	119	4
4	2000	Rockies	968	131	3
5	1998	Yankees	965	153	2
6	1996	Rockies	961	201	1
6	2003	Red Sox	961	88	9
8	1996	Indians	952	160	2
9	2000	Indians	950	113	5
10	1996	Orioles	949	76	12
11	2000	A's	947	40	14
12	1999	Rangers	945	111	6
13	1998	Rangers	940	82	13
14	2000	Astros	938	114	5
15	1996	Red Sox	928	91	8
15	1996	Rangers	928	83	11
17	2001	Mariners	927	174	1
18	2000	Giants	925	79	13
18	1997	Mariners	925	89	10
20	1997	Rockies	923	137	6

There looks to be a little more of a relationship here, which can be attributed to good offenses having more runners on base and therefore more opportunities to steal. Certainly, though, a number of these teams eschewed the stolen base and yet still ranked among the best offenses of the period.

One last note that deserves mention: for all the attention the running teams of Whitey Herzog got—teams that were successful more because of their high OBPs than their stealing—the unheralded master of the running game is Lou Piniella. In his career as a manager, Piniella's teams have almost always been among the league leaders in stolen-base percentage.

Piniella identifies the guys who can steal bases at a high rate of success and lets them run, while not wasting outs with the other guys. That's how you use the stolen base as a weapon.

Piniella managed the Yankees for their first 93 games. Stats listed are for the full season.

Year	Team	SB	CS	Pct.	Rank	Lg.
2003	TBY	142	42	77.1%	3	70.0%
2002	SEA	137	58	70.3%	5	68.1%
2001	SEA	174	42	80.6%	1	71.0%
2000	SEA	122	56	68.5%	7	68.8%
1999	SEA	130	45	74.3%	3	68.0%
1998	SEA	115	39	74.7%	1	69.0%
1997	SEA	89	40	69.0%	5	67.3%
1996	SEA	90	39	69.8%	6	69.6%
1995	SEA	110	41	72.8%	3	69.4%
1994	SEA	48	21	69.6%	8	69.0%
1993	SEA	91	68	57.2%	12	64.0%
1992	CIN	125	65	65.8%	8	67.8%
1991	CIN	124	56	68.9%	3	67.1%
1990	CIN	166	66	71.6%	6	71.1%
1988*	NYY	146	39	78.9%	1	68.7%
1987	NYY	105	43	70.9%	6	69.2%
1986	NYY	139	48	74.3%	1	65.9%
	TOT	1903	808	70.2%		

SCHRODINGER'S BAT
The Running Man
Dan Fox

As exciting as the stolen base can be, there's much more to baserunning than simply swiping bags: how a player handles himself on the bases when the ball is in play matters, too. In the piece reproduced below, Dan Fox explained his framework for evaluating a player's total contributions with his legs and identifies the best and worst on the bases.

> "When I got hurt this year I feel that really affected me, took a lot away from me. I wasn't able to steal bases. Every time I hit the ball in the hole I wasn't able to run. I just couldn't run. It's kind of frustrating because you feel like you would have done a better job. To me this year has been a learning experience about a lot of things, about knowing where I'm playing, knowing the city of New York, knowing myself. I feel good with it."
> —Carlos Beltran on his 2005 season

So we've finally reached a turning point in our series on quantifying baserunning. Since mid-July we've developed a methodology and framework for crediting baserunners for advancing on ground outs (Equivalent Ground Advancement Runs, or EqGAR), advancing on outs in the air (Equivalent Air Advancement Runs, or EqAAR), and attempted stolen bases as well as pick-offs (Equivalent Stolen Base Runs, or EqSBR). This week we'll look at the total picture and evaluate which players got the most and least from their legs over the past six years.

Adding to the Toolbox

To get those readers up to speed who may not have seen this framework before, the final piece of the puzzle is crediting runners with advancing on hits. To that end we can use the same basic methodology we did when creating the other metrics by relying on the Run Expectancy matrix. Simply put, we'll credit or debit runners for changes in Run Expectancy in the following scenarios:

- Runner on first, second not occupied, and the batter singles
- Runner on second, third not occupied, and the batter singles
- Runner on first, second not occupied, and the batter doubles

In each scenario we create a table that shows how often runners typically advance to each subsequent base or get thrown out; this will be broken down by the number of outs, handedness of the batter, and the position of the fielder who fielded the ball.

As we saw with advancing on ground and air outs, the probabilities of advancing and the number of bases a runner can advance change dramatically as the number of outs and the position of the fielder change. For example, when a batter singles with nobody out and a runner on second, the runner reaches third around 55 percent of the time and scores 45 percent of the time. With two outs, however, those probabilities change to 6 percent and 89 percent, respectively, with an increasing percentage of the runners getting thrown out (less than 1 percent up to 5 percent).

Totaling the credit assigned to each opportunity (and not crediting the runner for advancing the minimum number of bases) for players and teams allows us to assign a number of theoretical runs above and beyond what a typical player or team would have contributed given the same opportunities. Finally, as we did when looking at advancing on outs in the air, we apply a park factor in order to take into account the fact that at some parks it is easier or more difficult to advance given the dimensions or configuration (wall height, for example).

Some readers will recall that this is essentially the framework I published last fall in an essay in *The Hardball Times Baseball Annual 2006* with the metric called Incremental Runs (IR) and its associated rate statistic, Incremental Run Percentage (IRP). Since that time, I've made a couple small refinements to the framework and have recalculated the park factor to equally weight all of the previous six years' worth of data in order to smooth it out a bit. Along with those changes, we'll also take this opportunity to rechristen IR, Equivalent Hit Advancement Runs (EqHAR) so that it fits nicely into our toolbox.

It should be mentioned that EqHAR is essentially the same in both methodology and in what it attempts to quantify as James Click's metric discussed in the 2005 Baseball Prospectus annual. Both systems were being developed at the same time.

Let's take a look at the leaders and trailers in EqHAR for 2005, as well as the individual leader and trailer for each of the six seasons in our study. The table below lists the number of opportunities, the number of times the runner was thrown out advancing, the number of runs we credited them with, and a rate statistic that removes the bias associated with a greater number of opportunities.

2005 Leaders and Trailers in EqHAR

Name	Opp	OA	EqHAR	Rate
Carlos Beltran	45	1	3.53	1.66
Robinson Cano	54	1	3.36	1.49
Edgar Renteria	49	0	3.21	1.37
Grady Sizemore	59	0	3.14	1.31
Darin Erstad	59	0	2.99	1.38
David DeJesus	50	0	2.99	1.47
Scott Podsednik	45	0	2.98	1.43
Rafael Furcal	52	0	2.94	1.38
Julio Lugo	58	0	2.85	1.40
David Wright	41	0	2.82	1.39

Name	Opp	OA	EqHAR	Rate
Pat Burrell	34	4	-5.60	0.17
Luis Gonzalez	44	4	-5.33	-0.05
Lance Berkman	37	3	-4.56	0.00
David Ortiz	41	1	-4.12	0.25
Bengie Molina	34	0	-4.06	0.22
Mark Loretta	46	4	-4.02	0.58
Matt Lawton	49	3	-3.70	0.40
Kevin Millar	47	1	-3.59	0.34
Aramis Ramirez	45	2	-2.82	0.57
Rickie Weeks	30	5	-2.81	0.46

Yearly Leaders and Trailers in EqHAR

Year	Name	Opp	OA	EqHAR	Rate
2000	Luis Castillo	57	0	4.78	1.52
2001	Juan Pierre	41	0	4.04	1.81
2002	David Eckstein	60	0	3.66	1.52
2003	Raul Ibanez	55	0	4.75	1.54
2004	Vernon Wells	34	0	4.90	1.73
2005	Carlos Beltran	45	1	3.53	1.66

Year	Name	Opp	OA	EqHAR	Rate
2000	Joe Randa	50	2	-3.91	0.42
2001	Adrian Beltre	25	4	-4.59	-0.14
2002	Frank Thomas	40	4	-5.17	0.08
2003	Jim Thome	51	3	-5.15	0.49
2004	Bill Mueller	47	3	-5.17	0.29
2005	Pat Burrell	34	4	-5.60	0.17

From these lists it's apparent that at the extremes EqHAR falls roughly in the +5 to -5 range, or the equivalent of about one win, putting it in the same category as EqSBR in terms of magnitude, as shown below.

Magnitude of Baserunning Metrics / Single Player, Single Year

Metric	Min	Max
EqGAR	-1.50	4.00
EqAAR	-3.00	2.00
EqSBR	-6.00	5.00
EqHAR	-5.00	5.00

Interestingly, EqSBR actually has a slightly larger range on the negative side since there are more potential opportunities for stolen base attempts, coupled with the fact that some players don't know when to quit (see Guerrero, Vladimir). Both EqSBR and EqHAR, however, have larger ranges than EqGAR and EqAAR. This reflects two primary factors. First, there are a greater number of opportunities available to runners in terms of stolen base attempts and advancing on hits. The leaders in EqHAR and EqSBR typically had more than 50 opportunities in the 2000-2005 time period while those for EqGAR had slightly fewer; for EqAAR it's in the 30s.

Second, the success rates for EqHAR and EqSBR are such that good (or bad) baserunners have a bit more room to distance themselves from the pack. For example, with EqAAR almost all runners score from third on fly balls and so the difference between a good runner and one who is merely average is compressed to less than 5 percent. On the other hand, with EqHAR a good runner may take 16 to 20 percent more bases than an average one in a given scenario (for example, when advancing from first to third on a single).

But as we mentioned earlier in this series, those seasonal ranges don't mean that the best players and worst baserunners over the six-year span will be credited with -30 to +30 runs. As with any metric, part of the derived value simply reflects random variation, and that variation—combined with the fact that the same players don't necessarily end up at the top and bottom each season—means that over the entire period that span between the leaders and trailers is on the order of 25 to 30 runs, or three wins:

Leaders and Trailers in EqHAR for 2000-2005

Name	Opp	OA	EqHAR	Rate	Name	Opp	OA	EqHAR	Rate
Juan Pierre	315	4	15	1.41	Edgar Martinez	178	3	-13	0.58
Luis Castillo	331	6	15	1.32	Rafael Palmeiro	231	9	-12	0.63
Rafael Furcal	272	3	12	1.33	Dmitri Young	181	10	-11	0.60
Ray Durham	249	0	12	1.37	Richie Sexson	153	6	-11	0.53
Mike Cameron	188	2	12	1.37	Juan Encarnacion	201	12	-11	0.66
Darin Erstad	288	6	11	1.23	Carlos Delgado	237	8	-11	0.73
Jay Payton	201	3	11	1.36	Rich Aurilia	185	9	-10	0.62
Carlos Beltran	253	1	11	1.27	David Ortiz	172	5	-10	0.63
David Eckstein	280	4	11	1.30	Bill Mueller	168	9	-10	0.58
Cristian Guzman	226	3	10	1.37	Luis Gonzalez	266	10	-10	0.77

Finally, and as mentioned previously, EqHAR also has a rate stat (calculated as the ratio of actual runs to expected runs); if we want to see which runners performed the best regardless of the quantity of opportunities (and remember, we've already controlled for the quality of those opportunities by comparing what they did against the league average for each situation they found themselves in and then park-adjusting the results) we can rank them according to rate:

Leaders and Trailers in EqHAR rate for 2000-2005 (100 or more opportunities)

Name	Opp	OA	EqHAR	Rate	Name	Opp	OA	EqHAR	Rate
Timo Perez	100	1	5	1.42	Richie Sexson	153	6	-11	0.53
Juan Pierre	315	4	15	1.41	Kevin Millar	163	3	-9	0.56
Raul Mondesi	126	1	6	1.38	Edgar Martinez	178	3	-13	0.58
Scott Podsednik	132	1	7	1.37	Bill Mueller	168	9	-10	0.58
Mike Cameron	188	2	12	1.37	Dmitri Young	181	10	-11	0.60
Cristian Guzman	226	3	10	1.37	Bengie Molina	140	1	-9	0.61
Ray Durham	249	0	12	1.37	John Olerud	130	5	-7	0.62
Jay Payton	201	3	11	1.36	Javy Lopez	104	4	-6	0.62
Miguel Cairo	125	1	5	1.36	Rich Aurilia	185	9	-10	0.62
Felipe Lopez	110	1	5	1.34	Rafael Palmeiro	231	9	-12	0.63

Of active players with fewer than 100 opportunities, Robinson Cano (1.49), David DeJesus (1.46), and Ryan Freel (1.46) also all come out very well.

This list once again highlights the situation where a player like Cano does well in one metric but poorly in others. In Cano's case, his EqHAR was among the leaders in 2005 at 3.36, while his EqGAR, EqAAR, and EqSBR values were at -1.13, -0.93, and -1.5 respectively, putting him on the negative side (-0.21) when you add it all up. This may reflect the fact that different skills are required to do well in the different metrics (for example, judgment may be more important in EqGAR and EqSBR than in EqHAR, where sheer speed is what counts most), or simply that random variation and small sample size is at work—after all, Cano had just four stolen base attempts in 2005. I would bet on a mix of the two, although it will be interesting to see how Cano stacks up this season.

And because I know I'll be asked, Bobby Abreu and Juan Encarnacion lead all players in getting thrown out on the bases in these scenarios at 12, with Lance Berkman and Matt Lawton close behind at 11.

Contributing with their Legs

Finally, we can now provide a more complete picture of baserunning. Today we'll focus on individuals, and next week we'll take it to the team level. First, here are the individual leaders and trailers for 2005:

2005 Leaders in Total Baserunning

Name	Opp	EqGAR	Opp	EqAAR	Opp	EqSBR	Opp	EqHAR	Total
Chone Figgins	53	4.52	39	1.79	80	-0.30	58	2.27	8.29
Jose Reyes	52	1.76	33	1.34	77	1.73	50	1.98	6.81
Juan Pierre	54	3.52	30	-0.07	75	0.82	56	2.25	6.52
Alfonso Soriano	31	-0.08	45	-0.07	32	4.92	42	1.10	5.86
Jason Bay	20	0.82	29	1.02	22	2.39	54	1.39	5.63
Marcus Giles	27	-0.59	41	1.75	18	2.04	42	2.29	5.49
Johnny Damon	42	0.66	54	1.66	19	2.84	66	0.04	5.20
Carlos Beltran	19	1.16	22	0.24	22	0.14	45	3.53	5.07
Rafael Furcal	41	0.32	38	-0.71	57	2.36	52	2.94	4.90
Ichiro Suzuki	47	0.55	38	1.49	42	1.23	63	1.34	4.61

2005 Trailers in Total Baserunning

Name	Opp	EqGAR	Opp	EqAAR	Opp	EqSBR	Opp	EqHAR	Total
Pat Burrell	19	-0.48	25	-0.69	1	-0.46	34	-5.60	-7.23
Brad Wilkerson	48	-0.80	26	0.09	19	-6.23	43	0.31	-6.64
Matt Lawton	35	-0.12	38	-0.30	28	-1.91	49	-3.70	-6.03
David Ortiz	22	-1.16	34	-0.73	1	0.09	41	-4.12	-5.92
Mark Loretta	20	-0.33	29	0.02	12	-1.29	46	-4.02	-5.62
Bengie Molina	14	0.51	16	-0.80	2	-1.07	34	-4.06	-5.41
Oscar Robles	20	-0.59	19	0.46	8	-4.26	26	-0.23	-4.63
Luis Gonzalez	16	-0.47	32	1.44	4	-0.03	44	-5.33	-4.39
Jeromy Burnitz	17	-0.28	35	0.41	12	-4.02	61	-0.40	-4.29
Carlos Lee	18	-0.78	21	-1.27	18	0.61	29	-2.64	-4.07

Again, you can see that although some players do well in all categories (Jose Reyes and Jason Bay, for example) there are others who excel in just one, like Alfonso Soriano.

You'll also notice that in total, the player who comes out on top contributes about 7 runs and those who do poorly cost their teams about 7 runs; historically, as shown in the next table, the leaders and trailers have a span of more like -8 to +8.

Yearly Leaders in Total Baserunning

Year	Name	Opp	EqGAR	Opp	EqAAR	Opp	EqSBR	Opp	EqHAR	Total
2000	Tom Goodwin	41	0.94	34	1.38	66	4.66	40	3.45	10.43
2001	David Eckstein	44	1.17	41	0.35	33	2.68	51	3.75	7.95
2002	Derek Jeter	34	-0.61	39	1.55	35	4.20	56	2.70	7.84
2003	Scott Podsednik	38	1.66	29	1.21	54	3.14	44	3.16	9.16
2004	Tony Womack	46	1.59	33	0.68	33	2.12	55	2.55	6.94
2005	Chone Figgins	53	4.52	39	1.79	80	-0.30	58	2.27	8.29

Yearly Trailers in Total Baserunning

Year	Name	Opp	EqGAR	Opp	EqAAR	Opp	EqSBR	Opp	EqHAR	Total
2000	Vladimir Guerrero	27	-0.07	40	-1.00	22	-4.87	30	-1.77	-7.72
2001	Doug Mientkiewicz	31	-0.75	25	0.62	9	-3.23	43	-3.50	-6.86
2002	Deivi Cruz	27	-0.97	18	-2.08	4	-1.56	31	-0.75	-5.35
2003	D'Angelo Jimenez	30	-1.11	24	-3.51	19	-1.97	52	-1.04	-7.62
2004	Jim Thome	19	-0.41	28	-3.04	2	-1.41	60	-3.38	-8.24
2005	Pat Burrell	19	-0.48	25	-0.69	1	-0.46	34	-5.60	-7.23

To wrap up, we want to provide a first-order answer to the question of just who might be the best and worst overall baserunners in baseball since 2000. And so, without further ado, the following tables list the top and bottom 10 in total runs from the combination of all four metrics:

2000-2005 Leaders in Total Baserunning

Name	Opp	EqGAR	Opp	EqAAR	Opp	EqSBR	Opp	EqHAR	Total
Carlos Beltran	126	0.66	169	1.80	204	11.75	253	11.23	25.44
Derek Jeter	218	-0.51	252	6.93	149	10.59	317	8.09	25.09
Johnny Damon	258	1.78	265	3.15	217	9.03	322	9.40	23.36
Rafael Furcal	224	3.17	192	2.58	246	2.76	272	12.09	20.60
Tom Goodwin	90	2.59	83	3.74	147	5.15	97	7.43	18.91
Juan Pierre	279	9.37	204	2.91	378	-8.85	315	15.22	18.64
Tony Womack	201	4.26	178	3.18	219	2.68	224	7.65	17.77
Jimmy Rollins	212	3.49	180	3.28	223	1.69	243	8.62	17.08
Scott Podsednik	126	2.43	103	1.95	227	4.52	132	7.03	15.94
Darin Erstad	176	1.04	195	-2.23	136	4.10	288	11.43	14.35

2000-2005 Trailers in Total Baserunning

Name	Opp	EqGAR	Opp	EqAAR	Opp	EqSBR	Opp	EqHAR	Total
Jorge Posada	158	-2.67	149	-1.46	26	-8.08	199	-8.18	-20.39
Jim Thome	139	-3.12	129	-4.07	10	-3.74	222	-8.22	-19.16
Carlos Delgado	141	-1.06	177	-3.55	8	-3.65	237	-10.71	-18.95
Richie Sexson	104	-1.60	100	-1.73	14	-3.78	153	-10.83	-17.94
Paul Lo Duca	154	-4.16	133	-2.91	30	-6.09	190	-4.07	-17.23
Luis Gonzalez	133	-3.41	170	0.02	36	-4.00	266	-9.58	-16.97
Edgar Martinez	113	-2.97	142	-0.56	12	-0.55	178	-12.50	-16.58
Dmitri Young	132	-3.14	119	2.62	22	-4.95	181	-11.04	-16.51
Matt Lawton	185	1.65	198	-3.48	164	-9.32	258	-5.13	-16.28
Rafael Palmeiro	129	-3.92	159	0.22	15	-0.90	231	-11.50	-16.10
Juan Encarnacion	145	-1.61	145	1.60	113	-5.16	201	-10.73	-15.90

Carlos Beltran came out on top at +25.44 by virtue of his ability to steal bases at a high percentage and advance on hits. Meanwhile, Jorge Posada had trouble in all departments and ended up at -20.39. You'll notice that had Juan Pierre at least come out neutral in EqSBR, he would have taken the top spot. But still, the difference between the top and bottom is on the order of four to five wins, a difference far smaller than that between the best and worst offensive players and best and worst fielders. The upshot is that while good baserunning pays off and is repeatable (more on that next week) to a certain extent, its primary uses from an offensive perspective are probably more strategic than general—even the best baserunners seemingly cannot contribute a significant number of wins in the long haul. Not a surprising conclusion, to be sure, but one that is often forgotten.

Interestingly, although Beltran's injury last season affected his stolen bases and despite his comments to the contrary, it didn't appear to have quite the same effect on other parts of his running game, as his totals from each season show:

Year	Opp	EqGAR	Opp	EqAAR	Opp	EqSBR	Opp	EqHAR	Total
2000	7	-0.11	12	0.10	14	1.29	33	0.30	1.57
2001	29	0.20	31	-0.09	34	3.20	43	0.75	4.06
2002	18	0.38	26	-0.88	45	-0.33	39	2.47	1.64
2003	28	-0.80	31	1.80	44	3.69	42	2.40	7.08
2004	25	-0.17	47	0.63	45	3.76	51	1.79	6.01
2005	19	1.16	22	0.24	22	0.14	45	3.53	5.07

Alas, by adding up the metrics as we've done here, those on this list are heavily influenced by the number of their opportunities. To correct for this, next week we'll develop a rate statistic that encompasses all four metrics, discuss the relative importance of each, and perhaps even delve into aging patterns, how teams stack up, and any other interesting avenue we happen to wander down.

SCHRODINGER'S BAT
The Whole, the Sum, and the Parts
Dan Fox

Having developed a sophisticated system for evaluating the basepath contributions of individual players, Dan Fox turned his eye to the team level, identifying the best and worse baserunning teams and explaining the importance of baserunning in general.

> "This is not just a day off. Good baserunning is just as important as good hitting to win baseball games."
> —Lou Piniella, Mariners manager, on sitting infielder Jeff Cirillo following baserunning errors in 2002

When last we were together, we added up the various baserunning metrics we've been formulating all summer to come up with a total number of theoretical runs contributed on the bases for individual players. This included runs from advancing on ground outs, air outs, and hits, and runs contributed from stolen base attempts (and pick-offs).

What we found was that in a single season a baserunner may contribute from 8-10 runs over and above what would be expected or may forfeit an equal number, meaning that the spread between the best and worst runners was on the order of two wins. Over the course of the six seasons that were examined (2000-2005), a runner may contribute up to 25 runs and give up about 20. Using those raw numbers, we christened Carlos Beltran the best baserunner of the past six years at +25.44 runs, and Jorge Posada as the worst at -20.39.

However, we left unexamined two things: team-level performance, and what these numbers tell us about baserunning in general. As Socrates taught us, "the unexamined life is not worth living," so we'll delve into those topics this time around.

Pieces of the Pie
All fans love to grouse at the tube when their team has runners gunned down on the bases, picked off, doubled up, and thrown out stealing. But which fans have suffered the most (and the least)?

Best of Baseball Prospectus: 1996-2011

Part 1: Offense

The following tables list the top and bottom 20 teams in total number of runs contributed on the bases over the past six seasons First, the good:

Rank	Year	Team	Opps	EqGAR	Opps	EqAAR	Opps	PO	CS	EqSBR	Opps	OA	EqHAR	Total
1	2004	SLN	319	2.59	282	4.46	159	4	51	-5.76	447	6	9.19	10.47
2	2000	KCA	326	2.68	307	4.33	156	4	39	-0.68	461	8	3.48	9.81
3	2001	SEA	297	-1.06	320	2.80	212	7	49	-0.83	421	6	8.67	9.57
4	2005	NYN	289	2.40	246	-2.57	194	8	48	2.60	372	5	6.86	9.28
5	2005	ATL	313	-1.32	269	0.61	125	3	35	-0.09	392	4	7.99	7.19
6	2000	CHA	330	0.10	286	2.23	163	7	49	-3.35	390	6	7.70	6.67
7	2004	ANA	325	5.08	268	0.57	187	6	52	-0.98	489	13	1.96	6.63
8	2001	COL	354	3.13	251	0.74	188	10	64	-9.03	379	8	11.47	6.31
9	2000	COL	315	5.35	299	1.93	191	7	68	-12.45	445	7	11.28	6.12
10	2004	MON	316	2.54	236	-5.13	147	3	41	-0.50	373	4	9.16	6.07
11	2001	TEX	252	-1.33	305	4.24	130	8	40	-1.20	372	9	4.34	6.05
12	2005	TEX	244	-1.71	276	3.58	84	3	18	1.38	402	6	2.68	5.94
13	2003	OAK	289	-2.49	299	2.26	61	2	16	-0.25	401	11	5.23	4.75
14	2005	TBA	283	-1.66	277	-2.49	201	7	56	-5.33	447	6	12.42	2.93
15	2005	SLN	308	3.94	253	4.46	118	4	40	-8.83	448	6	2.62	2.19
16	2003	SLN	325	2.96	301	2.39	107	3	35	-6.60	478	11	2.74	1.50
17	2001	OAK	238	-0.95	275	2.58	98	4	33	-5.41	341	4	4.93	1.15
18	2004	ATL	299	-1.35	228	4.52	119	1	33	-1.72	428	8	-0.51	0.94
19	2003	NYN	322	2.14	240	3.29	105	6	37	-7.22	379	7	2.68	0.89
20	2000	CIN	304	2.43	295	4.49	139	7	45	-5.91	382	7	-0.45	0.56

Then the not-so-good:

Rank	Year	Team	Opps	EqGAR	Opps	EqAAR	Opps	PO	CS	EqSBR	Opps	OA	EqHAR	Total
1	2001	NYN	259	-1.16	297	-8.34	120	7	55	-20.72	328	12	-2.42	-32.64
2	2001	SFN	267	0.57	281	-4.68	103	5	47	-13.65	332	11	-12.23	-29.99
3	2002	MIL	339	-1.21	241	-4.92	155	13	63	-17.51	317	12	-4.51	-28.15
4	2001	BOS	266	-1.07	249	-3.03	83	4	39	-12.77	356	13	-10.39	-27.27
5	2005	WAS	326	-0.18	237	0.58	97	10	55	-22.49	392	7	-4.42	-26.50
6	2004	BOS	255	-4.67	299	1.12	100	4	34	-6.60	484	12	-14.80	-24.95
7	2001	MON	325	0.08	252	-2.74	154	8	59	-16.85	310	6	-3.74	-23.24
8	2001	PIT	299	3.61	255	-4.43	170	9	82	-26.71	285	8	5.72	-21.81
9	2005	LAN	312	-3.00	255	0.19	95	4	39	-9.71	396	12	-9.25	-21.78
10	2000	BOS	282	-0.96	324	-3.86	78	5	35	-9.97	381	10	-6.73	-21.52
11	2001	MIL	269	2.41	222	0.97	108	8	44	-12.72	311	13	-12.07	-21.41
12	2005	SDN	298	0.03	297	-1.23	153	12	56	-12.36	427	13	-6.51	-20.07
13	2002	CHA	254	-1.48	307	-3.35	116	13	44	-12.54	329	12	-2.60	-19.98
14	2002	SDN	312	-0.96	254	-3.91	114	5	49	-15.11	337	10	0.00	-19.96
15	2001	CIN	302	-1.09	231	1.04	161	8	62	-16.18	331	12	-2.22	-18.45
16	2005	PHI	302	-1.65	304	-2.37	144	7	34	2.17	447	18	-16.35	-18.20
17	2003	CHN	301	-2.22	273	1.50	110	8	39	-6.97	409	15	-10.33	-18.02
18	2002	ARI	304	-1.13	281	1.25	142	6	52	-12.35	340	11	-5.57	-17.79
19	2002	ATL	320	-2.81	272	-1.57	118	4	43	-11.67	337	8	-1.41	-17.45
20	2004	SEA	333	0.00	260	0.46	152	8	50	-8.23	488	10	-9.06	-16.84

First, it's apparent that looked at this way, teams don't really gain much from all their work on the bases. The top team, the 2004 Cardinals, came out just 10 1/2 runs to the good, or the equivalent of about a win. In fact, of the 180 teams in the study, only 23 accumulated positive totals. A quick glance at the list reveals that this is the case because the aggregate values for EqSBR are almost always negative and can be quite large in comparison to the other metrics. The reason? As a general-purpose strategy, stealing bases turns out to be a high-risk and low-reward endeavor, as evidenced by the matrix showing the positive and negative run values associated with stolen base attempts in the previous column. This means that in order to accumulate runs, an individual or team is required to be successful a very high percentage of the time.

Only seven of the 180 teams came out on the plus side in EqSBR (as shown below), with the average team losing a bit more than eight runs.

Year	Team	Opps	EqGAR	Opps	EqAAR	Opps	PO	CS	EqSBR	Opps	OA	EqHAR	Total
2004	NYN	320	-2.19	240	-1.79	132	3	26	4.47	360	11	-5.79	-5.30
2005	NYN	289	2.40	246	-2.57	194	8	48	2.60	372	5	6.86	9.28
2005	PHI	302	-1.65	304	-2.37	144	7	34	2.17	447	18	-16.35	-18.20
2004	PHI	315	0.77	269	-1.23	129	3	30	1.95	425	12	-9.30	-7.81
2005	TEX	244	-1.71	276	3.58	84	3	18	1.38	402	6	2.68	5.94
2000	CLE	280	-1.67	290	-6.41	143	2	36	0.44	395	11	-2.43	-10.07
2004	TBA	279	-0.30	293	0.31	175	5	47	0.40	398	6	0.06	0.47

The recent versions of the Mets and Phillies, along with these other three clubs, are the only ones to keep their heads above water in this regard, by minimizing their caught stealing and pickoffs and by selecting higher percentage running opportunities. Teams that run a great deal, like the Marlins of 2000-2003, usually do poorly and often come out with EqSBR values in the -5.00 to -10.00 range or worse. The poorest thieves were the 2001 Pirates, who in 170 opportunities were caught stealing a remarkable 82 times and picked off another nine times, which amounted to an EqSBR of -26.71.

That doesn't mean that stealing bases is always a bad idea. On the contrary it's a strategy that is sometimes the best option. It's knowing when to take those opportunities and with whom to take them that is the trick. In fairness (and as pointed out in a previous column), these raw stolen base numbers also include busted hit-and-runs, since there is no way to differentiate based on the play-by-play data, and that automatically drags down every team's numbers.

Getting back to the first table above, on the negative side, the 2001 Mets were at -32.64 runs on the strength of an EqSBR of -20.72. This points out that the range for EqSBR is on the order of +10 to -30 runs, repeating the point that the upside is clearly not as high as the downside is low. At first glance, the implication here is that even if a team works to inculcate good baserunning in general—as suggested by Lou Piniella at the start or by the attempt to do so earlier this season when the Rockies benched Matt Holliday and Jason Smith after their carelessness on the bases—

the advantage can easily be wiped away by attempting to steal bases in low-percentage and poor-leverage situations.

Attentive readers may have noticed that EqSBR is calculated slightly differently than the other metrics here. Remember that EqGAR, EqAAR, and EqHAR all are measured in terms of runs contributed above what would be expected, given the specific opportunities that each team encountered. In contrast, EqSBR is simply an accounting of total runs and is not base-lined by looking at what the average team would have done with the same opportunities. For most of the analysis, this is exactly what we want, since stolen base attempts are purely at the discretion of the offense. But if we wish to get a feel for the total magnitude of these metrics, we can instead simply show the total number of runs contributed in each area and reformulate our top and bottom 20 list in the following table where, for example, GAR simply stands for Ground Advancement Runs.

First, the good:

Rank	Year	Team	Opps	GAR	Opps	AAR	Opps	PO	CS	EqSBR	Opps	OA	HAR	Total
1	2000	KCA	326	26.75	307	46.66	156	4	39	-0.68	461	8	76.54	149.28
2	2001	SEA	297	23.04	320	46.11	212	7	49	-0.83	421	6	78.83	147.16
3	2000	COL	315	29.32	299	45.68	191	7	68	-12.45	445	7	74.96	137.51
4	2004	SLN	319	26.17	282	40.09	159	4	51	-5.76	447	6	75.75	136.25
5	2004	SDN	315	26.10	333	39.12	78	3	28	-6.16	490	9	74.70	133.77
6	2004	ANA	325	30.19	268	28.44	187	6	52	-0.98	489	13	74.57	132.22
7	2003	BOS	260	15.49	318	42.96	126	4	39	-4.76	475	7	76.75	130.43
8	2003	KCA	304	22.54	284	35.62	165	9	51	-3.54	490	10	72.26	126.88
9	2005	TBA	283	18.26	277	32.05	201	7	56	-5.33	447	6	81.32	126.31
10	2003	OAK	289	20.32	299	33.76	61	2	16	-0.25	401	11	72.16	125.99
11	2001	COL	354	31.04	251	30.64	188	10	64	-9.03	379	8	73.30	125.95
t12	2003	TOR	283	19.52	324	35.86	63	2	27	-7.63	463	9	76.84	124.58
t12	2000	CHA	330	20.81	286	37.57	163	7	49	-3.35	390	6	69.27	124.30
14	2005	OAK	259	14.38	320	28.15	54	1	23	-5.79	478	3	86.70	123.44
15	2005	ANA	321	33.55	265	24.34	218	5	62	-10.44	474	10	75.66	123.11
16	2004	COL	351	26.83	249	24.28	81	4	37	-10.34	445	10	82.27	123.03
17	2003	SLN	325	25.08	301	37.03	107	3	35	-6.60	478	11	67.34	122.86
18	2003	MIN	338	25.46	280	32.64	145	10	54	-8.88	461	8	72.78	121.99
19	2002	ANA	306	26.93	357	42.25	169	5	56	-8.71	437	8	60.10	120.57
20	2004	PHI	315	23.93	269	32.27	129	3	30	1.95	425	12	61.89	120.04

Then, the bad:

Rank	Year	Team	Opps	GAR	Opps	AAR	Opps	PO	CS	EqSBR	Opps	OA	HAR	Total
1	2002	MIL	339	24.05	241	21.53	155	13	63	-17.51	317	12	36.63	64.71
2	2001	NYN	259	16.21	297	19.67	120	7	55	-20.72	328	12	51.66	66.82
3	2001	MIL	269	20.84	222	25.44	108	8	44	-12.72	311	13	35.43	68.99
4	2001	MON	325	21.49	252	28.00	154	8	59	-16.85	310	6	37.80	70.44
5	2001	BOS	266	18.03	249	27.47	83	4	39	-12.77	356	13	37.72	70.45
6	2001	PIT	299	24.37	255	19.77	170	9	82	-26.71	285	8	53.90	71.32
7	2001	LAN	274	16.64	257	25.14	134	6	48	-8.60	292	13	38.40	71.59
8	2002	PIT	272	19.35	267	25.24	132	5	54	-12.50	294	5	39.83	71.92
9	2002	CLE	292	16.73	228	25.89	91	2	39	-11.20	319	8	41.02	72.44
10	2002	OAK	247	13.46	273	24.00	67	4	24	-5.24	351	7	41.57	73.79
11	2005	LAN	312	19.30	255	22.32	95	4	39	-9.71	396	12	44.75	76.66
t12	2001	SFN	267	18.98	281	32.20	103	5	47	-13.65	332	11	40.70	78.23
t12	2002	SDN	312	21.26	254	21.81	114	5	49	-15.11	337	10	50.27	78.23
14	2001	CIN	302	23.06	231	24.51	161	8	62	-16.18	331	12	46.86	78.24
15	2002	CHA	254	17.61	307	32.58	116	13	44	-12.54	329	12	42.25	79.90
16	2002	BAL	285	19.81	266	30.96	161	5	53	-7.11	297	11	37.39	81.04
17	2002	HOU	268	14.73	235	22.62	102	6	33	-7.63	365	13	51.80	81.52
18	2000	TBA	292	19.25	282	26.82	135	2	48	-7.65	352	11	43.95	82.36
19	2002	ATL	320	19.94	272	29.72	118	4	43	-11.67	337	8	44.57	82.56
20	2000	TOR	274	15.82	267	23.83	128	6	40	-4.01	385	10	47.29	82.94

One could interpret the tables above as indicating that the 2001 Royals cashed in approximately 150 runs with their baserunning, while the 2002 Brewers got only about 65. Unfortunately, that's not quite right. A better interpretation is that the aggregate of the actions by Royals baserunners in 2001 put their team in a position to score 150 more runs than they would have otherwise had they never advanced on the bases, tagged up, attempted a stolen base, or been picked-off—in other words, had they played absolute station-to-station baseball. The actual number of runs individual teams did gain from their baserunning is not what is being measured, since the run values used in the calculations are taken from the overall Run Expectancy matrix for the period and therefore simply help us model the impact of baserunning actions.

This does, however, give us the opportunity to sum each run value across all teams to get a feel for how important each metric is in its contribution to the running game. When this is done, you can chart the results to show the contribution that each makes to the total picture.

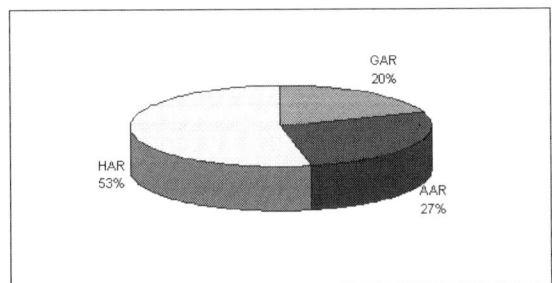

EqSBR is not in the total pie, since it turns out to be negative to the tune of 7 percent. The interesting aspect of this graphic is that while air advancement makes up a greater percentage of the pie than does ground advancement, air advancement is both more variable (and hence less impacted by skill) and has a smaller range which makes it more difficult for teams to capitalize on their opportunities. Advancing on hits is where the real opportunity lies, since it is a repeatable skill to a larger degree, and it provides the chance for teams to increase their run-scoring. That said, it should be remembered that the contribution of the running game pales in comparison to hits and walks, Piniella's quote above notwithstanding, and according to the analysis above, using the totals across all teams accounts for only 13 percent of the offensive output over the past six years.

Getting Older and Smarter?

Throughout this series, we've seen that players that do better in these metrics are generally faster than those who don't. During my chat session earlier this week one reader suggested correlating these metrics with BP's Speed Scores in order to find the speed threshold at which risk-aversion becomes the optimal strategy. Although I didn't appreciate it at the time, doing so would allow us to see which metrics are most dependent on pure speed and which on other attributes such as judgment. Alas, time pressures did not permit that analysis to be done this week.

Another way to do this, perhaps, albeit a little less directly, is to look at how aging affects the metrics based primarily on the assumption that speed decreases with age. To do this, we can simply group all the players by age and compare the rate statistics for each measure. This was done for ages 21 through 39 (those are the ages between which there were more than 1,200 opportunities), and is presented in the accompanying three graphs with the best-fit linear regression line thrown in for good measure.

As you can see, all three of these metrics show a downward slope, indicating that the younger a player is, generally speaking, the better he'll do. Looking more closely, you'll also notice that the slope of the line for EgHAR (advancing on hits) is greater than that for the other two, with EqGAR (advancing on grounders) coming in second, followed by EqAAR (advancing on flyouts). In fact, the correlation coefficients with age for the three measures pictured previously are:

Metric	r
EqHAR	0.86
EqGAR	0.80
EqAAR	0.48

This provides support for the view that speed is more important when advancing on hits than when advancing on ground and air outs. This makes sense intuitively, since players have more opportunities to take multiple bases on hits, which can better exploit their speed. As mentioned previously, the correlation between EqAAR and age is lower because there's simply more variability inherent in that metric. On the other hand, it might also indicate that judgment is more important when advancing on ground and air outs and is therefore a skill less diminished by the effects of aging.

We don't see quite the same kind of smooth trend for EqSBR as shown below using EqSBR per opportunity (since we have no rate statistic for EqSBR).

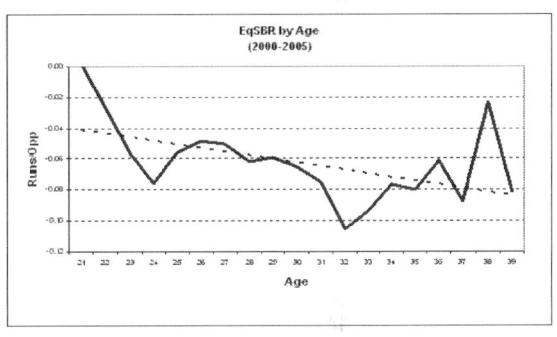

The likely reason for this bumpy track is that the combination of running only when the odds of success are good and running in higher leverage situations plays a larger role as a player ages. The increase after age 32 likely reflects a selection bias, as some players who remain in the league past that age continue to be productive (at least in terms of the league as a whole), if not prolific, base stealers, while the guys who can't run, don't.

Under the Tag

In an early article in this series, we began with a quote from Bill James from the *1984 Baseball Abstract* in which he lamented the fact that baserunning would be perfectly measurable if we simply tracked game events differently from the start. The last 20 years have seen revolutions in the collection of play-by-play data and in our ability to analyze that data. The happy result is that baserunning can be explored in more depth than ever before.

Part 2
PITCHING
Introduction by Mike Fast

From time to time, someone will write that baseball analysis has reached the point of diminishing returns, that we have learned nearly everything that we can learn about how the game works and that we are simply fine-tuning a few decimal places on our models. Is this so? I argue here that it is decidedly untrue, particularly in the arena of pitching analysis. The sweeping changes in our understanding of the game over the last decade ought to be enough to challenge the idea that we have arrived at the summit of knowledge. The articles in this section contain theories and knowledge from the mundane to the transformative, much of which was previously unknown.

The biggest, of course, is Vörös McCracken's discovery that the batting average on contacted balls in the field of play against a pitcher in one season is not very predictive of his performance in future seasons, as compared to the stronger predictiveness of his strikeout, walk, and home run rates—the Defense Independent Pitching Statistics (DIPS).

Much of the discussion in the 10 years that followed has tried to digest, expand, or qualify the DIPS theory. That might give the impression that we are mostly fine-tuning the work that McCracken did. Even if that is so, it is hardly an indictment, given the leap in knowledge that it represented. However, I believe that pitching analysis in particular, and perhaps baseball analysis in general, is on the cusp of great advances. Let me outline a few areas of potential progress for the future of pitching analysis.

First and foremost is injury prevention. Injuries have long been the bane of pitchers, and so they remain to this day. I do not hold out the hope of eliminating them, but any reduction or mitigation of pitchers injuries would be very valuable. The last decade was one of reduced pitch counts by starting pitchers, driven in no small part by the Pitcher Abuse Points theory detailed in this section. Another trend is the improved success in surgical repair of injuries, most notably Tommy John surgery for elbow ligaments.

The next decade holds the promise of better injury prediction from detailed and digitized quantification of pitcher mechanics on every pitch thrown in game action. Combined with wider availability and usage of high-speed video to measure pitcher kinetics, either in the game or in a laboratory setting, the prospects for better understanding of injury causes and danger signs is good.

These techniques are currently in their infancy. Some analysts have already studied injury predictors using the detailed PITCHf/x trajectory data available for almost every pitch thrown in the major leagues since mid-2007. As the PITCHf/x data set grows, our ability to examine pitcher trends, both within games and over the course of a season, also grows. Changes in fastball speed are a prime indicator of injury, and this is an area ripe for study to determine the telltale signatures. We can also study changes in a pitcher's release point or pitch movement for injury prediction. The TrackMan pitch tracking radar system also shows promise for learning about pitching mechanics, though the data from this system is not currently public.

Another frontier is the collection and digitization of high-speed video of pitcher deliveries in order to measure pitcher kinetics with precision. Dr. Glenn Fleisig and Dr. James Andrews at the American Sports Medicine Institute in Birmingham, Alabama pioneered the research in this area. Their research has led to video evaluation such as that offered by former pitching coach Rick Peterson's 3P Sports, and to high-speed video biomechanics labs for amateur athletes such as those offered by Doc Schoenhals at Scientific Baseball in Oklahoma City, Oklahoma, and by Kyle Boddy at Driveline Baseball in Seattle, Washington.

As high-speed video analysis proliferates, multiple cameras one day may record major-league game pitching action at the high frame rates necessary to evaluate the biomechanics of pitchers for every pitch they throw. Such data would be an amazing boon for injury analysis.

A second area of potential progress is in better understanding of the optimal roles for pitchers. Bullpen roles have been the subject of a great deal of research and controversy over the past decade, and the controversy, at least, is unlikely to abate soon. However, an emerging area of research is in the reliever-to-starter transition.

Recently, the Texas Rangers garnered a great deal of attention, first with the successful switch of C.J. Wilson from the bullpen to the starting rotation, and then with the attempted move of their closer Neftali Feliz into the rotation. Feliz quickly found his way back to the bullpen, while Alexi Ogando took his place as reliever-turned-starter. In New York, the Yankees moved young stars Phil Hughes and Joba Chamberlain from bullpen to rotation and back.

Common wisdom is that starting pitchers need a good changeup and breaking ball to complement their fastball and that pitchers who lack quality secondary pitches or stamina are destined for the bullpen. With detailed PITCHf/x data now available for a number of pitchers who have made the transition from reliever to starter, or the other way around, further study of this topic begs to be done.

THE LINEUP

How Much Control Do Hurlers Have?
by Vörös McCracken..........................95

Another Look at Pitchers Preventing Hits
by Keith Woolner..............................102

Does Vörös' Theory Work on the Farm?
by Clay Davenport............................108

Any Such Thing?
by Nate Silver..................................113

The Origins of the Closer
by Nate Silver..................................120

The Support-Neutral Stats
by Michael Wolverton........................124

Thirty Years of Fixing Pitchers
by Thomas Gorman..........................127

How We Measure Pitch Usage
by Rany Jazayerli.............................132

Discussing Jonathan Papelbon's Worth
by Marc Normandin and Tommy Bennett....136

Cliff Lee
by Marc Normandin, Eric Seidman, and Kevin Goldstein...141

Park Effects on Pitcher Type
by James Click.................................147

Adventures in Consulting
by Gary Huckabay............................151

Adventures in Consulting, Part Two
by Gary Huckabay............................154

Adventures in Consulting, Part Three
by Gary Huckabay............................157

C.J. Wilson
by David Laurila...............................160

Craig Breslow
by David Laurila...............................166

Brian Bannister
by David Laurila...............................171

Jim Palmer
by David Laurila...............................178

Why the "Earned" Run Needs To Go
by Michael Wolverton........................185

The Real Strike Zone
by Mike Fast....................................189

How is fastball speed affected by the transition between roles, and why is the effect different for some pitchers than others? Do pitchers really need good changeups and breaking balls more in the rotation than in the bullpen, and if so, do certain combinations of pitch types augur greater success as a starter? Can we measure how fatigue affects starters and relievers differently? Why do starters perform worse the second and third times through the lineup, and are certain types of pitchers immune or less vulnerable to this effect?

Another major area of ongoing research is the quantification of pitcher effectiveness, in at least two general areas. One is the measurement of pitcher skills, and the other is projection of future performance. The two are related, of course.

Detailed pitch data has made possible the measurement of pitch speed and movement on a scale unimaginable five years ago. There has been a great deal of research in the past five years into what makes pitchers effective, either as individuals or collectively across the league. The topic is challenging enough that though analysts have accumulated many pieces of knowledge, they have formulated few grand unified visions of pitcher effectiveness. The gradual systemization of this knowledge over the next few years is one of the most promising fields of baseball analysis.
Speed and movement, often described collectively as a pitcher's "stuff," are critical factors for the success of a pitch. Detailed pitch speed and trajectory data has taught us a great deal about what makes each pitch type most successful. We have quantified the value of speed for a fastball, identified the optimum speed separation between the fastball and changeup, and identified optimal spin-induced movement for various pitch types. Further research could greatly enhance our understanding of these topics. Investigation of the vertical and lateral components of a pitch's velocity as it crosses the plate shows promise for evaluating a pitcher's stuff.

Moreover, location, command, and deception are important factors for the success of a pitch. Though analysts have conducted some initial research into each of these parameters, further study is needed. The optimum location balances the likelihood of a strike call with the best chance to make the batter swing and miss or to induce weak contact. The strike zone itself is an ongoing topic of research—it is an area of complex interplay between pitcher, catcher, batter, and umpire. Analysts have developed methods for measuring pitchers' command by inferring the likely pitch target from the pitch location distribution. Companies are now tracking catchers' targets by video, and this data holds great promise for measuring command more directly if it becomes publicly available. Current measures of deception rely largely on comparisons of the similarities of pitch trajectories of different types of pitches when viewed from the batter's vantage point. It may be possible in the future to incorporate elements of deception involved in the pitcher's delivery as recorded by video.

Furthermore, by tracking a pitcher's release point with great accuracy, an analyst can measure the pitcher's mechanical consistency and determine how this relates to various aspects of performance, whether pitch speed, movement, location, or command. We currently have little knowledge of why a pitcher's pitches sometimes work well for him and other times do not.
A better understanding of pitcher effectiveness at the skill level would drive improvements in our ability to project pitcher performance in the future. Most projections are done based upon the results of past plate appearances. Strikeout rates, walk rates, home run rates, and batted ball types and results are weighted together to produce a picture of a pitcher's skills. A more granular picture of a pitcher's skills that described attributes of various pitch types would add knowledge of significant value for predicting future performance. A granular picture would also help accurately identify groups of similar pitchers, which would be useful for future projection.

As our understanding of pitcher skills grows and the timeline of detailed pitch data extends a few more years, we will develop a much better understanding of how pitcher skills age. How do pitcher fastball speeds change with age, and are certain types of pitchers better able to compensate for this than others? Do pitchers lose movement on their pitches with age? Do they gain command, and if so, is that mainly a mental process, or is there an accompanying improvement in mechanical consistency? Do the effects of fatigue and injury vary with age, and if so, how?

A final area of great interest for pitching research lies at the very heart of baseball itself: the battle between the pitcher and the batter. What we learn about pitcher skills and what makes a pitch effective will also teach us about the batter-pitcher confrontation. The batter's job is, as Pete Rose said, "See the ball; hit the ball." The pitcher's job is to keep the batter off balance by making him swing either over or under the ball because of unexpected or unusual movement, or early or late by changing speeds, or by locating the ball where it is hard to hit or in a different location than the batter is prepared to hit it.

Pitch sequencing and game theory are topics for future investigation. We know little about whether pitchers use and mix their pitch types optimally. Pitch type run values are currently widely reported, but these values are deceiving without the context of usage. Pitchers presumably use their best pitches the most often, such that batters expect them and adjust their approach accordingly. Similarly, batters face the pitches that exploit their weaknesses more often than the pitches they can drive. To the extent that pitchers and batters can optimize their behaviors and adjust to each other's approaches, pitch type frequencies may tell us more about pitcher and batter strengths and weaknesses than the resulting run values. Further research can illuminate how quickly and to what extent this adjustment and optimization occurs.

Data on batted ball trajectories, whether from HITf/x video or TrackMan radar, can be combined with pitch trajectory data to tell us whether batters are swinging under or over the pitch and early or late. This data can give us a great deal of insight into how the battle between pitcher and batter plays out. Trajectory data on foul balls would be extremely valuable for this purpose, as well. Ultimately, we could gain insight into the control that the batter and pitcher have over the quality of batted ball contact. This would help us measure batter and pitcher skill more quickly and accurately than we currently do. We might also be able to understand how pitchers and batters are able to use their strengths and weaknesses against each other and why this is or is not repeatable in future matchups.

Though some forms of detailed tracking data are current proprietary, technological trends are moving toward making this data more available to the fan. PITCHf/x data is the most obvious example. Rob Neyer has predicted that in the future, broadcasters will make available detailed slow-motion, high-definition replays of every play in a baseball game, viewable at the discretion of the fan. As this sort of video record becomes available and computing power increases, the ability of the analyst to make a detailed analysis of every play will only continue to increase. Interviews, game photos, and video have all become more common, more accessible, and more detailed. There may be little outside of the players' minds that remains out of bounds for analysis, and even there, we will study behavior records to gain a window into players' thinking.

If the inner workings of the game of baseball intrigue you, there is plenty of information available, and many stones remain unturned. This is the golden age of baseball analysis, particularly for those who are interested in learning how pitching works. The past decade of research has yielded some fascinating and groundbreaking discoveries. The coming decade promises to yield no fewer.

PITCHING AND DEFENSE

How Much Control Do Hurlers Have?

Vörös McCracken

Separating the effects of pitching and fielding has been one of the peskiest problems in sabermetrics. The finding that most pitchers exert little to no control over what happens to balls in play proved to be one of the keys to solving that puzzle, making it one of the most important discoveries in the annals of baseball analysis and revolutionizing the way in which teams and fans alike evaluate players. The landmark article that cracked the code and ushered in a wave of fielding-independent pitching statistics is reproduced below.

"You're insane." That's generally the response I get when I present the information you're about to read. I've been accused of being the "epitome of 'pseudo-stat fan' gibberish." I've even been accused of being Aaron Sele writing under a pseudonym. I'm not entirely sure why my little way of doing things stirs the emotions of people to such a large extent, but apparently it does.

My belief? Well, simply that hits allowed are not a particularly meaningful statistic in the evaluation of pitchers.

Now before you accuse me of being Aaron Sele, please bear with me for a few paragraphs as I explain how I reached this point, and where it led from there.

One of the basic issues in evaluating pitchers is to what extent the defense behind them is responsible for the results. In fact, in *Baseball Prospectus 2000*, one of Keith Woolner's "Hilbert Problems" for baseball was the issue of separating defense and pitching. As he put it, "Pitching and fielding are so intertwined that they seem impossible to separate."

Around the end of the 1999 season, I started to think about that problem. My plan was to go about dividing a pitcher's stat line into what the defense can't affect and what it's possible that it can:

Defense Independent:
Walks, Strikeouts, Home Runs (essentially), Hit Batsmen, Intentional Walks

Defense Dependent:
Wins, Losses, Innings, Runs, Earned Runs, Hits Allowed, Sacrifice Hits, Sacrifice Flies.

Any stats derived from the defense-dependent ones like OPS against or ERA would also be defense-dependent.

The idea was to express the things the defense can't affect in one area and check the results, then check those areas where it's possible the defense can have an effect and analyze how much of the performance is pitching and how much is defense.

The first thing I did was create something called "Defense Independent Pitching Stats." DIPS are the representation of a pitcher's stat line without any possible influence from the defense behind the pitcher. I calculated the various rates for walks, strikeouts, home runs, hit batsmen, etc. as a function of batters faced and inserted them into the pitcher's line. Then I calculated how many batters faced were remaining, and assigned league-average rates for all of the other component stats: innings, hits, doubles, triples, etc. So for all the stats that it was possible that the defense could affect, every pitcher was now on equal footing. The results, using Dave Burba's line in 2000, looked something like this:

Actual

BFP	IP	H	HR	ER	BB	SO	ERA
848	191	199	19	95	91	180	4.48

Defense Independent

BFP	IP	H	HR	ER	BB	SO	ERA
848	195	185	18	89	93	179	4.13

As you can see, the home runs, walks, and strikeouts changed little (they changed at all only due to park effects and a few other minor factors). But hits and innings pitched changed by a decent amount, at least in this case.

The next step was to look at the rest of a pitcher's stat line and somehow divine how much of it was the result of the pitcher's work. To do this, I looked at the range of values for Defense Independent ERA and compared how close they were to the range of values of actual ERA. For example, if the range of Defense Independent ERA was between 4.00 and 5.00, it would be a good indication that there's a lot about pitching not covered in the stat, because ERAs have a much larger range than that.

That didn't happen. The range was virtually the same as actual ERA, with the best pitchers having DIPS ERAs near 2.40 and the worst having DIPS ERAs up near 7.00. I found this surprising, as I expected the range to narrow quite a bit more than that.

Then, I looked at the behavior of Hits Per Balls in Play [(H-HR)/(BFP-HR-BB-SO-HB)]. That's where the trouble really started. I swear to you that I did everything within my power to come to a different conclusion than the one I did. I ran every test, checked every stat, divided this by that and multiplied one thing by another. Whatever I did, it kept leading back to the same conclusion:

There is little if any difference among major-league pitchers in their ability to prevent hits on balls hit in the field of play.

It is a controversial statement, one that counters a significant portion of 110 years of pitcher evaluation. Let's go over the facts that led me to this conclusion:

1. As we discussed, the range of ERAs for pitchers is almost as large without defense-dependent statistics as it is with them. This speaks to the fact that there can be massive differences in the ability of pitchers before even considering the impact of defense.

2. The pitchers who are the best at preventing hits on balls in play one year are often the worst at it the next. In 1998, Greg Maddux had one of the best rates in baseball, then in 1999 he had one of the worst. In 2000, he had one of the better ones again. In 1999, Pedro Martinez had one of the worst; in 2000, he had the best. This happens a lot.

3. There is little correlation between what a pitcher does one year in the stat and what he will do the next. In other words, what Eric Milton's hits per balls in play was in 2000 tells us next to nothing about what it will be in 2001. This is not true in the other significant stats (walks, strikeouts, home runs). Walks and strikeouts correlate very well and homers correlate somewhat well.

This is a crucial fact. One of the more critical aspects of statistical analysis is determining how well a statistic reflects an ability. It's the test given to clutch hitting, catcher game-calling, pitcher won/loss records, and so on. One of the first things asked when addressing this is, "Does the stat correlate well with itself from year to year?" One reason clutch hitting is questioned is that the "clutch hitters" change from year to year, which indicates that it probably isn't the hitter as much as it's other factors. The answer to whether hits per balls in play correlates well from year to year is a fairly solid "no."

4. You can better predict a pitcher's hits per balls in play from the rate of the rest of the pitcher's team than from the pitcher's own rate. This is pretty self-explanatory. The effects of having the same team defense and home park appear to be significant determinants in creating what little correlation there is in the stat.

5. Take pitchers with similar stats in every other component category (and other peripheral factors like age, throwing hand, team hits per balls in play rates, etc.) but large differences in hits allowed (and therefore in innings pitched). When you group the pitchers into two categories—high-hits and low-hits—the following year the high-hits pitchers do not give up significantly more hits per balls in play (.292 to .291) than the low-hits pitchers, and the groups have identical ERAs.

This is a difficult point to overcome if you want to show that preventing hits per balls in play is a significant ability of pitchers. If, when all other things are equal, there is no difference, the conclusion becomes clearer.

6. Similarly, if you take pitchers with comparable stats in every other component category, but have as large as possible a difference in strikeouts, then separate the pitchers into high-strikeout and low-strikeout categories, the high-strikeout pitchers continue to strike out more hitters, while also giving up far fewer hits and having significantly lower ERAs. This is the natural opposite of the fifth point. If number five is true, then logically number six ought to be true as well. It is.

7. The range of career rates of hits per balls in play for pitchers with a significant number of innings is about the same as the range you would expect from random chance. This is true even though we know that some pitchers may have had consistent advantages over others, as these rates are unadjusted for park or league. The vast majority of pitchers who have pitched significant innings have career rates between .280 and .290.

8. When you adjust for environmental advantages (the DH, park effects, and so on) the range becomes even smaller. The leaders in this stat (Pete Harnisch) have had significant environmental advantages, while most of the trailers (yup, Aaron Sele) have had disadvantages. After these adjustments, the range is well within the realm you could expect from chance alone.

9. A stat like Component ERA (or any similar stat that calculates ERA from the rest of a pitcher's performance), while correlating better with next-year ERA than ERA itself, does not correlate nearly as well with next-year ERA as it does if you perform the same calculation while using the average hits-allowed rate of the team for which a pitcher pitched. This advantage of "team average" rate grows to rather large proportions as the number of innings pitched in the season shrinks more and more.

Two key points here: one, there doesn't appear to be any "hidden quality" aspect to the stat. The numbers come out as they should if the above are all true: you can better predict

ERA without hits allowed than you can with them. The other key point is that using a reliever's hit rate seems to be an extremely suspect way of evaluating relievers. One of my favorite examples of this is Bobby Ayala in 1998 and 1999.

There are a few lesser and somewhat anecdotal points to be made that, while not critical, are nonetheless good concepts to understand:

1. People have a hard time diagnosing who the pitchers are that are very good at preventing hits on balls in play. You'll often hear people use names like Randy Johnson, Jamie Moyer and Andy Pettitte in protest of the concept, but by any definition you want to use, these guys are not particularly good in the stat.

2. Pitchers like Pedro Martinez and Greg Maddux have, at times, expressed thoughts on the matter. Martinez has been quoted as saying that the batter determines what happens once he hits the ball. Maddux described his scoreless-inning streak last year as "mostly luck" as hard-hit balls that had been falling in were being caught.

3. We only have 38 innings' worth of non-pitchers' pitching (like Brent Mayne). That's too small a sample on which to draw conclusions, but it is something to think about that these non-pitchers were not any worse than regular pitchers in the stat. In fact, they were a good bit better.

4. Pitchers are often dubbed as "unpredictable," and hits allowed is by far the most unpredictable of the component stats. In other words, it is one of the main culprits of pitcher unpredictability.

5. There is no significant cross-correlation. That is, a high number of home runs allowed doesn't really mean anything in determining how many hits per balls in play the pitcher will allow. The closest is an inverse relationship with strikeouts (lots of strikeouts means fewer hits per balls in play) but that relationship is very weak and could be the result of unrelated factors. There was no significant hits-per-balls-in-play advantage found in the strikeout study above.

Many people, after reading these points, think I'm saying that all pitchers give up the same amount of hits. That's not true, and of course it's not what I'm saying. Randy Johnson gives up fewer hits than Scott Karl. That's not because batters hit the ball harder off Karl than Johnson, but because they hit the ball more often off Karl than Johnson.

Aside from walks, there are two basic outcomes for a pitcher: batter hits the ball or batter strikes out. With the latter, the result is almost always an out. With the former, all sorts of things can happen, including a base hit.

So why is this all true? All I can advance are theories, some that can be checked out and some that are more difficult to verify. I'll end this article with a list of some of the more popular ones:

1. Scouting. The MLB scouting network is set up to sift through an enormous pool of potential players to get to the group that might be MLB pitchers. To do this, scouts often employ tactics that many might call unfair in an effort to reduce the pool to a manageable number. So they don't take guys under 5'10" and every pitcher has to throw a certain speed fastball and so on. One of these factors may be weeding out a subset of pitchers for which the theory is not true.

2. High talent level. This theory is that there's a certain limit to how good you can get at preventing hits on balls in play, and that in order even to come close to the major leagues, you have to have reached this. This theory often comes up in clutch-hitting discussions.

3. Too many variables. This suggests that the ability may or may not exist, but that the number of variables involved in the outcome of balls in play are so numerous and so difficult to control for that any ability gets lost. In other words, the noise completely masks any signal.

4. A misunderstanding of how the batter/pitcher dynamic works. Some people will argue that despite all the numbers, the above can't be true because it means that a screaming line drive hit into the right-center-field gap is as likely to be an out as a pop-up to the shortstop.

This point deserves further discussion. One of the critical points of misunderstanding is the issue of "blame." When a ball gets crushed into the gap in right-center, some think I'm saying that the defense deserves the blame, not the pitcher. When I counter with "Neither the pitcher nor defense is to blame, it's the batter who is to blame," I lose some people.

Consider this example:

When I was a kid, we used to go to the cemetery (this was our playground) and play a game called Lob-League. The makeup of this game was mostly offense and some fielding, with little to no pitching effects. The pitcher's job was to lob the ball over the heart of the plate and let the batter hit it as hard as he wanted.

Now, let's suppose we're playing Lob-League and the pitcher lobs one right in the batter's wheelhouse, but the batter pops it up to the shortstop. Who deserves credit for the pop-up? The blame argument would indicate that the pitcher deserves credit for inducing a pop-up despite the fact that all he did was lob the ball over the plate. No credit or blame would belong to the batter who popped up the pitch.

A more relevant MLB example might be the Home Run Derby at the All-Star festivities. I encourage you to watch next year's contest, or, if you have it, a videotape of past contests. Watch for batted balls that would clearly be outs. The pitcher is trying to give up home runs, so does he deserve credit for a pop-up?

In MLB, a pitch could result in a pop-up or a line drive. It all depends on what the batter does with it. I think the conventional wisdom on the dynamic between pitcher and batter may be slightly inaccurate.

The critical thing to understand is that major-league pitchers don't appear to have the ability to prevent hits on balls in play. There are many possible reasons why this is the case, and I don't really have a concrete idea as to why it is.

But the one thing I do know is that it is the case.

COUNTERPOINT: PITCHING AND DEFENSE
Another Look at Pitchers Preventing Hits
Keith Woolner

Vörös McCracken's important discovery that pitchers have little control over what happens to the ball once it's put into play was so counterintuitive that it required independent investigation and verification. Keith Woolner followed up with an article that largely confirmed McCracken's findings but also added some nuance to his conclusions.

Intro
Vörös McCracken's article on the BP website has generated a tremendous amount of attention, including at least two columns by Rob Neyer on ESPN.com. Vörös's research, as presented in the article, contains the remarkable result that "major-league pitchers don't appear to have the ability to prevent hits on balls in play."

In other words, when you remove defense-independent outcomes such as strikeouts, home runs, and walks from the batters a pitcher faces, the resulting batting average on "balls in play" (those handled by the defense) is not affected by the pitcher himself—Pedro Martinez is the same as Jose Lima.

Extraordinary claims require extraordinary proof, and Vörös has done an exemplary job setting forth evidence for his conclusions. In the interest of putting his results under the scrutiny of peer review, I've been doing some work inspired by Vörös's article to see if it was possible to poke holes in it.

Sample Sizes and Statistical Noise
I started by considering the amount of statistical noise present in measuring the ball in play average over the course of a season.

Consider a pitcher with the following typical seasonal pitching line:

GS	IP	H	HR	BB	SO
33	200	200	24	78	122

Let's estimate the balls-in-play average for this pitcher:

Total Batters Faced ~= 3*IP + H + BB = 3*200 + 78 + 200 = 878
Defense-Independent Outcomes = HR + BB + SO = 24 + 78 + 122 = 224
Non-HR Hits allowed = H - HR = 200 - 24 = 176

Balls In Play = TBF - DIO = 878 - 224 = 654

Ball-in-play Average = Non-HR Hits / Balls In Play = 176 / 654 = .269

Let's assume that .269 represents the pitcher's (or the league's) true ability to prevent hits on balls in play. What is the expected variance around this number that we'd expect to see over the course of a typical season?

We look to a statistical concept called standard deviation to help us quantify this range. We can treat a ball-in-play as a binomial variable consisting of two outcomes: 1 if a hit, 0 if not. The probability of being a hit is the ball-in-play average of .269.

Though we expect to see 176 hits over the 654 balls-in-play, statistical theory allows us to calculate the variance and standard deviation associated with this expectation. In particular:

Variance = (# trials) * (probability of a hit) * (probability of an out)
= 654 * .269 * (1-.269) = 654 * .269 * .731 = 128.602

Standard Deviation = SQRT (Variance) = 11.34 hits

We expect to see a standard deviation of about +/- 11 hits over the course of a season, simply by the statistical noise of a sample size of 654 balls-in-play. What effect does this have on the observed ball-in-play averages?

If you look at hundreds of pitchers with a .269 ball-in-play average, about two-thirds of the seasons will be within a single standard deviation, and 95 percent of seasons will be within two standard deviations.

```
(176 - 11.34) / 654 = .252
(176 + 11.34) / 654 = .286
```

One standard deviation yields a range of [.252, .286]

```
(176 - 2*11.34) / 654 = .234
(176 + 2*11.34) / 654 = .304
```

Two standard deviations yields a range of [.234, .304]

Simple statistical noise coming from a single season's worth of data will obscure true variations between pitchers over a pretty wide range of possible abilities. Failure to detect year-to-year consistency in ball-in-play average (as Vörös has found) could be the result of there being no differences in ability (as he concluded), or that the range of abilities is smaller than the statistical noise, making detection difficult.

Characteristics of Ball-in-Play Batting Average over a Career

To see which of these possibilities is true, we can look at pitcher performance over multiple seasons to reduce the amount of statistical noise.

I looked at play-by-play data for all pitchers between 1979 and 1999 and computed actual batters faced, hits, home runs, strikeouts, and walks for each season. I wanted to divide a pitcher's entire career into two halves to see if the ball-in-play hit rate from one half was correlated at all with that in the other half.

I could have simply taken the first 50 percent of a pitcher's career and compared it to the latter 50 percent. However, there is the possibility that if an ability exists, that it could improve or decline as a pitcher's career evolves. Age, maturity, learning how to pitch, velocity, etc. could all change the relationship between the pitcher's first and second halves of his career. Therefore, I chose to divide his career into even and odd halves, according to the year of that particular season. Thus a pitcher's 1990 season was in the "even" group, and 1991 was in the "odd" group, 1992 in the "even" group, and so on. By mixing seasons throughout a player's career into different groups, I could minimize the possibility that a pitcher's ability could be different at different ages, confounding the analysis.

The next thing I wanted to do was control for the overall quality of the pitcher's team defense. A pitcher who spent his entire career with a poor defensive team may show a spurious correlation between portions of his career, simply because the team was allowing more hits than the league as a whole. To control for this, I expressed a pitcher's ball-in-play average as a percentage of his team's total defensive ball-in-play average (similar to Bill James's defensive efficiency). Thus, a pitcher with a ball-in-play average of .270 on a team whose total ball-in-play average was .280 would have his ball-in-play average expressed as the ratio of .270/.280, or 0.96. This is similar to how Total Baseball expresses OPS as Adjusted Production (PRO+) where a value of 110 represents 10 percent above the league average, or a value of 80 is 20 percent below league average.

Having divided a pitcher's career into two halves (using even/odd seasons), and controlling for his team's defense, I totaled each pitcher's half-career ball-in-play ratio, as in this data sample:

PITCHER	EVEN_AVG	EVEN_RATIO	EVEN_BIP	ODD_AVG	ODD_RATIO	ODD_BIP
Jack Morris	.268	-0.9%	5945	.268	-0.6%	5420
Dennis Martinez	.266	-3.0%	5410	.273	-0.2%	6166
Frank Viola	.280	-1.7%	4450	.287	1.5%	4481
Bret Saberhagen	.288	1.6%	3670	.270	-6.3%	4296

I looked at all pitchers who had at least 3000 balls in play in both the even and odd halves of their careers—roughly five full seasons in each half (thus at least a 10-year career). I then looked at the correlation between the ratios of their ball-in-play averages to their team's average. A perfect correlation of +1.00 would indicate a totally predictable linear relationship between ball-in-play rates in the two halves of pitchers' careers, whereas a value of 0.00 would indicate that there is absolutely no statistical relationship. Values in between would indicate the degree to which knowing the value in one half would help you predict the value in the other half.

The correlation among the 70 pitchers who met the threshold was +0.53. Not a perfect correlation, but well above the level at which one could claim that there's no relationship. Some level of innate ability seems to be appearing in our sample.

We can further test the theory that all differences are due to chance by looking at the distribution of observed ball-in-play averages for the pitchers in the sample. Comparing the distribution of measured ball-in-play averages versus what the null hypothesis that all observed differences are due to chance, we find the following results:

40% exceed one standard deviation away from the mean (versus ~32% predicted by chance)
24% exceed two standard deviations away from the mean (versus ~5% predicted by chance)

This shows us that a significant number of pitchers are further away from the mean than we'd expect from simple randomness. With the relatively high correlation, and the number of pitchers falling outside the range attributable to chance, the evidence is starting to show that, at the very least, pitchers with long careers in the majors do have distinct abilities to prevent balls in play from becoming hits.

We can see this more clearly by looking at a chart plotting even-year rates vs. odd-year rates:

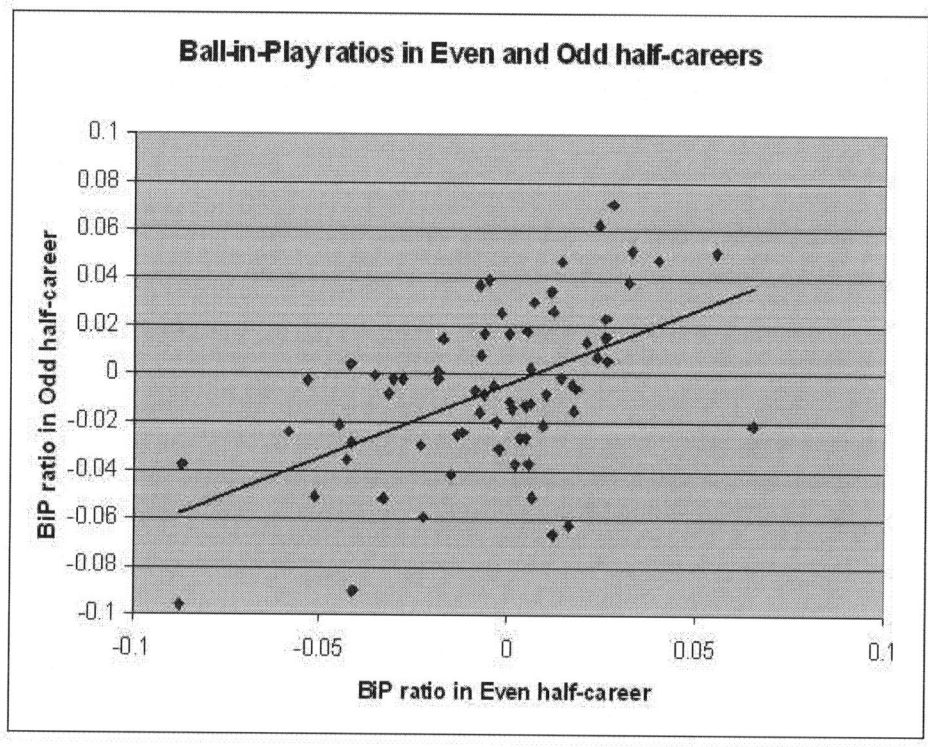

There is a distinct linear trend showing a relationship between the distinct halves of a pitcher's career. Though there is clearly a lot of variance around that line, some level of ability to influence ball-in-play rate is demonstrated by the chart above.

Looking at the range of ball-in-play rates for the 70 pitchers in the sample, the span from best to worst is roughly .251 (Charlie Hough) to .303 (John Burkett). If we expand the data set to include pitchers with at least 1000 balls-in-play in both halves of their careers (a total of 338 pitchers), the range is .242 (Mike Norris) to .317 (Aaron Sele). It's reasonable to estimate that the range in ability between the best and worst pitchers is around 50-60 points of batting average on balls in play. Consequently, though the pitcher's previous season may not be particularly useful in predicting future ball-in-play averages, using the pitcher's career ball-in-play average may be more accurate, especially for pitchers who have several major-league seasons under their belt (though additional research will be needed to demonstrate or refute this theory).

Analysis & Conclusions

How, then, do we reconcile Vörös's findings with the new results presented above? There are several alternatives, including:

> **1.** As suggested by the analysis of the standard deviation over a single season, one year's worth of data may not be sufficient to discern a pitcher's true level of ability with regard to ball-in-play average. It's only when many years of data are examined that the trends become clearer.
>
> **2.** Another possibility is that while the majority of pitchers have no such ability to affect ball-in-play average, a few special pitchers do have such an ability. Those whose ability allows them to systematically reduce their ball-in-play average below the overall league average would have a survival advantage and therefore would be more likely to be the pitchers whose careers are long enough to be detected in a 10-year sample. Slightly more than half (56 percent) of the longer-career, 70-pitcher sample had ball-in-play rates below the median rate of the 338-pitcher sample that includes shorter careers. This lends some support to the notion that the long-career pitchers are somewhat better at reducing balls-in-play than their more typical counterparts. However, the evidence for this theory is not overwhelming.
>
> **3.** Another line of reasoning might go as follows: when pitchers first arrive in the majors, they are still learning their craft, and in particular have not yet learned how to tailor their pitching to the defense behind them. Over time, playing with various teammates and parks over the years, pitchers learn more about how to maximize the benefit they get from their defense. Pitchers who've mastered this skill get more effective defensive play behind them than less experienced pitchers on the same staff. This wisdom that comes with experience allows veteran pitchers to systematically do better with their defense. Thus, a skill related to preventing balls in play from becoming hits emerges.

Additional research and analysis will be needed to determine whether options two or three (or another theory) are supported by the evidence. At the moment, the simplest explanation that is consistent with the facts should be favored, and thus the idea that the statistical noise in one year's worth of data obscures a relatively small true difference among pitchers may be the most likely explanation.

None of the preceding should be taken as diminishing Vörös's work at all. Indeed, it is his pioneering work and startling conclusion that led to widespread interest in and further analysis of the topic. Even if the conclusion is not quite as radical as saying pitchers have no influence on ball-in-play batting averages, the observation that differences among pitchers in batting average on balls-in-play are as little as 50 points (and require several years of data to discern) is a remarkable, counterintuitive result for which we gratefully acknowledge Mr. McCracken.

MINOR LEAGUE BATTING AVERAGES ON BALLS IN PLAY
Does Vörös' Theory Work on the Farm?
Clay Davenport

Vörös McCracken's surprising discovery of BABIP's variability seemed to suggest that all pitchers had the same inherent ability to prevent hits on balls in play, but it was possible that the results looked as they did because pitchers with lesser ability simply got weeded out on the way to the Show. Clay Davenport backed up that theory by confirming that BABIP does indeed follow a smooth downward progression as pitchers prove themselves worthy of advancing from the lowest level of the minors to the major leagues.

At feeds, signings, and any other meeting I happen to attend, it is clear that Vörös McCracken's observations on pitching and defense still generate intense disbelief from many, if not most, fans.

First of all, let us be clear on what Vörös actually said. He initially claimed that pitchers have no control over whether balls in play turn into hits or outs; after more work, he refined his claim to say that the differences between major-league pitchers are much smaller than commonly believed, and small enough to be insignificant information. It is convenient shorthand—an exaggeration, if you will—to continue with the original idea of there being no differences, and that the differences we do see can be attributed to luck. Here at BP, we'll describe a pitcher as being "hit-lucky," for instance; admittedly, from the data, you would have a hard time showing that it isn't luck.

Quite a few people have challenged Vörös' original article and subsequent follow-ups, with the best response probably being Tom Tippett's. However, even Tom's article still shows that most pitchers, indeed, have almost no effect. This still runs so contrary to most people's expectations that some more explanation is in order.

First, I have to say that most people are interpreting the proposition in light of their own direct playing experience—which, for the vast majority of us, does not extend beyond Little League or perhaps high school baseball. They know pitchers have some ability to be harder to hit because they have experienced it themselves, and no statistics can convince them otherwise. The trick here is to understand that major-league baseball is a different game from the one you played in high school. Some of the things we talk about at BP—a strikeout is no worse than any other out, for example—are not universal baseball truths, but are only true when the skill levels involved are at or near major-league levels. A strikeout is worse than other outs because it doesn't advance a runner and doesn't give the other team as much of a chance to make an error; it is better than other outs because it doesn't give the other team a chance to make a double play. You have to get somewhere in the high minors before the ability of the defense is high enough, both to turn a double play and to not make errors, to tip the scales from strikeouts being a really bad event to being no worse than other outs.

Hits per ball in play may be another one of those truths. Suppose that there is a clear ability to make batters hit a ball weakly, and that teams can recognize it; clearly, this would be a valuable ability for a pitcher to have. Other things being equal, it would give a pitcher an advantage, like height in the NBA. Assuming that teams can recognize it and select for it, you would produce a major league where the selected population is better than its selection group—just as NBA teams are taller, on average, than NCAA teams (its principal recruiting pool), major-league pitchers should be better than minor-league pitchers, and you should be able to demonstrate a weeding out of the less able. Reaching the major leagues is a sensational example of Darwinian survival.

The first question is easy to answer—Do major-league pitchers give up hits (per ball in play) at a lower rate than minor leaguers? And, ideally, does BABIP increase in a steady progression by minor-league level? At first glance, the answer is, "sort of."

All data from 1996-2004. BABIP = (H-HR)/(2.75*IP+H-HR-SO)

Level	Avg.	Leagues
Major Leagues	.309	
Triple-A	.322	(International, PCL, AA)
Double-A	.318	(Eastern, Southern, Texas)
High-A	.323	(California, Carolina, Florida)
Mid-A	.321	(Midwest, SAL)
Low-A	.327	(New York-Penn, Northwest)
Rookie	.348	(Pioneer, Appalachian)

The majors are lowest, the rookie leagues are highest, but the rest is muddled. It turns out, though, that the muddling is likely to be the result of another effect on balls in play, namely altitude.

As we know from the Rockies, averages go up in thin air. If we cut the list of leagues down so that we're only talking about those who play at essentially sea level—losing the PCL, Texas, California, Northwest, and Pioneer leagues—we get the following modified list of BABIPs.

Level	Avg.
Majors	.309
IL+AA	.314
Eas+Sou	.316
Caro+FSL	.316
SAL+ML	.321
NY-P	.323
App	.340

That, folks, is a smooth progression. Major-league pitchers do allow fewer hits per ball in play than minor-league pitchers. However, that doesn't prove the pitchers are responsible—it could simply be that the fielders are improving, not to mention the fields; smooth fields make fielding easier. We need to see if the pitchers themselves are being selected for this property.

To do that, I looked at every minor league from 1996 to 2000 and simply divided the pitchers into two groups: those who have played in the major leagues as of 2004, and those who haven't. One would expect that the major-league group would be better than the non-major group. Not 100 percent of the time; there's always a Ryan Anderson type who, despite being one of the best pitchers in his league, blows out his arm before pitching in the majors, and there are pitchers like Jorge Julio who were lousy minor-league starters and only made it to the majors after switching to the bullpen. The only massaging I'm doing to the numbers is normalizing them to a league with nine hits, one home run, three walks, six strikeouts, and 4.5 runs per nine innings, so that I can add the various leagues together; just think of 6.6 strikeouts not as 6.6 actual strikeouts, but 10 percent above average, and you'll be fine. I set the relative BABIP figure to a nice, round .300.

Triple-A

	IP	H	R	HR	BB	SO	BABIP
Majors	150067	8.88	4.36	0.97	2.92	6.10	.299
Non-majors	30387	9.60	5.21	1.13	3.39	5.52	.300

83% of the innings pitched in Triple-A were by pitchers who either had pitched in the majors before or would pitch in the majors later. Because it is the major-league group that dominates the league, their numbers are close to the league average, while the non-major leaguers show up as substantially worse pitchers overall. As expected, they give up more runs, more homers, more walks, strike out fewer—and they give up more hits per ball in play.

Double-A

	IP	H	R	HR	BB	SO	BABIP
Majors	81760	8.68	4.20	.94	2.81	6.30	.296
Non-majors	93872	9.28	4.76	1.05	3.16	5.74	.300

The major-league percentage of innings drops to 47 percent at Double-A, and now the two sides roughly straddle the means. Again, the major-league pitchers are superior in all phases of performance.

High-A

	IP	H	R	HR	BB	SO	BABIP
Majors	57441	8.55	4.05	0.91	2.69	6.49	.296
Non-majors	144201	9.19	4.69	1.04	3.13	5.79	.300

The major league-percentage is now only 28 percent, but the patterns are the same as before.

Middle-A

	IP	H	R	HR	BB	SO	BABIP
Majors	42045	8.64	4.15	0.94	2.74	6.34	.297
Non-majors	130670	9.12	4.62	1.02	3.09	5.88	.300

Percentage down to 24 percent. BABIP advantage still present, but weaker.

Low-A

	IP	H	R	HR	BB	SO	BABIP
Majors	11355	8.38	3.97	0.90	2.73	6.44	.292
Non-majors	63029	9.11	4.60	1.02	3.05	5.92	.300

Rookie

	IP	H	R	HR	BB	SO	BABIP
Majors	6466	8.24	3.82	0.84	2.58	6.53	.291
Non-majors	47849	9.10	4.59	1.02	3.06	5.93	.301

The major-league percentages for the short-season leagues are down to 15 percent and 12 percent of the total; those will probably go up, as more players from 2000 graduate to the majors in years to come (overall, these four leagues had a graduation rate of 16 percent in 1996 and 1997, 15 percent from 1998 and 1999, but only 7.5 percent from 2000). That means the difference is probably going to get a little narrower, since presumably only the very best pitchers were the ones who rocketed through the system. The difference between BABIP for the two groups is larger than for any other leagues.

Overall, the results are clear. The pitchers who made the major leagues are, not surprisingly, better than their counterparts who did not, by every measure of pitching you may desire—including giving up fewer hits per ball in play. Looking at the data for all 72 leagues, there were six leagues where the non-majors pitchers had a better BABIP than the major-league pitchers, just as there were six leagues where the non-majors allowed fewer home runs. Strikeouts broke "wrong" once; walks never did. The margins were not as large—the major-league pitchers were typically

10-15 percent better in home runs, walks, and strikeouts, but only about 3 percent better in BABIP—but they were present and consistent. Just as Tom Tippett concluded, based on looking at pitchers by the length of their major-league careers, one has to say that BABIP looks like just as much of a skill as home run, walk, or strikeout rates.

One other thing. Looking at the league figures, there was a correlation of .64 between BABIP and runs allowed—a much stronger correlation than either walks or strikeouts. There was, not surprisingly, a moderate correlation with home runs allowed, at .42—the biggest surprise may be that it isn't stronger. Pitchers who allow higher BABIPs have a strong tendency to give up more runs, something that any talent evaluator is going to notice pretty quickly, which makes it more likely to be a factor in their promotion—or release.

LIES, DAMNED LIES
Any Such Thing?
Nate Silver

The popular acronym TINSTAPP ("There is No Such Thing As A Pitching Prospect") refers to the fact that pitching prospects are much less dependable than prospects at other positions. But why do promising pitchers so often fail to live up to their potential? Nate Silver investigated why it's so much safer to count on position player prospects.

"There's No Such Thing As A Pitching Prospect" has become such a catch phrase that even pitching prospects are using it. Of course, the pithy phrase can't be entirely true. If not for pitching prospects, where would major-league pitchers come from? Does a stork, his beak shaped like Leo Mazzone's nose, swoop down from the heavens to deliver fully-formed pitchers to the majors?

Everything in prospect analysis is relative. Pretty much everyone agrees that some discount needs to be applied to pitching prospects. *Baseball America* isn't treating Mike Pelfrey like he's Justin Upton, and rest assured that we wouldn't trade Matt Cain for Trevor Plouffe. But figuring out exactly what the discount rate should be is something that hasn't really been resolved. Traditional prospect analysis almost certainly isn't discounting enough, and I've come to believe that Baseball Prospectus isn't discounting enough, either. Although the amateur draft has seen a substantial correction—perhaps even an overcorrection—pitching prospects are still treated in trade talks like they're black chips at the Bellagio.

PECOTA needs to tackle this question head-on, and the results are going to be a little shocking. Before we get into the details, however, we should take a step back and think about those things that make developing pitchers different than developing hitters.

1. Pitchers get injured more often than position players do.

This is the best understood and least disputed plank in the TNSTAAPP platform. PECOTA addresses the injury question by means of an Attrition Rate, which tracks substantial drops in playing time among a player's comparables. Attrition Rate is an imperfect measure—it will reflect a drop in playing time for reasons unrelated to injuries, such as being moved to the bullpen or a utility role, or being traded to Japan. Still, it ought to provide us with some useful information.

Following are the PECOTA attrition rates in 2010, five years out from today, for the hitters and pitchers ranking in *Baseball America*'s Top 50 list. We've excluded players like Pelfrey and Troy Tulowitzki who haven't played a significant amount of professional ball.

Player	Attr	Player	Attr
Delmon Young	13%	Francisco Liriano	30%
Brandon Wood	27%	Chad Billingsley	44%
Jeremy Hermida	24%	Justin Verlander	35%
Stephen Drew	48%	Matt Cain	47%
Lastings Milledge	38%	Jon Lester	37%
Prince Fielder	15%	Scott Olsen	36%
Howie Kendrick	17%	Joel Zumaya	58%
Andy Marte	23%	Jon Papelbon	67%
Ryan Zimmerman	20%	Bobby Jenks	48%
Ian Stewart	43%	Homer Bailey	56%
Conor Jackson	24%	Philip Hughes	37%
Jarrod Saltalamacchia	33%	Anibal Sanchez	43%
Andy LaRoche	27%	Anthony Reyes	42%
Carlos Quentin	36%	Mark Rogers	65%
Nick Markakis	39%	Adam Loewen	58%
Chris Young	31%	Adam Miller	64%
Joel Guzman	29%	Dustin McGowan	41%
Felix Pie	35%	**AVERAGE**	**48%**
Daric Barton	28%		
Billy Butler	28%		
Hanley Ramirez	35%		
Carlos Gonzales	26%		
Russell Martin	42%		
Neil Walker	35%		
Erick Aybar	12%		
AVERAGE	**29%**		

There's room for debate about the attrition rates attached to particular players. PECOTA does not know about a guy's injury history—it can only make inferences, and some of its inferences are going to be better than others. Regardless, the overall trend is plenty clear: PECOTA's attrition rates are 66 percent higher for pitchers than they are for position players.

We can cross-check PECOTA's estimates against a slightly more tangible data source. A scan of MLB.com's transaction wire reveals that there were 64 pitchers who spent some part of the 2005 season on the 60-day DL, versus 44 position players. The way that the Disabled List rules are set up, teams will usually place any player on the 40-man roster on the 60-day DL if he suffers a serious injury, whether he's presently in the majors or the minors. Also, 40-man rosters usually contain about an equal number of pitchers and hitters. Thus, these injuries are drawn from a base of about (20 players x 30 teams) = 600 pitchers and position players, respectively. Doing the long division:

Hitters: 44 / 600 = 7.3 percent chance of serious injury per season
Pitchers: 64 / 600 = 10.7 percent chance of serious injury per season

These numbers are broadly consistent with the Attrition Rate figures. A pitcher is about 45 percent more likely than a position player to be placed on the 60-day DL during the course of a major-league season. Note also that these are one-year numbers. If we multiply each of those numbers by five—and I realize that this is sidestepping a lot of discussion about the interaction of injuries from one season to the next—we come up with a 37 percent rate for hitters and a 52 percent rate for pitchers, quite close to the rates that PECOTA identifies.

In any event, it seems safe to say that a pitching prospect is 50-70 percent more likely to be injured over the near-to-medium term than a comparably regarded hitting prospect. This is necessarily going to have a rather profound impact on their respective valuations.

2. Pitchers face a "wall" when adjusting to the major-league level that position players do not.

Here are the maximum number of innings pitched in any professional season for the starting pitchers in the *BA* Top 50.

Player	Max IP
Cain	192
Liriano	192
Zumaya	151
Lester	148
McGowan	148
Billingsley	146
Papelbon	144
Loewen	142
Reyes	142
Olsen	136
Sanchez	136
Miller	134
Verlander	130
Bailey	104
Rogers	99
Hughes	87
AVERAGE	139

A healthy major-league starter might be asked to pitch 200-220 innings over the course of a full season. With rare exception, however, pitching prospects do not accumulate more than 140 or 150 innings in a typical season. Some of this is because the minor-league season is a month shorter, but most of it is because teams, quite rightly, want to protect their premium young arms from overwork. Either way, a young pitcher promoted to a major-league rotation might be asked throw 50 percent more innings than he ever has before, and that's a lot to ask. That jump has to occur sooner or later for a pitcher to mature into a #1-#3 starter, but some guys are not going to make it, or are going to see their performance atrophy along the way.

What's more, the pitcher not only has to throw more

innings once he hits the majors, but he'll have to throw more difficult innings. Major-league lineups filled with smart hitters will require more pitches to be retired, and the pitcher may need to turn to his breaking stuff or tertiary pitches more often, which means more strain on his arm. I believe that this "wall" effect is substantially responsible for the "injury nexus" phenomenon that Will Carroll and I documented three years ago. Our study was based on an evaluation of pitchers who had pitched effectively at the major-league level. Although our conclusion was that pitchers before the age of 23 were more likely to be injured, what we may really have been observing is that pitchers are more likely to be injured shortly after pitching their first full major-league season, because that season will involve throwing many more pitches than they ever have before.

3. Young pitchers do not experience the same predictable, age-related improvement that position players do.

If you've looked at enough Five Year WARP charts, you may have observed that many pitching prospects actually have their valuations go down over the course of their next five seasons. Put another way, PECOTA wouldn't trade today's Francisco Liriano for tomorrow's. This is partly a consequence of pitchers' high Attrition Rates: if a pitcher was healthy last year, we can say with more confidence that he'll be healthy in 2006 than in 2010.

While hitting prospects face injury and attrition risk—moreso than the TNSTAAPP cliche would imply—they counteract it by continuing to develop their talents up until the age of 26 or 27. Pitchers do not have this luxury. In fact, most pitchers flatline from about the age of 21 onward.

I went into our DT database, which covers all major- and minor-league pitchers since 1996, and evaluated the change in equivalent strikeout rates (EqK9) from one season to the next for pitchers of different ages. The ground rules for the study were as follows:

- Only pitchers who reached at least full-season ball were included.
- Strikeout rates were weighted based on the minimum number of innings pitched between the current and immediately previous season. This is the same weighting method that Clay uses in his translations system, and I'm convinced that it's the best way to account for selection effects.
- Pitchers were only included if at least three-quarters of their appearances came as a starter in both the current and previous seasons. This might seem like a meaningless detail, but it's essential to doing a study like this correctly. Almost all young pitchers begin their professional careers as starters, but as time passes, more and more of them are converted to the bullpen. Pitching in relief, however, is much easier than being a starter, and the typical pitcher can expect about a 25

percent jump in his strikeout rate if he switches from one role to the other. Superficially, it looks like the pitcher has had a "breakout" season, but in fact he's just made a natural adaptation to his easier role.

Here is the percentage change in strikeout rate (EqK9) according to this methodology. As we see, strikeout rates begin a slow, steady decline as early as age 22.

Age	EqK9 Change
20	3.4%
21	2.0%
22	-0.2%
23	-1.2%
24	-0.6%
25	-0.8%
26	-0.8%
27	-2.2%
28	-3.1%
29	-2.5%
30	-2.8%
31	-3.9%
32	-2.8%
33	-5.5%

This is easier to envision in the form of a career path graphic. Suppose that a pitcher's first professional season comes at the age of 19, when he posts an EqK9 of 6.0. This number is the major-league average, which would be a very impressive performance. Here's how we'd expect his strikeout rate to progress from there forward.

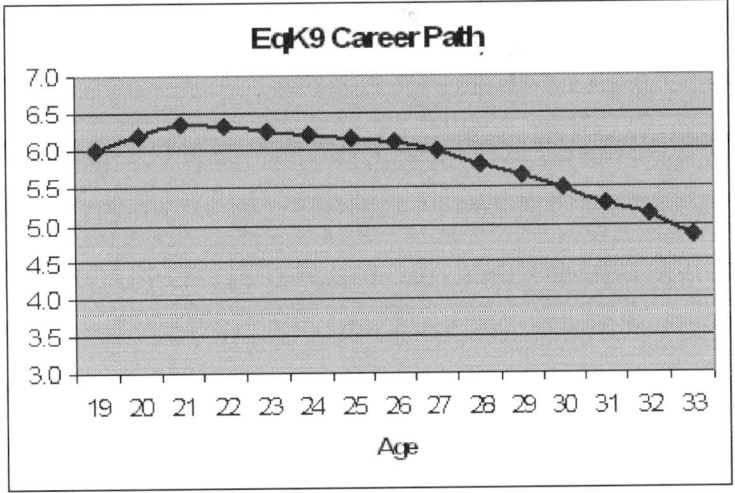

Now, there isn't a lot of downward momentum on strikeout rate until age 27 or so. But strikeout rates are certainly not improving, at least when we look at pitchers en masse, whereas a hitter might improve his productivity by 20-30 percent from age 21 to his peak.

Strikeout rates aren't everything, and young pitchers can expect to see improvement in their command. Indeed, the pattern that success stories like Rich Harden have followed is to cut out a walk or two per game while holding their strikeout rates steady. But a pitcher certainly faces an uphill climb to get better overall when his strikeout rate is on the decline, and the good majority of pitching prospects can't do much better than hold steady.

4. The quality of hitting probably improves more than the quality of pitching as a player moves up the developmental ladder.

This is certainly the most conjectural point, and I'm sure that it reads counterintuitively for people who are used to hearing about the dearth of quality arms. But there are a couple of strong inferential reasons to think that it's correct.

The first is related to the point that we've made above. Hitters, as a group, develop quite a bit during their early twenties, whereas pitchers as a group do not. Although the average pitcher in the International League is certainly much better than the average pitcher in the Midwest League, this is more a result of selecting out the better performers (this is, after all, the primary function of the minor leagues) than inherent, age-related improvement in the quality of individual performances. Think of it this way: the median age of a pitcher in the International League is 26, whereas the median age of a Midwest League pitcher is 22. But while 26-year-old hitters are quite a bit better than 22-year-old hitters, 26-year-old pitchers are not really any better than 22-year-old pitchers.

The second reason stems from an informed read of minor-league statistics. Following are untranslated strikeout rates per nine innings at the various professional levels.

The next time that you hear about some minor-league stud who struck out a batter an inning in his professional debut in the Pioneer League, keep in mind that this is barely better than league average down

Level	K/9	Level	K/9
Rookie League			
Appy	8.4	Double-A	7.3
Pioneer	8.4	Eastern	7.5
	8.5	Southern	7.4
		Texas	6.8
Short-Season A	8.0		
Northwest	8.2	**Triple-A**	7.1
NY-Penn	7.9	International	7.0
		PCL	7.1
Full-Season A	7.6		
Midwest	7.7	**MLB**	6.4
Sally	7.5	American	6.1
		National	6.6
Advanced A	7.5		
Cali	7.5		
Carolina	7.6		
FSL	7.5		

there. This is one of the reasons that I believe that pitchers like Jon Lester and Jon Papelbon are overrated, at least on a purely statistical basis. People "read" Lester's stat line like they would a major-league stat line: he struck out 163 batters in 148 innings—that's outstanding. What kind of crack is PECOTA smoking? Well, strikeout rates are 23 percent higher in the Eastern League (the most strikeout-friendly of the Double-A levels) than they are in the American League—and that's before accounting for the fact that the pitchers doing the striking out are a lot better in the AL than the EL. Striking out a batter an inning is not the benchmark for dominance in the middle minors—it's the benchmark for being on the prospect radar screen.

But we've strayed from our main point. Strikeout rates are one of the cleanest indicators of who is dominating the batter-versus-pitcher matchup, particularly since they are not highly impacted by ballpark effects. The evidence suggests that pitchers are getting the better of it more often in the minors, particularly the lower minors, and less often in the majors. A lot of minor-league hitters have holes in their swings and either can't hit a breaking ball or don't have the bat speed to catch up with a fastball. These players are weeded out before they get to the majors.

We can observe a similar pattern in home run rates; this is the number of home runs hit per game in 2005.

The pattern here isn't quite as steady, particularly at the Appalachian and Pioneer League levels, which are played almost uniformly at hitter-friendly, higher-altitude environments. Power becomes much more a part of the game as we move up the ladder. There are a finite number of baseball players who can drive a decent fastball 390 feet; a minor-league lineup might feature three or four real home-run threats, and a major-league lineup seven or eight. This, too, is a consequence of players getting progressively older at each level, since power is the skill that shows the most significant age-related development. It's also the reason that we've always paid a lot of attention to minor-league home run rates, and that we're paying more and more attention to groundball/flyball numbers. In any event, pitchers not only have a higher mountain to climb, but a steeper path.

Level	HR/9	Level	HR/9
Rookie League	.80	**Double-A**	.80
Appy	.80	Eastern	.84
Pioneer	.80	Southern	.69
		Texas	.88
Short-Season A	.59		
Northwest	.63	**Triple-A**	1.02
NY-Penn	.56	International	.98
		PCL	1.05
Full-Season A	.73		
Midwest	.70	**MLB**	1.05
Sally	.73	American	1.09
		National	1.01
Advanced A	.84		
Cali	1.02		
Carolina	.84		
FSL	.70		

LIES, DAMNED LIES
The Origins of the Closer
Nate Silver

Closers have a lot of cachet, but few players are born into the role. As Nate Silver discovered in the process of debunking the myth of the "proven closer," many successful firemen come from humble origins.

One of baseball's great unsolved mysteries is just where great closers come from. Although it might seem like a J.J. Putz or a Jonathan Papelbon or a Bobby Jenks beams himself straight down from the Great Closer Factory in the Sky, elite relievers have to have some way to get from there to here. That route can alternately involve a resurrection from middle relief, a conversion from a starting role, or an exaltation from the minor leagues. What we do know is that, as far as closers go, the exceptional journeys are the norm. Few closers fit into the Gregg Olson category of a player who was born and bred into his role in the minor leagues, and fewer still of these pitchers were relievers as amateurs.

This article is not going to directly attack the question of the origin of the closer species. But by making a few observations about the closers who have made the leap, we can at least understand the issue a little better. Before we proceed, let's concoct a quick-and-dirty way to evaluate a closer's effectiveness. We can define a Closer Efficiency Index (CEI) as...

$$CEI = RA+ \times (Saves \times 2 - SvOpp) \times (162 / TeamG)$$

...where RA+ is a pitcher's run average relative to his league and park average, and TeamG is the number of games that the pitcher's team plays during the regular season (this term is intended to put pitchers from strike-shortened seasons on equal footing).

CEI is not intended to replace something like WXRL, which is a far more informative metric, but it should do well for our purposes. John Smoltz in 2004 had an RA+ of 1.66 (his RA was 66 percent better than league average) and 44 saves in 49 opportunities; this produces a CEI of 64.8. This is an outstanding score—anything over 50 might be considered a great season, while anything over 100 is a Hall of Fame type season. The highest CEI's of all time are as follows:

Pitcher	Year	CEI
Jose Mesa	1995	183.7
Dennis Eckersley	1990	178.3
Eric Gagne	2003	171.1
Rollie Fingers	1981	163.5
Mike Jackson	1998	155.9

Jon Papelbon is within striking distance of this group; his CEI is 165 as of this writing.

Since 1985, when reliever usage patterns began to coalesce more or less into their present form, there have been 131 pitchers who posted a CEI of 50 or higher. Of those 131 seasons, 32 (24 percent) came from pitchers who had never recorded as many as 20 saves in any major-league season previous. This is a pretty remarkable statistic: nearly one in four great closer seasons are recorded by pitchers who have no track record whatsoever as a major-league closer. How many home run titles are won by players whom most casual fans hadn't even heard of the year before? How often is the batting crown won by a player who spent his previous season doing middle infield duty in the International League? Is the closer mystique all it's cracked up to be?

What's more, this type of season is becoming more common. Here is a chronological list of the 32 pitchers since 1985 who came from nowhere to have a great season (50+ CEI) as a closer.

Nearly half of these seasons have occurred since 2000. We may see as many as five more in 2006, between Papelbon, Putz, Jenks, Chris Ray, and possibly Takashi Saito. Of

Year	Pitcher(s) from nowhere to 50+ CEI
1985	(none)
1986	Todd Worrell
1987	Tim Burke
1988	Dennis Eckersley, Doug Jones, Randy Myers
1989	Gregg Olson, Jeff Russell
1990	(none)
1991	Doug Henry
1992	(none)
1993	Rod Beck, Roberto Hernandez
1994	(none)
1995	Jose Mesa
1996	Troy Percival
1997	Mariano Rivera, Jeff Shaw
1998	Mike Jackson, Tom Gordon
1999	John Rocker
2000	Keith Foulke, Derek Lowe
2001	Jeff Zimmerman
2002	Eric Gagne, Eddie Guardado, Byung-Hyun Kim, John Smoltz
2003	(none)
2004	Francisco Cordero, Brad Lidge, Joe Nathan
2005	Chad Cordero, Dustin Hermanson, Francisco Rodriguez, B.J. Ryan, Derrick Turnbow

course, there is a logical enough explanation for this: teams are looking at the instant success achieved by pitchers like Eric Gagne and Joe Nathan and are becoming more willing to experiment with in-house options, rather than turning the closer's job over to the usual crusty, overpaid alternative. And it's been working.

We can also examine the background of these 32 pitchers. Major-league closers can have essentially one of four pedigrees: they can be minor-league relievers (like Gregg Olsen), minor-league starters (like Papelbon), major-league starters (like John Smoltz), or middle relievers (like B.J. Ryan). Although these definitions are somewhat subjective—someone like Derek Lowe might belong in any one of three or four different groups—I'd divide the pitchers up as follows:

- MLB Middle Relievers (7): Burke, F. Cordero, Foulke, Guardado, Jackson, Ryan and Shaw.
- MLB Starters (8): Eckersley, Gagne, Gordon, Hermanson, Lowe, Mesa, Russell and Smoltz.
- Minor-League Relievers (9): C. Cordero, Henry, Jones, Kim, Olson, Percival, Rodriguez, Turnbow and Zimmerman.
- Minor-League Starters (8): Beck, Hernandez, Lidge, Myers, Nathan, Rivera, Rocker and Worrell.

Great closers are about as likely to come from the major leagues as the minors and are also about as likely to have spent their recent past as starting pitchers than as relievers. The latter fact might be surprising—people often talk about pitchers like Dennis Eckersley as though they are once-in-a-generation flukes—but it really shouldn't be. Almost all pitchers begin their careers as starters and convert to relief as a result of injury or ineffectiveness—not usually characteristics that would lend themselves to closing games for your favorite team.

Do these groups show any differences in their ability to sustain their effectiveness after their initial success? Let's look at the average CEIs in the three years following the breakout season:

Category	n+1	n+2	n+3	Total
MLB Starter	68.4	50.9	20.9	140.2
Minor League Starter	48.4	43.9	31.2	123.5
MLB Reliever	54.0	20.8	32.0	106.7
Minor League Reliever	27.8	22.6	16.9	67.3

(Methodological note: although it is technically possible to have a CEI below zero, negative CEIs are treated as zeroes for this article).

Although the sample sizes are small, it appears that 'new' closers with some major-league experience are more likely to sustain their success than minor leaguers, and that converted starters are quite a bit more likely to sustain their success than pitchers who were already working in relief. In particular, minor-league relievers don't do very well as a group. Once again, selection effects are important here: if a pitcher is throwing in relief at the age of 22 or 23, it usually means that he has been selected out for his lack of durability. Thus, it shouldn't be a surprise that pitchers like Olson or Byung-Hyun Kim burn themselves out after a couple of seasons' worth of high-stress innings.

Finally, regardless of their background, how do the breakout closers hold up as compared to the experienced closers? Here are the CEI progressions for the 32 breakout closers, and the control group of experienced closers who posted a CEI of at least 50 in year n.

Category	n+1	n+2	n+3	Total
New Closer	50.2	35.8	24.8	110.8
Experienced Closer	37.3	34.2	27.8	99.3

Not only do the breakout closers keep pace with their experienced counterparts—they actually outperform them (although not by a statistically significant margin). Part of this is because the breakout closers are younger as a group. Nevertheless, this qualifies as a statistical anomaly. Normally, a player who has demonstrated a skill (such as closing ballgames) on multiple occasions is much more likely to repeat that performance than someone who has demonstrated that skill just once. Not so here.

The idea of the proven closer is a myth. This is not to suggest that a pitcher like Mariano Rivera is not extremely valuable. But Rivera is valuable precisely because he is virtually unique in the baseball universe: a closer who gets great results year after year. Most of the time, closers are fickle, and past results are no strong guarantee of future success.

The flip side of this, however, is that it is surprisingly easy to find elite closers from almost literally out of nowhere. While these closers are vulnerable to burnout, too—Jeff Zimmerman didn't exactly set the world afire after his breakout in 2001—they are no more vulnerable to burnout than their veteran counterparts. The club is small, but the apprenticeship is short.

BASEBALL PROSPECTUS BASICS
The Support-Neutral Stats
Michael Wolverton

Pitcher wins and losses have proven difficult for most fans to abandon. To correct some of the glaring problems with pitcher wins and losses while preserving their appearance, Michael Wolverton developed the Support-Neutral Win-Loss record (SNWL), which he explained in the article below.

> "...and the tough-luck loser in tonight's game is..."

We hear the above quote in dozens of post-game wrap-ups every year. A starting pitcher goes seven or eight innings and gives up only one or two runs, but his team's offense can't produce anything, so he gets stuck with an "L" next to his name in the box score. The fact that "tough-luck loser" is such a commonly invoked cliche suggests that it's widely recognized that the "L" isn't doing a very good job of measuring the starter's contribution, at least in those situations. But that still doesn't stop the W/L record from being possibly the most prominently used statistic to evaluate starting pitchers in major media baseball coverage.

The idea behind the pitcher's W/L record is flawed on its face. Wins are a team thing, after all, not a pitcher thing. If the offense fails to put runs on the board, or if the bullpen melts down in the late innings, the starter won't get the win no matter how well he pitches. Conversely, if the offense is having a great night (or if it's going up against the Rangers, which is pretty much the same thing), the starter doesn't have to do anything more than last five innings to get the W.

And it's not like the luck always evens out over the course of a season. Just ask any member of last year's Tigers rotation. Even over a long career, offense and bullpen support can significantly distort a pitcher's W/L record. Just ask Lew Burdette. Or Bob Friend.

The pitcher's role is pretty much limited to keeping as many runs off the board as possible. That may sound obvious, but it goes against the notion that "pitching to the score" is an important part of a pitcher's job. Plenty of people have looked for a significant ability to pitch to the score without finding it (most notably Greg Spira). And Bill James found that this year's ERA is a better predictor of next year's W/L record than this year's W/L record is.

Toward that end, there's been a gradual (very gradual) movement among baseball fans over the past 20 years to pay less attention to W/L record and more to ERA in pitching evaluation. And that's a good thing, since ERA is a good statistic. It's measuring more of what it's supposed to be measuring—the performance of the pitcher—and less of the performance of his teammates.

Still, as good a statistic as ERA is, it's not without its limitations. Some of those limitations are:

- It doesn't take into account the scoring environment—park, league, and era—in which the pitcher is performing. A 3.00 ERA in Coors Field in 2000 is radically different from a 3.00 ERA in Dodger Stadium in 1968.
- The rule for eliminating "unearned" runs is silly, and it serves only to remove an arbitrary subset of the runs the pitcher gave up.
- Since ERA is a rate stat, it doesn't incorporate playing time. It's easy enough to conclude that a 3.00 ERA over 180 innings is better than a 3.00 ERA over 120 innings. But how do we compare 180 innings of a 3.50 ERA to 120 innings of a 3.00 ERA?
- It includes the runners allowed to score by the starter's bullpen successors. Really good bullpen support—i.e., stranding a lot of inherited runners—can chop a quarter or even a half a run off a starter's ERA. Really bad bullpen support can add about as much.
- It treats all runs as equal. More on this in a second.

To address these limitations, I developed the Support-Neutral Win-Loss (SNWL) record, which we've been tracking at Baseball Prospectus since the 1997 annual. The idea is to measure starting pitchers' performance on the familiar and understandable W/L scale, but without the distortions of run support and bullpen support that plague the traditional W/L record.

A starter's SNWL record is his expected (in the statistical sense) W/L record—how many games he would be expected to win and lose given his pitching performances, assuming he had a league-average offense and bullpen behind him. An additional statistic, Support-Neutral Value Added (SNVA), measures the total number of extra games his team would be expected to win with his pitching performances instead of an average pitcher's.

The calculations are adjusted for park and league scoring level, they're based on runs allowed rather than earned runs, and they're based on the situation in which the starter leaves the game (before, not after, his relievers finish with the runners he turns over), so they're not subject to the problems with ERA we noted above. I won't go into the gory details in this article.

One other benefit of the Support-Neutral numbers is that they look at each start's contribution to winning individually rather than a season's run total cumulatively, so a single disastrous outing can't have the disproportionate impact that it can have on a starter's ERA. Consider a simple example:

	Start 1	Start 2
Pitcher A	0 IP, 10 R	8 IP, 0 R
Pitcher B	4 IP, 5 R	4 IP, 5 R

Their ERAs are equal, but Pitcher A's starts are likely to lead to more wins than Pitcher B's. An average team has a good chance of going 0-2 behind Pitcher B's two starts, but that same team is almost guaranteed to win Pitcher A's second game. The Support-Neutral stats account for the fact that the 10 runs concentrated in Pitcher A's one start don't do the same amount of damage as the 10 runs spread among Pitcher B's two starts.

Are the Support-Neutral stats the be-all and end-all in assessing pitching performance? Of course not. There are many different goals for pitching evaluation, and many different tools that are useful for achieving those goals. If you're doing short-term prediction, for example, you're certainly better off looking at the components of run-scoring rather than a stat based on runs allowed itself. And we haven't even touched the nasty question of separating pitching from fielding.

However, if you're looking to determine a pitcher's contribution toward winning, the Support-Neutral numbers have a lot going for them. They correct for both the big distortions of the traditional W/L record and the small distortions of ERA.

INSIDE TOMMY JOHN SURGERY
Thirty Years of Fixing Pitchers
Thomas Gorman

Since the procedure was first performed in 1974, "Tommy John" (or ligament replacement) surgery has saved countless careers, enabling pitchers to overcome injuries that would have left them much diminished or forced them into early retirement in the past. Thomas Gorman provided a helpful primer on the mechanics and history of the surgery itself.

> *Since the invention of the breaking ball, there has been no more significant development in baseball than Tommy John surgery." —Will Carroll,* Saving the Pitcher

Kerry Wood. Matt Morris. John Smoltz. Mariano Rivera. Tom Gordon. Eric Gagne. Other than an ability to throw a ball past the best hitters in the world, what these hurlers have in common is a four-inch scar on their pitching arms. They're not the only ones. *USA Today* reports that in the 2002 and 2003 seasons, 75 of the almost 700 pitchers who appeared in the majors were Tommy John surgery survivors. That's approximately one in every nine pitchers.

Tommy John surgery—technically an ulnar collateral ligament replacement procedure—has saved the careers of hundreds of major-league players. It may one day make a Hall of Fame case for its inventor, surgeon Frank Jobe (who was Hollywood enough to trademark the name "Tommy John procedure"). Thirty years after Jobe was told by his patient to "make something up," we take a closer look at the surgery that changed the game and some of the recent advancements that have made it such a medical wonder.

First some anatomy: the elbow is a hinge joint, moving in only one dimension (flex or extend), making it relatively simple from an architectural and functional standpoint. The humerus bone in the upper arm connects to the two bones of the forearm by means of various connective tissues. For a pitcher, one of the most important of these connections is the ulnar collateral ligament (UCL). The UCL offers much of the stability that is necessary for the elbow to withstand the extreme stresses created by throwing a baseball at high velocity. Its function is to stabilize against lateral forces and keep the arm connected across the joint space.

Pitching overhand is a particularly stressful motion; the strain it puts on a player's joint is commonly injurious. Sometimes the UCL will weaken and stretch (technically a sprain), making it incompetent. Other times a catastrophic stress will cause the structure to "pop" or blow out. The injury isn't tremendously painful, and it can be incredibly difficult to diagnose without sophisticated imaging (such as an MRI), but an incompetent or blown-out UCL will prevent a player from throwing at full velocity or with effective control.

Until recently, a UCL injury was career-ending or, at the very least, a major detour in a career path. Some believe that Sandy Koufax's "dead arm" in 1966 was simply a case of a damaged UCL. It is unknown how many pitchers prior to 1974 could have benefited from this type of procedure, but given the rate of surgeries today and what we know about the workloads of the past, it is reasonable to assume that one out of every ten or so pitchers who burned out or simply faded away might have been saved.

Crudely described, what Jobe did was build John a new ligament. Since no artificial tissue can fully approximate the function of the body's own connective tissues, and since the body doesn't have a whole lot of spare ligaments lying around, Jobe began by harvesting a healthy tendon. In most cases the tendon is harvested from the forearm of the patient, one attached to the palmaris longus muscle. This tendon is not crucial for anatomical function, and in fact, 15 percent of people do not have the tendon. To see your palmaris longus tendon, look at the palm-side of your forearm. Touch your thumb and little finger and then make as much of a fist as possible. Eighty-five percent of you should be able to see this tendon running down your arm.

San Francisco Giants team orthopedist Ken Akizuki reports that when the palmaris longus tendon is unavailable, the surgeon will often use the plantaris tendon in the ankle or a small part of the hamstring tendon in the leg. Usually this tendon will be harvested from the leg that is not used as the plant foot in the pitcher's delivery. The removal of either of these tendons has a negligible effect on function.

Next, the surgeon has to open up the elbow. In the original procedure, Frank Jobe used a large incision to get exposure to the joint. For an idea of the size of this incision, hold your right arm out from your body with your palm pointed upwards. With your other hand, feel along the inside of the elbow until you can find what feels like a hard round nub. That's the proximal end of your ulna bone. The incision would have taken place along the inside of the arm, beginning several inches above the elbow and ending several inches below.

More recently, Kris Benson used his webcam to document the healing of his own Tommy John scar. In the first image you can actually see the two incisions in his forearm that were used to remove his palmaris longus tendon. Benson's elbow incision is quite a bit smaller than the scars left by early Tommy John procedures.

As Dr. Akizuki explains, "In order to get exposure to the joint you used to have to detach the entire flexor attachment [the muscles that flex the elbow, which you can feel along the incision site]. You used to just fillet that open."

Once inside the elbow the ulnar nerve is recognized, lifted out, and moved to provide greater access to the joint. This is the "funny bone" nerve, and it runs inside the ulnar groove.

Dr. Tim Kremchek, Medical Director of the Cincinnati Reds and one of the four doctors who do most of the Tommy John surgeries on major-league pitchers, explains that in early versions of the procedure this was a problematic part of the surgery. "Sometimes the movement of the nerve would cause scarring and you would need to go back in and re-release it." This was the case for Tommy John. A second procedure to correct his nerve problems guaranteed that his DL stint would last the entire 1975 season.

With the muscle separated and the ulnar nerve safely out of the way, the surgeon would then locate the damaged ligament. After scraping out the damaged tissue, the next step is to drill tunnels in the elbow. If you were imagining a Makita with a quarter-inch bit you wouldn't be too far off. Two different drill passes are made through the humerus in a V-shape aimed at the ulna, and one more tunnel runs through the ulna at approximately a perpendicular angle to the humerus. The result is a pattern that allows for the surgeon to loop the harvested tendon through the various holes in a series of figure-eight patterns.

Over time, the transplanted tendon "ligamentizes," which basically means it learns to become a ligament. There is a healthy blood supply from the muscle above the surgery site (the one the surgeon had to cut through), and there is also a hope that the drilling will give the harvested tendon access to the vascular supply of the humerus and ulna. It is not completely clear how it is that a tendon becomes a ligament, although Dr. Akizuki thinks that range-of-motion exercises help the tendon learn that it is being used as a ligament now and that it needs to adopt. Surgeons don't go back in to biopsy the repaired elbow to see how the tissue has changed, but follow-up MRIs do show that the new tissue is maturing and functioning as a ligament should.

That's basically it. Or at least, that would be it if surgeons and trainers and pitching coaches and GMs weren't the tinkering sort and didn't try to keep one-upping each other.

Dr. Kremchek, who does some 120 UCL replacements a year, detailed some of the many improvements in the surgical technique that have been made since the original procedure. After noting that the drill equipment they use is more sophisticated, he explained, "the entire procedure is less invasive. We leave the ulnar nerve, and we leave the damaged ligament."

Making the procedure less invasive isn't about having a smaller, prettier scar; it's about doing as little damage as possible to the surrounding muscles and tissues. Leaving the ulnar nerve in place reduces the risk of scarring or permanent nerve damage. Scarring would require a second procedure to re-release the nerve, whereas nerve damage could leave a pitcher with permanent numbness or tingling in part of the hand, a condition that would make pitching tricky.

Leaving the damaged ligament in place can help in a couple of ways. First, like any ligament, the UCL has nerve receptors. These receptors allow for proprioception, which is a fancy name for the body's ability to sense the position, location, orientation, and movement of its parts. If you close your eyes, you can still tell what position your body is in due to proprioception. A damaged ligament can no longer serve its stabilizing function, but its nerve receptors can still contribute to the elbow joint's combined ability for proprioception. If the damaged ligament is removed completely, the new ligament must develop its own proprioception, a long and complicated process that physicians don't completely understand.

Another reason for leaving the damaged ligament in place is that the structural attachments of the old ligament are still there. As Dr. Akizuki explained, "It you look at a biomechanics study, the number of loops you put in is not as important as fixation at each end." (Someone tell Billy Koch to quit yapping about his six loops!) Dr. Akizuki detailed the way he uses the old ligament structures: "I split the old ligament longitudinally, peel it open from top and bottom so the attachments at the top and bottom are still intact, even though they might be loose. I free it up distally and proximally, pass the new ligament across, and suture it. The priority is on the new ligament first. You may have to debride out some of the old ligament, but if it's just loose you can overlap it."

No one is exactly sure whether the proprioception advantage or the structural advantage is more important. What the surgeons do know, though, is that leaving in the damaged ligament doesn't make the procedure any harder. After leaving the damaged ligament in place, what some have called an "overlay Tommy John," the cutting edge is probably the use of bio-absorbable screws instead of drilling tunnels through the bone for attaching the harvested tendon, but the use of such screws is still experimental.

Yet Dr. Kremchek is adamant that we understand that surgery is not the most important part of the equation. In fact, he says that post-surgical rehab makes up at least 55 percent of the solution for an elbow injury and that the "difference maker is the rehab people, not the surgeon." Shocking words from a man whose profession is not well known for deferring credit or modesty.

Kremchek explains, "The crucial element is communication between the surgeon, therapist, trainer, and pitching coach. When you diagnose a UCL injury you don't want to waste a ton of time with the rehab. Go straight into surgery." BP's Injury Database concurs. Surgery produces a much higher success rate than just straight rehab. "Keep the communication lines open. Everyone gets my cell phone number: players, agents, coaches, GMs. Progress safely, and if everything falls into place, these ultra-fast returns are possible."

As a case study, consider Ryan Dempster. Dempster was placed on the DL on August 1, 2003, a Friday, and on the following Monday he was under Dr. Tim Kremchek's knife in Cincinnati. The

Reds released Dempster in November; by January his agent was talking with the Chicago Cubs.

Cubs GM Jim Hendry was involved in negotiations with Jon Lieber before George Steinbrenner's pocketbook knocked him out of the picture, so the idea of signing a pitcher with a serious arm injury was not completely foreign. As Hendry explained it, "We had a good relationship with Dr. Kremchek. We've had him look at our guys before. Our staff liked him. We called him in the past for other players and our medical team thought his diagnosis was dead-on. I don't think we assumed a lot of risk. We felt comfortable with our talks with Dr. Kremchek. We felt Dempster was on or ahead of schedule in the winter."

All throughout Dempster's rehab, Dr. Kremchek was in constant communication both with Dempster and with Larry Rothschild, the Cubs pitching coach who was helping to manage Dempster's progress. Available by cell phone, Kremchek could help the team make quick decisions about advancing the hard-tossing righty. Dempster was throwing in extended Spring Training and Class A ball in May; he was in Triple-A in June and July; and on August 1, exactly a year to the day from when was first put on the DL, he was called up to the Cubs' 25-man roster.

Hendry, for one, says he wouldn't be surprised to see more and more teams regularly signing guys with elbow injuries. "Our situation in our minor-league system is that we've had a lot of success with rehab from elbow surgeries."

There are always surgeons working on more advances, as well. Several teams are working on techniques that would allow the operation to be performed arthroscopically, reducing the stress on the arm. There are amazing advances in the rehabilitation process, most notably by Kevin Wilk and his team from ASMI. Even the material used is being re-considered, with "cloned" ligaments built from stem cells and grown in a dish being considered as an alternative to the harvested tendons used today.

That Tommy John surgery seems all too common is perhaps the best measure of its success. While there is still a failure rate of 10 to 15 percent, most of these happen on younger subjects. It would be more accurate to say that the pitcher fails himself in most cases, rather than the surgery being the problem. Some think the procedure is becoming too common, with younger and younger patients electing to undergo it. Others want to have their "prospect" son given the procedure when young so as to avoid it later.

While there are faults, the surgery and the team behind the procedures have made baseball better. One in nine pitchers would not be on the field without it, which would further dilute the pitching population. Frank Jobe's experiment on a desperate pitcher has become a part of America's game, a routine procedure taken for granted. That alone is pretty amazing.

MARCH 3, 2004

http://bbp.cx/a/2633

BASEBALL PROSPECTUS BASICS
How We Measure Pitch Usage
Rany Jazayerli

Baseball Prospectus made a major contribution to the movement toward lower pitch counts by pioneering the Pitcher Abuse Points, or "PAP" system. In the article reproduced below, Rany Jazayerli, PAP's creator, outlined the principles behind its approach to assessing workloads.

To understand the methods we use to analyze pitcher usage, it's important to appreciate that while every team in baseball today employs essentially the same usage pattern—starting pitchers work in a five-man rotation, with four or five days of rest between starts, and never relieving in between—that usage pattern is far from the norm historically.

- As recently as 30 years ago, starters were expected to start every fourth day, with only three days of rest between starts. This does not appear to have had a detrimental effect on the pitchers of that era; in fact, over half of the 300-game winners of the live-ball era were in the prime of their careers in the early 1970s.

- There is no definitive proof that pitching in any kind of rotation is a necessary ingredient for successful pitching staffs. Through the 1950s, starting pitchers would routinely get six or seven days off to pitch against a team they matched up favorably against, then return to the mound on just two days' rest for their next start.

- There is no evidence that starting pitchers who relieve on their days off between starts suffer adversely for doing so. Starting pitchers routinely made 10 or 15 relief appearances a season for the better part of half a century.

So if starting pitchers have been used in many different ways over the years, and there's no hard evidence that any one usage pattern was more likely to keep pitchers healthy, how do we determine whether a pitcher is being used in a manner that's likely to get him hurt?

One thing we have learned is that for starting pitchers, how many days off they get between starts does not seem to correlate with injury risk. One series of articles carefully looked at the track record of pitchers working in a four-man rotation vs. pitchers in a five-man rotation and found that pitchers who worked in a four-man rotation stayed just as healthy as pitchers working every fifth day. It also showed that a pitcher working on three days of rest is no less effective than when he works on four days of rest, and in fact that he might have better command on less rest.

What seems to matter isn't how often a starter pitches, but how much he pitches when he does take the mound. About five years ago, we unveiled a system known as Pitcher Abuse Points (PAP for short) that attempted to measure just how much is too much. The system is based on the following principles:

1. While pitching is an inherently unnatural motion, throwing a pitch does not necessarily do permanent damage to a pitcher's arm. It's only when fatigue sets in (and a pitcher's mechanics start to waver) that continued pitching can result in irreversible injury.

2. There is a certain number of pitches that a pitcher can throw before that fatigue sets in.

3. Once a pitcher is fatigued, each additional pitch causes more damage and results in more additional fatigue than the pitch before.

The original version of PAP operated under the assumption that fatigue set in at 100 pitches, and after 100 pitches a starter was awarded Abuse Points for each additional pitch. The number of points he received per pitch slowly increased as he threw more pitches.

Two years later, Keith Woolner performed the definitive study that examined the relationship between high pitch counts and injury risk. First, Woolner looked at whether there was a relationship between high pitch counts and decreased effectiveness over the pitcher's next few starts. What he found was that, while the relationship was there, the formula for PAP needed to be changed—that until that point, the system did not penalize pitchers enough for really high pitch counts (120 and up) compared to a 105 or 110-pitch outing.

Then using the new, refined formula for PAP, Woolner showed that there was, indeed, a link between high PAP scores and future injury risk.

The way PAP scores are calculated is quite simple. Simply take the number of pitches thrown in any given start, and subtract by 100. (If the pitcher threw fewer than 100 pitches, he automatically receives zero PAP for that outing.) Then the resultant number is cubed to arrive at the PAP score for that start:

100 pitches - 100 = 0^3 = 0 PAP
105 pitches - 100 = 5^3 = 125 PAP
115 pitches - 100 = 15^3 = 3375 PAP
130 pitches - 100 = 30^3 = 27000 PAP

As you can see, by this method a 130-pitch outing is eight times more damaging than a 115-pitch start and 216 times worse than throwing 105 pitches.

There's one other factor that needs to be considered when evaluating whether a starting pitcher is throwing too many pitches. As first explored by Craig Wright in his landmark book, *The Diamond Appraised*, starting pitchers under the age of 25 appear to be particularly sensitive to how many innings they are allowed to throw. Some of the most talented young pitchers of the last forty years—from Gary Nolan and Don Gullett in the 1970s, to Dwight Gooden in the 1980s, to the Mets' "young-guns" trio of Bill Pulsipher, Paul Wilson, and Jason Isringhausen in the 1990s—went on to suffer career-threatening injuries that prevented them from ever reaching their full potential. Conversely, two of the most durable starters of our generation, Nolan Ryan and Randy Johnson, weren't even full-time starters in the majors until they turned 25.

Indeed, when 21-year-old Kerry Wood blew out his elbow, the spring after one of the most exhilarating seasons ever by a rookie pitcher, it proved to be the spark needed to convince major-league organizations that lowering the pitch counts of their starting pitchers might prevent a significant number of injuries—and save them millions of dollars in the process.

So to recap, here's everything we know about the usage of starting pitchers:

- There is no evidence that the current system of employing a five-man rotation is any better at accomplishing what it was created for—keeping pitchers healthy—than the four-man rotation. It appears that most pitchers simply don't need more than three days of rest between starts.
- In the era of the four-man rotation, teams were able to get six or seven more starts, and 50-75 more innings, out of their best starters than teams do today.
- Starting pitchers have, historically speaking, thrived without use of a fixed rotation at all.
- Starting pitchers have, historically speaking, been used as relievers between starts without adverse consequences.
- What seems to put starters at risk of injury is throwing too many pitches per start.
- Roughly speaking, "too many pitches" seems to translate to "over 100."
- Once a pitcher hits his fatigue point, his risk of injury goes up very quickly with each additional pitch.
- Pitchers under the age of 25 are exquisitely sensitive to overuse.

The ideal usage pattern—something I think we'll see some teams try to emulate over the next decade—would probably look something like this:

- A reversion back to a four-man rotation, giving a regular starter 40 to 41 starts over the course of a season.

- More careful observation of pitch counts, with most pitchers probably averaging about 90-95 pitches a start and rarely going over 110 in any given outing. Older, more established pitchers might average closer to 100 pitches a start, with a soft limit of 120 pitches in an outing.

- Judicious use of a starting pitcher on his standard throw day between starts could net another seven or eight appearances and 10-15 innings over the course of a season.

Individual starting pitchers throw fewer innings, and therefore have less overall value, today than at any point in baseball history. But it doesn't have to be that way. By following these guidelines, teams should be able to get 280-290 innings out of their #1 starter safely, instead of the 220-230 innings we see today.

GIVE AND TAKE
Discussing Jonathan Papelbon's Worth
Marc Normandin and Tommy Bennett

Jonathan Papelbon claimed that being converted to closing hurt his future earnings potential (at least, he did before signing a mega-deal with the Phillies after the 2011 season). Marc Normandin and Tommy Bennett went back and forth on whether Papelbon would have made more as a starter.

Marc Normandin: Jonathan Papelbon once again waited until the last minute to avoid arbitration and signed a one-year deal with the Boston Red Sox. His reasoning for delaying the proceedings has been pointed out in the past, by Papelbon himself—it boils down to the fact that Paps, a closer, feels monetarily slighted after being removed from a career path as a starting pitcher. The following quotes come from early in the 2007 season, his second full campaign as a reliever, and the first in which it was guaranteed by the Red Sox that relieving was his role for the future:

> I'm here to get my fair share of money. My main priority is to stay healthy and be able to make money, not to go out and try and hurry up and win a championship this year [at the risk of injury]. It's not like I'm hurrying up and going back to the closer's role because we have a good team this year and I'm going to blow [my arm] out and try and win as many games as we can [at any cost]. No, it's not going to happen.
>
> I've got a lot of money to be made in this game, whether it's with Boston or not. My goal is to make sure I'm ready to play every day and to make money, and you can't make money if you're sitting on the bench. That's the way I look at it.

Papelbon has been vocal about his desire to climb the salary ladder through one-year deals, either through arbitration or by inking a deal right before he goes to arbitration as he has these past two seasons. The goal is to take away the sting of missing out on the contracts starting pitchers get in the open market by ratcheting up the value of his relief contracts—it sounds like a chip-on-his-shoulder situation, if you read what Rob Bradford had to say about it prior to this new deal.

Here's one take on it, though: Papelbon is now making and will continue to make more money in the future as a relief pitcher than he would have as a starting pitcher. There are various lines of reasoning that support this stance, from pitcher health to the starter market to the Red Sox and Papelbon themselves, but seeing as this exercise is hypothetical in nature, we're going to flesh out the arguments for and against it.

Tommy Bennett: Let's first figure out the implied free-market value of Papelbon's services from his arbitration deals. Then, we can work backward to calculate the approximate number of wins Papelbon would need to produce as a starter in order to earn the same amount.

A handy rule of thumb for arbitration cases holds that players earn 40 percent of their free-agent value in their first year of eligibility (for non super-two players), 60 percent in their second year, and 80 percent in their third year. We can divide Papelbon's earnings in years one and two of arbitration by the percentage players typically earn of their free-agent value. That will give us the implied free-market value of Papelbon's services. Here's a table:

	Salary	Implied FA Salary
Arb. Year One	$6.25 million	$15.625 million
Arb. Year Two	$9.35 million	$15.58 million

The Red Sox and Papelbon seem to have a pretty clear agreement on his value being somewhere around $15.5 million. Next year, assuming he stays healthy, Papelbon can look forward to earning approximately $12.4 million.

Next, let's see if we can figure out how much value Bizarro Papelbon would have to provide as a starter to earn the equivalent of $15.5 million of value. Last year, A.J. Burnett, CC Sabathia, Tim Hudson, Jason Schmidt, and Derek Lowe all earned approximately the same amount. However, for various reasons (especially that Schmidt did not even pitch 20 innings), this is not a good way of calculating how many wins Papelbon would have to be worth.

One way of doing this would be to find a comparable player. Earlier this offseason, the Red Sox signed John Lackey to a deal that pays him an average of $16.5 million for the life of the deal. PECOTA's weighted mean projection for Lackey's WARP value in 2010 is 4.1. Simply dividing his average salary by his projected 2010 WARP implies the Red Sox are willing to pay approximately $4.1 million per WARP. This is not the most rigorous of calculations, since the Red Sox are actually paying Lackey $18 million in 2010, and a proper analysis would consider all five years of the contract. However, the difficulty of projecting pitcher performance five years into the future make this a reasonable approximation of their willingness to pay.

By analogy, in order to earn $15.5 million, Papelbon would have to be a slightly worse pitcher than Lackey. Using Boston's implied willingness to pay, Papelbon would need to be worth about 3.9 wins. Something like 200 innings of 3.80 ERA would get the job done. Does that sound like the kind of projection that would be reasonable for Bizarro Papelbon as a starter?

MN: While it seems easy enough to say yes to the above, given how much Papelbon has thrived in the role of fireman, the relationship between his performance as a starter and a reliever is littered with question marks. Back when Papelbon was first officially made a reliever, Nate Silver wrote that the average difference in ERA between a starter and reliever was 25 percent—you could expect a pitcher to move from relief to starting and have that significant a change in his ERA for a variety of reasons, such as the need for fewer pitches and increased velocity.

Papelbon is a special case, though, given his status as a reliever—he's one of the league's elite in that regard, and adding 25 percent to his ERA makes him appear as if he would be one of the league's best starting pitchers as well. It's more likely that Papelbon is on the high end of that scale, as a pitcher who picks up far more than the average improvement in ERA by virtue of closing. In his best days, he used a splitter with fantastic drop alongside a blazing fastball that ticked ablove triple digits in order to put hitters away. The splitter's effectiveness has dropped with time, as the opposition is more likely to sit on it and wait for another fastball—Papelbon's mentality is that if the 95-mph heater didn't finish them, the 97-mph one should do the trick. While he has flirted with a changeup that he uses off and on, generally he's a one-trick pony these days, though his record still shows him to be more Seattle Slew than Elmer's Glue.

The point is that he never fully developed a consistent, valuable third pitch, and because of the way he uses the ones he does possess—his splitter is predictable in that it's always down in the zone, falling out of it—it's hard to believe he would have breezed through starts as well as he has relief outings. Let's assume he did work on that change, though, giving him the repertoire he would need to get by. Without the extra velocity on his fastball, you still lose something in the performance.

My own thinking is that Papelbon would have a ceiling somewhere around a 4.00 ERA as a starter, which is not bad by any means, but as Tommy pointed out, that probably wouldn't get him the kind of money he has found as a relief pitcher. That's just my informed opinion, though—luckily, we can step into the wayback machine and have a look at what his PECOTA forecast as a starter looked like in 2005 and 2006, courtesy of Clay Davenport:

Year	Age	GS	IP	H	BB	SO	HR	GB%	BABIP	WHIP	RA	ERA	PERA	WAR
2005	24	24	122.2	124	49	109	16	44%	.309	1.41	4.65	4.42	4.50	1.5
2006	25	24	126.1	125	48	108	17	44%	.301	1.38	4.52	4.30	4.41	1.8

Those projections are a long way off from where he needs to be in order to get the same kind of money, and his comparables don't do much to bolster confidence in his getting significantly better: for 2005, Carlos Fisher, Ben Shaffar (never made it out of Triple-A), Boof Bonser, and James Shields show up, with Shields being the one optimistic case in the bunch due to his late bloom. For 2006, we see Gavin Floyd, Bonser once again, Brett Tomko, and Roy Smith. These are, for the most part, average to below-average starters who didn't have very long or productive careers. Floyd and Shields are the two most interesting names from an optimism standpoint, but it's hard to envision either of them pulling in the kind of value Papelbon has in his time as a reliever.

TB: One valid gripe that Papelbon might have is that he was never given a chance to succeed as a starter. This can work against him in two ways. First, we are assuming that Papelbon wouldn't be able to match his value as a reliever if he were pitching in the rotation. Some of the reasons for this, like health concerns, are separate from the statistical expectations. But some of it also is based on our backward-looking understanding of just how great Papelbon has been as a reliever. In 298 innings since coming to the major leagues, Papelbon has been good for a 2.11 RA. Now, our estimation of his true talent level has to be a little lower than that (as it would be for any pitcher who put up such a good RA in his first five seasons), but it seems silly to suggest that Papelbon hasn't performed better than anyone expected when he made his debut. How can we be sure he wouldn't have outperformed expectations at least as much as a starter? The evidence about his pitches seems compelling, but I worry that it may just be a way to justify our observations.

Another way Papelbon is hurt by never getting a chance to start in the majors is that he was doomed by his own success. I don't just mean that being so good in the bullpen meant he made himself irreplaceable there (although I think that's a factor at work). A pattern that we've seen with nearly every power pitcher who makes his debut in the bullpen is that commentators immediately discount his ability to make it as a starter. Very few observers questioned Joba Chamberlain's ability to survive as a starter until he was dominant in the pen. The same thing is currently happening with Neftali Feliz, whose dominance as a starter in the minor leagues was basically unparalleled last year, and yet many now say doesn't have the stamina to survive in the rotation. I think it's similar by analogy to Nichols' Law of catcher Defense, in that the more dominant a young pitcher is in the bullpen, the more people wonder about his ability to survive under a starter's workload.

These two separate reasons combined mean that Papelbon may have missed out on some of his upside potential. Since he has already been almost as good as a reliever can possibly be, he can't really have realized much extra upside from here. Can you really imagine many closers with a 10-percent better RA in his first five years? (Keep in mind, Mariano Rivera's RA for his first five full bullpen seasons was 2.24.) However, if Papelbon was a starter, he would have more room to succeed—say as a 3.50 ERA guy—since that's a relatively common level of success.

MN: I think you're right on the nose when it comes to pitchers in these roles like Feliz, but Papelbon is once again a special case. He's a college closer converted to starting in the minors, who was converted back to relief for two reasons: bullpen stabilization and health. The Red Sox were loathe to convert him back to starting once again after watching Papelbon essentially work like a Phoenix Down for the beleaguered pen, and based on the fact that Paps is on a throwing program that, in his own words, is meant to extend his career past 10 years, we can safely assume that the cries about his lack of stamina in the rotation are warranted.

Could the Red Sox have given him a throwing program that extended his career as a starter? I don't see why not, but why waste him in that role if he's as good as he is in the bullpen? I concede that he could have been a bit better than we expected in a starting role, but given what we know about his shoulder and his repertoire, I find it hard to believe he would be much better than that 4.00 ERA or so ceiling mentioned earlier.

PLAYER PROFILE
Cliff Lee
Marc Normandin, Eric Seidman, and Kevin Goldstein

At Baseball Prospectus, we prefer to combine a number of different approaches in forming our evaluations of a player, rather than limiting ourselves to either what our eyes or our spreadsheets tell us. The following profile, in which two of our authors approached a player profile from the statistical side and another offered a scouting perspective, was a perfect example of this multidisciplinary approach.

In the wake of his recent campaigns, Cliff Lee's 2008 season looks to have come completely out of the blue. What began as a productive year that many thought would fade with more innings has instead withstood the test of time, at least within the limits of this single season. What many people have forgotten is that there was a time when Cliff Lee was considered a quality prospect in the Expos' and Indians' systems, before fatigue, an inability to translate his pure stuff into results, and injuries all derailed what seemed like a promising career. Today we'll have a go at what we might expect from this new-look Lee going forward.

Clifton Phifer Lee was selected three times before finally signing with the Montreal Expos in the 2000 amateur entry draft; the lefty had also been chosen by the Marlins (#246, 1997) and the Orioles (#609, 1998) before signing as an Expos fourth-rounder (#105) and heading to Cape Fear in the Sally League. While Lee's walk rate (7.4 per nine) was atrocious during his 44 innings there, he did strike out nearly 13 batters per nine innings. The 22-year-old would spend the entirety of his full-season debut in 2001 at High-A Jupiter in the Florida State League, where he would put together a much more impressive showing: Lee struck out 10.6 per nine, walked a much more acceptable 3.8 batters per nine, and proved difficult to hit, giving up just 6.4 safeties per nine at a level of play where poor defensive support makes that difficult. If not for a stiff shoulder that forced him to miss a month, he most likely would have walked away with the league's ERA title.

Baseball America would rank Lee the 11th-best prospect in the then-stacked Expos organization—this is an organization that had Brandon Phillips, Brad Wilkerson, and Grady Sizemore as its top three—mostly based off of his pure stuff and his recent FSL performance. According to BA, the Expos believed that they had gotten a steal in the fourth round when selecting Lee, as they felt he was one of the top three college southpaws in that year's draft class. Lee was known for having four above-average offerings, but his problem to that point had been consistent command of all of them; here was a pitcher who could struggle due to his lack of command, or absolutely dominate when he was on. *Baseball Prospectus 2002* mentioned that the Expos wanted their young hurlers pitching to contact, and that despite this, Lee led the FSL in strikeout rate, "showing how tough he is to hit."

As for the 2002 season itself, Lee moved up to Double-A Harrisburg and continued to show off his stuff. He struck out 11 per nine while lowering his walk rate to 2.4 per nine, and though an increase in home runs (1.3 HR/9) was worrisome, he once again used his strikeouts and the Expos' pitch-to-contact style to hold the opposition to 6.4 hits per nine. Those low hit rates probably didn't help Lee in the long term, though, as they made him appear to be a more accomplished and polished pitcher than really he was at that stage.

Lee was a piece in the blockbuster deal that Nationals fans might have nightmares about (who knows what Expos fans think these days), since that was the exchange in which Grady Sizemore, Brandon Phillips, and Lee, the current Cy Young candidate, were all swapped for a few months of Bartolo Colon (and Tim Drew). The Indians plopped Lee onto their own Double-A affiliate for all of three starts, then moved him to Triple-A. He didn't set the world ablaze there, striking out just 6.3 per nine and walking 4.6, a big increase over his previous marks. Despite this, the Indians called him up to the big leagues at the end of the year, where he posted a 1.77 ERA in 10 1/3 innings, even though he had more walks (8) than strikeouts (6).

Baseball America was excited by Lee's potential, ranking him the third-best prospect in the Indians' stacked farm system—they'd ended up stealing most of the best of the Expos' system, adding Phillips, Lee, and Sizemore to Victor Martinez, Jeremy Guthrie, Travis Hafner, Jhonny Peralta, Ryan Church, Coco Crisp, Ben Broussard, and Josh Bard among their top 30. *Baseball Prospectus 2003* pegged Lee perfectly:

> ...Lee has a variety of brutal pitches ... and he can throw all four for strikes. Which is not to say that he does throw them for strikes ... but it happens. Lee is pure stuff at this point, with his control coming and going. He's a guy who could find consistent command and be a great pitcher, or he could be one of the majors' flakiest starters and would still be a guy I'd buy a ticket, and a OSHA-approved hardhat, to go see...

Lee would begin the season in the minors after straining his abdomen during camp, and in spite of pitching in pain—he required hernia surgery after the season ended—he did pretty well for himself. He was able to improve on his strikeout rates from his last time at the level (8.7 per nine), but his walk rates (4.4 per nine) still left something to be desired. Lee was called up to the majors and slotted into the rotation on August 16, and he would pitch well, except for two starts where he was forced out early. *Baseball Prospectus 2004* said he could end up "somewhere between Steve Trout and [Sid] Fernandez, either merely succeeding or flat-out torching the league, but it will be fun to see which way he goes, starting this year."

Sadly for Lee, he was the one getting torched during his first full year in the majors. He threw 179 innings, and though the front half of those went well (3.77 ERA, 7.3 K/9, 4.3 BB/9, and 1.0 HR/9 in 107 1/3 IP), his second half was downright awful, resulting in a 5.79 ERA thanks to 2.3 HR/9 and 11 hits per nine in spite of more strikeouts (9.3 per nine) and fewer walks (3.8). *Baseball Prospectus 2005* noted that this was a case of a "dead arm" that caused his mistakes to end up in orbit rather than as outs.

Essentially, we had a young power lefty coming into his own slowly during the first 153 2/3 innings of his career who was then derailed by fatigue during the second half of 2004. He would give us something closer to his minor-league performances and his early time in the majors in 2005, delivering a 3.79 ERA and 202 innings pitched. He managed to reduce his walk rate significantly, cutting it down to 2.3 per nine; the only negative that came from this was a drop in his strikeout rate as well, although it was a still-respectable (but not dominating) 6.4 per nine. His 2006 campaign was a lot like his 2005, with an above-average strikeout rate and a low walk rate making him a quality pitcher. It was easy to lose hope about Lee heading into the 2007 season, as he had just posted a career-low in strikeout rate, and despite the improvement in the walks and control department, he had also given up more hits and homers than was normal for him. Pitching through an abdominal strain in 2007 did nothing but harm his reputation further, as he posted a 6.29 ERA over 97 1/3 innings pitched, with 1.6 HR/9 and a slight uptick in walks to 3.3 per nine.

Lee should have been better than he was that year, at least based on his quality walk and strikeout rates as well as his excellent stuff, but the homers were a problem that weren't going to go away unless his high fly-ball rate came down. That appeared easier to say than do; Lee was an extreme fly-ball pitcher, and the 2006-2007 seasons, the ones where his homer rates exploded, were his most fly-happy yet.

The first step in recognizing Lee's genuine improvement as a pitcher in 2008 comes from taking a look at his batted-ball data, as Lee has given the Indians something closer to the average G/F ratio, coming in at 1.3 rather than an extreme like 0.7. Unsurprisingly, dropping his fly-ball rate by nearly 15 percent also means that his homer rate has cratered, as he's given up just 0.4 per nine on the year, and just 3.8 percent of his fly balls have gone for homers. While that's so low as to be unsustainable, chances are good that this new approach that's earning him more grounders will keep him from the ridiculous rates of homers allowed he was suffering through before.

Lee also improved further on the command that he had developed during his time in the majors, and a look at his strikeout and walk rates leaves you with the sense that he puts the ball wherever he wants to. He's striking out nearly seven per nine, standard fare for him, but he's walking just 1.3 per nine. If we were to adjust his BB/9 to his career rate of 2.7, his QERA would still call for a pitcher deserving of an ERA in the 3.47 range; since QERA is based off of components that aren't as susceptible to luck as others—more on that later—it's something we can trust more than his current (or past) ERA figures. It would be nice for the Indians if he could post an ERA of 2.28 every year, but they should be satisfied with a legitimate ace in the 3.50 range as well. Amazingly enough, that 3.47 QERA is not all that far off from his 90th-percentile PECOTA forecast this year: that had him down for an ERA of 3.81, 6.1 K/9, and 2.9 BB/9 with 1.0 HR/9.

A power lefty who took some years to put things together—that's not exactly an oddity, given the tendencies of many power lefties from the past. Think of Floyd Bannister, Mark Langston, Randy Johnson, Frank Viola: all of those pitchers had to get over some hiccups before turning into the quality pitchers we remember them as. The career arc for a power lefty is something we may forget, as there aren't that many of them for us to analyze; without a constant stream of them to remind us of situations like Lee's, we may forget that they very well may turn into the pitchers we always thought they could become. Lee always had the stuff, and now he has the numbers working in his favor as well.—*Marc Normandin*

Performance Evaluation

Last week we looked at Ryan Ludwick, a player whose success has been deemed a great story. Even comparitively, Cliff Lee's incredible performance this year is nothing short of unbelievable. For the record, I mean unbelievable in the very literal sense of the word, as the large majority of baseball fans simply cannot believe that Lee has been *this* good. In fact, one of my favorite things to do following a Lee start is to check for blog posts wondering whether or not he is "for real." What does that even mean?

My inclination is that being "for real" would involve a performance line more talent-driven than the result of luck. Is this the case for the Indians lefty? Well, I am forced to give an ambiguous "yes and no" answer, since there are many aspects of his success directly related to talent or a change in approach, but there is at least one red flag that should regress either over this next month or next season.

In April, Lee was performing better than Pedro Martinez circa 1999-2000, with numbers largely built upon a ridiculously low—unsustainably low—sub-.200 BABIP. He had always struck batters out at a respectable rate, but his rates of walks and home runs were high enough to prevent him from being a very successful pitcher. That inaugural month saw Lee walk next to nobody and vastly limit his home runs, allowing all of... well, one. The extremely low BABIP was begging for subsequent regression, so he naturally had a significant number of doubters.

As more starts passed and more statistics accrued, it became clear that Lee had turned himself into a different pitcher. He'd sustained high strikeout rates in the past, but now he was doing so while limiting his walks to an extent that his K/BB stayed above 4.5, steadily rising to its current 5.5. So, he was striking batters out, avoiding free passes, and keeping the ball in the yard, all controllable skills for a hurler, and elements of performance that are that much more impervious to luck than success based on balls in play (i.e., based on how well his teammates field). His BABIP soon regressed to .298, right around the league average, but lo and behold, he still kept delivering tremendous performances. Even his rate of stranding runners normalized to a still above-average but sustainable 78 percent.

These signs pointed towards this being a legitimate improvement, but there's still the question of *why* he's improved. For starters, some of the first numbers to stabilize are rates of balls in play. In every year prior, Lee had produced ground-ball rates between 33 and 36 percent and fly-ball rates around 45 or 46 percent. This year, however, his ground balls are at a career-high 46 percent, while his fly balls allowed are at a career-low 35 percent. On top of that, his rate of home runs per fly ball is at a (likely unsustainable) four percent. Given that the league average hovers around 11 percent, this is one luck-based indicator that is sure to regress over this final month, not to mention next season. However, along with this rate-based improvement, his fastball has gained velocity, but he's also mixing in more curveballs.

With all of that in mind, I feel confident that Lee can continue to be successful, but it is not very likely that he will post numbers like this next year. The common misconception is that this slight decline would mean he is not a good pitcher, but nothing could be further from the truth. If he truly has become a different pitcher with a different approach, based on his location, sequencing, and an improved ability to keep the ball on the ground, then he would have the ability to post solid numbers in the future. For all we know, his luck-based indicators could lead to some unlucky runs next year that, when coupled with a higher home-run rate, might inflate his ERA, but Lee's performance this year has definitely been more attributable to a change in approach than luck.—*Eric Seidman*

Scouting Report
When people ask me to explain the difference between Cliff Lee circa 2007 and the one we're seeing now, I have two answers. The first one is based on pure scouting and is therefore scientific and easier to understand, and perhaps even to agree with. Beyond Lee's much-improved physical conditioning, the Indians simplified Lee's mechanics by focusing on getting the left-hander to use the same release point on all of his pitches and achieving what he does with his secondary pitches with only grip and arm action. That's the explanation for improved command—one delivery to commit to muscle memory, one delivery to perfect and gain consistency with. That aspect of Lee's transformation has been a rousing success.

The second aspect is a bit more abstract, and not something that can be explained with any kind of metric or spreadsheet. I still remember a conversation that I had with a scout, and while I don't even remember who we were talking about, the point stuck with me. A significant percentage of pitching has little to do with radar guns, but rather involves fearlessness and confidence. Lee had very little of either last year, and this year he started out well, built them back up, and they have soared from there. Believe it or not, sometimes that can mean all the difference in the world. He doesn't have monster stuff, but depending on how you count pitch variations, he has up to five offerings, as well as the confidence to use any of them (four-seam, cutter, curve, slider, changeup) at any point in the count and in any situation. He's not aiming for the perfect spot any more; he's simply aware of where he wants each pitch to be and letting it fly.

Lee recognizes what's working and what's not in any single start, and he now makes adjustments to accentuate the positive and eliminate the negative on a start-to-start basis instead of pitching to a template. He's pitching smarter, and he's now attacking hitters as opposed to defending against them. It's one of the hardest things in the world to teach a player, and it may sound like a bit too much of that old-time religion, but that's been the real key to Lee's remarkable season. It's much deeper than Crash Davis' advice—"don't think, just throw"—that works when you have closer stuff in your arsenal. This is more, "Think, but not too much, and just throw."—*Kevin Goldstein*

CROOKED NUMBERS
Park Effects on Pitcher Type
James Click

Prompted by Derek Lowe's signing with the Dodgers, James Click looked into whether the performance of groundball pitchers is less influenced by stadium dimensions than that of their flyball-prone counterparts, with surprising results.

After taking a detailed look at the Dodgers' acquisition of Derek Lowe, a number of readers wrote in to discuss the hundreds of new field-level seats being added to Dodger Stadium. The general question was: Did I consider this in my research, and if not, how did I think it would affect Lowe and the Dodgers in general? The answers I provided over e-mail were: "No, I didn't, and it should increase general offense in the park. Because that should mainly be a result of a few more foul pop-ups lost to the seats, Lowe would be affected less by these changes than other pitchers because he's such an extreme groundball pitcher."

This got me wondering about parks and the application of park factors. Park factors are not simply for adjusting runs; they can also be applied to individual statistics such as singles, doubles, triples, home runs, etc. While most parks see a consistent difference in most offensive categories (Coors Field and Bank One Ballpark increase all offensive measures while decreasing strikeouts), some stadiums have differing effects on similar parts of offense. As I discussed last time, Dodger Stadium differs from Fenway Park in that it suppresses doubles and triples but allows more home runs. Additionally, Comerica Park and SBC Park allow nearly double the league-average triple rate while suppressing all other forms of offense.

Generally what happens at this point is people look at those factors and say, "Well, that makes sense. Fenway Park's Green Monster and cavernous center field should increase doubles and triples while Dodger Stadium's shorter center field allows the center fielder to play more shallow and cut off a few more drives to the power alleys." Everyone nods in agreement, noting how that makes sense.

Of course, the one thing people rarely talk about with park factors is the infield, because it's the only part of the ballpark mandated to be exactly the same dimensions everywhere. Outfields can be all sorts of sizes and shapes within the league guidelines (and sometimes not), but it's always 90' to first, 60'6" to the mound, and, if my math is correct, 127'3" from home to second. While the surface can be different, and while some teams intentionally keep their grass short or long, infields are all very similar and generally considered not to have as much of an effect on park factors as outfield dimensions.

It stands to reason, then, that groundball pitchers should be less affected by park factors than flyball pitchers. By keeping the ball on the ground, groundball pitchers should see significantly more balls fielded in the more regulated infield and fewer balls rattling around the unique confines of each outfield.

While park factors for left- and right-handed players have been used in the past, groundball/flyball ratio is not the same binary system that lefty/righty is. There's no clean cutoff for differentiating groundball pitchers from flyball pitchers. Simply using players above or below league average every year likely would not yield enlightening results, because groundball/flyball rates form a nice bell curve with most of the league within a very small range around the mean. Putting players with a GB/FB ratio .01 higher than the mean on one side and those .01 lower on the other would give us two groups of very similar pitchers.

Instead, looking at only players on the extremes of the groundball/flyball scale will give us a better idea of whether or not groundball pitchers are less affected by park factors than flyball pitchers. Thus, for the past four seasons, I've compared the home and road stats of all pitchers who threw at least 20 innings both at home and on the road. From that group, I've then broken them into three groups for each season: groundball pitchers, neutral pitchers, and flyball pitchers. These groups have been defined by being one standard deviation either above or below the mean for each season.

For example, of the pitchers who met the innings qualifications in 2004, the mean GB/FB ratio was 1.30 with a standard deviation of .55. Thus, all pitchers with a GB/FB ratio above 1.85 are part of the groundball group, while all pitchers below .75 are part of the flyball group. Everyone in between those numbers is in the neutral group. Generally, one standard deviation above and below the mean will encapsulate about 65 percent of the sample, so each extreme group has only about 17-18 percent of the total sample. There's some concern about small sample size, but I'm more concerned with each group having too many pitchers with more neutral splits.

With the groups established, we now need to establish how to determine if the groundball group is less affected by park factors than the flyball group. To answer this question, I've computed each pitcher's individual park factors, comparing his performance at home versus his performance on the road, weighted for playing time and centering the park factors around 1.00. Thus, if a pitcher were completely immune to park factors, he would have a 1.00 park factor for every statistic examined. Obviously, no pitcher fits that bill, but if groundball pitchers are less affected by park factors than flyball pitchers, their park factors should be closer to 1.00 than those of flyball pitchers.

There's one additional small issue with this method. If the sample of pitchers happens to be from a more extreme set of parks than the other groups, the variance found between the pitchers' performances might be the result of a more extreme park rather than the groundball/flyball tendencies of the group. For instance, Coors Field had a runs park factor of 1.31 in 2004 (increasing run-scoring by 31 percent) while Turner Field was exactly neutral at 1.00. Two sample pitchers, one a groundball pitcher and one a flyball pitcher and each with runs park factors of 1.10, would appear to support the idea that both groundball and flyball pitchers are equally affected by park factors. However, the pitcher in Coors has been affected significantly less than the pitcher in Turner Field.

To correct for this, each pitcher's individual park factor will be compared to their composite park factor for that season. Comparing on a ratio basis would not only skew results but would also yield division by zero, so differences in actual performance and park factors will be compared on an absolute basis. Taking our above pitchers, the pitcher in Coors Field would have a value of 0.21 whereas the Atlanta pitcher would have a value of 0.10. Negative values indicate the pitcher was less affected by the park than expected.

Here's how each group averaged in each of the last four seasons for a variety of park factors:

Group	Year	H	ER	R	BB	HR	SO
GB	2001	.23	.57	.57	.32	.41	.11
GB	2002	.14	.29	.22	.19	.61	.19
GB	2003	.13	.25	.27	.35	.55	.17
GB	2004	.21	.51	.47	.25	.34	.22
FB	2001	.19	.30	.31	.40	.31	.11
FB	2002	.22	.56	.53	.31	.82	.13
FB	2003	.17	.75	.79	.39	.48	.16
FB	2004	.18	.54	.44	.31	.49	.13
Diff	2001	.04	.27	.26	-.08	.10	.00
Diff	2002	-.08	-.27	-.31	-.12	-.21	.06
Diff	2003	-.04	-.50	-.52	-.04	.07	.01
Diff	2004	.02	-.03	-.03	-.05	-.15	.09

Each number in the chart is the average of how much more variable each group was than the league-wide park factor that season. Because individual pitchers are much more variable than a three-year park factor, all of the numbers for the two groups are positive. In the third section (marked by "Diff"), the two groups are compared, subtracting the flyball group from the groundball group. If the groundball group were less variable than the flyball group, the numbers in this section would be negative.

One look at those final four rows doesn't yield the results I was expecting to find. The groundball group is less variable than the flyball group in 13 of the 24 samples, barely over half. Because our sample of extreme groundball pitchers appears to show as much variance in performances at home and on the road as the extreme flyball pitchers, we cannot conclude from this analysis that groundball pitchers are less subject to the adjustments of park factors than flyball pitchers. Even when looking at categories like doubles and triples, the groundball group doesn't show significantly less variance than the flyball group.

I must admit that I'm a little surprised that this appears to be the case. Intuitively, it seems that keeping the ball on the ground and in the infield more often should leave pitchers less exposed to the unique features of each park's outfield. With GB/FB ratio appearing to have no effect on park factors, we must concede that the other unique aspects of each park—weather, hitting background, surface, altitude, etc.—cause similar amounts of variance for both types of pitcher.

Getting back to Lowe, while I had been e-mailing that I didn't believe the extra seats in Dodger Stadium's foul ground would affect him as much as flyball pitchers, I can't find any information in this analysis to support that claim. Instead, it appears that those seats should affect Lowe as much as any other pitcher in Chavez Ravine, despite his noted extreme groundball tendencies. It appears that Lowe will be able to take advantage of the rest of the offense-destroying influences of Dodger Stadium. That still does little to justify his contract.

MARCH 14, 2008
http://bbp.cx/a/7237

SIX-FOUR-THREE
Adventures in Consulting
Gary Huckabay

In part one of his series on consulting, Gary Huckabay addressed the edge that can be gained through a proper appreciation for platooning and pitcher workloads.

I think it was Einstein who said, "Answers to questions should be as simple as possible, but no simpler." Almost every job I've ever had involved finding answers to operational questions. One of the the most interesting projects I ever worked on was for a major-league organization that didn't just want an answer—-it wanted the question, too. The engagement was pretty simple; I can't identify the client, nor can I use specific data, but I think this is still an interesting case study. I hope you'll find it worth your time to read; if not, you might as well skip the next 6-4-3, too, since it's going to be Part Two. So let's dive in...

We'll cover how we arrived at the question in another column, probably during the Thanksgiving season, when only the truly deranged are reading or writing for Baseball Prospectus. But let's address the question at hand, which is: How can a club best use its pitching staff?

It's a fairly simple question, but one that dominates a fair number of games, particularly once you get past the first three or four innings. Traditionally, teams use a rotation of starting pitchers, usually five, who go out there, throw somewhere around 100 pitches or so (hopefully), then give way to the guys in the bullpen, who work somewhere between one batter and perhaps 10 or 12, depending on the circumstances of the game, pennant race, or acute team need.

By and large, this structure of pitching staffs drives a surprisingly high number of decisions within an organization. It also drives the market for free agent pitchers, the roster structure for most clubs, and even team staffing decisions, like those involving trainers, coaches, etc. On a more tactical level, managers work really damn hard to eke out every little matchup advantage they can get, resulting in a lot of left-handed relievers pitching something like 80 games and 45 innings during a season. Much to the screaming horror of people like me, multiple factors, mostly human frailty and hardwiring, lead clubs to use a closer in games that they're winning by an arbitrarily small margin very late in the game. (I'm narcissistic enough to believe that most managers do this just to piss me off and vent my spleen at random people with no interest in the topic.)

That's tradition, and it probably works better than I'd like to admit. But consider this—let's say you're running a mediocre club, one that just isn't going to win more than, say, 82 games, and that's only if a couple guys in the lineup go all Brady Anderson for you. Looking at reasonable expectations of your players' performance, you're just not going to finish very high. Realistically, you're going to win 70-something games, and your attendance after the All-Star break is going to be way too close to 10,000 a game for your taste. If you take a look at the last several decades, even teams in this circumstance stick with tradition.

So you're in that spot, and you ask someone to come in and provide a fresh, outside perspective, hoping to find some knob or lever you can adjust to get into the race in the short term while you rebuild your talent through the farm system and draft. One of the things you ask them to look at is, vaguely enough, "pitcher usage." You do some really basic research, doing your level best to throw conventional wisdom and the sometimes weighty assumptions that come with it out the window. You come across a very basic question: What drives pitcher usage, specifically bullpen usage? Just then, you glance over at what happens to be a Cardinals game, and Tony La Russa is making his 17th pitching change of the night, bringing in the lucky fan in Section 206, Row 9, Seat M into the game, because there's a chance he might be left-handed. Hey, there's a big part of your answer: platoon advantages drive the bus, often along with conditional fatigue.

So you start to do some actual number-crunching, and as it turns out, there's actually a lot of advantage to be earned not just by exploiting platoon effects, but by drawing upon the specific performance histories of your pitchers, based on how recently they pitched, and for how long. You can get another one percent efficiency out of a complicated metric that involves more than just the last outing, but for a start, this seems a pretty good one. Being a weaselly consultant, you resist the urge to put together a lengthy PowerPoint presentation on the topic and instead present the data to your liaison at the club, consisting entirely of a worksheet for each pitcher on his staff. It looks something like this:

Pitches	Days Rest				
	0	1	2	3	4+
0-14	94	98	104	100	
15-29	83	92	112	109	
30-44		80	96	97	
45-59				98	102	130
60-74				70	
75+					78

It's a simple concept, simplified yet again for brevity's sake. Each cell represents a performance index for this specific pitcher, with 100 representing the three-year average. (For this exercise, the metric doesn't matter. It could be ERA, or WHIP, or VORP, or whatever.)

OK, so you've now had a little bit of an opportunity to take a look at some alternative ideas. The context in which this research exists is in a front office in the major leagues. So, to prep the ground for the second piece of this column, I'd like you to consider how this story actually played out in the real world. I encourage you to take a few moments to review the organization of the various MLB clubs for some inspiration regarding potential pros and cons for this type of approach.

SIX-FOUR-THREE
Adventures in Consulting, Part Two
Gary Huckabay

In part two of his series on consulting, Gary revealed that teams aren't always receptive to input from a number-crunching outsider.

Time for a quick "Previously, on Adventures in Consulting…" (read using your best Don LaFontaine voice…)

In part one, I set the scenario: a consulting engagement with a team that pretty much knew it had little chance to be a contending, or even competitive, team during the upcoming season. What it was looking for was a method to try to genuinely outperform reasonable expectations based on its actual talent level. To that end, the consulting team laid out a proposed deliverable to their primary team contact, which consisted primarily of a grid for each member of the pitching staff. That grid had one axis consisting of the number of pitches in that pitcher's last appearance, with the other axis showing the number of days of rest since that last outing. In the (x,y) cell was a measurement of that pitcher's performance in that circumstance, using data over the previous three years. The chart looked like this:

Pitches	Days Rest				
	0	1	2	3	4+
0-14	94	98	104	100	
15-29	83	92	112	109	
30-44		80	96	97	
45-59			98	102	130
60-74				70	
75+					78

The value in each cell was an index, where 100 equals overall average performance for the pitcher in question. (No specific metric was used; it's largely irrelevant, but you could picture ERA, or Opponent's OPS, or even VORPr, or whatever.)

You, the BP readers, were invited to comment on what you thought would happen next. This isn't just a clever work-avoidance mechanism by your friendly author; it's a way to get perspectives that I otherwise would never have considered. I originally had Part Two (of a planned two) largely done, and was planning to simply fill in the gaps with the predicted responses and have it out for your enjoyment in a few days. I would submit that my plan and forecast turned out to be far superior to others throughout history, specifically "Computers will lead to a paperless society." Instead, what I received in the mail reflected the heavy leaning of our readership towards the law, consulting, baseball operations, and scouting professions. I had intentionally left significant information out to see what people would assume where information was scarce.

You're pretty much up to date, so let's go to the responses from BP readers, and, where appropriate, the full e-mail exchange...

From Reader RMD:

> "I'm assuming that your contact in the organization was at too low of a level for your engagement to be effective. Rarely would someone at the ultimate decision-making level allow such a broad scope to the engagement. If that's the case, they had a limited budget to work with, and wanted enough of a platform built so they could take a proposal up the chain and make a big splash."

Good call, RMD. I had expressed concerns about this from the very beginning, and I accepted verbal assurances that there was not only buy-in but active participation from the very highest levels of the organization. Rookie mistake on my part, but I was, in part, blinded by the hourly rate I was offered for the engagement. This was, if memory serves, my second job for an MLB club, and the highest hourly rate I would ever be offered. The money probably affected my judgment, and not for the better. Can you tell me what happened next? Reader SM took a shot and did pretty well:

> "I've been there, but not in baseball. Let me guess. You showed the deliverable to a middle manager type as a proof of concept, verbally warning him that the charts weren't finished, and weren't ready for a higher audience until they were fine tuned, right?"

That's correct. Please go on.

> "So the middle manager takes the idea and shows it to his boss as an example of either his brilliance or his leadership skills. The manager above him looks at the presentation incredulously, and can't believe what a moron you and your liaison in the organization are. Then one of two things happens. Either he reads your liaison the riot act, and tells him to cut off the engagement immediately and burn this poop before anyone sees it, fearful that the incompetence might rub off on him, or he says nothing, and your liaison's career is on the bullet train to nowhere, given fewer assignments and projects, of lesser and lesser importance."

Both excellent guesses, but neither one quite hits the mark. Full credit for part one of your answer, though, so let's pick up from there with reader AB:

> "You are so screwed. Your contact with the club probably convinced his immediate boss that these were real game changers, so to speak. They then decide that the strange intern that never goes home can create these sheets for every pitcher in the majors and minors, pretty them up, and show them to the big bosses."

Ding! Ding! Ding! Ding! We have a winner! But in fairness, the person wasn't strange, and I don't know if he or she was an intern.

So we end up with a not-ready-for-prime-time deliverable, copied using the original as a template and included as part of a larger presentation from an upper-middle-management type to an upper-management type. From the perspective of this humble author, I have no visibility at all into this process. My last conversation with anyone from the org is a few days ago, talking in broad terms about the limitations of this information, and how it might realistically be used on the field. Come to think of it, even that conversation lasted a grand total of about four minutes, ending with "We can talk more about this when you come south to meet with us."

In Part Three, we'll go over the ultimate outcome and how it played out, but I will leave you with a couple of pieces of information. One is the chart (slightly modified to protect the innocent) for one pitcher, which ended up being the string hanging off the sweater, and the other a particularly insightful comment from a reader who didn't leave a name. First, the chart:

Pitches	Days Rest				
	0	1	2	3	4+
0-14	111	127	103		
15-29	94	112	33		
30-44			70	82	
45-59					
60-74					209
75+					61

And finally, I leave you with this comment, from a reader who chose not to reveal his or her name:

> "You might be the stupidest person on the Internet. There aren't many people who could think any of this is interesting to read on a baseball site, and none of those people would be stupid enough to think it justifies making it a two-part article. Stick to baseball, and put this kind of [stuff] in the Wall Street Journal."

Thanks for writing in, Mom!

SIX-FOUR-THREE
Adventures in Consulting, Part Three
Gary Huckabay

In the final installment of his series on consulting, Gary recounted how a little communication goes a long way.

So, it's time to check back in to see how the story ends, and my thanks to those of you who have stuck around for the full ride. In short, there's kind of a Dilbertesque house of cards that I've built as an illustrative abstraction, with a consultant, some middle management, budgetary constraints, and uneven communication, all taking place in the front office of a club that wants to find a way to be competitive and outperform reasonable expectations. I realize this is a little bit like asking a new viewer to start watching *Lost* for the first time about 50 episodes in (and insisting that they do so while sucking down an unholy blend of Jagermeister and Oxycontin), but bear with me for a bit. If you can, please take a couple of moments to go back and read at least one of the previous two parts to the series, and hopefully, things will become a bit more understandable and interesting.

In the last installment, you may remember that I left the following chart for all of you to peruse and consider prior to this delayed follow-up:

| | Days Rest | | | | |
Pitches	0	1	2	3	4+
0-14	111	127	103		
15-29	94	112	33		
30-44		70	82		
45-59					
60-74					209
75+					61

To refresh your memory, each cell of the grid is a performance index. The pitcher's average performance over the recent past is equal to 100. The left-hand column indicates the number of pitches thrown in the most recent outing. The top row indicates the number of days of rest since the last outing. So, for example, the upper left cell populated with the value "111" indicates this pitcher was 11 percent more effective pitching on consecutive days when held to 14 pitches or fewer than he was overall. You can check out the previous articles for more information, but the key things to understand is that we're working with a baseline where 100 is normal performance for a given pitcher, and that the cells represent pairings of pitch counts and days of rest.

When we left the case study, I had not been in regular communication with anyone from the club. My liaison with the organization had created cards like this for pretty much everyone in the system, from the majors ranging all the way down to Low-A. To make things slightly more Hitchcockian, the entire concept was in its infancy, with me believing we were going to work backwards from the decisions they'd be used to inform. Instead, they were rolled in, in their current state, to an amalgam of information passed up to senior management. Meanwhile, back at the batcave, I was over-patiently waiting to connect with my liaison to get to work on this. Whoops. Consider this an attack of rookie mistakes.

Reader AB writes in with this observation:

> I don't understand this pitcher. It looks like you never want him to go more than one inning, at the very most. It must be a left-handed reliever, used in very short bursts, right?

And RS follows up with an insightful rejoinder:

> Please tell me that you weren't collectively stupid enough to not go into significant detail on the power of sample size. Did these oafs try to put this Tony Fossas clone into the rotation based on one emergency start two years ago?

To their credit, no, they did not. Instead, there was a meeting with about six people, including myself, the liaison, the pitching coach, one assistant who had actually created the cards for each pitcher, an Assistant General Manager, and a scout. At this point, I've been in the area for a couple of days to meet with people, nail down a bunch of details, and weigh in on a couple of topics. It's a very informal setting, and the conversation does turn to the cards, and that's when I had a day not unlike that bird had when it happened to cross the path of that Randy Johnson fastball a few years back.

The tone was immediately not one I would have chosen. It was clear after about ten seconds of cursory conversation that the expectations were that I had created this wonderful new tool that would allow better use of the pitching staff and might even allow a weak pitching staff to become a strength. That wasn't where I had wanted to go at the outset; I had instead prepared for more of a brainstorming session aimed at addressing big-picture questions like "What do you need to make these decisions that you don't currently have?" and "Here's some interesting findings that I think we can find an advantage in if we're lucky—which ones do you want to examine first?" My recollection of the specific events here gets hazy, probably due to the human body's remarkable penchant for protecting itself from scarring pain.

I was torn between two very disparate paths—on the one hand, wanting desperately to distance myself from using a strawman deliverable as something to base million-dollar and multiple-win decisions on, but on the other not wanting to throw my liaison under the bus, thereby making both of us look like incompetent yutzes. There weren't a whole lot of good options, and my instinct to say "No habla Engles!" would be neither credible nor helpful. So instead I fell back on, "Holy crap. I apologize for not being in touch as much as I should. This isn't meant as something to use in the fashion you're talking about. It's only the basis for us to start talking about some options that you really want. I didn't make this clear to all of you, and this is all my bad. Let's start over here, and I can show you some findings from some studies that I think can be used to steal a win here and there without spending any more cash."

The groveling and apologizing took a fair amount of time, and at the end of it, I expected to hear righteous indignation and to receive a hearty chastising. Instead, it went something like this:

"Thank God. I was wondering what I was missing, because I saw this to say that we should keep using [Tony Fossas Clone] as a lefty specialist, which isn't exactly too shocking." That was from the pitching coach, and things really moved forward from there.

One of the key things I learned (or, more accurately, re-learned) is that one of the great things about working with dedicated people is that you're throwing at a moving target. It's not throwing through a tire at 40 feet like some highly creepy Levitra ad; it's like throwing to a gifted wide receiver who will contort his body eight ways from Sunday and stretch out to make sure the throw is caught. The result of the engagement was actually very productive and ended up significantly different from what any of us thought we were getting into in the beginning. I can't go into the types of specifics that would satisfy everyone, but we ended up developing a slightly different method for examining pitching performances for the purposes of forecasting. Without giving away too much, there's some interesting data that points to a greater probability of a significant performance drop-off among pitchers, and it's something that I hadn't considered before getting in the room with a bunch of people with different approaches to answering these kinds of questions.

I still get emails from people all the time talking about stats vs. scouts in terms of "ideology," for lack of a better term. As has been stated many times, there never was a beer vs. tacos question. Dayn Perry may not be an attractive man, his morals may be questionable, and he may pay slightly too much attention to his hair care, but he's always stated that truth very well: it's beer *and* tacos. My fear and panic in this would have been lessened significantly had I kept that in mind and had a little more faith. But not on issues of testable fact, of course. X-Rays do work.

PROSPECTUS Q&A
C.J. Wilson
David Laurila

At Baseball Prospectus, we don't just speculate about what players are thinking—sometimes, we meet face-to-face and ask them. David Laurila unearthed an analytically-minded interview subject in C.J. Wilson, who was as familiar with Moneyball as he was with the American League.

C.J. Wilson has a unique approach to pitching. The Rangers' southpaw is both "a math guy" and a student of biomechanics, and the melding of the two helps create a thought process that is as esoteric as it is analytical. There is certainly a method behind the madness, as the 29-year-old Loyola Marymount product has held opponents to a .206 BAA and a .306 SLG in his first season as a member of the Texas rotation. No American League starter has been better against left-handed hitters, who have gone just 9-for-97 against his slants. One negative is walks allowed, as his 60 free passes are the most in the league. Overall, Wilson is 8-5, with a 3.23 ERA in 19 starts.

David Laurila: You're pretty numbers-savvy. Did you read *Moneyball*?

C.J. Wilson: Yes, I read it when it first came out. I was pretty familiar with statistics already, because I'm a math guy and have always been interested in the different parts of the game. Growing up, I used to memorize batting averages and slugging percentages, and stuff like that, although I guess I never really thought about on-base percentage as much, as a team concept, until I read that book. As a hitter in college, I always took pride in having a really high on-base percentage. That was before it was in vogue, I guess.

DL: Did it impact the way you think as a pitcher?

CJW: No, not at all. My pitching thing has always been… the battle has been to stay healthy and wrangle my movement. I've always had so much movement on my pitches that it has been maybe difficult to command the ball as much as other guys.

DL: Do you use statistics to prepare for a game?

CJW: I look at scouting reports a lot. I'll look online and see stats—I'll look at guys and see trends. If a guy starts walking more often, it presents a dual effect, because it's kind of like the better hitter you are, the fewer good pitches you're going to get to hit, so then you can kind of just narrow down your strike zone. I used to call it the Barry Bonds effect, because it was like people had to work so hard to throw him strikes. His strike zone was so small that you couldn't really nibble and get [strikes], but in turn that led to them being behind in the count more, being less likely to throw him a hittable strike. At that point, he either hits a home run or he walks.

I became really aware of that back then, when he was really on a tear in '01, '02, '03, when I was coming through the minors. I started looking at that as an indicator when I would see other hitters around the league. If I was going to have to face a guy with a high on-base percentage, or a low on-base percentage, relative to his batting average, he's either going to chase or not chase. That affects my strategy in terms of how I'm going to pitch him with two strikes, or whatever.

DL: How much does data influence your pitch selection?

CJW: I really am a super number-cruncher and I use our video system, which is like a statistics video matrix where you can kind of narrow down where pitches are that you gave up hits on, or that you got strikeouts on, or whatever. I've noticed a ton of trends, for me personally, based on location of pitches and particular pitches that maybe goes against the grain a little bit sometimes. I do pitch to my own scouting reports at times.

DL: Did that change in any way when you moved from the bullpen to the rotation?

CJW: As a starter, you just do it less often, because you're trying to minimize pitches so that you can throw more innings. As a closer, or whatever, you're going for 0 percent; you're pitching for 0 percent. I was always trying to pitch for 0 percent and pitch to the ultimate hole—my strength versus their weakness, my strongest point against their weakest point. As a starter, you just kind of take your strengths against whatever. You just stick with your strengths, which is a little bit different, because you don't really have the luxury of nibbling or taking so much time.

DL: Do your strengths differ as a starter?

CJW: Yeah, they're totally different; it's weird. They're completely different. As a reliever, I would throw harder, so effort-wise it was more adrenaline. I threw 95-96 and I would pound guys inside. I'd just force them to hit the ball. As a starter, I don't have to do that as often, so I can use both sides of the plate and kind of take a little bit off and change speeds, and that's created a whole different dynamic for how I throw. It's like you go from the Billy Wagner model of hard fastball and then a breaking ball, trying to make guys swing and miss, to a Mike Mussina where it's like a cutter on both sides, a sinker, a curveball, a changeup—all these different speeds of pitches—and keeping guys off balance overall.

DL: Is there ever a disconnect between you and your catchers because of the way you use data and approach pitching?

CJW: Not because of that. It's more for me, because of the fact that I'm kind of newish at starting; I haven't done it for about seven years, so it's like a learning process all over again. I'm always trying to get the most out of myself, like I get really upset—I get really frustrated with myself when I walk guys. That's the thing that is always the bane of my existence—the walk. I feel that if I can reverse that trend, it would improve my other numbers a lot. Despite that, all of my peripheral stats are pretty good to this point, relative to how people probably thought that I was going to transition as a starter.

DL: Do you pitch to contact as a starter more than you did as a reliever?

CJW: You know, I've never really liked that phrase, because I just throw to a zone. I can't control if the hitter swings the bat or not. I'm looking at a particular guy, and let's say that he's a dead fastball hitter, inside. Well, I'm just going to throw him fastballs away, like over and over and over again. It's not necessarily pitching to... I mean, yeah, he has a chance to hit that, if he compromises, but I don't really think of it as pitching to contact as much as I consider it pitching to a zone, if that makes sense.

The thing is, I was a hitter my whole life. I didn't really become a pitcher until I got drafted and so, for me, I still have that sort of hitter mentality of pitching against slugging percentage, like the low slugging percentages—controlling the bat head by keeping hitters off balance. That's my No. 1 goal, keeping hitters off balance. It's not pitching to contact, because to me that idea is so vague. You can throw the ball down the middle and people are going to whack it. That's contact, but what does it even mean? It's not good pitching; it's really just throwing.

DL: To what extent can you control the movement on your pitches?

CJW: It depends on the situation I have with things like my blisters and calluses and all that stuff. And for me, my delivery is a constant work in process—I completely changed it in the offseason to make it easier on my arm and my body—so the better the delivery is, the more I can control anything. I can cut the ball and sink the ball—I throw a cutter and a sinker anyway, but then I can make my sinker go more down or more sideways, or whatever, if I'm really locked in with my delivery.

DL: If your ball is moving so much that you're having trouble keeping it in the zone, what sort of adjustments do you make?

CJW: I just start throwing four-seamers. I just say, "OK, maybe what I need to do is use my other pitches to get my release point and targeting good." Then when I use that other pitch I can use it almost like another breaking ball. When my sinker moves too much, I think of it as a slider to the point where I'll use it as a two-strike pitch, as opposed to saying, "Oh, I'm going to throw this pitch on 2-0, even though I have no idea where it's going to go." I'll throw the four-seamer, because I know where it's going to go, and then I'll throw the two-seamer to create some kind of vector. I think of pitching a lot differently than everybody else I talk to. I don't know anybody who thinks about it the way I do about it.

DL: What is it that makes you unique?

CJW: I guess I feel that I'm sort a hodgepodge of various different pitches from other people that I've learned from, and different biomechanical stuff that I've picked up over the years. My whole life growing up I was a hitter, which is what I always really wanted to do, and I didn't pitch until I was older, and as I transitioned from being a hitter in college to a pitcher in pro ball, I found that I had a much different outlook on things. A lot of that is based on somewhat of a scouting analysis of the hitters that I face. I feel that, based on how a hitter is built, or his stance in the box, there is going to be a weakness to where... like, he won't be able to drive the ball over the fence if [the pitch] is in a certain location, or a certain speed, based on how he reacts. That's the stuff that I try to pick up. A lot of guys feel that it is unnecessary to get to that level, to where you're trying to figure out where a hitter's A-swing is versus his B-swing, and stuff like that. That's kind of something I've always worked on, even when I was younger.

Now, with video, we're really able to archive whatever sort of statistical information it is that we want to compile and give us sort of a visual to it. It's pretty interesting, but I guess that when I look at a hitter... I've talked to some pitchers about it before and they're like, "I just sort of see what he swings at early in the count and I don't throw that," or "I see what kind of pitches he hits for home runs and I don't throw that." For me, I look at things like where he stands in the box. I might overcomplicate things at times, but I feel like it allows me to have a longer memory chain on each guy.

DL: It sounds like when you mentioned biomechanics, you were talking about your opponents' mechanics rather than your own?

CJW: Well, that's the thing, as well. On my mechanics, I'm physically limited to being a certain height and having a certain stride length and I have to basically just repeat my delivery within certain parameters. But every hitter that I face is a different size; every hitter that I face is a different hand speed, foot speed, tendency to swing at the first pitch or try to hit the ball to right field or try to hit the ball to left field. Every guy has a different swing. It's very rare that you face a team where you have more than three guys with a similar enough approach to hitting that you can pitch them the same way if you're really trying to get to the point of fully neutralizing their attack.

I've always felt that if I over-prepare, by over-analyzing, then when I get into the game, what I would revert to would be a step below over-analysis, which would still be analysis as opposed to just heaving the ball in there and hoping. I don't believe in hope at all. Hope isn't a very good strategy when you're out there pitching and trying to get guys out.

DL: As a starter, you're facing hitters multiple times in a game. Can you attack the same weaknesses in the same way, every at-bat?

CJW: It just depends on the quality of the hitter. You have different strata, statistically speaking. You have your just-kind-of-scraping-to-get-by .200-.230 hitters; then you have the .230 hitter with a lot of pop, where if you make a mistake he might hit it over the fence. Then you have your guys who are .250, .260, .270 hitters, and then you have your guys who are kind of .280-.300, then you have your guys who are .300-plus.

You'll have a guy like Joe Mauer or Justin Morneau, who is a power-line-drive hitter, or a Derek Jeter who is a really-high-batting-average hitter, or Ichiro, who is high-batting-average because he has this foot-speed thing, and you have to pitch against the foot speed as well. A guy like Jason Giambi, it's more like if you get him to hit the ball on the ground you did your job.

With Ichiro, that could be a hit and it could turn into a double, because of the stolen base thing. I factor that in as well and try to get Ichiro to hit the ball to a certain part of the field. I think about his swing and how it works as opposed to just saying, "Oh, I'm going to get him to hit the ball on the ground," because he's going to beat out a lot of stuff that he hits to the six hole. He's going to beat out every single ball that the third baseman has to go to his left on; every ball.

DL: To what extent do you pitch to your team's defensive strengths?

CJW: Based on what kind of stuff that I have, and the way that my ball moves, certain defenders are going to field the ball more often than not. I feel that a lot of times the defense is set around the hitters, like "this guy is a pull hitter," but to me, the defenses could be set around the pitcher. For instance, a guy like me who has a heavy sinker and a cutter is going to force the ball to the corners of the field more; the ball is going to be hit more to the three hole and the six hole as opposed to up the middle. The ball doesn't get hit up the middle on me a lot, unless it's a complete rocket, so I prefer to have the fielders play in the hole on the left side. Having Elvis Andrus and Mike Young, who are really sure-handed, on the left side makes it easy for me. If one of those guys wasn't sure-handed, it would complicate my strategy a lot more. Now I can just say, if a righty is up, "OK, if he hits a ground ball, I just want him to pull it." That's how I think about changing speeds on the baseball, or changing the different types of movement.

DL: Can you say a little more about biomechanics and the movement you get on your pitches?

CJW: A hard thing for some people to judge, and gauge, is how their anatomy is going to affect the flight of the ball. The reason why some guys are able to throw only one pitch, let's say a slider or a curveball, but they can't throw the other one, is all based on the ratio—in my opinion—of your finger length to your palm, and the width of your palm to the length of your fingers. If you're able to grip the ball and you have medium-sized hands, then you have more flexibility because you can make the ball go sideways, because there is less deflection, distance-wise, from your same release point.

If you have really, really long hands, then it's kind of like having more whip, so you might throw harder and make the ball spin more, but you're not going to be able to throw the big variety of pitches without some sort of visual deflection from a hitter. That's why... Greg Maddux didn't have very big hands, but he was able to make the ball move in every direction and it looked kind of the same coming out of his hand. That's because he could be on almost the entirely different side of the ball, but his release point would never change.

DL: Had you been born 20 years earlier, would you be a different pitcher?

CJW: I wouldn't have been a pitcher; I would have been a hitter. The damage that I did to my arm as a Little Leaguer, throwing too many breaking pitches and stuff, would have been irreversible and I probably wouldn't have been able to make it through the Tommy John surgery that I had as a 22-year-old. I knew that I'd eventually need that, because my arm hurt all the time when I was growing up.

DL: I was referring more to the detailed information and video than wasn't readily available until more recently.

CJW: It would have been the same; I just would have had a thicker notebook. I've always kept notes. Even when I was in the minor leagues, I kept these huge notebooks on every hitter where I drew their feet and drew their swing path. I had the four-colored pen, and all that stuff. The technology that we had in the minor leagues, when I was in A-ball, was probably like what everybody in the big leagues had 20 years before I got there. So, I was the same pitcher then that I am now, if that makes sense. Like I said, I don't know any pitchers who think like I do.

PROSPECTUS Q&A
Craig Breslow
David Laurila

Some pitchers go about their business without thinking about what they're up to on the mound. Craig Breslow, whom David Laurila spoke to about mechanics and the physics of pitching, wasn't one of them.

Craig Breslow has both a major-league resume and a biochemistry degree from Yale. Originally a 26th-round pick by Milwaukee in the 2002 draft, the 26-year-old left-hander made his big-league debut in 2005, appearing in 14 games for the Padres. Signed by Boston in January as a minor-league free agent, the native of Trumbull, Connecticut, saw action in 13 games out of the Red Sox bullpen last year, going 0-2 and posting a 3.75 ERA in 12 innings. David Laurila sat down with Breslow for BP to talk about how the Ivy League graduate views pitching philosophy, mechanics, and the genetic predisposition of arm-slots.

Baseball Prospectus: You studied molecular biophysics at Yale. Can you make a good analogy between that and baseball?

Craig Breslow: Boy, probably not. Biochemistry is such a specific science—it's so analytical and methodical, and that kind of mentality can actually hurt in baseball. The specificity of what you do in the lab is something you can't take to the mound with you. Maybe it's similar in the preparation, but on the mound you need to make adjustments and don't want to be too predictable. You can't do that in the lab.

BP: What about finger placement and finger pressure on the seams when you release the ball? How precise do those need to be on each pitch?

CB: Well, in terms of repeating pitches and particularly movement on pitches, then of course pressure must be precise and consistent from pitch to pitch. Finger pressure impacts the spin of the ball, which translates into breaking pitches breaking, sliders sliding, etc. I know from experience that I rarely throw two pitches identically, but that tends to help me in that some pitches move earlier, some later, more, less, etc.

BP: You often hear pitchers talk about how the ball comes out of their hand. What does that actually mean?

CB: The way a pitcher releases a ball has a drastic effect on the spin that is derived. Commonly pitchers talk about staying behind or on top of the baseball, meaning that the fingers are behind the ball and true four-seam spin is achieved. When pitchers tire or get mechanically neglectful, the hand tends to get under the ball and the plane and trajectory are altered.

BP: Once the ball leaves a pitcher's hand, he no longer controls what is going to happen. Prior to it leaving his hand, what separates a big-league pitcher from a minor-league pitcher?

CB: I think, interestingly, that mechanically there is little that separates a big-league pitcher from a minor-league pitcher, with perhaps the exception that big-league pitchers have mastered the ability to repeat their deliveries from pitch to pitch. While the ball is still in a pitcher's hand, I think the fundamental differences between minor leaguers and big leaguers are not mechanical, but instead mental. Big-league pitchers show an ability to make adjustments quickly and to maintain a level of concentration, focus, and confidence that is sometimes elusive to minor leaguers.

BP: Players drafted out of high school face the decision of signing a pro contract or going to college. While the quality of on-the-field instruction is arguably better in pro ball, a college education offers insights to the world you can't experience in the minor leagues. Is baseball a game where that type of personal growth is important?

CB: Coming from Yale, I am a strong proponent of the college experience. I am well aware that college is not for everyone, and it is becoming increasingly difficult to convince young athletes to turn down lucrative offers to go to college. However, baseball is a game of maturity, and a game which requires both physical and mental discipline to succeed over the course of a season. I believe that college offers athletes a chance to foster some of the responsibility and independence it takes to be productive as a professional.

BP: Bill James was once quoted as saying, "Pitchers, basically, like to throw fastballs...They are proud of the fact that they can throw hard. They like it." What are your thoughts on that?

CB: I think it is true that pitchers primarily take pride in the gun-readings they garner. That so much emphasis is placed on velocity is not attributable to pitchers only, though. When is the last time a pitcher threw 80 miles per hour, kept hitters off balance, threw strikes, changed speeds, and got drafted? It doesn't happen. I look at it this way: velocity will get you a foot in the door, perhaps even give you a few more chances, but ultimately, it takes the acquisition of the skill of pitching to be successful.

BP: How much should an individual hitter dictate how you pitch?

CB: I think each at-bat requires a combination of recognizing your skills and coupling that with the knowledge of a hitter's weakness. Ideally those match up, however often they don't. In those scenarios I think it is more important to pitch to your strengths than to a hitter's weakness.

BP: Left-handed hitters historically like the ball down-and-in, while the same isn't true for right-handed hitters. Have you ever heard an explanation for why that is, or do you have your own theory?

CB: That is a question for which I don't know the answer. Garnering a guess, I would propose that perhaps since hitters generally face right-handed pitching growing up, perhaps right-on-right fastballs down-and-in are typically rarely thrown, while to lefties, right-handed pitchers may come inside more often. From seeing that pitch regularly, perhaps left-handed hitters have adapted a suitable swing. Just a guess.

BP: When you're watching a hitter from the bullpen, or on video, what are you looking for?

CB: I typically watch the way hitters approach at-bats. We get a general scouting report that may dictate some holes, tendencies, etc. I like to be aware of guys that bunt, go the other way, move runners, that sort of thing. Video is available almost immediately—definitely by the end of the game—and since that offers the ability to be slowed down, repeated, etc., I think it is a great tool, though I caution myself against becoming overly analytical.

BP: Does a young pitcher learn more from an experienced and well-prepared catcher like Jason Varitek, or from other pitchers?

CB: A combination of both. I think that throwing to Tek has been invaluable to my transition to the major leagues. He is one of the most focused and prepared players I have ever met. It is a privilege to play with him. In-game, I rely greatly on his pitch-calling ability and his ability to read situations. While sitting in the bullpen, and in between outings, I try to talk with some of the veteran pitchers as much as possible and see the way they approach certain hitters—certainly situations—that sort of thing.

BP: When you meet the pitching coach of your new team, what are the first things you talk about?

CB: Generally, I think we try to get a feel for each others' styles. Not every coach is the same, and similarly not every pitcher is. I think we try to determine mutually what works best for each player, what pitches we like to throw in certain situations. That way, it becomes easier for a coach to identify what may be going wrong when things start to run amok.

BP: You've pitched for both the Red Sox and Padres, and before that spent time in the Brewers system. How does the pitching philosophy differ between those organizations, at both the minor-

and major-league levels?

CB: I think that the philosophies in the minor leagues have primarily been the same. At the lower levels, there is a focus on some fundamental tenets; learning the professional game, working ahead, and mastering a secondary pitch. At the big league level, I would say there is less hands-on mechanical tinkering but more result-oriented instruction. More time is spent on the intricacies; holding runners, fielding bunts, etc.

BP: In an interview with *Baseball Prospectus* last summer, pitching instructor Tom House said, "Leave the throwing arm alone; it's genetically predetermined." Do you agree with that, and have you ever had anyone suggest that you change your own arm-slot?

CB: I think that to some extent we are genetically predisposed to certain traits, arm-slot, velocity, breaking ball spins. For me to lower my arm-slot—and I have tried—feels as foreign as throwing right-handed. I actually tried lowering my arm-slot slightly, to increase my success against left handed hitters. The results are still pending...

BP: If Warren Spahn and Juan Marichal can combine to throw over 400 pitches in a game, why can't today's pitchers do the same? Shouldn't advancements in training and sports medicine make it easier to throw a lot of innings?

CB: This is obviously a heated debate. Unequivocally, the pitchers of earlier eras threw more, far more, than today's pitchers do. I think that the effects of the advancements in sports medicine and training are somewhat ambivalent. On one hand, pitchers are bigger, stronger, and throwing harder than ever before. However, for this reason, I think they are putting increased strain on the body as well. Perhaps because of strength training and an increased understanding of the anatomical demands of pitching, I can throw 90 miles per hour today, but along with that comes the stress, torque, and wear of a 90-mile-per-hour fastball. Additionally, I think that kids are pitching, not throwing, more at an earlier age, and athletes are specializing in one sport at an earlier age—two factors that could lead to injuries.

BP: With your background in biochemistry, what can you tell us about the dangers of anabolic steroids, and has anyone ever approached you for advice about their effects?

CB: Actually it's kind of funny that you would ask. I guess either fortunately or unfortunately, simply because of where I went to school, many of my teammates have deemed me an expert on such subjects from drugs to the weather. As far as steroids, I think the dangers are pretty well documented, from short-term acute injuries to longer-term, more serious damage. Some people have asked some general questions, but just out of curiosity, and not with intent. The problem with steroids is the same as the attraction—they work, and for that reason I am not sure they will ever be completely abandoned.

BP: Do you plan to go to medical school someday?

CB: That was the contingency plan if baseball didn't work out, but it kind of gets tucked further away as I have more success. I guess it still is, but hopefully I'll have 15 years in the game and I won't have to think about it for awhile. That said, I've always felt strongly about medicine, and it's something I'll keep as an option. We'll see when the time comes.

PROSPECTUS Q&A
Brian Bannister
David Laurila

Brian Bannister became a sabermetric celebrity by discussing his affinity for PITCHf/x and defense-independent statistics while pitching in the major leagues. In an interview with David Laurila, Bannister explained his analytical approach to pitching.

Brian Bannister is a thinking man's pitcher. Known more for his guile and pitching acumen than for his stuff, the 26-year-old right-hander has established himself as a mainstay in the Royals starting rotation in his first full major-league season. Originally a seventh-round pick by the Mets in 2003, Bannister was acquired from them last December in exchange for reliever Ambiorix Burgos. The son of former big-league pitcher Floyd Bannister, the USC product has started 17 games for Kansas City and is 7-6, 3.45 in 107 innings.

David talked to Bannister about his cerebral approach to pitching, the major-league strike zone, and how he views his VORP and PECOTA projection.

David Laurila : Who is Brian Bannister?

Brian Bannister : Brian Bannister is a student of the game of baseball. I've known for a long time that I wasn't blessed with the greatest amount of ability, but what your future is based on is more than just your physical talent. I've always believed there are guys who learn certain aspects of the game that allow them to play at a level above their physical talent. Some guys survive on future projections for awhile, and then, as they don't live up to those projections, their careers come to an end. I've always wanted to be known as a guy who got the most of his ability—someone who maximized his potential—because to me that's the true measure of success.

DL: What approach do you take with you to the mound?

BB: I obviously didn't get to the major leagues on my fastball velocity. I learned early on, through guys like Maddux, Glavine, and Schilling, that locating your fastball is the single most important aspect of pitching. It's about fastball command. Beyond that, it's the ability to throw alternate pitches in hitter's counts, like 2-0, 2-1, and 3-1. There's a hidden side to the approach of a pitcher, which includes the ability to throw a first-pitch strike—something Schilling is a huge advocate of. There's also the ability to throw a strike on 1-1, which is one of the fundamental principles of Rick

Peterson, who was my pitching coach with the Mets. By going to a 1-2 count, as opposed to a 2-1 count, a hitter's batting average in the major leagues drops by over two hundred points. Those are the kind of hidden things that I think the mainstream media and the average fan doesn't pick up on. I believe that pitching is all about giving yourself the best odds of success—not just finding the guy with the best stuff and sending him out there to compete. It's the guys with the best stuff who understand the odds and percentages of pitching that become the Hall of Famers.

DL: Is it possible to think too much on the mound?

BB: I think it's possible to think too much about the wrong things. You're thinking about things you can't control, like who is standing in the batter's box, or maybe drifting off about something like what your ERA will be if you give up a home run to the next hitter. I think every pitcher has been guilty of thinking thoughts like that—about what will result if something negative happens. When you do, it ultimately comes out in the next few pitches or over the course of the game. The negative will transcend into your results. That is why being mentally tough is such an important aspect of pitching. It takes training and preparation to achieve that, which is why your bullpen sessions are so important. You're training your mind to get ready for the game, and also to react to situations that might come up.

DL: Can you normally sense when a hitter is about to adjust to how you're working him, and if so, do you wait for him to prove that he is or do you try to beat him to the punch?

BB: One of the hardest things about pitching, and one of the reasons no one will ever have a zero ERA, is that while you're trying to play the odds in your favor, there are no certainties. If a hitter has a reputation of always taking the first pitch, as a pitcher you're only hurting yourself by not taking advantage of that and throwing a strike. But I remember that Ted Williams, who almost always took a strike, hit a first-pitch home run once and the pitcher yelled at him while he was running around the bases that he never swung at the first pitch. Those are the types of things that a pitcher needs to study and learn about a hitter, because at the major-league level a lot of hitters change when there are men on base or in scoring position. That's why a lot of young pitchers struggle, because they don't recognize that good hitters change their approach in certain situations. For a pitcher, it's a guessing game as to how you want to attack a hitter in a given at-bat, and you can't always be right.

DL: Hitters typically hit mistakes. How would you define a mistake?

BB: It's not only a pitch that's not well-executed, which, in general, could be a hanging curveball or a fastball over the heart of the plate. A mistake can also be a pitch to a hitter that has one strength, and pitching directly into that strength. It's a mistake because every hitter has weaknesses, and it's a pitcher's job to exploit them, hopefully matching them with his own strengths. By not taking advantage of that, and pitching into his strengths, you're just increasing the probability that the hitter will be successful.

DL: Two nights ago you allowed home runs to Dustin Pedroia, Manny Ramirez, and David Ortiz. What was your intent on each pitch, and why were they hit out of the park?

BB: I'll take you through each one. On the 3-2 count to Pedroia, just in my own research, my own study of him, it was a case of where throwing a strike doesn't always mean throwing a pitch in the strike zone. If you know that a hitter has a tendency to swing at a pitch out of the zone, to a pitcher that's a strike. What I was trying to do with that pitch, which ninety-five percent of the time is going to be a fastball—and the hitter knows that—was to throw a pitch that was elevated. Getting a hitter to swing at a pitch that's elevated will help you get him out, because it's a ball—it's a lower-percentage pitch to hit. In my research, that was the pitch to get him out on; he just did a good job of getting on top of the ball. He hit the pitch I was trying to throw.

DL: How about the pitches to Ramirez and Ortiz?

BB: With Manny, it was a 2-1 fastball, and I missed out over the plate. That's a pitch that a major-league hitter should hit, so it was simply a mistake pitch—my worst pitch of the night. The 3-2 pitch to Ortiz was also a mistake, but it was a mistake for a different reason. I had thrown him seven pitches, and we decided to throw him a changeup. The best changeup is one that's below the knees—below the strike zone for a ball—because it has the best action and movement on it, but I decided to throw it for a strike. I threw it up in the strike zone, and he managed to hit it to the shortest part of the park. [*Editor's note: Ortiz lined the ball just inside the Pesky Pole, 302 feet from home plate.*]

DL: Joe Mauer recently said that when he's going well with the bat, the ball almost seems to be coming toward the plate in slow motion. As a pitcher, what do you see, or feel, when you're in the zone?

BB: I think that what happens—to me, besides a hitter's past performance, what's most significant is the confidence level. For both a hitter and a pitcher, confidence translates into a subconscious ability to relax. Whether you call it being in your zone, on fire, or anything else, as an athlete it's that ability to relax. As a pitcher, it allows you to grip the ball looser, which allows you to finish a pitch, to impart more spin on it, and to keep it lower in the strike zone. In general, your muscles react quicker than when you're tense. It's the same thing with a hitter. Being relaxed allows the muscles to be looser and your swing to follow a more natural arc; your hands to be quicker, and the bat barrel to release quicker. That translates to more bat speed and a swing with better timing. I always try to be aware of that on the mound, because to me a .250 hitter who is in the zone hits more like a .350 or .400 hitter, whereas a guy who's hitting .350 but is struggling might be hitting worse than someone who is a .200 hitter.

DL: What you're saying is that a lesser hitter may be more dangerous on a given day?

BB: Yes. You have to know the lineup, one through nine, but at the same time you have to know that, at some point, a three- or four-hole hitter might be a weaker hitter than the ninth-place hitter. That's based on his recent performance, because even though his overall numbers may not show it, they're an average—they're based on the entire season. Recent performance can have a real impact on what a hitter is likely to do in a given game. One of the biggest tells of a hitter is that when he's tense, or if he's injured and not playing at 100 percent physically, he starts cheating on balls. He's struggling, and not as quick, so mentally he's not as relaxed. That causes him to cheat, which makes him more susceptible to breaking balls. You see him fly out a lot, because he's trying to get the bat head out. That, along with a hitter's body language after a swing, or after his at-bat, is a very telling sign.

DL: How would you describe the major-league strike zone?

BB: Compared to other levels, it's clearly defined, and it's enforced better because the umpires are better. The QuesTek system basically enforces the accuracy of the strike zone and helps make the umpires better. But I think what you see, coming up from high school, college, and the minor leagues, is that it gets narrower at the corners. You don't get wide strikes. Even compared to the 1980s, it's a slightly narrower zone. You hear older pitchers talk about expanding the zone, but it's very hard to do that nowadays because of the enforcement of the QuesTek system and the evaluations they do. However, I also think that an inch or two has been added at the top of the zone, which has historically been from the bottom of the letters. Of course, even though that's how it's drawn, it's never really been enforced that way. It's been more from the waist to the knees.

DL: You feel that the strike zone is somewhat higher now?

BB: I think it's compensation for it being narrowed, and I see more pitchers and hitters surprised at strike calls on balls above the waist. You see it most often on a bad curveball, a hanging curveball, where the hitter traditionally takes it because coming in he registers it as a ball. Sometimes you'll notice the pitcher react like he's surprised that the umpire calls it a strike.

DL: How much do the strike zones of individual umpires vary?

BB: I think, at the major-league level, it's been extremely consistent, and I give a lot of credit to the umpires. I think the only variation I've seen, umpire to umpire, is their determination of a strike on a breaking pitch. A strike, by definition, is where the pitch crosses the plate, and from pitcher to pitcher the break of a breaking pitch is different. Some guys have more of a vertical break on a curveball, and some guys have more of a horizontal break on a slider. It's a judgment call for each umpire, because even though it might cross the plate, it finishes outside of the strike zone where the catcher catches it. Do they call that a strike or not? The one variation I see is how they make that determination.

DL: When you go over scouting reports before a game, do they include the tendencies of that night's plate umpire?

BB: It's something that's discussed among pitchers. Is he a so-called pitchers' umpire, or is he a hitters' umpire? But I think the only real difference is whether your percentages, with a specific umpire, increase or decrease with getting strikes called on certain breaking pitches. That's it, really.

DL: Does that impact pitch selection at all?

BB: It can be talked about ahead of time, but I don't think it can be determined until you actually go out there with your own selection of pitches and see the results. It can be told to you that someone is a pitchers' umpire, but if he's not calling strikes on certain pitches you have to react accordingly to the zone he has that night.

DL: Jim Palmer pitched almost 4,000 innings and never allowed a grand slam. With that in mind, how do you approach a situation where the bases are loaded with two outs and the count is 3-2 on the hitter?

BB: I actually gave up my first grand slam in pro ball this year. I also gave up one in college. As to the question, I think you have to weigh the slugging percentage of the hitter you're facing. There are some hitters where the odds of him not hitting a home run are in your favor so much that you have to be aggressive. But if it's a cleanup hitter who has tremendous power, you're probably more likely to go outside the zone because a walk is a much better option than a hit. A single is two runs, a double is most likely three, and a home run is obviously four. So once again, you're playing with the percentages of how you match up with that hitter. That's how you make your determination of what to throw.

DL: What is your repertoire right now?

BB: A fastball, of course. I used to throw a cut fastball, which was kind of my signature pitch in the minor leagues, but I've turned it into a slider, which I've found is more successful at the major-league level because it has a slower velocity and a deeper break. I'm also throwing an overhand curveball and a circle change.

DL: How much does the feel of individual baseballs matter to you?

BB: I don't find that there's much of a variation with the seams, but there is, from stadium to stadium, a variation with how the balls are rubbed up. I know there's a consistency with the type of substance used to rub them up, but there's also a variation from person to person and how they're rubbed up. It's the extent to how much it's dirtied up, or soiled, before it's determined to be game ready. With some balls you receive there's a layer of dirt, like a slippery layer, and at some fields you get one that has a different tackiness because it's a drier ball. The humidity is one thing that plays into it. The one location where all the pitchers notice it is in Colorado, with the humidor they use, where every pitcher talks about the different feel. Of course, pitches obviously break differently there because of the altitude, especially breaking balls.

DL: Does the pitch you're planning to throw ever dictate whether or not you ask for a different ball?

BB: In general, if I'm throwing a pitch other than a fastball, I'll focus more on the ball not being slippery. If I need my hand directly behind the ball it's more likely to slip out if it's not rubbed up properly. Of course, I try not to give a tell by throwing a ball back, or rubbing it up, before I throw a certain pitch. I try to stay the same so I'm not giving the hitter any advantage by showing him what I might be throwing. Even if a ball feels fine, I still like to rub it up.

DL: We're at Fenway Park. How different does it feel standing on the mound here than it does in Tampa Bay or Colorado?

BB: There's a special significance to playing in Fenway, because it's a link to the past and the tradition of the game. It's always a fear of older players that young players will forget what they did for the game—their contributions, both on and off the field. Being a player and helping to carry that torch—that mystique—is a tremendous honor. You're there knowing that Ted Williams stood in that batter's box, and Babe Ruth stood on that mound. It's something you don't experience everywhere you play.

DL: The Brooklyn Cyclones honored you with a Brian Bannister bobblehead night last year. Where does that rate among your career highlights?

BB: They retired my number too, and it will always be special to me, because every player has an attachment to the team he was drafted by and the team he came up with. It's almost like it is with your own family, with the memories and emotions. It's the start of a journey, and Brooklyn will always be my first professional experience, which is what makes it special. It's also such a great baseball town, with the history of the Dodgers there—the love and passion that the fans have for the game.

DL: Denny McLain intentionally grooved pitches to Mickey Mantle, allowing him to homer in his final game. Can you see yourself doing something similar?

BB: I don't think so. The game has a special integrity, and I feel that all historical numbers should be put up in a fair and competitive environment. I don't think I could essentially throw batting practice to a hitter so another record could be achieved. Of course, if he did it in the normal sequence of the game, I'd tip my hat to the guy. And I'd never intentionally walk someone to try to avoid a record. I'd never deny myself my competitive side. The game means too much to me.

DL: Last one—when you come to BP and look at your VORP and PECOTA, what do you think?

BB: Every publication that's ever tried to project me has been wrong. I think that's because they use my current repertoire of pitches, and I'm unique as a player in that I continue to grow and evolve, always trying to refine and add new ways to help me get hitters out. That's why I think I'll always continue to surpass my projections. At the same time, I always use statistics—non-standard statistics that you'll find outside of a box score—as a way to improve myself as a player. I know my weaknesses. I know that I have a tendency to give up more fly balls than ground balls. I'm also very aware of my WHIP, my on-base percentage against, my slugging percentage against, my home runs per nine innings, my strikeouts-to-walks ratio. I look at those things to see how I compare to other players in the league, and also to try to make myself a better pitcher. Like I said, I consider myself a student of the game. Numbers are important.

PROSPECTUS Q&A
Jim Palmer
David Laurila

David Laurila sat down with Hall of Famer Jim Palmer for a revealing talk about his influences and approach on the mound, the hitters who gave him the most trouble, his favorite catcher, and more.

A lot of great pitchers have worn an Orioles uniform over the years, but none has been better than Jim Palmer. Inducted into the Hall of Fame in 1990, Palmer won 268 games over 19 seasons, winning 20 games or more eight times and twice leading the American League in ERA. Signed by Baltimore as an amateur free agent in 1963, Palmer made his big-league debut in 1965 and went on to play his entire career with the Orioles, pitching 3,948 innings and earning three World Series rings. In Game Two of the 1966 Fall Classic, Palmer became the youngest pitcher to throw a World Series shutout when he defeated Sandy Koufax and the Dodgers 2-0 at the age of 20. The winningest pitcher in team history, Palmer is currently an analyst for Orioles TV.

David Laurila: What kind of pitcher was Jim Palmer?

Jim Palmer: I was a fastball pitcher with three other pitches: a slider, a curveball, and a changeup. I had a four-seamer and a two-seamer... four seams early on. I didn't turn my two-seamer over, but it had a little different look, so it was a pitch I could use. If you throw enough four-seamers away to lefties, it is a pitch you can throw where the ball has a little different movement to get them to maybe roll over, especially when they're trying to hook a ball in the hole with a runner on first base. But I was primarily... even when I was throwing 90-whatever, upper 90s or upper 80s, I was still pretty much the same pitcher.

DL: A lot of veteran pitchers talk about the point where they went from being a thrower to being a pitcher. When did that happen for you?:

JP: Well, it certainly didn't happen until... probably my third or fourth year, in the early '70s. I came up in '65, but I was hurt. In '66, I was a thrower. I came back from an arm injury after two years running around the minor leagues, or whatever. In '69, even though I led the league in ERA, I was still pretty much a thrower, but I had pretty good stuff. I wasn't a command guy until probably 1973. I mean, there's a big difference between throwing strikes and commanding the strike zone. You can be wild in the strike zone, and a lot of guys, if they don't have great stuff, they're not able to pitch in hitter's counts. They don't walk people, but they get hit very hard, because they're constantly behind and their stuff just isn't good enough. Like I said once to Tim McCarver, the key to pitching is to throw enough strikes to get them to swing at balls. Most pitchers want to do that. Very few guys can pitch successfully inside the strike zone.

DL: Who most influenced you as a pitcher?

JP: Well, from a pitching-coach standpoint, it was George Bamberger. I had George after the Northern League, I think. I was one of the leaders in ERA and strikeouts, but I was also one of the leaders, or led the league, in wild pitches and walks. So I went to instructional league and worked every day on my windup. The Orioles had told me that I might be a guy they'd have to protect the following year, and that's how I got to the major leagues at 19. Back then you didn't have a 40-man roster, you had a 25-man roster and one guy that you can protect, so you really could only protect 26 guys out of your whole roster—minor league and big league. I was the one guy they took to the big leagues.

The whole winter, in Clearwater in 1964, I worked on my windup and it allowed me to... I still had a high leg kick, but it was more controlled. George taught me to throw the ball through the hitter, to the catcher. I think that a lot of people know who is up at the plate, but they don't understand the dynamics of throwing a baseball. You have to be able to load, you have to be able to get over your front side, and you have to have extension. Throwing to the opposite side of the plate... if you have a right-handed hitter standing up there, I would work on throwing the ball down and away, because to do that... George's philosophy, and it seemed to make a lot of sense, was that you had to have about as good a windup as you were going to have.

DL: Who was the best catcher you threw to over the course of your career?

JP: Elrod Hendricks caught my no-hitter, and we had a great understanding. He pretty much told people, as Rick Dempsey did... you know, Demper threw much better. He turned out to be a very good catcher. Of course, he had to learn our program when he was traded over from the Yankees. So I guess it was Dempsey and Elrod Hendricks. They would pretty much sit on the corner until... I mean, you have to understand, signs are just suggestions. You have a game plan, and it changes from the time you warm up until the game progresses. Sometimes you have good stuff. You might have an overpowering fastball and you have to be able to trust that whoever is catching you is able to tell you what your stuff is. A lot of times you can see the way a hitter reacts to your stuff, like where the bat head is, if you've been taught... if you understand how to do that. You can see when you're on the mound where the bat head is. If it's late, you obviously don't want to speed it up, because some guys have slider-speed bats; they don't have particularly quick bats, so breaking balls are advantageous to them. They give them a little more bat speed than they can generate normally.

My first roommate was Robin Roberts, who had 270-some wins, and I didn't have any. Right back here at Fenway, 44 years ago yesterday, I came in with the bases loaded to face Tony Conigliaro, the first guy I ever faced in the big leagues. Hank Bauer was the manager, and he said, "Are you nervous?" I said, "Well, I've never done this before," because I was a starting pitcher in A-ball the year before. I said, "What do I do with this warm-up ball?" I had brought the warm-up ball in with me because I was so nervous. But I struck out Conigliaro, and 3,948 innings later I had never given up a grand slam. That could have happened with the first guy I ever faced. I struck him out on three pitches. He swung at two high fastballs and John Flaherty called him out on a knee-high fastball low and away. Not that I meant to do that, it just went there.

DL: Carl Yastrzemski had 169 official at-bats against you, the most of any hitter you faced in your career. How did you pitch to Yaz?

JP: Well, I knew he was a great hitter, until his later years. I threw him primarily fastballs and maybe some curveballs. I never threw him a slider. I maybe threw him some changeups. But he was going to have a home-run swing on anything you threw. Later on he would cheat a little bit, when his bat slowed down, but he could hit any pitch you threw. I was pretty much going to try to not let him pull the ball, although one of the reasons he's a Hall of Fame hitter is that he took such good advantage of the Green Monster. But I didn't want to speed up his bat. He was a good fastball hitter, but I was a good fastball pitcher. At the end of the day, you have to... it's funny, we come up to the big leagues and sometimes we have a tendency to forget how we got here. You come up and you want to work on your breaking stuff, you want to work on your fielding or holding runners, and you want to work on the fact that you have a number of pitches, but at the end of the day you still have to understand what you do best. I threw the fastball. That doesn't necessarily mean that you're overpowering, even though I had a pretty good fastball. I'd try to strike guys out when I needed to.

DL: How did you work Jim Rice?

JP: Well, a lot of solo home runs. Rice would like the ball out over the plate, and I would throw him fastballs. I threw him some breaking balls, but I didn't want to speed up his bat either. Jim Rice could hit fly balls to right-center field with the best of them. I think he hit 10 home runs against me, nine solos, and I hung one slider in September of, I think, 1978. He hit a three-run homer against me in Baltimore, and I didn't like that.

DL: The number of home runs you allowed to Rice is interesting, given that you struck him out 24 times in 87 at-bats.

JP: But they were solo home runs. He hit .216, or maybe .219, against me. Kaline... my first home run in the big leagues was Moose Skowron, and it went about 445 [feet] to center field in Chicago, but Kaline hit a home run in my first start. I struck him out the first time on three pitches. Then, strike one, strike two, the catcher called for a changeup, and I was 19, and he hits it off the foul pole in Baltimore for a home run. Later I threw him about a 97-mph fastball down and away and he hit it into right field for a single, and I realized that Al Kaline may be better than I was. It's funny, when you look at a lineup you have to see which guy, if you're doing the things you're supposed to do well, that you should be able to get out. And there are some guys that you can't. People go, "Who was the toughest hitter in the American League?" It was Rod Carew, but Rod Carew hit singles and he didn't steal bases. Even though he could steal bases, he didn't steal bases off me. Once you know that, part of pitching, and being successful against teams he played on, was to get the guys out who hit in front of him and behind him. Of course, when he played for the Twins, he had Oliva and Killebrew coming up, which made it a little bit harder. When he played for the Angels, I could usually get the guys out behind him.

DL: Who didn't you like to face? Who had Jim Palmer figured out?

JP: Oh, a lot of guys had me figured out. Brett had good numbers. A second baseman for the Red Sox, Doug Griffin... I used to pitch away, and he liked the ball away. I'd throw pitches outside, two or three inches off the plate, and he'd hit them down the right-field line. Then Nolan Ryan hit him in the head, and that changed his approach. He didn't dive anymore. I didn't feel good about that, because you don't want to see anyone get hit in the head, but it changed his approach at the plate. Paul Blair is another example. After Paul got beaned by Ken Tatum in Anaheim, he was never the same hitter. Those are tragic things that happen in the game, and I'm sure Nolan didn't try to hit him in the head, and I'm sure that Ken Tatum didn't try to hit Paul Blair, but it happens, and when it does it can change a hitter's approach at the plate.

DL: Four at-bats into your career, you were a Hall of Fame hitter. What happened to you?

JP: I was in Cleveland, Ken Suarez was catching, and I had faced him when I got out of high school and went up to the Basin League in Winner, South Dakota, and he played for Valentine. He looked up at the scoreboard, and he goes, ".750?" Sonny Siebert was pitching and I go, "Oh, no. That's a mistake." Three curveballs later, I was 3-for-5. That's what happened.

DL: Gates Brown had a lot of success against you. Why was that?

JP: Here's the deal with Gates. If you went back and actually examined those numbers, every time Gates would hit a home run it would be a solo home run, and every time he hit a home run off me, which was probably four or five times, I won the game. I never lost a game where he hit a home run. Why? Because they were solos. Gates Brown stood right up on top of the plate... and he was a terrific guy. I love Gates. I didn't like to face him, but he stood on top of the plate, I pitched away, and he wanted the ball out over the plate. It was a game of, was I going to be able to make good enough pitches to get him to hit it to center field? When I didn't, he was going to try to pull the ball, and that's how he hit his home runs. But they were all solo home runs. One time he hit four rockets in Tiger Stadium, and then he didn't hit a home run the next time, but he hit a couple of loopers, and I don't think I beat the Tigers that night. But that one game he almost killed

Frank [Robinson] in right, and he hit a couple of BB's to center that Blair ran down, and one to Buford, so he was four rockets and 0-for-4. So statistics are a funny thing. They don't always tell you the story. To me, Gates was the kind of hitter... he'd had some problems with the law—I don't know if he was a convicted felon—but he was standing on the top of the plate and I wasn't going to hit him. He might come out and get me! Come on! But no, Gates was a great guy.

DL: What do you remember about facing Reggie Jackson?

JP: Reggie hit two home runs in the playoffs, which I won 5-3, giving up three solo home runs on 169 pitches. That was a playoff game in 1971. But I think Reggie hit two or three home runs off of me in 14 years? He didn't have a very high batting average. Reggie said that I used to pitch him like there was a little rectangle up and away.

DL: That's how you liked to work Jackson, up and away?

JP: Most hitters. Again, if you're throwing the ball through the hitter, to the catcher, your intent is not to throw... I mean, I could throw the ball down, but I could make the ball... Elrod Hendricks used to always say that I had some deceptiveness in my windup that made hitters think they could hit the ball, but it used to have a little bit of hop, kind of Koufax-like. His last game was my first World Series game, and his ball jumped, and his curveball started around eye level, and Roseboro would catch it on the ground. But I could make the ball go up, whether I was throwing 88 or 98, and I felt like, okay, that's what I did best. It's not like you're trying to throw it to get it by people, you're trying to throw pitches in an area of the plate where they're going to have to go out... I mean, [Graig] Nettles had real good numbers against me, and thinking back I probably should have just thrown him hanging sliders right down the middle, because he couldn't have hit them any harder than he did with my approach. Even if you're in the Hall of Fame, you think back, and there are probably some adjustments you should have made.

DL: You've mentioned solo home runs a couple of times. Was going right after hitters with the bases empty a team-wide approach with the Orioles?

JP: Nah, it just made sense. I mean, I was pretty good at math. If you're going to pitch a lot of innings, if you're going to be out there... I never worried about the tying run. In my era you pitched extra innings, and I played for a lot of great teams, so the only run that ever bothered me was the run that was going to beat me. Solo home runs... they just didn't mean anything. Obviously, if you're on the road... Jimmy Hall, in my first loss in the big leagues, I pitched like four and two-thirds innings on a Tuesday, and on Wednesday they said they weren't going to use me. Dick Hall gives up six hits and it goes from 2-2 to 5-2, and I came in and struck out two guys to get out of the inning. Dick Brown hits a three-run home run while I'm taking my clothes off. I come back out and Jimmy Hall hits a 2-1 fastball, down and away, down the left-field line, and the wind blows it into the first row of the old park in Minnesota, and I lose for the first time in the big leagues. It was a solo home run, but it was a very good pitch. The guy had hit 33 home runs the year before, so it wasn't like he was an out. And Brooks [Robinson] had to take me off the field because I didn't realize the game was over, because I had never done that before. But most of the time, solo home runs... they don't mean much. There's usually a reason. Maybe you're behind a guy. But not too many guys hit low-and-away pitches for home runs. But if you get behind a guy... to me, the odds of putting the ball in play favor walking a guy and letting the next guy hit a two-run home run. So when I walked guys... yeah, sometimes I was wild. But home-run guys, it's usually when they get a good pitch to hit.

DL: Can you talk a little about Mike Cuellar and Dave McNally?

JP: They were unbelievable. Cuellar was as good a left-handed pitcher as there was in baseball for five or six years. He won the Cy Young in 1969. He tied with McLain. He should have won in 1970, but Jim Perry won because we split the votes in the East. I think he was 23-8, or something like that, that year. Weaver would take him out early in the season, and then he'd come back and pitch with two day's rest. Mike was an incredible pitcher. We were very lucky to get him, and that's why we had so many great teams. McNally was a warrior; he won 20 games four times. He pitched through sore arms and elbows and all that stuff. Both of them were great guys. One of the great comforts pitching for the Orioles was that if I didn't win on Monday, one of those guys was going to pick me up on Tuesday or Wednesday. Then, when Dobson came in 1971, that made it even easier.

DL: If you were a young pitcher in the big leagues today, what would be different for you?

JP: It's a lot easier for the hitters now to know your tendencies. There are the hitting drills, and I think they're better prepared. You have hitting instructors and strength coaches. We went through the Steroid Era, and when people ask me about Mussina, he won 270 games pitching in an era when the strike zone was the size of an 8-by-10 paper, in Camden Yards before the football field was put in, where the ball carried and guys were cartoon characters. Plus, he won Gold Gloves and had the consistency. To me, he's a Hall of Famer. But if I was pitching now, guys can hit the ball fair inside, because they're much shorter to the ball. I think the hitting approaches are better.

But at the end of the day, while the hitters are still better, you are... the key to pitching, and I prided myself in having a low earned run average, because to me that meant you were consistent, month after month, week after week, year after year, but just think about it. At the end of the day, even though you don't pitch complete games now—even though I think you should be prepared to—and hand the ball to your closer, you still have to beat the guy you're pitching against. That's the key to pitching. You have to be better than the opposition... the guy you're facing. Obviously, it helps if you have a closer better than their closer, the way the game is played now. But hitters are very well prepared now. They can do the statistical readouts, where most guys said, "Palmer is going to start us off with fastballs."

Jim Spencer, who passed away, he was from Baltimore and I kept him from hitting .300 two years in a row. He hit .280-something and he was 0-for-32 against me. I'd see him on Monday in Texas, when I'd be pitching on Wednesday, and he'd say, "I'm laying off that high fastball." On Tuesday, I'd be out shagging and he'd run by and say, "I'm laying off that high fastball." Wednesday I'd throw the first high fastball and he'd pop it up. So, in the 12th inning, he's 0-for-32 over two years, and I figure, 'OK, where can I go where he's not going to hit a home run?' He's a great low-ball hitter, so I throw him a fastball up and away and he hits a little, soft single to left. I go, "You could have been doing that the last two years." So just like you kind of have to subjugate your ego on the mound, I think you have to do that as a hitter, and some hitters didn't do that. The guys that did... the Kansas City approach, where they hit the ball where you pitched, it was very tough to pitch against those teams.

DL: What was your preparation? Was it all memory?

JP: Weaver came out to me in Yankee Stadium once. I had a 4-1 lead and threw a ball about 12 inches inside to Dave Winfield that he hit about 430; he must have been looking in. It was a solo home run, and the only one he hit off of me. I had pitched very well. It was toward the end of my career, probably 1982. Earl came out, and he says, "Two outs, infield hit in the ninth, I'm bringing in Tippy [Martinez] to face Nettles." He said, "He's only 2-for-23 off of him." I said, "Yeah, but he was 0-for-21 and he beat us with a 2-run single to left field when Tippy was well rested, because he went up there and looked for a curveball. Then he beat us in that 11-inning ballgame when first base was open, and Tippy had pitched five straight days, and he looked for one and hit it into the upper deck." So numbers don't mean a whole lot, but I was very happy. Whatever. Part of pitching is... to bring in Tippy Martinez and say that he's 2-for-23 is one thing, but he was really 2-for-2 in my mind.

What have you done for me lately? I look at numbers every day when I'm broadcasting, and what do they mean? Ryan Freel played last night against Brad Penny, and he's 8-for-19, but that was when he was playing every day in Cincinnati. That doesn't mean he's not a good player, it's just that those numbers don't mean anything when you're sitting on the bench and not playing. What numbers mean is, who is pitching, what kind of stuff does he have, what is the situation, is he rested or not rested, did he make good pitches? Some guys can't make good pitches to hitters, so they have a problem. To me... memory served me pretty well.

DL: Would it be accurate to say that you believe numbers have their place, but they aren't always used correctly?

JP: It depends on who is using them. It's just like being an accountant. You can manipulate numbers. When Mark Teixeira is 6-for-10 with six home runs off of Bruce Chen, I think it's pretty safe to say that if you have first base open, you better walk him. There just might be a trend there. But trends don't always... numbers are very important, but they don't tell you the whole story.

NOT EARNING ITS KEEP
Why the "Earned" Run Needs To Go
Michael Wolverton

In another seminal BP piece intended to cut a sacred cow down to size, Michael Wolverton enumerated the shortcomings of the "Earned Run," a statistic that most fans believe to be simple but which is actually both misleading and overly complicated.

We at Baseball Prospectus occasionally hear the complaint that we make the game too complicated, with all the numbers and bizarre acronyms we throw around. So today I'm going to do my part to simplify the game. I'm here to suggest that baseball and its fans would be better off without one of its most fundamental, and most complicated, scoring rules. It's time to ditch the "earned" run.

The earned-run rule is widely accepted, or at least tolerated, throughout the baseball world, even in sabermetric circles. There are several reasons for that. For one thing, there's 116 years' worth of tradition behind the rule. I learned the rule because my dad learned the rule because his dad learned the rule, etc. ERA is on the back of every pitcher's baseball card, and it pops up in nearly every baseball-related article or news report you'll see. For another thing, believing in "earned" and "unearned" runs isn't nearly as harmful as, say, believing that RBI are meaningful for evaluating hitting. You have to pick your battles, and in the big scheme of things, this one may not be a battle worth fighting.

Perhaps most importantly, the earned-run rule might have gotten a pass because it's designed to achieve what everyone agrees is a noble goal: separating pitching from fielding. But good intentions aren't enough. The earned-run rule is a lame and counterproductive attempt at solving the pitching/fielding conundrum, one that deserves to be put out of its (and our) misery. There are many angles from which to attack the idea of "unearned" runs. Here's the one that works best for me:

Pretend for a second that the earned-run rule hadn't been invented over a century ago. In this alternate reality, baseball is played the same as it is now, except there's one fewer column in the box score for pitchers. Pitchers are charged with all the runs they allow, and RA rather than ERA is the de facto standard for evaluating them. Everyone recognizes that good or bad fielding can affect a pitcher's RA, but no one has come up with a good solution to the problem.

Then one day, an enthusiastic columnist writes:

> I've done it! I've solved the problem of removing the corrupting influence of fielding on pitchers' RA. We simply pay a sportswriter to sit in the press box, munch Cheetos, and decide which safeties came on plays that should have been made with normal fielding effort. Whenever one of these "errors" occurs, we reconstruct the inning—not the game, mind you, just the inning—pretending as if the error never happened. Count up the runs that would have scored in this hypothetical reconstructed inning, and you have a revised run total for the pitcher. Things get a lot more complicated for relievers and team totals, and we'll broaden the "plays that should have been made" definition a little bit, but you get the idea.

For me, shifting the rule's invention into the present day helps illustrate just how absurd it is. If it were proposed today, this idea would be dismissed out of hand, no matter who advanced it. If it had come from the blogosphere, people would use it as an example of the inferiority of the Internet. If it had come from a respected columnist like Peter Gammons or Thomas Boswell, people would wonder if senility was setting in. Absolutely no one would take this idea seriously. So why should it be any different just because the idea originated in 1888 instead of 2004? It could be construed from our fictitious columnist's quote above that the main problem with the earned-run rule is its reliance on errors. And it's true that errors are one of the problems with the rule. The well-discussed shortcomings of errors as a defensive measurement—their miniscule coverage of defensive plays, their subjective nature, etc.—suggest that ERA isn't doing much to eliminate fielding from pitching numbers.

But focusing on errors is really missing a bigger problem. Even if errors were somehow the perfect measure of fielding performance, the earned-run rule would still be wrong-headed. The main problem with unearned runs isn't errors, it's the notion that the pitcher's job ends whenever an error is made.

The most glaring example of this problem is that the earned-run rule allows the pitcher to give up runs with impunity after the third out "should have" been recorded. We've all seen these kinds of situations. An error allows Michael Tucker to reach with two outs, and Barry Bonds comes up next to deposit one in McCovey Cove. The result: two runs, none earned. That's nuts. Never mind Tucker's run; you're telling me that Bonds wouldn't have hit his homer leading off the next inning if Tucker had been put out? In this situation, the earned-run rule essentially allows the pitcher to skip Bonds in the lineup, as far as his ERA is concerned.

OK, you might say, why not hypothetically reconstruct the entire game, rather than just the inning? That way, Bonds' homer would count as earned. But of course, that would be even more ridiculous than the current rule. Besides the fact that it's way too complicated to reconstruct an entire game this way, you'd frequently end up with absurd situations where the pitcher is charged with more earned runs than actual runs. It's possible, in hindsight, for errors to save you runs, if you buy into this hypothetical reconstruction philosophy.

No, the right solution to this problem is to recognize this simple baseball truth:

Errors will happen. Good pitchers will minimize the damage caused by them. That is, a good pitcher will allow fewer runners on base before the errors happen (so there aren't runners to score on the errors) and will allow fewer hits and walks after errors happen (so the runners who reached on errors won't score).

This isn't a hypothesis, it's a fact. Preventing unearned runs is a skill that pitchers have, and it usually comes hand-in-hand with the ability to prevent earned runs. I took all the pitchers since 1900 who pitched more than 2,000 innings and compared their earned run averages (ERA) to their unearned run averages (UERA). (In both cases the values were normalized to the league averages for the years in which they played). A couple of results:

- The correlation between ERA and UERA was 0.36—not overwhelming, but pretty strong. That means that pitchers who are good at preventing earned runs are also generally good at preventing unearned runs.
- Of the top 50 pitchers in career (normalized) ERA, 46 of them were better than average at UERA.

What this means is that when you throw out unearned runs, you're throwing out part of the pitcher's performance. In other words, ERA is understating the run prevention abilities of the best pitchers in the league and overstating it for the worst. Measures based on ERA, such as Pete Palmer's Pitching Runs from the Total Baseball books, are going to underestimate the seasonal and career values of baseball's all-time greats.

We noted above that the correlation between ERA and UERA wasn't perfect, so let's look at some of the exceptions. Here are a few of the pitchers who had average-to-excellent ERAs combined with terrible UERAs, along with their rankings (out of 317 total pitchers) in both categories. You may notice from the list of names that they also have something else in common.

Pitcher	Rankings out of 317 ERA	UERA
Hoyt Wilhelm	4	295
Dutch Leonard	36	307
Tom Candiotti	115	310
Phil Niekro	125	297
Wilbur Wood	126	302

Coincidence? Not bloody likely. Knuckleballers are a huge exception to the "good pitchers prevent unearned runs" rule. Despite being good pitchers overall, these knuckleballers were all among the worst all-time at surrendering unearned runs. Joe Niekro was the only long-time knuckleballer I could think of who didn't fit the pattern, finishing about average in both categories. (And Joe threw the knuckleball far less often than any of these other guys.) The reason is obvious: knuckleballers produce a lot of passed balls, and passed balls count the same as errors in the unearned-run rule, hence a bunch of unearned runs.

So now the situation is even worse than what we saw above. Not only does the unearned-run rule generally undervalue good pitchers, it's also systematically biased in favor of a particular type of pitcher. Phil Niekro, for example, looks quite different when you evaluate his career based on RA rather than ERA. He's a Hall of Famer either way, but he's not the inner circle guy that Total Baseball makes him out to be if you take his unearned runs into account.

The bottom line is that there's little evidence that unearned runs have much to do with fielding, and there's plenty of evidence that they have a lot to do with pitching. ERA has a long tradition as a pitching metric, but if we replaced it with simple RA, we'd be getting a more accurate measure of a pitcher's contribution. And if the average baseball fan would free up the brain cells he's using to store the complicated earned-run rule and use those cells to learn about other elements of the game, baseball would be the better for it.

SPINNING YARN
The Real Strike Zone
Mike Fast

The strike zone does have rulebook dimensions, but as Mike Fast discovered, a number of surprising factors determine how it's actually called.

Ever since the PITCHf/x system debuted in the 2006 playoffs, people have been interested in what it says about the strike zone that the umpires call.

John Walsh and Jonathan Hale provided some of the seminal work on the topic. John observed how the umpires called a strike zone that was wider than the rulebook definition but not as tall and that it was shifted toward the outside for left-handed batters. Jonathan also looked at the umpire zones and broke down the results by umpire and pitcher.

Jonathan and recent BP addition Dan Turkenkopf built on this work by examining how the strike zone changed in a variety of situations: by inning, by pitcher age/experience, by pitcher control, by home/away team, etc.

More recently, John Walsh and J-Doug Mathewson raised the profile of the discussion with articles about how umpire zones change based on the ball-strike count and other factors. Jonathan Hale and Dave Allen had observed many of these effects previously, but John and J-Doug's work got the attention of Rob Neyer, and with that attention came a lot of criticism of umpire abilities from Rob and others. Unfortunately, the focus was more on inflaming hysteria about bad umpiring than on thoughtful sabermetric questioning:

> From Major League Baseball's perspective, it doesn't matter why it's happening. It shouldn't be happening, and we can only hope that something's being done. The strike zone should be the strike zone, regardless of the count. If the umpires call it the same way every time, the players will adjust accordingly. And it's worth pointing out that the games would go just a little quicker if umpires weren't consistently extending plate appearances based on the count.

Why would umpires be influenced to change their strike zones in so many different ways? What physical or mental factors influence them, and is there any evidence to support those theories?

Are the umpires really as inconsistent as the data presented by the articles to date would suggest?

I have spent portions of the last couple years investigating the data about the strike zone and puzzling over those questions, mostly without finding answers I considered satisfactory, until recently, when a number of separate ideas coalesced into a theory about how umpires actually call the strike zone. Most of the ideas are individually well known in baseball and will not come as a surprise. What came as a surprise to me, however, was how they fit together to explain with one consistent theory a great deal about the data that has been observed about the umpire strike zone.

Individual Batter Zones

As mentioned above, several analysts have found that different pitchers have different strike zones called by the umpires. It turns out that batters also have their own individual zones. That this is true in the vertical dimension is not surprising, of course. Batters are of differing heights, from David Eckstein at 5'7" to Adam Dunn and Corey Hart at 6'6", and their crouches are more or less extreme, leading to varying vertical boundaries even for the rulebook strike zone. However, individual batter strike zones, like individual pitcher strike zones, also vary by an inch or two on the inside and outside edges.

In aggregate, this shows up as the previously observed difference between left-handed and right-handed batters, but it also extends to differences among individual batters of the same handedness.

The first theory I examined as an explanation for this variance among batter zones was that batters who stood closer to the plate had their zones shifted outside as a consequence of the umpire using the batter's body as a reference point. It is true that there is a correlation between batters who stand closer to the plate, as measured by how often they are hit by inside pitches, and those whose strike zones are shifted outside. However, the correlation is not perfect, and the counter-examples are particularly instructive as to the true cause of shifted strike zones. For example, Jason Kendall hangs over home plate and is among the batters with the highest hit-by-pitch rates. Nonetheless, his strike zone was shifted almost an inch inside relative to the average right-handed batter. On the other end of the spectrum, Nelson Cruz has a very upright stance that keeps him away from the plate, and he is near the low end on hit-by-pitch rates. However, his strike zone was shifted almost an inch outside relative to average. What could be causing this disparity?

You might know that Kendall displayed the last vestiges of a power stroke during final years of the Clinton administration, while Cruz had a slugging percentage of .555 over the last three years. Despite Kendall's tendency to crowd the plate, pitchers are unafraid to come inside and over the plate to him, whereas low and away is the favorite spot for a hurler confronting Cruz.

The typical pitch location seen by the batter has a strong correlation to the horizontal shift in his strike zone. Batters who see more pitches on the outside edge also see their strike zone boundaries shift farther away on both the outside and inside edges of the plate. Batters who see more pitches on the inside edge see their strike zone boundaries shift toward the inside.

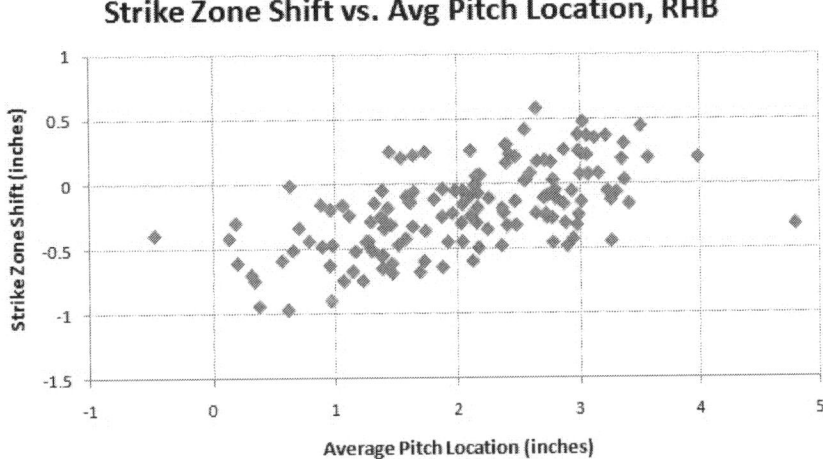

The question, then, is whether the umpire calls the strike zone differently because the pitcher and catcher are aiming the pitches differently to the batter or whether the causality runs in the opposite direction. If the pitcher and catcher are adapting to an already existing umpire-specific zone for each batter, that still leaves us with the unanswered question of why the umpire zone differs from batter to batter, and batter positioning at best offers only a partial answer to that question.

I was unable to definitively answer the question of the direction of causality, but a mountain of circumstantial evidence points to the umpire zone being influenced by the location of the catcher's target, rather than the other way around. Thus, I propose that the catcher target is the driving factor in how umpires call balls and strikes.

The Catcher Target Theory
In June 1993, Baseball Digest quoted Matt Nokes with his views on how umpires call the zone.

> "Predictability is the key to getting borderline calls," says Matt Nokes of the Yankees. "If the pitcher is consistent, then the umpire knows where to be looking. But if the catcher is jerking all around the plate and the ump does not know what is coming in where, it's going to be harder for him to focus on those close pitches and you won't get them. If the pitcher is throwing consistently where the catcher is setting up, he doesn't have to be so fine. But if I set up inside and the pitch is on

the outside corner, even if it is a strike, we're not likely to get that call. Even if the pitch is over the outer half of the plate, it will be called a ball, because it missed the catcher's target so bad. That's just the way it is."

If the umpires adapt their strike zones based on the location of the catcher target, it explains with one consistent theory many of the heretofore observed phenomena regarding the zone. If the catcher changes his target based on shifting umpire zones, these phenomena remain a collection of unrelated and unexplained oddities requiring a variety of unsubstantiated and sometimes contradictory theories about umpire motivations.

For example, as mentioned earlier, the zone for left-handed batters is shifted toward the outside. Do umpires have some bias against left-handed hitters? If so, why? Perhaps a more likely explanation is that they simply call more strikes outside to lefty hitters because that's where the catchers are setting their targets, and the umpires are using the target as a cue. While right-handed batters see 58 percent of pitches outside of the midpoint of the plate, left-handed batters see 66 percent of pitches on the outside half. The average pitch to a left-hander is 2.4 inches farther outside than the average pitch to a right-hander, which dovetails nicely with John Walsh's finding that the average strike zone for a left-handed batter was shifted 2.3 inches farther outside than the average zone for right-handed batter.

If umpires are influenced by the catcher target, it also explains why individual pitchers see such different zones. J-Doug Mathewson's research placed Livan Hernandez and Felix Hernandez at opposite ends of the spectrum in benefiting and suffering from changing umpire zones. Look at where those two pitchers locate. (Pitches where the batter swung are not shown.)

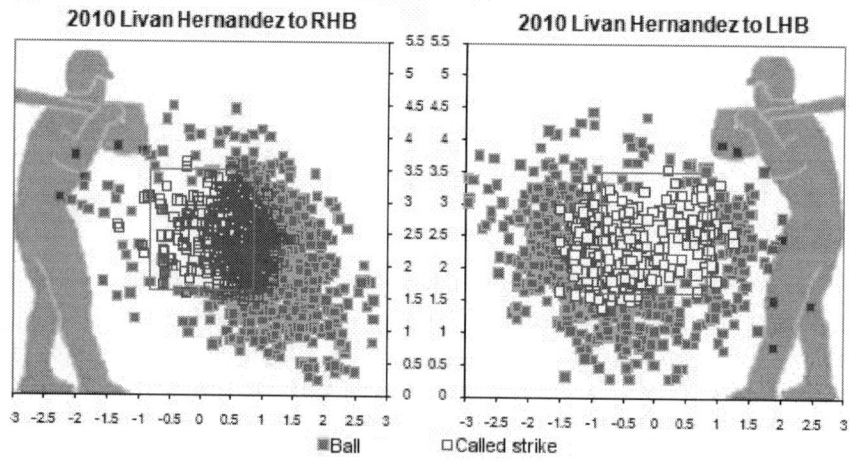

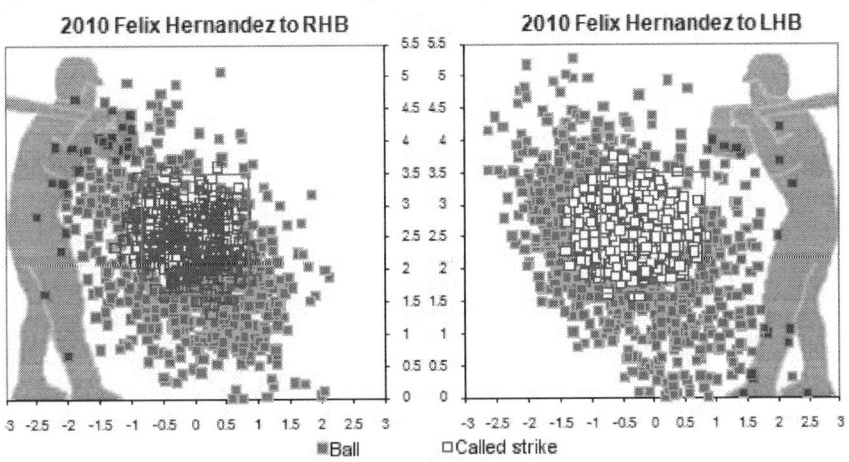

Livan Hernandez aims toward the very edges of the zone, or even a little outside, both to righties and lefties, and it appears that the umpires give him the strike call when he hits the middle or inside of the catcher target. Felix Hernandez, on the other hand, aims closer to the middle of the zone. If he locates a pitch at the edge of the zone, he's very likely to have missed his catcher target, and the umpires don't give him the strike call in those cases.

Similarly, one of the variations in umpire zones that Dan Turkenkopf identified can be explained by variations in the locations that pitchers and catchers are targeting. Dan found that the older (or more experienced) a pitcher was, the bigger the zone he got from the umpires. It also happens to be true that the older a pitcher is, the more he pitches to the outside edges.

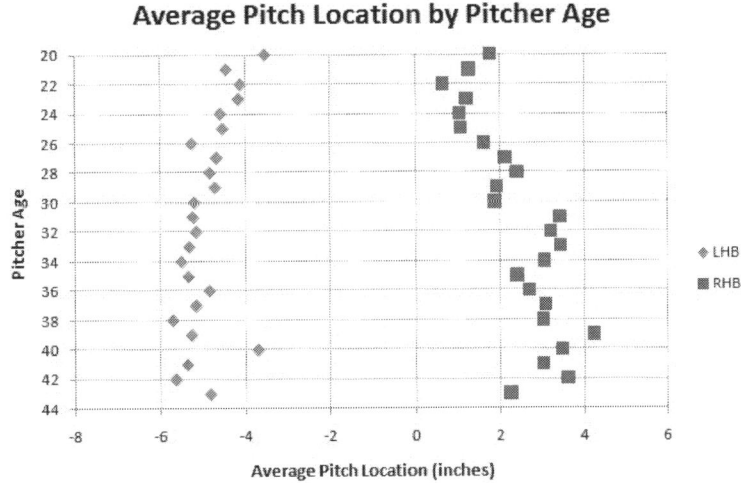

Why older pitchers pitch more on the outside edge is a question for further investigation, but it's no accident that this affects the strike zone that pitchers see. This is another piece of circumstantial evidence that umpires are giving pitchers strikes on the edges when they hit the catcher target.

Catcher Framing
We can even look at pitchers who live on the edge of the zone and see some surprising differences among their receivers. Livan Hernandez got a bigger strike zone in 2008 with Joe Mauer behind the plate than he did when Mike Redmond was his catcher. In 2009, Hernandez got a bigger zone with Wil Nieves than with Omir Santos behind the dish. The effect is not huge, but it's noticeable —the difference of a couple strikes per game. Other pitcher-catcher pairs demonstrate this effect, as well.

Compare the strike zones that Javier Vazquez saw with Jorge Posada and Francisco Cervelli catching him in 2010.

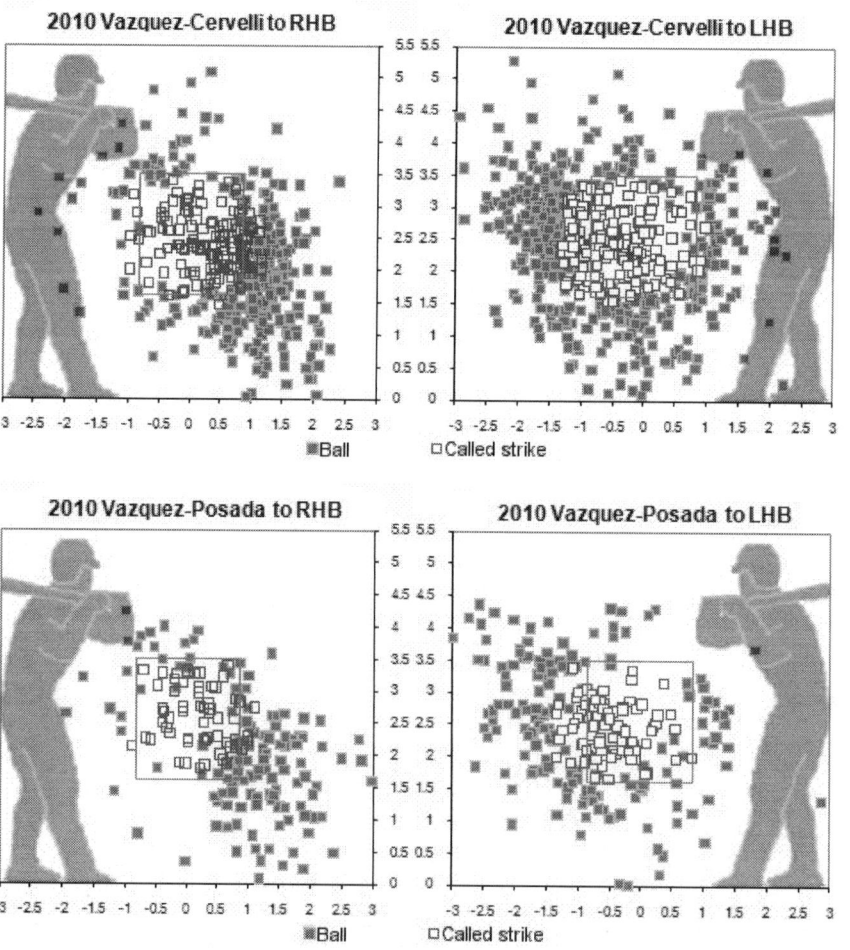

Vazquez saw a slightly larger zone on the outside edge to left-handed batters and especially to right-handed batters when Cervelli was catching.

Analysts such as Dan Turkenkopf and Bill Letson have looked at the issue of catcher framing using the PITCHf/x location data. They found dramatic and repeatable differences in framing performance among catchers, to the tune of 50 runs per season or more. Our catcher target theory of the zone would suggest, however, that a large part of this difference may be due to the typical pitch distributions thrown by pitchers and seen by batters. The differences in batter pitch distributions would probably mostly wash out over a season-size sample for a full-time catcher, but the pitcher sample for each catcher could remain highly biased and have a large effect on the framing measurement.

When Bill's catcher framing numbers for 2008-2009 are normalized by pitcher, the best and worst catchers are around +/- 20 runs per season. This method could benefit from some additional fine-tuning, but at least the size of the effect is now in a range much more compatible with the size of the catcher ERA effect that Sean Smith found by studying catcher-pitcher pairs in the Hardball Times 2011 Annual.

This is an effect that has been observed at least far back as 1989, if not earlier. In *The Diamond Appraised*, Craig Wright discussed catcher framing skills.

> Surprisingly, one of the key differences between the best and the worst is a mechanical factor. A catcher can get more strike calls on borderline pitches by not showing the umpire his glove as a target, or at least by drawing it back after the target is given. The best catchers—particularly the ones who call fewer walks in the matched innings—tend to give a full open-faced target to the pitcher and hold the glove closer to their body (watch Boone and Gary Carter). Holding the glove in toward the body is partially a physical reaction. Holding the glove perpendicular to the ground is a strain on the wrist and the forearm; holding the glove closer to the body eases the tension in the arm.
>
> At first, the technique may seem counterproductive, giving a better target to the pitcher, but at the cost of losing the umpire by taking the glove out of his view. It would also seem to hurt your chances of getting a strike call by making you move more to go after bad pitches, particularly the low ones.
>
> But that isn't the way it works. It's easy enough to handle the pitches around the strike zone with the glove held close to the body. The excess movement going after a bad pitch doesn't make a difference, because those are obvious ball calls anyway. It may even help emphasize to the umpire that if the catcher has to move a lot, it's a ball. Now consider the borderline pitch. Along with his natural

judgment, the umpire is instinctively looking for clues. If he can't see the glove clearly, he may rely more on the catcher's movement; he didn't move, so it's a strike.

Not every strike zone variation can be explained by the catcher target theory, however. For example, there is a small but significant portion of the home field advantage (around 15 percent, according to Dan and J-Doug's research) which derives from the strike zone. Average pitch distributions are very similar between home and visiting pitchers, implying that there is a different cause for the variation in umpire zone in that case.

The Effect of the Ball-Strike Count

Let's dive in deeper on another source of strike zone variation that doesn't seem to be explained by the catcher target theory: the changing strike zone by ball-strike count.

To recap, Jonathan Hale, Dave Allen, John Walsh, and J-Doug Mathewson have all observed that the strike zone is bigger in ball-strike counts that favor the hitter and smaller in counts that favor the pitcher. Since pitchers tend to pitch more to the edges in pitchers' counts and more to the middle of the zone in hitters' counts, our catcher target theory of the strike zone would suggest the zone should get bigger in pitchers' counts and smaller in hitters' counts. But that's not what happens. What gives?

This is not a question to which I have an answer yet. However, it is instructive to look at the detailed location data by count. Though Dave conducted a regression that indicated that pitch type had no significant impact on the size of the zone at different counts, I found that pitch type and pitcher handedness did have a noticeable impact.

I compared mid-height pitches on the outside edge to right-handed batters at the 0-2 and 2-0 counts. The outside edge of the strike zone at 2-0 is about an inch and a half farther outside than it is at 0-2, as defined by the point where the umpire calls 50 percent balls and 50 percent strikes on average.

At this boundary, changeups were highly likely to be called strikes, especially from left-handed pitchers. Changeups made up about nine percent of the mid-height pitches on the outside edge at 2-0, but only three percent at 0-2. Sinking fastballs displayed a similar effect. On the other hand, sliders and curveballs were highly likely to be called balls, especially from left-handed pitchers. Breaking balls made up about eight percent of the mid-height pitches on the outside edge at 2-0, and 24 percent at 0-2.

Nonetheless, even if only four-seam fastballs are considered, the strike zone is still larger at 2-0 than it is at 0-2, still by about an inch and a half, and the reason for this remains unclear. I did not find any significant bias in the sample of batters or pitchers between the 0-2 and 2-0 counts in terms of their pitch location distributions. The differences were less than one tenth of an inch, which is a small fraction of the observed effect.

Even if the sample of players is relatively unbiased, the PITCHf/x data itself may be biased. There is some error associated with all measurements, and though the PITCHf/x plate location measurements are highly accurate, they are not perfect. Umpire ball-strike calls give us some information about the likely direction of this measurement error. The effect is usually not large, but small distinctions can become very important at the edge of the strike zone. Thus, corrected PITCHf/x plate location measurements may be needed for some types of strike zone research.

I have previously speculated in response to the findings about the zone and the count that PITCHf/x measurement errors could be playing a role in the measured size of the zone. However, this effect turns out to also be a fraction of the observed effect. Moreover, it actually operates to exaggerate the difference in the size of the zone. After accounting for PITCHf/x measurement error, the actual strike zone edge is about 0.4 inches closer to the plate on the 0-2 count and about 0.2 inches closer to the plate on the 2-0 count.

A better understanding of how and why the zone changes size by count awaits the results of further research.

What's Next?
Anyone researching the performance of umpires in calling balls and strikes is strongly encouraged to consider the catcher target theory. It does not fully explain every umpire variation, but it appears to be the primary factor in many cases.

Catcher framing is also an important topic in its own right. The specifics of what catchers do is worthy of further research with the PITCHf/x data. Noting that the catcher target affects the umpire zone is one thing; identifying and quantifying the effect of specific catcher mechanics is another. In any case, the ability to better quantify this aspect of catcher fielding is very important. Whether baseball benefits from umpires adapting their zones to the catcher's target is not necessarily a question with a simple answer. Umpires are rewarding pitchers for accuracy and command and penalizing them for being inconsistent and missing their target. Pitchers and catchers presumably expect this, and in *As They See 'Em*, Bruce Weber argues that coaches and players in the dugout also judge balls and strikes in relation to the catcher target.

> [Umpires will] say calling strikes is paramount, but they'll withhold a strike call from time to time—if the pitcher badly misses the catcher's target, for example, even if the ball might still graze the zone. If the catcher sets up outside and the pitch is up and in, the umpire ethos says the pitcher doesn't deserve a close call for doing a poor job. Besides that, he's made the catcher lunge; his glove probably moved out of the strike zone, which means it'll look like a ball from the dugout,

which means the umpire will be getting an earful if he calls a strike.

Is it a good thing or bad thing that some pitchers, like Livan Hernandez, are able to make a living by persistently targeting the edges of the zone? Similarly, some catchers can help their pitchers and their teams by gaining strike calls from the umpire through superior receiving mechanics. The umpire zone affects the career prospects of some players positively and others negatively. There is undoubtedly skill involved from both the pitchers and the catchers who are able to expand the strike zone. Such skill would be lost if the umpires were replaced with pitch-calling robots or were retrained to call the exact same size of zone for every pitch, regardless of the catcher target. Some people would find such fairness laudable; others would lament the passing of valuable baseball skills.

Even if it were desirable, it may not be possible for the umpires to cease using the catcher target as a physical reference point. It might be difficult for umpires to change that behavior, whether it is conscious or unconscious. The Zone Evaluation system, which is based upon PITCHf/x data and is used by Major League Baseball to grade umpires, takes into account the catcher target, according to statements made by Sportvision representatives at the 2008 PITCHf/x Summit. (The details of how catcher target is included in the umpire grading process were not given. It may be similar to the process used with Questec data, which is described in As They See 'Em, pp. 198-199.)

In the cases where the catcher target theory does not appear to explain the strike zone variation, it's worth taking a deeper look to see if the mix of pitch types and pitcher and batter handedness are concealing instances of the catcher target theory in operation in canceling directions. Moreover, the pitcher, batter, or even catcher samples may be biased toward types of players who throw or see atypical pitch distributions.

Even if the sample of players is relatively unbiased, the PITCHf/x data itself has measurement error which may bias the results. Thus, corrected PITCHf/x plate location measurements may be needed for some types of strike zone research.

Umpire grading, whether individually or collectively in various game situations, is a tricky task. Umpires appear to call a zone that is very dependent on the location of a pitch relative to the catcher's target. Sample bias and PITCHf/x measurement are also confounding factors. One may wonder how well Major League Baseball's umpire grading accounts for these factors.

Many fans and writers rush to stick negative labels on umpires and to jump to conclusions of incompetence without carefully investigating the data. It's not enough to throw up a PitchTrax graphic of the strike zone with a strike call shown outside the box in order to declare an umpire an incompetent idiot better replaced with a machine.

PITCHf/x data has been a great boon for baseball analysis, including the analysis of umpires and the strike zone, but it requires careful analysis if we are to come to conclusions that will stand up to scrutiny. The strike zone is an important topic, and the quality and motivations of umpires are worth investigating deeply. Let's not stop with half answers and then delude ourselves that we are ready to sit in judgment of the umpires.

Part 3
FIELDING
Introduction by Christina Kahrl

"If then, Sir William Jones, who read in thirty languages, could not read the simplest peasant's face in its profounder and more subtle meanings, how may unlettered Ishmael hope to read the awful Chaldee of the Sperm Whale's brow? I put that brow before you. Read it if you can."—Moby Dick

No different from literature, the field of sabermetrics has its white whales to goad, inspire, and frustrate those seeking answers. But from among those fields of inquiry, there is perhaps none greater—and more greatly frustrating—than the subject of defense.

At its most basic level, the game rests on three skills: pitching, hitting, and fielding. The entire field has done a great job of parsing offensive value to the last decimal and delivering a varied and equally comprehensive range of interpretive schemes to evaluate pitchers. It is fielding that has still managed to keep one foot firmly planted in the realm of speculation.

This isn't simply a matter of fiction or faith, or even a debate over scouting vs. science. Instead, it goes back to a matter of original sin: in his Adamian responsibility for naming and codifying the game, Alexander Cartwright gave us very little to work with in terms of data to conjure up interpretations of fielding performance. Worse yet, his inheritors saw very little cause to improve matters; 140 years ago, Cartwright suggested that what we've come to know as Range Factor might be a nice thing to have to tell us something about defensive skill. That notion fell on deaf ears, and had to be re-discovered a century later by Bill James.

Even then, as sabermetrics became a going concern in the '70s, it was following trails blazed by Earnshaw Cook in the '60s—and assiduously bricking up the cul-de-sacs that a few of his assertions represented. That was thanks to the wealth of interpretive data available to describe hitting or pitching outcomes, and with founding fathers like Pete Palmer, Dick Cramer, Barry Codell, and James, the horizon of discovery has proven limitless.

But fielding has had nothing like the same splendor of study and results. The limited range of tools to work with—putouts and assists, errors and double plays—has long left us with a stunted vocabulary to describe a huge range of abilities and skills. Take answers to questions we might all want the answers to, like, "Who was the greatest shortstop of all time?" or "Who had the best outfield arm ever?" If you wanted to argue for Ozzie Smith in the '80s to answer the first question, and Bob Meusel in the '20s the second, you might have a lot of people willing to sign on, but even the best researchers, men like Palmer and later Clay Davenport, were working with the tools that Cartwright gave them. And even then, pursuing those answers risks ignoring the basic fact that, where fielding and pitching events can be neatly segregated in terms of who did what, fielding will forever be synergistic, with players operating interdependently.

However, working from such examples as James' rediscovery of Range Factor and his introduction of Defensive Efficiency, as well as Palmer's interpretive system of Linear Weights, the next generation of statheads was suitably inspired to try to create a new language to describe defensive value, at Baseball Prospectus and elsewhere. Whether as far-reaching as Clay Davenport's founding efforts to put all leagues ever from everywhere on the same scale to arm himself and his colleagues with perspective on fielding feats, or James Click's later discoveries of park-effect impacts on defensive units as a whole, we've helped advance the conversation, even as we've run up against the limits of what's possible.

With that in mind, Click's BP Basics column from 2004, "Evaluating Defense," provided readers with a nice summary of the virtues of Clay's system of Fielding Runs as an interpretive scheme, talking about the adjustments involved to provide a sense of player performance: rates and types of balls in play, park factors, baserunners, and pitcher handedness, among other basics.

Click expands on his own discoveries about the importance of park factors in interpreting team-level fielding performance and employing that knowledge within Bill James' Defensive Efficiency. By good fortune, this became one of those rare metrics with an acronym worth remembering: PADE, for Park-Adjusted Defensive Efficiency, making for easy deployment of maximum snark with his initial piece from October 2003, "Getting PADE," followed by its perfected sequel in November 2004, "Time to Get PADE Again." (Never let it be said that we've left a dead horse unbeaten.) As Click notes, PADE is "a purer metric of a total team's defensive performance that does not punish or reward teams for playing in certain parks." As such, it was subsequently handy for describing the development in the late Aughties as the Rockies became one of the best defensive teams in baseball while playing at altitude, a key factor in their 2007 pennant-winning season.

Because we started out as a company with Clay's commitment to interpret the major and minor leagues (and foreign leagues, and independent leagues) on the same scale to get a sense of defensive performance and then try to use that information in the annual, it was perfectly natural for us to be excited by Dan Fox's research on Simple Fielding Runs, which initially ran in January 2008 (and was prosaically titled "Simple Fielding Runs Version 1.0" in Dan's regular column,

THE LINEUP

Evaluating Defense
by James Click..206

Simple Fielding Runs Version 1.0
by Dan Fox...209

Reminiscing with SFR
by Dan Fox...220

Improving on Defensive Efficiency
by James Click..231

Park Effects on Team Defense
by James Click..235

What Would Bacon Do?
by Dan Fox...239

Adventures in Team Fielding
by Ben Lindbergh..244

What Do We Really Know About Defense?
by Colin Wyers..251

Looking Farther Afield
by Colin Wyers..255

How Do You Solve a Problem Like Derek Jeter?
by Colin Wyers..261

"Schrodinger's Bat"). Like Clay's original Fielding Runs metrics, Dan's work addressed the majors and minors and had the virtue of his characteristic thoroughness, because he didn't just create a system that defined individual fielding performance, he also tackled direct comparisons to popular fielding metrics like UZR and Plus/Minus. Dan then gave us something that tickled everybody's history bone in March 2008, "Reminiscing with SFR," which applied SFR's algorithms to the period of 1988-1998 to give us some insight into who was really good (or bad) over that period of time.

As the Rays went about winning the American League pennant in 2008, an improved defense was obviously one of the basic components of their massive improvement from an epically awful showing in 2007. (It probably also comes as no surprise that Click, long since graduated from BP's ranks, was to be found in their front office.) Diagnosing and describing the extent of their improvements was taken up by Ben Lindbergh in February 2009, in his brilliant essay "Getting Defensive: Adventures in Team Fielding." What was critical then, and remains important to recognize now, was Ben's insight into how much of the lesson the Rays of '08 represented was a unique example, and how much of it might be reproducible elsewhere, something too often forgotten in the industry-wide rush to try and ape a success that owed much to the Rays' singularly awful starting point.

A year and a half later, Colin Wyers posited the important question, "What do we really know about defense?" in his "Manufactured Runs" column. As is his wont, Colin tested a lot of the assumptions many of us would like to operate from, asking about reliability across simultaneously existing data sets describing identical groups of events and reminding us of the uncomfortable truth that these do not provide us with as much certainty as we would wish for. What might get lost about his observation's significance is that it came as a necessary prescription against the creeping, unquestioning faith being invested in interpretive metrics like UZR; what was becoming sabermetric canon for some might more properly be consigned to the pile of things that are interesting but inconclusive.

Two short weeks later, Wyers amended his concerns over the state of defensive analysis with his own effort at interpreting defensive performance, "Looking Further Afield." Focusing on shortstops, Colin broke out an elegantly simple-sounding method for interpreting performance before breaking down whom it described as the best ever. (Yes, it *was* Ozzie Smith after all; score one for deeply held articles of faith.)

A few months later, Colin moved on to tackle one of the most desperate and dangerous subjects in the field of fielding: Derek Jeter, and the damning consistency with which the Captain winds up at the bottom of almost every scale for defensive performance ever invented. And perhaps consistent with Colin's facility with uncomfortable truths, he winds up determining that we may have understated the scale of the problem Jeter represents, then, now, and into the future.

In retrospect, it might seem that BP's work on defense and defensive metrics over time has been decidedly spare. It's a fair criticism, but it also reflects the downside of a number of long-standing commitments.

First, there's the aforementioned institutional commitment to interpret the majors and minors across all time, the original challenge that Clay Davenport set for himself and pursues to this day. That allowed us to explore broader historical questions as well as address the likely outcomes of players' minors-to-majors jumps, but it also meant never setting that task aside to focus strictly on the immediate present or the major leagues alone. Despite that larger challenge, Clay's work and the subsequent adaptations reflected in that of Click, Fox, and Wyers reflects how well it has withstood the test of time.

Second, there was the matter of not consciously limiting the conversation about metrics to strictly sabermetric columns. Here again, you consider this simultaneously a strength and a weakness of the original design of Baseball Prospectus as a going concern. We conceived ourselves not simply as a generator of metrics, but as a writing project that would achieve the other critical component of Bill James' success by giving you stuff you enjoyed reading. Whether within Jay Jaffe's work with JAWS or in performance analysis columns by Jay, Joe Sheehan or myself, or fantasy commentary by Marc Normandin—just examples, because the list goes on—the conscious goal with any new BP metric was to integrate it into broader applied sabermetrics reflected in all or most of the writing on BP.com. That can be successful on an intra-organizational level, but for all the benefits that come with a pay wall, in retrospect effective web-wide proselytization wasn't always among them.

Finally, it's important to credit the extent to which great work outside BP informed the conversation on defensive statistics, not simply among ourselves, but also with you as readers and independent thinkers. We were never the only kids on the block, and we have all profited from the output of effective analysts like John Dewan, Mitchel Lichtman, Dave Smith, Tom Tippett, and many more besides. That's without getting into the sticky subject of those whose work is invisible to most of us, because they're behind the highest pay wall of all—they work for teams from the outset of their careers as sabermetricians, as industry output has long since lapped sabermetrics' original open-source splendor. The field would no doubt be more fun if more information were more broadly available, and we're all looking forward to what's going to be available from the camera-driven data streams of the future.

But for all those discoveries we won't see because they're made in the name of one team's success instead of everyone's edification, I say more power to those making them. If nothing else, sabermetrics was supposed to educate, not just you or me, but more importantly *them*, those who run the teams we root for, in the game we love. The white whale of sabermetrics may already be caught, but don't hold your breath waiting to see it on display.

BASEBALL PROSPECTUS BASICS
Evaluating Defense
James Click

The first two chapters of this book taught you plenty about hitting and pitching, but how can we get a handle on the most elusive element of a team's play—its performance in the field? James Click's summary of the subject described the difficulties of proper fielding evaluation and also proposed some solutions.

It is one of the most suspenseful moments in a baseball game. There's a smash to the second baseman, he slides, knocks it down, picks up the ball, throws from his knees, and the first baseman can't dig it out. The crowds waits, and then the message appears on the scoreboard "On the last play, the official scorer has ruled: HIT."

Many of the problems inherent in evaluating defense are evident in the situation above. The first, and most crucial, is the fact that one of the most basic statistics involved in defense, the error, is assigned by one of baseball's loosest rules, left to the interpretation of the various official scorers. While the league has struggled for the past few seasons to remove the subjectivity inherent in calling the strike zone, it has done nothing to remove the same from the assignment of errors. Rules 10.05.a-e discuss in detail what is to be considered a "base hit"—essentially any ball that could not be fielded with "ordinary effort," a phrase that is never defined or clarified. In any field, statistics are only valuable if they are consistent and accurately reflect the action on the field. Errors, especially recently, have become assigned in such an ad hoc fashion as to relegate the statistic to nearly unusable status.

Second, the conclusions about defensive performance we draw with our eyes are often based on insufficient or severely flawed evidence. Rey Ordonez made more than his fair share of exciting plays at shortstop over the past few seasons, but while they certainly look impressive, you must ask yourself if the same plays are made by other fielders more consistently without the all the spins and ninja rolls, either because of greater range or better positioning before the play. Distinguishing between the economically boring and the inefficiently flashy is simultaneously essential and difficult.

Finally, defense is intrinsically a team activity, and thus metrics assigning individual credit or debit can be as deceptive as RBIs and other team-dependent hitting measurements. Statistics like Range

Factor are largely based on the number of balls fielded by a particular player. However, the fact that a right fielder, for example, doesn't field as many balls as other right fielders in the league may be the result of many other factors besides actual defensive ability; he may be playing next to an extraordinary center fielder, in a park with a small or irregular rightfield area, or playing behind a pitching staff that gives up significantly fewer flyballs than a league-average staff. As with virtually all metrics in baseball, the context is the key, not the actual statistic.

When analyzing defensive performance, the most important mental adjustment to make is to hold the defense accountable for every hit on balls that could have been fielded. Initially, this does not seem fair—defense and pitching are almost inseparably entangled. Determining whether the causality lies with the pitcher or the fielders is even more perplexing than drawing conclusions about the play itself. This approach certainly requires some refinement, but it removes the decisions of the official scorer from the equation. Bill James suggested this approach in one of his Abstracts in the 1980s, calling the new metric "Defensive Efficiency (DE)." It is, quite simply, the percentage of balls in play fielded by the defense. The best teams are usually around .7300 with the worst around .6900.

While DE works fine for entire teams, it doesn't yield any information about individual defensive accomplishment. To that end, BP's Clay Davenport has developed several metrics that allow us to better evaluate each fielder. First and foremost, these metrics are based on range, complimenting players more for the plays they make than the plays they screw up. The reason for this is quite simple: there is no difference between reaching a ball and dropping it and letting it drop in for a hit. It's like the old axiom in golf: 97 percent of the putts that don't make it to the hole don't go in; in baseball, if you can't get to a ball, you can't field it. To determine the number of opportunities the player had to make a play, we start with the league-average defensive performance at that position and adjust it for the player's particular situation. There are five key adjustments:

- Park Factor: This affects outfielders more than other positions since infield size is strictly regulated while outfields seem to be turning more into amusement parks than playing surfaces. Other factors, such as the amount of foul territory, can also have profound effects on fielding performance, at least until baseball allows players to enter the stands to make plays. Imagine if the Cubs had built Wrigley Field with just a little more space in left field—Steve Bartman wouldn't have been able to reach out and grab his fateful ball.
- Balls in Play: Certain teams allow more balls in play than others. Teams with staffs heavy on power pitchers (again, the Cubs come to mind) see many more strikeouts than an average team, yielding fewer balls in play. Fielders should not be penalized for not making an out when the pitcher does it all himself.
- Ground balls and fly balls: Having the best outfield in the league means less if you've got a groundball staff. Since the GB/FB ratio listed for pitchers is based on outs, some slight adjustments have to made to estimate how many of the hits allowed were ground balls with eyes and how many were liners and flies.

- Left/right balance of the pitching staff: Left-handed pitchers face more right-handed batters—something that generally leads to more balls hit to short, third, and left field, and vice versa. After adjusting for strikeouts, better estimates of batted-ball distribution can be made.
- Men on first base: With the exception of the rare triple play, the double play is one of the most impressive defensive feats in baseball. Obviously, though, certain teams have more opportunities for double plays than others, so knowing the raw number of double plays isn't nearly as helpful as knowing what percentage of double play opportunities were actually converted.

Using these factors, it's possible to estimate the performances of individual fielders compared to the league average. From there, the number of runs allowed above or below average can be determined for each fielder. In *Baseball Prospectus 2004*, the "Defense" column for fielders contains values like "154-1B 3"; this indicates that the player played 154 games at first and was 3 runs above average (FRAA). You can also see these numbers on BP's PECOTA Cards.

Davenport Fielding Runs are a major step up from other widely available defensive statistics such as Fielding Percentage, Range Factor, and the enigmatic Zone Rating, but statistical analysis of baseball defense is still in its infancy. Front offices have access to much more advanced metrics than the public, some specifically charting where each batted ball is hit, how hard, and how high. As that wealth of data expands and reaches the public, it will be possible to better evaluate individual defensive performances. For the time being, however, just try to use an objective eye the next time ESPN's Web Gems comes on.

SCHRODINGER'S BAT
Simple Fielding Runs Version 1.0
Dan Fox

Baseball Prospectus has employed a few different systems to evaluate defense over the years. One of those was Simple Fielding Runs, or SFR, a methodology developed by Dan Fox that straddled the line between statistics steeped in traditional fielding stats and those based on zone data.

> "Let him hit it, you've got fielders behind you."
> —Alexander Cartwright, attributed by Bob Chieger in *Voices of Baseball*

When it comes to fielding analysis, there really is no such thing as simple. Be that as it may, in this space during the last month and a half we've been exploring a nascent fielding system I developed based on play-by-play data: "Simple Fielding Runs," or SFR, for those who aren't totally nauseated by yet another TLA (three-letter acronym).

Simply put, the main advantage of developing such a system is that it claims the middle ground between systems that are based on traditional fielding statistics (such as the Davenport Translations, or the subsequently-developed fielding component of Bill James' Win Shares), and those based on zone data tracked for every ball put in play, notably Mitchel Lichtman's Ultimate Zone Rating [UZR] or John Dewan's Plus/Minus system (as described in the initial 2006 edition of *The Fielding Bible*). As we'll see, each approach has its advantages, and we'll exploit one of those where SFR is concerned in the final section of today's column.

While the idea of creating a system based on play-by-play records turned out not to be very original, the implementation of SFR is unique, and it has been interesting to see how the two systems fare when compared to those based on more granular data. To that end, and in the formulaic threefold manner that defines so many of these columns, this week we'll briefly recount the refinements that have been made in SFR over the last month, then make a few comparisons between SFR, UZR, and the Plus/Minus system, and wrap up by applying SFR to the 2007 minor leagues to take a look at who is flashing the leather down on the farm.

Evolution Not Revolution

We'll lead off with a quick recap of where we've been with SFR and how it has evolved. Regular readers will recall that the original version discussed in early December had three core components.

First, a baseline for each position is created that specifies how frequently and at what cost balls of different types (line drives, groundballs, popups) hit "near" a fielder were turned into outs. The second step is to make the same calculations for each fielder and compare their results to the matrix to determine how many balls above- or below-average the fielder either turned into outs or let past him (assuming all else was equal). The final step is to convert the difference into a run value, which we did using values derived from linear weights. The rub in all of this is in determining just what a ball hit "near" a fielder actually means, since we don't have hit location data broken down into zones. In the first iteration, very simple partitioning rules were used to come up with the "virtual area of responsibility" for each position; and by "simple," I mean static, as in "for shortstops, all ground balls fielded by the shortstop and left fielder are considered, as well as half the groundballs fielded by the center fielder."

We then compared SFR to UZR for 2005 and 2006 data and computed a correlation coefficient of 0.75, which was high enough to justify continued development of the system.

Our next step was taken a week later and primarily incorporated two refinements that most readers likely thought obvious: batter handedness and bunting. In taking the first into consideration, we're controlling for fielders facing a disproportionate number of batters from one side that may in turn skew the overall difficulty of turning batted balls into outs. In the latter case, we're affecting corner infielders who usually end up fielding bunts, since treating bunts like normal ground balls is clearly not sufficient. In addition, this second attempt eliminated from consideration for middle infielders all line drives that resulted in extra-base hits, since the odds of a line drive catchable by an infielder resulting in a double or triple are negligible. One final refinement in the second beta version of the system involved introducing more sophisticated partitioning rules. These rules were based on the proportion of batted balls that we find "in the wild" for balls we know were fielded by the positions participating in the split (i.e. between third and short, and second and first) with the split between short and second handled as a 50/50 division. The new partitioning rules also put an end to the double-counting of batted balls where, for example, the same grounder to the outfield was assigned to both the third baseman and shortstop. Instead, each ball was assigned using the proportion calculated in the partitioning rules.

After applying these changes, we once again ran our comparison with UZR and found that our correlation coefficient rose slightly, from 0.75 to 0.78, in addition to bringing SFR in line with UZR in terms of range and standard deviation. It should be noted that while I'm effectively using UZR as a baseline for comparison, that doesn't mean that UZR is a perfect system. My use of it is based on the principle that all other things being equal, a system like UZR based on more detailed data should, in theory, give us results that are closer to reality.

While those changes were certainly beneficial, I quickly discovered (and have not yet discussed in this space) a few more tweaks that could possibly make a substantive difference.

First, I considered the additional context for all infielders depending on whether first base was occupied and added this to the baseline used for comparison. It turns out that for first basemen, on groundballs hit by lefties, the percentage of runners who reach via hit or error goes from 16 percent to 24 percent when first is occupied, and from 20 percent to 29 percent for right-handers. For second basemen in the same scenarios it goes (respectively) from 27 percent to 29, and from 30 percent to 34. For shortstops, interestingly, the trend is the opposite, as it declines from 34 percent to 30, and 32 percent to 31. Finally, for third basemen it's pretty steady—an unchanged 27 percent on lefties, and from 24 percent to 26 against right-handers. Although a far smaller percentage of fielded balls, the differences are significant for bunts when first is occupied, since the vast majority of such attempts are sacrifice bunts instead of bunt hit attempts, which have a higher success rate.

Secondly, the partitioning rules for determining which balls are assigned to first and third basemen were once again altered. In the previous attempts, all balls in the shared areas of responsibility—except as noted above for middle infielders when a line drive resulted in an extra-base hit—were partitioned according to the split percentages. This was changed to exclude bunts from the calculation of the partitioning percentage and, more importantly, all extra-base hits on groundballs to left field are now assigned to the third baseman, and all extra-base hits on grounders to right are assigned to the first baseman. This is done based on the assumption that these are hits down the line that naturally would fall within the corner infielder's area of responsibility.

Based on some correlation results shown in the second article, we also no longer partition any popups, fly balls, or line drives to the outfield, since by doing so we didn't seem to be adding much information to what we already knew. Fielders still get credit, however, for balls of these other types that they field. And as noted above, we were using a 50/50 split on groundballs up the middle. Shortly after publication, this was changed to partition these balls based on the percentages of grounders actually fielded by the shortstop and second baseman. Finally, in just the last few days, a small error in attributing popups, line drives, and fly balls for shortstops was corrected.

The end result of all of these changes and refinements is that we're ready to—in the words of my field of software development—ship the code and stamp the current version for infielders as version 1.0 of SFR. What that means is that you can now download a spreadsheet containing the 2005 through 2007 data for all infielders. Enjoy.

Like Two Peas in a Pod?

In order to provide just a little more context for this first version, let's run a few more comparisons to UZR and the Plus/Minus system. As we did before, we can compute correlation coefficients for SFR and UZR and break it down by position. This time, though, we'll use all seasonal data for 2003 through 2006 for players who played in 50 or more games at their position. The results are shown in Table 1:

Table 1. Correlation Coefficients for SFR vs. UZR, Seasonal 2003-2006 for >=50 Games Played

Pos	Seasons	r
All	549	0.80
1B	143	0.68
2B	132	0.81
SS	141	0.81
3B	133	0.82

From this it appears that our latest set of changes bought us a slight rise in correlation coefficient, increasing the similarity slightly for first basemen, second basemen, and shortstops. It's still interesting to note that first basemen lag behind the other positions, although I still have no solid reason why this should be the case. It certainly could be that the style of play varies more for first basemen in terms of positioning and allowing or not allowing a second baseman to field certain types of balls that a more granular system can take into account. It should also be noted that in this version of SFR the context of whether first base is occupied is taken into account, although the state of second base is not. This may have a larger effect than one might think. This whole question is obviously one ripe for further research.

In addition to running correlations based on seasonal data, we can also see how our metric performs across a span of a few seasons for players with significant playing time. Sean Smith reported his findings for TotalZone+ (the analogous system referenced in the introduction) recently, so we'll take a similar tack here. In Table 2 you'll find the correlations by position for all players who played in 162 or more games (Sean filters by 500 or more chances) at their positions from 2003 through 2006:

Table 2. Correlation Coefficients for SFR vs. UZR, Aggregated 2003-2006 for >=162 Games

Pos	Players	r
All	156	0.87
1B	38	0.78
2B	40	0.88
SS	41	0.86

To give you a feel for what this looks like graphically, Figure 1 shows the scatter plot colored by position (and yes, that blue dot in the upper right hand corner of the graph is new Twins shortstop Adam Everett, which SFR has at +81 runs in 481 games, and which UZR has at +104):

Figure 1. SFR vs. UZR for players with >=162 G from 2003 through 2006

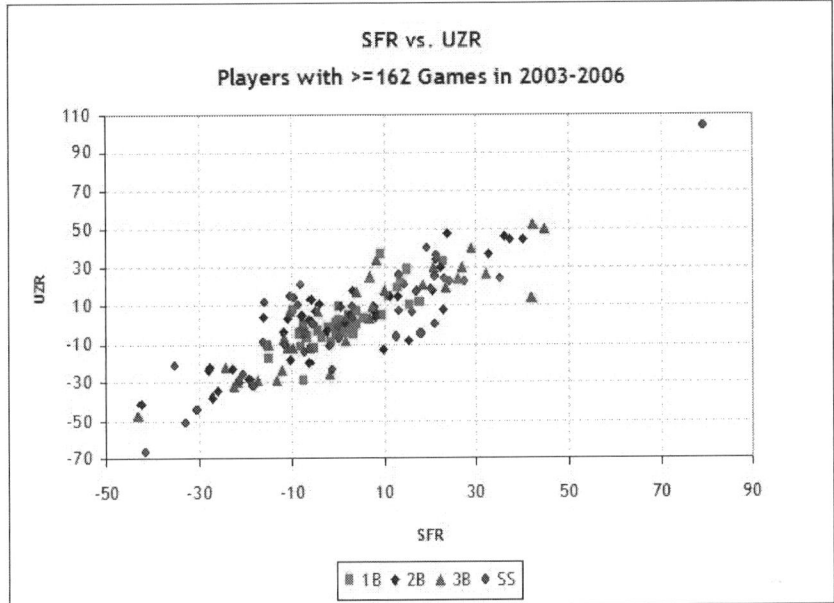

In addition to comparing SFR to UZR we can also compare it, at least in the aggregate, to the Plus/Minus system developed by Baseball Info Solutions. I used the caveat "at least" since full data for 2006 and 2007 is not available, although summary data as well as leaders and trailers have been published in *The Hardball Times*' annual and *The Bill James Handbook 2008*.

In THT's published work, we find the aggregated team totals for 2007 broken down by middle and corner infielders, which we can compare to the SFR totals for those positions, as shown in Table 3 ordered by total SFR:

Table 3. Comparison of SFR to Plus/Minus, 2007 Team Totals

Team	Middle SFR	+/-	Corner SFR	+/-	Total SFR	+/-
TOR	42	56	5	25	47	81
COL	35	46	9	-16	44	30
SDN	30	0	8	-6	38	-6
SFN	19	1	18	46	37	47
BOS	15	3	15	14	30	17
OAK	21	14	8	8	30	22
CHN	11	3	3	13	14	16
SLN	-15	-17	28	58	13	41
BAL	17	3	-5	-5	12	-2
ATL	11	-5	1	4	12	-1
NYN	15	15	-3	11	11	26
KCA	6	25	5	24	11	49
PHI	17	25	-6	-2	11	23
MIN	-6	14	11	16	5	30
ARI	2	19	3	-18	5	1
ANA	0	8	1	27	1	35
TEX	4	-9	-3	-14	0	-23
NYA	-8	-20	3	17	-6	-3
DET	-26	0	16	29	-10	29
WAS	-11	-33	0	-8	-11	-41
LAN	-5	-8	-8	-20	-13	-28
CLE	-10	5	-5	-9	-16	-4
SEA	-7	-11	-10	-14	-17	-25
HOU	-3	-5	-15	17	-18	12
PIT	-23	-4	2	18	-22	14
CIN	-13	7	-13	-29	-26	-22
CHA	-19	-38	-9	-15	-28	-53
TBA	-39	-51	-4	-17	-43	-68
MIL	-16	-5	-33	-41	-49	-46
FLO	-43	-54	-20	-44	-64	-98

Keep in mind that while SFR is denominated in runs, Plus/Minus is simply counting the difference from expected in the number of balls fielded (although for corner infielders Plus/Minus does have a concept termed "Enhanced +/-" that considers balls hit down the line for corner infielders to give them added weight, although I can find no evidence that the numbers presented here are

"Enhanced"). This means that the Plus/Minus numbers will have a larger magnitude. A quick translation would multiply the Plus/Minus number by something like 0.44 for middle infielders and 0.50 for corner infielders to convert them to runs.

The lists agree substantially, with 13 of the 16 teams that SFR pegs as above-average also rating as such in Plus/Minus. Overall, a regression between the totals results in a correlation coefficient of 0.79 with no discernible difference between middle infielders (at 0.78) and corner infielders (at 0.78). Once again, to give you a visual, the following graph depicts how the two systems see the teams overall in terms of their infield defense:

Figure 2. SFR vs. Plus/Minus for 2007 Teams

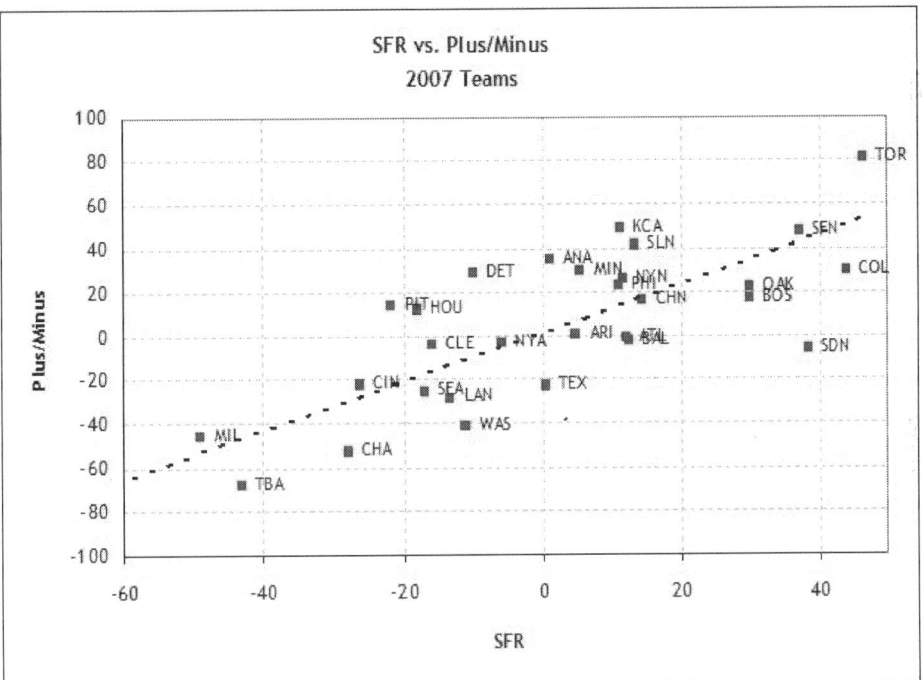

There are clearly differences between the systems—for example, the cluster of Detroit, Pittsburgh, and Houston, which SFR sees as below-average, while Plus/Minus has them in the black—but the similarities and the fairly tight correlation between both UZR and Plus/Minus should give us some confidence that the system is indeed measuring fielding prowess to a substantial degree.

We can't perform the same kinds of correlations for Plus/Minus using player seasons as we can for UZR, since the data is not available, but we can sample the leaders and trailers for 2005 through

Best of Baseball Prospectus: 1996-2011   Part 3: Fielding

2007 as published in the Handbook. What follows is a series of tables that shows the top and bottom five in Plus/Minus, along with the SFR value computed for the player. I've also added a few notable players who may have done well in one metric but not the other (blank values for Plus/Minus indicate that the player did not appear in the leaders or trailers lists).

Table 4. Leaders and Trailers in Plus/Minus Compared to SFR, 2005-2007

First Base			Second Base			Shortstop			Third Base		
Player	SFR	+/-	Player	SFR	+/-	Player	SFR	+/-	Player	SFR	+/-
Albert Pujols	22	72	Chase Utley	29	64	Adam Everett	64	92	Pedro Feliz	30	64
Casey Kotchman	7	31	Orlando Hudson	19	53	Jason Bartlett	22	45	Brandon Inge	33	61
Doug Mientkiewicz	8	31	Aaron Hill	36	48	Clint Barmes	17	43	Scott Rolen	27	50
Lyle Overbay	14	24	Mark Ellis	42	43	Jimmy Rollins	22	42	Joe Crede	24	44
Kevin Youkilis	10	19	Mark Grudzielanek	27	36	Jack Wilson	11	41	Adrian Beltre	7	42
...			...			...			...		
Mike Jacobs	-7	-25	Jorge Cantu	-29	-29	Marco Scutaro	-15	-33	Garrett Atkins	6	-21
Richie Sexson	-4	-25	Jose Vidro	-13	-31	Felipe Lopez	-20	-34	Edwin Encarnacion	-26	-25
Carlos Delgado	-11	-26	Craig Biggio	-3	-33	Hanley Ramirez	-23	-43	Hank Blalock	-8	-28
Adam LaRoche	-7	-28	Jeff Kent	-13	-36	Michael Young	-26	-64	Mark Teahen	-22	-30
Prince Fielder	-21	-33	Rickie Weeks	-45	-41	Derek Jeter	-37	-90	Miguel Cabrera	-16	-37

Notables			Notables			Notables			Notables		
Player	SFR	+/-	Player	SFR	+/-	Player	SFR	+/-	Player	SFR	+/-
Mark Teixeira	16	15	Jamey Carroll	32	17	Omar Vizquel	45	31	Nick Punto	19	28
Nick Johnson	7	6	Placido Polanco	10	28	Jose Reyes	30		Eric Chavez	30	27
Justin Morneau	5	14	Brian Roberts	8	25	John McDonald	20	33	Ryan Zimmerman	9	24
Olmedo Saenz	-8		Jose Castillo	-22		Rafael Furcal	18	36	Morgan Ensberg	16	16
Jason Giambi	-11		Brandon Phillips	-24		Troy Tulowitzki	10	30	Ryan Braun	-28	
			Dan Uggla	-30		Angel M. Berroa	-27	-33	Alex Rodriguez	-19	
						Carlos Guillen	-2				

Defense in a Minor Key

Because of the confidence we've gained through the comparisons to UZR and Plus/Minus, we can now begin to take the next step and apply the SFR methodology to data sets where we do not have numbers generated from a more granular system. To wrap up today, let's review the leaders and trailers for all of the minor leagues (except the Mexican League) for 2007 by position.

First, let's tackle the first basemen:

Table 5. Minor League SFR Leaders and Trailers at First Base, 2007

Player	League	Team	SFR
Brandon Snyder	SAL	DEL	9
Daric Barton	PCL	SRC	9
Yurendell De Caster	INT	IND	8
Larry Broadway	INT	COH	8
Todd Self	TXS	COR	7
...			
Lars Anderson	SAL	CAP	-6
Jeffrey Cunningham	PIO	CAS	-8
Logan Morrison	SAL	GBO	-9

Our top slots go to Orioles farmhand and converted catcher Brandon Snyder, playing in A-ball, and Daric Barton, playing at Triple-A for the A's organization. Snyder just missed Kevin Goldstein's list of top Orioles prospects, while Barton (another converted catcher), after being named the top prospect before the 2007 season, didn't disappoint with the bat and remains at the top of the Oakland stack.

On the flip side, 20-year-old left-handed slugger Logan Morrison, toiling in A-ball for the Marlins, had a good year with the bat by smacking 24 home runs despite struggling against southpaws. However, he did not turn in such a good season with the glove. Another big slugger in the Rockies system, Jeffrey Cunningham, got his first taste of professional baseball in Casper and rated at -8 runs in just 59 games.

Now it's on to the second basemen:

Table 6. Minor League SFR Leaders and Trailers at Second Base, 2007

Player	League	Team	SFR
Adam Davis	SAL	LCO	17
Jayson Nix	PCL	CSP	16
Jose Vallejo	MDW	CLI	15
Luis Valbuena	SOU	WTD	15
Miguel Abreu	SAL	DEL	14
...			
Chih-Hsien Chiang	SAL	CAP	-14
Brooks Conrad	PCL	RRE	-14
Chase Fontaine	SAL	ROM	-15

Grabbing the top spot at +17 runs is Adam Davis, playing in Low-A for Cleveland. Not exactly a prospect at 22 years old, he split time between second (104 games) and third base (25 games) where he also rated +2. At runner-up we find the Rockies' 2001 first-round pick, Jayson Nix, shining afield at Colorado Springs. After delivering his best season with the bat since 2003, he's in the running to win the second base job, where he'll be competing with Marcus Giles, Ian Stewart, Clint Barmes, and Omar Quintanilla, among others. He will have a leg up defensively.

Chase Fontaine was promoted from the Sally League to the Carolina league, and in both stops was tried at short, third, second, and the outfield. While I haven't run the outfield numbers, it's clear that the Braves are trying to find him a position where he can do the least damage. When you add it all up, in his two stops his infield "contribution" totaled -27 runs.

While never touted for his glove work, Brooks Conrad's 2007 season was a disaster on both sides of the ball. His .218/.305/.420 performance at Round Rock for the Astros will be an impediment now that he's a minor-league free agent. His -14 SFR at second base to go along with a -2 at third base in just 13 games won't help either.

On to the shortstops...

Table 7. Minor League SFR Leaders and Trailers at Shortstop, 2007

Player	League	Team	SFR
Hainley Statia	CLF	RCQ	21
Ramon Santiago	INT	TOL	21
Clint Barmes	PCL	CSP	19
Jonathan Herrera	TXS	TUL	16
Juan Sanchez	DSL	DTW	15
...			
Jeffrey Dominguez	CLF	HDM	-16
Dylan Johnston	NWN	BOI	-16
Neil Walton	FSL	VBD	-17

At shortstop, our leader is Hainley Statia playing his first full season at High-A. According to Baseball America, Statia's "an instinctual middle infielder with plus defensive skills." SFR agrees, as he was +14 at two stops in 2006 and +16 at two stops in 2005. In second and third places, we find a couple of Triple-A veterans, Detroit's Ramon Santiago and Colorado's Clint Barmes, both of whom will be competing for utility roles on their respective clubs in 2008.

Prior to the 2006 season, Neil Walton was ranked by *Baseball America* as the top defensive middle infielder and the player with the best infield arm in the Rays' system. His 2006 SFR of +5 seems to support that, but in 2007 he committed 25 errors in 88 games and showed decreased range on his way to a -17 SFR. Dylan Johnston was drafted by the Cubs in 2005, has played nothing but shortstop in his three seasons, and reportedly has average range with a quick release. In 2007 he was promoted from Boise to Peoria, but before moving east, he committed 28 errors in 56 games, leading to an SFR of -16. He wasn't done, however, and after moving to the Midwest League he totaled -8 by committing 18 more miscues for a 2007 SFR total of -24.

Finally, at the hot corners of the minors, the best and worst...

Table 8. Minor League SFR Leaders and Trailers at Third Base, 2007

Player	League	Team	SFR
Ryan Rohlinger	SAL	AUG	35
Mario Lisson	CRL	WIL	16
John Contreras	DSL	DCU	15
Andrew Davis	NWN	SKV	15
Mike Hessman	INT	TOL	14
...			
Michael Grace	SAL	KAN	-11
Matthew Sweeney	MDW	CED	-17
Mat Gamel	FSL	BRE	-24

As a 24-year old who hit .235 in Low-A, Ryan Rohlinger is not exactly high on most peoples' radars, but his SFR of +35 ranked the highest of any player. Although he did play second and short in college, one wonders whether there is a data problem (although in looking at the other infielders at Augusta, nothing jumps out) or if this is just something of a fluke in the system. We'll give Ryan the benefit of the doubt for now and crown him with the title of best infield defender in the minors in 2007.

In the runner-up slot we find Royals third sacker Mario Lisson, who played at High-A Wilmington as a 23-year-old. Lisson is acknowledged as a good defender—as you might expect of a converted shortstop—and he's on the 40-man roster, since the Royals opted to protect him in the Rule 5 draft.

On the bottom, we find Brewers farmhand Mat Gamel, who purportedly has plus arm strength but poor footwork that leads to poor throws. He made an astonishing 53 errors in 113 games in 2007, and since 2005 has committed 91 errors in 229 professional games at third base, good for -34 runs on his career. Can you spell DH?

Finally, we have 19-year-old Angels prospect Matthew Sweeney, who in his first full season in Low-A committed 28 errors in 85 games at third, leading to his -17 SFR. Although he has decent arm strength, a move to first base seems to be in his future.

SCHRODINGER'S BAT
Reminiscing with SFR
Dan Fox

Having developed his Simple Fielding Runs framework for assessing individual performance on defense, Dan Fox put the system to the test by seeing what SFR thought of past players at each position.

> "He (Ozzie Smith) plays like he's on a mini-trampoline or wearing helium kangaroo shorts."
> —Andy Van Slyke

When I began looking at creating a fielding system based on Retrosheet-style play-by-play data, there were two primary sets of data for which it seemed ideally suited. First, since fine-grained hit location data in the form of zones is not recorded at the minor-league level, the system—if indeed it could be proven accurate enough—seemed ideal for measuring defense below the majors. Two things validate that: comparisons with UZR at the major-league level, and a recent column exploring how the system stacks up against scouting judgments of the best defensive players in each organization. In the end, the three different methods largely agree. The second set of data is historical play-by-play data at the major-league level that contains the crucial pieces of information needed to run the system as is. It is this data set that today's column will focus on.

In short, there is a subset of the historical play-by-play data set that contains nearly complete records, with reference to which fielder fielded the ball and the particular hit type (line drive, grounder, fly ball, popup). Armed with this information, the SFR algorithms can be executed against data from 1988 through 1998 without having to make any corrections or allowances for missing data. Earlier this week, that's exactly what I did, and so we'll get into our Wayback Machine and sift through the results for that particular 11-year period. Hopefully we'll bring to mind a few fond—and perhaps not-so-fond—memories of players from that era.

So let's start our look at the decade-plus-one in Table 1, with the overall SFR leader from each season (for a single team), regardless of position:

Year	Player	Team	Pos	Age	Balls	Runners	Diff	SFR
1988	Ozzie Guillen	CHA	SS	24	804	155	36	27.0
1989	Ozzie Smith	SLN	SS	34	709	143	33	24.6
1990	Ozzie Smith	SLN	SS	35	532	92	36	27.3
1991	Ryne Sandberg	CHN	2B	31	721	162	27	19.7
1992	Craig Grebeck	CHA	SS	27	393	86	28	20.9
1993	Scott Fletcher	BOS	2B	34	522	96	27	20.2
1994	Cal Ripken	BAL	SS	33	459	105	20	15.1
1995	Cal Ripken	BAL	SS	34	574	121	27	20.5
1996	Mark Lemke	ATL	2B	30	533	111	24	18.0
1997	Rey Ordonez	NYN	SS	25	488	95	28	21.0
1998	Robin Ventura	CHA	3B	30	458	73	28	22.2

As a quick refresher: Balls is the number of balls allocated to the fielder's virtual area of responsibility. Runners is the actual number of runners who reached base. Diff is the delta between the number of runners who would have been expected to reach versus the number who actually did, and SFR is a conversion of that difference (broken down into one- and two-base components) into runs saved above or below what an average fielder would have done.

Those players who bubble up to the top in Table 1 don't really come as a surprise, which gives us confidence that the system does indeed function as expected against this data set. The list has three Hall of Famers who were certainly no slouches with the glove in Ozzie Smith, Ryne Sandberg, and Cal Ripken, in addition to highly-regarded defenders like Ozzie Guillen, Rey Ordonez, and Robin Ventura.

Now we'll examine each of the four infield positions in a little more detail...

Shortstops

What's most interesting about the shortstops shown in Table 1 is that Ozzie Smith put up those seasons of around +25 runs at the relatively advanced ages of 34 and 35. Although I haven't run SFR for earlier seasons—for reasons explained in the introduction to this column—one wonders whether this represents a significant decline from his peak and, if so, what his peak would look like under this system. In any case, Table 2 shows the full data for the Wizard of Oz:

Table 2. Ozzie Smith 1988-1996

Year	Balls	Runners	Diff	SFR	Rate
1988	768	163	24	18.0	1.15
1989	709	143	33	24.6	1.23
1990	532	92	36	27.3	1.39
1991	638	183	-3	-2.5	0.98
1992	676	177	13	9.7	1.07
1993	692	167	9	6.7	1.05
1994	464	135	-9	-6.9	0.93
1995	178	44	7	5.0	1.15
1996	253	52	11	8.1	1.21

SFR records a decline immediately after that 1990 season, as he never topped +9.7 runs again in his final six seasons. Still, to be worth over 13 runs in less than a season's worth of play at ages 40 and 41 (1995 and 1996) is pretty special. You'll also notice in Table 2 that we've included a Rate in the final column that is simply calculated as the ratio of expected to actual baserunners for the chosen time period. Perhaps surprisingly, in 1995 and 1996 in limited playing time, Smith's rate was actually higher than it had been since 1990. Overall during this timeframe, Smith was +90 runs at shortstop, which places him second behind only Cal Ripken's +112.

Since Ripken is the leader, it's worth taking a look at his numbers as well:

Table 3. Cal Ripken at Shortstop 1988-1997

Year	Balls	Runners	Diff	SFR	Rate
1988	673	155	5	4	1.03
1989	756	166	22	16	1.13
1990	643	137	18	13	1.13
1991	785	182	25	19	1.14
1992	688	178	17	13	1.09
1993	717	176	12	9	1.07
1994	459	105	20	15	1.19
1995	574	121	27	20	1.23
1996	666	168	4	3	1.02
1997	3	1	-1	0	0.35

One of the main differences in looking at Ripken versus Smith is that this timeframe covers Ripken's age-27 through age-36 seasons, so we might expect his values and his rates to be consistently a little higher. When Ripken moved to third base full time in 1997, he rated at +5.5 SFR / 1.08 Rate and performed equally well in 1998 at +8.7/1.15. Taken together, Ripken is by far the fielder who contributed the most runs over that time span at +127, with Mark Lemke second at +93, followed in turn by Smith.

But these questions about rates lead directly to wondering which shortstops (and, by extension, fielders at other positions) rated the best and worst in terms of rate over this time period. Table 4 provides the answer for those shortstops who had 1,000 or more balls assigned to their area of responsibility, and it's not surprising that Ripken and Smith occupy two of the top four spots:

Table 4. Top and Bottom Shortstops by Rate, >= 1,000 Balls 1988-1996

Name	Span	Balls	Runners	Diff	SFR	Rate
Rey Sanchez	1991-1998	1723	388	74	55.1	1.19
Deivi Cruz	1997-1998	1184	299	36	27.0	1.12
Cal Ripken	1988-1997	5963	1389	149	111.6	1.11
Ozzie Smith	1988-1996	4911	1157	121	90.2	1.10
John Valentin	1992-1996	2361	561	58	43.6	1.10
Alan Trammell	1988-1996	3234	744	61	45.9	1.08
Greg Gagne	1988-1997	5777	1388	111	82.7	1.08
Jose Valentin	1993-1998	2513	619	45	33.7	1.07
Nomar Garciaparra	1996-1998	1336	334	24	18.1	1.07
Ozzie Guillen	1988-1998	5749	1349	97	72.1	1.07
...						
Edgar Renteria	1996-1998	1715	504	-38	-28.1	0.93
Andres Thomas	1988-1990	1674	439	-39	-29.5	0.91
Rafael Ramirez	1988-1992	2061	562	-51	-38.1	0.91
Jose Offerman	1990-1996	2597	775	-72	-54.3	0.91
Wil Cordero	1992-1995	1689	513	-48	-35.8	0.91
Chris Gomez	1993-1998	2620	792	-77	-57.7	0.90
Dale Sveum	1988-1997	1149	333	-34	-25.7	0.90
Andujar Cedeno	1990-1996	2391	762	-90	-67.3	0.88
Kurt Stillwell	1988-1996	2214	646	-82	-62.3	0.87
Ricky Gutierrez	1993-1998	2084	684	-104	-78.2	0.85

Although Rey Sanchez also played a significant amount at second base during this period (part-time in 1994 and 1997, and full-time in 1995 for the Cubs) covering his age-23 through -30 seasons, he ends up rating the highest of any shortstop, allowing 19 percent fewer runners to reach base than would have been expected. He rated especially well in 1992 (+16/1.38), 1996 (+13/1.20), and 1998 (+13/1.29). At second base, Sanchez placed eleventh overall in Rate at 1.06 with 1,043 balls assigned to his area.

Deivi Cruz takes second on the strength of just two seasons (1997 and 1998 with the Tigers) when he rated at +20/1.23 and +7/1.05. Special mention here should also be made of Craig Grebeck, who took the top spot overall in 1992 for the White Sox at +20.9 runs. From 1990 through 1998 he was at +32 runs and, if the threshold were lowered to 500 balls fielded, would rank second in Rate at 1.21, just slightly behind Mike Benjamin at 1.27.

On the flip side, we find Ricky Gutierrez at the bottom of the heap at -78.2 runs and a rate 15 percent below average. Although he played a smattering of games at second and third for San Diego and Houston during this period, he was nothing if not consistent defensively, putting up SFR numbers of -8, -12, -17, -12, -10, and -19 in consecutive seasons. Many of the remaining names on the bottom of this list—perhaps with the exception of Edgar Renteria who, it should be remembered, is represented in only three of the overall sample's seasons—should come as no surprise to those who saw them play. It should also be mentioned here that Chris Gomez and Kurt Stillwell recorded the two lowest seasonal SFR totals at shortstop for a single team, with Gomez at -25.8 in 1997 and Stillwell at -24.2 in 1991.

No doubt I'll field some questions this week about Derek Jeter if I don't show his numbers as well, so Table 5 includes his 1995 through 1998 seasons:

Table 5. Derek Jeter 1995-1998

Year	Balls	Runners	Diff	SFR	Rate
1995	61	19	-3	-1.9	0.86
1996	704	191	-9	-6.9	0.95
1997	702	213	-30	-22.4	0.86
1998	589	158	9	6.7	1.06

With a good rating in 1998, he comes out at only -25 runs during the time period.

Second Base

Moving on, Table 6 lists the top and bottom second basemen in terms of Rate, once again looking only at those fielders who've been assigned 1,000 or more balls.

Table 6. Top and Bottom Second basemen by Rate, >= 1,000 Balls 1988-1996

Name	Span	Balls	Runners	Diff	SFR	Rate
Mike Gallego	1988-1997	1936	393	65	48.3	1.17
Jose Oquendo	1988-1995	2318	464	72	53.9	1.16
Mark Lemke	1988-1998	3576	780	118	87.6	1.15
Tony Phillips	1988-1997	1330	268	37	27.2	1.14
Manuel Lee	1988-1995	1001	184	21	15.7	1.11
Scott Fletcher	1989-1995	2516	527	58	42.6	1.11
Lou Whitaker	1988-1995	3494	760	60	44.8	1.08
Ryne Sandberg	1988-1997	5207	1199	83	61.8	1.07
Luis Alicea	1988-1998	2612	591	38	27.8	1.06
Jim Gantner	1988-1992	1941	410	25	19.1	1.06
...						
Jeff Frye	1992-1997	1655	431	-26	-19.7	0.94
Ray Durham	1995-1998	2310	602	-45	-33.4	0.92
Mariano Duncan	1989-1997	2110	549	-50	-37.2	0.91
Tony Womack	1994-1998	1277	372	-34	-25.6	0.91
Terry Shumpert	1990-1998	1046	293	-28	-21.4	0.90
Nelson Liriano	1988-1998	1867	474	-47	-35.5	0.90
Juan Samuel	1988-1998	2160	574	-61	-46.0	0.89
Joey Cora	1989-1998	3313	888	-102	-76.7	0.89
Carlos Garcia	1992-1998	2076	568	-71	-53.0	0.87
Gregg Jefferies	1988-1993	1230	326	-51	-38.3	0.84

Mike Gallego and Jose Oquendo take the top two spots at second base, but Mark Lemke logged much more time there and did almost equally as well from a rate perspective, topping the charts with a SFR of +87.6 runs. Interestingly, his career line shown in Table 7 reveals no apparent age-related decline from ages 22 through 32.

Table 7. Mark Lemke at Second Base 1988-1998

Year	Team	Balls	Runners	Diff	SFR	Rate
1988	ATL	80	17	-1	-0.9	0.93
1989	ATL	56	12	1	0.7	1.09
1990	ATL	161	28	8	5.5	1.27
1991	ATL	306	67	10	7.2	1.14
1992	ATL	530	152	7	5.4	1.05
1993	ATL	571	114	24	17.5	1.21
1994	ATL	412	90	12	9.1	1.14
1995	ATL	429	88	12	8.8	1.13
1996	ATL	533	111	24	18.0	1.22
1997	ATL	415	90	13	9.7	1.14
1998	BOS	84	12	9	6.6	1.73

Perhaps fittingly, Ryne Sandberg and Lou Whitaker are virtually tied, with Whitaker edging Sandberg in Rate, but Sandberg played significantly more, resulting in 17 additional runs saved. Whitaker had his best season in this period in 1990, putting up a +20/1.35, while Sandberg had two seasons of approximately +20 runs, at +20/1.16 in 1991 and then +21/1.16 in 1992, which ranked second and fifth among the single-season leaders. However, the top single season by a second baseman goes to Jose Oquendo, who recorded an SFR of +23.8 in 1990 for the Cardinals.

Readers will no doubt recall that Greg Jefferies was moved around a bit in an effort to hide his glove, thereby giving him significant time at both third and first base as well as in the outfield. He did his damage at second base putting up -16/0.81, -14/0.85, and -7/0.89 from 1989 through 1991 at ages 21 through 23.

Although Carlos Garcia rated more poorly, Joey Cora logged the most time at second base of any of the bottom ten. He racked up a significant percentage of his -76.7 total runs (most for a second baseman) with four consecutive consistently poor showings from 1995 through 1998 after being acquired by Seattle. In those years—which were his age-30 through -33 seasons—he rated at -19/0.80, -16/0.84, -18/0.83, and -17/0.83.

The lowest single-season total by a large margin belongs to Tony Womack, who put up a -29.2 in 1997 for the Pirates. The next-closest competitor is Todd Walker's -24.3 in 1998 for the Twins.

Third Base

As we move to the hot corner, consider Table 8, which lists the top and bottom third basemen, once again in terms of Rate.

Table 8. Top and Bottom Third basemen by Rate, >= 1,000 Balls 1988-1996

Name	Span	Balls	Runners	Diff	SFR	Rate
Edgardo Alfonzo	1995-1998	1018	187	35	27.7	1.19
Scott Brosius	1991-1998	1533	282	49	38.1	1.17
Matt Williams	1988-1998	3757	678	97	74.9	1.14
Robin Ventura	1989-1998	3660	676	85	66.5	1.13
Gary Gaetti	1988-1998	3825	727	90	70.4	1.12
Brook Jacoby	1988-1992	1526	286	30	23.4	1.10
Chris Sabo	1988-1996	2287	440	44	34.6	1.10
Tim Wallach	1988-1996	3368	633	61	47.2	1.10
Scott Cooper	1991-1997	1366	284	27	21.0	1.09
Wade Boggs	1988-1998	3680	698	65	51.3	1.09
...						
Sean Berry	1990-1998	1688	401	-24	-18.1	0.94
Bobby Bonilla	1988-1998	2619	585	-35	-27.5	0.94
Dave Magadan	1988-1998	1307	303	-19	-14.5	0.94
Leo Gomez	1990-1996	1619	374	-30	-24.1	0.92
Mike Blowers	1989-1998	1534	368	-35	-27.1	0.91
Todd Zeile	1990-1998	3282	803	-76	-60.4	0.90
Dean Palmer	1989-1998	2491	623	-67	-52.4	0.89
Gary Sheffield	1989-1993	1458	357	-40	-31.8	0.89
Howard Johnson	1988-1995	1396	338	-44	-34.3	0.87
Jim Presley	1988-1991	1121	266	-41	-31.9	0.85

During this time period, Edgardo Alfonzo and Scott Brosius both did very well from a rate perspective, but a trio of third sackers—Matt Williams, Robin Ventura, and Gary Gaetti—played significantly more often, and each saved their teams roughly 70 runs over those years. Of those three, Williams stands a little above the others in both rate and total SFR; we can see in his career line that SFR recorded only one subpar season (1996, his final year with the Giants) out of those 11. Once again, there is no age-related decline to speak of.

While Williams' rates were consistently higher (outside of 1996), Ventura recorded two of the top seven SFR seasons during this period, with his +16

Year	Team	Balls	Runners	Diff	SFR	Rate
1988	SFN	135	21	4	3.2	1.20
1989	SFN	206	23	15	11.9	1.65
1990	SFN	483	74	18	14.4	1.25
1991	SFN	488	94	2	1.5	1.03
1992	SFN	444	83	7	5.6	1.09
1993	SFN	429	87	6	4.6	1.07
1994	SFN	357	65	16	12.1	1.24
1995	SFN	274	55	5	3.6	1.08
1996	SFN	296	66	-5	-3.5	0.93
1997	CLE	442	76	18	13.9	1.23
1998	ARI	202	33	10	7.6	1.29

in 1992 and a +22 in 1998 at the age of 30. Ventura also ranked above average in each of his ten seasons at third base, while Gary Gaetti did so in ten of 11 seasons. Honorable mention goes to Chris Sabo, whose 1988 SFR of +24.3 with the Reds was the single highest total for a third baseman for a single team, with Terry Pendleton's +23 in 1989 for the Cardinals a close second.

Gaetti, Ken Caminiti, and especially Tim Wallach were all particularly good at fielding bunts, with respective SFR totals and opportunities of +11/178, +12/194, and +14/166. On the other side of the coin, Dave Magadan (-8/61), Jim Thome (-7/67, before being shifted permanently to first base in 1997), and Kevin Seitzer (-7/80) were... not so good.

At the bottom of the stack we find a collection of notably poor defenders, including a young Gary Sheffield, who was tried at third by the Brewers, Padres, and Marlins after recording a collective -14/0.84 at shortstop for the Brewers in 1988 and 1989 at the tender ages of 19 and 20.

In terms of total runs, Todd Zeile is our "winner" at -60.4, having managed to record subpar SFR totals and rates in all 11 seasons. He was particularly poor on bunts, recording an SFR of -9 in 157 opportunities—the lowest total among third baseman. His work at catcher and first base drops his overall total to -65 runs and, when combined with his baserunning efforts (an EqBRR of -38), during this time period he cost his teams on the order of 100 runs in these "secondary" skills.

Although Zeile's -15.2/0.86 performance for the Cardinals in 1993 was among the poorest showings by a third baseman during this period, it was Russ Davis playing for Seattle in 1998 who almost lapped the field, recording an SFR of -25.8 and a Rate of 0.73. The next-closest competitor was Howard Johnson at -16.4 in 1989 for the Mets.

First Base

Finally, we'll wrap up with a look at first basemen, as shown in Table 10.

Table 10. Top and Bottom First Basemen by Rate, >= 1,000 Balls 1988-1996

Name	Span	Balls	Runners	Diff	SFR	Rate
John Olerud	1989-1998	2433	295	73	58.7	1.25
Sid Bream	1988-1994	1163	122	25	19.3	1.20
Jeff King	1989-1998	1072	142	27	20.7	1.19
Rafael Palmeiro	1988-1998	3299	440	63	49.4	1.14
Pete O'Brien	1988-1993	1369	161	23	18.1	1.14
Mark Grace	1988-1998	4122	528	73	57.0	1.14
Ricky Jordan	1988-1996	1167	134	15	12.0	1.11
Glenn Davis	1988-1993	1101	135	11	8.2	1.08
Wally Joyner	1988-1998	3132	432	34	26.3	1.08
Jeff Bagwell	1991-1998	2644	376	29	22.7	1.08
...						
Randy Milligan	1988-1994	1221	177	-6	-5.2	0.97
Fred McGriff	1988-1998	3158	470	-17	-12.4	0.96
Will Clark	1988-1998	3537	521	-23	-19.0	0.96
J.T. Snow	1992-1998	1499	228	-11	-7.7	0.95
Rico Brogna	1992-1998	1126	186	-10	-7.9	0.95
David Segui	1990-1998	1712	287	-23	-17.7	0.92
Cecil Fielder	1988-1998	1771	290	-26	-20.3	0.91
Paul Sorrento	1989-1998	1617	266	-27	-22.0	0.90
Frank Thomas	1990-1998	1694	294	-40	-31.1	0.87
Pedro Guerrero	1988-1992	1033	170	-28	-21.8	0.84

Keep in mind that SFR does not include a key component of first base defense—fielding throws from other infielders. Even so, notable scoop artist John Olerud comes out well on top at +58.7 runs and a rate of 1.25, having scored positively in every season from 1991 through 1998. His top season came in 1998 at the age of 29, when he was with the Mets and recorded a +17/1.50. Both Rafael Palmeiro and Mark Grace played more, as did Wally Joyner and even Jeff Bagwell. Grace's seasonal totals are shown here.

Year	Team	Balls	Runners	Diff	SFR	Rate
1988	CHN	300	45	-7	-5.2	0.85
1989	CHN	396	53	2	1.2	1.03
1990	CHN	468	59	3	2.3	1.05
1991	CHN	489	59	12	9.4	1.20
1992	CHN	451	45	21	16.9	1.47
1993	CHN	370	42	10	7.9	1.24
1994	CHN	247	37	3	2.2	1.08
1995	CHN	322	43	5	3.6	1.10
1996	CHN	341	37	11	8.4	1.29
1997	CHN	367	41	12	9.7	1.30
1998	CHN	369	66	1	0.7	1.01

Both Grace and Olerud capture three of the top ten seasonal totals during the time period, with Olerud's 1998 season topping the charts, followed by Grace in 1992. One of the seemingly clear differences between Olerud and Grace is that Grace performed much better on bunts, recording a total SFR of +8 runs in 280 opportunities, far outdistancing Andres Galarraga (+4/192) and Jeff Bagwell (+4/223). Meanwhile, Olerud recorded just +1 runs in 102 opportunities.

Pedro Guerrero, playing for the both the Dodgers and Cardinals, recorded the lowest rate: just 0.84 in 1,033 opportunities at first base. Interestingly, he still ranked last despite a healthy positive contribution on bunts at +4 runs in 57 opportunities. When you also consider his 1988 experience at third for the Dodgers—where he recorded a -9/0.65—his total in the infield drops to -32 runs.

Will Clark and Fred McGriff logged the most time at first base, and Clark recorded the single lowest SFR total at first in 1998 with the Rangers at -15.2/0.77.

In perusing this table, one might be surprised (like I was) that J.T. Snow appears on the bottom, since he developed a good defensive reputation over the years. In fact, SFR overall doesn't like him very much, recording negative values in six of the eleven seasons on which it has data (1992-1998 and 2003-2006) with a whopping -10 in 1995. In only one season was his SFR above 5, when it was +5.6 in 1998.

GETTING PADE
Improving on Defensive Efficiency
James Click

Park effects on hitters and pitchers are fairly easy to see with the eye, if only when a home run barely scrapes over a fence it wouldn't have cleared in another stadium. However, as James Click noted in the course of introducing Park-Adjusted Defensive Efficiency, or PADE, ballparks have effects on fielders, too.

Evaluating defense has always been one of the more difficult tasks for performance analysts. The first reason for this is that looks can be deceiving. Sure, that acrobatic shortstop playing in the country's largest market might appear to be a superior defender to the untrained eye, but all too often we draw our conclusions by putting emphasis on the outcome rather than the process of fielding the ball. The second source of difficulty stems from the still-severe limitations we face with regard to collecting data and properly interpreting that data once we get a meaningful amount of it. Granted, there are some statistics that can be used when evaluating defense—errors, fielding percentage, Range Factor, Zone Rating, etc.—but none of them is without its flaws.

Which bring us to one of Bill James' measures for quantifying defensive performance: Defensive Efficiency (provided here by Keith Woolner). Defensive Efficiency is a metric that measures a team's ability to turn balls-in-play into outs, using the formula...

$$(\text{TotalOuts} - \text{Strikeouts})/(\text{BIP-HR})$$

Despite being raw and only applying to entire teams, Defensive Efficiency is a fair measure of overall defensive performance. But that doesn't mean it can't be improved.

Defense can be broken down into several facets, primarily *pitching*, *ballpark*, and *actual defensive performance*. While we've conceded that pitching and defense are extremely difficult to separate, it's much easier to take into account the venue in which the game took place. For example, looking at this season's numbers, Defensive Efficiency rates the Rockies as one of the league's worst defenses, while the Dodgers have one of the best. But how much of that is actual performance, and how much of that is simply a function of each team's playing environment? Can we determine how the Rockies would perform if they played someplace else?

We already use park factors when adjusting hitting and pitching statistics, and they can be applied to defense as well. However, using established park factors to adjust our defensive statistics would yield skewed results, as they take into account the full slate of offensive statistics, most notably home runs. Smaller ballparks are the main concern, as they yield a higher park factor, mostly thanks to home runs. But the fact of the matter is that many small ballparks might actually be easier to play defense in, since their outfields are much smaller.

Since we can't use established park factors, the first step has to be to establish a defensive baseline for each park in the majors. There are several ways to do this. One would be to generate a Def_Eff number for each park in the majors, using James' formula but applying it to parks instead of teams, and using statistics over a wider range of time (say, three-to-five years). However, doing so would still allow various defenses too much input on the park factors. For instance, how would Turner Field's park factor look if Andruw Jones hadn't been patrolling center field the entire time? Or Torii Hunter in the Metrodome or Ichiro Suzuki and Mike Cameron in Safeco? Even when allowing for visiting teams' numbers, those star defensive players make up half of the available statistics for a park and could skew the numbers.

Instead, at Keith's suggestion, we'll use the ratio of each team's home Def_Eff to its away Def_Eff, using numbers for the last three years where applicable. There are some adjustments to be made, particularly in Cincinnati, where the Great American Ballpark has been open for only one season, and in Puerto Rico, where there were a mere 22 games played in Hiram Bithorn Stadium. Though a small sample size flag should go up for both of those, it shouldn't increase the amount of statistical noise (the nice way of saying "error") in our numbers. The results are to the right, complete with Clay Davenport's full park factors for 2001-03. Note that with DE Park Factor, the lower the number, the harder it is to play defense in a particular park, whereas with Clay's Full Park Factor, the higher numbers

Park	DE Park Factor	Full Park Factor
Coors Field	.9544	1112
Kauffman Stadium	.9773	1100
Fenway Park	.9779	1010
Ballpark at Arlington	.9779	1053
Bank One Ballpark	.9782	1060
Metrodome	.9875	1009
Minute Maid Park	.9880	1038
Olympic Stadium	.9898	1067
Tropicana Field	.9899	997
Sky Dome	.9915	1034
Edison Field	.9953	987
PNC Park	.9955	1009
Pac Bell Park	.9984	942
Jacobs Field	1.0021	997
Pro Player Stadium	1.0027	955
Busch Stadium	1.0028	974
Turner Field	1.0038	986
Hiram Bithorn Stadium	1.0092	1120
Comerica Park	1.0093	966
Great American Ballpark	1.0097	998
Wrigley Field	1.0098	976
Shea Stadium	1.0104	950
New Comiskey Park	1.0113	1018
Miller Park	1.0127	995
Network Associates Col.	1.0161	1003
Qualcomm Stadium	1.0169	918
Yankee Stadium	1.0173	976
Camden Yards	1.0206	959
Veterans Stadium	1.0216	939
SafeCo Field	1.0218	949
Dodger Stadium	1.0294	917

indicate advantages to the hitters.

There are a few notable parks that move up or down the list. Pac Bell Park, normally one of the game's most pitcher-friendly parks, is actually slightly tougher-than-average on defense, likely owing much to its expansive outfield. Pro Player Stadium falls into this category as well. Fenway Park, despite having a park factor almost identical to Network Associates Coliseum, is actually one of the most difficult parks on defenders—but for slightly different reasons than Pac Bell. While the Coliseum is a symmetrical ballpark, Fenway's nooks, crannies, and monsters turn many routine fly balls into singles and doubles (or for Bucky Dent, home runs). For the most part, the results hold true to our previous thinking—Dodger Stadium is up at the top, while Coors is way off the bottom—but the adjustments will make our measurements more accurate.

Now that we've established a general idea of how difficult it is to play defense in each park, we can see how teams perform against that average. To do so, we need to establish a team baseline for the season. By multiplying the number of games a team plays in each park by that park's defensive average and then dividing by the total number of games played, we can establish a baseline for how difficult a team's schedule was on the defense. To save some space, we won't include those numbers here, but if you really want them, let me know.

Then, quite simply, we divide James' raw Defensive Efficiency for each team, re-centered around the league average, by each team's schedule-adjusted Defensive Efficiency. This calculation yields a percentage that gives us an idea of how each team's defense performed against the expected league average, given their schedule. We'll clumsily call this metric PADE—Park Adjusted Defensive Efficiency—and will now open the floor for suggestions for a new acronym. Here are the results for 2003.

A league-average defense will yield a rating of 0.000. A team with a PADE of 1.000 turns one percent more BIP into outs than an average team in its schedule—not an insignificant amount.

There aren't many teams that suddenly appear to be significantly better or worse defensively than with James' original metric. However, there are a few interesting moves to note.

Team	PADE
Tampa Bay Devil Rays	2.141
Seattle Mariners	1.887
Houston Astros	1.831
San Francisco Giants	1.774
Oakland Athletics	1.522
Anaheim Angels	1.067
Cleveland Indians	1.020
Chicago White Sox	.756
Arizona Diamondbacks	.752
Minnesota Twins	.570
Atlanta Braves	.552
Kansas City Royals	.512
Los Angeles Dodgers	.148
St Louis Cardinals	.064
Montreal Expos	.049
Pittsburgh Pirates	-.081
Colorado Rockies	-.171
Philadelphia Phillies	-.324
Boston Red Sox	-.390
San Diego Padres	-.517
Chicago Cubs	-.679
Detroit Tigers	-1.061
Florida Marlins	-1.116
Cincinnati Reds	-1.162
Toronto Blue Jays	-1.208
New York Mets	-1.226
Milwaukee Brewers	-2.141
Texas Rangers	-2.332
New York Yankees	-2.497
Baltimore Orioles	-2.690

- Colorado, originally ranked second-from-the-bottom, appears to be much closer to league-average.
- The Rangers, Yankees, and Orioles don't get any help, remaining cellar-dwellers.
- The Dodgers drop significantly down the list, moving from the fifth-best team to only slightly above average—obviously due to playing so many games in extreme pitchers' parks like Dodger Stadium and Pac Bell Park.
- Those kids in Tampa can play, jumping ahead of the Mariners and A's for the top spot in this year's list.

So what is PADE good for? Primarily, it's a purer metric of an entire team's defensive performance that does not punish or reward teams for playing in certain parks. Using PADE does not account for how individual players affect a team's defense, but it can, among other things, give a better estimate of which pitchers benefited the most from nifty glovework, yielding more accurate appraisals of individual pitching performances. There are still many improvements that can be made to our defensive statistics, but removing park factors is a good first step.

TIME TO GET PADE AGAIN
Park Effects on Team Defense
James Click

A year after developing Park-Adjusted Defensive Efficiency (PADE), James Click revisited the system to refine it further and explain what it revealed about each team's performance in the field.

Now that baseball's coaches and managers have weighed in on their favorite defensive players, and Clay Davenport has unveiled his champion glovemen of 2004, I though I'd bring back an old friend for a fresh look at this year's defensive performances.

Last year, I introduced some changes to Bill James' Defensive Efficiency, a metric that measures the percentage of balls in play that the defense converts into outs. While it eventually ended in a measure intended to be free of both park and pitching factors called Team Adjusted Defense (TAD), I'm uncomfortable with the process of removing pitching from the operation, so for now I'll stick to the original update: Park Adjusted Defensive Efficiency (PADE).

There will be one major improvement over last year's version. In 2004, PADE will include instances in which a player reached on an error against the defense. For long and drawn-out reasons from which I will spare you, PADE missed that last season, but now it has been added, and the metric is more accurate for it.

The first thing PADE does is generate defensive park factors for each ballpark. These will be slightly different from full park factors, since defensive park factors do not include home runs. Instead, by comparing how each team plays defense at home and on the road, we can gain an estimate of how difficult each park is for defenders. These will be three-year factors to eliminate some of the variance for year to year, with the obvious exception of the parks that have been open less than three years in Philadelphia, San Diego, and Cincinnati.

Here are the 2004 defensive park factors. The lower the factor, the more difficult it is to play defense:

Ballpark	Park Factor
SBC Park	.9780
Coors Field	.9796
Sky Dome	.9857
Fenway Park	.9861
The Ballpark at Arlington	.9882
PNC Park	.9898
Shea Stadium	.9908
Metrodome	.9954
Edison Field	.9957
Jacobs Field	.9961
Kauffman Stadium	.9980
PETCO Park	1.0025
BankOne Ballpark	1.0038
US Cellular Field	1.0060
Wrigley Field	1.0139
Citizens Bank Park	1.0150
Turner Field	1.0152
Yankee Stadium	1.0152
Comerica Park	1.0157
Minute Maid Park	1.0162
Olympic Stadium	1.0164
SafeCo Field	1.0208
Busch Stadium	1.0233
Tropicana Field	1.0238
Dodger Stadium	1.0250
Camden Yards	1.0251
ProPlayer Stadium	1.0255
Miller Park	1.0262
Network Associates Coliseum	1.0312
Great American Ballpark	1.0370

There is quite a bit of interesting movement on this list with another year of data and the addition of reaching on errors. For example, SBC Park actually comes out as a more difficult venue in which to play defense than the vast expanses of Coors Field. I would assume that most of this is due to the staggering size of the outfield in SBC Park, the high wall in right, the small foul area, and the age of the Giants' outfield. Perhaps the San Francisco outfielders have a more difficult time than younger players in compensating for the extra area in the outfield by the Bay. None of these reasons constitutes an actual explanation on its own, but together, the four seem plausible.

Also interesting is PETCO Park's very average park factor despite the vehement protests of many San Diego players about the park's ability to suppress offense. It's just one year of data, but it appears at this point that PETCO's main offensive suppression comes from turning home runs into very long flyball outs, making things easier on the defense, but much harder on Padres hitters' agents.

Getting on with things, let's see how teams fared this year. Here are the raw Defensive Efficiency numbers and PADE. PADE is presented as a percentage. For example, a PADE of 1 means that a team converts one percent more balls in play into outs than an average defense, given its park environment.

Team	Def_Eff	PADE
Dodgers	.7147	1.548
Cardinals	.7126	1.398
Giants	.6957	1.302
Mets	.6964	.912
Red Sox	.6944	.879
Phillies	.7040	.829
Blue Jays	.6934	.792
Marlins	.7033	.405
Padres	.6949	.352
Mariners	.7009	.325
Cubs	.6980	.271
Devil Rays	.7013	.264
White Sox	.6955	.292
Rangers	.6879	.150
Expos	.6964	.027
Pirates	.6871	.013
Angels	.6883	-.072
Twins	.6876	-.132
Rockies	.6809	-.252
Athletics	.6982	-.287
Indians	.6855	-.367
Braves	.6901	-.558
Brewers	.6922	-.715
Yankees	.6883	-.736
Astros	.6871	-.889
Diamondbacks	.6825	-.930
Tigers	.6859	-.991
Orioles	.6871	-1.182
Royals	.6766	-1.323
Reds	.6896	-1.324

As expected, while there's a little bit of shuffling in the middle, there's quite a bit of movement at the extremes. The Reds, by virtue of their venue, suddenly and narrowly pass the Royals as baseball's most defensively inept team. Conversely, the Rockies, as usual, move up to near average defensive performance.

What I found most interesting, however, was that the Dodgers and Cardinals—baseball's two best defensive teams—managed to hold their top spots despite park factors that suggest that some of their prowess is a result of friendlier confines than other teams. Also, despite some of the more well-publicized gaffes of the post-season, the Red Sox come out in the top tier of defenders. If the Sox's braintrust truly was focusing on defense this season, they accomplished their goals, as Boston's new World Series champions flashed a great deal more leather than could have been expected.

The rest of the playoff field seems to run the full range of defensive ability, as the Cardinals, Dodgers, and Red Sox finished well ahead of the pack, while the Yankees, Astros, and Braves finished well behind. With the Angels and Twins both slightly below-average, we can chalk up another point for those who feel that defense isn't a good predictor of who will reach the playoffs. However, considering how well the Cardinals and Red Sox did in October with their superior defenses, the idea that defense wins in the playoffs could be argued. Of course, considering some of the "defense" we witnessed in these playoffs, it's tough to say that that had anything to do with who won the games.

SCHRODINGER'S BAT
What Would Bacon Do?
Dan Fox

Derek Jeter's defense has long been a point of contention between fans who see his obvious athleticism as a sign of fielding prowess and those who contend that he misses many balls hit up the middle—and have the stats to support their assertion. Using Simple Fielding Runs and other defensive metrics, Dan Fox attempted to determine whether the evidence was overwhelming enough to conclude that Jeter's glove definitely didn't measure up to his bat.

> "It is the peculiar and perpetual error of the human understanding to be more moved and excited by affirmatives than by negatives."
> —Francis Bacon (1561-1626)

Since everyone else seems to be chiming in on the fielding prowess of Derek Jeter, perhaps it's relevant to pause and ask the question, what would Sir Francis Bacon, the English philosopher and statesman, have thought of Jeter's defense? That question may be more relevant than it would first appear, since not only did Bacon popularize what we now call the scientific, or Baconian method, but he also, in his wildly ambitious quest to categorize all of human knowledge in a 1620 book called *Novum Organum* (meaning "New Instrument"), classified intellectual fallacies into what has been called "the four idols." Both his method and *Novum Organum* have a bearing on the question of Jeter's ability at shortstop.

First, of course, there is the question of whether one can objectively evaluate Jeter's defensive ability, or that of any shortstop. The question of defensive analysis has been a stickler for most of major-league history due primarily to a lack of creativity in determining what to track; the same six official fielding stats—games played, total chances, putouts, assists, errors, and fielding percentage—adopted by the National League in 1876 are the same six in use more than 100 years later. However, the ease with which new kinds of data can be collected and analyzed in recent years has made the task far easier.

Building off of a wealth of new data that includes play-by-play records of each and every one of the almost 200,000 events in a major-league season, complete with observational recording of each batted ball and its location on the field, researchers have constructed sophisticated systems (although based on straightforward and accessible ideas) that probabilistically debit and credit fielders for making or not making plays judged as similarly difficult, as compared to their peers.

University of Pennsylvania professor Shane Jensen's Spatial Aggregate Fielding Evaluation system (SAFE) has certainly grabbed the attention of the media after he revealed at a meeting of the American Association for the Advancement of Science in Boston that Jeter ranks at the bottom of the list of shortstops in the 2002-2005 period, averaging nearly -14 runs per season. Only Michael Young of the Rangers was even close, at -13 runs. But Jensen's system is only one of several built on similar principles, all of which rank Jeter poorly, and some of which are shown in the following table. A quick confession: while also relying on play-by-play data, SFR does not use as fine-grained data as the other systems, but I place it here alongside these other metrics to make a comparison.

Year	SAFE (Runs)	UZR (Runs)	PMR (Outs)	Plus/Minus (Balls Fielded)	SFR (Runs)
2003	-16	-21	-13	-14	-15
2004	-11	3	-30	-16	2
2005	-19	-11	-41	-34	-9
2006	n/a	-15	-18	-22	-8
2007	n/a	-7*	-40	-34	-20

First half of the season only

There is clearly a decent amount of variation in the numbers from year to year and from system to system (even taking into account the fact that PMR and Plus/Minus are based on balls fielded, while the others are calculated in terms of runs). But even so, a clear trend emerges from the table—Derek Jeter simply does not rate well in these systems when compared to his peers.

Bacon was one of the first observers to realize what the trend in the previous table might signify. After all, in *Novum Organum*, he also had this say about his new-fangled inductive method of reasoning from observation to fact, rather than from general principles to particular truths:

> There are and can be only two ways of searching into and discovering truth. The one flies from the senses and particulars to the most general axioms, and from these principles, the truth of which it takes for settled and immovable, proceeds to judgment and middle axioms. And this way is now in fashion. The other derives axioms from the senses and particulars, rising by a gradual and unbroken ascent, so that it arrives at the most general axioms last of all. This is the true way, but as yet untried—Aphorism 19

In the case of Jeter, those "particulars" of the various fielding systems do indeed tend to rise in a "gradual and unbroken ascent" to arrive at the general axiom that the Captain is simply not the defensive wizard that his Gold Gloves might otherwise indicate he is.

Of course, Bacon might go further and wonder whether, in designing the "particulars" of the various systems, these researchers have made accurate-enough observations to warrant the inductive conclusion. Both Jeter and his defenders have picked up on this idea several times, with Jeter most recently noting:

> Every [shortstop] doesn't stay in the same spot, everyone doesn't have the same pitching. Everyone doesn't have the same hitters running, it's impossible to do that.

And with Yankees senior advisor Gene Michael observing:

> First of all, what pitching staff was out there? Each team has a different staff. Derek doesn't really have a sinkerball pitching staff, whereas other shortstops, you sit behind certain pitchers, you're going to get a lot of ground balls... You simply can't do that by those charts, that's a bunch of baloney... You have to use a scout's eye to determine range.

There is certainly something to consider in these criticisms. For example, none of the systems takes into account the starting position of the fielder on individual plays, and so all are making an assumption that over the large number of observations—a shortstop would be expected to field somewhere between 350 and 425 balls a year—positioning evens out. That said, the systems also assume (not unfairly, in my view) that positioning is a part of what being a good defender is all about. So, if a fielder is claiming that his positioning is making him look bad defensively, which boils down to his not making as many outs in the field as he should, thereby costing his team runs and wins, it's incumbent upon him to change whatever failed strategy is being employed.

These systems do take into account a large amount of context upon which these criticisms are based, however. From the distance the ball traveled, to both how the ball was hit (grounder, line drive, fly ball, popup) and how hard, to the number of outs and the occupied bases (which affects positioning), to the handedness of the batter, to the ground-ball tendency of the pitcher on the mound, and even to the park itself, context is carefully accounted for. No disrespect to Gene Michael intended, it appears you actually can "do that by those charts." In fact, in what may come as some consolation to Jeter fans, breaking down the data in this fine-grained fashion reveals that several of the systems see Jeter as an above-average fielder on balls in the air.

Even so, critics might further contend that some of that context is recorded by human observers, so it is therefore subject to bias and simple human error, anticipating one of Bacon's favorite themes (which will be further developed in a bit). That too is a fair criticism, although it should be remembered that for the various metrics shown in the table above, there are multiple forms of data collection represented, and that each employs multiple observers (typically based on park), with turnover in those positions. As a result, it seems highly unlikely that over the course of several years and thousands of balls in play, there exists some kind of systematic bias that works against Jeter.

Perhaps the final word on the objective analysis of Derek Jeter's defense was had by Tom Tango. In a recent essay from the most recent *The Hardball Times* annual, Tango uses a more direct method of neutralizing those factors discussed above by comparing the percentage of outs on all balls in play with and without Jeter on the field in a variety of scenarios. For example, with Jeter on the field, the shortstop makes an out on 11.6 percent of balls in play. However, when looking at how the pitchers whom Jeter has played behind did with other shortstops in the field, the rate goes up to 12.5 percent—that's a difference of 38 plays over a full season, and the second-worst mark for a regular shortstop in baseball, behind only Young. Tango then does likewise controlling for batters (Jeter is 25 plays worse, fourth from the bottom), a runner on first base (11 plays worse, ahead of only Felipe Lopez), and park (18 plays worse, ranking in the bottom half).

Indeed, the evidence is such that Bacon could only conclude that Jeter is not even an average defender. What then accounts for the vast difference between many of the subjective views of Jeter's abilities, and the objective view, as represented by the advanced fielding systems?

Here's where Bacon again may offer us a clue. In *Novum Organum*, he identified several impediments (which he called "idols" in aphorisms 38-44) to human reasoning in the pursuit of a correct interpretation of nature. Some of these idols, "Idols of the Tribe" (idola tribus), are impediments grounded in ways of thinking common to the human species. Bacon says these are:

> ...inherent in human nature and the very tribe or race of man; for man's sense is falsely asserted to be the standard of things; on the contrary, all the perceptions both of the senses and the mind bear reference to man and not to the universe...

One might say that idols of the tribe reflect weaknesses in reasoning that are common to all people. Among those weaknesses can be included the problem of affirmation bias, looking for only those examples that reinforce our preconceived opinion, and the related inability to deal with large sample sizes only through observation.

Related to this first weakness, in support of their man fans of Jeter might point to the way which he makes hustling, diving plays (who can forget his dive into the stands against the Red Sox on July 1, 2004, or "the flip" in the 2001 ALDS?) and his patented jump-throw from deep in the hole at short. Leaving aside the actual efficiency of the latter (which Bill James touched upon in a fine essay in *The Fielding Bible*, and David Pinto discussed more recently), the common thread is that both are infrequent and isolated instances of Jeter's fielding ability. Bacon recognized that such positive events, although rare and not necessarily indicative of a general trend, can strongly color our overall perception. While this need not always be the case, in the case of Jeter one suspects that it plays a role.

Looking only for affirming examples is actually a product of the second weakness, where we are unable to discern real differences in results when those differences are spread over so many individual observations. For example, who can tell a .300 hitter from a .270 hitter by observing even several hundred at-bats from the two? Should we be less surprised that most of us can't tell the difference between good and bad shortstops, even after faithfully watching them all season? Our minds are simply not designed to collect, categorize, and compare at that level of detail. Not to put too fine a point on it, in contrast, computers are ideally suited to do so.

Ultimately, we all have to make our own decisions about how we want to look at the world. For my money and understanding, and in full appreciation of the frailties of human reasoning and the power of inductive reasoning, I'd have to conclude that while Francis Bacon would appreciate the many wonderful qualities of a superb player like Derek Jeter—especially his leadership, dedication, baserunning, and offensive prowess, to name but a few—he would have to conclude that when compared with other major-league-quality shortstops, when it comes to defense, Jeter leaves something to be desired.

FEBRUARY 24, 2009 — http://bbp.cx/a/8549

GETTING DEFENSIVE
Adventures in Team Fielding
Ben Lindbergh

In the wake of the Tampa Bay Rays' on-field reversal of fortunes in 2008—which Baseball Prospectus' proprietary projection system, PECOTA, foresaw—Ben Lindbergh examined whether teams could still get the most bang for their buck by investing in good gloves.

What *Moneyball* did for on-base percentage, the Rays' 2008 triumph may have done for defense—even if the book on the latter has yet to be written (although it's reportedly on its way, courtesy of BP alum Jonah Keri). Of course, the importance of avoiding outs at the plate, and of accumulating them in the field, was as clear to F.C. Lane and Henry Chadwick, respectively, as it is to Billy Beane and Andrew Friedman; the rest of the class merely needed a little prodding to send it plunging past the tipping point. Unfortunately for those prematurely in the know, these watershed moments often mark the end of their salad days, as other prospectors make inroads on their fertile claims. The rubes are growing scarce: just ask Manny Ramirez, Adam Dunn, Bobby Abreu, and the other defensively challenged sluggers who failed to douse themselves with eau de Ibañez before seeking long-term relationships this winter.

An appreciation for on-base percentage could have yielded a competitive advantage at any point in the game's history, but until fairly recently, fielding skills remained relatively impenetrable, even to those with the inclination to evaluate them. However, as defensive metrics improve and become increasingly reliable (a process that the imminent arrival of the HITf/x system promises to accelerate), the leathery component of run prevention will assume an even greater significance in player evaluation and analysis (while remaining an area in which scouting insight can elucidate persistent quirks in the numbers). In order to determine just how large a slice of the run-prevention pie defense deserves to consume, we might take a quick look back at an earlier investigation.

Steven Goldman devoted a chapter of *Baseball Between the Numbers* to examining the relative importance of run scoring and run prevention in an attempt to answer the question, "Can a team have too much pitching?" The abridged version of his answer, as one might expect, was "no." His more nuanced conclusion, however, stated that "you can't have too much pitching—except when you don't have enough of everything else." For the purposes of his essay, "everything else" was limited to offense, but we can take some limited steps to extend the discussion to defense—in

Steven's words, "the invisible hand that affects much of what we perceive as pitching"—despite the difficulty of separating the pitcher's work from that of the fielders behind him.

As part of our inquiry, we can assess the relative impacts of pitching and defense on run prevention, and, by extension, winning. A one-point swing in defensive efficiency, in either direction, constitutes a difference of roughly four hits over a full season. Assuming a typical distribution of singles, doubles, and triples (and multiplying by their respective expected-run values), those four hits amount to approximately 2.2 runs. To analyze pitching's effects without muddying the waters with defensive contributions, we'll use QuikERA, a handy tool developed by Nate Silver that estimates a pitcher's ERA based solely on his defense-independent strikeout rate, walk rate, and GB/FB ratio. A .01 addition or subtraction in QERA translates to a difference of approximately 1.77 runs allowed by a team over the course of a season, or almost exactly four-fifths that of a .001 fluctuation in defensive efficiency. The following graphs display the payoff in wins as a factor of improvements in defensive efficiency and QERA, according to Bill James' simple Pythagorean expectation formula:

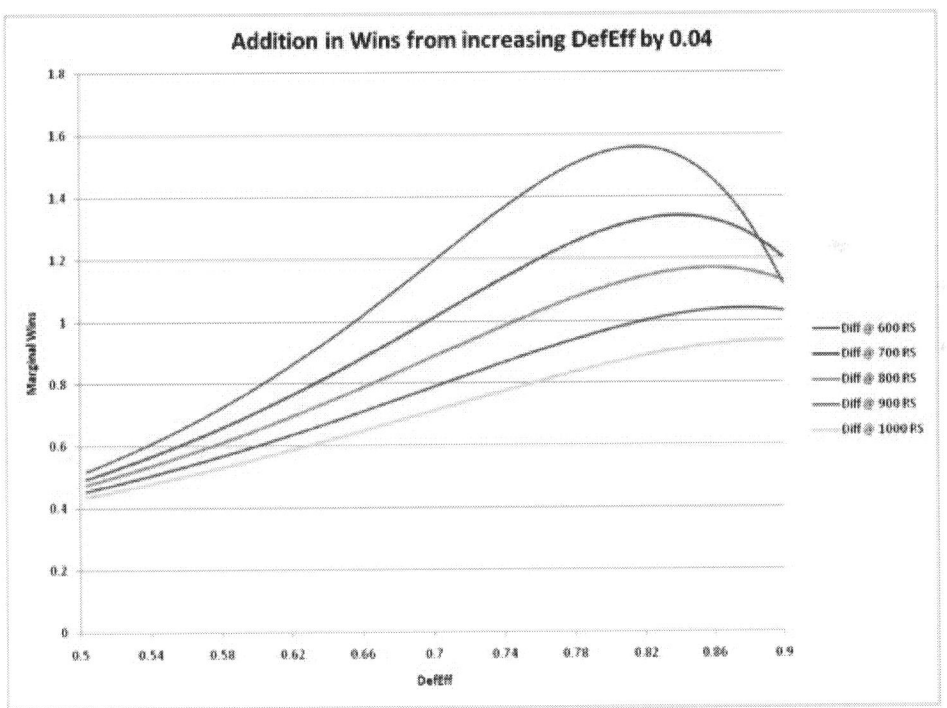

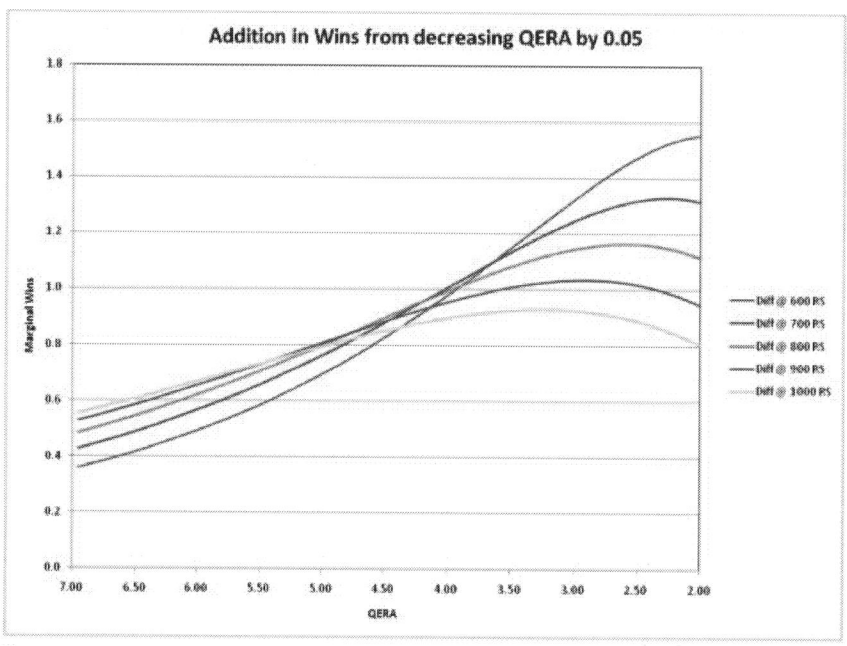

Since fluctuations in both defensive efficiency and QERA affect only the "runs allowed" portion of the run-expectation formula, these graphs have little comparative value, but it's still helpful to visualize the gains that even modest improvements in either category can yield. The fewer the runs that one can hope to receive from one's own batters, the more valuable the suppression of the opposition's lineup becomes.

Teams that dramatically improved their defensive efficiency or QERA in a single year provide real-world examples of the benefits awaiting aspiring run preventers. Here are the top 20 teams in each category since 1954, along with their average improvements in winning percentage:

Year	Team	Def Eff (Difference in)	Wpct (Difference (in)
2008	Rays	.054	.192
1980	Athletics	.048	.182
1981	Rangers	.046	.071
1981	Tigers	.035	.031
1991	Braves	.035	.179
1988	Brewers	.033	-.025
1971	Giants	.032	.025
2008	Marlins	.031	.084
1955	Cubs	.030	.050
1997	Tigers	.029	.161
1991	Angels	.028	.006
1971	Astros	.027	-.001
1965	Pirates	.027	.062
1985	Giants	.027	-.024
1992	Brewers	.027	.056
1998	Red Sox	.026	.087
2001	Twins	.026	.099
1968	Indians	.026	.071
1982	Padres	.025	.127
2005	Indians	.025	.080
Average			.076

Year	Team	QERA (Difference in)	Wpct (Difference in)
1963	Indians	-0.88	-.006
1997	Brewers	-0.86	-.010
2001	Athletics	-0.85	.065
2001	Yankees	-0.84	.054
1974	Rangers	-0.83	.170
1997	Tigers	-0.81	.161
2001	Cubs	-0.78	.142
1984	Mets	-0.76	.136
1963	Cubs	-0.75	.142
1994	Expos	-0.74	.069
1993	Mariners	-0.72	.111
2001	Astros	-0.72	.130
1997	Blue Jays	-0.70	.012
1994	Padres	-0.70	.025
1971	White Sox	-0.69	.142
1958	Braves	-0.69	-.021
1997	Mariners	-0.69	.028
2004	Tigers	-0.68	.179
1977	Dodgers	-0.67	.037
1998	Padres	-0.67	.136
Average			.085

The teams that recorded historically large one-year boosts in QERA enjoyed slightly higher gains than those that tallied similarly pronounced increases in defensive efficiency. However, like most "before and after" tableaux, this juxtaposition omits a portion of the story: in a sample of this size, offensive disparities may account for some, or all, of the difference between the groups.

Setting offense aside for the moment, we might ask whether it's wiser for a team to invest its fortunes in one element of run prevention, in pursuit of a stunning reversal like those above, or to distribute its finite resources in a more even-handed manner. Again, history supplies us with a possible answer. One hundred and twenty-seven teams in baseball history have finished with the same league ranks in defensive efficiency and QERA, posting a collective winning percentage of .504. The 127 teams with the greatest disparity between their league ranks in defensive efficiency and QERA have registered a slightly higher .507 winning percentage. Of course, these numbers are misleading, because the list of the 127 most balanced teams also includes teams that were balanced in a bad way—near the bottom of the league in both categories. All of the 127 least-balanced teams, in contrast, were at or near the top of their leagues in one of the categories.

The worst average rank ((defensive efficiency rank + QERA rank)/2) of any of these least-balanced teams was 10.5 (the 2006 Washington Nationals, who ranked 16th in the NL in QERA and seventh in the NL in defensive efficiency). Only three had an average rank of 10th or worse. In contrast, two of the most-balanced teams finished with average ranks of 16, and twenty-three of them finished with average ranks of 11 or worse. If we eliminate these twenty-three well-balanced failures, we're left with 104 well-balanced teams with an average rank less than or equal to 10th, and a collective winning percentage of .518. The 104 least-balanced teams, on the other hand, amassed a collective winning percentage of .506. Again, offense plays a role here, but these findings suggest that it pays, albeit slightly, to devote equal care to both aspects of run prevention, rather than placing one's fate entirely in either the hands that throw the ball or the hands that catch it.

This conclusion is borne out by a survey of some of the last decade's most successful squads. Most of the 22 pennant-winners since the last round of expansion in 1998 have ridden balanced approaches to run prevention deep into October:

Year	Team	DefEff (Diff. In rank)	QERA (Diff. In rank)
2008	Rays	1	6
2007	Red Sox	1	3
2006	Tigers	1	7
2005	White Sox	2	4
2004	Red Sox	5	1
2003	Yankees	13	1
2002	Angels	1	7
2001	Yankees	9	1
2000	Yankees	4	6
1999	Yankees	2	2
1998	Yankees	1	1
Average		4	4

Year	Team	DefEff (Diff. In rank)	QERA (Diff. In rank)
2008	Phillies	6	8
2007	Rockies	4	10
2006	Cardinals	6	10
2005	Astros	1	1
2004	Cardinals	2	3
2003	Marlins	9	5
2002	Giants	4	12
2001	D'baks	2	1
2000	Mets	4	4
1999	Braves	6	2
1998	Padres	7	2
Average		5	5

Since 1954, 111 teams (counting ties) have topped their leagues in defensive efficiency, racking up a collective .563 winning percentage along the way. As it happens, an identical number of squads have paced their circuits in QERA during the same period, finishing at .558. The moral of this story? Preventing scoring is a winning strategy, no matter what route one takes to pursue it.

Although Steven was referring to offense when he wrote that "in the absence of available pitching, making other changes will work just as well," the same statement holds true for defense. Still, while the evidence suggests that improving team defense can be an effective alternative to hoarding hurlers, whether a team should elect to invest its available funds in pitching or defense depends largely on the state of the talent market and the unique circumstances of the club in question. The graphs above evince the benefits of improving defensive efficiency and QERA, but they can't tell us which of the two is easier to fortify.

A vote for pitching usually funnels aid through the proper channels without springing a leak elsewhere on the roster, while the addition of a defensive whiz often exacts a toll on the offensive side of the ball. However, even in these more enlightened times, a mediocre moundsman may command a higher price than a superlative defender, whose contributions might be more easily overlooked or underestimated. The window may be closing, but as long as this state of affairs persists, teams with average run production, pitching, and defense would be wise to channel their resources along the path of least resistance. Moreover, as Keith Woolner and Dayn Perry observed in a separate *BBTN* chapter, the pitcher that you get only rarely becomes the pitcher you paid for, "given the precision demanded by pitching, the ability of opposing hitters to crush weak pitches, and the risk of injury inherent in the physical act of throwing a baseball." The greater consistency offered by defensive acquisitions represents a compelling argument in favor of making them the foundation of a winter's retooling.

Furthermore, good defense makes pitchers look better, a phenomenon which has implications not only for fantasy baseball, but for the genuine article. Pitchers whose traditional stats are inflated by the human safety nets surrounding them may bring a greater return in trade than they deserve, especially from those who fail to examine their underlying performance closely. It's not difficult to imagine a scenario in which a superior defensive team could consistently mint superficially league-average starters, only to convert them into more valuable commodities by convincing gullible takers in more hostile environs to roll out the welcome mat; witness Greg Smith's inclusion as a nominal piece of the return in the deal which sent Matt Holliday from Colorado (14th in the NL in defensive efficiency) to Oakland (third in the AL).

It's also worth noting that while the presence of a superior pitching staff bestows little or no advantage on its supporting fielders (all anecdotal reports of efficient workers "keeping fielders on their toes" aside), the construction of a capable fielding unit can confer tangible benefits upon a team's valuable arms beyond those merely cosmetic perquisites mentioned in the preceding paragraph. As noted in the Rays team essay in *BP2008*, a strong defense can hasten and enrich the development of a young pitching staff, "with effects on the order of 20 to 30 points of long-term ERA." In addition, adept glove work enables pitchers to work more efficiently, reducing the incidence of wasted pitches over the course of a season and indirectly reducing the workload shouldered by a team's complement of relievers.

Last year's Rays vaulted to the top of the defensive efficiency differential leaderboard—and, despite posting a QERA nearly identical to their 2007 mark, the AL East—primarily by re-shuffling assets (B.J. Upton, Akinori Iwamura, and Evan Longoria) that were already under club control; the team's primary outside defensive acquisition, Jason Bartlett, failed to perform as expected in the field. Other organizations have taken note: the new Mariners regime's emphasis on outfield defense in the face of a largely inflexible starting rotation smacks of a lesson well-learned, and the Yankees' fixation on high-strikeout starters, who minimize the damage done by porous defensive units, represents something more than a visceral reaction to an overdose of Sidney Ponson (landing Mark Teixeira and allowing Jason Giambi and Bobby Abreu to do what they do best—walk —should compound the benefits). The allure of the Rays' resounding success will continue to encourage copycats, especially if the defending AL champions manage to power through the plexiglass this season.

Next offseason's weak free-agent class might provide further inducement to pursue the stealth approach, as the teams that miss out on the few choice cuts available scramble for the most savory gristle. Since fielding contributions remain the most difficult to quantify, as well as the least easily observed with the naked eye, defensive specialists may find themselves riding home in a number of doggy bags—and, perhaps to the surprise of their new owners, feeding the whole family.

The Tampa Bay approach isn't suited to every roster, and most teams that adopt it will find the path from ignominy to respectability far smoother than the one leading thence to contention. Still, good gloves tend to sprout more readily on the farm than do MLB-ready arms, making it a sound strategy in the aggregate. Which is not to suggest that the Orioles may have stolen away with the annual AL East arms race by eschewing the likes of Sabathia and Smoltz in favor of Cesar Izturis— the big-ticket items usually do reserve admittance to the most desirable show. Nonetheless, as last year's high-QERA, low-defensive efficiency Yankees, Diamondbacks, and Reds discovered, procuring pitching without addressing underlying defensive woes is like using an HDTV to display SD sources: you simply won't end up with the pretty picture you thought you were paying for.

INDEFENSIBLE
What Do We Really Know About Defense?
Colin Wyers

In developing the latest implementation of BP's advanced fielding metric, Fielding Runs Above Average (FRAA), Colin Wyers questioned some of the assumptions made by zone-based systems, discovering that they were built upon biased data and might not represent a significant step forward from the systems that ruled the roost in the 1980s.

Occasionally, I get asked—what's going on with my attempts to make a defensive metric? I started off working on a Loess-based defensive metric, and then efforts just stalled. Because of the stall, it's a fair question, and one that's harder to answer than I think the questioners realize, because I've been slowly coming to some realizations about defensive metrics in general, and they aren't encouraging.

The short version: I'm not really sure that we've gotten any further than where we were when Zone Rating and Defensive Average were proposed in the '80s. And if we have gotten further, I'm not sure how we would really tell. I've discussed some of this recently, first in a rather sprawling discussion at Tom Tango's blog, and then in a conversation with Kevin Goldstein and Jason Parks on the BP podcast. But now's a nice time to sort of take some time and compose those thoughts.

Let's start with first principles, I mean really basic stuff: What is sabermetrics? Bill James proposed a definition—"the search for objective knowledge about baseball." And—that really does say a lot, doesn't it? It defines sabermetrics as the search, not the result. It tells us we are looking for knowledge. And it tells us we want to be objective about it.

Now the question comes: Are we being objective about fielding analysis? In other words, do we know what we think we know?

The Trouble with Defense
For the most part, those who are inclined to the sabermetric world view have come to a consensus on the evaluation of offense. There are occasional arguments, but over what I would call "little things." There is more agreement than disagreement, by a long shot.

But now imagine for a second that managers no longer got to set the lineup order. Maybe the umpire throws dice to determine who the next batter is. Or he has a spinner, stolen from a game of Chutes & Ladders. And then imagine that nobody is recording how many times a hitter came to the plate, simply how many innings he played and how many hits, walks, etc. he got.

What would our analysis of offense look like then? Probably a lot like range factor, for example—you'd simply have to hope that over time, the number of plate appearances per inning played approached the average. And over time, you might even be right. (Of course, there's no guarantee that a single season is enough time for this to happen; actually, you'd expect it not to even out for a substantial number of players in any one season.)

And that's where we've been for the longest time when it comes to measuring defense. The solution to this has been to use batted-ball data (both an indicator of how the ball was hit—ground ball, line drive, fly ball, popup—and where it was hit) to approximate chances.

What the Data Says

Now, I've spent a lot of time writing about the data that we're using. To be rather indulgent and quote myself:

> A baseball fact is, simply put, something where the decision has a direct outcome on the game. Changing a strikeout into a walk has a very large effect, for instance—it provides both a baserunner for the offense and prolongs the inning.

The batted-ball data we have doesn't conform at all to the definition of baseball stats proposed above, so it's very difficult to say how well those measurements are describing the essential reality on the field of play. I have been studying differences in the data, and it seems to shed very little light on the subject. What I can say with some certainty:

- There are definite differences in how different data providers are defining the events that are occurring.
- We have not yet established which of the data providers are correct, or more appropriately, we haven't established which are more correct.
- To the extent that the data providers are erring, it seems that some of the errors are systemic—that is to say, they can be counted upon to repeat themselves in a similar fashion over a long period of time.
- When multiple data providers are in agreement, we can say only that it is due to something in common between them—we cannot necessarily assume that the underlying reality is the only common element. There is a potential for shared bias, so that multiple data providers are wrong in similar fashions over time.

It's the third point that actually provides the biggest problem for us. If the errors were simple, isolated mistakes, then we could simply address them by adding more data. Over time, we would expect the errors to "wash out." But that is not how bias behaves—we cannot assume that bias will wash out, no matter what the sample size is, or how much we regress a sample to the mean.

And so when we look at repeatability of metrics, we run into a problem that we don't know how much of that repeatability is due to underlying skill, and how much is due to bias.

I've focused on the potential for bias in the batted-ball classifications, largely due to the availability of the data. But there are certainly other ways the data could potentially be biased. Commenter Guy at Tom Tango's blog notes:

> The most likely systematic bias in the data will be exacerbated, not remedied, by regression. That is the bias toward rating plays as "easier" when they become outs, or when fielders get to them quickly. Imagine having people rate the difficulty of 200 GBs into the 3B-SS hole from video. Now, imagine that the fielders are digitally removed, and the video stopped before it's clear whether the ball reaches the OF, and the plays are scored again. Does anyone doubt that the balls that became hits will on average be rated as easier in the second scoring, while the outs become more difficult.

Or, as I put it on the podcast—imagine a ball hit between the shortstop and third baseman. Or imagine several, some where the shortstop gets to the ball, some where the third baseman does, some where it goes past them for a hit. What are your frames of reference, watching on video?

For example, if you watch a play by Ryan Braun from the All-Star Game, what do you see when the ball is caught, other than Braun, some grass, and maybe a little bit of the outfield fence? And that's a highlight-reel play, where you're getting multiple angles. What about a routine catch? Another clip from the All-Star Game—Marlon Byrd's throw to get David Ortiz at second. How much of a frame of reference are you getting to determine the location of the ball?

One can suppose a range bias for the location data, where a fielder's ability to get close to the ball (much less field it) influences the scoring of where the ball was on the field. Is there any evidence for this sort of a bias? Perhaps. What I did was take all players with at least 100 innings played in back-to-back seasons and look at their plays made and balls in zone as defined by Baseball Information Solutions (from the leaderboards at Fangraphs.com). This is based upon the same BIS data that is fed into UZR or the *Fielding Bible* Plus/Minus stats. The data ran from 2003-09.

So I looked at BIZ and total plays (Plays plus OOZ, or "out of zone" plays, as defined on Fangraphs) per inning and divided that by the positional average for that season. Then I looked at the correlation between years.

	BIZ	AllPlays
All	0.14	0.23
IF	0.14	0.26
OF	0.15	0.19

The autocorrelation for how many plays a player makes isn't really that much higher than the autocorrelation for chances, as defined by BIS. This is especially true for outfielders.

So we have questions about the data quality, as yet unresolved. And I wonder—what conclusions can we draw from the data when we don't know these things?

Method Man
Even using the same data, though, you can come up with drastically different results. Fangraphs publishes two defensive metrics, UZR and Defensive Runs Saved. These are both derived from the same BIS batted-ball data and purport to measure the same thing (a fielder's value above average, compared to his peers at his position). The correlation between the two for 2009 for qualified starters, as reported by Mitchel Lichtman, UZR's creator, is .79.

Compare that to the correlation between the primary offensive rate stat on Fangraphs, wOBA, and a pretty crude bases per plate appearance measure—(TB+BB+HBP)/PA. For qualified starters in 2009, the correlation is .94.

So you have two methods that seem to disagree quite a bit, at least compared to offensive metrics. And that agreement seems to be driven largely by the underlying data—using the plays and ball-in-zone data from BIS, I constructed a quick-and-dirty runs above/below average metric. That rubric, with almost no adjustments, correlated with DRS at 0.76 and with UZR at 0.65. It seems that simply using the same batted-ball data (and the same set of underlying facts—so-and-so made so many plays and was on the field so often) will get you most of the way to that level of agreement, regardless of method.

So our metrics don't do a very good job of agreeing. We don't know which methods are "better," only which ones we like more. And our data hasn't been validated against some objective standard.

To me, this opens up a simple question—how good are our defensive metrics? Are they useful? How useful?

And if we go back to the beginning, where we talked about what sabermetrics is about, it doesn't seem to me to be good or valid sabermetrics to accept these metrics without some sort of evidence, some objective facts that show they measure what we think they measure. And I think the burden of proof is on those who are making claims based upon these metrics to provide that evidence.

MANUFACTURED RUNS
Looking Farther Afield
Colin Wyers

Having identified the problems with zone-based defensive systems in his previous article, Colin Wyers proposed some solutions of his own with a revamped version of FRAA.

I have been making something of a ruckus recently about where I feel the state of current defensive analysis is. I have been long on listing problems and short on proposing solutions.

Well, allow me to make amends there. I don't pretend to have the problem solved. I'm not sure any of us will ever see it truly solved. But I think—or at least hope—that this can point us in the right direction.

The Two Problems
We can really subdivide our problems neatly in two. One is the issue of bias, the other of uncertainty.

Let us start with the latter. What we are trying to do here is measure, and then compare, two things:

1. How many plays a player has made, and

2. How many plays we think an average player at that position would have made, given the same chances.

The first, we all think we can measure directly—given the record, we can readily come up with a total. We may have some disagreement over what to count, but if we agree on what we should be counting, we can come to an agreement. The second is an estimate and, as such, is subject to error. Over time, the error in our estimate should come down (as a proportion of our estimate, that is).

Now, what modern defensive metrics (ones based on observational data, like batted-ball types, hit locations, etc.) are trying to do is to cut down on the effects of measurement error on our estimate of plays made by an average player.

By attempting to reduce measurement error, those metrics have introduced the potential for bias into their estimates, however. The two key ones are:

1. Park-scorer biases. To the extent that a park influences the scoring of batted balls, that has an impact on our estimates. It could have to do with the identity of the scorer in different parks. It could relate to the vantage point of the scorers in each park. Regardless of the source, it distorts the estimates of a fielder's chances.

2. Range biases. To the extent that a fielder's range (or the range of his teammates) influences the scoring of batted balls (either by type or location), that also distorts the picture of a fielder's abilities. The most obvious possible effect is that a good fielder will raise the number of estimated chances he gets by getting to more balls (or at least getting closer to them)—and vice versa for a poor fielder. This would both artificially compress the observed spread of fielding performance and systemically underestimate fielders with good range (and overestimate fielders with poor range).

So what we have is some presumption of increased accuracy, in exchange for additional bias. What we do not know, as of yet, is how much accuracy we are gaining, at the expense of how much bias. And I think that's an important thing to know—if your gain in accuracy is less than the amount of bias you're introducing, you haven't actually gotten better, you've gotten worse.

And we know how to solve the accuracy problem—get more data! Over a long enough timeline, the estimates will improve on their own. Adding more data doesn't make bias any better, though—in fact, over time, the effect of bias becomes more powerful.

Just the Facts, Ma'am
So let's take a different approach. Let's try to design a fielding metric with no bias—or, at least, attempt to minimize the effect of bias. What we can do is:

1. Restrict ourselves to looking at only factual data—data we can validate objectively. That means no batted-ball data, no hit location data, etc.
2. For estimating the amount of plays an average player at that position would have made, ignore data about the outcomes of batted balls whenever possible.
3. Err on the side of caution when deciding whether or not to adjust—in other words, make as few adjustments as possible. We can allow the data to be expressive by getting the metric out of its own way whenever we can.

Over time, the potential inaccuracies of our data should wash out, and because we think we are minimizing our potential for bias, over a long period of time we should be able to be confident of our measure of a fielder's ability.

Figuring Plays Made
Looking at play-by-play data available from Retrosheet, we can start off with counting the plays a player actually made on the field.

Ideally, what we would do is separate the fielding of balls hit on the ground (OK, OK—ground balls) from balls hit in the air (pop-ups, liners, and fly balls). But we've already committed to not using that sort of data. Is there anything we can do, simply looking at facts, to determine what sort of plays a player made?

For outfielders, it's a simple matter. We just count an outfielder's unassisted putouts as his plays made. (His assists we can examine separately at a later date.)

For an infielder, how are we to determine whether he caught the ball on the fly or fielded it on the ground, without resorting to batted-ball categorizations? It's simple (if a bit messy for first basemen and pitchers):

1. An assist by the infielder who first fielded the ball counts as a play made on a "ground ball." (This is not always the case—a fielder who deflects a ball that is then fielded by another player for an out is credited with an assist. But this is rare enough that over time we can ignore it, and in the short run we can do little about it.

2. An unassisted putout of a baserunner, other than the batter, by an infielder is a play made on a "ground ball." For catchers, second basemen, third basemen, and shortstops, an unassisted putout of the batter is a play made on an "air ball." There are rare occasions, mostly for second basemen, where this isn't the case, but again, over time we shouldn't have to worry about this.

3. For first basemen, an unassisted putout of the batter is a "ground-ball" out when it was either on a bunt attempt or hit by a left-handed batter. For pitchers, an unassisted putout of the batter is a "ground-ball" out on a bunt attempt only. All others are classified as "air-ball" outs. This is probably the least-confident part of the system, but for now we'll leave it as it is.

This gives us, at the team level, outs on the ground versus outs in the air. And what we see is a strong negative relationship between ground plays and air plays, with a correlation of -0.77. So when a team makes a lot of ground-ball plays, the most likely explanation is that they saw a lot of ground balls.

Let's adjust for that. What we can do is look at how many plays a team made in total, compared to the average team, and then look at how many ground-ball plays a team made compared to how many air-ball plays they made. A team with superior ground-ball fielders will not only have more ground-ball plays but likely more plays made overall.

So for a team that's above-average on making ground-ball plays but below-average in making total plays, we "shift" the responsibility toward the ground-ball plays (in other words, inflate the amount of ground-ball plays we think the team should have made, but deflate the amount of air-ball plays we think the team should have made), while keeping the total number of plays we think the team should have made constant.

This is, for lack of a better term, our "ground-ball rate" adjustment. It's a bit of a misnomer, because we ignore any scorer data on the number of ground balls a defense saw. And it is possible that including that scorer data could improve the process here as well. But for now, let's err on the side of excluding that data.

Breaking Down the Fielders
What we do now is apply the process from above to individual fielders. As we did for teams, we break down outfielder plays, infielder plays on the ground, and infielder plays in the air. That tells us how many plays each fielder made.

Then we look at each batted ball and estimate the likelihood that each fielder makes a play on it. The only data we are considering right now are the handedness of the batter who hit the ball. (For first basemen, we're also considering whether or not they had to hold a runner at first.) We aren't considering who eventually fielded the ball, whether or not the ball was an out or a hit, etc. Why? Because the outcome of the batted ball is a potential source of bias. By giving up some accuracy in the short run, we allow truly great fielders to look truly great—otherwise, we artificially compact the spread of the impact of top fielders over time.

So we have our measure of plays made and our estimate of chances. We can leave off there, at least for infielders. (Outfielders will require a bit more work, I'm afraid—and that will have to wait for another day.) But we discussed uncertainty—can we at least try to measure it?

Ignore, at least for now, uncertainty about actual plays made—for first basemen and pitchers, especially, we do have some, but enough that we can afford to at least set it aside for a while. But for our estimate of how many plays a fielder should have made, we know there is a margin of error. What we can do is calculate the uncertainty of our estimate per ball in play and use that to figure our total uncertainty for any given player.

What I did is figure the root mean square error between the average number of plays made and the actual plays made, on an individual basis.

For example: in 2009, with a right-handed hitter batting, a shortstop will make a play on a ball in play roughly 12 percent of the time. (For a left-handed batter, a shortstop will make a play on a ball in play roughly six percent of the time.) But the margin of error around our estimate of how often a shortstop will make any single play is about 30 percent. (Notably, the error is asymmetrical—obviously, there is no chance of a shortstop making a negative play, even if in exasperation I may have accused Alex Gonzalez of it during the '03 playoffs.)

To attribute that margin of error over a number of chances, we take:

$$\sqrt{BIP * MOE^2}$$

What's interesting about this is that the margin of error per BIP drops, the more BIP we observe. So, after 100 BIP, the margin of error for any one play drops all the way to three percent.

That's why, to me, uncertainty is preferable to bias—with enough statistical power, we can plow through uncertainty readily. Without an accounting of what the bias is, we're essentially powerless against it.

Some Examples

After taking you all this way, surely I wouldn't leave you without something to look at, would I? Here are the top 10 seasons by a shortstop since 1950, according to our new fielding metric:

Name	Year	Chances	Plays	AvgPlays	+/-	MOE	+/-R	MOE_R
Guillen, Ozzie	1988	4480	515	442.3	72.7	19.5	55.9	15.0
Ryan, Brendan	2009	2507	325	259.0	66.0	14.5	53.7	11.8
Fermin, Felix	1989	4217	480	411.0	69.0	19.0	53.3	14.7
Belanger, Mark	1975	3996	467	403.9	63.1	18.0	49.2	14.7
Tulowitzki, Troy	2007	4294	490	432.0	58.0	19.1	48.4	15.9
Sanchez, Rey	1999	3666	391	336.9	54.1	17.5	46.4	15.1
Thon, Dickie	1983	4271	481	423.0	58.0	19.3	45.5	15.1
Smith, Ozzie	1980	4618	570	512.0	58.0	20.2	45.2	15.7
Martinez, Felix	2000	2818	318	265.8	52.2	15.4	45.2	13.4
Sanchez, Rey	2000	3785	394	342.8	51.2	17.9	44.3	15.5

I've provided a tentative conversion of plays to runs, although it still needs a little work. Note, for instance—Ozzie Guillen is being credited with about 73 plays above the average shortstop for 1988. That's pretty impressive. It's also pretty imprecise, with a margin of error around 20 plays.

What's important to note is that the error is not symmetrical—we think there's practically no chance that Guillen really made over 90 plays above average, for instance.

So, on a single-season level, we see some quizzical results. (Brendan Ryan? Really?) The important thing to remember is—we aren't very confident in those results! Our confidence increases as we move to the career level, though.

It isn't to say there's no uncertainty. We can say, given the statistical evidence we have at hand, there's a small (but not impossible) chance that Mark Belanger saved more runs compared to the average shortstop than Ozzie Smith did. And after that, well, nobody else is in the running.

Name	+/-R	MOE_R
Smith, Ozzie	332.1	61.4
Belanger, Mark	237.2	50.1
Sanchez, Rey	217.7	37.6
Russell, Bill	190.6	49.7
Valentin, Jose	177.4	43.3
Guillen, Ozzie	168.3	52.3
Templeton, Garry	150.3	53.2
Groat, Dick	144.0	49.0
Maxvill, Dal	139.3	37.5
Gagne, Greg	130.4	49.8

Nobody has really disputed how good Ozzie Smith was—but other metrics haven't fully captured the magnitude of it. Our own FRAA, for instance, gives Smith 266 runs above average. Sean Smith's TotalZone says 239 runs above average. In reality, Ozzie was better than that—a lot better.

What's Next

Well, obviously I have to produce outfielder measurements, as well. And there are probably still some tweaks to be made to this system that could improve it.

But past that—these values cannot simply be used in place of FRAA to calculate WARP the way we're doing it now. We have this measure of uncertainty. We can similarly compute uncertainty for our offensive metrics (and it's quite a bit smaller on a per-play basis). We cannot, in coming up with a single value to express a player's season, add defense to offense as though we are equally certain of both.

So we're going to be revising WARP to account for this uncertainty. Along the way, we'll be adding some other enhancements to WARP as well. And we'll be looking at pitching—after all, a lot of what we've always thought was pitching is fielding, isn't it? And so any uncertainty we've had in measuring fielding spills over into pitching as well.

So, consider this a beginning, not an end.

Notes and Asides

I should give a nod to Bill James' Fielding Win Shares, which served as an inspiration for some of my efforts here. I should also give a nod to the work Smith has done on TotalZone, which was also something I spent a lot of time thinking about.

MANUFACTURED RUNS
How Do You Solve a Problem Like Derek Jeter?
Colin Wyers

Appraising Derek Jeter's defense is a rite of passage for any new defensive metric. Just as Dan Fox had done with Simple Fielding Runs a few years earlier, Colin Wyers took his new version of FRAA for a spin by examining how it felt about Jeter, and why.

One of the things about being a baseball analyst as a writer is that I have the luxury of taking the broad view. If I am right about most players, I'm doing a pretty good job. If I miss on a player here or there...I don't enjoy it, and I try to learn from it, but it's not devastating.

A general manager, on the other hand, is responsible for about 25 players or so—more if you include everyone who could conceivably play on a team in one season, fewer if you limit it to players who will end up having (or missing) enough playing time to have a real impact. Missing on one player can, in fact, be devastating.

All of which is to say—I don't envy Brian Cashman right now. He has a lot of tough choices to make about Derek Jeter—and if he slips up, Yankees fans aren't likely to be forgiving. Even if he does the right thing, Yankees fans may not be understanding.

While none of us shares Cashman's unique burden, the outright refusal of MLB to play even a single game between now and March means a lot of us will satisfy our desire for baseball by following the Hot Stove League, and Jeter's contract negotiation figures to be the star attraction. So, let's ask, how much is Jeter worth?

Figuring out how much Jeter's bat has been worth is relatively trivial; it's also pretty uncontroversial. Here's runs above replacement player for Jeter over the past five seasons from us, Baseball Reference, and FanGraphs, excluding defense.

Year	RARP	rRAR	fRAR
2006	61	67	71.7
2007	43	61	53.6
2008	29	32	37.2
2009	55	62	64.7
2010	25	24	28.4
Total	*213*	*246*	*255.6*

Everyone seems to be using subtly different definitions of replacement-level offense, but past that there is solid agreement between the three as to what Jeter has been worth with the bat.

The question the Yankees have to answer, at least in terms of batting, is this: was 2010 simply an aberration for an otherwise exceptional hitter, or was 2009 an Indian summer masking Jeter's age taking its toll? What our projections can tell us is the most likely answer (or, more accurately, the answer with the least presumed error), but there's still uncertainty around that forecast, and that uncertainty compounds the more years you tack onto the contract.

(The Yankees also need to come to grips with where in the lineup Jeter's bat belongs. Barring a substantial bounce-back, it's hard to make the case that the Yankees are best served with the Captain leading off every game).

But still, looking simply at Jeter's bat and his position, he seems like an average to above-average player over the next few seasons, and the Yankees seem to lack decent alternatives (either internally or available through free agency). It seems like a simple decision to retain Jeter in pinstripes, doesn't it?

The trouble is fielding.

Let's look at several common fielding stats, all expressed in terms of runs saved compared to the average player at the position—Defensive Runs Saved as published by Baseball Info Solutions, Ultimate Zone Rating (based on the same BIS data as DRS), Sean Smith's TotalZone, BP's current implementation of FRAA, and our forthcoming overhaul of FRAA. Looking at years for which all of those metrics are available:

Year	DRS	UZR	TZ	FRAA1	nFRAA
2003	-13	-4.0	-14	-23	-38
2004	-12	-0.7	5	-9	-17
2005	-28	-14.9	-5	-5	5
2006	-18	-7.3	-3	-11	-30
2007	-23	-17.9	-14	-19	-27
2008	-9	-0.3	-5	-9	-33
2009	2	6.4	4	-11	-34

Someone relying on UZR or TotalZone might reasonably conclude that Jeter's defense was subpar but unlikely to deter the Yankees from wanting him to return. Looking at DRS and FRAA1, one might be more skeptical.

New FRAA, however, casts more substantial doubts on the question.

I've discussed what new FRAA does before, but a refresher is probably in order. Simply put, we count how many plays a player made, as well as expected plays for the average player at that position based upon a pitcher's estimated ground-ball tendencies and the handedness of the batter. There are also adjustments for park and the base-out situations; depending on whether there are runners on base, as well as the number of outs, the shortstop may position himself differently, and we account for that in the average baselines.

The other metrics use other data to come to their estimate of expected outs—in the cases of UZR and DRS, it's batted-ball and hit location data measured by BIS video scouts. In the cases of TZ and FRAA, it's data collected by press box stringers working for MLB's Gameday product. (TotalZone and FRAA1 both incorporate some batted-ball data from MLB's Gameday product from 2005 on; this means that what we're calling TZ and FRAA1 aren't exactly the same thing depending on season. Guy Molyneux has explained why range bias seems to exist in pre-hit location metrics, which is probably beyond the scope of this discussion).

So let's examine nFRAA for all seasons Jeter played in the majors:

Year	CH	PM	AVG_PM	PAA	MOE_PM	RAA	MOE_RUN
1995	385	33	36.1	-3.1	6.0	-2.7	5.0
1996	4069	403	402.2	0.8	19.0	0.7	16.3
1997	4149	407	424.3	-17.3	19.3	-14.5	16.1
1998	3837	349	374.4	-25.4	18.3	-21.3	15.3
1999	4081	335	386.1	-51.1	18.4	-44.2	15.9
2000	3900	300	353.7	-53.7	18.1	-46.8	15.8
2001	3749	308	350.2	-42.2	18.0	-35.1	15.0
2002	4135	339	394.8	-55.8	19.0	-45.9	15.6
2003	1878	173	218.1	-45.1	14.0	-37.6	11.6
2004	4100	344	364.5	-20.5	18.3	-17.1	15.3
2005	4173	400	394.1	5.9	18.7	4.9	15.3
2006	3941	338	373.8	-35.8	18.3	-30.2	15.5
2007	4046	335	366.5	-31.5	18.4	-26.5	15.5
2008	3738	307	347.4	-40.4	17.5	-33.4	14.5
2009	3563	301	342.2	-41.2	17.4	-33.8	14.3
2010	3703	315	342.8	-27.8	17.7	-22.3	14.2
Total	57447	4987	5471.3	-484.3	70.2	-405.7	58.8

Over the course of his career, Jeter has made nearly 500 fewer plays than we would expect a shortstop to have made. MOE_PM represents the margin of error around our estimate of an average shortstop's plays. What I want to re-emphasize is that the margin of error doesn't scale linearly—the margin of error for three seasons is smaller than the margin of error for each of those seasons added together.

Looking only at 2003-2010, the cumulative MOE (expressed in runs, not plays) for those seasons is 41.209. In other words, 68 percent of shortstops with that number of chances will have their "actual" value within 41 runs of the value estimated by FRAA—that's one standard deviation.

Assuming a normal distribution, 99.73 percent of players will have their actual value within three standard deviations of the estimate.

The estimates of Jeter's defense provided by UZR and TZ are about 3.7 standard deviations away from what nFRAA says. It is staggeringly unlikely that Jeter would end up with a batted-ball distribution that cost him so many opportunities based upon random chance alone. DRS is just under two SDs away (roughly, the 95 percent confidence interval)—still very, very unlikely.

If not random chance, then what else might it be? Is there something else that could be so consistent across Jeter's career? We've already controlled for park factors, ground-ball tendencies of the pitchers, and the handedness of opposing hitters. He's played in nearly 40 ballparks (including two home parks), behind nearly 80 starting pitchers, with two managers (one of whom was still catching for the Yankees when he started playing). Since Jeter became the full-time shortstop for the Yankees in 1996, the team has had six different starting second basemen and five different starting third basemen (not to mention the numerous backups to each). The single greatest constant in Derek Jeter's career has been, well, Derek Jeter.

The appropriate response is that the probabilities assume we've plucked Jeter at random; of course we haven't. But we haven't cherry-picked Jeter because he's an isolated case. He's an example of a systemic problem with fielding metrics based on observational data—range bias.

It's a fairly straightforward matter to determine whether a play was made or not—primarily, you figure out if the batter was safe or out after putting the ball in play. It's nearly as simple to figure out who made the play; typically the idea of "first touch" is used—who was the first fielder to contact the ball? So "plays made" is mainly an assertion of fact. Expected outs, derived from observation of where the ball was hit and how it traveled there, is more difficult. Here's a still frame grabbed from a highlight of Jeter making a play.

What I want to emphasize is that, other than Alex Rodriguez, the only real reference point to where the ball is when it reaches Jeter is Jeter himself. Because of the way baseball telecasts are shot, this isn't an isolated incident—this is how baseball looks on TV. And companies like BIS get the same video feeds the rest of us get.

So a player's range seems to influence his expected outs. How can we tell this? The first data point we have is the spread of observed fielding performance—the spread of observed performance in metrics like UZR and DRS is much, much smaller than that of metrics like nFRAA (or Tom Tango's With Or Without You system, which is similarly down on Jeter's fielding ability).

The other thing we see is that a player's expected outs as a share of team balls in play (or "balls in zone," a proxy measure for expected outs) persists from season to season, even when looking only at players who switch teams. In other words, the identity of the player seems to change the recorded batted-ball distribution. (We have no mechanism that would allow us to explain how a fielder could dramatically change the actual distribution of batted balls; it seems much easier for him to be impacting the estimates.)

All of the available evidence seems to suggest that Jeter is a worse fielder than most defensive metrics indicate, perhaps on the order of 20 to 30 runs below the average shortstop. This makes it possible that Jeter, in 2010, was performing at roughly the same level as a typical replacement—in other words, his ability to hit like something resembling an average shortstop doesn't offset his inability to field like one. And while Jeter's bat may improve next year from a disappointing 2010, over the next three years it's a fair bet that his hitting will continue to erode. That's what happens to baseball players as they get closer to 40.

No, I don't envy Brian Cashman at all.

Part 4
HISTORY
Introduction by Steven Goldman

Like a mad scientist, John McGraw, the manager of the Giants from 1902 to 1932, liked to build his own monsters. Baseball took place in a smaller, slower world then, and McGraw could function not only as the team's on-field boss but also as a part-time general manager, scout, and instructor: acquiring, developing, and training his own prospects without recourse to the minor leagues. Not every youngster McGraw picked up got this kind of specialized, hands-on treatment, just the special ones. One such player was Frankie Frisch, the "Fordham Flash."

A native of the Bronx, in 1919 the 20-year-old Frisch went right from the campus of Fordham University to the Polo Grounds, where McGraw tutored him on the finer aspects of the game. As pupils go, Frisch wasn't perfect but was pretty darned close; in short order he evolved into a true switch-hitter who could hit for average with pop, ran the bases well, and was not only excellent with the leather at second base but could fill in at third base and shortstop without hurting you. He was also a natural gamer whom McGraw soon named team captain. If you crossed Roberto Alomar's results with a Derek Jeter's work ethic, you'd have something like Frisch.

As with the literary Dr. Frankenstein, McGraw had a perverse tendency to reject his own creations. Having built Frisch up, he seems to have presumed that he had the right to tear him down as well. For McGraw, Frisch being captain meant that everything that happened on the field was his fault. If the team lost a game because an outfielder dropped a ball, it was Frisch's fault. If the pitcher balked home the winning run, it was Frisch's fault as well. Perhaps McGraw felt that if the less-talented remainder of the roster saw how high his expectations were of his favorite player, they would be motivated to play that much harder—or perhaps McGraw was just a hard, irritable man with medical and financial problems whose own abusive upbringing had finally expressed itself in his becoming a petty tyrant in his 50s. Whatever the reason, whether the Giants won or lost, whether the game was cleanly or sloppily played, Frisch was in for a banquet of verbal abuse when it was over.

Frisch absorbed this punishment for eight years, but by 1926 he had had enough. He was playing hurt—McGraw was not overly sympathetic to an injury short of a bullet wound—but that wasn't the most serious of the club's problems. Southpaw Art Nehf, a two-time 20-game winner for the Giants in the 20s, saw his career ruined by neuritis and was sold to the Giants, while Ross Youngs, one of the best hitters in the National League, was sidelined by Bright's disease about two-thirds of the way through the season. He would die a little more than a year later.

Despite these losses, McGraw continued to goad his club and Frisch in particular. A late-August loss to the Cardinals, not long after Youngs' final departure, resulted in another vicious tongue-lashing. Frisch later recalled:

> Tommy [Thevenow] was a right-handed batter and I was the man to cover second on a steal. But it was a hit-and-run play, Thevenow hit a grounder to my left as I was moving to second, and I couldn't have swetopped the ball if I'd had a net on a long pole.
>
> McGraw called me a dumb Dutchman, with a lot of profane trimming, a concrete-head, and asked me what I was doing—trying to give away the ball game? I said, "Mr. Mack, you don't mean that." But he got on me harder than ever and kept it up in the clubhouse after the game, which we lost.

Frisch walked out and stayed away for almost three weeks, a brave move at a time when a player had no union rights and could easily be blacklisted. Though he did finally return and finish out the season before such an action could be taken, it was clear that the relationship was irreparable, and that December, McGraw traded him to the Cardinals for Rogers Hornsby. In retrospect, the deal signaled that a rapidly-aging McGraw was losing his grip. His great years were over, while a period of Cardinals ascendancy that had begun with a World Series victory that fall would be cemented and sustained by Frisch's arrival. They would win four more pennants and two championships between 1928 and 1934. Frisch was voted the National League MVP in 1931, the year of the first championship, and served as player-manager for the second. McGraw didn't see that last World Series—he died that winter, embittered emotionally, corrupted physically.

All of the foregoing is invisible from the statistics, and yet several National League pennant races, World Series, and Hall of Fame careers were affected by the McGraw-Frisch relationship. The publication of *Moneyball* started a long public debate about the value of statistics versus scouting, but this construction is inadequate. A thoroughgoing understanding of baseball rests on a tripod in which scouts and stats are joined by a third leg, story. The first two legs tell us, in different ways, what happened on the field and how it was accomplished. Story endeavors to tell us why it happened.

Without story, which you could also refer to as "history," we might miss how fate intervened to save the Yankees franchise from its own worst instincts in 1996. First, owner George Steinbrenner second-guessed his own decision to let go of manager Buck Showalter and replace him with Joe Torre, contacting the former and offering him a chance to wait in the wings in case Torre faltered.

THE LINEUP

Interleague Numerology
by Jay Jaffe..................271

Consider the K
by Jay Jaffe..................274

The Myth of the Golden Age
by Dan Fox..................279

Tilting the Playing Field
by Dan Fox..................288

The Burgess Shale and Other Weighty Matters
by Dan Fox..................302

Age Before Beauty
by Dan Fox..................310

Prestige, D, and Derek Jeter
by Christina Kahrl..................323

Penning a New Recipe
by Jay Jaffe..................326

Oh Rickey, You're So Fine
by Jay Jaffe..................332

Throwing Rice
by Jay Jaffe..................339

Gamesmanship, Dammit
by Steven Goldman..................345

Infinite Edition #4
by Steven Goldman..................350

Position Changes
by Steven Goldman..................356

Judge Landis on Steroids Edition
by Steven Goldman..................360

Why Babe Phelps and I Weren't in St. Louis Last Week
by Steven Goldman..................364

Enhanced?
by Steven Goldman..................369

The Statheads vs. Blondy Ryan
by Steven Goldman..................375

Dusty Baker and the Johnny Oates Affair
by Steven Goldman..................381

Odds and Ends
by Christina Kahrl..................386

A Peach of a Deal
by Christina Kahrl..................393

The New Guys
by Christina Kahrl..................399

Harden-ed
by Christina Kahrl..................406

Teixeira Two-Step
by Christina Kahrl..................412

Is Moneyball Dead?
by Derek Jacques..................417

Cardinals' Special Era Reaches a Crossroads
by Bradford Doolittle..................421

Meanwhile, Torre, who in December of 1995 had said, "Derek Jeter is going to be our shortstop going in. We may have to suffer through some growing pains early on, but that's our plan," arrived at spring training and begin backtracking, saying only that the rookie would be given the "opportunity" to win the job. Simultaneously, general manager Bob Watson observed that incumbent shortstop Tony Fernandez, "is part of the New York Yankees. Until we're shown the other man is the best thing since sliced bread, we want Fernandez around."

Fortunately for everyone involved, Fernandez was seriously injured that spring, and Jeter was prevented from being the best shortstop ever to spend the first 10 years of his professional career in Columbus, Ohio. He was the Rookie of the Year, Torre, who (like Steinbrenner) never had much use for young players, looked like a genius and would eventually ride Jeter into the Hall of Fame, and Steinbrenner didn't have to summon Showalter back from exile. It was only Fernandez's season-long injury, rather than great baseball judgment or forbearance of impatience by the Yankees, that made possible two plaques in Cooperstown. Despite the old Latin proverb, sometimes fortune favors the feckless, not the bold.

Story makes us think critically and try to interpret sometimes shadowy decision-making processes on the part of people who are often no longer around to explicate their thinking. This is challenging and by its nature imprecise, which is why so many of us would prefer to let the numbers do our thinking for us. If the player has 3000 hits, 500 home runs, or 300 wins on his resume, we don't have to evaluate, we can just wave him on into the pantheon, and if not, forget him altogether. For too many, the question of whether Fred McGriff should be in the Hall of Fame is difficult because he has 493 home runs. We trip over ourselves to venerate round figures, forgetting that these qualifiers are entirely arbitrary.

In the essays that follow, you will see the writers of Baseball Prospectus stripping away those arbitrary distinctions and getting at story, the decisions, accidents, coincidences, and yes, emotions, that motivated the events on the field—and in one case (mine) ourselves.

PROSPECTUS HIT AND RUN
Interleague Numerology
Jay Jaffe

League strength isn't static over time, but as Jay Jaffe observed, the AL held a significant advantage over the NL in the late 2000s, as revealed by its teams' performance in interleague play.

The National League may lay claim to two of the last three World Champions, but little doubt exists in most observers' minds that the American League has become the superior circuit in recent years. Not only does the AL have a 13-year undefeated streak in the All-Star Game (including the infamous 2002 tie), but it has gotten the upper hand on the senior circuit in interleague play, winning at a .522 clip since it was instituted in 1997. The AL has held an even bigger advantage in each of the past five years, posting a .566 winning percentage over that span.

Whether that's due to the designated hitter, the evolutionary pressure of trying to keep up with the Yankees and Red Sox, the abject fate of the Expos/Nationals and the thoroughly mismanaged Pirates, or some other reasons is a conversation I'll leave for another day. Having confronted this problem in the context of strength-of-schedule issues and in Baseball Prospectus Hit List power rankings, I'm simply trying to get a feel for the magnitude of the gap.

Here's the year-by-year breakdown of interleague results, not only the actual ones but also the Pythagenpat projected marks, with the winning percentages as seen from the AL's vantage.

That 56-ish percent figure holds up pretty well across a few different samples. The AL has won at a .560 clip in interleague play from 2007-09, a figure that winds up being

Year	AL	NL	Win%	AL Runs	NL Runs	Pyth%
1997	97	117	.453	994	1007	.494
1998	114	110	.509	1089	1078	.505
1999	116	135	.462	1246	1374	.452
2000	136	115	.542	1278	1233	.517
2001	132	120	.524	1175	1175	.500
2002	123	129	.488	1127	1097	.513
2003	115	137	.456	1239	1267	.489
2004	127	125	.504	1252	1210	.516
2005	136	116	.540	1230	1056	.571
2006	154	98	.611	1336	1116	.585
2007	137	115	.544	1352	1172	.568
2008	149	103	.591	1249	1014	.596
2009	137	114	.546	1201	1061	.558
Tot	1673	1534	.522	15768	14860	.528
05-09	713	546	.566	6368	5419	.576

identical using a typical 5/4/3 weighting system, with the most recent result weighted the most heavily. But winning at a .560 clip doesn't mean that we can simply say that the AL is a .560 league and the NL a .440 circuit, with a 120-point gap between the two leagues.

To figure out what the strength of the two "teams" are that could produce a result where one won at a .560 clip, we turn to what Bill James called the Log5 method, one I've referenced in my articles on schedule strength, and one that Clay Davenport uses literally millions of times a day to generate the daily Playoff Odds reports at Baseball Prospectus. The formula boils down to Winning percentage = .500 + A - B, where Winning percentage is the observed outcome percentage (.560) and A and B are the two teams. Since we also know that in this case the winning percentages are complementary (A + B = 1.000), it's simple algebra to determine that a .530 team playing a .470 team would produce that observed .560 winning percentage.

When I did the strength-of-schedule pieces, I used 2006-2008 results, which produced an AL winning percentage of .582, to apply a 40-point bonus to the AL team in each head-to-head matchup and a 40-point tax to the NL one. (I stuck with round numbers for the purposes of demonstration.) Now that the 2009 results are almost entirely in the books, that estimate winds up on the high side, as the 2006 results were the most lopsided to date.

One revealing aspect of the AL's advantage over the NL is that even the lousier junior circuit teams are beating the senior circuit's weak sisters consistently. Sticking with the last five years of data (including this unfinished season) and splitting each league into upper and lower halves in terms of interleague records—the 35 best (or worst) team-seasons in each half in the AL, 40 in the NL—we find that the AL's better half, which won at a .561 clip in those intraleague games, boosted their winning percentage to .610 in interleague games. The lower half, which produced a measly .438 winning percentage in intraleague play, kicked NL tail at a .523 clip. The NL's better half posted a .551 winning percentage in intraleague play but just a .447 mark in interleague play, while the lower half dipped from .450 to .421.

This tendency persists if we break the teams into smaller groups. Here it is in quintiles.

Granted, we're not talking about huge sample sizes here (14 seasons apiece in the AL groups, 16 in the NL groups), but... wow. Every NL grouping, from the best 20 percent to the worst, won significantly less than 50 percent of its games against the AL. The top three AL groupings dominated interleague play, and while the fourth AL group won less than half its games, the bottom grouping won at a robust .556 clip, thanks to a couple recent Orioles teams going 11-7, a couple of Royals teams posted winning records (including 13-5 in 2008), and just two of the 14 teams in

Group	Intra	Inter
AL1	.594	.595
AL2	.550	.627
AL3	.504	.587
AL4	.458	.466
AL5	.392	.556
NL1	.580	.439
NL2	.538	.449
NL3	.503	.461
NL4	.460	.408
NL5	.418	.414

the group finishing below .500 in interleague play.

Via linear regression (and the much-appreciated assistance of my colleague, Eric Seidman), we can express the predicted relationship between intraleague and interleague winning percentage over this five-year period as follows:

```
AL_Inter = 0.353 + 0.427*AL_Intra
NL_Inter = 0.324 + 0.221*NL_Intra
```

So, an AL team that goes .450 in intraleague play would be expected to post a .545 winning percentage in interleague play; for a .500 team, it's .567, and for a .550 team, it's .588. For a .450 intraleague team in the NL, the expectation is for a .423 winning percentage in interleague games; for a .500 team, it's .434, for a .550 team, it's .446. By this reckoning, the Dodgers (.605 in intraleague) would produce a .458 winning percentage against AL competition, about what the Blue Jays (.464 in intraleague) have done, and the Jays would produce a .551 winning percentage in the NL, good enough to contend for the Wild Card.

That seems fairly extreme, and it's worth remembering that the individual interleague samples are fairly small. Still, it's quite clear that the AL's advantage is a very real one that cuts even the best NL teams down to size. The four 2008 NL playoff teams went a combined 22-38 in interleague play last year, including 4-11 by the eventual World Champion Phillies, and this year's three division leaders were a combined 24-27. That doesn't mean the senior circuit can't win the World Series, but via this way of looking at things the odds aren't stacked in its favor.

PROSPECTUS HIT AND RUN
Consider the K
Jay Jaffe

JUNE 23, 2010   http://bbp.cx/a/11277

Strikeout rates have steadily increased over the past two decades, prompting Jay Jaffe to attempt to determine why.

Last week, I explored the frequently-voiced claim that we're experiencing another Year of the Pitcher. Digging into the numbers, I noted that while scoring was down about three percent from 2009 and had dipped to its lowest rate since 1993, a more intriguing facet of the current crop o' stats is that strikeout rates are at an all-time high. This year, batters are whiffing in 18.1 percent of all plate appearances, up one tenth of a percent from last year, over one percent higher than 2007, and over two percent higher than 1994. Where are the strikeouts coming from?

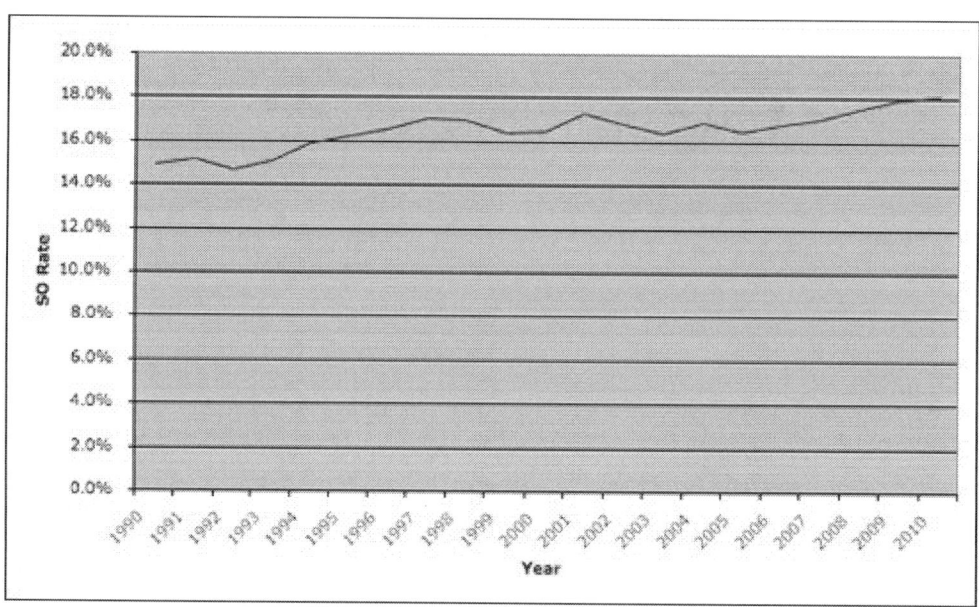

While scoring has been all over the map over the past two decades, strikeout rates have crept upwards at an increasingly accelerated pace. Examining the annual pitch data at Baseball-Reference.com, which goes back to 1988, yields some subtle insights. The full data culled from B-R is here, but allow me to summarize:

Year	R/G	Pit/PA	Str%	B/PA	S/PA	L/Str	I/Str
2010	4.47	3.84	62.5%	1.44	2.40	29%	30%
2009	4.61	3.89	62.4%	1.44	2.39	28%	30%
1996	5.04	3.71	61.4%	1.43	2.28	26%	32%
1990	4.26	3.61	61.7%	1.39	2.23	24%	34%
90-10	4.9%	6.4%	4.0%	7.6%	21%	-12%	-5%
00-09	-8.5%	3.2%	0.4%	4.8%	8%	-6%	-3%

I've isolated two time spans here. The first one runs from 1990 through Sunday, a range chosen to provide a sample which includes pre-expansion, pre-strike data. The other runs from 2000 through 2009, to sidestep the 1994-1995 strike and the currently incomplete campaign in favor of a contiguous decade which began when scoring was at its highest level since 1930, more than 10 percent higher than it is today.

Pitches per plate appearance have risen slowly but steadily over the past two decades, spending more than half that time in the 3.7-3.8 range. While the overall percentage of pitches which were strikes has barely moved, what's interesting is that the number of balls per PA has increased at only about half the rate of the number of strikes per PA over the longer span (4.0 percent compared to 7.6 percent). Over the shorter span, the number of balls has actually decreased, which does jibe with what we'd expect as offense has deflated. In fact, of all of these various rates, B/PA is the only one which has a substantial correlation with scoring rates, r = .53, compared to .12 for S/PA, .15 for looking strikes (L/Str), and -.33 for in-play strikes (I/Str).

Breaking this down further, while the rates of swinging strikes (14-15 percent) and foul strikes (27 percent) have varied so little they're not worth including in the table above, the rate of looking strikes has risen by over 20 percent, to an all-time high ("all-time" in this particular instance meaning "since 1988"). Correspondingly, the rate of in-play strikes has decreased by about 12 percent.

What's behind all of this? My theory is that two forces are in play here. First, Major League Baseball has spent the past decade attempting to enforce the official definition of the strike zone, directing umpires to call pitches strikes in a higher, narrower zone than they had been doing before. In 2001, MLB even introduced the controversial QuesTec pitch-tracking system in order to grade umps on their compliance, quietly replacing that with a newer and more widespread system called Zone Evaluation in 2009. According to a *New York Times* article about the latter, the Elias Sports Bureau's analysis of 2008 data concluded that umps in QuesTec parks called strikes slightly more often—a few pitches per game—than those not in such parks. Second, we've seen an evolution in the way strikeouts are understood within the game, at least beyond the Big Apple sports pages and their concern for David Wright. Thanks to statheads inside and out of front offices, we know that hitter strikeout rates correlate with a number of useful attributes, namely hitting for power and drawing walks. Furthermore, the accounting shows that hitters' failures to move runners over via "productive outs" are cancelled out by the decreased possibility of double plays, making a whiff no worse than any other kind of batting out.

Consider for a moment the history of Bobby Bonds' single-season record of 189 Ks, set in 1970. Players such as Three True Outcomes patron saint Rob Deer, Jose Hernandez and Preston Wilson gave chase to Bonds' record, but such was the stigma that their managers sat them down late in the year to avoid breaking the record. Deer played in just five of the Brewers' final 12 games in 1987, settling for the AL record of 186. Hernandez played in just one of the Brewers' final four games in 2001, finishing at 185, and more dubiously sat for all but three of his team's final 11 games the following year, including games with playoff implications, while stuck at 188. Wilson had 185 Ks with six games remaining in 2000, but his pace was slowed by pinch-hitting in two games and missing the final game of the year to finish with 187.

Since all of that silliness, Bonds' record has been topped seven times by four men: Adam Dunn, Jack Cust, Ryan Howard, and Mark Reynolds. Dunn broke Bonds' record in 2004, finishing with 195. Howard topped it with 199 in 2007, and Mark Reynolds blew through the 200-strikeout barrier in 2008 and 2009. This Magnificent Seven of Swish averaged 41 homers and 94 walks during those years, and none of the players who surpassed Bonds was reduced to parading around in public wearing a scarlet letter K.

While hitter strikeouts have become less stigmatized, pitcher strikeouts are valued ever more highly. For pitchers, missing bats means avoiding the largely inescapable vagaries of balls in play, a key element in preventing runs; if a hitter doesn't make contact, he can't even reach on an error, let alone collect a base hit or a homer. Furthermore, higher strikeout rates are tied to pitcher longevity and long-term success.

Recent work by researchers such as Tom Tango and J.C. Bradbury has shown that as far as strikeout rates go, hurlers tend to peak in their early 20s, somewhere between 20 and 25 years old according to Tango, depending upon the set of assumptions regarding regression which are used. A younger population of pitchers, it stands to reason, would generate higher strikeout rates, and as it turns out, the population of pitchers has indeed gotten ever so slightly younger in recent years.

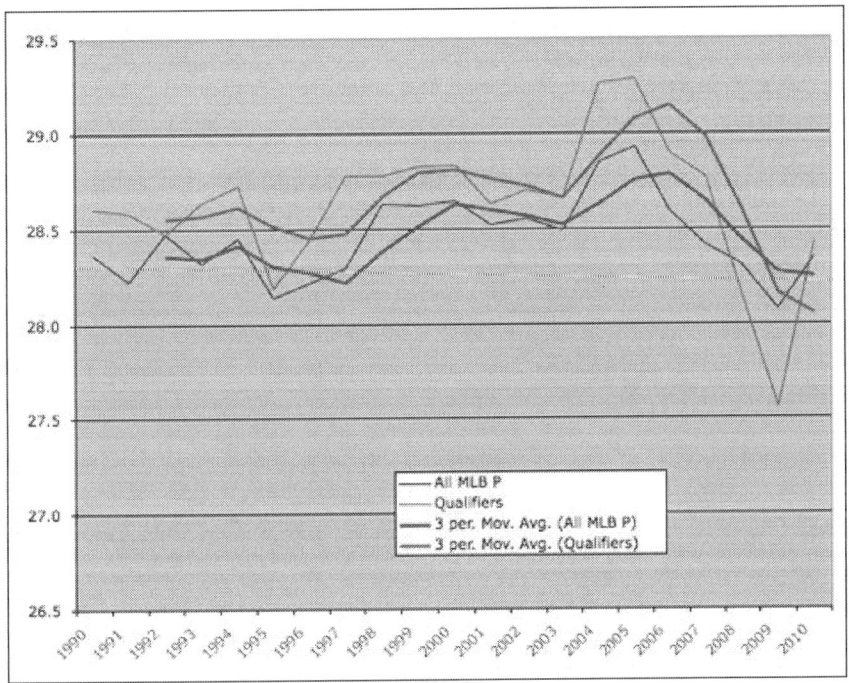

From 1990 through 1997, the average pitcher age—July 1 age, weighted by innings pitched that season—hovered in the range between 28.1 and 28.5 years old. From 1998 through 2006 it fluctuated in the 28.5 to 28.9 range. It's dipped back below 28.5 for the past four years, the period when strikeout rates have risen most rapidly. The correlation between the average age and the fluctuating strikeout rates from 1990-2010 turns out to be almost nil (r = .01), though if we ditch the pre-expansion, pre-strike, pre-juiced-ball years and isolate 2000-2009, it shoots up (r= -.78; strikeout rates are rising while age is falling, remember). The youth movement is even more apparent if we limit the selection to ERA qualifiers (one inning pitched per team scheduled game), as the average pitcher age fell nearly two full years from 2005 (29.3) to 2009 (27.6). It's back up this year, but hey, Stephen Strasburg is just getting started, and there are likely more minor-league promotions to follow.

Where this becomes somewhat interesting, if not exactly a model of scientific rigor, is on the leaderboards. The average age of qualifying pitchers with above-average strikeout rates—say, 7.5 percent higher than league average (ignoring the relatively minor effects of park adjustment)—is dropping, and at a rate considerably faster than both the overall population of pitchers and the qualifiers.

Year	All	High K	Dif
2000	28.6	29.4	0.8
2001	28.5	29.3	0.7
2002	28.6	29.1	0.5
2003	28.5	28.4	-0.1
2004	28.9	28.4	-0.4
2005	28.9	28.4	-0.5
2006	28.6	28.4	-0.2
2007	28.4	26.9	-1.5
2008	28.3	27.2	-1.2
2009	28.1	26.9	-1.1
2010	28.3	26.9	-1.4

Year	Qual	High K	Dif
2000	28.8	29.4	0.6
2001	28.6	29.3	0.6
2002	28.7	29.1	0.4
2003	28.7	28.4	-0.3
2004	29.3	28.4	-0.8
2005	29.3	28.4	-0.9
2006	28.9	28.4	-0.5
2007	28.8	26.9	-1.9
2008	28.2	27.2	-1.0
2009	27.6	26.9	-0.6
2010	28.4	26.9	-1.5

Granted, we're talking about only 20 to 30 high-strikeout pitchers per year and ignoring park effects, but the charts above suggests we're seeing a larger-than-normal influx of young high-strikeout pitchers, a class who by and large we can expect to be successful. Consider that the majors' current top 30 in strikeout rate (SO/PA) contains 11 pitchers 25 and younger, just seven 30 and over, and just one older than 33. Dial back to 2005, and you've got nine pitchers 25 and younger, 10 who were 30 and over, with four of those over 33 and two of them (Randy Johnson and Roger Clemens) over 40. Dial back to 2000, and it's 10 in the 25-and-under bucket, but 15 in the 30-and-over one. The trend is probably more cyclical than linear, but it's certainly visible. Not all of those 11 youngsters (Clayton Kershaw, Mat Latos, Tommy Hanson, Yovani Gallardo, Phil Hughes, Felix Hernandez, Brandon Morrow, Ricky Romero, Max Scherzer, Ian Kennedy, Chad Billingsley) in this year's high-strikeout group are household names, but some of them will be someday, grabbing the headlines the way the 26-year-olds in that group (Ubaldo Jimenez, Josh Johnson, Tim Lincecum, Jon Lester, Francisco Liriano) are today.

My guess is that this is where a good bit of the talk about the Year of the Pitcher comes from. An especially large cohort of quality young hurlers who weren't on center stage a few years ago—not just high-strikeout pitchers 25 and under, mind you—is tasting success at a time when scoring is returning to levels not seen in almost two decades and strikeout rates are at an all-time high. Other changes in the game may be contributing to both trends, but they're the faces of the phenomenon, this so-called Year of the Pitcher.

JANUARY 18, 2007 http://bbp.cx/a/5813

SCHRODINGER'S BAT
The Myth of the Golden Age
Dan Fox

Utilizing a number of approaches, Dan Fox demonstrates that despite widespread nostalgia for earlier eras, today's players are better than ever before.

The golden age was first; when Man yet new,
No rule but uncorrupted reason knew:
And, with a native bent, did good pursue.
Unforc'd by punishment, un-aw'd by fear...

- Ovid, from his *Metamorphoses* (A.D. 8)

Throughout much of history, humans have looked back on the remote past as a time of peace and plenty. As in the Roman poet Ovid's verse above, containing ideas that can be traced directly back to Hesiod writing in the late eighth and early seventh centuries B.C., peace and harmony prevailed during this Golden Age, when the remote ancestors of the Greeks never aged and the earth brought forth food without effort.

That basic idea is repeated around the world. From the "First Time" of Osiris when abundance characterized the now-dry Egyptian landscape, to the "Reign of Saturn" when Jupiter's father ruled Italy, to the days when Krishna walked in India, to the rule of Quetzalcoatl and Viracocha in the Aztec, Mayan, and Incan domains, and finally to our more familiar Garden of Eden.

It is only much more recently that humanity, aided in no small part by the Enlightenment and the insight of biological evolution, has adopted a more or less linear view of history that poses its own dangers. Under this view the future is generally bright and the lives of our ancestors are often viewed as "nasty, brutish, and short," a view C.S. Lewis labeled "chronological snobbery" when used to characterize more recent generations.

But be that as it may, the myth of the golden age in baseball has proven harder to shake. From Ty Cobb to Ted Williams to Joe Morgan (but notably not Casey Stengel), both the players and those who write about the game hearken back to the good old days when players were smarter, the level of play supposedly better with a greater emphasis on fundamentals, and when giants like

Ruth, Johnson, and Gehrig "roamed the earth," as the book of Genesis says. Williams himself summed up the view nicely in 1992:

> Modern players are stronger, bigger, faster, and their bodies are a little better than those of 30 years ago. But there is one thing I'm sure of, and that is the average hitter of today doesn't know the little game of the pitcher and hitter that you have to play. I don't think today there are as many smart hitters.

This week we'll review the arguments that show us, with all due respect to The Splendid Splinter, that there was, in fact, no golden age in baseball.

A Full House of Variation

Perhaps the most complete argument for the position that the general level of play in baseball has improved and not declined over time was articulated by the late paleontologist and baseball fan Stephen Jay Gould in his 1996 book *Full House: The Spread of Excellence from Plato to Darwin*.

Gould devotes six short chapters to arguing that the disappearance of the .400 hitter, rather than documenting a decline in excellence, paradoxically records an ever-increasing level of play. Essentially his argument for why .400 hitters have become extinct can be broken down as follows:

- One set of conventional explanations for the disappearance of the .400 hitter employs the "tougher conditions" argument—that too much travel, too many night games, and too much publicity and media exposure have led to a lesser level of play. Those explanations don't hold water, as train travel and doubleheaders were likely every bit as exhausting as coast-to-coast flights, and night games offer an escape from the heat and, for some players, better visibility.

- Another set of explanations (more promising, in Gould's view) stems from "tougher competition" and includes better pitching (the development of the slider is often cited), better fielding (equipment and positioning), and better managing (defensive charting and the employment of relief specialists). However, if pitching and defense had gained the upper hand over hitting, then the fact would be evident from the fall of league batting averages as hitters struggled to keep pace. In fact, league averages have remained relatively constant over time, and, as we all know, have actually jumped up in the last decade. Further, the powers-that-be have actively maintained some semblance of balance through subtle (changing the definition of the strike zone) and not-so-subtle (changing the height of the mound) rule alterations, the one primary exception being the prolific offensive environment ushered in by Babe Ruth that was not squashed due to the threat posed by the Black Sox scandal.

    The idea that somehow today's baseball players, as opposed to athletes in all other sports, would be unable to keep up with players from a generation ago just doesn't make logical sense. The combined forces of the increasing population pool from which athletes are drawn (which in baseball includes African-Americans since 1947, the influx of players from Latin America since the early 1960s, and now the Pacific Rim) far outstrips the effects of expansion. Better training and medical care, a general increase in size and strength (the average player today is over two inches taller and 20 pounds heavier than the average player in the dead-ball era), and the improvement in absolute records in other sports such as running, swimming, and jumping, all point to the conclusion that baseball players as a group must be better athletically and therefore able to outperform players from previous generations. Ty Cobb, Walter Johnson, Babe Ruth, and yes, even Ted Williams, were the outliers in populations characterized by a lower general level of ability.

- The relative stability of batting averages then allows for the possibility that .400 hitting has disappeared because the amount of variation in batting averages among players has shrunk. In other words, batting averages are distributed in a bell curve, and the spread of that curve has been restricted over time. To test this hypothesis, Gould calculated the standard deviation of batting average over time for all regular players. What he produced was a graph like that shown below, which I updated to include data through the 2006 season for players with one or more at-bat per scheduled game and which uses the coefficient of variation (CV) rather than simply standard deviation in order to account for the small differences in league batting average across seasons.

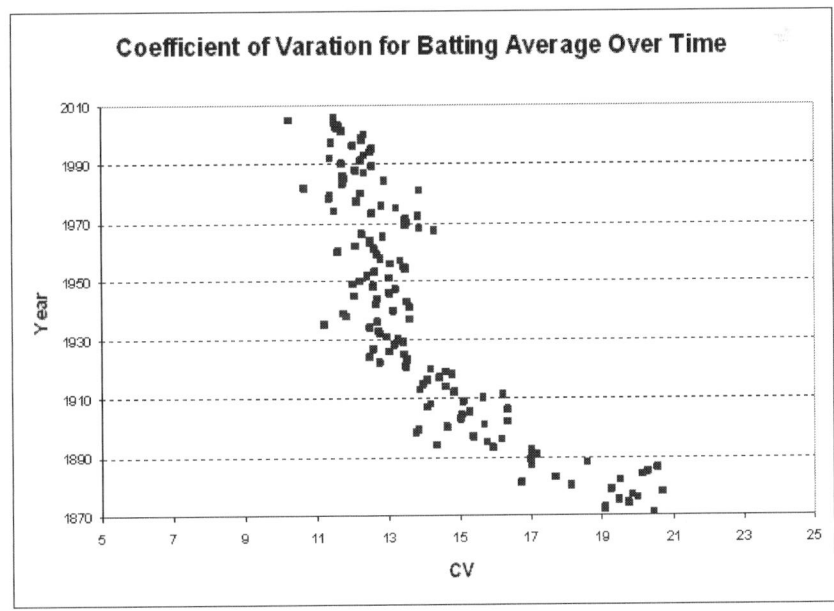

As you can see from the graph, the CV shrinks over time. Gould, almost giddy with the regularity of the decreasing variation, concludes that his "general hypothesis is confirmed again: variation decreases steadily through time, leading to the disappearance of .400 hitting as a consequence of shrinkage at the right tail of the distribution." He also notes that this method reveals that while variation decreased rather rapidly and in lock step through the early years of the game, the rate of decline decreased in the 20th century and began to stabilize after 1940. However, when viewed by decade, along with the CV for both slugging percentage and OPS, it's clear that the variation in all three seems to have declined over the past three decades as well (Gould's original data went to only 1983 or so), as shown below.

- Finally, Gould provides two arguments to support his contention that the shrinking variation documents a general improvement in play. First, he argues that complex systems improve when the best performers play by the same rules over extended periods of time. In his view, this permits the system to equilibrate and decrease variation. In essence, the argument is that baseball has been around long enough that strategies for everything from defensive positioning and turning the double play, to fielding the bunt and pitching mechanics, to pitch selection and batting swings and stances have been refined to the point where they are increasingly becoming optimal and therefore essentially standardized. In short, an elite player like Tony Gwynn "lacks the space for taking advantage of the suboptimality in others."

Although not discussed by Gould, Bill James echoes many of the arguments related to population and player size, while adding the increased ability to select good players within the population due to the development of the minor leagues in his book *The New Bill James Historical Abstract*. In addition, James acknowledges the wider variation in past performance by applying a rudimentary "Time Line Adjustment" based on year of birth to his player ratings, since great players before 1950 "dominated their game to a greater extent than more recent players." Even that adjustment doesn't fully compensate. Only 34 of his top 100 players came to the majors since 1960.

This shrinking variation can also be seen at the team level in the decreasing variation in winning percentage, as shown in the graph below.

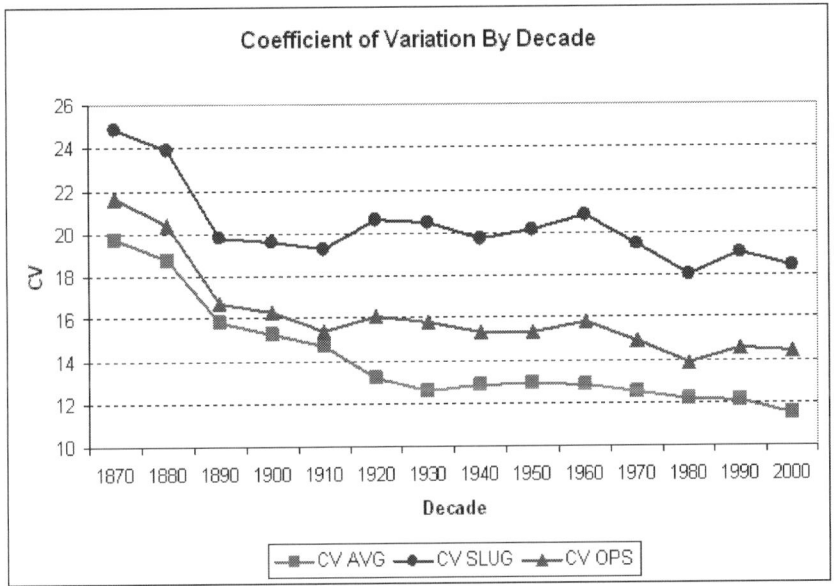

Secondly, as play improves, the bell curve moves towards the "right wall" of human ability, causing the right tail to shrink and variation to decrease. There is a limit to what human bones and muscle can do (Sidd Finch excepted), and as play improves, the general population of players moves closer to that limit, or "right wall." The approach to that wall can more easily be seen in other sports, where incremental improvements in records such as the hundred-meter sprint decelerate over time and eventually almost stop as we reach the limits of human performance.

In baseball, the human limits of what hitters can do in an environment where pitchers and fielders are also closer to the "right wall" will restrict the variation. This makes it ever more difficult for hitters to attain a .400 average as long as the mean stays in the .260-.270 range. Mathematically, this can be illustrated by pointing out that in the 1920s, players with two at-bats per game were 2.7 standard deviations away from .400. By the 1990s, the analogous set of players were 3.98 standard deviations away, which explains why there were seven .400 hitters in the 1920s and of course none in the 1990s. Gould also supports this argument with an illustration of how fielding percentages (a more "absolute measure of changing excellence over time") have increased over time, particularly from 1870 through the 1960s.

Gould then summarizes by saying that hitting .400

> is not a *thing*, but the right tail of a full house for variation in batting averages. As variation shrinks because general play improves, .400 hitting disappears as a consequence of increasing excellence in play.

Although this conclusion is generally accepted and is supported by the data that shows decreasing variation, it doesn't tell us how much the level of play has improved.

Measuring the Rising Tide
Fans of Baseball Prospectus, especially those who have read *Baseball Between the Numbers*, will no doubt find many of Gould's arguments familiar. In the introduction to the book, titled "Batting Practice," Nate Silver discusses the idea that players of today are better for many of the same reasons discussed here. He then introduces a procedure called the "Baseball Time Machine" which uses EqA to compare players who remain in a league from one season to the next. This calculates a league difficulty factor normalized for the 1975 American League.

What is produced is a graph that shows a steady rise in difficulty over time, with a small blip for World War II. It also shows the NL stronger than the AL from the mid-1950s through the mid-1980s, thereby confirming Gould's thesis. For example, the 1927 AL is credited with a factor of 0.846, while the 2005 NL is at 1.167. These factors are then used to translate statistics and illustrate how a Honus Wagner (EqA 0.354 in 1908) might translate to the modern game (EqA 0.232, or roughly a Neifi Perez). Interestingly, the graph shows the same stabilization in the 1940s that was noted by Gould, as the slope of the trend noticeably decreases.

A more subtle approach then employed by Silver—termed simply the "Time Machine"—intended to level the playing field a bit in terms of equipment, training, and medical advances (and, one would assume, styles of play and strategy), lays a simple trend line over the league difficulty factors since World War II and then extends that line backwards through time. This results in a much more gently sloping line and so treats Wagner and Ruth more kindly in their comparison to Barry Bonds. The general conclusion remains, however, that there has been a steady improvement in the level of play over time.

This same methodology was previously used in a study by SABR's Dick Cramer in the 1980 *Baseball Research Journal*, where he compared batting averages for players who remained in the league and produced a similar graph with a similar trend line as the league difficulty factors.

Some have argued, however, that this general approach will always show such a trend regardless of whether one really exists because of the twin problems of skills deteriorating over time and regression to the mean. The first problem can be adjusted for by applying an aging curve, while the second must take into account the fact that players who remain in the league and are selected for inclusion in studies like these do so because they receive at-bats, and those at-bats are predicated on performance that is more likely to be better than their actual talent.

Applying both adjustments has led Tom Tango, co-author of *The Book*, to conclude that the level of improvement has decelerated over time, particularly in the last 30 to 40 years, but that "Babe Ruth would not be BABE RUTH, but more like a great hitter."

But is this approach the only way to approach the question of measuring the change in level of play over time?

I got to thinking about this question this week while reading a comment from SABR member Stew Thornley related to the hitting feats of pitchers of old on the SABR list server, which was in response to the contention from another member that pitching is so highly specialized in the modern game that pitchers don't have time to learn hitting. Rather than look at the issue as one of practice, Stew pointed out that it is more likely that if pitcher's hitting relative to the league has decreased over time (an assumption on his part but one that appears to have been researched by others), it is likely due to an increasing level of play.

Pitchers are increasingly selected from the amateur ranks based on their extreme right-hand-tail-of-the-distribution excellence in pitching. While there is certainly some athletic and experiential crossover that allows them to hit better than the general population (as evidenced by the best players at early ages being both the best hitters and pitchers), their hitting skill is not selected for in the evolutionary sense and so should remain relatively constant over time. In other words, pitchers simply don't hit as well in the modern game, not because they are not just as skilled (or slightly more so) with the bat as their predecessors but because the selected skills of all players have increased over time.

Incidentally, this is why it has been increasingly difficult for pitchers to transition to position players over time, a fact I documented in a 2005 article titled "Rube Bressler Redux?" which discussed the career of Rick Ankiel. The rarity of crossover skills, in the words of Thornley, is "something to celebrate in that it is an indication of how much better the players are" today. And rather than posit that the designated hitter is responsible for the decline in pitcher's hitting, under this view the increase in level of play can be seen as a contributor to the introduction of the designated hitter.

It turns out Thornley's intuition is correct. Pitcher's offensive output relative to that of position players has declined over time. In the following graph I show the OPS of pitchers (defined as players who appeared in more than one game as pitcher) relative to non-pitchers in all major leagues since 1871 using the pink line and the y-axis on the left side of the graph, and the percentage of plate appearances that pitchers consumed during those years on the gray line tracked on the y-axis on the right side of the graph.

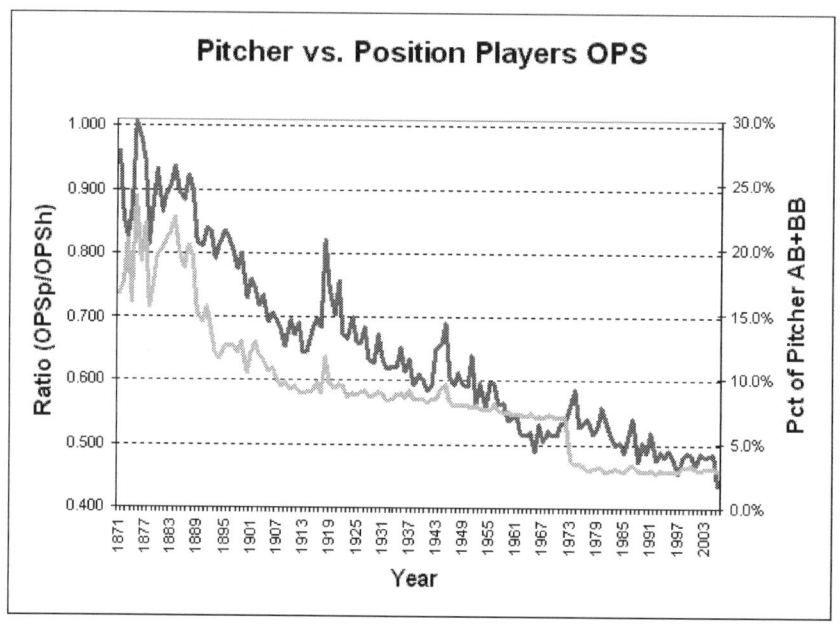

What is immediately obvious from this graph is that pitcher hitting has followed a workmanlike decline over the years as depicted with the pink line, with the increase during World War II consistent with the idea that the level of play was lower as minor leaguers took the place of major leaguers in the service. The large blip around 1920 is partly accounted for by the presence of Babe Ruth (1915-1919, 1921) and George Sisler (1915, 1916, 1918)—who count as pitchers since they appeared in multiple games as pitchers during that time.

The gray line illustrates the increasing specialization of the game, which was accelerated by the moving of the mound back to 60 feet 6 inches from 50 feet in 1893, causing pitchers to play other positions less frequently. The appearance of the designated hitter also is prominent.

What is more difficult to discern is that, as Gould found with decreasing variation in batting average over time and Silver with the "Baseball Time Machine," the slope of the line changes around 1946, with pitcher hitting decreasing at less than half the rate it did before World War II. The same graph with the two distinct trend lines is shown below.

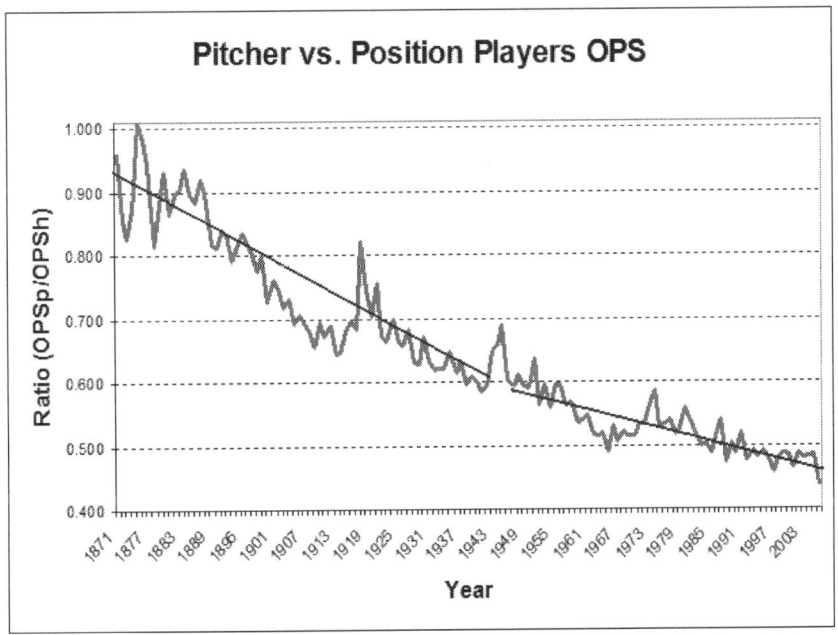

While there may be other interpretations of the trend, the underlying regularity suggests a systemic cause, such as a generally increasing level of play.

The End of an Age
There may be those who still argue that players of the past were every bit as good as players today. For my money, however, the combined evidence of demographics, other sports, technology, shrinking variation, and direct (albeit relative) measurement make for an enormously difficult circumstantial case to overcome. And while we may long for a golden age somewhere deep in our soul, we can be comforted by the fact that we get the privilege of watching the game played at an unparalleled level of excellence.

SCHRODINGER'S BAT
Tilting the Playing Field
Dan Fox

Not all baseball players are big and muscle-bound, but that doesn't mean they haven't made physical gains as a group, as Dan Fox explained with a clever look at pitchers' performance at the plate.

> "It is the best game because the players look like us. They are not seven feet tall, they don't weigh 350 pounds, and they don't bench-press 650. We can relate to them. We can see them—they're not obscured by some hideous face mask, and they don't play behind a wall of Plexiglas—we can touch them and we can feel them. I see Greg Maddux with his shirt off, with his concave chest and no discernible muscles, and I marvel: This is one of the six greatest pitchers in the history of the game? I see Tony Gwynn with his shirt off and I see a short, fat guy with the smallest hands I've ever seen on an athlete, and I wonder: 'This is the best hitter since Ted Williams?'...They are regular guys, at least most of them, who just happen to be really, really good at something that everyone else is not."
> —Tim Kurkjian, from chapter one of *Is This a Great Game, or What?: From A-Rod's Heart to Zim's Head—My 25 Years in Baseball*

This fan certainly agrees with Mr. Kurkjian that baseball is indeed the best game. Where opinions start to diverge is in the related claim that because players "look like folks," there is little difference between the players of, say, 60 years ago and today. If we could bring players from the past back to life and suit them up, so the argument goes, Ted Williams would still be walking down the street hearing people call him the greatest hitter who ever lived and Babe Ruth would still be, well, Ruthian.

The perception that this view is on the money is fueled not only by the accessibility and appearance of many players, but by the statistics that we use to record their performances on the field. Unlike in swimming or sprinting, accomplishments in baseball are recorded in a relativistic manner, with the credits of hitters perfectly balancing with the debits of pitchers and defenders, as in an accountant's ledger book. In addition, the powers-that-be have ensured that the balance between offense and defense has never swayed too far from a historical norm; with some exceptions, individual performance data can be reasonably compared across eras by the average fan. As a result, similar stat lines from different eras can mask underlying differences in the skills and abilities of players that would be otherwise evident if they played side by side.

As I discussed in a column last January titled "The Myth of the Golden Age," the same processes that drive improvements in other systems and sports are at work in baseball. Chief among these are that complex systems improve when the best performers play by the same rules for an extended period of time, permitting the system to reach equilibrium and allowing various strategies and techniques to be discovered, selected, and optimized. In baseball, this manifests itself in everything from defensive positioning and technique to batting stances and pitching mechanics that have improved over time through a process of trial and error. Secondly, as in all sports, today's athletes are superior to those of the past in size, speed, and strength, as evidenced by contests where an absolute—rather than a relative—measuring stick is used (as in track and field). When combined with the advantages of modern medical care, nutrition, and training regimes, this improvement has pushed the average major-leaguer closer to the absolute right wall of human ability. These processes have had the consequence of decreasing the variation between players. In short, the greats of the past were outliers who could take advantage of the sub-optimal play among populations characterized by a lower general level of ability.

But in addition, baseball has also benefited from an ever-increasing population pool from which to draw—first via African-American integration, and later through the influx of Latin and, more recently, Asian players. More players to choose from will ensure that the quality of those players is higher. And this was on the heels of a minor-league and scouting system that has been developing since Branch Rickey increased the efficiency of discovering and cultivating talent.

All of this adds up to an increasing excellence in play on the field. In the previous article we discussed several attempts to detect the magnitude of that increase using various lines of evidence; before closing my off-season ruminations in late February, I promised readers that we'd have one more installment related to this topic. And so for those who have been on pins and needles since before the snow melted and the games began, this is your lucky day. Today we'll take one of those techniques and apply it to position players in order to tilt the stat lines away from the forces that have conspired to level the playing field.

A Lack of Selection Pressure
As discussed in the previous column, we'll use the offensive production of pitchers relative to position players as a measure of the increasing level of play over time. As the game evolved from where pitching was throwing underhand with a straight arm (as in "pitching" horseshoes) in the 1850s, to a variety of submarine and sidearm deliveries in the 1860s and 1870s, and finally to the full overhand delivery after 1883 in the National League (NL) and 1884 in the American Association (AA), pitchers were selected primarily for their pitching and not their hitting ability. In an evolutionary sense, batting skills of pitchers did not undergo the same selection pressure as their pitching skills.

The consequence of substantially lowering or removing this selection pressure is that the actual or true hitting ability of pitchers should have remained relatively constant throughout the history of baseball. By comparing the offensive production of pitchers to position players who do face the rigors of selection, we should be able to measure the increase in the level of play. This is the case since the factors mentioned previously are all constantly contributing to a subtle rise in the talent level of the environment in which pitchers as batters find themselves less and less able to successfully compete. Ironically, their frustration as a group is in large part a consequence of their own ever-increasing ability to execute their craft.

As I showed in the previous column, the results from making this comparison do indeed show a decrease in offensive output for pitchers over time. Unlike in the previous column, however, the following graph breaks down park-adjusted normalized OPS for pitchers relative to hitters by league.

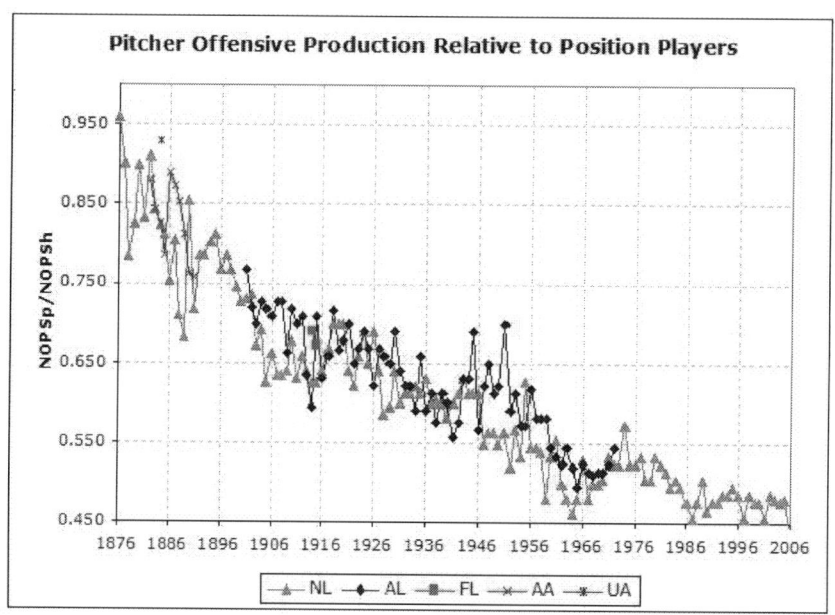

Pitchers as a group were pretty similar to position players in terms of offensive output in the 1870s, often producing in the range of 80 to 95 percent. That started to change relatively quickly in the 1880s; by 1901 pitchers would see their last season at 75 percent or above as recorded in the nascent American League (AL). The ratio fell from around 70 percent in the first decade of the twentieth century to under 50 percent most recently, as illustrated in the following table (AL and NL only), with only a small bump in the 1970s.

Pitcher Production Relative to Hitters

Decade	Ratio
1900s	.694
1910s	.662
1920s	.653
1930s	.612
1940s	.606
1950s	.574
1960s	.510
1970s	.526
1980s	.494
1990s	.478
2000s	.465

The trend by decade shows a fairly steep decrease from the 1900s through the 1920s, a leveling off in the 1930s and 40s, and then another steep decline in the 1950s and 1960s before the increase in the 1970s followed by smaller declines in the 1980s, 1990s, and the first decade of this century.

In one sense this is what we might expect. For example, we could easily imagine that this tracks with the following five-era chronology:

- Rapid improvement initially, with a slowing as the game evolved and stabilized (1901-1929) in any number of ways, from rosters to the role of relief pitching and pinch hitting.
- Improvement again picks up speed with the efficiencies produced by the advent of the minor-league system (1930-1949) but is then slowed due to the effects of World War II.
- The integration period (1950-1969) raises the level of play as black and Latin players are given opportunities, again leading to rapid improvement.
- Feeling the effects of two rounds of expansion (1970-1979), the game experiences a slight decrease in the level of play, perhaps with assists from some really bad uniforms and disco music.
- A slower but still-steady improvement as the game continues to draw players from Latin America and Asia (1980-2006).

The other interesting aspect of this graph that may be unexpected is that it shows pretty clearly the differences in the leagues themselves. For example:

- In its only season of 1884, the Union Association (UA) scores higher than both the NL and AA, consistent with its oft-considered status as a minor league.
- The AA itself had scores tied with or higher than the NL in seven of its 10 seasons, also

indicating that the NL was the stronger league.
- The more mature NL recorded lower relative values than the AL in 11 of the twelve seasons from 1901 to 1913, indicating that it was the stronger league at this time.
- The Federal League (1914-1915) recorded relatively high values in its two seasons, besting only the 1915 AL, indicating its weaker status.
- The NL appears to have been the stronger league from 1947 through the early 1970s (when pitcher hitting data for the AL disappears with the advent of the designated hitter), posting lower scores in all but four seasons, often by margins similar to those during the NL's dominance during the first decade of the 20th century. This too coincides with the common wisdom.

Where things appear less clear, the data indicates that from 1914 through 1926 the leagues appeared fairly evenly matched, but then the tide turned back to the NL again through the early 1930s. Beginning around 1934 the balance again returned and stayed through the end of World War II.

Upside Down and Backwards

So if we're correct in our assumption that pitcher hitting records the rate at which the level of play has increased, we can use that data to construct an index of level of play over time. However, since the data from the plot above has a lot of noise in it and slopes in the wrong direction, we'll apply a couple of transformations. By combining both the NL and AL, applying a moving average, inverting the ratios from the above plot, and finally normalizing each year relative to 2006, we can smooth out the rough edges and come up with the following graph, which shows the "Level Index," or LI, for each year beginning in 1876:

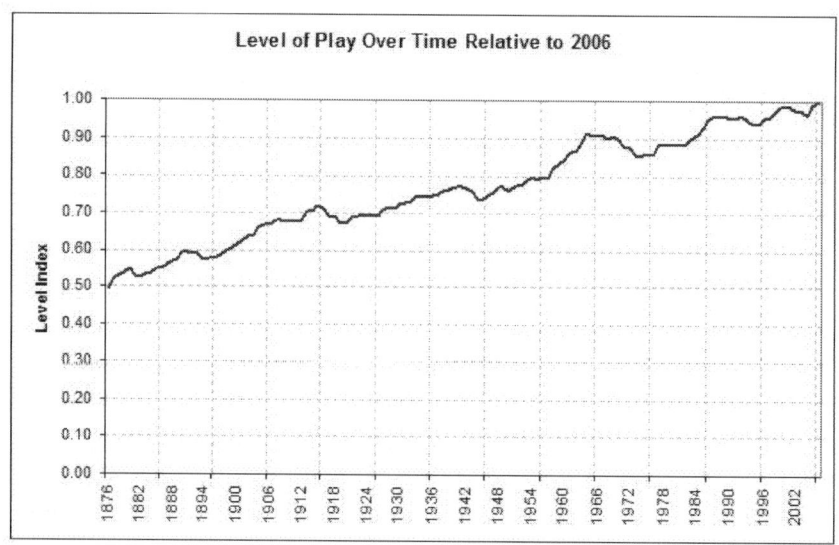

You'll notice that this graph follows the trends noted earlier, in addition to picking up the effects of both World Wars, which interrupted the upward march temporarily.

Readers somewhat familiar with this discussion will note that earlier this summer David Gassko wrote a three-part series of articles in which he used a different technique to develop a similar index and compare that to the methods used in both Dick Cramer's original 1977 study and by Clay Davenport's *Baseball Between The Numbers* essay. That methodology relies on direct comparisons of player performance from year to year and is somewhat more difficult to sort out, since there are conflating factors at work.

Gassko's version of that technique—after a critique by our own Nate Silver—accounts for regression to the mean using a player's predicted career performance based on plate appearances, as well as neutralizing the effects of aging by using only 26- to 29-year-olds (who show no overall performance change during that time span). In his addendum on the subject, Gassko produces a graph that depicts his final attempt along with Davenport's method, and which looks similar to the graph above. A quick side-by-side comparison reveals that the LI line we've drawn here has a slightly larger slope, thereby somewhat splitting the difference between Davenport and Gassko, although ending up much closer to Gassko. If you review his graph, you'll also notice that the dip during World War II in all the lines shown by Gassko is more pronounced than shown here. The reason is that we've used a moving average, which tends to smooth out the data. While that's good for most of the graph, it underestimates the magnitude of the talent loss during the war.

There is now one final adjustment to make. If we're going to tilt the playing field, we'll also need to adjust for the differences between leagues. As mentioned previously, the chart of pitcher versus position player hitting provides us with some data to use to create separate LIs for the AL and NL. The way this was done was to note that relative percentage difference between the leagues, again using a moving average, and then to calculate how that difference would be reflected if it were applied to the previous graph.

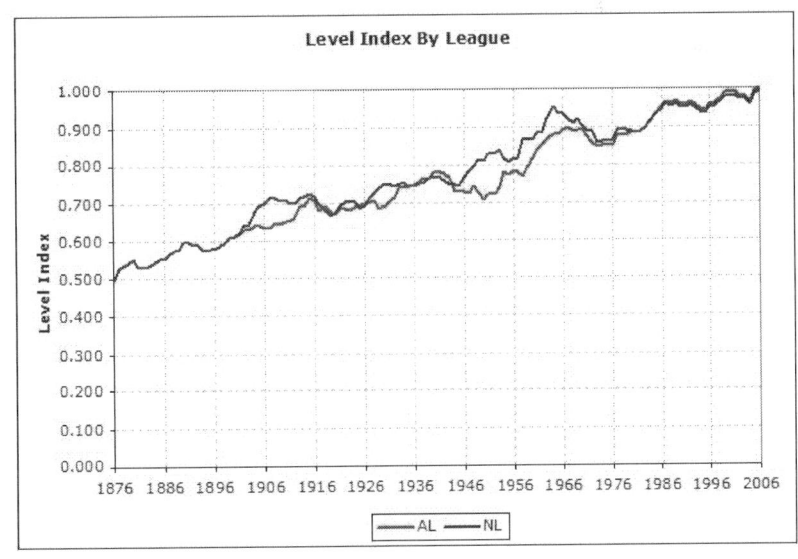

Based as it is on the relative performance of pitcher hitting, it includes the same differences noted earlier, namely the strength of the NL in the 1900s, and again in the post-integration era. The weakness of his approach is that since pitcher hitting data dries up after 1972, we need to estimate the league differences after that time. I've done this by showing a slight advantage for the NL through the 1970s, introducing parity in the mid-80s, and then giving the AL a slight advantage through the present. Surely this isn't a perfect system; in simply eyeballing the results, it probably overestimates the difference between the leagues in the late 40s and early 50s.

Tilt!

Finally, we're able to use the previous graph to tilt the playing field. To take this final step we'll use Keith Woolner's Win Expectancy (WX) framework and the derivative WX1 that I discussed in a column last year.

In short, the WX framework allows for the aggregation of all events that a batter was responsible for and debits or credits the player corresponding to how much that event pushed his team either towards winning or losing. It does not include defense or baserunning. The derivative WX1 relies on the same concept, although instead of being calculated using individual plays complete with their base, out, inning, and run environment attributes, it uses general coefficients for each offensive event based on the run environment of the league and the player's home park. This provides an overall picture of the win contribution of a player. Basically, WX1 is a shorthand way of getting to WX when you don't have play-by-play records available, as we don't prior to 1959.

When we calculate WX1 for all AL and NL seasons going back to 1876, we find the top and bottom 15 seasons to the right.

Bonds, Ruth, and Williams dominate the list, taking 11 of the top 15 spots, with Gehrig, Mantle, Cobb, and Hornsby each grabbing a spot. Bonds is the only player to amass 10 wins, doing so in both 2001 and 2002. On the other end of the spectrum, the only players not from the 19th century include Neifi the Terrible and Jim Levey; the latter played shortstop for the 1933 St. Louis Browns in what would be, at age 26, his final year in the big leagues. That season he hit .195/.237/.240 in those 564 plate appearances and was

Year	Name	PA	WX1
2001	Barry Bonds	655	11.3
2002	Barry Bonds	603	10.6
1923	Babe Ruth	695	9.7
1921	Babe Ruth	689	9.5
1920	Babe Ruth	612	9.4
1927	Babe Ruth	691	9.2
1926	Babe Ruth	649	9.1
1927	Lou Gehrig	714	9.0
1946	Ted Williams	670	8.9
1941	Ted Williams	603	8.9
1957	Mickey Mantle	623	8.7
1917	Ty Cobb	665	8.6
2004	Barry Bonds	608	8.5
1924	Rogers Hornsby	638	8.4
1942	Ted Williams	667	8.4
...			
1891	Lou Bierbauer	528	-4.7
1890	Germany Smith	523	-4.8
1884	Jim Lillie	476	-4.8
1891	Germany Smith	550	-4.8
1892	Joe Quinn	567	-4.8
2002	Neifi Perez	585	-5.0
1885	Joe Gerhardt	423	-5.1
1894	Chippy McGarr	551	-5.2
1895	Jack Boyle	620	-5.2
1890	Bob Gilks	576	-5.2
1894	John Ward	574	-5.3
1893	Joe Quinn	580	-5.5
1886	Jim Lillie	427	-5.5
1933	Jim Levey	564	-5.9
1894	Jiggs Parrott	533	-6.1

20 runs below average on defense for good measure.

Because the bottom of the list is dominated by 19th-century players, we'll re-run the bottom 15 starting at 1901, thereby allowing Neifi to sneak in there one more time, along with the immortal Rob Picciolo of the 1977 A's.

Year	Name	PA	WX1
1902	John Gochnauer	506	-4.1
1977	Rob Picciolo	445	-4.1
1901	John Ganzel	553	-4.1
1936	Skeeter Newsome	507	-4.3
1937	Jackie Hayes	629	-4.3
1901	Bill Hallman	521	-4.4
1999	Neifi Perez	731	-4.5
1909	Bill Bergen	372	-4.5
1931	Jim Levey	538	-4.5
1934	Ski Melillo	588	-4.5
1932	Ski Melillo	657	-4.5
1953	Billy Hunter	602	-4.6
1933	Art Scharein	521	-4.6
2002	Neifi Perez	585	-5.0
1933	Jim Levey	564	-5.9

Now, applying our Level Index, we'll run the top and bottom 15 seasons again, this time accounting for the difficulty of the league. Keep in mind that this adjustment treats every player as if he were transported to the 2006 AL with his hitting skills from the season in question intact.

Year	Name	PA	WX1
2001	Barry Bonds	655	11.0
2002	Barry Bonds	603	10.3
2004	Barry Bonds	608	8.2
1998	Mark McGwire	675	8.0
2001	Sammy Sosa	705	7.6
1993	Barry Bonds	672	7.1
2003	Albert Pujols	675	7.0
1992	Barry Bonds	607	7.0
1941	Ted Williams	603	6.9
2003	Barry Bonds	540	6.8
1957	Mickey Mantle	623	6.8
1923	Babe Ruth	695	6.6
2001	Jason Giambi	658	6.6
1961	Mickey Mantle	646	6.6
1942	Ted Williams	667	6.5
...	...	...	...
1897	Germany Smith	449	-8.0
1894	Germany Smith	523	-8.0
1886	Joe Gerhardt	448	-8.1
1891	Germany Smith	550	-8.1
1892	Joe Quinn	567	-8.2
1879	Will White	300	-8.6
1890	Bob Gilks	576	-8.8
1884	Jim Lillie	476	-8.9
1895	Jack Boyle	620	-8.9
1894	Chippy McGarr	551	-9.0
1894	John Ward	574	-9.1
1885	Joe Gerhardt	423	-9.2
1893	Joe Quinn	580	-9.3
1886	Jim Lillie	427	-10.1
1894	Jiggs Parrott	533	-10.6

Not surprisingly, Bonds still dominates, this time adding his 2004, 1993, 1992, and 2003 campaigns to the list in capturing six of the top 15 slots. Ruth is left with just his 1923 season (although he does claim two more spots in the top 20) making it the least recent, while Williams hangs on to two spots and Mantle actually adds his 1961 effort in the 15th slot. New to the list are recent stars McGwire, Sosa, Pujols, and Giambi. Derrek Lee's 2005 season also ranks 25th.

To give you a feel for the magnitude of the adjustment, you'll notice that Ruth, Giambi, and Mantle are all tied at 6.6 wins and each separated by about 40 years. Their unadjusted batting lines for those three seasons are:

Year	Name	PA	AVG/OBP/SLG	HR	BRAA	EqA
1923	Ruth	695	.393/.545/.764	41	120	.405
1961	Mantle	646	.317/.448/.687	54	96	.379
2001	Giambi	658	.342/.477/.660	38	85	.369

Obviously the worst players from the remotest time period will do the most poorly, and now the entire list contains 19th-century players. Poor Jiggs Parrott put up a .248/.274/.333 line playing for the Chicago Colts in the highest-scoring league (7.36 runs per game per team) in our data set.

Next, we'll look at WX1 from the perspective of entire careers, with the unadjusted leaders and trailers in the following tables.

Name	Start	End	PA	WX1
Babe Ruth	1914	1935	10573	116.2
Barry Bonds	1986	2006	12026	108.6
Ty Cobb	1905	1928	12978	102.1
Ted Williams	1939	1960	9752	97.3
Hank Aaron	1954	1976	13908	89.3
Stan Musial	1941	1963	12659	86.0
Willie Mays	1951	1973	12449	83.8
Mickey Mantle	1951	1968	9896	81.8
Lou Gehrig	1923	1939	9615	78.1
Rogers Hornsby	1915	1937	9427	76.8
Tris Speaker	1907	1928	11885	73.9
Mel Ott	1926	1947	11273	70.2
Frank Robinson	1956	1976	11545	67.1
Eddie Collins	1906	1930	11960	62.4
Honus Wagner	1897	1917	11614	61.3
...				
Davy Force	1876	1886	3081	-30.0
Fred Pfeffer	1882	1897	6544	-30.2
Herman Long	1890	1904	7798	-30.3
Ed Brinkman	1961	1975	6600	-30.8
Bones Ely	1884	1902	4991	-31.0
Ozzie Guillen	1985	2000	7126	-32.0
Malachi Kittridge	1890	1906	4438	-32.4
Bill Bergen	1901	1911	3228	-33.3
Kid Gleason	1888	1912	8160	-33.9
John Ward	1878	1894	7455	-34.6
Germany Smith	1884	1898	4638	-34.8
Alfredo Griffin	1976	1993	7305	-35.1
Bobby Lowe	1890	1907	7670	-35.9
Joe Quinn	1885	1901	6304	-39.5
Tommy Corcoran	1892	1907	8252	-41.8

Next, we'll make the adjustment by evaluating each season of their careers in the context of the 2006 AL.

Bonds takes over the top spot by a large margin, while Cobb falls from second to seventh. Ruth remains somewhat Ruthian but is now coupled with Aaron. In the first list, the third through sixth spots were occupied by Williams, Aaron, Musial, and Mays, while in the adjusted list the order is now Aaron, Williams, Mays, and Musial. Meanwhile, Gehrig falls only one spot, while Tris Speaker (now 16th), Eddie Collins (23rd), and Honus Wagner (24th) drop out of the top 15 altogether, with Rickey Henderson, Frank Thomas, and Jeff Bagwell taking their places. In addition, active players Gary Sheffield (18th), Manny Ramirez (27th), Chipper Jones (28th), and Mike Piazza (30th) all move up considerably.

Name	Start	End	PA	WX1
Barry Bonds	1986	2006	12026	104.6
Babe Ruth	1914	1935	10573	80.4
Hank Aaron	1954	1976	13908	78.9
Ted Williams	1939	1960	9752	73.7
Willie Mays	1951	1973	12449	73.4
Stan Musial	1941	1963	12659	69.3
Ty Cobb	1905	1928	12978	68.4
Mickey Mantle	1951	1968	9896	66.2
Frank Robinson	1956	1976	11545	59.2
Lou Gehrig	1923	1939	9615	55.9
Rogers Hornsby	1915	1937	9427	53.6
Rickey Henderson	1979	2003	13248	52.1
Mel Ott	1926	1947	11273	51.9
Frank Thomas	1990	2006	9084	51.8
Jeff Bagwell	1991	2005	9303	50.8
...				
Jack Burdock	1876	1891	3747	-48.1
Tom Burns	1880	1892	5190	-48.7
Pud Galvin	1879	1892	2402	-48.7
Bill Bergen	1901	1911	3228	-48.7
Herman Long	1890	1904	7798	-50.5
Bones Ely	1884	1902	4991	-52.0
Malachi Kittridge	1890	1906	4438	-53.9
Fred Pfeffer	1882	1897	6544	-53.9
Kid Gleason	1888	1912	8160	-55.4
Davy Force	1876	1886	3081	-56.3
Bobby Lowe	1890	1907	7670	-59.4
Germany Smith	1884	1898	4638	-59.7
John Ward	1878	1894	7455	-62.8
Tommy Corcoran	1892	1907	8252	-67.9
Joe Quinn	1885	1901	6304	-68.0

Once again, to get a feel for the adjustment, take a look at the career lines of Cobb and Musial, whose adjusted wins are very close at 68.4 and 69.3 respectively:

Name	PA	AVG/OBP/SLG	HR	BRAA	EqA
Cobb	12978	.366/.433/.512	117	1206	.335
Musial	12659	.331/.417/.559	475	1083	.332

In absolute terms, the adjustments cost Ruth the most (more than 35 wins), while also being hard on Cobb (34), Speaker (25), Williams (24), and Hornsby (23).

Finally, let's take a look at the unadjusted leaders in WX1 per 600 plate appearances for those players with 2000 or more plate appearances in their careers:

Name	Start	End	PA	WX1Rate
Babe Ruth	1914	1935	10573	6.6
Ted Williams	1939	1960	9752	6.0
Barry Bonds	1986	2006	12026	5.4
Albert Pujols	2001	2006	4014	5.0
Mickey Mantle	1951	1968	9896	5.0
Rogers Hornsby	1915	1937	9427	4.9
Lou Gehrig	1923	1939	9615	4.9
Ty Cobb	1905	1928	12978	4.7
Joe Jackson	1908	1920	5631	4.3
Stan Musial	1941	1963	12659	4.1
Willie Mays	1951	1973	12449	4.0
Hank Aaron	1954	1976	13908	3.9
Johnny Mize	1936	1953	7319	3.8
Mel Ott	1926	1947	11273	3.7
Tris Speaker	1907	1928	11885	3.7
Dick Allen	1963	1977	7298	3.7
Mark McGwire	1986	2001	7585	3.7
Joe DiMaggio	1936	1951	7625	3.6
Jimmie Foxx	1925	1945	9657	3.6
Frank Thomas	1990	2006	9084	3.5

Ruth and Williams are well ahead of the pack, although Pujols ties with Mantle for fourth place, while Frank Thomas slides in at number 20. This list also contains our first glimpses of Joe DiMaggio, Dick Allen, Jimmy Foxx, Johnny Mize, and Joe Jackson.

Name	Start	End	PA	WX1Rate
Barry Bonds	1986	2006	12026	5.2
Albert Pujols	2001	2006	4014	4.9
Babe Ruth	1914	1935	10573	4.6
Ted Williams	1939	1960	9752	4.5
Mickey Mantle	1951	1968	9896	4.0
Willie Mays	1951	1973	12449	3.5
Mark McGwire	1986	2001	7585	3.5
Lou Gehrig	1923	1939	9615	3.5
Frank Thomas	1990	2006	9084	3.4
Rogers Hornsby	1915	1937	9427	3.4
Hank Aaron	1954	1976	13908	3.4
Dick Allen	1963	1977	7298	3.3
Lance Berkman	1999	2006	4414	3.3
Stan Musial	1941	1963	12659	3.3
Jeff Bagwell	1991	2005	9303	3.3
Travis Hafner	2002	2006	2065	3.2
Ty Cobb	1905	1928	12978	3.2
Chipper Jones	1993	2006	7528	3.1
Mike Piazza	1992	2006	7386	3.1
Frank Robinson	1956	1976	11545	3.1

As you would expect, several active players jump into the list; perhaps most surprisingly, Lance Berkman coming in at 13th, and Travis Hafner at 16th.

Wrapping Up
So in the end, what does all of this tell us?

I think it's important to note that while adjusting these statistics using the LI method certainly makes a difference, it does not wipe out the greatness of past stars by equating them to reserve players in today's game. Yes, they're knocked down a few pegs, but the adjusted lists are not populated only by active and recently-retired players. For example, Honus Wagner's fabulous 1908 Deadball Era season—in which he hit .354/.415/.542 with a .362 EqA—is adjusted to 5.5 wins, dropping it from the 28th-greatest offensive season of all time to the 62nd; it's still in the company of Sammy Sosa's 2000 campaign in which he hit .320 with 50 home runs, Ruth's 1928 season, and Frank Thomas's 1991 efforts. Wagner would still be a star, simply one who couldn't dominate so completely.

Secondly, it should remind us that we have the privilege of watching players like Albert Pujols, who are among the most skilled hitters who have ever put on a uniform.

But finally, while analyses like these are interesting, ultimately they're not a complete answer to the question, since they have nothing to say regarding some of the more interesting speculations. For example, how would Ruth have done with the aid of modern medicine, training programs, and especially nutrition? How would Pujols or Bonds perform without those aids and with inferior equipment, facilities, and the rigors of train travel? These are questions for which there can never be a complete answer; perhaps that's just fine, since it continues to leave us room for arguing about who was the greatest.

SCHRODINGER'S BAT
The Burgess Shale and Other Weighty Matters
Dan Fox

Dan Fox's look at player demographic data uncovered a crucial formative period in the game's growth early in the 20th century.

> "Inasmuch as all base ball managers are imitative all clubs now carry at least one pinch-hitter. For this may the Lord forgive [John] McGraw, as there is no doubt that the system has added to the expense of the clubs, the length of the box scores, and the vexation of the scorers; while there is much doubt as to the practical value of the system."
> —*Sporting Life*, August 30, 1913

Before my brief hiatus last week the topic of this column turned back to triples, as we explored whether it was the case that the ever-increasing bulk of players could be responsible for the steady decline in three-baggers since around 1930. It turned out that even when normalizing for the distribution of Body Mass Index (BMI) that prevailed in the 1920s when leaner players were more prevalent, the triples rate still declined, albeit slightly less dramatically. Given the other probable causes for the decline in triples, we concluded that in the aggregate the increasing scarcity of triples over time is a residue of the ever-increasing level and standardization of play.

As interesting as all that was, it was the following paragraph that engendered the largest volume of comments from readers.

> As an aside, I'd be interested to hear reader theories as to why average height and especially weight dipped in the period from 1910 through the 1920s and then picked up where it left off in the 1930s. No systemic cause or data problem jumps out at me, and it doesn't seem likely that the slashing style of play popularized by the Baltimore Orioles of the 1890s would have such a latent effect.

I asked the question because one of the graphs I built indicated that height, and more dramatically weight, decreased for players who debuted in the 1910s and 1920s before resuming a steady upward trend in the 1930s. A more detailed graph below with weight graphed on the Y-axis on the left and height on the Y-axis on the right shows the same basic picture.

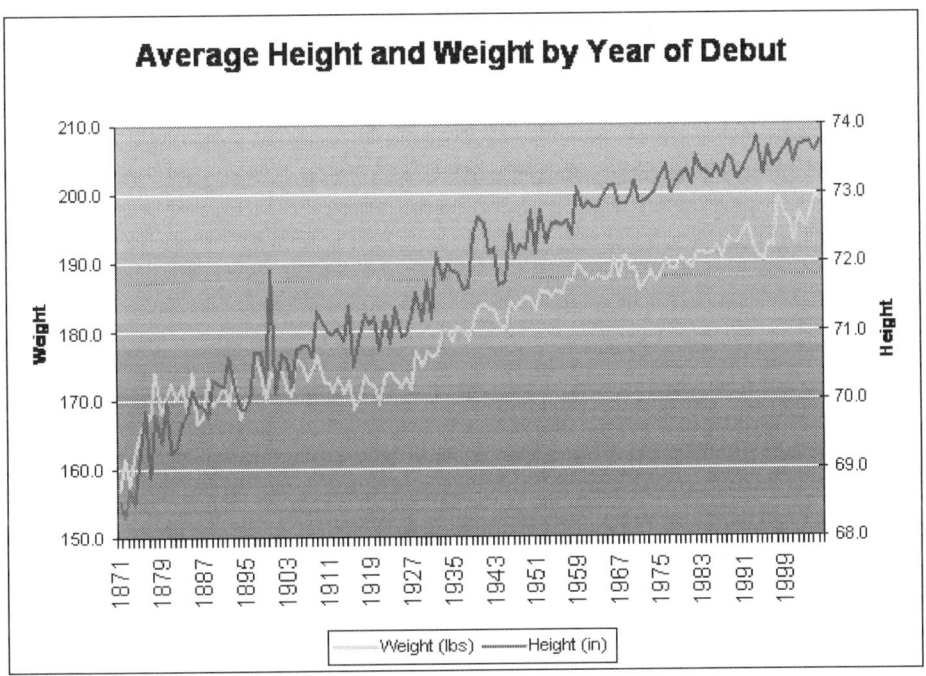

When looked at in more detail, it's clear that weight decline was more acute than height, and in fact, average height increased in each of the first three decades of the 20th century, while weight decreased in the period 1910-1919 before rising slightly from 1920-1929 to just under its level from 1900-1909.

What I found most interesting was the variety of responses articulating theories to explain the trend, the most frequent of which were:

- Immigration. Some readers speculated that a spike in eastern and southern European immigration in the early years of the century might be responsible as more players with those backgrounds entered the league. This would be the case, so the theory goes, since the general health and nutrition (and hence height and weight) might be lower for those immigrants than it had been for players born in America.

    Country of birth is available in the database, but calculating the percentage of players born in the US versus those outside by debut decade revealed that by the 1910s 97 percent of players were born in the United States. That percentage did not begin to shrink until the 1950s (92 percent) and has since accelerated with the larger influx of Latin and Asian players in the 1980s (87 percent) and 1990s (78 percent) to the point we're at now, where in the 2000s the percentage of US-born players was 72 percent. It is perhaps the case that the data for country of birth is incorrect for players from that period, or that there is a residual generational effect in play, but absent more data there is no hard evidence that country of birth or ethnicity is the cause of the trend.

- The Flu. It occurred to me, as it did to several readers, that the inappropriately named (since it started in the U.S.) Spanish Flu pandemic of 1918 might in some way play a role here, since it was paradoxically hardest on otherwise healthy young adults and killed between 500,000 and 675,000 people in the United States. That large a disruption might have affected the population from which baseball players were pulled and led to a decline in the average weight and height.

    It turns out, however, that while there were certainly flu outbreaks in eastern cities as early as 1916, the trends we see (as revealed in the more granular graph above) began as early as 1910. That's not to say that the flu might not have reinforced the trend in some way, since it obviously had a devastating effect on the entire population, only that it couldn't have been the initial or major cause.

- The Great War. As with the flu, the effect of World War I on the pool from which players were selected was too late for the trend we see. Once again, however, the war clearly had an effect later in the decade of the 1910s and probably into the 1920s and may have helped perpetuate the trend. This is suggested by the fact that in World War II we see decline in height and weight from 1942 through 1945 before both resume their upward march in 1946.

- A Competing League. Although not mentioned by many readers, I thought perhaps the rival Federal League might have had an effect whereby the introduction of eight additional teams might have depressed the size of players available to the American and National Leagues. Once again the timing is not quite right, since the Federal League did not come online until 1914, and the trend had clearly begun before then.

The Young and the Restless

After cogitating on these theories for several days and satisfying myself that none was the underlying cause, I went back and took a second look at the data. Thinking that perhaps there was something wrong with the data itself, I began to look at the players who debuted during the upturn in the trend. What struck me was that the number of players who debuted in a given season rose from 99 in 1907 to 221 in 1912 and 201 in 1913. Since the number of teams remained constant during this period (at 16), this more than doubling of the number of rookies in the game aroused my suspicion that this trend and the trend for decreasing height and weight were related.

But first, to confirm that teams made historically liberal use of players during this time, I created the following graph.

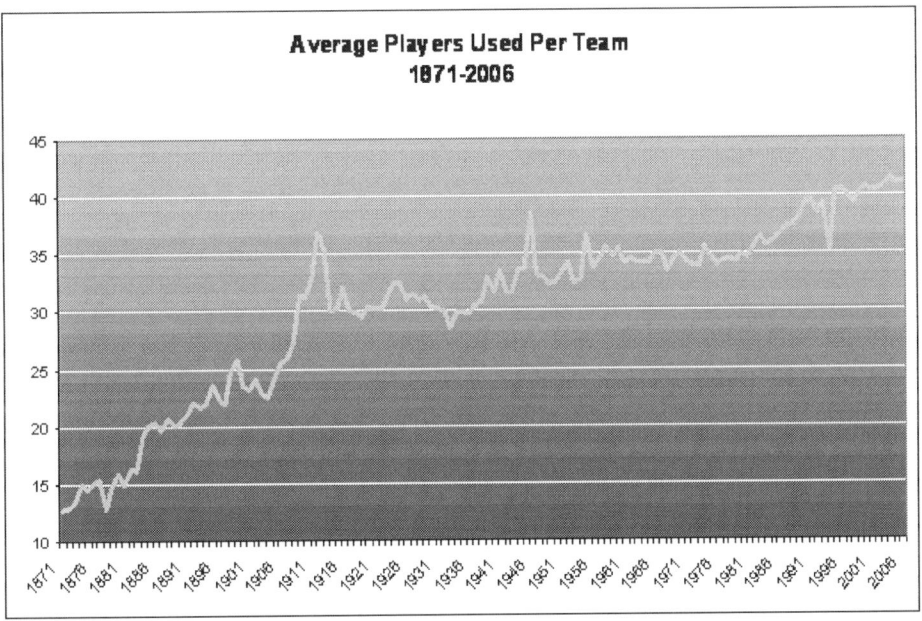

The average number of players employed per team rose sharply between 1904 (when it was 22.6) to 1912, when it topped out at 36.9. For the next 78 years, only in 1946—in the wake of World War II, as players returned from the service—was there a total number of players used (38.6) that eclipsed that 1912 high. Of course, in recent years teams have increasingly exercised their 40-man rosters to the point where the average per team has topped 41 since 2003 (excluding 1994, when the strike wiped out September call-ups).

And now we come to the link between the two. In looking closer, we find that the average age of players who debuted also fell coincident with the 1908-1919 period, as shown in the graph below.

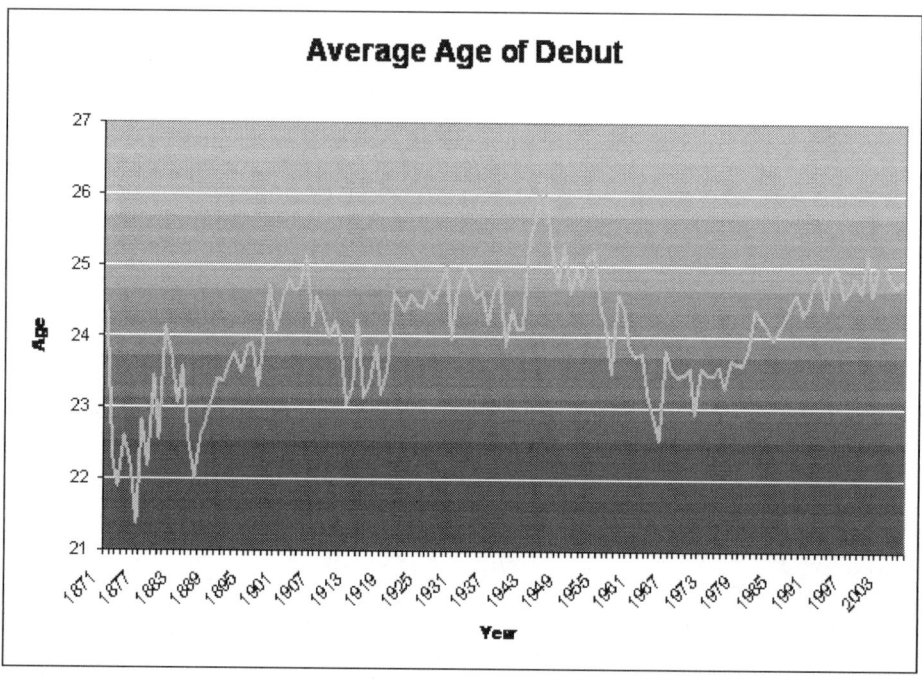

In other words, as teams employed more players during this period, they were also selecting players who were slightly younger than players who had debuted in the previous decade and who would debut in the 1920s and 1930s. Assuming that height and weight were recorded early in a player's career (remember, we have only one data point for each player) it would also be the case that they would likely trend lower, especially in weight, which is precisely what we see. Here, then, we likely have the primary cause. Players who debuted were slightly smaller because they were slightly younger.

Two additional points can be added. First, the impact of the war may also be evident here, although having the opposite effect of World War II, where the average age of a player at his debut increased to more than 25 years from 1943 through 1946 while height and weight decreased. Additionally, the average age dropped precipitously through the 1950s and bottomed out in 1965, when 117 players debuted who averaged 22.6 years of age. Since then, the average age has increased and stabilized at just under 25 years old since the mid-90s.

The question then becomes, "Just why did so many more players break in during this time?" I posed the question to Steve Treder (he was after all, a finalist in the trivia competition at last year's SABR convention), who reminded me that Bill James had written on the subject in last year's *Hardball Times* annual.

In his article titled "Young Pitchers," James shows that the percentage of innings pitched by young pitchers (age 25 or younger) in the decade 1910-1919 was 42 percent, the highest of any decade, with the 1960s coming in second at 37 percent. The percentage then drops sharply to 24 percent in the 1920s and 23 percent in the 1930s. As to why this occurred, James wrote that:

> The pitching patterns of the 1910-1919 era were abnormally simple. At that time the pitcher was allowed to abuse the baseball—scratch it, rub it in the dirt, spit licorice on it—and then pitch with it... You just rear back and throw hard, and the baseball itself will take care of the rest... Pitchers in that era threw fewer breaking pitches and fewer off-speed pitches than ever before or since, and this obviously worked to the advantage of young pitchers. After 1920 the salaries of players grew rapidly, which probably accelerated the trend away from younger pitchers.

But an increased reliance on young pitchers isn't the entire story. As James himself recounts in *The New Bill James Historical Baseball Abstract*, the 1910-1919 period was also one where managers began to use players for more diverse reasons.

For example, as told by Peter Morris in *A Game of Inches: The Stories Behind the Innovations that Shaped Baseball Volume 1, The Game on the Field*, pinch hitting began in 1905 when Giants manager John McGraw purchased the contract of veteran Sammy Strange, who would be called upon in both utility infield and pinch-hitting (in the sense of hitting "in a pinch") roles. The trend caught on, and by 1909 the *New York Telegram* observed that "Almost all teams in the National and American leagues carry some player these days who is supposed to be able to take his place at bat in an emergency..." As documented in the quote I led off with today, this was the case, and Ham Hyatt for the Pirates and Dode Criss for the Browns, and later Moose McCormick with McGraw's Giants, became successful pinch-hitters. By 1914, Hyatt had 58 at-bats as a pinch-hitter, whereas James mentions that in 1904 several AL players tied for the league lead in pinch hits with a paltry two.

In part, this trend was driven by the increased demand on pitchers to specialize at their craft, and as a result become less effective offensive players. The graph of Pitcher vs. Position Player OPS over time presented in a previous column bears this out. At the same time, pinch-runners became fashionable, and once again it was McGraw who was the innovator and took it to the limit 72 years before Charlie Finley later would with Herb Washington, when he used Sandy Piez in that role full-time in 1914.

Entangled with the development of pinch hitting, removing starting pitchers and thereby necessarily developing a demand for the first true relief pitchers (such as Sad Sam Jones in 1915 and Dave Danforth in 1917) was an innovation characteristic of the era. As early as 1902, White Sox manager Clark Griffith was reported to be toying with the idea of removing his starter when he showed signs of fatigue after the sixth inning. In January of 1913, *The Sporting News* reported that, "The pinch hitter is becoming a factor in the big league races, and it may be only a short time until teams will have to carry great one and two-inning pitchers—men that hurl shut-out ball for a couple of rounds." Although it would take almost another 60 years for this concept to be cemented in the game in the form of the closer, the trend can be seen in the following graph that tracks the percentage of appearances that were made in relief by year.

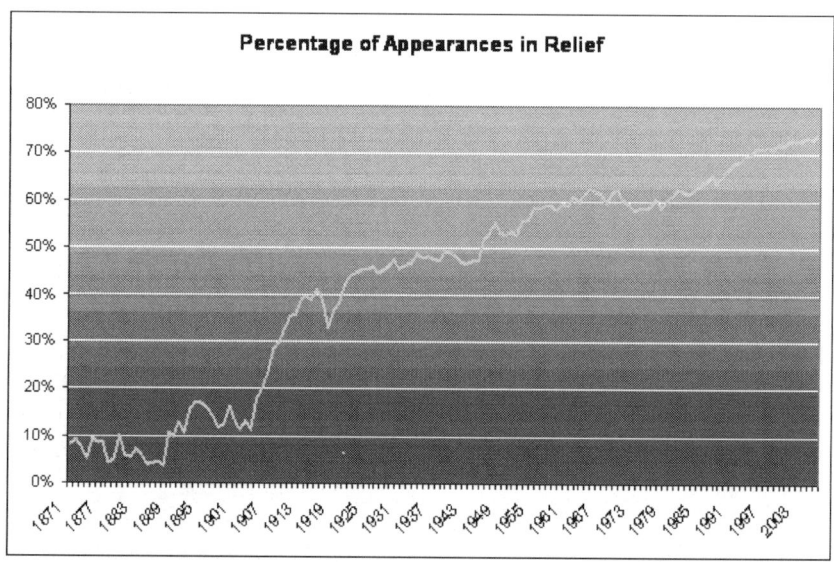

The big jump takes place between 1904, when 11.3 percent of the appearances were in relief, to 1916, when 41.1 percent were.

And finally, as is widely known, the adoption of extensive platooning following its successful employment by George Stallings as manager of the 1914 Miracle Braves served to increase the number of players teams employed. Platooning reached its heyday by around 1919 and enjoyed a resurgence following World War II, in no small part because of the return of Casey Stengel to the major-league managerial ranks. As a player, Stengel had been platooned by McGraw, as documented by Retrosheet event files from 1922 (incomplete though they were when I downloaded them, but accounting for 89 percent of Stengel's plate appearances).

Casey Stengel, 1922

	PA	AB	H	2B	3B	HR	SO	BB	IBB	HBP	SH	SF	AVG	OBP	SLG
R	246	216	82	7	9	6	15	19	1	7	1	2	.380	.439	.579
L	6	6	3	0	0	0	0	0	0	0	0	0	.500	.500	.500

James also notes that roster sizes must have become standardized around 1917 in order to control expenses and to limit the number of players who could be controlled by a single team in light of the developing minor leagues. Unfortunately, I can't seem to find any documentation to back that up, and the data on players used per team would tend to support a slightly earlier date around 1914 or 1915.

The Cone Inverted

The flowering of strategies and the increase in the usage of players brings to mind an analogy from the world of paleontology. In 1909, Charles Doolittle Walcott discovered a treasure trove of wonderfully unique fossils preserved in a layer of shale near the town of Field in British Columbia, specimens that would become known simply as the Burgess Shale. While Walcott placed his specimens in familiar phyla that were known to exist during the period (Middle Cambrian, 505 million years ago), it was a reinvestigation by Harry Blackmore Whittington, Derek Briggs, and Simon Conway Morris of the University of Cambridge in the 1980s that upended that traditional interpretation of the fossils' place in the evolution of life. By inverting the familiar iconography of the cone of increasing diversity in life forms, Whittington, Briggs, and Morris reinterpreted the Burgess Shale as replete with creatures in phyla that are now extinct. In other words, rather than life becoming increasingly more diverse in terms of its basic body plans over successive geologic periods, the Burgess Shale records an initial flowering of experimentation in structures just after the dawn of life before a later decimation or winnowing into the few surviving phyla we see today. Stephen Jay Gould devoted an entire book to this theme as an illustration akin to his theory of punctuated equilibrium in his 1989 book *Wonderful Life: The Burgess Shale and the Nature of History*.

This pattern from the history of life is akin to what we see in the history of baseball, as ideas (usually after being initially successful) spread throughout the game and are either adapted into its fabric, standardized, and carried forward, or discarded. The period of 1910-1919 was one particularly active time of experimentation.

The analogy fails, however, in one crucial respect. In the history of life, once a phyla becomes extinct it cannot be recovered, since major body plans, as expressed through genes, lose their flexibility for major reorganization. That's fortunately not the case in baseball, where although some experiments are discarded forever (courtesy runners, "plugging" baserunners, legal doctoring of baseballs), styles of play that were once innovations can come back in vogue. Platooning in the 1950s and base stealing in the 1970s and 1980s are two examples, and some of us are hopeful for the return of the four-man rotation as another. Even so, the overall trend is towards standardization, as more effective strategies and techniques are adopted, resulting in an ever-increasing level of play. In that sense we can look at something as innocuous as a blip in the average weight of rookies as recording the continual evolution of the game.

FEBRUARY 15, 2007 — http://bbp.cx/a/5873

SCHRODINGER'S BAT
Age Before Beauty
Dan Fox

Youth movements are often greeted with great fanfare, but Dan Fox found that age and experience often trump fresh faces.

> "Men do not quit playing because they grow old; they grow old because they quit playing."
> -Oliver Wendell Holmes

Before we get to the topic at hand, I want to offer an additional insight on last week's column, related to the influx of players in the early 20th century.

In that column, I observed that the average weight of players who debuted during this time (roughly 1910-1919) dropped fairly sharply, and that the average age of those players also dropped. From this I concluded that if it were the case that weight were recorded early in each player's career, the drop in mean weight for new players could be explained by younger—and therefore, on average, lighter—players entering the population pool. That would be relative to players who had debuted at other times, who were older and therefore generally heavier.

Reader Guy Molyneux challenged that line of thinking by drawing my attention to two important points. First, as shown in one of the graphs in that piece, mean age at debut fell fairly precipitously in the late 1950s and 1960s as well, yet the graph showing average weight at debut does not indicate the same kind of downward trend as seen in the early part of the century. Second, he noted (as I also mentioned) that average weight fell during World War II despite the fact that the average age of players who debuted during that time increased greatly.

Guy then offered what I now feel is probably a major reason (and simpler, with a nod to Occam's razor) for the decline in weight during the 1910-1919 period. Simply put, as the number of players used drastically expanded, teams were forced (in general) to add inferior players, and those inferior players tended to be smaller. (Nate Silver did a good study on the interrrelationship on size and performance.)

In regard to the first point above, in looking at the data more closely it is apparent that weight flatlines from 1961-1965 and then spikes in 1966 before falling back to the line in 1967. In other words, while the decreasing age of rookies may have kept the average weight from increasing (in other words, decreasing age may still have been a contributing factor), it did not cause it to fall, indicating that some other factor is probably at work in the 1910-1919 period. Secondly and more convincingly, Molyneux's theory fits very nicely with the trend we see in 1943-1946, where weight decreased despite a skyrocketing average age. If World War II meant anything, it meant an influx of inferior players, and those inferior players were smaller despite being older.

Now back to our regularly scheduled topic...

In his 2005 book, *The Singularity is Near: When Humans Transcend Biology*, inventor and futurist Ray Kurzweil predicts that big changes are ahead for the human race in the next 20 to 30 years. In short, "The Singularity" is the point at which the three already exponentially growing and overlapping revolutions of genetics, nanotechnology, and robotics converge to usher in a fusion of biology and technology that will ultimately result in saturating the universe with a combination of our biological and non-biological intelligence. In essence, the law of accelerating returns will create "a rupture in the fabric of human history."

Along the way, "minor" problems such as disease, pollution, and the topic of this column, aging, will be overcome by the applications of that convergence. For example, Kurzweil notes seven key aging processes ranging from mitochondrial mutations to cell loss and atrophy that he expects will be stopped or reversed through techniques such as therapeutic cloning and the introduction of nanobots that perform a kind of maintenance into the bloodstream. Using some of these techniques "radical life extension has already been achieved in simpler animals," and Kurzweil expects that once successfully applied to higher animals like mice, there will be no stopping their application in humans 20 to 25 years in the future.

Interestingly, until the technology is available, Kurzweil takes 250 supplements a day, a half-dozen intravenous therapies a week, drinks eight to 10 glasses of alkaline water and 10 cups of green tea per day, a regimen which he reports has lowered his biological age to 40. Not bad for a 56-year-old.

In the face of those kinds of advances, I'm afraid Nate Silver is going to have to recode his PECOTA spreadsheets if he wants to remain "deadlier than ninja accurate." But I'll leave Nate and Will Carroll (since nanobots coursing through the body will surely be able to repair shoulder and elbow injuries on the fly as well) to think through the implications of those kinds of advances on baseball.

Last week's peripheral discussion on aging and Clay Davenport's fascinating report of organizational ages did, however, get me to thinking about how the player population has aged over time and what that means, especially for teams. So this week, while it's still relevant anyway, we'll explore aging in a little more depth.

Tipping the Scales

First, though, we need a consistent and relative way to measure the age of teams. To that end, I calculated two measures.

- Weighted Age (WA): This measure is calculated by first creating separate ages for position players and pitchers, weighted by plate appearances and innings pitched, respectively. The fractional age of players is calculated as of July 1st of the year in question. Then, the weighted age of position players is multiplied by .6, and that of pitchers multiplied by .4 and then summed to calculate the WA for the entire team. Obviously there are other ways to weight playing time (by games played to weight relief pitchers and pinch hitters more heavily, or innings in the field) and there may be quibbles with the weighting (keep in mind the 60 percent also takes defensive playing time into account), but overall this approach provides a reasonable indication of team age.
- Normalized Weighted Age (NWA): As you can imagine, the average weighted age for teams has changed over the course of time and differs by league, so we can normalize the WA by dividing it by the mean weighted age for the year and league. To illustrate why this is necessary, consider the graph below, that tracks average mean WA for teams in the American and National Leagues. While absolute team age has generally increased since the early 1970s (with a large increase with the advent of free agency as teams invested in older players for the longer term), team age was also high from the middle of the 1920s until the 1950s. The graph also indicates that the AL went younger in the 1910-1919 period, and that the NL was younger in the 1950s and 1980s, although more recently the AL has literally been the junior circuit. By normalizing for the average age of teams in the league, we'll later be able to examine how being relatively old or young correlates with winning on the field.

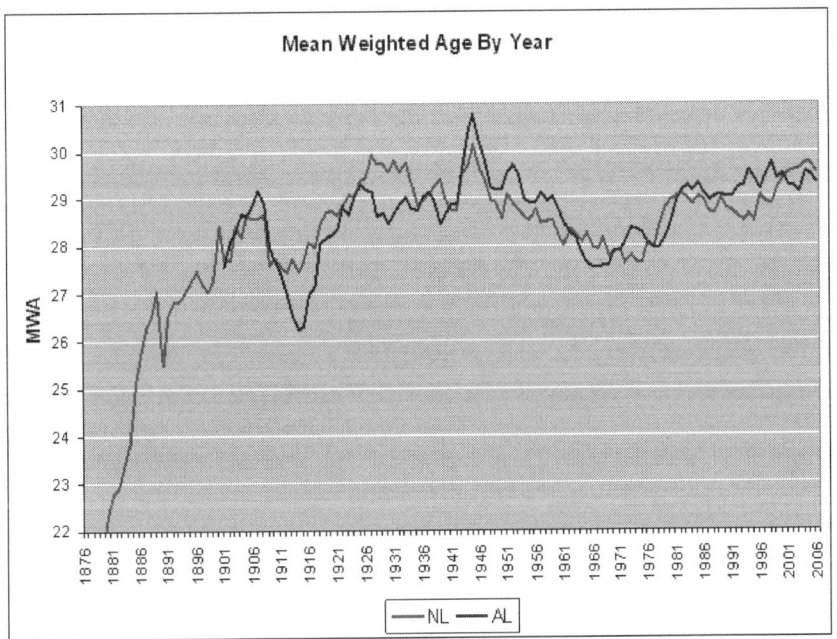

Using WA and NWA, we can now determine the oldest and youngest teams in history based on these measures. First, the absolute oldest and youngest teams since 1901 using Weighted Age are shown in the table below, where WA is the Weighted Age of the Team, NWA is the Normalized Weighted Age, and LgWA is the average WA for teams in that league.

Best of Baseball Prospectus: 1996-2011

Oldest and Youngest Teams Since 1901 Using Weighted Age

Year	Team	Lg	HitterAge	PitcherAge	WA	NWA	LGWA
2005	NYA	AL	32.81	34.68	33.55	1.137	29.51
2004	NYA	AL	32.76	33.49	33.06	1.119	29.55
2005	BOS	AL	31.98	34.19	32.86	1.114	29.51
1982	CAL	AL	32.94	32.39	32.72	1.123	29.15
2002	ARI	NL	32.38	33.01	32.63	1.102	29.60
1998	BAL	AL	33.88	30.71	32.61	1.096	29.76
1983	CAL	AL	32.01	33.37	32.55	1.113	29.26
2001	ARI	NL	32.82	32.11	32.53	1.102	29.53
2006	SFN	NL	34.54	28.98	32.32	1.094	29.53
2000	NYA	AL	31.85	32.81	32.23	1.092	29.51
1988	DET	AL	32.61	31.61	32.21	1.110	29.02
2003	NYA	AL	30.82	34.23	32.18	1.104	29.14
1945	WAS	AL	31.77	32.76	32.17	1.046	30.76
1983	PHI	NL	32.66	31.24	32.09	1.107	28.98
2006	NYA	AL	31.42	32.97	32.04	1.093	29.32
1945	CHA	AL	32.39	31.51	32.03	1.041	30.76
1984	CAL	AL	32.36	31.42	31.98	1.097	29.16
1982	PHI	NL	31.58	32.46	31.93	1.097	29.10
1999	BAL	AL	33.18	29.81	31.83	1.083	29.40
2005	SFN	NL	32.89	30.24	31.83	1.071	29.73
...							
1967	KC	AL	25.28	23.84	24.70	0.897	27.53
1915	CLE	AL	25.03	24.45	24.80	0.942	26.32
1968	OAK	AL	25.19	24.30	24.83	0.901	27.57
1915	PHA	AL	26.99	22.38	25.15	0.955	26.32
1921	PHA	AL	25.58	24.98	25.34	0.894	28.36
1901	CLE	AL	28.33	20.96	25.38	0.921	27.56
1966	KC	AL	26.03	24.48	25.41	0.923	27.54
1916	PHA	AL	26.65	23.62	25.44	0.944	26.95
1920	PHA	AL	25.33	25.62	25.45	0.901	28.24
1911	BOS	AL	25.27	25.72	25.45	0.928	27.42
1914	BOS	AL	25.84	25.14	25.56	0.974	26.24
1998	FLO	NL	26.01	24.89	25.56	0.885	28.88
1972	SDN	NL	25.43	25.81	25.58	0.926	27.64
1917	PHA	AL	26.00	24.99	25.60	0.942	27.16
1973	SDN	NL	25.57	25.73	25.63	0.922	27.80
1914	WAS	AL	27.38	23.02	25.64	0.977	26.24
1974	SFN	NL	25.67	25.66	25.67	0.928	27.66
1982	MIN	AL	25.73	25.62	25.69	0.881	29.15
2006	FLO	NL	25.82	25.62	25.74	0.872	29.53
1910	BOS	AL	25.92	25.53	25.76	0.932	27.65

Five of the last seven Yankee teams make the top 20, with the 2005 version taking the top spot. Some other notably old teams include the California Angels led by the aged trio of Tommy John, Rod Carew, and Reggie Jackson, and the Philadelphia Phillies (Pete Rose, Tony Perez, Joe Morgan) of the early 1980s. The 1998 Orioles (Jesse Orosco, Harold Baines, Joe Carter), the 2001-2002 Diamondbacks (Mike Morgan, Randy Johnson, Mark Grace), the 1988 Tigers (Darrell Evans, Doyle Alexander, Fred Lynn), and the Giants of the past two seasons also are prominent.

You'll also notice that in addition to a strong representation of recent teams, two teams from 1945 make the list, since both periods feature historically high average team weighted ages.

On the other side of the spectrum, the 1967 A's (Rick Monday, Catfish Hunter, Bert Campaneris) take the distinction as the youngest team since 1900, with the franchise's 1966 and 1968 squads also making the list. It should also come as no surprise that the post-fire-sale Marlins of 1998 (Mark Kotsay, Brian Meadows, Derrek Lee) and 2006 make the list, as do five versions of Connie Mack's Philadelphia A's. After Mack released or traded most of the stars from his 1914 pennant winner, the A's teams on the list (1915, 1921, 1916, 1920, 1917) never won more than 55 games, and it wouldn't be until 1925, with an older team (WA of 28.06), that they would again break .500.

In order to account for the age of the league, let's next take a peek at the oldest and youngest teams using Normalized Weighted Age.

Oldest and Youngest Teams Since 1901 Using Normalized Weighted Age

Year	Team	Lg	HitterAge	Pitcher Age	WA	NWA	LgWA
2005	NYA	AL	32.81	34.68	33.55	1.137	29.51
1982	CAL	AL	32.94	32.39	32.72	1.123	29.15
2004	NYA	AL	32.76	33.49	33.06	1.119	29.55
1973	DET	AL	32.26	30.78	31.67	1.116	28.38
2005	BOS	AL	31.98	34.19	32.86	1.114	29.51
1983	CAL	AL	32.01	33.37	32.55	1.113	29.26
1988	DET	AL	32.61	31.61	32.21	1.110	29.02
1983	PHI	NL	32.66	31.24	32.09	1.107	28.98
1979	NYA	AL	30.85	31.71	31.20	1.107	28.18
2003	NYA	AL	30.82	34.23	32.18	1.104	29.14
1960	CHA	AL	31.16	32.51	31.70	1.103	28.75
2002	ARI	NL	32.38	33.01	32.63	1.102	29.60
2001	ARI	NL	32.82	32.11	32.53	1.102	29.53
1905	BOS	AL	31.94	30.77	31.47	1.099	28.64
1998	SFN	NL	31.23	32.42	31.71	1.098	28.88
1982	PHI	NL	31.58	32.46	31.93	1.097	29.10
1984	CAL	AL	32.36	31.42	31.98	1.097	29.16
1988	NYA	AL	31.10	32.91	31.82	1.096	29.02
1998	BAL	AL	33.88	30.71	32.61	1.096	29.76
2006	SFN	NL	34.54	28.98	32.32	1.094	29.53
	...						
2006	FLO	NL	25.82	25.62	25.74	0.872	29.53
1982	MIN	AL	25.73	25.62	25.69	0.881	29.15
1998	FLO	NL	26.01	24.89	25.56	0.885	28.88
1999	FLO	NL	25.71	26.59	26.06	0.893	29.19
1921	PHA	AL	25.58	24.98	25.34	0.894	28.36
1999	MON	NL	26.18	26.06	26.13	0.895	29.19
1967	KC	AL	25.28	23.84	24.70	0.897	27.53
1968	OAK	AL	25.19	24.30	24.83	0.901	27.57
1920	PHA	AL	25.33	25.62	25.45	0.901	28.24
2000	MON	NL	26.55	26.51	26.53	0.902	29.41
1999	CHA	AL	26.28	26.96	26.55	0.903	29.40
1998	MON	NL	26.15	26.12	26.14	0.905	28.88
1936	PHA	AL	26.24	26.45	26.33	0.906	29.04
1956	PIT	NL	25.45	27.08	26.10	0.907	28.79
2000	FLO	NL	26.52	26.91	26.68	0.907	29.41
1983	MIN	AL	26.48	26.76	26.59	0.909	29.26
2000	MIN	AL	26.92	26.75	26.85	0.910	29.51
1950	SLA	AL	25.96	27.50	26.58	0.910	29.20
1914	CHF	FL	26.29	25.82	26.10	0.911	28.66
1981	TOR	AL	26.46	26.31	26.40	0.912	28.94

Once again, the Yankees of 2005 come out on top, almost 14 percent older than the average team in the American League that season, while many of the same teams from the first list find themselves on this one as well. Looking a bit out of place, the 1905 Boston Americans make an appearance with a team that featured 38-year-old Cy Young (who would throw 24 percent of the team's innings), 36-year-old outfielder Jesse Burkett, and 35-year-old third baseman Jimmy Collins.

The 2006 Marlins make their way to the top as the relatively youngest team in history, with the 1982 Twins led by Tom Brunansky (21), Kent Hrbek (22), Brad Havens (22), and Gary Gaetti (23) taking the runner-up spot.

Because position hitters' and pitchers' ages were calculated separately, we can take a quick look at the youngest and oldest teams in each category.

Oldest and Youngest Hitters by Weighted Age

Year	Team	Lg	HitterAge	PitcherAge	WA	NWA	LgWA
2006	SFN	NL	34.54	28.98	32.32	1.094	29.53
1998	BAL	AL	33.88	30.71	32.61	1.096	29.76
1999	BAL	AL	33.18	29.81	31.83	1.083	29.40
1945	DET	AL	33.01	28.53	31.22	1.015	30.76
1985	CAL	AL	32.98	28.51	31.19	1.064	29.30
...							
1915	CLE	AL	25.03	24.45	24.80	0.942	26.32
1975	MON	NL	25.10	27.22	25.95	0.939	27.65
1973	CLE	AL	25.11	29.36	26.81	0.945	28.38
1968	OAK	AL	25.19	24.30	24.83	0.901	27.57
1911	BOS	AL	25.27	25.72	25.45	0.928	27.42

It's not surprising that the 2006 Giants and their collection of obscenely geriatric position players took the top spot. What is somewhat confusing is that in their stated effort to "get younger and healthier" in 2007, they've added a 35-year-old center fielder, a 32-year-old catcher, and a 29-year-old starting pitcher whom they signed for seven years to go along with their 42-year-old left fielder and 40-year-old shortstop.

By contrast, the 1915 Indians did not have a starting position player who was 30 years old and were led by 24-year-old shortstop Ray Chapman, while the 1975 Expos featured a pair of 21-year-olds, Gary Carter and Larry Parish.

Oldest and Youngest Pitchers by Weighted Age

Year	Team	Lg	HitterAge	PitcherAge	WA	NWA	LgWA
2005	NYA	AL	32.81	34.68	33.55	1.137	29.51
2003	NYA	AL	30.82	34.23	32.18	1.104	29.14
2005	BOS	AL	31.98	34.19	32.86	1.114	29.51
2002	NYA	AL	30.48	33.63	31.74	1.085	29.24
1935	BSN	NL	29.63	33.58	31.21	1.081	28.88
...							
1915	PHA	AL	26.99	22.38	25.15	0.955	26.32
1914	WAS	AL	27.38	23.02	25.64	0.977	26.24
1916	PHA	AL	26.65	23.62	25.44	0.944	26.95
1967	KC	AL	25.28	23.84	24.70	0.897	27.53
1901	NY	NL	27.83	23.95	26.82	0.948	27.72

Three recent Yankee teams make the top five, along with the Red Sox of 2005, while the 1935 Boston Braves, losers of 115 games, sneak into the fifth slot by virtue of 40-year-old Bob Smith's 203 1/3 innings pitched and 38-year-old Huck Betts' 159 2/3 innings.

The 1915 A's had the youngest pitching staff, as 23-year-old Weldon Wyckoff threw 276 innings and 20-year-old Rube Bressler threw 178 1/3.

The Wisdom of Age

Having these measures in hand gives us the tools for answering several interesting questions. I'm sure most BP readers are familiar with the normal career trajectory (or, if you prefer by position, the trajectories for different types of players). This can be graphed to illustrate that offensive production increases rapidly from ages 20 through 25, peaks between the ages of 26 and 28, and then declines more gently through the mid-30s. Given that the 26 through 28 age range registers the peak of individual performance (on average), the question is whether or not that's the case for teams as well. In other words, do teams with WAs between 26 and 28 outperform younger and older teams?

To examine this, we can simply calculate the aggregate winning percentage for all teams of a certain age. The graph below does this on the blue line, while the red bars represent the number of teams that fell into each age range (i.e. the bar representing 26 includes all teams whose WA rounded to 26).

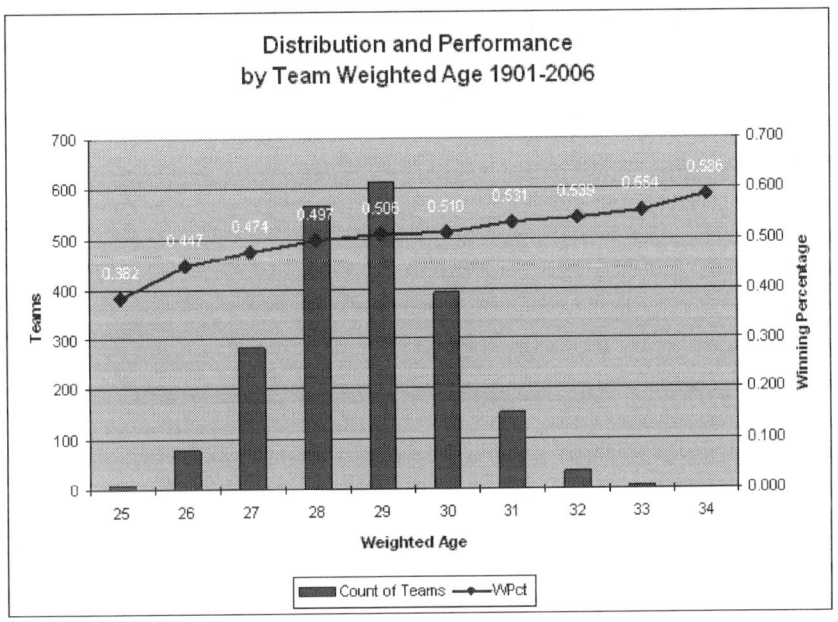

What is clear from this is that a minority of teams (42 percent) fall into the 26-28 age range, and those teams in the aggregate do not win half of their games. Teams who are 29 and older are the ones who perform better (which the attentive reader probably noticed from the tables presented above). Interestingly enough, the trend continues with each successive year, even up to the single team, the 2005 Yankees, who round to a collective 34 years old while posting a .586 winning percentage. The correlation coefficient between winning percentage and team age for all 2,136 teams was also calculated at .227, which also illustrates the relationship.

This result is confirmed by a study done by Chip McNamara in 2003 titled "Does Team Age and Success Correlate in Major League Baseball?" Although the methodology was slightly different, McNamara produced a table that shows regular-season winning percentage increasing steadily from a team age of 25 through 31 and then slightly decreasing at age 32. Contrary to the popular notion that younger is always better, when it comes to winning games on the field it appears that age trumps youth.

But perhaps these results are skewed by the underlying differences in league age? To correct for that we can produce the same graph, this time using Normalized WA, and the results look very familiar:

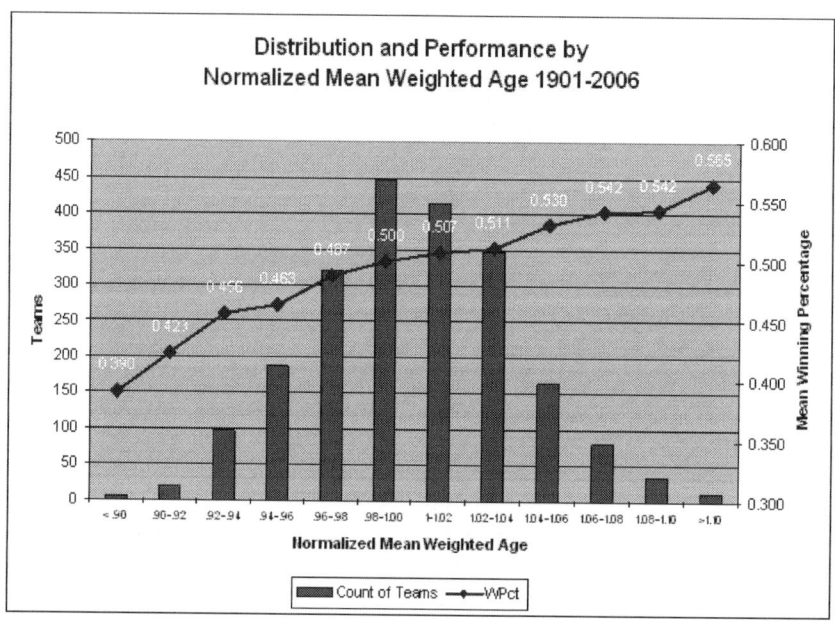

Once again, teams that are relatively older than other teams in their league perform better. The correlation coefficient in this case is slightly higher at .272 and goes up to .373 when considering only teams from 1977-2006.

So, we're left asking, why is it that old or older teams perform better? I believe there are two primary reasons.

First, as is evident in the aging curve discussed earlier, the slope of the curve at younger ages is steeper than it is for later ages. A team that is heavily populated with young players (in the 21-25 age range, for example) will therefore likely have more players who are still developing and therefore generally don't perform quite as well as established veterans. In large part this is probably due to the twofold effect of younger players getting acclimated to the league while honing their skills, the greater variability in the performance of younger players as they adjust, and to some extent reflects the promotions of young players to The Show who simply don't succeed at the major-league level for whatever reason.

Secondly, old teams retain old players in large part because those old players are productive players and help produce winning records on the field. In other words, the teams that continue to employ older players have selected the best older players (perhaps the only older players, as the others are forced into retirement), so there is less space in the universe of teams for those who are old and yet not very good (the 1935 Boston Braves are a stunning exception to the rule). This effect has intensified in the free agent era, and even more so in the recent past, as wealthier teams are able to retain the services of the best veteran players. Once those older and productive players reach the end of their careers, the team is often forced to retool to some degree, getting younger and typically worse in the process. The current Yankees are the exception, having remained a relatively old team since 1994 while putting up good records.

An illustration of these trends can be seen in the recent history of the Detroit Tigers:

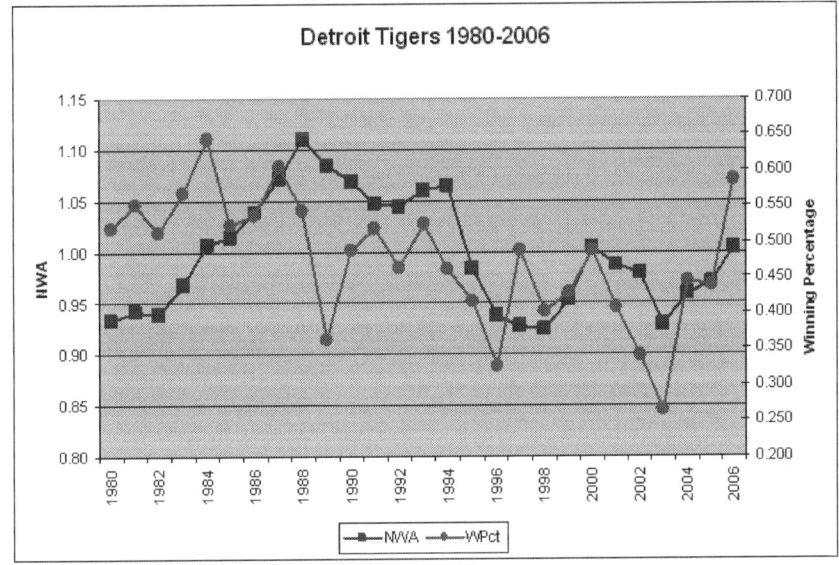

The Tigers reached their peak winning percentage in 1984 with a team that had aged steadily since 1980 and was at that time slightly above the mean age. That group continued to age, and while the team performed well through 1988, they went over the cliff in 1989 as veterans like Darrell Evans moved on and Chet Lemon became unproductive. They retooled with the likes of Cecil Fielder and Travis Fryman in the early 1990s and remained competitive until the decline and retirement of first Lou Whitaker and then Alan Trammell following the 1996 season. They rebuilt again with Bobby Higginson, Jeff Weaver, and Tony Clark before turning wholesale to the youth movement as Dave Dombrowski took the reigns in 2002. Since then the team has gotten older with aggressive free agent signings prior to the 2004 season and progressively better as the youngsters jelled with the veterans in 2006, winning 95 games with a team whose age was slightly higher than average.

Maturing
Is there a lesson here? If anything, these results should simply serve as a reminder that youth (at the team level anyway) is not necessarily all it's cracked up to be. While young teams can win (the 1928 New York Giants, 1948 Brooklyn Dodgers, and 2001 Twins are three examples), they're often battling uphill against teams with a substantial veteran presence. Maturing that young talent and supplementing it with veterans at the appropriate time, like the recent Tigers, is what can make for a formidable combination.

CAPTAIN, OH CAPTAIN
Prestige, D, and Derek Jeter
Christina Kahrl

Riffing on Derek Jeter's declining defense at shortstop, Christina Kahrl noted that certain players' iconic standing can get in the way of what's best for their teams.

One area in which the present really shouldn't compare poorly with the past is in legend-making. However much how the story that gets told might be different, we still have heroes on the diamond whose reputations transcend what they do and how well. Nowhere is that more apparent than in the case of "The Captain," Yankee great Derek Jeter, future Hall of Famer.

A long-running debate over Jeter's virtues as a defender has been a basic touchstone of the sabermetric landscape for almost as long as Jeter has been a major leaguer, and assessments of his value with the glove mark one of the most startlingly specific divisions between analysts and scouts, between performance and anecdotal observation, between documented statistical evidence and reputation. In his prime, the argument was relatively pointless, as Jeter's tremendous position-relative value helped power the last Yankees dynasty. When Jeter was able to provide a Wins Above Replacement mark of 6.9—a mark that includes his defense—as recently as 2006, the debate was puerile, if not downright academic. Ask any GM if he'd like a seven-win player at shortstop, and he'll say yes. Players this good, statistically or in the flesh, don't grow on trees.

However, with Jeter's WARP down to 3.5 in 2007 and 2.5 last season, and with his overall offensive contributions coming down from MVP-worthy to "merely" very good, especially in the power department, we start getting into questions over whether or not his recent decline as a defender might really re-spark the question of whether or not Jeter really belongs at short, or if the Yankees might not be better off putting him at another position. While the arguments over how descriptive and effective different contemporary defensive metrics are rage for good reason, their near unanimity on The Captain's limitations should be damning. Clay Davenport's new play-by-play metric that debuts in this year's edition of the BP annual sees Jeter's work with leather costing the Yankees 18 runs in 2007 and another 12 in 2008. John Dewan's Plus/Minus system from the *Bill James Handbook* rates Jeter the worst shortstop in total Plus/Minus of the last three years. Other metrics have seen his fielding value move around a bit, but what they have to say about Jeter's leather work is rarely complimentary. On a scouting level, as strong-armed as he is, his range afield has become an obvious issue, just as it did for Cal Ripken in his mid-30s.

The problem with suggesting such a thing, of course, is that playing shortstop for the Yankees has become a thing of celebrity unimagined in the days of Alvaro Espinoza or Bucky Dent or Gene Michael, and that's because Jeter has been so good for so long that there shouldn't be any question that he's the best shortstop in the history of the franchise. This association of a high-profile player—indeed, a celebrity ballplayer in his own right—with his position is seen as a major factor militating against even suggesting that Jeter move to some other spot on the field.

Where this over-developed sense of some slight being associated with recognizing the obvious and moving a great player to another position came from, I don't know. The recent controversy over the Rangers asking Gold Glove winner Michael Young to move from short to third in camp this spring makes it clear that players of lesser stature than Jeter can, after all, be asked by their teams to do something that fits within the ballclub's long-term planning. If prestige associated with position is the problem, since when did playing center field for the Yankees become an indignity? What, Mickey Mantle or Joe DiMaggio or Bernie Williams were nobodies playing nowhere? Perhaps only until very recently, center field in the Big Apple used to be baseball's highest-profile piece of real estate, going back for generations.

There was a point in time when Robin Yount was every bit the signature franchise player for the Brewers that Jeter is for the Yankees today, a winner of the AL MVP Award in 1982, and one of the game's trinity of great shortstops of that period, along with Ripken and the Tigers' Alan Trammell. By 1985, however, persistent shoulder problems forced Milwaukee to start thinking in terms of moving Yount to the outfield, and by the age of 30, he'd settled in as their center fielder, filling a position at which the team had an obvious need. (Skip rhyme schemes, there's a reason why nobody's singing songs about where Paul Householder has gone.) This wasn't the downslope of the man's career or a case of his being put out to a figurative pasture as well as a literal one, as Yount won another AL MVP Award in 1989.

There are risks, of course. There's the cautionary tale of the Brewers' attempted shift of infielder Bill Hall to center in 2007, which inspired them to go get Mike Cameron (a name that coincidentally seems to come up a lot as a proposed short-term solution for the Yankees' problem in center). Also, asking a player in his age-35 season to move from shortstop to center very obviously isn't like the storied switch of Mickey Mantle as a teenager in the minors, or even Bobby Murcer's move from short to the outfield in the late '60s. But maybe just framing the proposition within the context of those switches and their place in Yankees history might help engender some acceptance of a move certain to elicit months of howling on sports radio or on sports pages. (If fear of that howling is a factor in not making a change, that would be an unfortunate abdication of responsibility from the people paid to make these kinds of calls.)

Obviously, getting Jeter's buy-in is a real-world problem for a team with a real-world need for a center fielder, because the margins are too thin in the tough AL East for the Yankees to rely on the wrong Cabrera in the lineup. Crying over last year's spilled Melky won't help you catch up to the Rays and Red Sox, but signing Orlando Cabrera, providing the team with a useful-enough hitter and a slick-fielding asset at short could make a small but important difference to a bad defensive ballclub. Last season's Yankees ranked 25th in the major leagues in Defensive Efficiency (their ability to convert balls in play into outs) and Park-Adjusted Defensive Efficiency, and no positions see more chances than the middle infield.

Swapping Jeter out at short to address the team's need for a center fielder would be the sort of win/win move that can let the Yankees return to the top of the standings while breaking in their new stadium, and it does nothing to damage the Captain's place in franchise history. If Yount or Ripken, MVP winners and top stars in their day, could agree to help their teams and themselves to make these switches, you need to ask yourself why Jeter should be any different, especially when the need has gone from debatable to obvious.

🕗 OCTOBER 21, 2008   http://bbp.cx/a/8235

PROSPECTUS HIT AND RUN
Penning a New Recipe
Jay Jaffe

The 2008 Rays benefited from vastly improved defense, but Jay Jaffe noted that that wasn't the only historic improvement that catapulted them to the World Series.

You wouldn't know it given the way that their bullpen pitched at times during the latter portion of the American League Championship Series, but the Rays likely wouldn't have reached this year's World Series without the remarkable turnaround achieved by that unit. By a couple of measures, the performance of the Tampa Bay bullpen qualifies as historically significant.

In 2007, the Rays' bullpen finished dead last in the majors with -1.8 WXRL. As if that weren't bad enough, the bullpen's Fair Run Average—adjusting its runs allowed per nine innings for its performance in handling inherited runners—virtually tied for the worst of all time at 6.80. Roughly speaking, that's about three runs allowed for every four innings, a long night of watching a relief corps fritter away a shaky starter's five-inning effort. Here's a quick look at the relievers most responsible for this debacle (all stats for relief appearances only):

Pitcher	IP	FRA	WXRL	LEV
Gary Glover	77.1	4.45	0.7	1.12
Brian Stokes	62.1	6.75	-1.3	1.15
Al Reyes	60.2	5.18	2.6	1.78
Shawn Camp	40.0	8.36	-0.9	0.98
Juan Salas	36.1	5.42	0.0	0.67
Scott Dohmann	32.2	2.87	1.1	0.96
Dan Wheeler	25.0	7.73	0.2	1.75
Casey Fossum	24.2	9.92	-0.9	1.02
Jae Kuk Ryu	23.1	7.41	-0.7	0.75
Grant Balfour	22.0	7.39	-0.4	0.77

Pretty ugly, isn't it? Rays manager Joe Maddon had just two pitchers whose FRAs were below 5.00, workhorse Glover and journeyman Dohmann, the latter of whom didn't arrive until the second half. So bare was the cupboard of reliable relievers that Maddon was often stuck using ones with FRAs above 6.00 in higher-leverage roles, virtually guaranteeing disaster. The team had overseen the recovery of Reyes from Tommy John surgery in 2006, and he rewarded that patience by getting off to a hot start by compiling a 2.17 ERA through mid-June, converting his first 17 save opportunities, but he was rocked for a 7.39 ERA the rest of the way while converting 10 of 14 opportunities. On the other hand, there weren't all that many leads to risk being blown.

Maddon and GM Andrew Friedman couldn't be blamed for wanting to burn the bullpen to the ground and start over, and that's almost what they did. They signed free agents Troy Percival and Trever Miller and shifted 2007 starters Jason Hammel and J.P. Howell to the bullpen. Here's what they got (relief stats only):

Name	IP	FRA	WXRL	LEV
J.P. Howell	89.1	2.78	4.6	1.41
Dan Wheeler	66.1	2.94	2.1	1.84
Grant Balfour	58.1	0.96	3.4	1.34
Jason Hammel	50.2	5.81	0.7	0.84
Troy Percival	45.2	5.26	1.7	1.51
Trever Miller	43.1	3.32	1.5	1.07
Gary Glover	34.0	6.21	0.5	0.81
Al Reyes	22.2	4.86	0.0	0.98
Chad Bradford	19.0	2.65	0.8	1.53
David Price	8.2	1.20	0.1	0.60

Percival, who'd come out of retirement to put together a nice second half in St. Louis in 2007, was installed as the closer, and despite serving stints on the DL in June and July, he saved 27 games and put up a 3.69 ERA into mid-August before injuring his knee while fielding a bunt. He was rocked for seven runs in his first four appearances upon returning, lost his closer job and pitched sparingly while dealing with assorted maladies, and was left off of the post-season roster. Balfour and Wheeler, acquired in separate deals near the 2007 trade deadline, both filled in for Percival, with the former coming up from Triple-A Durham and carving out a roster spot for himself in the closer's absence. Howell emerged as a multi-inning lefty stopper, giving Maddon a much more versatile palette to draw on for the late innings, while Miller did solid work as a lefty specialist. Meanwhile, 2007 mainstays Glover and Reyes both struggled with injuries and ineffectiveness and were cut loose in midseason as more effective pitchers were added to the roster; Reyes was designated for assignment shortly after the team traded for Bradford in early August.

It all worked like a charm, as the Rays led the majors in WXRL with 15.2 and finished fourth in reliever FRA at 3.70. Their improvements in both categories qualify as the largest year-to-year gains in our database, which now goes back to 1954. Here are the top 20 in year-to-year change in WXRL:

Team	WXRL	Prev	Diff
Rays	15.2	-1.8	17.0
Indians	13.5	-1.5	15.1
Padres	16.0	1.3	14.7
Phillies	11.3	-2.7	14.0
Astros	13.3	-0.4	13.7
Twins	16.7	3.5	13.2
Dodgers	11.8	-1.1	12.9
Indians	10.4	-2.4	12.8
Mets	17.8	5.0	12.8
Cardinals	15.0	2.4	12.6
Braves	5.9	-6.6	12.5
Braves	7.8	-4.6	12.4
Yankees	14.2	1.8	12.3
Padres	15.9	3.8	12.1
Royals	10.4	-1.6	12.0
Cubs	8.8	-2.4	11.2
Braves	18.9	7.9	11.0
Padres	11.0	0.6	10.4
Astros	11.1	0.8	10.4
Mariners	12.0	1.8	10.2
Braves	11.4	1.2	10.2

As usual, there are plenty of good stories to be told starting from such a list. Fourteen out of these 21 teams made the postseason, and five of them, including the Rays, won pennants: the worst-to-first 1991 Braves, the 1996 Yankees, the 1998 Padres, and the 2004 Cardinals.

The 1990 Braves had tallied the third-worst WXRL total in our database, and managers Russ Nixon and Bobby Cox had used nine different pitchers to close out ballgames, with Joe Boever leading the pack with eight saves but a 5.92 FRA and -1.2 WXRL before being mercifully traded to the Phillies. The 1991 Braves benefited greatly from the arrivals of grizzled veteran free-agent Juan Berenguer and rookie Mike Stanton, and sealing the deal was one of the great waiver-period acquisitions of all time, Alejandro Pena. Acquired from the Mets on August 28 for Joe Roa (who never threw a pitch for New York), Pena saved 11 games and put up a 0.18 FRA and 2.0 WXRL over the last five weeks of the season. The Braves won the NL West by a single game and went all the way to Game Seven of the World Series.

The 1995 Yankees had returned the storied franchise to the postseason despite a bullpen that finished second to last in the league in WXRL. Although John Wetteland had saved 31 games, a rocky two-week period in August saw him turn three save opportunities into losses, and he finished with just 1.6 WXRL. His set-up men weren't much to write home about either, but that changed for the better the following year, when a second-year pitcher named Mariano Rivera emerged as one of the league's top relievers, striking out 130 hitters in 107 2/3 innings and finishing second in the AL in WXRL at 6.9. Wetteland himself finished fourth at 6.0. That combo played a huge role in the Yankees' first world championship in 18 years under new manager Joe Torre; in fact, they're the only team on this list to win it all.

Speaking of all-time greats like Rivera, the ups and downs of Trevor Hoffman play a role in no fewer than three separate appearances for the Padres on this list, including the 1998 pennant-winners. The future all-time saves leader had topped the 30-save mark for the first time in his career in 1995, but thanks to seven blown saves, he totaled just 0.7 WXRL while sporting a flabby 4.14 FRA amid an awful bullpen. Relying on a much-improved changeup, Hoffman increased his strikeout rate from 8.8 per nine to 11.4 in 1996 and led the league with 7.7 WXRL, while set-up men Tim Worrell and Doug Bochtler finished 10th and 11th, helping the Pad squad to the third-best turnaround of all-time, not to mention the second playoff berth in franchise history. All three pitchers fell off in 1997, with Worrell ending up south of replacement level at -0.3, one of three Padre pitchers to total at least 50 relief innings and a negative WXRL. Hoffman rebounded in 1998, not only leading the league in WXRL again, but also setting a career high with the seventh-best total of all time. Dan Miceli augmented that work by placing ninth, tops among NL set-up men.

The 2003 Cardinals were hamstrung by the fact that Jason Isringhausen missed the first 63 games of the year recovering from off-season shoulder surgery. Steve Kline, Cal Eldred, and Jeff Fassero tried to hold down the fort with predictably bad results; none of them managed even 1.0 WXRL for the year. Izzy rebounded to put up 4.9 WXRL in 2004, good for sixth in the league, while Ray King—acquired over the winter along with Adam Wainwright and Jason Marquis in a deal for J.D. Drew—pitched in with 3.1 mark, a high total for a lefty specialist. Additionally, Kiko Calero and Julian Tavarez both cracked the top 30 to round out the pen. The Cardinals finished second to the Eric Gagne-led Dodgers in WXRL and won 105 games—the fifth-highest total of any post-war NL team—and the pennant, before falling to the Red Sox in the World Series.

The 2006 Mets and 2007 Indians both came within one win of joining the above ranks, but their bullpen turnarounds were nonetheless noteworthy. The former got a huge shot in the arm by upgrading from Braden Looper to Billy Wagner at closer; Wagner finished second in the league in WXRL, while Aaron Heilman and Duaner Sanchez cracked the top 15, and Chad Bradford placed 27th. All told, those Mets posted the fourth-best team WXRL total in our database. The Tribe rebounded from an ugly 2006 thanks to the stellar work of set-up men Rafael Betancourt (second in the league in WXRL) and Rafael Perez (13th despite being a mid-season call-up); much-maligned closer Joe Borowski ranked 16th despite a 4.84 FRA inflated by some early-season woes. Alas, all three tailed off dramatically in 2008; Borowski was released in early July after struggling with triceps issues, while Betancourt saw his FRA rise from 1.07 to 5.43. The team's 2008 falloff ranks as the fourth-worst in history, and it's an all-too-familiar story in Cleveland; their 2006 falloff ranks as the third-worst.

Cherry-picking a few highlights among the rest: the 1974 Braves represent a rebound from the second-worst WXRL total in our database. Phil Niekro had led the club in WXRL in 1973, compiling 0.9 WXRL after beginning the year in the bullpen due to shoulder stiffness. Tom House, who was below replacement level in 1973, rebounded to lead the league in WXRL the following year... The 2002 Braves own the second-highest WXRL in our database. In his first full year as closer, John Smoltz finished second to Gagne in WXRL, while Mike Remlinger and salvage-job Chris Hammond—who hadn't pitched in the majors since 1998—placed in the top 10... The 2002 Twins boasted five of the league's top 20 relievers, with lefty J.C. Romero (5.5 WXRL) ranking third in the league and closer Everyday Eddie Guardado placing seventh... The 2007 Royals rank as high as they do thanks in large part to GM Dayton Moore hitting the Rule 5 jackpot by plucking Joakim Soria from the Padres; the rookie ranked fifth in the league in WXRL and topped that by finishing third this year... The 2000 Mariners represent the team that rebounded from a 6.80 FRA the year before, the mark with which the 2007 Rays virtually tied.

On that note, here's a quick look at the teams that put up the biggest year-to-year Fair Run Average improvements:

Year	Team	FRA	Prev	Diff
2008	Rays	3.73	6.80	-3.07
1974	Braves	3.47	5.79	-2.32
2005	Indians	3.10	5.40	-2.30
1972	Yankees	3.11	5.37	-2.26
1960	Cardinals	3.40	5.58	-2.18
1979	Orioles	3.12	5.23	-2.11
1998	Padres	3.65	5.74	-2.09
1988	Brewers	3.16	5.20	-2.04
2001	Phillies	4.28	6.29	-2.01
2004	Cardinals	3.29	5.29	-2.00
2001	Blue Jays	4.23	6.23	-2.00
1963	Athletics	4.25	6.25	-2.00
1958	Reds	3.52	5.51	-1.99
2000	Mariners	4.89	6.80	-1.91
1967	Red Sox	3.38	5.27	-1.89
1960	Tigers	3.69	5.58	-1.89
1991	Braves	4.18	6.01	-1.83
2001	Astros	4.11	5.90	-1.79
2001	Mariners	3.14	4.89	-1.75
1971	Mets	2.90	4.64	-1.74

Not only do the aforementioned 2000 Mariners make the list, but the 2001 Mariners do as well; they improved by nearly as much while helping the M's to their 116-win season. Closer Kazuhiro Sasaki and set-up man Arthur Rhodes, both of whom arrived prior to the 2000 season, were the biggest keys to those improvements, with Jeff Nelson putting up an excellent 2001 to push them even further.

Overall, this list is less playoff-centric than the previous one, as just nine out of the 20 teams made the playoffs. Unlike the other list, several teams from the Fifties and Sixties turn up here. Teams didn't use their bullpens as often back then, preventing large year-to-year WXRL fluctuations, but shifts in performance as captured by FRA could still be dramatic. Of the older teams on this list, the standout is the 1967 Red Sox, the "Impossible Dream" team that returned the Sox to the World Series for the first time since 1946. Along with a stellar year from John Wyatt (2.76 FRA, 3.7 WXRL), they got outstanding work from mid-season call-up Sparky Lyle (1.20 FRA, 1.2 WXRL), who allowed just three out of 28 inherited runners to score. The pennant roll also include the 1979 Orioles, who benefited greatly from the rebound of Tippy Martinez (5.66 FRA in 1978, 2.61 in 1979) and the work of rookies Tim Stoddard and Sammy Stewart, as well as mainstay Don Stanhouse.

Personnel turnover is a recurring theme of these reversals. That may seem like an obvious point, and it's certainly not uniform across the board; some of these turnarounds were based simply on improvements or rebounds from the pitchers already on hand. Nonetheless, in general the teams who enjoyed the most dramatic bullpen turnarounds did so by shaking things up, whether that meant going the free-agent route to find proven talent and stability, working youngsters into the mix, or overturning rocks to find the next Hammond or Soria. The 2008 Rays did a little of each, showing some creativity by relying on 38-year-old comeback kid Percival at the start of the year, and later turning to top 2007 pick David Price, who made just his eighth big-league appearance to close out Game Séven of the ALCS in an "October Surprise" for the ages. That outside-the-box thinking, as much as anything else, is why they're playing in a World Series for the first time in their 11-year history.

PROSPECTUS HIT AND RUN
Oh Rickey, You're So Fine
Jay Jaffe

DECEMBER 15, 2008 • http://bbp.cx/a/8375

When Rickey Henderson became eligible for the Hall of Fame, Jay Jaffe used the Jaffe WARP Score system (JAWS) to put the Bill James' "If you could split him in two, you'd have two Hall of Famers" line to the test.

Last week, I discussed the Hall of Fame Veterans Committee ballot results and previewed Clay Davenport's revisions of the Wins Above Replacement Player system, the underlying currency of my JAWS Hall of Fame analysis system. Today, I begin tackling the 2009 Baseball Writers Association of America ballot.

For those tuning in for the first time, this marks the sixth year in which I've used the very self-consciously named Jaffe WARP Score system (JAWS) to examine the ballot. The goal of JAWS is to identify candidates who are as good or better than the average Hall of Famer at their position, a bar set so as to avoid further diluting the quality of the institution's membership. WARP totals are the coin of the realm for this endeavor because they normalize all performance records in major-league history to the same scoring environment, adjusting for park effects, quality of competition, and length of schedule. Pitchers, hitters, and fielders are thus rated above or below one consistent replacement level, simplifying cross-era comparisons. JAWS does not incorporate non-statistical considerations—awards, championships, post-season performance, rap sheet, urine test results—but that's not to say they should be left by the wayside. They're just not the focus here, though they'll be discussed in the context of the various candidacies.

Election to the Hall of Fame requires a player to perform at both a very high level and for a long time, so JAWS identifies a player's peak using his seven best WARP scores (for this exercise, WARP refers exclusively to the adjusted-for-all-time version, WARP3). Effectively, a player's best seasons get double-counted, an appropriate strategy given what we know about pennants added and the premium value of star talent: individual greatness can have a non-linear effect on a team's results both in the standings and on the bottom line.

The career and peak WARP totals for each Hall of Famer and candidate on the ballot are tabulated and then averaged [(Career WARP + Peak WARP) / 2] to come up with a candidate's JAWS score.

JAWS averages for the enshrined are calculated at each position to provide a baseline for comparison, but the lowest-ranked player at each position (and four pitchers) are omitted before that calculation. Invariably these are Veterans Committee selections who lag far behind the pack, lowering the bar with scores that might be one-third of the position leader.

As noted last week, Clay is in the process of implementing two major changes to the WARP system. First, he's raised the replacement-level floor by about 20 runs per player, lifting it significantly beyond the level of the bottom-of-the-barrel 1899 Cleveland Spiders or a current Double-A player to conform to a more modern definition of the major-league replacement level. Second, he's adding a play-by-play-based fielding component for the years where it is available, the "Retrosheet Era" which—for the purposes of our database at least—goes back to 1954.

Alas, the tail end of Clay's R&D effort is taking place during the chaotic and often stressful period known around these parts as "book season," where our authors and editors are slaving away on player comments and essays for our 2009 annual. The vanguard of Clay's fielding changes are geared towards the book, and as such, the fielding side of things for earlier years is not ready for prime time yet. Despite this awkward situation, I've decided that the new replacement level itself is an important enough step forward to merit incorporation into this year's JAWS evaluation. The downside is that the data used here is not yet on the DT player cards available on our site, making it impossible for readers to play along at home. Furthermore, it's still using a derivative of the older version of the fielding system that will soon be replaced for the years in which we have enough play-by-play data. As acknowledged with regards to the VC ballot, we're on the bleeding edge of a new ballgame here. When necessary, we'll refer back to past years' results for perspective and guidance.

We'll cut through further minutiae to save space; additional details on the nuts and bolts can be found here. Below are the JAWS benchmarks, the adjusted positional averages once the low man on the totem pole is removed, to which I'll refer throughout the series:

Pos	#	EqA	BRAR	BRAA	FRAA	Career	Peak	JAWS
C	13	.286	420	210	77	78.3	50.9	64.6
1B	18	.306	742	487	-10	75.8	48.4	62.1
2B	18	.288	569	299	86	84.9	54.6	69.8
3B	11	.294	653	374	108	89.4	56.1	72.8
SS	21	.275	435	159	117	79.5	52.2	65.9
LF	18	.303	743	473	2	76.8	48.2	62.5
CF	17	.307	733	484	10	84.2	52.5	68.4
RF	23	.306	804	526	35	87.9	52.2	70.1
CI	29	.301	709	445	34	80.8	51.3	66.1
MI	39	.281	494	221	103	81.9	53.2	67.6
IF	68	.290	586	317	74	81.5	52.4	66.9
OF	58	.305	764	498	17	83.4	51.0	67.2
Middle	69	.288	540	285	75	81.8	52.6	67.2
Corners	70	.303	749	479	26	82.2	50.8	66.5
Hitter	139	.296	646	383	50	82.0	51.7	66.8

Other abbreviations: EqA is Equivalent Average. Batting Runs Above Replacement (BRAR) and Batting Runs Above Average (BRAA) are both included because they make good secondary measures of career and peak value. Fielding Runs Above Average (FRAA) is a bit more comprehensible to the average reader than measuring fielding from replacement level.

Not every position is represented on this year's ballot, and many candidates have been addressed at length in prior years. In the interest of leading with the good stuff, I'm starting with the 2009 ballot's marquee addition, a man who is in a class by himself:

Rickey Henderson

H	HR	RBI	AVG	OBP	SLG	ASG	MVP	GG	HoFS	HOFM	Bal	2008%
3055	297	1,115	.279	.401	.419	10	1	1	52.6	183.5	0.0	---

	EqA	BRAR	BRAA	FRAA	Career	Peak	JAWS
Henderson	.316	1285	906	194	155.7	74.9	115.3
AVG HoF LF	.303	743	473	2	76.8	48.2	62.5

Henderson's Hall of Fame-ready credentials would dwarf the rest of the BBWAA field on the ballot in nearly any year. Widely acknowledged as the greatest leadoff hitter of all time, he's the all-time leader in both stolen bases and runs scored as well as being a member of the 3,000 Hit Club. "If you could split him in two, you'd have two Hall of Famers," wrote Bill James in his *New Bill James Historical Baseball Abstract* before anointing him "the greatest power/speed combination of all time (except maybe Barry Bonds)." Indeed, Henderson's dazzling speed and derring-do on the basepaths obscured the other facets of his game. He certainly had pop, setting a record with 81 career leadoff home runs and barely missing out on the 300 Home Run Club. He had range afield, if not a great arm. He was a complete ballplayer, something of a sabermetric ideal; while he may have led the league in OBP only once, he finished in the top three nine times, and 16 times in the top 10. When the gold-plated Baseball Prospectus skyscraper is eventually built in a major metropolis to be named later, a 20-foot-tall bronze statue of Henderson will undoubtedly adorn its entrance.

Chosen in the fourth round of the 1976 amateur draft out of Oakland Technical High School by the hometown Athletics, Henderson was just 20 when he was called up to the majors by the A's, debuting on June 24, 1979. He led off the bottom of the first inning with a double off of John Henry Johnson but was thrown out at home plate before he could score his first run. Later in the game he would single and steal second base. From that day forward, he was off to the races. Despite Henderson's arrival, the 1979 A's were a wretched ballclub, finishing 54-108. Their fortunes turned the next year, when former Yankees manager Billy Martin brought to town an aggressive style of play that gave Henderson the green light on the basepaths. In 1980, as the A's climbed to second in the AL West with an 83-79 record, Henderson hit .303/.420/.399 and drew 117 walks (second in the AL), thanks in part to the exaggerated crouch of his batting stance. "Rickey Henderson's strike zone is smaller than Hitler's heart," wrote the great sportswriter Jim Murray. Henderson explained his stance to *Sports Illustrated*'s Ron Fimrite a few years later:

> Anyway, I found that if I squatted down real low at the plate, the way I do now, I could see the ball better. I also knew it threw the pitcher off. I found that I could put my weight on my back foot and still turn my hips on the swing. I'm down so low I don't have much of a strike zone. Sometimes, walking so much even gets me mad. Last year Ed Ott of the Angels got so frustrated because the umpire was calling balls that would've been strikes on anybody else, that he stood up and shouted at me, "Stand up and hit like a man." I guess I do that to people.

Once Henderson got on base, it was showtime. In 1980, he became just the third player of the 20th century to steal 100 bases, though he was caught 26 times, for a 79.4 percent success rate. Urged on by Martin, he reached the century milestone by swiping an astounding 34 bags from September 1 onward. It was the first of seven straight years in which he'd lead the AL in stolen bases; he did so 12 times in all. It was also the first of five times Henderson would top 10.0 WARP, according to the new baseline; he finished with 10.8.

In 1981, the A's reached the playoffs for the first time since their mid-'70s dynasty by dint of being in the AL West lead when the strike hit. Henderson swiped 56 bags during the shortened season and hit .319/.408/.437, good enough to help him place second to Rollie Fingers in the league's MVP voting. The team slumped to 68-94 the following year, as the pitchers that Martin had pushed to finish what they started in 1980 and 1981 began to break down. Henderson kept things interesting, setting a modern single-season record that year by swiping 130 bases, breaking Lou Brock's 1974 mark of 118. He was also caught a record 42 times, for a success rate of 75.6 percent. He would become more efficient in the years to come; in 1983 he was successful on 108 out of 127 attempts, an 85.0 percent clip.

Henderson was traded by the A's to the Yankees as part of a seven-player deal at the Winter Meetings in December 1984, in part because the A's felt they couldn't afford him, and in part because his contract status was perceived as having affected his availability. "Henderson had filed for arbitration three straight years, and when he lost last season and had to struggle along with a $950,000 salary, he let the decision affect his play," wrote *Sports Illustrated*'s Henry Hecht. "Quite simply, he dogged it at times, and of the 20 games he missed, probably half were for no apparent reason." More than two decades before Manny Being Manny, Rickey was accused of being Rickey.

Henderson signed a five-year, $8.6 million deal with the Yankees upon being acquired. Shifting to center field on a full-time basis as a Yankee in 1985, he put up a monster season, hitting .314/.419/.516, stealing 80 bases in 90 attempts, and setting new career highs with 24 homers and 146 runs—a performance good for 10.8 WARP3. Alas, he finished just third in the MVP balloting behind teammate Don Mattingly (who drove in 145 runs while hitting .324/.371/.567) and George Brett. Where did the BBWAA voters think Mattingly's high RBI total came from? Rickey topped his '85 totals for home runs and stolen bases the following year, but his .263/.358/.469 was a major step down. By 1989 the Yankees felt his skills had begun to fade. Unable to complete a new three-year deal, they sent him back to Oakland for three players on June 21 of that year. As with any escape from the orbit of Dallas Green, the move rejuvenated Henderson, who joined Tony La Russa's defending AL champions, a club that needed an offensive infusion due to the injuries and subpar performances of the Bash Brothers, Mark McGwire and Jose Canseco. Henderson hit .294/.425/.438 and stole 52 bases in 85 games after being traded, helping the A's to their second straight division title and then winning MVP honors in the ALCS by hitting .400/.609/1.000 with two homers and eight stolen bases. He hit .474/.524/.895 in Oakland's four-game sweep of the Giants in the "Bay Bridge Series," but the victory was overshadowed by the Loma Prieta earthquake, which forced a 10-day suspension of play mid-Series.

Henderson helped the A's to their third straight pennant in 1990 with a season worth a career-best 13.8 WARP. He hit .325/.439/.577 with a career-high 28 homers and 65 steals and earned the MVP award (his first and last), but despite his playing well in the World Series, the A's were swept by the Reds. The following year, he stepped into the all-time record books for the first time: on May 1, 1991, at the age of 32, he broke Brock's carer record of 918 stolen bases. In celebrating the record during a stoppage of play, he raised the hackles of some observers by declaring, "Lou Brock was a great base stealer, but today I am the greatest of all time," as Brock stood by. While he would add another 487 when all was said and done, putting the record out of reach for a long,

long time, the comment provided ammunition to critics only too ready to accuse him of cockiness. Henderson would earn another World Series ring with the Blue Jays in 1993, when he was acquired via a deadline-day trade from the A's. That deal began the peripatetic phase of his career. He would serve two more stints in Oakland while making stops in San Diego, Anaheim, Los Angeles, Seattle, Boston, and New York. His greatest success during those years came with the 1999 Mets; at the age of 40, he hit .315/.423/.466 for a club that advanced to the NLCS. Alas, Henderson's year was overshadowed by a report that he had joined teammate Bobby Bonilla to play cards in the clubhouse after being removed from the game in the eighth inning of the decisive Game Six.

Indeed, stories about Rickey Henderson often tend to obscure his greatness as a player, much as they did with Yogi Berra. Everybody's got their list of favorite Rickeyisms, starting with his tendency to talk about himself in the third person. ("Illeism? Rickey's not sick...") It didn't even matter if the stories were true, or, like the John Olerud helmet tale, demonstrably false. My own favorite example of the mainstream media being content to print the legend instead of the fact came when none other than Peter Gammons tried to explain away then-Padre Henderson's role in inciting a 2001 blowup with Brewers manager Davey Lopes when he stole a base in the seventh inning with a 12-5 lead:

> What precipitated the Davey Lopes-Rickey Henderson blowup was that Rickey was sick and had been sleeping in the clubhouse when he was told he had to pinch-run for Tony Gwynn. Henderson, who is trying to get the career runs record, went to first base not knowing the score, looked around and saw second base empty and asked first-base coach Alan Trammell how many outs there were.
>
> "Two," replied Trammell.
>
> "Rickey can't score from first base," said Henderson, who proceeded to take off for second base and thus incurred the wrath of his former mentor.

It's a bit funny, at least until you spend two seconds looking at the box score to see that Henderson didn't enter the game as a pinch-runner—he was the starting left fielder. Furthermore, the "stolen base" was ruled defensive indifference. But skip the facts, we need a colorful anecdote!

Back to Henderson's playing, his 2001 season with the Padres was rich in milestones, as he broke Babe Ruth's all-time record for walks, Ty Cobb's record for runs, and, on the final day of the season, collected his 3,000th hit. His final big-league appearance was with the Dodgers in 2003, but he spent the 2004 and 2005 seasons playing in independent leagues in the hope that he might get one last shot at the majors.

As if his greatness needed any further proof. Via the revised replacement level, Henderson's career WARP total and JAWS score both rank ninth all-time, and his peak score ranks 12th. With the caveat that the new defensive system could bump that ranking up or down, the important point is that Rickey Henderson is in the class photo of the greatest ballplayers of all time:

Player	Career	Peak	JAWS
Babe Ruth	195.8	93.4	144.6
Barry Bonds	192.6	88.7	140.7
Willie Mays	177.5	80.4	129.0
Walter Johnson	169.2	87.7	128.5
Roger Clemens	162.0	78.3	120.2
Honus Wagner	158.8	76.2	117.5
Ty Cobb	158.5	76.4	117.5
Hank Aaron	159.6	72.4	116.0
Rickey Henderson	155.7	74.9	115.3
Stan Musial	152.7	75.7	114.2
Greg Maddux	141.6	76.7	109.2
Mel Ott	141.4	72.2	106.8
Tris Speaker	143.8	68.8	106.3
Eddie Collins	137.9	72.7	105.3
Pete Alexander	132.3	76.6	104.5
Rogers Hornsby	128.6	76.6	102.6
Cy Young	139.4	63.1	101.3
Ted Williams	128.2	74.2	101.2
Joe Morgan	127.5	73.5	100.5
Mickey Mantle	124.9	73.1	99.0

Not only is Henderson overwhelmingly worthy of a vote for the Hall of Fame, but it's hardly hyperbole to suggest that a ballot sent back without his name on it constitutes mail fraud. Given the blank-ballot protests of the past few years, it's unlikely that he'll be the first player ever to be elected unanimously, but he could challenge for the highest vote percentage of all time. Rickey Henderson will slide into Cooperstown head first and without a throw.

DECEMBER 29, 2008 http://bbp.cx/a/8394

PROSPECTUS HIT AND RUN
Throwing Rice
Jay Jaffe

Shortly before Jim Rice was inducted into the Hall of Fame, Jay Jaffe evaluated Jim Rice's candidacy and found his qualifications lacking.

In evaluating the Hall of Fame candidacies of Rickey Henderson and Tim Raines recently, I made a point of avoiding any discussion of Jim Rice for a simple reason: his candidacy doesn't merit being mentioned in the same breath. That's not to say that Rice wasn't an excellent ballplayer, but his relatively short career and the context surrounding it simply leave his case wanting. The BBWAA clearly feels otherwise, as Rice polled 72.2 percent of the vote last year, the ninth straight year he's received above 50 percent. Still, he fell 16 votes shy in his second-to-last year on the ballot. With his candidacy in its final year and surrounded by such controversy, we'll take a closer look at his case.

	H	HR	RBI	AVG	OBP	SLG
Jim Rice	2452	382	1,451	.298	.352	.502
Rickey Henderson	3055	297	1,115	.279	.401	.419
Tim Raines	2605	170	980	.294	.385	.425

	AS	MVP	GG	HOFS	HOFM	Bal	2008%
Jim Rice	7	1	0	42.9	147	14	72.20
Rickey Henderson	10	1	1	52.6	183.5	0	---
Tim Raines	7	0	0	46.8	90	1	24.30

	EqA	BRAR	BRAA	FRAA	Career	Peak	JAWS
Rice	.293	627	359	-41	55.1	39.6	47.4
Henderson	.316	1285	906	194	155.7	74.9	115.3
Raines	.309	905	608	8	94.3	54.9	74.6
AVG HOF LF	.303	743	473	2	76.8	48.2	62.5

HOFS & HOFM: Bill James' Hall of Fame Shares and Monitor.
Bal: How many years the player has appeared on the ballot.
2008%: The player's share of the vote in 2008.

Jim Rice was Boston's first pick in the 1971 draft, the 15th pick overall, passed over in favor of such luminaries as Danny Goodwin, Jay Franklin, Condredge Holloway, and Tom Veryzer. Not that the first round was entirely a bust, as Frank Tanana was taken just two picks ahead of Rice by the Angels, and Rick Rhoden was chosen five picks behind him by the Dodgers. Though he hit just .256/.311/.408 as an 18-year-old in the New York-Penn League, Rice climbed quickly through the Red Sox system, reaching Triple-A Pawtucket in late 1973 and Boston in late 1974 after a season at Pawtucket in which he won the International League Triple Crown and would earn *The Sporting News* Minor League Player of the Year honors. He made his major-league debut on August 19 and hit .269/.307/.373 in 24 games, mainly as a DH and pinch-hitter.

Just over two weeks later, fellow rookie Fred Lynn would debut as well. The following year the two players would help Boston win their first pennant since 1967, with Lynn winning both Rookie of the Year and MVP honors, a then-unprecedented feat; for the year, Lynn hit .331/.401/.566 with 21 homers, a season worth 8.3 WARP, using Clay Davenport's revised replacement level. Rice finished second in the Rookie of the Year balloting and third in MVP on the strength of a .309/.350/.491 line with 22 homers, but his season was worth only 4.1 WARP due to his lesser defensive value and much lower OBP and SLG numbers. Already he was overrated.

In any event, Rice missed the final week of the season and the entirety of Boston's post-season run due to a wrist injury. The Sox made it all the way to Game Seven of one of the greatest World Series ever played before finally falling to the Big Red Machine. It doesn't take much imagination to think that had he been available, Sox fans might have been spared three decades of misery awaiting that elusive World Championship.

Rice soon emerged as one of the league's top sluggers; he would place either first or second in slugging percentage in each of the next four years while leading the league in home runs in 1977 (39) and 1978 (46). He earned MVP honors for his 1978 performance, in which he hit .315/.370/.600 and finished with 406 total bases, the only other player besides Hank Aaron to reach the 400 plateau between 1949 and 1997. Rice's performance that year was worth a career-high 8.4 WARP. Alas, it wasn't quite enough to put the Sox over the top in an AL East race that came down to a Game 163 play-in, where Mike Torrez served up a meatball to Bucky Dent. You may have heard about it at some point.

Rice enjoyed another strong season in 1979 (.325/.381/.596, 39 HR, 7.1 WARP) but another hand injury cost him a month in 1980 and sapped his performance (.294/.336/.504, 24 HR, 3.0 WARP). He wouldn't reach a .500 slugging percentage in either of the next two seasons, though his 1982 performance heralded a rebound the following year: .305/.361/.550, with a league-leading 39 homers. However, his minimal defensive value kept his WARP at just 4.3.

That was the last time Rice's slugging percentage topped .500, but after two more down seasons, he had one more big year in 1986, hitting .324/.384/.490 with exactly 200 hits but "only" 20 homers, a season worth 5.5 WARP. At 33 years old, Rice's power may have been waning, but he was growing more disciplined as a hitter, setting career bests with 62 walks and that OBP. He finally made the postseason, hitting just .161 but homering twice in the ALCS against the Angels, then hitting .333/.455/.444 in Boston's traumatic seven-game World Series loss to the Mets.

Rice would never again come close to even his 1986 level. Over his final three seasons, he slugged a feeble .395, never topping 15 home runs. Knee problems were a factor, but surgery after the 1987 season failed to solve the problem. New manager Walpole Joe Morgan, who took over from John McNamara in mid-1988, made a power play shortly after taking the job by sending Spike Owen up to pinch-hit for Rice in the eighth inning of a close game. A shoving match ensued in the dugout and Rice was suspended for three games. The handwriting was on the wall, though he would linger on the roster for one more dismal year before finally drawing his release.

The proponents of Rice's Hall of Fame candidacy point to the way his power dominated his era, the respect he drew for his performances, and the fear he elicited. They have something of a point on the first two counts, which have their basis in fact. From 1976 to 1983, Rice finished either first or second in the league in slugging percentage five times, led the league in total bases four times and in home runs three times, and salted those accomplishments with several other top-10 finishes. He placed in the top five in MVP balloting six times, and made eight All-Star teams. Just about all of that is captured in his Hall of Fame Monitor Score, as noted above. According to that Bill James metric, Rice scores 147 points, where the average Hall of Famer—average at the time James was creating his system some 25 years ago, at least—scores 100. He did a ton of things that typical Hall of Famers do, basically.

As for the fear factor, there's a lot of hot air in circulation, and plenty of anger directed at those who would try to debunk the myths surrounding the truth. Rice may have intimidated the writers who covered him; Howard Bryant's *Shut Out: A Story of Race and Baseball in Boston* goes into great and painful detail on that front, unraveling Rice's tumultuous relationship with the media who covered him and the complex dynamics in play regarding his team and his city, and I strongly suspect at least some of the increased momentum his candidacy has received relates to some guilty consciences over the way things unfolded at the time.

Getting a raw deal from the beat reporters and columnists does not, however, change the facts surrounding his case, and any case one wishes to make about "fear" simply isn't reflected in the statistics. Opposing pitchers didn't pitch around Rice they way they pitch around Barry Bonds or Albert Pujols; Rice is tied for 179th in intentional walks, a stat that would seem to indicate some measure of fear. Among those tied with him at 77 intentionals are Fred Lynn, Geoff Jenkins, Claudell Washington, Terry Pendleton, Jerry Grote, and Clay Dalrymple. Hmmmm. In fact, Rice didn't walk much at all. Of the 118 players with at least 300 career home runs, he has the 14th-lowest walk rate per plate appearance:

Player	BB	PA	BB/PA	HR
Andre Dawson	589	10769	0.055	438
Vinny Castilla	423	7384	0.057	320
Joe Carter	527	9154	0.058	396
Lee May	487	8219	0.059	354
Matt Williams	469	7595	0.062	378
Juan Gonzalez	457	7155	0.064	434
Gary Gaetti	634	9817	0.065	360
Al Simmons	615	9515	0.065	307*
Andres Galarraga	583	8916	0.065	399
Dave Parker	683	10184	0.067	339
Orlando Cepeda	588	8695	0.068	379**
Ruben Sierra	610	8782	0.069	306
Ernie Banks	763	10395	0.073	512*
Jim Rice	670	9058	0.074	382
Willie Horton	620	8052	0.077	325

*: BBWAA-elected
**: VC-selected

That list contains some very good players, Hall of Famers as well as contemporaries of Rice who are currently on the BBWAA ballot, but none had to make his Cooperstown case on some intangible factor that wasn't represented in the stats. On the contrary, there are also free-swinging hackers like Joe Carter, Juan Gonzalez, and Ruben Sierra on that list—players who had some pop, but also a very large hole in their game regarding plate discipline. Rice actually has the second-highest OBP of the above group behind Hall of Famer Al Simmons, but it's a distant second, 28 points. He may have been slightly more disciplined than Orlando Cepeda, and he was certainly faster than Ernie Lombardi and taller than Rabbit Maranville. This isn't a strong building block for a vote.

The real problem, beyond the fact that concepts like fear aren't well-captured in baseball statistics and are prone to distortions of memory among those passing on the legend, is that Rice's offensive accomplishments received a considerable boost from playing half of his games in Fenway Park. For his career, Rice hit .320/.374/.546 with 208 homers in Fenway, but just .277/.330/.459 with 174 homers on the road. Taking advantage of one's home park is no crime; quite the contrary, most great sluggers get such a boost. But once you adjust for his park and league scoring environments via the WARP system, a good amount of the air is let out of the tires.

Rice's .293 EQA is an impressive figure, but it's still 10 points shy of the average Hall of Fame left fielder. His monster 1978 showing was good for a .314 EQA, which ranked third behind Ken Singleton's .323 and Amos Otis' .316, neither considered a dominant hitter at that point or any other. Rice's 130.7 Equivalent Runs paced the circuit, but he also used up more outs than all but three hitters, because again, he didn't actually walk very often (just 58 times in 746 plate appearances, including seven intentionals), and because he also grounded into a ton of double plays (15). Indeed, on the latter score, Rice ranks sixth all time, and in some pretty fair company—Cal Ripken, Hank Aaron, Carl Yastrzemski, Dave Winfield, and Eddie Murray—until you consider that all had at least 35 to 55 percent more plate appearances in their careers than Rice.

That short career is the other thing that dooms his candidacy. Rice's last productive season came at the age of 33, and he was done by 36. He thus falls more than 100 runs shy of the JAWS standards in Batting Runs Above Average and Batting Runs Above Replacement. Worse, he falls 21.7 WARP shy on the career front and 8.6 WARP shy on the peak front; as "dominant" as he was in his heyday, he was worth an average of 1.2 wins per year less than the typical Hall of Fame left fielder. Repeating the chart from the last time around, his JAWS score ranks only 35th among left fielders and ahead of only four Hall of Famers.

Rk	Player	Career	Peak	JAWS
1	Barry Bonds	192.6	88.7	140.7
2	Rickey Henderson	155.7	74.9	115.3
3	Stan Musial	152.7	75.7	114.2*
4	Ted Williams	128.2	74.2	101.2
5	Pete Rose	106.7	56.2	81.5
6	Tim Raines	94.3	54.9	74.6
7	Carl Yastrzemski	94.7	50.9	72.8*
8	Ed Delahanty	84.7	59.6	72.2**
9	Jim O'Rourke	94.3	46.5	70.4**
10	Willie Stargell	82.2	54.1	68.2*
11	Fred Clarke	81.1	43.9	62.5**
12	Jose Cruz	72.7	47.7	60.2
13	Jesse Burkett	72.1	47.5	59.8**
14	Al Simmons	71.6	47.0	59.3*
15	Tony Phillips	69.0	49.3	59.2
16	Albert Belle	61.9	53.2	57.6
17	Joe Medwick	67.1	46.5	56.8*
18	George Foster	62.7	50.8	56.8
19	Jimmy Sheckard	63.9	42.8	53.4
20	Bob Johnson	63.7	41.7	52.7
21	Goose Goslin	61.9	43.1	52.5**
22	Joe Kelley	59.9	44.9	52.4**
27	Zack Wheat	61.8	38.2	50.0**
29	Billy Williams	59.2	38.8	49.0*
35	Jim Rice	55.1	39.6	47.4
38	Ralph Kiner	47.9	43.4	45.7*
39	Lou Brock	54.6	36.0	45.3*
75	Chick Hafey	31.8	28.9	30.4**
81	Heinie Manush	31.3	27.1	29.2*

It's instructive to compare Rice's Hall of Fame case to that of another slugging left fielder who came along 15 years later and who was similarly dominant in his era, thanks in part to his park and league environments, while offering a similarly intimidating persona that brought the word "fear" into play on multiple levels. Said slugger, whom we'll call Player X for the bare moment it takes to make this comparison, also saw an early end to his career (after his age-33 season) and accumulated similar credentials:

	H	HR	RBI	AVG	OBP	SLG	AS	MVP	GG	HOFS	HOFM
Rice	2,452	382	1,451	.298	.352	.502	7	1	0	42.9	147.0
Player X	1,726	381	1,239	.295	.369	.564	5	0	0	36.1	134.5

	EqA	BRAR	BRAA	FRAA	Career	Peak	JAWS
Rice	.293	627	359	-41	55.1	39.6	47.4
Player X	.315	647	454	-50	61.9	53.2	57.6
AVG HOF LF	.303	743	473	2	76.8	48.2	62.5

Player X was in fact a better hitter of the pair after adjusting for context, and not by a little; his peak was worth two wins per year more than Rice. That player, who fell off the ballot after just two rounds of voting, was Albert Belle, and however feared he was as a hitter and a human being, the BBWAA voters have definitively decided that Albert Belle is not a Hall of Famer.

Neither is Rice, at least according to any comparison that rests on fact as opposed to legend. The BBWAA may well feel otherwise, however, and I strongly suspect he'll receive enough votes to get over the top. He won't be the worst mistake they've ever made, but he would be close, with the fifth-lowest JAWS score of any hitter ever voted in by that august body:

Player	Career	Peak	JAWS
Rabbit Maranville	49.8	32.2	41.0
Lou Brock	54.6	36.0	45.3
Ralph Kiner	47.9	43.4	45.7
Luis Aparicio	57.5	36.1	46.8
Jim Rice	55.1	39.6	47.4
Bill Terry	53.9	41.4	47.7

As good a player as he may have been, Rice's admission to Cooperstown would flatter neither the institution or the process. I suspect we'll have to learn to live with it nonetheless.

JUNE 2, 2004   http://bbp.cx/a/2926

YOU COULD LOOK IT UP
Gamesmanship, Dammit
Steven Goldman

As Steven Goldman made clear via a textual trip to the 1930s, a keen awareness of the rulebook and a willingness to exploit any edge often come in handy on the field.

In this week's Pinstriped Bible (one of the other columns in the Steve Goldman media empire, the entirety of which can be yours for a song), a reader takes your host to task for suggesting that an incident that took place last week involving Gabe White should be a hint to managers to pay attention to the rule book for bonus competitive advantages. Around here we take any excuse to delve further into a worthy thesis, in this case, that gamesmanship is, or should be, a major component of the manager's job.

The White situation was very simple. The Yankees lefty entered the team's May 26 game at Baltimore in the sixth inning with the Yankees leading 7-6. The game was momentarily delayed when the umpire asked White to remove a gold chain. With the chain removed, White gave up consecutive hits, allowing another run to score and setting up a blown save for future Hall of Famer Tanyon Sturtze. After the game, White claimed that he had pitched badly because he'd been unnerved by the umpire's request.

In forcing White to divest himself of shiny accouterments, the umpire was enforcing rule 1.11. Here are some highlights:

> 1.11
> (a) (1) All players on a team shall wear uniforms identical in color, trim and style... (3) No player whose uniform does not conform to that of his teammates shall be permitted to participate in a game... (2) No player shall wear ragged, frayed or slit sleeves. (d) No player shall attach to his uniform tape or other material of a different color from his uniform. (e) No part of the uniform shall include a pattern that imitates or suggests the shape of a baseball. (f) Glass buttons and polished metal shall not be used on a uniform... (h) No part of the uniform shall include patches or designs relating to commercial advertisements.

Section h isn't really relevant, but I left it in as a reminder of the egregious "RICOH" patches the

Yankees wore during their fan-unfriendly visit to Japan back at the beginning of the season. As for the rest, players are pretty much unaware of the rule's existence and tend to get offended if they're called on it, as several relatively recent incidents suggest, including Arthur Rhodes blowing a fuse over being told that he had nothing to lose but his chains, David Wells being asked to remove Babe Ruth's cap from his unworthy head, and White's reaction last week. You can also throw in rulebook matters that have nothing to do with the uniform, such as Carl Everett's inability to cope with the batter's box and even the infamous Pine Tar game of 1983, in which George Brett did an incredible impression of a Norse warrior experiencing berserker rage while under the influence of rapturous Odin-love and hallucinogenic mushrooms.

All of this stuff falls under the heading of, "You should have known better." However, the fact is that they don't, and the end result is that the player is often run from the game or plays with reduced effectiveness due to emotional duress. Because of this opposing teams can gain an advantage in a given game not due to good pitching or timely hitting, but simply because they encouraged an umpire to enforce the rules.

The yanking of White's chain was motivated by the umpire. He acted on his own, apparently without impetus from Baltimore manager Lee Mazzilli. This is unusual. The umpire is a bit like the rhinoceros, a lumbering creature with poor eyesight which is happy to quietly do his job (which entails grazing, grazing some more, and quietly humming Hank Williams tunes to itself) until someone runs up and bothers it. An umpire may be aware that a minor uniform code violation is talking place, but until a manager complains, the umpire is going to remain benignly indifferent because he knows that any action he takes is going to lead to two ejections: the affected player and the affected player's manager. The rhino/ump does not want the headache.

This means that every manager must know the rulebook, so that if a rare chance to win one from the bench comes along, he can recognize it. Last season the Orioles batted out of turn in a game against the Yankees, and both Joe Torre and his valuable bench coach Don Zimmer slept through it, passing up the chance for a free out. Hall of Fame manager Leo Durocher once said: "As long as I've got a chance to beat you I'm going to take it." That was a chance, and they didn't take it.

The best example of what can be gained from knowledge of the rules should have been the pine tar game, but baseball dropped the ball on that one. (Yes, it was a stupid rule, but it was a rule nonetheless. If you want to drop the rule, you do it after the fact, not retroactively.) Instead, the best example is the one that inspired section 2 of rule 1.11 above, the case of Johnny Allen and the frayed shirt sleeves.

Righty pitcher Allen (1932-1944) was one of baseball's more unique characters, an incredible hothead, a bad loser who was frequently injured and yet always effective. A typical 1935 Allen start was perfectly encapsulated by John Drebringer in the *New York Times*: "Johnny Allen, his prominent jaw squared off at a very pugnacious angle, fought with all three umpires impartially as he hung up a five-hit shutout to record his seventh victory of the campaign." In his autobiography, Durocher, who managed Allen in the 1940s, described what happened on May 27, 1943, when third base umpire George Barr called a balk on Allen, allowing a run to score. Allen went berserk. Durocher recalled:

"Before I could get to him, he had a headlock on Barr and he was pounding on top of his bald head with the ball... Barr is flat on his back and Johnny has him by his necktie... I give you my word of honor that his tongue was hanging out and he was turning purple. He was choking him. Choking him! ...It took half the team to pull him away."

Contemporary newspaper reports hint that Durocher's version contains its fair share of hyperbole, but overall it was a typical day with Johnny Allen.

Allen broke into the majors with the Yankees. That the New Yorkers had him at all was the result of pure good luck. Allen began his career in obscurity, living in North Carolina while perfecting a pitch that had little currency in the majors at the time, the slider. In 1927, top Yankees scout Paul Krichell, the man who had discovered Lou Gehrig and many other pinstriped stars, checked into a Sanford, N.C. hotel on a scouting mission. The bellboy, a young man of 22, off-handedly mentioned that he pitched a little. Krichell undoubtedly heard this line from every bellboy, porter and steward he ran into, but this time the clerk showed off a wicked breaking pitch. The next day Johnny Allen was property of the New York Yankees.

For the first seven seasons of his major-league career—until the slider ruined his arm—Allen won a greater percentage of his decisions than any other pitcher in the majors. Contemporaries Lefty Grove, Carl Hubbell, Dizzy Dean and Red Ruffing all took a back seat to him in this department. Left to his own devices, Allen did not lose games.

Unfortunately for Allen, once the league figured out that he was so easily riled, he was rarely left to his own devices. In 1936 the Yankees dealt Allen to the Indians after manager Joe McCarthy decided that between injuries and temper tantrums, Allen was both unreliable and annoying. McCarthy didn't like southerners, didn't like players who argued with the umpires, and didn't like pitchers with bad arms, and Allen generally answered to at least two out of three.

His first year with the Indians, Allen "struggled" to a 20-10 record, the victim of his own reputation. "Knowing that his patience was limited," wrote Franklin Lewis in *The Cleveland Indians*, "other clubs spread the word that Allen 'couldn't take it.'" Allen was pursued around the junior circuit by accusations of scuffing and other more extreme forms of heckling. When Indians general manager Cy Slapnicka wrote a letter to the league office accusing the competition of "poor sportsmanship" where Allen was concerned, the epithet "crybaby" was added to that of "cheat." By June 4, Allen was only 4-5.

That night Allen tried to channel his frustration in a productive direction by trashing his hotel room. He also attempted to assault a waiter with a fire extinguisher. Somehow escaping incarceration, Allen returned to the mound and went 16-5 over the rest of the season.

June 7, 1938 saw the incident that would put Allen's underwear in the Hall of Fame. That day, the first-place Indians took on the fourth-place Red Sox at Fenway Park. Allen pitched against rookie Jim Bagby. Allen took the mound wearing a sweatshirt with "three gaping holes in each sleeve, just below the elbow." Allen claimed he had cut the holes to give the shirt some ventilation and that he had been using it since 1937. Red Sox manager Joe Cronin didn't see it that way and complained to umpire Bill McGowan that the garment was a distraction to the hitters.

McGowan asked Allen to go to the clubhouse and put on another shirt. Allen stalked off the mound. It was thought that he would swap shirts and be right back. Minutes ticked by. Indians manager Oscar Vitt sent a batboy in to see what was keeping Allen. He quickly reported that Allen refused to come back unless he was allowed to wear the shirt. Vitt ran into the clubhouse and explained to Allen, probably none too calmly, that it was his job to decide when a pitcher came out of the game. Allen refused to change his shirt. Vitt fined him $250 and went back to the game. Left alone in the clubhouse, Allen repented, but by that time another pitcher was on the mound.

Later, Allen said he would wear the same shirt the next time he pitched and that he would again quit if ordered to change it. Allen did pitch again, but the shirt never played again. Allen sold it to a Cleveland department store owned by his general manager for $500, where it was put on display. Eventually the Hall of Fame claimed the shirt and it vanished into the holdings of a museum that currently has nothing on display.

Considering the shirtsleeves game, Stuart Bell of the *Cleveland Press* wrote: "There may be no hard-and-fast rule governing the cut, width, length, size and general consistency of undershirts, but Johnny Allen didn't do himself any good by wearing a shirt that the law ruled against. John thinks that he is being ganged... but the ganging is pretty much John's own fault. He has a bad temper, players know it and they do everything they can to excite it... It is not a very favorable commentary on the managers and players of the American League that they goad any pitcher on such gossamer digressions, but it also is a very unfavorable commentary on Allen that he falls for the guff and gets mad."

Bell had it right, because Allen was nearly impossible to beat. In 1937 Allen had come as close to a perfect season as any in the history of the game. Kept to a shortened schedule by a holdout and a bout with appendicitis, he was nonetheless perfect whenever he took the mound. After going 4-0 prior to the medical emergency, he returned to action on Aug. 15 and won 11 straight games to post a 15-0 record.

Allen took the mound on the last day of the season looking to tie Walter Johnson's record for consecutive wins. It was not to be; the Indians had a third baseman named "Bad News" Hale, and he lived up to his rep, allowing a Hank Greenberg grounder to go through his legs for an RBI. Allen lost 1-0, finishing the season at 15-1. His .938 winning percentage remained the major-league record until Elroy Face of the Pittsburgh Pirates went 18-1 in 1959. It's the American League record to this day.

Allen was gracious in defeat. "I ought to kill him," Allen said of Hale. "Any bush-league third baseman would have made that play." Only intervention by his manager and teammates saved Hale from bodily harm.

Despite frequent arm problems, through 1938 Allen's career record was 99-38 (.723) with an ERA of 3.61, vs. a league ERA of 4.63. Some of Allen's magic was attributable to strong run support from strong Yankees and Indians clubs. The combination of Allen's bulldog attitude, his slider, and good hitting made for a combination that was very hard to beat. The only sure way to defeat him was to get him to self-destruct.

If, like Allen, a player is willing to fall apart in a key spot because of an over-attachment to a garment, a piece of jewelry or a place in the batter's box, why wouldn't you take advantage of that?

YOU COULD LOOK IT UP
Infinite Edition #4
Steven Goldman

In Steven Goldman's hands, the career of Don Padgett, catcher of the 1930s and 1940s, became a lesson about the importance of appreciating what you have.

In the titanic team-up you asked for but never thought you'd get, the current members of Baseball Prospectus have crossed dimensional boundaries to meet their predecessors from Golden Age Baseball Prospectus. The resultant "Crisis on Earth-BP" had many ramifications, not the least of which was the recovery of BP player comments for players who predated the first Baseball Prospectus book in 1996. These are those comments.

The previous installment featured players from the K through O section of the alphabet. This week, we're departing from the format slightly to take an extended look at one player from the land of P. In the next chapter, which you should see before the next Harry Potter book, we'll resume with shorter observations of players from Q through U.

DON PADGETT
OF/C ST. LOUIS CARDINALS, 1937-1941
There is a reason catcher isn't on the defensive spectrum.

When Bill James laid out the defensive spectrum, he left catcher off. The positions, in order of difficulty, went:

DH - 1B - LF - RF - 3B - CF - 2B - SS

Players could move leftward along the spectrum but rarely moved rightward. As for catcher, it was a box of its own that required special skills. Getting out once you were in was difficult. Getting in if you weren't born there was nearly impossible. Trying can destroy your career. This is the story of Don Padgett.

Padgett, 25, hit his way onto the St. Louis Cardinals' roster in spring 1937, after only two years as a pro. The outfielder was signed out of Lenoir Rhyne College of Hickory, North Carolina as a 21-year-old in 1935 and rapidly ascended through the Cardinals chain, making stops with Bloomington, Beatrice, Sioux City, and Houston (where he hit an uninspiring .268) before rising to Columbus of the American Association midway through the 1936 season. Padgett batted .329 and slugged .461 with an approximate on-base percentage of .347 (just 10 walks in 81 games) for the Columbus Redbirds of the American Association in 1936. This is based on six home runs in 362 at-bats; another source claims that Padgett hit 22. Just to place that offense in context, the league as a whole batted .295/.350/.431. Padgett's teammate, Tom Winsett, batted .354/.417/.731 with a league-leading 50 home runs (a season that would help to firm up Winsett's standing as one of the great busted prospects). Whatever his numbers, the lefty, pull-hitting Padgett had established himself as a top prospect in the eyes of Cardinals mastermind Branch Rickey.

Padgett had a promising National League debut, batting .314/.357/.457 with 10 home runs (.284 EqA) against league averages of .272/.332/.382. He played 102 games in right field, pushing the incumbent, the popular Pepper Martin, into a part-time role.

After the season, Padgett was secure enough in his major-league career to think about taking up golf in the offseason. What he didn't quite realize was that 102 games in right field was enough to convince Rickey that he should never be allowed to play there again. Padgett showed off a good arm, killing eight base runners. He had five double plays, just one short of tying for the league lead. Still, 10 errors in so few games was off-putting (siding with Rickey, BP's Davenport translations show Padgett to have been worth -10 runs on defense). Two days after Christmas 1937, a crate filled with catching gear was delivered to Padgett's house. This was his first notice that he was changing positions. The day after that, Padgett received a letter from Rickey suggesting that he get out in the backyard and practice.

The Cardinals had a strange spring in 1938. They were trying to make a shortstop out of third baseman Don Gutteridge, a catcher out of right fielder Padgett, an infielder out of center fielder Terry Moore, and a third baseman out of Washington Redskins quarterback Sammy Baugh. Padgett was made to catch two games a day so as to speed up his learning curve. He was virtually never seen without the tools of ignorance. Teammate Martin once asked him, "Hey, how do you sleep in those things?"

Padgett's primary instructor that spring was Mike Gonzalez, the longtime National League catcher, coach, and manager. Yankees catcher Bill Dickey also tutored Padgett informally and even gave him a pair of his shin guards. Dickey later taught Yogi Berra as well, "learning him" all his experiences. The lesson backfired. "Put me back in the outfield!" Padgett told manager Frankie Frisch. "After watching that guy, I know I'll never be anything but a clown behind the plate."

Padgett proved to be adept at calling a game and made strong throws to second base. Pop-ups, though, were an adventure, and balls in the dirt inevitably got by him. "Of course you can't make a catcher in two weeks," Rickey temporized. "It takes time, and if Don does catch this year, it may be some time before he gets on to all the fine points of the position. But he has made progress, decided progress. He likes to play the position."

That was a lie. Padgett hated catching. His move was complicated by his own reluctance and manager Frankie Frisch's resistance to it; Rickey had come up with the transfer without consulting his skipper. On opening day, Padgett played right field; that's what you call a vote of confidence. By mid-April, the Cardinals were on their way to another experiment. Moore, the strong defensive center fielder (+28 FRAA career), was moved to third base. Padgett went to center field. Mickey Owen, who would shortly become to the Dodgers of the 1940s what Joe Girardi was to the Yankees of the late '90s (or at least what those teams claimed they were besides out sponges) got to catch. Stress or sophomore slump, Padgett slumped to .271/.303/.425 and lost playing time to rookie Enos Slaughter.

Held back by Frisch, Padgett caught just six games that year. When Frisch attempted to move Padgett from right field to catcher as part of a late-inning switch in one contest, Padgett even refused to come in from the outfield. But Frisch was let go late in 1938. The new manager, Ray Blades, was more amenable to the Rickey plan, and the Cardinals revived the experiment in 1939 despite Padgett's protests. "I think Branch is right in his plans for Padgett," said Cards owner Sam Breadon. "We've got too many outfielders and there's no chance for him in that department. Of course, Padgett doesn't have to catch if he doesn't want to." Yes he did, as long as Rickey was convinced. "If Blades can keep that fellow behind the bat for 100 games this year, we'll win the pennant," Rickey said.

The prospect mavens, such as they were, were split on Padgett. "His .271 batting average last year makes one wonder why the powers-that-be insist on finding a spot for him, either behind the bat or in the outfield, both of which he plays with only fair success," wrote *The Sporting News* editor E.G. Brands that spring. Yet that same spring, in that same paper, J. Roy Stockton wrote, "Padgett has many advantages over any other receiver candidates on the squad. He is highly intelligent, on and off the field. He has splendid team spirit, loves to play every day, and most important, he can rattle base hits against the most distant fences."

The second iteration of the catching experiment was delayed when Padgett fell on his left elbow while rounding second base in a spring training game, dislocating his shoulder. Though there was no break, he would miss the first 62 games of the season. Simultaneously, Padgett was effectively frozen out of the Cardinals outfield. He was not going to displace veteran left fielder Joe Medwick, the 1937 MVP and Triple Crown winner. Center fielder Terry Moore could hit and was considered one of the premier ballhawks in the league. Right field was manned by sophomore Slaughter, who was rapidly establishing himself as both and offensive and defensive threat. With the benefit of hindsight it is apparent that Padgett was a corner outfielder of moderate skills who was blocked by an older Hall of Famer at one possible position and had been passed by a younger Hall of Famer at another. First base was covered by Johnny Mize, another future Hall of Famer. It was a bad time to be Don Padgett.

Stymied, he rededicated himself to catching. "I'm going to make it, accident or no accident," he said, referring to catching. "I didn't care about it all last year, but I like it fine now. And I think I can do everything. You know, I wasn't a helluva outfielder. I know that. But I think I can whip this catching business." (*TSN*, 3/23/39). When he made his 1939 debut on June 11 he had two singles and threw out a basestealer. That was merely the beginning; Padgett initially had trouble getting into the lineup, but he rapidly hit himself into a starring role. By July 20 he was hitting .427 (32-for-75). A month later, he was up to .431.

The Cardinals now had Mize, Medwick, Padgett, and Slaughter in the middle of their order. This was potent stuff. On June 10, the team was 25-20 (.556), but as Padgett heated up so did the team, pushing its overall batting average to nearly .300 and going 44-19 (.698) in August and September.

On September 26, 1939, the Cardinals were 3 1/2 games behind the front-running Reds with just seven games to play, but the two teams had four head-to-head contests remaining. That day at Cincinnati the Reds carried a 3-1 lead over the Cardinals into the ninth. With two outs, Johnny Mize singled, bringing Padgett to the plate. Pitcher Gene Thompson was on the mound. Just as Thompson was going into his motion, Cards manager Blades decided he'd better use a pinch-runner for Mize. "Time!" he shouted. The umpires heard him, but Thompson was already pitching. He fired to the plate. Padgett laced a single to right field, keeping St. Louis's pennant hopes alive. The umpires conferred. Time had been called. The single hadn't actually happened. Padgett got back in the box, swung, and grounded out 4-3. Ballgame over. Season, for all intents and purposes, over. The Cardinals finished second, 4 1/2 games behind the pennant-winning Reds.

Padgett had cooled slightly in September, batting .359 over his last 20 games. He finished the year at .399/.444/.554. Though he didn't qualify for the batting title (Mize's .349 won it), no other player was close to him. He did this while catching 61 games and making no appearances in the outfield. Rickey's mission, it seemed, had been accomplished.

Manager Blades lasted a year and change with the Cardinals. Early in the 1940 season he was fired and replaced by Billy Southworth. Blades had gone along with Padgett as his catcher though he generally sent in a defensive replacement in the late innings. Southworth was different. Like Frisch, he refused to buy into Rickey's experiment and declared that Padgett was, had always been, and forever more would be, an outfielder. Midway through the 1940 campaign, Padgett had lost his job. There was still no room in the outfield. Nor was Padgett making the case that he could out-hit his glove if assigned to the pastures. For the season he batted a weak .242/.321/.388, never raising his averages far above that level. Padgett never made an appearance in the outfield in 1940. Once Southworth had formed his opinion he mostly sat, watching proto-Girardi Mickey Owen get most of the playing time behind the dish.

For reasons known only to himself, Rickey decided that he wouldn't give in that easily. On December 4, 1940, he traded Owen to Larry MacPhail's Brooklyn Dodgers for veteran catcher Gus Mancuso, a minor-league pitcher, and cash. Mancuso, 35, hadn't been a regular in years and lacked power. As Rickey had deprived Southworth of his one viable catcher, this should have made Padgett a backstop again. It didn't. Southworth stuck to his guns. He preferred to start Mancuso and a rookie catcher named Walker Cooper.

Padgett was a homeless man on the Cardinals. What to do with him was something of a mystery, as *New York Times* columnist John Kieran observed that spring: "He used to be an outfielder and a hitter. As a catcher last season he wasn't much of a hitter. Or much of a catcher, either, if it comes to that. He doesn't like the job. He was in it with both feet but no part of his heart. His heart was in the outfield all the time they had him shackled behind the plate with a lot of cumbersome upholstery draped over his manly form."

Walker Cooper would soon prove to be a very effective hitter, but not in 1941. He struggled at the plate, then broke his shoulder, leaving the field to Mancuso, who batted .229/.309/.293. The Cards finished second to the Dodgers that season, missing the pennant by 2.5 games. Padgett played the outfield occasionally, caught 18 games, and didn't hit, got sick, and sulked. With tonsillitis, inactivity, and depression, he gained weight.

MacPhail, president of the Brooklyn Dodgers and a former Rickey associate, openly coveted several Cardinals, including Medwick and Padgett. It was expected that the two would go together in any trade, but when the trade for Ducky Wucky had finally been swung on June 12, 1940, Padgett was not included. A trip to Brooklyn waited for over a year. On December 10, 1941, the Dodgers bought Padgett for $30,000. Padgett promised MacPhail he would slim down, but in the end the Dodgers got their money back: Padgett was called into the military and the contract stipulated that if he didn't start the season with the team, the deal was off. Inducted into the Navy, Padgett joined the Great Lakes Baseball team under manager Mickey Cochrane. He would remain in the military for the duration of the war.

The war accomplished one thing: it made Padgett a catcher for good. There were 174 games left in his career, and he never played at another position. The Dodgers welcomed him back in 1946, decided he had nothing left, and quickly sold him to the Braves. Branch Rickey had by this time moved from the Cardinals to the Dodgers, so he got the opportunity to pull the plug on his

Frankenstein's monster for a second time. The Braves traded Padgett to the Phillies for pitcher Andy Karl. Padgett played parts of two seasons in Philadelphia and was gone from the majors for good.

There are many morals to this story. One is that not even Branch Rickey knew everything. Second, unremarked upon here, is that poor plate judgment/high batting average players are going to suffer wide fluctuations in performance. Padgett fits that description. Third, in baseball, as in life, it is very easy to fail to appreciate what you have. Finally, while one may doubt Bill James on many things, the defensive spectrum is not one of them.

FEBRUARY 24, 2006
http://bbp.cx/a/4797

YOU COULD LOOK IT UP
Position Changes
Steven Goldman

After digging through baseball's back pages for examples of defensively shaky infielders who found success in the outfield, Steven Goldman recommended that error-prone shortstop B.J. Upton follow in their footsteps, which he ultimately did with great success.

One of the reasons a familiarity with history is valuable is that, though every situation is different and every individual unique, situations will recur, perhaps not identical, but strongly similar in their broad outlines. The Devil Rays are a new franchise, so perhaps that's why they don't recognize an old problem when they see one.

B.J. Upton is an old book with a new cover. The Jeter-worshipping athlete very much wants to make it as a major-league shortstop. He has the bat, as his minor-league career rates of .304/.396/.474 attest. His weighted-mean PECOTA projection for 2006 is .270/.348/.425. These aren't All-Star numbers, not yet, but Upton is just 21 years old, so they'll do for now. Upton also has great speed and should be a successful basestealer in the majors. With a good enough knowledge of the strike zone to take an above-average number of walks, Upton may prove to be the rare young player with leadoff skills who can actually function as a leadoff hitter.

The problem is that his glove isn't major-league-ready and may never be. Upton makes a lot of errors by current standards. His 53 errors at Triple-A Durham last season are nothing compared to the 72 that Joe Tinker made at the same age, but that was 1902, and he was wearing a glove the size of a baby's sock while playing on infields that not only had pebbles and potholes but ravines and gullies. Nor was this anything new for Upton—he made 56 errors at two levels in 2003 and 44 at three levels, including the majors, in 2004.

Many young shortstops compile high error totals. Some grow out of it and go on to be excellent major-league shortstops. As an 18-year-old professional freshman at Bluefield of the Appalachian League, Cal Ripken Jr. made 33 errors in just 63 games, fielding .900. Ripken slowly tamed his great arm; in 1982, his first full season in the bigs, he made just 19 errors. Conversely, 21-year-old Jose Offerman, splitting his time between Bakersfield of the California League and San Antonio of the Texas League in 1989, made 50 errors in 130 games. Three years later, in the majors with the Dodgers, Offerman earned the appellation "E-6" after being officially credited with 42 miscues.

Errors are in and of themselves not damning if the shortstop is doing enough other things with the glove—showing exceptional range, for example—to make up for his mistakes. In Offerman's case, the errors were indicative of a player who just couldn't play shortstop. In 1992, he was 27 runs below average at short. In 1993, he was 23 runs below average. Worse, the heat Offerman was taking for his defense was affecting his offensive development, where thanks to his ability to hit for average, his advanced strike-zone judgment and his speed, he showed a good deal of potential. It took a change of positions for him to reach it.

Knowing which young, error-prone shortstops are going to go the Ripken route of improvement and which are going to careen down the Offerman path of career stagnation is something that can't be gleaned from the statistical record. That determination is more of an art than a science. It requires a scout's practiced eye to make the evaluation, and even that asset doesn't come with a guarantee. Of the Orioles personnel asked to evaluate Ripken, only Earl Weaver thought he could be a big-league shortstop. The decision-makers in the Dodgers organization thought that Offerman could be developed as a shortstop, and they were wrong. So much for the intuition of the trained observers, at least in that case.

What we do know from the historical/statistical record is that the Upton-model player—good bat, good speed, shaky defense—comes along very frequently. Upton's protestations to the contrary, many players drafted as shortstops don't get to play there in the majors. The benefit of drafting players from the right side of the defensive spectrum is that if they prove to be inadequate defenders at their original positions, they can move leftwards, whereas a second baseman who can't play second probably doesn't have the bat to play first base or left field, and a first baseman who doesn't have the bat to play first doesn't have the defensive ability to play anywhere else. Prospective shortstops with questionable range who can hit and have an accurate arm and good reactions generally get moved to third base. For example, Mike Schmidt was drafted as a shortstop, as were George Brett and Paul Molitor. Those who have some defensive ability but don't have the bat to play the hot corner move across the bag to second base.

Prospective shortstops with great speed tend to go to the outfield, often to center field (Schmidt, Brett, and Molitor could have done that too, had their organizations not found more demanding uses for them. In fact, Molitor played center field in the majors for part of one season). Some terrific players, including a number of Hall of Famers and near-Hall of Famers, began life as middle infielders but quickly took their bats to the outfield. Mickey Mantle, Hank Aaron, and Carl Yastrzemski played shortstop their first year in organized ball, but they are special cases at any position.

Some of the "lesser" players to make the move:

- Jimmy Wynn: The top comparable on Upton's PECOTA list, "The Toy Cannon" played second, third, and short in two minor-league seasons and also played 21 games at shortstop during his rookie year in Houston. Wynn was a little guy (5-foot-9) with a howitzer of an arm (hence the nickname), power, plate discipline, and speed. He wasn't the error machine that some of the other players on this list were, but the combination of an above-average number of errors and limited range dictated a move to center field.
- Bobby Murcer: Murcer made his pro debut at 18, playing shortstop for Johnson City of the Appalachian League, and made 34 errors in 32 games for a .775 fielding percentage. We should pause here to note that although fielding percentage has been discredited as a measure of defensive ability, and properly so, for the purposes of this discussion it is a useful shorthand for the degree to which errors affected a player's game. Murcer returned to shortstop in the Carolina League and led the league with 55 errors, fielding .898. He made another five errors in a September cup of coffee with the Yankees that fall but did seem to be improving—in 29 major-league games, Murcer made "only" 11 errors. That is a common thread with the players in this group: given major-league trials, they almost always field a bit better than they would have been expected to given their minor-league numbers. This may be due to several factors, including better-maintained infields, superior lighting, and paralysis induced by sheer terror. You can't make errors if you're too scared to touch the ball.

    Murcer played a full season at short with Toledo and again led his circuit in errors, making 36 in 133 games. Murcer then missed two years in service to Lyndon Johnson. When he came back, the Yankees no longer considered him a shortstop, ultimately moving him to center.
- Roy White: A statistical ringer for Bernie Williams through the mid-1990s, White was signed as a second baseman in 1962 and played the position through 1965. The error totals stayed high, and after the Yankees briefly and disastrously moved White to third, he made his way to left field and five seasons of eight-plus WARP.
- Reggie Smith: Smith played 66 games as an 18-year-old shortstop at Wytheville of the Appalachian League in 1963 and led the league in both assists and errors (41) for an .851 fielding percentage. The next season he was briefly tried at third but made nine errors in 17 games (.750), and the march to the outfield was on.
- Chet Lemon: Lemon was Oakland's first-round pick in the June, 1972 draft. Signed as a shortstop, he spent the first several pro seasons bouncing between short and third, generally fielding below .900. He was moved to the outfield after a 1975 trade to the White Sox. Lemon somehow never won a Gold Glove despite a reputation as one of the best center fielders of his day.

- Tim Raines: Drafted as a shortstop in 1977, Raines was tried there as well as second base, third base, and the outfield before finally drifting to left field for good.
- Von Hayes: Cleveland drafted him as an "infielder" in 1979 and played him at third base and shortstop in 1980. He split time at short and third base his first year, then gradually became an outfielder, starting in both center and right field.
- Eric Davis: Drafted as a shortstop in 1980, Davis split 33 games between second and third in his first season, fielded .843, and was in the outfield the next season.
- Gary Sheffield: The sixth player taken in the first round of the 1986 draft was a high-school shortstop who stuck at the position into his second major-league season. It wasn't errors that moved him to third and then the outfield as much as it was a pronounced lack of range.

The point I'm making is not that if a team converts a shaky shortstop into an outfielder an Eric Davis automatically results, but rather that these teams were confronted with a choice about how to best deploy these players. The scarcity of hard-hitting shortstops means that any team that can play one reaps a significant competitive advantage. There is no doubt that these teams were aware of that. Having evaluated each player's skill set, they made a determination that the players were better suited to the outfield. Productive center fielders being almost as hard to find as punchy shortstops, they still had a high likelihood of benefiting from the repositioned player. They could have waited and hoped that the shortstops improved, but they ran the risk of getting neither benefit.

The Devil Rays have a choice to make. They can consign themselves to an indefinite wait for Upton to settle in at shortstop, or they can pull the plug and potentially develop a superior outfielder along the lines of Wynn, White or Smith. In choosing to wait, the Rays—or at least Ye Old Regime—would unsurprisingly point to Jeter, who made 56 errors as a minor leaguer in 1993. The Yankees, they'd say, didn't move him, so they shouldn't move Upton. This is a spurious bit of reasoning: what Jeter did as a 19-year-old Sally Leaguer has no relevance to Upton's innate ability to play, or learn to play, shortstop. Further, any argument that rests on the suggestion that Jeter is a defensively accomplished shortstop is ignorant at best, misguided at worst.

Billy Martin used to say that some players were mules and some were racehorses, and no matter how much you beat the former they weren't going to turn into the latter. The Rays are experiencing that dilemma with Upton, but only because they've misread the situation. They can still get a racehorse, but only if they choose correctly and decisively.

YOU COULD LOOK IT UP
Judge Landis on Steroids Edition
Steven Goldman

Well before the Mitchell Report saw the light of day, Steven Goldman envisioned baseball's steroid scandal unfolding much as one much earlier in its history had.

**JUDGE LANDIS ON STEROIDS EDITION
(OR, RIVER DEEP, KENNESAW MOUNTAIN HIGH)**

Last weekend Chris Kahrl, Cliff Corcoran, Neil deMause and I spent a pleasant evening answering questions at Coliseum Books in Manhattan. Actually, we didn't answer questions, we answered question, because all anyone wanted to talk about was Performance-Enhancing Apple Jack, Barry Bonds, and *Baseball Between the Numbers*' take on the latter. As we do radio spots around the galaxy talking about our vast array of spring products (Two books! Branded Horse Blankets! Will Carroll's All-Ages Slumber Party!) all anyone wants to do is engage us in judging players and handing out asterisks. We're the stats guys, after all—we must know Where They Should Go.

If you're fair, though, you have to admit that you don't know where or how to apply the asterisks. If half or a third of the players were using, and all of them were using a different combination of chemicals to hulk out, and each one derived a different benefit from doing so, it becomes difficult or impossible to figure out to what degree the statistics were perverted. The best you can do is shrug your shoulders and hope that the various distortions washed out in the mix.

This is exactly what happened in 1926 when Judge Kennesaw Mountain Landis, the first commissioner, found various parties picking at the scab of the 1919 World Series scandal. In November, 1926, Ty Cobb, who was still a vital ballplayer at 39 (he had just batted .339/.408/.511 in a half-season of play) was terminated as Tigers manager and released, ending an association with the Detroit club over two decades old. Not long after, Tris Speaker, player-manager of the Indians and also still a potent hitter (.304/.409/.469 in 150 games) at 38, was let go in similar fashion. Two of the game's most enduring stars had disappeared in a puff of smoke. No explanations were given.

Eventually it was revealed that a pair of letters, one sent by Cobb to Smokey Joe Wood, the other from Wood to Dutch Leonard, implicated Cobb in fixing, or at the very least betting on, the Cleveland-Detroit game of September 25, 1919. Speaker wasn't mentioned in the letters but when Leonard turned the letters over to the American League he fingered Speaker as being part of the plot. Once the truth was out, Cobb and Speaker demanded a full investigation—the letters were vague and didn't specify what, if anything had happened. Cobb was ready to admit that he had helped Leonard and Wood get a bet down, but, Pete Rose-like, insisted that he had always played to win. Nor did he have any money on the game itself.

The revelation opened up the quintessential can of worms, with players coming out of the woodwork to report other fixes or cases of one team paying another a "gift" to "bear down" against a key opponent. Even Chick Gandil and Swede Risberg, the Black Sox's top scumbags, appeared to trash the integrity of the 1917 American League race won by the White Sox, with the Tigers supposedly rolling over for the Pale Hose in some key games. Others called aspects of the 1921 and 1922 seasons into question. The Judge was now swamped with gambling scandals, and it appeared that the game's reputation was about to take another big hit. Congress began talking about regulating baseball (in American politics, nothing ever changes and nothing ever gets done), and all of the other typically self-serving hysterics got to caterwauling.

Landis held open hearings before the press, calling over 30 players to respond to the various charges. In the cold light of day, Gandil and Risberg's charges seemed easy to dismiss because they appeared to be so stupid. Directly after he and Risberg testified that in 1919 they had played out of position in games against the Tigers in return for favors done in 1917, Gandil and the Judge had this exchange, as reported in J.G. Taylor Spink's biography of Landis:

GANDIL: I want to ask you, Mr. Landis, why, after I was dragged through a court trial and acquitted in the 1919 Series, is it that I was blacklisted?

LANDIS: Do you want to be reinstated?

GANDIL: No, I don't. But I want to know why I was blacklisted.

LANDIS: I couldn't pass on that unless I could ask you some questions about the 1919 World Series.

GANDIL: I don't want to go back to that Series.

LANDIS: Well, if you want an answer right now, you have just testified that you played out of position in two games in 1919. That would cause you to be placed on the ineligible list.

GANDIL: ...Oh.

That last "Oh" isn't part of the official record, but what else could he possibly have said? Surely nothing we could print here.

During the proceedings, pitcher Bernie Bolland, a member of the 1917 Tigers, got in Risberg's face and said, "You're still a pig."

"I am not a pig," Risberg cleverly replied.

Despite such high camp fun, Landis wished all of them would just go away. There were a number of suspicious things about the games brought up by the besmirched duo. Even squeaky clean Eddie Collins had admitted he paid $45 into a gift fund for the Tigers as incentive to beat the Red Sox during the tight 1917 race. At least that's what Collins understood the fund to be, as opposed to a bribe for the Tigers laying down against the White Sox in consecutive doubleheaders played on September 2 and 3, 1917. Indeed, the Sox had run wild on the bases against the Tigers, stealing up to eight bases in the games. In fact, it was Landis himself who had published the incriminating Cobb and Wood letters, perhaps with an eye towards deflating rampant rumors about the reason for Cobb and Speaker's releases and eventually reinstating the pair. Landis then exacerbated the situation by holding off any ruling on the Cobb-Speaker matter until after he had dealt with the Risberg-Gandil accusations. "Won't these God damn things that happened before I came into baseball ever stop coming up?" he said privately, while at the same time dragging the events out in public.

In the end, Landis employed a magic wand solution, making all of the past gambling problems disappear. He decided that Risberg and Gandil were lying, said that the practice of giving gifts, "was an act of impropriety, reprehensible and censurable, but not an act of criminality." He imposed penalties for all future infractions, then declared a statute of limitations on baseball offenses. If it happened before Landis became Commissioner, he didn't want to know about it.

Within a few days, American League president Bancroft Johnson, Landis's mortal enemy, forced the Commissioner's hand on the Cobb-Speaker matter by giving an interview in which he said:

> Tris Speaker and Ty Cobb never again will play ball or manage an American League club. They were given positions of trust and they failed to keep that trust. No matter what Landis rules, the American League won't have them. Ty Cobb and Tris Speaker have been offered public hearings. Each of them declined. [Cobb and Speaker had insisted that they be able to confront Dutch Leonard in any hearing, but the pitcher refused to appear. Their attitude towards a hearing was also complicated by the possible damage that would be

done to Joe Wood, who likely had bet on the game. Now the baseball coach at Yale, he had a lot to lose.] In view of that, the public itself can answer the question whether the legal fight Cobb's and Speaker's attorneys have been talking about will materialize.

Landis wasn't about to let Johnson usurp his authority and called for a face-to-face showdown in the presence of the assembled owners. Within a few days, Johnson, who had dropped a few brain cells over the years, amended his story to say that Cobb and Speaker were thrown out of the league because they were bad managers—Cobb was too brutal with his players, while Speaker thought more about betting on horse races than managing his club. This was a new wrinkle—a manager could be banned from baseball just for being bad at his job? Did the Dodgers forget this when they hired Grady Little?

Johnson became the subject of the meeting instead of Cobb and Speaker. Johnson, the founder of the American League, was let go, the cover story being that his health was shot. "Johnson was twice near collapse" at the meeting, the *New York Times* was told by one of the attending owners, and had to be helped to a chair. "After the meeting he failed to recognize a close friend for almost a full minute. He was seen in the lobby of the club, walking as if dazed and talking in a mumble." Johnson very well may have had a breakdown at the meetings, but this represented a face-saving coincidence for the owners—this was the first time he was said to have had health problems. Landis said he would "take up" the Cobb-Speaker case shortly.

At the end of January, 1927, Landis finally cleared Cobb and Speaker. Landis was helped immensely by Leonard's adamant refusal to travel east from California and testify in person. The Judge declared the outfielders free to sign with any club—American League only (take that, Ban).

With two of the game's top-tier stars vindicated and the statute of limitations eliminating the possibility of anymore cases coming to light, the Commissioner was free to devote himself to things he really enjoyed, like persecuting Branch Rickey over his farm system and keeping African-Americans out of the majors. Everything had been whitewashed. If there were games fixed in the past, the policy was don't ask, don't tell.

In today's magic jellybeans scandal, the disincentives to mounting a full investigation are exactly the same as those confronted by Landis. Not only will an investigation be unable to come to any definitive or satisfactory conclusions, but it will implicate so many players, managers, coaches, and even front office personnel and owners along the way that the game's reputation will suffer worse damage than if the bodies are left buried.

That's why the only asterisk we are likely to see is the one denoting that steroids violations will be prosecuted from this* date forward, with all that went before officially sanctified as terra incognito.

YOU COULD LOOK IT UP
Why Babe Phelps and I Weren't in St. Louis Last Week
Steven Goldman

In an intensely personal piece, Steven Goldman tied his struggle with anxiety to that of past player Babe Phelps.

Last Thursday, Baseball Prospectus had its last event of the 2009 book tour in St. Louis. I was on the bill and greatly looked forward to being there. I had even arranged a press credential for that day's Mets-Cardinals game, intending to do some comparisons of the newish Busch with the new Yankee Stadium. I never got there, though not for lack of trying. I drove to the airport in plenty of time, patiently and calmly waited at the gate, and boarded my plane. I took my seat, buckled my seatbelt, and rapidly realized that I could not stay. Grabbing my bag, I lowered my shoulder, pushed back down the narrow aisle past passengers still trying to board, and fled.

As I sat at the gate at Newark Liberty Airport last Wednesday morning, excoriating myself, filled with self-disgust, watching my plane roll away, among the many things I said to myself is, "Congratulations. You've officially become Babe Phelps. Now you too are the Grounded Blimp."

Gordon "Babe" Phelps was one of the best-hitting catchers of all time, albeit in a very short career during that golden age of platoon catchers, the 1930s. In one small sense he was, at least for awhile, the greatest-hitting catcher of all time—playing for the Dodgers in 1936, he batted .367 in 349 plate appearances (.367/.421/.498 overall), and under the rules of the time was in contention for the batting title. It is still the second-highest batting average for a catcher in a season of 300 or more plate appearances, surpassed only by Smoky Burgess's .368 in 1954; Smoky got there in 392 plate appearances. (The highest batting average by a catcher in a full season is .362, a mark shared by Bill Dickey, who got there in 472 PA in 1936, and Mike Piazza, who reached that level in a more-impressive 633 PA.) Phelps was neck-and-neck with Paul Waner for the National League batting title until the last days of the season but refused to sit to protect his average, and Big Poison passed him, finishing at .373.

This wasn't the only strong season in Phelps' catalog, and except for a few problems—including my problem—he might have put together a truly remarkable career. Phelps made his minor-league debut at 22 years old in 1930, batting .376 with 38 doubles, 19 triples, and 19 home runs. The next season he batted .404 with 15 home runs. The Maryland native made his major-league debut with the Washington Senators that September, a three-at-bat cup of coffee. Though the Senators didn't have anything great at catcher—they would soon trade for Luke Sewell, who would be the receiver on their 1933 pennant winners—they sent Phelps back out. It's easy to imagine the reason. First, Phelps hadn't yet reached the high minors, so he was inexperienced. In addition, Phelps was never a polished defensive catcher and had only just been converted to the position from the outfield. It's likely that at this stage of his career his glove game seemed inadequate to those running the team at the time, the old pitchers Walter Johnson (then the manager) and owner Clark Griffith.

Phelps went back to the minors and kept socking, batting .373 with 47 doubles and 26 home runs in 1932. He would get the major-league call again the next season. Unfortunately, he was now the property of the Cubs, who had a future Hall of Famer behind the dish in Gabby Hartnett. Hartnett played every day and hit like an outfielder besides, so Phelps sat behind him for the entire 1934 season. They thought so much of his defensive work that that August they signed the 37-year-old catcher Bob O'Farrell to back up Hartnett, so for a while Phelps sank to third on the depth chart.

The Dodgers claimed Phelps off of waivers in January, 1935, but he again found himself stuck behind a veteran catcher eventually bound for the Hall of Fame, this time Al Lopez. Lopez couldn't hit like Hartnett, but was considered solid—in 1935 he was coming off of back-to-back seasons of .301/.338/.376 and .273/.349/.383; the aggregate was just a shade on the good side of league average. Lopez was also considered to be one of the best defensive catchers in the game, garnering frequent "honorable mention" votes in the MVP balloting, votes based purely on his glove work.

Unlike Hartnett, Lopez took the odd day off, so Phelps received 130 plate appearances, a career high to that point, and ran with them, batting .364/.408/.579. For the National League of 1935, where the rabbit-ball action of previous years had calmed down quite a bit, these were sterling numbers. That winter, Phelps caught another break—sort of—in that the Dodgers had quite literally reached the end of their financial string and needed to purge salaries. Their two best players, Lopez and second baseman Tony Cuccinello, were dealt to the Braves, giving Phelps a starting catcher's job, or at least a platoon share of it, as right-handed backstop Ray Berres (ironically one of the worst-hitting catchers of all time, with career rates of .216/.260/.255 in 561 career games) had come over from the Braves in the deal. Finally free to play, Phelps had his remarkable 1936 season.

For the next several years, Phelps settled in as a regular, giving the Dodgers enough above-average offense to make three All-Star teams. Defense and game-calling remained a problem. Casey Stengel, Phelps' 1935-36 manager, once asked him why he had failed to call for Dutch

Leonard's knuckleball in a crucial game situation, letting the pitcher get beaten on a secondary pitch instead.

"It's hard to catch," Phelps replied.

"Did it ever occur to you," Stengel asked, "that if it's hard to catch it might be hard to hit too?"

Phelps allowed he hadn't thought of that.

Phelps broke his hand three times in 1938, which seems to have affected his offense in 1939, when he had his weakest season at the plate, hitting .285/.336/.418, but he recovered his form in 1940, hitting .295/.349/.492. Phelps was already known as Babe, some say for the way his home runs resembled Ruth's, but this seems unlikely, as he wasn't that kind of power hitter. Any photograph of Phelps suggests a strong alternative reason—he was a heavy, round-headed man. Squatting behind the plate, he looked like a giant baby. By 1938, the weight had earned him a second nickname: "Blimp."

Ironically, Phelps didn't like blimps or any other form of air travel. "The train was fast enough for me," he once said. He was hypochondriacal by nature, with a habit of listening to his heart to make sure it was still beating. Planes frightened him; as it turned out, boats did too. When Larry MacPhail took over the Dodgers and inaugurated the age of air travel in baseball, Phelps' career began to unravel. He tried one flight, hated it, and after that he simply wouldn't get on a plane. The writers started calling him the Grounded Blimp. After 1939, the Dodgers flew to most away games. Phelps took a train and got there when he got there.

I have boarded many planes, though it has never been something I enjoy doing. I used to be afraid of crashing, but except for a brief moment or two of involuntary alarm during takeoff, I no longer worry about that, and once the plane is in the air I always feel fine. My problem is that I have an anxiety disorder centered around claustrophobia. I get into any small space, like a small airplane, and my limbic system goes haywire. My heart rate shoots up. My chest tightens. The ironically named flight response is incredible.

The plane to St. Louis was quite small, not quite a puddle-jumper, but the next step up. The low ceiling scraped my head. My overly large frame barely fit in the seat. The way the aisle was blocked by incoming passengers made me feel as if there was no exit. I imagined what I would feel like when they closed the door. The thought was terrible. I did not panic... but realized I probably would if I stayed, and that even if I was able to tough out the three-hour ride to St. Louis, I might never be able to convince myself to board the plane back home. I had taken two Xanax, an anti-anxiety medication, an hour before boarding, because I have been dealing with this stupid, frustrating, annoying thing for eight years now, and I knew it was possible that I might feel this way. The pills did not help. I felt helpless.

There is a classic Sly Stone song, "Thank You (Falletinme Be Mice Elf Agin)." I would like to be myself again. Until I was about 30 years old I led an anxiety-free life. I did what I wanted, when I wanted, and went where I pleased. One day, somewhere in the summer of 2000, I went out to run an errand and found I could not breathe. Frightened, I returned home, and the symptoms ebbed. This situation repeated itself periodically over the next several months. I went to doctors. They said nothing was wrong with me. One laughed at me and handed me a nebulizer. As the year went on, the feelings became more frequent, and I had an increasingly difficult time getting myself to leave the house. Even when I seemed to be breathing normally, I would start thinking about my breathing, and that was enough to trigger another attack. There were days when I could not only not bring myself to leave the house, but I had a difficult time convincing myself that it was safe to get out of bed.

In 1941, the Dodgers held spring training in Havana, Cuba. Phelps trained down in Florida but couldn't bring himself to get on the boat. His manager, Leo Durocher, later remarked that apparently Phelps wasn't cut out to be an amphibious blimp either. He waited in Florida for the team to come back. Injuries kept him shelved for the early part of the season, but he had barely gotten back into the lineup when his grounded blimp problems came to a head. Ironically, a plane wasn't even involved. On June 12, the Dodgers were to take a train to St. Louis. Phelps was late. Durocher held the train until it became clear that Phelps wasn't going to show at all. His roommate, third baseman Lew Riggs, confessed to Durocher that he and Phelps had shared a cab to the train station, but that when it came time to get out, Phelps had said he felt ill and wasn't going to go on the road trip. By the time the Dodgers found Phelps, he was back home in Maryland, worrying about his heart. The Dodgers, who had had the 33-year-old thoroughly examined at an earlier date, fined him $1,000, suspended him, and suggested to the press that he had a psychological problem.

When my world had shrunk to the size of a small room, I realized that I needed help. Thus began my eight-year pharmacological odyssey through the world of antidepressants, Paxil, Celexa, and so on. They have crazy side effects, which in my case have most visibly manifested themselves in the form of amazing weight gain. Unfortunately, they are necessary in my case, and they largely work. I still have a bad day every once in awhile, but on the whole I am back to going where I want to go and doing what I want to do. Sometimes I have to think about it a little beforehand, but I always go. I don't like to give in to this thing I have.

The frustrating thing is that I still feel like myself. I don't feel afraid inside. Even when I was in the grips of the worst of the attacks, the rational me was still in here, trying to manage the situation. On the plane to St. Louis I was, at least mentally, completely calm. The physiological reaction was like an overlay, a computer virus that was attacking the mainframe. I wasn't thinking, "Aaagh! Let me out of here!" I was thinking, "Okay, how do I deal with this? How do I overcome this feeling?" It was a measured weighing of pros and cons that led me, in this instance, to get off of the plane. It was the right decision, but I still felt immensely disappointed that I had not been able to push it away, to rise above.

From time to time, I try to quit the drugs that I am on. I hate the side effects, which disrupt my sleep schedule, my short-term memory, and other aspects of day-to-day living. Yet, when I have attempted to quit, as soon as the half-life of the pills has ended, I go back to not breathing again, to the inexplicable fear. "Inexplicable" really is the right word; I've been twice diagnosed with cancer and didn't have a panic attack either time, but stick me in an MRI machine, or Goldfinger's mini-plane, and I can't function despite having a rational understanding of everything that is happening. The chemical process of grounded blimpism overrides all else.

Babe Phelps refused to return to the Dodgers, preferring to load baggage instead. "Preferring" may not be correct, and neither may "choosing." Given his problems, he may not have had a choice. That December, the Dodgers traded him, along with three lesser players, to the Pirates in return for the future Hall of Fame shortstop Arky Vaughan, a heck of a deal for Brooklyn given Phelps's problems. Phelps got into 95 games for the 1942 Pirates, hitting a solid .284/.345/.440. This was his last season in the majors. He didn't play in 1943—I have not been able to ascertain if he was injured, and he doesn't appear to have been in the military. He was traded to the Phillies that December but did not report. The Blimp sailed—or perhaps more properly, walked—into the sunset.

As for this grounded blimp, I will persevere with air travel. I've not had a problem flying on larger planes, so I guess I'm more likely to appear at the next BP event on the West Coast than on anything that requires a short hop to the Midwest on an X-Wing fighter. I remain committed to losing my Paxil 50 (60? 70?) so perhaps one day I'll be more of a grounded balloon, or grounded sausage casing, or something like that. I'll never hit .367 like Phelps did, but looking on the bright side, being a pseudo-shut-in gives you plenty of time to write, and perhaps one day that will lead to a book of nearly that quality. Though the body can't fly, the mind remains untethered.

YOU COULD LOOK IT UP
Enhanced?
Steven Goldman

As Steven Goldman pointed out, kneejerk reactions condemning players' desire to self-medicate in order to return to the field overlook the fact that they have always done so—and that by refusing to do so, they could be depriving us of the pleasure of watching a Hall of Fame career unfold.

In the aftermath of Mark McGwire's confession, one of the more dubious reactions came, as you might expect, from the MLB Network's own Harold Reynolds. Reynolds said (I paraphrase) that even if you accepted McGwire's explanation that he received no performance benefit from his usage of so-called performance-enhancing drugs but rather was doing so to thwart his own physical frailty, then McGwire still did something wrong, because the marathon baseball season requires stamina. If you resort to taking a drug to stay on the field, you've cheated your way to overcoming a basic requirement of the sport.

As I've pointed out over at the Pinstriped Bible, anything a player might use to get through the drag of the season, from a cortisone shot (a legal use of steroids) to the ubiquitous greenies of the 1970s, to Joe DiMaggio's black coffee and cigarettes, is taking a drug to stay on the field. No player, whether he takes an aspirin to overcome a blinding headache or undergoes Tommy John surgery, depends only on his own internal powers of recuperation. Putting aside the question of whether McGwire did or did not see his level of production increase due to his usage, saying that his taking a particular substance to promote healing was wrong, when there are so many other substances and procedures available to players for the same purpose, is just drawing a boundary that arbitrarily and hypocritically separates one medicine or therapy from another. And before you reply, as some of my readers did, "Yes, but steroids have nasty side effects, so that's why they're bad," every drug has side effects, and most of them come along whether you've used them properly or not. There is a reason that drug commercials come with disclaimers like, "If you experience sudden death while using AsthmaMax, consult a medical professional immediately."

Try to imagine a world in which players could not take any action to accelerate their recovery from injury or fatigue. The disabled lists would swell; rosters would have to double in size to account for all of the wounded, and many would never come back. Of course, it never has been this way.

Players have always had some medical recourse for most injuries, however limited, except in one area: psychological illness. Antidepressants weren't widespread until relatively recently and, if a player had problems with depression or anxiety, his options were to deal with it somehow or to go find another line of work. Those that would condemn McGwire for pursuing a pharmaceutical solution to his injury problems would, of course, have it no other way, even if it would cost us the pleasure of watching a Hall of Fame career unfold. This has, in fact, happened.

After Ernie Banks, Charlie Hollocher was the greatest all-around shortstop in the history of the Chicago Cubs. Born in St. Louis in 1896, as an amateur Hollocher looked like a classic good-field/no-hit type, as a result of which both the local Cardinals and Browns organizations declined to sign him. Turning pro with Keokuk of the Central League in 1915, he began to work his way upward, reaching Portland of the Pacific Coast League in 1917. Along the way, he fulfilled the expectations of the St. Louis scouts, fielding well but not hitting with any particular impact. The PCL played a very long schedule thanks to the long western summer, so in 1917, Hollocher played in 200 games, hit .276, and slugged .342, recording 33 doubles, nine triples, and one home run in 813 at-bats.

The Cubs bought him for $7,500 anyway, as they had had a very difficult time finding a solid shortstop since they had traded Joe Tinker to the Reds after the 1912 season:

Does a Bear Boot Grounders in the Woods? Cubs Shortstops, 1913-1917

Year	Player	G	AVG	OBP	SLG	EqA	FRAA
1913	Al Bridwell	136	.240	.358	.316	.253	0
1914	Red Corriden	107	.230	.323	.318	.253	-7
1914	Claud Derrick	28	.219	.257	.271	.197	0
1915	Bob Fisher	147	.287	.326	.370	.260	-5
1916	Chuck Wortman	69	.201	.258	.261	.192	-9
1916	Eddie Mulligan	58	.153	.200	.212	.129	-7
1917	Chuck Wortman	75	.174	.245	.205	.174	-10
1917	Pete Killduff	56	.277	.324	.371	.265	-10

Hollocher would likely have been another infielder through the revolving door, but something changed when he reached the majors. According to SABR's Arthur Ahrens, who wrote one of the only full-length articles on Hollocher, "Realizing that his survival depended on his hitting ability as well as his glove work, Hollocher altered his batting stance." Whether this came as a result of Hollocher's own insight, good coaching at the major-league level, or simple maturation on the part of the then-22-year-old Hollocher, he was suddenly a completely new player.

The 1918 season was truncated due to the war—the government had issued a "Work or Fight" order to all able-bodied young men and told baseball to wrap up its season. Hollocher made the most of it, playing in a league-leading 131 games, hitting .316/.379/.397 (.293 EqA) as the Cubs' second-place hitter and leading the league in hits (161). "For a youngster playing his first season in the major leagues he has done better than surprisingly well and he is without a doubt the greatest young infielder the Cub machine has unearthed in years," the *Sporting News* gushed. "Throughout the league he is spoken of as the successor to Joe Tinker and Hans Wagner because his fielding has been brilliant his hitting the same." With Hollocher on hand, the Cubs improved from 74-80 and a fifth-place finish to 84-45 and the pennant.

Hollocher would disabuse some of those Wagnerian notions when he batted just .190 in the six-game World Series loss to the Red Sox, and again in 1919, when he sophomore-slumped to .270/.347/.347 (.265 EqA). He did have a reasonable excuse, as the deadly Spanish Influenza pandemic had caught him up during the offseason. He was limited to only 115 games, which must have seemed like a transient thing at the time but proved to be an omen.

In 1920, just as the lively ball was souping up offense throughout baseball, Hollocher first developed the stomach problems that would trouble him throughout the remainder of his life. He was in and out of the lineup starting in June. At the end of July, he was hospitalized for causes that were not publicly specified, although it is likely the stomach was to blame, as it would be on subsequent occasions. He never returned to the lineup, missing just over half the season, though he hit well when he played, batting .319/.406/.389 (.290 EqA).

Strangely, over the next couple of seasons, things settled down for Hollocher. Though he broke his nose in June of 1921 when a bad-hop grounder hit him in the face, he played in 140 games and hit .289/.342/.384 (.238 EqA). Despite what was a slow season (Hollocher was roughly a league-average hitter that year in terms of raw rates, but in a hitter's park), sportswriter John B. Sheridan, who had been a booster of Hollocher's since the latter was a kid playing on St. Louis sandlots, wrote in 1921, "I think Hollocher was the best and most valuable player in the National League." Others held differing opinions, noting that Hollocher, by now the Cubs' team captain, "seemed rather lackadaisical."

Even if that had truly been the case in 1921, no one could argue with Hollocher's 1922 season. Though he contracted tonsillitis in spring training, the 26-year-old shortstop played in 152 games and batted .340/.403/.444 (.265 EqA). It was an offensive-minded season in baseball, and Hollocher's batting average was good only for eighth in the league, his OBP ranked only sixth, and his 201 hits were just the seventh-most. The only category in which he led the league was caught stealing. Still, it was an unusual season by the standards of his position: in all the years of modern baseball, there have been just 22 campaigns of a .340 or better batting average in at least 400 plate appearances by shortstops, six of them by Honus Wagner, six in the years since 1995. Holly's

1922 season legitimately was record-setting, however. He came to bat 692 times (592 at-bats) and struck out five times. His 118.4 at-bats per strikeout remains the modern National League single-season record, and his career rate of 31.2 at-bats per strikeout ranks 15th among modern players. Charlie Grimm later recalled that Hollocher hit Dazzy Vance, the premiere strikeout pitcher in baseball at that time, "like he owned him."

Hollocher, listed at 5-foot-7 and 154 pounds, was also highly regarded defensively. His fielding percentage was the second-best in the National League from 1918-1924, trailing future Hall of Famer Rabbit Maranville .955-.954. He also participated in two triple plays. In 1922 he led the National League in fielding percentage (.965) and was +8 runs according to FRAA.

And there Hollocher stopped—well, there was more, but only a little. He reported late in 1923, in poor shape supposedly due to suffering from a cold or the flu, and was quickly sent home due to "illness," not playing until May. Hollocher's "forced departure was no surprise to those who watched him in the Cubs' camp," the *Sporting News* reported. "When he reached camp he appeared to be under weight, was lacking in color, and his usual smile was not much in evidence... He hadn't been at work more than a week before he was forced to ease up. His ailment was a form of stomach trouble, probably brought on by not giving the effects of the flu sufficient time to work out of his system."

Time did not heal whatever was ailing the shortstop, and in May the Cubs sent him to a specialist who determined through X-rays that there was nothing physically wrong with his stomach. Hollocher returned to the Cubs, but with the assurance that he could take a day off when he felt he needed it. He would play one day, then ask out of the lineup the next, saying, "I feel as if I was going to collapse." Despite the clean bill of health, the stomach drove him back to the bench for good in July. Shortly thereafter, he jumped the club and went home, leaving a note for manager Bill Killefer:

> Dear Bill:
>
> Tried to see you at the clubhouse this afternoon but guess I missed you. Feeling pretty rotten so made up my mind to go home and take a rest and forget baseball for the rest of the year. No hard feelings, just didn't feel like playing anymore. Good luck,
>
> As Ever,
>
> Holly

In late July, John Heydler, the president of the National League, went to St. Louis to try to persuade Hollocher to return to the club. The shortstop demurred. In the end, he played in only 66 games, batting .342/.410/.423 (.272 EqA).

Hollocher felt better in the spring of 1924 and, arguing with the Cubs about both how much of his salary he should have been paid while disabled and how much he should get to play, held out. He and the Cubs couldn't come to an agreement until May. "Holly" played well at first once he did get on the field in the middle of the month, hitting an inside-the-park home run in his first plate appearance (the ball rolled under the stands). Ominously, he missed his third game back so he could get a stomach X-ray. Shortly thereafter, he stopped hitting. In August, the Cubs sent him home, saying it was for his own good. He had hit .245/.292/.336.

There would be no return, though from time to time Hollocher would report he was feeling somewhat better. It was reported that the chief obstacle to his return was hotel food. On another occasion, Hollocher said that he had been advised by doctors not to play at all in 1923 and had permanently ruined his health by giving in to the Cubs and rejoining the club. "I miss baseball," he said in 1933, by then 36 years old. "When I quit, some writers hinted that there must have been other reasons besides my health. One story was that I had trouble with other players, another that I had made and invested enough money to enable me to retire. All of which is the bunk. If I had my health I would be playing baseball even if I had a million dollars. I love the game."

What he didn't love was going through life with the intense stomach pain that had destroyed his career, pain that no one, in fact, believed existed. On August 14, 1940, Hollocher got into his car, aimed a shotgun at his throat, and pulled the trigger.

Would Hollocher have made the Hall of Fame had he been healthy? Obviously there is no way of knowing for sure, but he retired a .304/.370/.392 hitter (.264 EqA). Among contemporary shortstops, only Joe Sewell out-hit him by a large margin, and he was roughly comparable with future NL Hall of Famers Maranville and Dave Bancroft during the time that the three were in the league—and neither of them hit .340. He was also five years younger than each, meaning he would have had more prime seasons in the lively ball era than either of them. Further, of the 10 retired shortstops who did hit .340 or better in a season, seven of them are in the Hall of Fame. The only exceptions are Cecil Travis, who very likely would have gone in had World War II not cut his career off in its prime, Alan Trammell, who has been inexplicably snubbed, and Hollocher himself (the Hall of Famers are Luke Appling, Lou Boudreau, Joe Cronin, Joe Sewell, Arky Vaughan, and Honus Wagner).

Unfortunately, baseball at the time was limited in what it could offer Hollocher to keep him on the field. Doctors couldn't find anything wrong with his stomach, but there was clearly something happening. Whether or not pain is physically or psychologically inspired, it feels real. His treatment at a dead end, a player in Hollocher's position could either attempt to soldier on or go home. He went home. Today, a player like Joey Votto who develops depression or anxiety can get appropriate treatment, which may include medication, and can return to the field.

Votto, a career .310/.388/.536 hitter at 25, might or might not make the Hall of Fame one day. Thanks to his being born at the right time, if he does not make it, it probably will be because his career did not deserve it on its merits, rather than because he was forced into an early decline or retirement because his brain chemistry betrayed him. Those who would condemn a player for resorting to a medical solution to stay on the field would plainly rather have it the other way—Hollocher's way.

YOU COULD LOOK IT UP
The Statheads vs. Blondy Ryan
Steven Goldman

As Steven Goldman clarified by recounting the tale of Blondy Ryan, statistically minded fans don't seek to dismiss the human side of players but to put it in the proper perspective.

Last week, the normally excellent LoHud Yankees Blog had an entry by a guest columnist named Yair Rosenberg. Rosenberg's topic is a sadly typical one, "the tendency of statistical measures to unintentionally obscure the human side of baseball." He proceeds to set up a straw man that he can knock down:

> The more statistically-minded baseball community has often adopted the following implicit assumption: Players are essentially machines, largely unaffected by clubhouse atmosphere, personal psychological factors or the day-to-day effects of real life. Columnists who refer to "team cohesion" or a player's "mindset" (think Alex Rodriguez) as factors in performance are treated with indifference, if not derision, and are considered a product of a bygone era where intuition trumped hard data. By contrast, a modern talent evaluator like Billy Beane looks at advanced metrics and finds the right players to draft without ever observing them in person. A player's performance can thus be predicted, fantasy baseball style, without reference to anything but the numbers.

Show me a statistically-minded fellow who has adopted these assumptions, implicitly or otherwise, and I will show you a statistically-minded idiot. Nevertheless, let's revisit a player whose "mindset" was credited as being a direct cause of "team cohesion" and then talk about the value that the player's team placed on his services. This was well before the "Moneyball-influenced era" decried by Rosenberg, taking place back in 1933.

The Great Depression year of 1933 should have been a transitional season for the New York Giants, not least because of the Depression itself. Teams, feeling the pinch of lowered ticket sales, were cutting back. Even the size of the rosters themselves would be diminished in an effort to save money. The Giants, though, were unsettled in ways that went beyond the global economy. For years the National League's most successful franchise was under the stewardship of John McGraw. However, the club hadn't won a pennant since 1924, and McGraw himself had quit 40 games into the 1932 season, naming the team's first baseman, Bill Terry, as his successor. The '32 team had gone on to finish in sixth place with a 72-82 record, one of just a very few second-division finishes the team would have in the McGraw years, which had begun in 1902; indeed, McGraw's average Giants team had a .591 winning percentage, equivalent to a 91-63 record in a 154-game schedule.

The talent on the field was less than stellar. Being elevated to manager would cost Terry the services of a good friend and productive player, the outfielder/third baseman Freddie Lindstrom. Lindstrom claimed he had been told he would be McGraw's successor, and when the job went to Terry instead he demanded a trade, a request Terry intended to honor. It was also unclear if the club's two-way shortstop, Travis Jackson, could be counted on for the upcoming season, or ever; in late June, he had caught his spikes sliding over the second base bag and gone out for the year. He had ultimately required surgery not just on the knee injured in the incident, but the other as well. Jackson was a defensive standout (from 1927 to 1931 he had averaged 18.4 FRAA per season), but he was also a career .299/.347/.450 hitter to that point, less than dominant numbers given the period in which he played (the NL averaged about .294/.354/.418 in those years), but extremely dominant numbers for a shortstop of the day. Jackson's absence compounded other problems on defense, and the club finished fifth in an eight-team league in defensive efficiency.

With Lindstrom about to be gone and Jackson's availability in doubt, the Giants would be down to just two standout offensive players, 23-year-old right fielder Mel Ott, coming off of a .318/.424/.601 season in which he led the league in home runs (38), walks (100), and on-base percentage, and Terry himself, a career .343/.395/.532 hitter to that point. Surveying the roster, Terry realized that the offense couldn't possibly be fixed in one offseason. He could build through pitching, but trying that presented a problem as well: the club had only two established pitchers, 29-year-old screwball expert Carl Hubbell, and 30-year-old right-hander Freddie Fitzsimmons, whose out pitch was a knuckle-curve. Terry chose a third path, one very much in vogue today: defense.

Terry would later tell F.C. Lane of *Baseball Magazine*, "The managerial policy which I have adopted is built upon defense rather than offense. The Giants do not usually need to score many runs. All that we must do is score more than the other fellow. Our system is built upon air-tight pitching. We commonly play for one run. I have said to the players many times, 'If we can hold them to the seventh inning, we can win.'"

It took some work to get the roster to the point that the foregoing would be true. He dealt a solid starting pitcher, southpaw Bill Walker, and three spare parts to the Cardinals for catcher Gus Mancuso, a weaker hitter but a far more agile defender than the team's incumbent backstop, the porcine Shanty Hogan, whom Terry subsequently sold to the Braves. Satisfying his promise to Lindstrom, a three-team trade was executed, with the disgruntled star going to the Pirates and the

Giants receiving 30-year-old sophomore center fielder Kiddo Davis from the Phillies, which was the best Terry could do with no leverage. Finally, in a deal that attracted little comment at the time, he dealt the player who had proved to be a weak substitute for Jackson, utility infielder Doc Marshall, to the Buffalo Bisons of the International League, receiving shortstop John Collins "Blondy" Ryan in return.

Blondy Ryan, a former quarterback at Holy Cross College, would prove to be a key pickup. He was mistakenly reported to be a young player, as his baseball age was two years younger than his actual age of 27. He had first reached the major leagues with the Chicago White Sox in 1930 but had batted only .207/.258/.333 in 94 plate appearances and had Luke Appling to compete with in any case. He was packed off to Atlanta of the Southern Association, then Buffalo, where he hit roughly .264/.295/.376 (some stats are unavailable) while playing second base and shortstop. Clearly this was no coming star. Yet, he had a good glove, and when Jackson proved unable to take the field regularly in early 1933, he ended up getting the bulk of the playing time at shortstop.

The changes to the roster created by Terry caused the defense to sparkle. The Giants' defensive efficiency rose from .687 to a league-leading .719. The outfield, which had to patrol the vast Polo Grounds pastures (roughly 430 feet to center field at that time, and 450 to each of the alleys), was terrific: Jo-Jo Moore was +20 FRAA in left field. Davis was +5 for 120 games in center, and Ott was +12 in right field. Terry wasn't a great glove man at first base, but he was adequate. Second baseman Hughie Critz wasn't much of a hitter; as pitcher Red Lucas once said, "There's no harm in Hughie." That was true insofar as batting went, but he was deadly to the opposition in the field at +35 FRAA. Third baseman Johnny Vergez had a tough year at -11 but incited no complaints. Finally, Ryan was +15 FRAA at short.

Terry later remembered, "For that one year, Ryan played the greatest shortstop I ever saw. He made impossible stops. Never better than a .240 hitter, if we needed a run he'd knock it in. You could play tight ball with those men because they knew what to do and you could depend on them. They were the right types. They had baseball brains. When we got a couple of runs, they knew it was our quota and held onto 'em."

As the quote from Terry suggests, the new lineup didn't hit much: as a club, the Giants batted but .263/.312/.361 in a league that hit .266/.317/.362, and their 4.1 runs scored per game ranked only fourth in the league. However, the superior defense more than evened things up on the pitching side. Today we take it for granted that Hubbell was a Hall of Famer, but through 1932, his age-29 season, he hadn't quite ascended to that level. To be sure, he had been very good, with a career record of 77-52 and an ERA of 3.13, more than a run below the NL average during that period. However, he had yet to win 20 games or lead the league in any major category. That changed in 1933. Between 1932 and 1933, the NL offensive environment dropped by about half a run, but Hubbell was riding the express elevator: his ERA dropped from 2.50 to a league-leading 1.66. He pitched 10 shutouts and led the league in wins with 23.

Fitzsimmons had been a career 109-61 (.641) pitcher through 1931, with a solid 3.56 ERA. The next season had been an off year, as a career high in hit and walk rates had increased his ERA to 4.43. In '33, he dropped back to 2.90. Further, the new defense allowed Terry to establish two young pitchers that McGraw hadn't quite had time to figure out before his departure, Hal Schumacher and Roy Parmelee. McGraw had kept the future "Prince Hal," 22, hopping between the bullpen and starting assignments as part of his major-league apprenticeship. Not even a two-hitter in April of '32 earned him a permanent spot. Terry put him in the rotation and got 19 wins and a 2.16 ERA. The Giants had been trying to get "Tarzan" Parmelee established in the majors for years but, as his nickname suggests, he was too wild for Gotham. In 1933, he led the league in hit batsmen and wild pitches, but with his walk rate at a livable 3.2 per nine (league average was 2.4), he was able to muster a 1.7 strikeout-walk ratio (sixth-best in the league) and a 3.17 ERA.

With the new alignment, the Giants got off to a solid start; on June 1, approximately a quarter of the way through the schedule, they were in third place with a 22-16 (.579) record but only two games behind the front-running Cardinals. The team would catch fire that month, going 19-9 overall. As the calendar turned to July, they stood in first place with a 57-37 record, 3.5 games ahead of the second-place Pirates and 6.5 games ahead of the third-place Cardinals.

During this phase, one of the stories of the season was the way that Ryan had been key to the team's resurgence. He was a cocky, likable player, one of those scrappy types the press and public always fall for. Later, Hubbell would tell of a close game he pitched in which Ryan's ninth-inning error had put the team in a difficult spot. He ran out to the mound, patted the veteran Hubbell on the back, and said, "Don't worry, old man, we'll get out of this. Remember, I'm behind you." Said the *Sporting News*: "Ryan of the Giants, while a weak batter, is credited with having 'made' Bill Terry's infield after Jackson's knees buckled in the spring."

Both Terry's new approach and Ryan's key role came together in a doubleheader at the Polo Grounds against the Cardinals on July 2. In what was undoubtedly one of the great regular-season pitching performances in history, Hubbell threw an 18-inning shutout, allowing six hits, no walks, and striking out 12. In the nightcap, Parmelee outdueled Dizzy Dean 1-0, allowing four hits, no walks, and striking out 13. Early in that game, there was a close play at second and Cardinals left fielder Joe Medwick spiked Ryan, opening a severe gash on his leg that required 10 or 13 stitches (depending on your source) to close. He would be out for an indeterminate time while some healing took place and he awaited the manufacture of a shin-guard. Meanwhile, the Giants headed out on an epochal, 21-game road trip.

Terry had no choice but to put Jackson back at shortstop. Physically, "Stonewall" just wasn't up to the job, and after beating the Braves on the first game of the trip, they dropped seven straight, getting swept out of Chicago. What had been a six-game lead shrunk to 2.5. It was at this moment that Ryan, finally ready, sent a telegram to his manager. There are many variations of its wording, but all sources agree it went something like this: "THEY CAN'T BEAT US. AM ON MY WAY. J.C. RYAN."

The note amused the heck out of Terry. Ryan surely hadn't meant to imply a cause and effect relationship, "They can't beat us [because] I am on my way," but it read that way to Terry. He made a point of showing it to his players, who all saw it the same way. "They can't beat us!" became the club's rallying cry, the "You gotta believe!" of 1933. The day Ryan arrived, the Giants broke their losing streak. They won three straight, then seven out of 10, then 13 out of 17. John Kieran of the *New York Times* proposed a new rule: "Any time that Blondy Ryan is not in uniform, it shall be illegal to hit a ground ball in the direction of shortstop when the New York Giants are in the field."

Although the club wavered again as July turned to August and the Pirates challenged, they never relinquished their lead, pulling away in August and finishing the year 91-61 (.599), five games ahead of Pittsburgh. They played a more offensively talented Washington Senators club in the World Series and licked them easily, winning the championship four games to one. "Didn't I tell you it would be just a breeze?" Ryan said after Schumacher won Game Two. He also singled in the winning run of Game Four. Despite hitting that was so weak (.238/.259/.293, worthy of a .199 EqA) that he was worth only 0.6 WARP, Ryan finished ninth in the NL MVP voting. Hubbell won the award, with Terry finishing fourth and Mancuso sixth. Arky Vaughan, who had hit .314/.388/.478 while playing shortstop for the second-place Pirates, finished 23rd.

Ryan was now a star, credited with being a key to the championship, the team's first since 1922. His celebrity was based partly on glove work but mostly on attitude and comportment, the intangibles that the statistical approach to baseball supposedly denies. Yet, he was also a replacement-level player, and while Terry was not thinking in those terms as the winter of 1933 turned into the spring of 1934, he understood the concept perfectly. In the spring of 1934, Jackson, now a year and a half removed from his knee surgery, was given back his old job. No competition with Ryan was held. Ryan worked off the bench, though he still got in a fair amount of playing time at third base as Vergez's career fell apart. The Giants were famously edged out for the pennant on the last day of the season, and giving 416 plate appearances to Ryan was one of the reasons why they lost. He and Vergez combined to hit .214/.271/.320 at the hot corner.

The Giants still had a problem at shortstop, however, because although Jackson played fairly well in 1934, if not up to his old standards, another leg injury meant that his days as a shortstop were over. He'd be a third baseman for the remainder of his career. Sparky, motivational Ryan was still on the roster, but Terry didn't look to him for a pick-me-up; he got rid of him in order to get someone better. In November, 1934, Ryan, Vergez, and two other bits of roster flotsam were dealt to the Phillies in return for All-Star shortstop Dick Bartell. Bartell fit the Jackson mold: he was an excellent fielder who was, for the most part, a poor hitter by the standards of the day, but as a .300/.360/.397 hitter (through '34), he was far more potent than most shortstops. The Giants would win two more pennants during the Terry years, and Bartell would be the shortstop for both of them.

Meanwhile, even the perennial dead-end Phillies realized that Ryan wasn't quite a major-league ballplayer. Partway through the 1935 season, he was replaced by rookie Mickey Haslin and optioned to Baltimore-if the Phillies were ever going to get out of the hole, they needed ballplayers, not characters. Ryan refused to report, saying he would quit baseball and study law. The Yankees bailed the Phillies out; their starting shortstop was injured and they needed a body to play the infield, so they sent the Phillies a few dollars for his services. He failed to convince Joe McCarthy that his .238/.259/.305 performance in 30 games was outweighed by his great clubhouse skills, and he was sold on to the Indians.

Ryan spent the entire 1936 season in the minors, and most of the 1937 and 1938 seasons as well. Terry briefly brought him back to the Giants in each of the latter two seasons, perhaps for old-times' sake, perhaps to see if some of his rah-rah-ism would rub off on his club in small dosages, but mostly he was content to let Ryan remain in places like Minneapolis, Milwaukee, and Baltimore. You see, in baseball, character suffices when you don't have players, as Terry did not in 1933 ("Everybody played every day," Terry said years later. "We had to. We had no reserves."), but both then and now it is much more likely your team will win if it plays fully-rounded talents. Terry clearly realized this after 1933 and again after 1934.

No one who watches baseball for any length of time with any real understanding of what it is they are seeing can come away with the perception that those who play it are in any way less than human in their reactions to happiness, to sadness, to fear, to stress. The goal of the statistical study of baseball is not to equate the players to automatons, but to get an objective record of what happens on the field. That's all. It is not to dismiss the intangibles, but to place them in proper perspective to the tangibles. That's all. If Bill Terry and the New York Giants were capable of seeing that distinction over 75 years ago, surely we are allowed to observe it in today's players without the more insecure among the audience feeling threatened by it.

YOU COULD LOOK IT UP
Dusty Baker and the Johnny Oates Affair
Steven Goldman

Manager Dusty Baker's tendency to put prolific out-makers at the top of his lineups frustrated and perplexed fans, but Steven Goldman proposed one solution to the mystery by looking back at Baker's playing career.

It's an affront to Managing 101: whether you look at the batting order as a way to set up the offense or simply as a vehicle for distributing the most plate appearances to your best hitters, it has long been accepted baseball doctrine that your leadoff hitter should have a high on-base percentage. Yet, every day you can look at the box scores and see Orlando Cabrera and his .276 on-base percentage taking the first hacks of the day for Dusty Baker's Cincinnati Reds. Drew Stubbs opened the season in the leadoff spot, occasionally yielding to Chris Dickerson, but when both started slowly, Cabrera got the nod and has been rooted at No. 1 ever since.

At .238/.276/.327 (.231 True Average), the 35-year-old shortstop is hitting well below his career rates of .273/.320/.395 (.250 TAv), yet as those rates suggest, even peak-form Cabrera isn't exactly Max Bishop or Rickey Henderson. His highest single-season on-base percentage was .347, recorded in 2003. He also reached his career high in walks that year with 52. Cabrera does have one small positive as a leadoff hitter. Since 2001, he has been an excellent percentage basestealer, swiping 193 bags in 232 attempts, an 83 percent success rate. This season (through Wednesday) he's nine-for-nine. Since, to invoke a cliché, you can't steal first base, and Cabrera has never been a high-volume basestealer in any case (averaging 21 per 162 games since 2001), his baserunning does not add to his credentials as a leadoff hitter.

Baker's inability to exploit the leadoff spot is nothing new. Now in his 17th season as a manager, the aggregate rates for a Baker leadoff hitter are .264/.327/.382. Baker leadoff hitters have drawn more than 87 walks in a season only once, in 1998. More often, they have drawn fewer than 60. Overall, his leadoff hitters have averaged 749 plate appearances and 61 walks per season. While we would expect leadoff hitters to have a higher walk rate than the average hitter, Baker's leadoff men have actually had a slightly lower walk rate than the average National League non-pitcher.

Despite Baker's oft-expressed disdain for slow runners who clog the bases no matter their other positives, it's not that he has been blinded by speed, choosing fast players to lead off, or if he has, it hasn't shown up in the results. Baker leadoff men have stolen as many as 58 bases and as few as 16 (with 12 caught stealing); the average has been 29. With the exception of his 2006 leadoff man, Juan Pierre, and the two half-seasons in which his teams traded for Kenny Lofton (with the 2002 Giants and 2003 Cubs), he hasn't had a classic burner at the top of the order, and by the time he got Lofton, the outfielder was 35 and his basestealing had been greatly curtailed.

Baker is not unique among managers in having trouble in finding an adequate leadoff hitter when the choice is not obvious. Think of Ralph Houk, who led off .261/.295/.316-hitting Bobby Richardson for the 1961 Yankees and got 90 runs out of the leadoff spot (80 of them belonging to Richardson, who had 706 PAs) despite having more home runs than any team in history coming up next. This was the kind of choice that Houk indulged in again and again during a 20-year managing career, but when he got to Detroit and had Ron LeFlore, he had an epiphany and stopped leading off the crappy second basemen (he batted them second instead). Casey Stengel once said that he didn't need his hair parted with an axe to get an idea from the outside. Houk needed the axe. Similarly, when Baker had Lofton, he knew what to do with him, but the rest of the time he couldn't sort out his options.

In Baker's defense, identifying the leadoff man on his roster hasn't always been easy. The big on-base threat on his first team was Barry Bonds, who seemed a more obvious three-four hitter (Baker batted him fifth, which suggests a problem greater than just his taste in leadoff men). A good, though unorthodox choice, would have been Will Clark, who had lost much of his home-run power at 28. Robby Thompson was having his best season (his last good one) but he hadn't been a great on-base threat at prior points in his career. Baker went with the veteran, Willie McGee, then the punchless outfield gloveman Darren Lewis. Result: abject failure. The first spot in the Giants' order hit .252/.301/.313 that year.

Baker stuck with Lewis in 1994 and was still using him in July 1995, at which point the Giants included him in a package that brought back Deion Sanders and four other players from the Reds. Though Sanders had hit only .240/.296/.326 to that point in the season, Baker made the football star his leadoff hitter. Sanders hit well enough in 52 games (.285/.346/.444; .273 TAv) that he qualifies as one of Baker's best choices, but he left as a free agent at the end of the year and was incapable of maintaining that level of production in any case.

For the next several years, Baker would devote himself to making Marvin Benard his leadoff man, but Benard's middling hitting and resultant inconsistency meant that the manager would have frequent recourse to Stan Javier, Darryl Hamilton, F.P. Santangelo, and Calvin Murray. For two years, 1998 and 1999, the aggregate result was quite good. In the former season, Giants leadoff hitters averaged .297/.392/.386; in the latter, .288/.368/.458. After that season, Benard's time as a useful hitter was over, while Murray's would never come, but it took Baker two years to be sure.

Since the Benard years, Baker's leadoff men have been a fascinating congeries of ill-fitting spare parts, including (but not limited to) David Bell, Tom Goodwin, Tsuyoshi Shinjo, Mark Grudzielanek, Lenny Harris, Jose Macias, Todd Walker, Corey Patterson (in three different seasons), Jerry Hairston, Neifi Perez, Ryan Freel, Jay Bruce, Willy Taveras, and the aforementioned Lofton, Pierre, and Dickerson. Baker's career is bookended by the disaster of his first-season and 2010 leadoff men, but those aside, the nadir of his mid-career choices came in 2005, when Hairston, Patterson, and Perez, the last two of which with career OBPs below .300, combined to hit .245/.299/.358 in the leadoff spot. Hitters at the top of the Cubs' order that year scored a grand total of 83 runs.

Sometimes, Baker's teams have even outsmarted themselves. In 2005, primary leadoff hitter Walker was hitting a solid .298/.346/.472 when Baker kicked him out of the top spot for good, first for Grudzielanek, then for the Moby Dick of Baker's career, his irresistible force, Patterson. The current Oriole led off for 55 of the final 58 games of the season, hitting .211/.263/.359 in the spot. Give Baker this much credit: Patterson's leadoff rates were better than his overall .215/.254/.348.

It is difficult to understand why a manager would choose to handicap his team the way Baker has in most seasons. He is clearly not a stupid man, and yet he continually makes batting order choices that are difficult to describe in any other way. It's as if some psychological trauma prevents him from seeing the errors in his thinking. It might be that his career provided poor role models, leadoff exemplars that he's still trying to find facsimiles of for his own batting orders, someone like Ralph Garr.

Baker played with Garr in the Braves' system and then again in the majors, where Garr was the leadoff hitter. Garr was a terrific hitter at his best, but his approach didn't leave much room for error. He was an Ichiro Suzuki-style hitter, averaging .306 for his career, peaking in 1974 with a league-leading .353. He had speed and a contact-oriented, line-drive approach which led to as many as 17 triples in a season. The downside was that he rarely walked, so when he didn't hit over .320, which was most of the time, he didn't contribute that much on offense. His career OBP was only .339.

At his peak, Garr would have made a fine third- or fifth-place hitter, but he spent his entire career hitting first or second. This was how baseball liked its leadoff men in the 1970s and early '80s; walks weren't important, but if you hit .290- or .300-worth of singles and threw in some steals, you were getting the job done. Garr wasn't very different from Mickey Rivers, Dave Collins, Willie Wilson, or Mookie Wilson, and McGee wasn't too far off either, though he spent more time hitting lower in the order (McGee's MVP-winning 1985 is a dead ringer for Garr's 1974). They almost exclusively hit their way on base rather than got there through a combination of hitting and selectivity.

Baker saw Garr at the height of his career. They were together at Triple-A Richmond when the latter hit .386/.426/.522, in the majors for part of the season in 1971, when Garr hit .343/.372/.441 in 154 games, shared the outfield with him as a regular in 1972 when Garr hit .325, and in 1974 when he won the batting title. In none of those seasons did Garr take more than 29 unintentional walks. Perhaps Garr remains Baker's leadoff role model. Yet, there are only so many .300-hitting line-drive hitters with speed, and Baker hasn't had them. Moreover, Baker's teams, in fact, any teams, are almost certainly not looking to draft them. If Ichiro had been born in the United States, he'd be a cornerback. Pure singles hitters who put the occasional liner in the gaps, no matter how fast, are not beloved of scouts and scouting directors.

Baker's subsequent career exposed him to a more rounded leadoff hitter in Davey Lopes, a terrific percentage basestealer who also had power and patience. He seems to have made less of an impression than his successor, Steve Sax, another player who sometimes hit his way on base, and Dan Gladden, who for a glorious half-season was Garr all over again. Baker went out with the A's, playing with them in 1985 and 1986. The A's employed three primary leadoff hitters in that period: Tony Phillips (career .374 OBP), Collins (.338, but fast), and Alfredo Griffin (.285, and perhaps the worst baserunner in modern history). If you not only saw but accepted Griffin as a leadoff man, it probably required no cognitive acrobatics to place Perez atop a batting order, for they were practically the same player.

As for the psychological insult that made Baker so wary of those "base-cloggers," there is no smoking gun, but perhaps the blow came on June 3, 1973. The Braves were managed by future Hall of Fame third baseman Eddie Mathews, who might have been a bit over his head. Garr was already established in the majors but had gotten off to a painfully slow start, hitting .234/.254/.292 through the end of May. At that point, Mathews decided to drop him out of the leadoff spot. Here is the lineup card that Baker saw on June 3, with the rates of the starters coming into the game:

#	BATTER	POS	RATES THRU 6/2/1973
1	Johnny Oates	C	.230/.282/.291
2	Mike Lum	1B	.290/.346/.411
3	Darrell Evans	3B	.251/.347/.514
4	Hank Aaron	LF	.237/.368/.548
5	Ralph Garr	RF	.249/.267/.318
6	Dusty Baker	CF	.259/.320/.411
7	Davey Johnson	2B	.249/.350/.410
8	Marty Perez	SS	.245/.345/.340
9	Ron Reed	P	.107/.107/.107

The late Johnny Oates, best remembered as the manager of the Orioles and Rangers, was a career platoon catcher who never hit much, batting .250/.309/.313 in a career that lasted 593 games and

11 seasons. He was best known not for getting on base but for having an excellent arm behind the plate, something attested to by his career 38 percent rate of throwing out basestealers. He was 27 and coming off of a season in which he'd hit .261/.332/.364 for the Orioles, a performance that was better than it looks given that the American League hit only .239/.306/.343 that year. Still, it was an 85-game, 288-PA performance that was just decent. It didn't mark Oates as the second coming of Ed Yost. In the game, Oates went 1-for-4 but didn't score a run—the Braves were shut out by the Cubs' Milt Pappas and Bob Locker.

June 3 wasn't the first time Mathews had led off with Oates; he tried it in early May, with Aaron hitting second and Baker hitting third. This was, however, the first time that he stuck with it, leaving the catcher at the top of the order for 10 of 12 games beginning a few days later. Oates hit .250/.321/.313 and a Braves team that went 76-85 overall went 8-4. Baker himself got crazy hot, going 17-for-40 (.425) and driving in eight runs, so it's not like he can harbor an irrational hatred of Oates for clogging up the bases so much that he himself somehow slumped.

No, the humiliation of hitting behind a journeyman catcher does not seem to be the source of Dusty's pain, but an antiquated sense of what makes a proper leadoff man might be the real source of the problem. A gar is a slippery fish that swims in brackish waters; for Baker, a Garr may be a slippery notion that swims in a troubled mind. Any leadoff man might be a Garr if he is fast enough and can be made to hit for a high enough average. Baker is forever seeking his old friend and teammate, and the potential damage to his team's standing is no obstacle to the continuation of that quest.

FEBRUARY 22, 2008

http://bbp.cx/a/7169

TRANSACTION ANALYSIS
Odds and Ends
Christina Kahrl

No Christina Kahrl Transaction Analysis column was complete without a reference to Napoleon, and the column reproduced below illustrated how an awareness of history could be used to deepen an understanding of the game's most recent moves.

CLEVELAND INDIANS
Signed OF-L Jason Tyner to a minor-league contract.

Kevin Goldstein IM'd me with this hot-off-the-wires story, alerting me to the fact that they'd be dancing in the streets of Buffalo because of the return of the mite-y Tyner. Lest we forget, the peerless punchless one was a key contributor down the stretch for the Bisons in 2004, and in something of an echo of those days when Buffalo was on the short list for an expansion team because of solid attendance, the enthusiasm generated for an International League playoff team and its heroes lingers on. Can you blame the people of Buffalo? Tyner is admirable as the anti-Branyan (more on him in a bit), a player of an extreme type who scraps, living up to Ozzie Guillen's comparison of him and his later Twins teammates to a riverine slaughterhouse. He may be less fond of the 2004 season than Buffalo seemingly is—for Tyner, it was his year in the Triple-A wilderness, time lost between his ignominious demotion before his own bobblehead day in Tampa Bay and his subsequent major-league resurrection with the Twins.

The Bisons are still operated by the Rich family, who were the driving force behind the attempt to get major-league baseball in Buffalo but who used to place a premium on fielding a competitive team. (Not too much unlike Rochester for ages, and perhaps now too for Sacramento in the PCL.) After ditching their affiliation with the Pirates after 1994—the Riches seem to have wisely anticipated how some things might be incompatible with winning—and hooking up with the Indians, Buffalo went to the playoffs in nine of its first 11 seasons as the Indians' top affiliate. That's changed, as the Bisons have been shut out of the International League playoffs in consecutive seasons in 2006 and 2007, a first for them in this relationship, and the first time it's happened since the honeymoon-killing '93-'94 double shutout from post-season play that killed off the partnership with the Pirates. As implausible as it might sound, bringing Tyner back is a win-now move, and in an organization that very much wants to win now—albeit not just in the AL

Central alone. If signing Tyner keeps people excited and coming to games in Buffalo, more power to them, and modest kudos to the Tribe for making it so; would that more teams were more responsive to the ambitions of their affiliates.

SEATTLE MARINERS
Signed OF-L Bubba Crosby to a minor-league contract with a spring training NRI.

TEXAS RANGERS
Signed 2B-R Ian Kinsler to a five-year, $22 million extension through 2012 with a $10 million club option for 2013.

This preempts his arbitration eligibility by a year and effectively takes him two years into his free agency eligibility, as well as past his 31st birthday. Kinsler probably suffers from some indifference because he's merely been very good as opposed to outstanding, but when you look at the components—the walks, the steals, the good (not great) glove work at the keystone—it's a decent package. Nevertheless, there is the matter of whether or not he's a park-inflated asset, because the discrepancy between his home rates (.314/.387/.537) and road (.234/.315/.359) is the difference between a down-ballot MVP and a Triple-A lifer.

In terms of what else happens at the plate, Kinsler is a bit above-average in delivering line drives (23.6 percent last year, against a 19 percent average for right-handed hitters over the last five) but is also above-average in hitting popups (10.3 percent, against 8.6) and fly balls (31.7 percent, versus 28.5). That's an interesting spread that equals a lot fewer groundballs than your average righty at the plate, but what I'm curious about is where they'll go from here—if he hits popups, will it be because he's connecting squarely even more often and delivering even more of his tasty line-drive power? Will the liners predictably "regress to the mean" (we use that phrase way too often here), or is that simply a reflection of what Ian Kinsler does? Certainly, if the rate drops, that would be a symptom of something going very wrong for him.

An interesting element of the deal is that final option year, where the buyout's an exceptionally cheap half-million; if Kinsler remains a half-useful player, the odds the option doesn't get exercised become a near-certainty. As good as Kinsler is, and as generically sensible as this kind of commitment is, there's work that remains to be done, and it'll be interesting to see whether it gets done, and what the upshot of it will be.

CHICAGO CUBS
Signed INF-S Alex Cintron to a minor-league contract with a spring training NRI.

Well, fiddle, no sooner do I want to add an amen to the idea that he might be a decent low-cost solution to the Orioles' shortstoplessness, and he decides he'd rather take his chances at Windy City cameos and a lot of time spent in the cornfields of Iowa. I wouldn't say it was a wise choice—Ronny Cedeno is out of options, Ryan Theriot isn't going anywhere, and Mark DeRosa's got to play, and that's all before we start drawing up scenarios that put Brian Roberts in the Cubs' middle infield picture. It's interesting that what went really wrong for him since that brief bit of sunshine in 2003 is that he was hitting a ton of line drives from both sides of the plate back then and never has since.

CINCINNATI REDS
Signed RHP Josh Fogg to a one-year, $1 million contract; placed LHP Bobby Livingston on the 60-day DL.

While the price might seem right and Fogg has plenty of experience pitching in hitter's parks, I guess I'm left wondering why you'd sign a veteran with next to no chance of pitching better than Matt Belisle. I suppose it notionally buys Johnny Cueto, Homer Bailey, and/or Edinson Volquez some quality time getting double- or triple-dipped in seasonings down at Louisville (and hopefully not getting battered as well). But if it's a win-now move to placate Dusty Baker by giving him somebody he's heard of, it doesn't really work, even by the relatively modest standards of the NL Central. One of the most noteworthy virtues of Fogg's performance record has been how he pitched against some of the Rockies' divisional rivals over the years, but that goes away in a different division with the unbalanced schedule, and you're left with a finesse righty with a track record of getting pasted by the Astros, Cubs, and Cardinals (and even the Pirates, but in only three starts). Add in that he's a fly-baller going to the Gap, and that Dusty might not be as quick on the draw getting him out of ballgames as the Rockies were, and I'll let you ink in the Batman-style "Kapow!" effects.

Nevertheless, Reds fans should consider this a win, if and only if this means that dealing far too much talent to the A's for Joe Blanton is now off the table. That doesn't necessarily mean Dusty's ever going to figure out what a Joey Votto is for, or that a Johnny Cueto can pitch, but it's better to have your own hatchlings on hand instead of growing up in someone else's nest. Consider the Fogg signing one cuckoo move that doesn't push anybody out of the nest.

HOUSTON ASTROS
Signed RHP Shawn Chacon to a one-year, $2 million contract.

One of the always-fun elements of having a new skipper running a camp is that it can fundamentally shake up a team's composition and just as radically alter player roles. In a situation as fluid as the Astros' pitching staff, bringing in a utility pitcher like Chacon, for this little money over just one season, fits in perfectly. At least two rotation spots, and perhaps three, are up in the air—and they should be. Woody Williams, Chris Sampson, and Brandon Backe haven't earned any consideration. Similarly, just about every spot in the bullpen beyond those of Jose Valverde and Doug Brocail could be up for grabs; sure, Geoff Geary and Oscar Villarreal seem likely, but a really bad camp might change matters. I'm not saying that Cecil Cooper's some sort of wild man, but he's got options, and given that even Williams has been told he has to earn his spot in the rotation, to Cooper's credit he seems willing to ponder them.

As a result, Chacon's sort of a Mr. Fix-It pickup, someone who could conceivably become Valverde's best set-up man at some point and who could just as probably be the team's third-best starter. I'm not saying he'll be good, mind you, but the talent's still there, and he has experience closing in Coors and starting in Yankee Stadium, and, at least superficially, that sounds like the breadth of experience that would make him a worthwhile pickup for the Astros' kamikaze run on contention this year. In an exercise of fun with statistically meaningless samples, in his four starts last year for the Pirates, Chacon threw an initial "pen start" of sorts, tossed one absolute gem, got let down by his bullpen after a decent outing, took a beating from the Yankees, and headed back to the pen, which adds up to mean exactly nothing. In 2006, his combined SNLVAR between the Yankees and Pirates added up to 0.7—not good, but to pick a weak-sister argument, that isn't really any worse than what they got out of Jason Jennings last season. I know, not exactly a ringing endorsement.

Some might quail over Chacon having walked a batter every other inning last season, but keep in mind that almost a quarter of his walks (11) were at the orders of Jim Tracy; take that out of Chacon's rate, and you've got a guy who walks just under 3.5 batters per nine—not bad, but not very good either. Survivable, and since he struck out more than twice as many, he's obviously still got stuff that fools a lot of the people some of the time. For the price and at this time of year, and given that the Astros' pitching might really only have four names that Cooper can put down in ink in terms of both spots and slots, a nice little pickup.

MILWAUKEE BREWERS
Signed 4C-L Russell Branyan to a minor-league contract without a spring training NRI.

"Look, it's the Russell Branyan action figure! 'He slugs!'"
"Hrm, 'Batteries not included.'"
"But he's on sale!"
"Son, he's always on sale."

Derision aside, I'm delighted to see the TTO demigod back in action at the site of some of his greatest mashing. It also isn't inconceivable that he might be able to crack the roster at some point this season. His primary opponent for a four corners reserve role might be the equally storied journeyman Joe Dillon, but in Branyan's favor, he has more major-league experience despite being four months younger. If Bill Hall's move to third goes especially badly, that might also help Branyan, but less helpful is the fact that Gabe Gross is out of options. The roadblocks that Dillon and Gross represent might be gone by Opening Day, however, as there's a chance that the Brewers might instead keep Kid Gwynn and the comebacking Gabe Kapler as their primary outfield reserves, putting Dillon in Nashville and Gross on somebody else's roster via trade or waiver claim. That latter possibility would be a nice break for Gross—he's too good to be a fifth outfielder, but he's not good enough to merit starting ahead of the Brewers' regular outfielders.

Outrighted OF-L Drew Macias outright to Portland (Triple-A) but didn't un-invite him from spring training.

ST. LOUIS CARDINALS
Signed LHP Ron Villone to a minor-league contract with a spring training NRI.

Not a bad little pickup. Although Villone might be considered a heavy as a result of his being named in the now-infamous Mitchell Report, the Birds don't exactly have a set situation among their options for southpaw specialists in the pen. Tyler Johnson should be a lock as the primary lefty-getter, and that's solid enough. After that, for the indispensable second lefty (this is a Tony La Russa team, after all), you get into picking one of the two Flores brothers, Randy or Ron, neither of whom is really a great choice. As a result, the hulking Villone might make an interesting as well as more effective alternative to Johnson.

WASHINGTON NATIONALS
Signed Nepotista-R Bret Boone and LHP Odalis Perez to minor-league contracts, but only Perez's comes with a spring training NRI.

I recently finished reading the late Gunther Rothenberg's last book, *The Emperor's Last Victory*, an account of Napoleon's first major battlefield defeat and last war-winning contest. As ever with the old master and his noted Austrophilia, Rothenberg's attention is more closely fixed on this latest mishap to befall the Habsburg empire, with particular attention to the fractious relationship between the emperor, Franz, his younger brother and battlefield commander, the Archduke Karl, and their younger brothers, the Archdukes Johann, Joseph, and brother-in-law Ludwig. Generally speaking, they were a collection of men supremely unqualified for the responsibilities given to them by their equally lackluster eldest brother. Franz feared that his brother Karl might have designs on the throne and so constantly spied upon and interfered with command and control of the army. Franz had reason for his suspicions, because Karl was a reluctant Generalissimus, preferring to treat with the French emperor he was supposed to be fighting against over secret peace offers. Karl had equal reason to despair over his ability to conduct the campaign with every possible resource for victory at his disposal; Ludwig may have sensibly scampered home early on, but Johann and Joseph were spectacularly uncooperative, and the lot of them anticipated that if they lost badly, the dynasty itself might collapse.

So, what came of family management? Generally, everyone managed their games to try to not lose as opposed to trying to win, while investing a huge amount of time in CYA-minded prevaricating and actions that fundamentally undermined the chances of success for any of the others. So they lost, but not as badly as they might have, and the penalty was tossing their nubile baby sister Marie Louise to the infamous "Corsican Ogre," who was craving the sort of validation that only a blonde trophy wife can really bring to a self-made emperor having a mid-life crisis. For his indeterminate loyalties, Karl was put out to pasture for the remainder of his adult life despite being the first general to have beaten Napoleon in the field at Aspern-Essling. He was replaced the next time Austria entered the lists against French domination by a non-family member, Prince Karl von Schwarzenberg. Schwarzenberg can be politely referred to as the entirely competent if cautious architect of total victory over Napoleon in 1813-14; this was before the game French emperor's last, doomed comeback attempt a year later, but that petered out well short of a full season at Waterloo. (Steve Carlton should have taken notes.)

Which brings me to this profusion of Boones in the Nationals organization, because like putting too many Habsburgs into the mix, it just doesn't seem like something with any kind of relationship to winning. Aaron was a bit of a stretch, but setting aside that he can't really play anywhere but first—although, like any archduke TBNL, he'll do more if asked, with not necessarily desirable results—he's been employed by somebody and done well enough to be seen as a decent enough replacement for Robert Fick; heck, he's even an upgrade on that guy, who wasn't even related by marriage. Signing Aaron might have been skeevy, insofar as proud pappy Bob Boone is part of Jim Bowden's retinue, but there's enough there to defend it conceptually as a baseball move.

But Bret? Bret abruptly walked away from the game in spring training 2006 after two mediocre years at the plate; his defense was already a problem, and if he couldn't hit well enough to make himself an asset at second base, there wasn't a whole lot else to recommend having him around. He'll be "only" 39 this year, so I suppose it's possible that he'll provide well-aged something or another at Columbus. Maybe this will be a way to have the Boone clan do a one-game reunion in spring, where failed manager Bob runs a squad that has son number one planted at second and son number two planted at third. Heck, maybe the old coot puts on the tools of ignorance; he was apparently cranky his games caught record bit the dust, and don't the Nats need a catcher?

See, that's my problem with nepotism in a nutshell—it's no longer about finding the best talent, it's about trying to work around people who clutter up an improving organization that has real-world tasks like winning more games. A plague of Boones has nothing to do with that, but the fact that this is being done here should make people wonder if this is the way life's going to be with the Lerner family in charge. What's next, a Stephen Larkin comeback? He's only been out of baseball for a couple of years too, so why not? To anticipate a complaint that I'm taking this a bit seriously, consider that this is the same game run by the same people who said they wouldn't let the White Sox put Minnie Minoso on the field because it was a travesty; it was, but either you have standards, or you don't, and this ranks with the career of Jim Morris among the proofs that there aren't standards, there are only agreed-upon conceits, and less agreeable ones.

Oh, and Odalis Perez? Long coveted by Bowden, he does have the virtue of not being related to anybody, except for his family, and they're apparently not baseball people, so that must not really count for much, does it now? It's hard to suggest there's much left in the tank after his recent failures—Perez didn't do well against righties or lefties, early in his games or late, on the road, at home, in interleague contests. With a train, in the rain, and you know the rest. If you're really struggling for a compliment, I suppose you can note that he did somewhat better with runners on base, but then he was also intimately familiar with throwing from the stretch, so that's not exactly the sort of silver lining you want to spin into something to dress up this move. However, with perhaps only two rotation slots set, and those only for as long as both Shawn Hill and John Patterson are healthy, I suppose there's always a danger that Bowden will inflict another ill-fated project on his staff, not unlike Zach Day or Ryan Drese or Brian Lawrence, all in his quest to find the next Jimmy Haynes.

TRANSACTION OF THE DAY
A Peach of a Deal
Christina Kahrl

When evaluating a trade, it's important to approach the comings and goings from a variety of angles, as Christina Kahrl made clear in her take on the departure of Javier Vazquez from Chicago.

CHICAGO WHITE SOX
Acquired C-R Tyler Flowers, SS-R Brent Lillibridge, 3B-R Jon Gilmore, and LHP Santos Rodriguez for RHP Javier Vazquez and LHP Boone Logan. [12/2]

While Sox fans have reason to be concerned that dealing Vazquez and not getting a starter close to ready coming back in the deal exposes them to a rotation of Danks, Buehrle, Floyd, humming a few bars, and getting back to Danks, Buehrle, and Floyd, let's remember that familiarity bred contempt for a few of the team's high-profile pickups of late, notably departing free agent Orlando Cabrera, but not excepting Vazquez.

Flowers is the obvious prize, though his glove work behind the dish is questionable enough that he's no sure thing. Which is not to say this is a bad pack, it's just that it's comprised of disparate parts, players on different trajectories moving at different speeds who might answer different needs at different times. Lillibridge can run, and he can handle short well enough, but he was also highly overrated after a batting average-inflated 2006 season, and there's a pretty good chance he's just a utility player who allows the Sox to wean themselves from the Age of Ozuna once and for all. He's not a bad add, but he's also probably not a starting shortstop that lets the Sox move Alexei Ramirez to third instead of short, which means the Ramirez-at-short experiment isn't being ended before it gets started. Lillibridge also doesn't pose much danger to Chris Getz at second. So, he's filler.

What about the young third baseman, Jon Gilmore? Although he got a taste of the Sally League last season before moving back down to short-season A-ball in the Appy League, Gilmore has yet to graduate to a full-season league. That's fine—as a 2007 supplemental first-round pick in his age-19 season, the goal was to see how well the athletic former high school shortstop and quarterback adjusted to the pro game. He gets plenty of credit for a quick bat, readily reflected in his peppering Appalachia at a .337/.365/.473 clip, or what might be more easily described as a lot of singles and doubles. His glove work at third is still a bit rough, but he has the hands, arm, and grace to handle the position. Maybe these gifts mean that the Sox have found their new Joe Crede type a few years down the line. Maybe, and it's worth waiting to see, but still only a 'maybe,' with the acumen of Sox scouting duly taken into account. In the meantime, it's still looking like Wilson Betemit and maybe Josh Fields at third, a solid bit of placeholding I like, but might do less for you.

I really don't have a lot to say about Rodriguez, who isn't exactly a tall drink of water out of the Dominican: 6'5" but listed at 180, he's more of a swizzle stick, but 45 strikeouts in 29 GCL innings has a way of really catching the eye on the printed page, and those are the product of an arm that delivers 90-93 mph heat. Despite what five wild pitches might convey, reports on his wildness are not to be exaggerated.

Which brings us back to the player who has to make this deal really work, Flowers. Getting a top catching prospect is a good idea in the abstract, and it's interesting (in light of all the attention) that Kenny Williams managed to pull it off with a team that wasn't the Rangers. What makes him a prospect is that he's a catcher who hits, and heading into what will be his age-23 season, he's also ready for Double-A, which puts him into the range of possibilities as far as arriving at the end of '09 if that goes really well, and perhaps more reasonably 2010. (Which matters, in light of the club's financial commitment to A.J. Pierzynski through that very season.) He put the hurt on the Carolina League as something more than just a Three True Outcomes type, thwacking 32 doubles from a .288 clip while also delivering 200 walks and strikeouts in 520 PA (split almost evenly, 98 walks and 102 whiffs). While everyone's worked up over his exceptional AFL performance, I wouldn't get worked up over the numbers there—I still have that James Mouton hangover to live down—as much as they represent a continuation of his second-half breakout for Myrtle Beach, hitting .328/.454/.586 after the league's all-star break. If you want to believe that might make him the new Piazza, you can be forgiven that—it's clear that he's breaking out and might climb the ladder fast.

In this organization, concern over his catching skills is less of a stumbling block than it was with a team that has Brian McCann. Even so, doubts about his receiving skills and his bulk should give his new organization pause; without improving his footwork and release times, throwing out 28 percent of opposing baserunners in the Carolina League seems likely to go down against more polished basestealers at higher levels. More interesting still in the winter of speculation over whether or not CC Sabathia's too big a signing to risk, in physical as well as financial dimensions, keep in mind that Flowers isn't simply big—listed at 6'4" and 245 pounds, he's taller and heavier than Lance Parrish, and heavier than Andy Allanson and Joe Mauer, the largest backstops of recent memory. Search through Baseball Reference (all hail Sean Forman), there have been only six catchers who were both 6'2" or taller and 230 or heavier since 1901: Ernie Lombardi, Javy Lopez, Pete Varney (briefly a White Sox backup backstop in the '70s), and three current catchers,

Ronny Paulino of the Pirates, A.J. Ellis of the Dodgers, and Colt Morton with the Padres. Lopez and Lombardi were never considered defensive assets, but the latter three get good marks. However, everyone on this list is smaller than Flowers, and as Kevin Goldstein noted in his Top 11 for the Braves, it's not a good weight.

To recap, I can accept a big bet on Flowers being something at the plate because of the development curve, even while I think that taking the risk that he could pan out at catcher is pretty speculative. Basically, the bat could play at first and DH, and in an organization employing Jim Thome for one more year and Paul Konerko for two, that has value to the Sox even if he doesn't pan out at catcher. Gilmore and Rodriguez are long-term markers, guys we won't really know whether the tools translate into high confidence-level projectable results for another couple of years, but both are worth having. Lillibridge might have the most name recognition; you'll get over that.

Was it worth tearing out one plank of the rotation that propelled the Sox to the postseason this year? I'm inclined to think so, because Vazquez wasn't cheap, the Sox need all kinds of talent, and this year's division title was something of a nice surprise that helps buy Kenny Williams and company breathing room and credibility as they embark on a rebuild. The real question is whether or not they could have gotten more, but that's speculative at best. If they were talking turkey with the Braves but couldn't land one of the center fielders, it's easy to suggest you take your Vazquez and go elsewhere, but given that a lot of teams don't have any more love for the well-traveled right-hander than the Sox had, that's easier said than done, and there's not much reason to anticipate he's got another 2007 season in him, not in light of his performance in the other four of the last five years.

ATLANTA BRAVES
Acquired RHP Javier Vazquez and LHP Boone Logan from the White Sox for C-R Tyler Flowers, SS-R Brent Lillibridge, 3B-R Jon Gilmore, and LHP Santos Rodriguez. [12/2]

The Braves haven't been to the playoffs since 2005, not for lack of trying. In that time, regearing the lineup with younger, better parts continued as smoothly as before, with prospects like Brian McCann, Kelly Johnson, Yunel Escobar, and seemingly Jeff Francouer all successfully integrated. Think about that for a second: three quality up-the-middle regulars, with Jordan Schafer and Gorkys Hernandez on the way up to potentially complete the set. Add that sort of good stuff to Chipper Jones on one corner or another, and you have a lineup that ought to be part of a contender. Same old Braves, right?

The problem's been the team's pitching.* However, last year's reunion rotation didn't solve all their problems, nor did the recent abandonment of what had been a decades-long experience with the fundamental replaceability of most relief pitching. Keeping the rotation going with thirtysomethings hasn't really worked out so well in the last several seasons: eventually, old men break down or peter out. Mike Hampton was less than what they needed, and then he wasn't even that the last four years. John Smoltz got old, Tim Hudson's busted, and bringing back Tom Glavine proved as lamentable in practice as it appeared at first blush. Anticipated retread successes, another regular feature in the glory days, with John Thomson and Jorge Sosa didn't work out. Home-grown hurler Chuck James disappeared under a welter of walks and homers before breaking down. Nabbing Jair Jurrjens from the Tigers and Jorge Campillo off the rejects pile kept things going nicely last season, but that did not a rotation make, and the Braves' unit finished 11th in the league in SNLVA Rate, 12th in Expected Wins, and next to last in starter innings pitched in 2008.

So yeah, they need starting pitching. They also have a gaggle of desirable prospects, and apparently they still want to give this contending thing a shot, rather than curl up for a year and wait for the kids. Like a lot of teams, the Braves aren't affording themselves the time to rebuild, and they're instead focusing on retooling. That can mean making space for the kids once they come, but it also means some more of the same, getting somebody else's thirty-something starter, somebody already under contractual control. Landing Vazquez is just the latest iteration of this particular play, and while I like the deal, it's important to recognize that this is an act of repetition to keep this club hanging around an 80-win talent level that automatically puts you in the playoff picture in the senior circuit.

Of himself, Vazquez is a decent enough pickup, a mid-rotation starter who's flirted with being slightly more than that at times. Last season's .504 SNLVA Rate doesn't sound great, rating 91st among all big-league starters with 100 IP, a big drop from his 2007 mark of .566 but of a piece with his 2006 mark of .500. Arguments that he'll be happier and perhaps more dominant in the NL have to go back to his Expos days more than five years ago and conveniently overlook that he was as adequate as ever in his season with the Snakes in 2005 (.531), which wasn't all that much better than his much-lamented season with the Yankees in '04 (.520). It's more important to accept that his range is as a guy who'll give you 30 starts or more of you solid performance, not dominance. That's entirely acceptable, of course, especially when the alternative might be a call to a tanned, rested, and forever unready Rick Behenna.

The change of leagues is going to help him of course, but not really because getting out of the Cell is going to make a big difference for him—in his three seasons in Chicago, he allowed 4.4 R/9 against 4.9 R/9 on the road. No, what's going to make a difference for Vazquez is his problem with getting through the sixth inning, which has been especially tough for him in recent seasons. As a matter of timing, that's usually around when a starting pitcher is seeing the heart of the order the third time, but in the NL, with the pitcher's slot generating easier outs, that might happen a little later in an individual start. If Vazquez's problem is a combination of the best hitters getting a good look at him and running out of gas around his 90th pitch, that can be mitigated a bit by a manager more inclined to recognize the need to hook him while the hooking's good, instead of a skipper who dares you to finish what you started and then gets understandably cranky when you predictably don't. Assuming the exchange of the pitcher for the DH helps avoid his past problems of hitting the wall against a lineup's best the third time through, Vazquez could wind up with a superficially excellent-seeming season if Bobby Cox hooks him after six innings. Cox wouldn't have to be obvious about it and insult Vazquez's dignity—NL skippers always have pinch-hitting and double-switch possibilities to bring into play—and Vazquez wouldn't really be a radically different pitcher. He'd simply be given the advantage of being lifted before he was pushed into too many of those unhappy third at-bats against the people who can hurt him.

The financial element of this deal shouldn't be underrated. While Vazquez isn't cheap—$23 million over 2009 and 2010—put that money in the context of the current market. You simply can't get a known quantity like Vazquez for a two-year deal from among this winter's free agents. Put this move up against spending more over three or four years for some mid-market rotation regular, and it comes across as especially inspired as an adaptation to what little time the Braves have left to run as Chipper Jones' ballclub. If they can't make a better play at contention in 2009 than they have the last three years, it won't be a matter of turning the page—it will have already been turned and glued shut.

Finally, on the most fundamental level, you have to credit the Braves for what this deal boils down to in terms of impact at the big-league level: they got a solid mid-rotation starter, and they didn't have to give up any of their better prospects in the deal. Sure, skip putting Jason Heyward or Tommy Hanson into an exchange of this nature, but they didn't even have to deal from their second rank, the guys like Jordan Schafer and Gorkys Hernandez, and this despite the fact that they're making a trade with a team that needs a center fielder? Admittedly, if the Sox had gotten Hernandez or Schafer, that would have been a real coup, but I don't mean to beat up on Kenny Williams in this space—he did apparently try to get them, and he didn't. The Braves were willing to deal from depth in prospects and take on salary, and working with an organization that could use the salary space and the talent. From Frank Wren on down, the Braves deserve credit in targeting Vazquez—rarely in Ozzie Guillen's favor for any great length of time—and getting him relatively reasonably with prospects they could afford to trade away.

As for getting Logan, I guess I'm of two minds on the subject. He's a lefty who cooks with gas, but he's also acquired a rep as a guy not especially gifted with a lot of aptitude. Maybe Roger McDowell will reach him where another good pitching coach, Don Cooper, apparently struggled, but I'm reluctant to get as enthusiastic about adding Logan as I was yesterday about the organization's grabbing Eric O'Flaherty on waivers. If I had to put O'Flaherty, Logan, and Jeff Ridgway in some particular order, that would be it, and it's nice that all of them have better-than-average velocity for southpaws. While I doubt that Emperor Charles V was talking about lefty relief help when he picked Plus ultra as his motto, I guess the Braves can take some satisfaction in achieving Redundancy plus ultra.

*: I know, as well as multiple meltdowns from among their non-Chipper options on the corners, but we'll set that aside for the time being—this is just my argument.

2006—SETTING THE STAGE
The New Guys
Christina Kahrl

Evaluating managers is difficult under any circumstances, even more so when a skipper takes a new job. Nonetheless, Christina Kahrl accepted the challenge and took a crack at predicting the performance of five new managerial hires before Opening Day of the 2006 season.

One of the most interesting periods in a team's construction and development is that moment when a new manager takes over a ballclub. Although most new guys are always going to be selected to serve as the factotum of the club's general manager, some new managers are placed in the position to make decisions which fundamentally change the fortunes of the team and the players. Certainly, one of the most interesting periods in a fan's experience is getting to watch what happens to your team when a new manager comes in. Approaching the talent on hand with a fresh set of eyes, he goes to work on deciding who's going to play, who isn't, and who's on the way out.

It's particularly interesting watching to see which players end up making good impressions on the new boss. While stathead orthodoxy might insist on some of sort of performance evaluation-minded determinism, as much as performance matters, so do first impressions and fresh starts. There's nothing like a camp with a new manager for out-of-nowhere success stories, for organizational soldiers or minor-league veterans who suddenly break through, and for opportunities given to players who were previously typecast, pigeonholed, or simply overlooked. A new manager has no particular loyalties: most of these guys haven't done anything for him before.

It's also sabermetric orthodoxy to deride the relative importance of the manager on what happens in terms of the results on the field. We're all familiar with Casey Stengel's observation on his relative importance, that "I couldn't have done it without the players." But these are the easy claims, and like pat assertions that team chemistry doesn't matter—because it isn't something we can measure—the maddening thing about denying that the manager is critical to what goes on in the field is that such a belief skips over the simple fact that managers are the people who choose who's on that field, managers are the people who design a player's usage patterns, and managers are the people most responsible for putting players into situations in which they help their teams.

No, they can't do it without the players, but they can put the players into situations where they're more likely to succeed, and through that, build a better ballclub.

As a group, managers have been pretty ill-served by performance analysts, particularly in terms of our creating statistics that might convey useful information about how they run their ballclubs. What is particularly frustrating about how managers get evaluated these days is the reliance on statistics that have next to no descriptive or practical value. Take platoon percentage: it seems sensible enough on the face of it, right? We know that righty-lefty platoon advantages exist, and it seems straightforward enough to "measure" the extent to which a manager exploits that in his lineups, right? But how then does such a statistic compensate for more basic, team-specific considerations? If you're the 2001 Astros, and you've got a lineup with seven right-handed regulars and Lance Berkman, then 'platoon percentage' doesn't tell us that Larry Dierker was ignorant of platoon splits any more than it suggests that he should have found more ways to get Daryle Ward and Jose Vizcaino into the lineup. It's a matter of the numbers being mute on the subject of a team-specific context and generating data that is, at best, uninformative. These are the sorts of frustrations that have fueled the interest of people like me or Steven Goldman in helping to craft a better collection of statistics to describe manager performance, but these will have to be created over time.

What needs saying is that when we're talking about managers, context matters. Whom they're managing, what kinds of teams, what sorts of assemblages of talent, young or old, rebuilding, retooling, contending, competing, all of that matters if we're ever going to get a good sense of which managers are doing good work, and which ones should be haunting network studios instead of clubhouses. It is a question of relying on data to tell us some things, but not everything. It's about studying a manager's history: whom he's used and how he's used them, what problems he's solved, what habits he likes to fall into, and which ones he shouldn't but does. It's about recognizing where the manager came from and understanding that he is the sum and product of his experiences up to that point. Whom a manager played for can matter, because his range of experiences as a player might lead to how he thinks a ballclub should be run and what tactics make the most sense.

Will a brand-new manager like Joe Girardi take his cues from what he saw and was asked to do when he was a Cub playing for Don Zimmer in 1989? Did he learn something from witnessing Don Baylor's mismanagement of the Rockies in the 1995 NLDS? Or does everything that he feels he needs to know about managing come from his four years with Joe Torre's Yankees? We don't know, and whatever Girardi might say on the subject, he may not know until he's confronted with specific problems whose answers can come only from the limited choices available to him with his team. Because what's really going to matter here is what the managers do with their new ballclubs, not what they say they're going to do.

If we're going to be serious about evaluating managers, we need to do so on a level more interesting and more telling than simply referring to the values we attach to on-field tactical events. It's about watching and learning how a manager runs a team, and how he gets good mileage out of his players. Because of that, it's particularly interesting when a new manager is dealing with a new group of talent, a new roster, players he may know only from scouting reports and stats and passing impressions from watching them play on other teams a few times per year. A new manager is in a position to shake things up, create new roles for some players, and discard others.

Setting aside the guys who, like Jerry Narron, Buddy Bell, or Sam Perlozzo, are running their first camps but already have the benefit of managing a good chunk of last season, what can we expect from the five new managers in MLB? Leaning on their histories, past patterns, past successes, past failures, what might we get to see once the games start counting?

Joe Girardi, Florida Marlins
- The Past: This is Girardi's first job as a manager, and like the Mets' Willie Randolph, he's someone who seems most closely associated with his years of work with the Yankees, first as a player, and later as a coach. But as mentioned before, he also played for Don Baylor and Don Zimmer for good stretches. Beyond those three, you get into brief periods with Jim Lefebvre, Tony La Russa, Bruce Kimm, Joe Altobelli, and Jim Essian. Girardi had a checkered career as a player, where he had to overcome Greg Maddux's preference to work with anybody else as well as his limitations as a hitter. In many ways, Giradi is a throwback to the '30s: Italian, famously good-natured, and a catcher who could at least bunt well. He's done television work, and media savvy is an underrated element of the manager's job these days—managing the Fourth Estate and keeping it in his face, instead of nagging after his players.
- What He's Got: Kids, lots of 'em, and it isn't a Catholic thing. Highly-rated prospects like Jeremy Hermida, Hanley Ramirez, and Scott Olsen, but also young stars like Miguel Cabrera, and even guys like Reggie Abercrombie in center and Dan Uggla at second getting their first (and perhaps only) big breaks. And very little veteran leavening. The absence of veterans might mean extra pressure on the coaching staff as far as running herd on new guys not used to larger per diems. Interestingly, Girardi did not find a famous ex-manager to be his bench coach for his rookie campaign, which can either be something about self-confidence, or that the staff's function is going to be more about really coaching.
- Who Might Catch a Break: Who won't might be the better question, because this is the best opportunity that guys like Eric Reed, Abercrombie, or Chris Aguila are ever going to get. Girardi's willingness to let Josh Willingham continue catching is a good choice; finding catchers who can hit is hard, and as Mike Stanley demonstrated, you really can make someone into an adequate catcher. Abercrombie and Reed both seem to reflect a fascination with slap-happy speed guys, but it's not entirely clear whether that's entirely

to Girardi's taste, or a matter of an organization being conditioned to believe that you want someone like Juan Pierre leading off.

- What to Watch For: With this sort of club, Girardi cannot afford to be like Randolph and mistake stubborn inflexibility for leadership. He's in the most low-pressure, low-expectations job in the major leagues, and he's going to have to admit mistakes and fix them while undergoing his OJT as a big-league manager. It'll be particularly interesting to see whether or not Dan Uggla holds onto the job at second base. What will Girardi do with any of the young hitters who struggle: let them play through it, demote them, or jerk them in and out of the lineup? How will he handle the pitchers who start trying to make perfect pitches to overcompensate for their lack of run support, or the ones who are simply in over their heads? Will his experience as a catcher help? Will he get too attached to the immediately available mediocre young pitchers, like Sergio Mitre, or will he be able to move them out of the way for the better talents should they be ready?

Jim Leyland, Detroit Tigers

- The Past: After coaching for Tony La Russa, Leyland enjoyed a brilliant career with the Pirates, helping take one of the game's most moribund franchises to three consecutive NL East division titles from 1990-92. Then a lot of misery as the Pirates slowly disintegrated, the decision to flit over to Florida to hook up with fellow former Sox staffer Dave Dombrowski and win a quick World Series, followed by the ugliness of having to manage the Huizenganated '98 Marlins, and then the odd decision to go to Colorado.

  As a manager, Leyland initially made himself famous for his willingness to bunt as a matter of reflex, but he eventually got away from that. He was unafraid to try some interesting things with his pitchers (like starting Ted Power in a playoff game, or starting pitchers on three days' rest with the Rockies) and had the flexibility to come up with some other novel solutions, like making Wally Backman a third baseman in 1990 or Darren Daulton a right fielder in 1997, because that's what he needed. He was able to cope with the annual question of where to put Bobby Bonilla, third base or the outfield, because he was willing to stomach the errors in exchange for the offense. He built effective, lasting platoons at first base and catcher in Pittsburgh, but platooned a bit in the outfield and third base as well, and continued to do so with Florida to some extent. If there's an ominous note to strike, it's that Leyland seems inclined to work some starters pretty hard, notably Alex Fernandez, Livan Hernandez, and Pedro Astacio.

- What He's Got: A team more like the Marlins '97 squad that was expected to win than the Pirates he started off with, certainly. But despite that, he's willing to trust some roles to the kids. Curtis Granderson and Justin Verlander might seem obvious, but Leyland hasn't been afraid of choosing them, and not everyone would be as calm about it.

- Who Might Catch a Break: Craig Monroe, of course, courtesy of the team's decision to cut loose Carlos Pena. That's a "sending a message" move, but it's also one that costs the

Tigers runs they won't make up with Monroe as an everyday player. Omar Infante, because Leyland always seems to find a way to use a multi-positional supersub in ways big and small, going back to Bill Almon in 1986, or someone like John Wehner, but also including stars like Bonilla or Jeff King.

- What to Watch For: Will he stick with Granderson and Verlander or not? Will Leyland's success with platoons lead to a decision to go looking for a left-handed bat for left field? When the Tigers are in fourth place on July 1, will his enthusiasm flag again, as it did in Colorado?

Grady Little, Los Angeles Dodgers

- The Past: We all remember the Pedro Game, right? Yankees fans have to hold onto something these days. But whatever the complaints about Little's failure to effectively manage a bullpen by committee or stand up to a veteran pitcher, he did manage two second-place finishes in the AL East in 2002 and 2003, no better and no worse than expected. Before that, Little coached for Bobby Cox in Atlanta. That sounds good, but keep in mind that Pat Corrales has coached for Cox for a long time, and nobody's itching to give him another shot.
- What He's Got: Not exactly an All-Star team, but not far short of that. It's a veteran club, and just about the only complicated significant choice to be made is in left field, where Little could safely stick with Jose Cruz Jr., or he could use Joel Guzman's spring to convince him to give the kid a shot. I wouldn't bet on it, though.
- Who Might Catch a Break: Ramon Martinez has already made the team, so he's one. Generally speaking, when you're expected to win, it takes a pretty bold manager (see Cox, Bobby) to keep a couple of rookies for anything from a key role to last man on the bench. Little's boldest surprise picks seem to be his sudden taste for Jason Repko, and the decision to keep Hong-Chih Kuo as the situational lefty. Also, if he's healthy enough, I wouldn't be surprised to see Eric Gagne flirt with breaking the saves record.
- What to Watch For: Push-button managing in a sense that's far more true to the term: scripted bullpen usage roles, scrupulous observation of veteran pecking order, and nothing resembling a tactical surprise being sprung on the other guys. But with a rotation that's relying on Brett Tomko and Aaron Sele, will he develop a quick hook this summer? Will the enthusiasm for Repko survive the return of veteran Jayson Werth from the DL?

Joe Maddon, Tampa Bay Devil Rays

- The Past: An upbeat coach from the Angels organization fresh from several years spent as Mike Scioscia's bench coach, which makes for a huge change of pace from the equally past-caring previous pair of managers, Lou Piniella and Hal McRae. Maddon came up the player development route, coaching and managing in the minors and doing stints as Minor League Field Coordinator and Director of Player Development. He was a catcher as a player and has done some time as a bullpen coach, and he was the Angels' interim manager during or after the tenures of John McNamara and Terry Collins. Basically, someone who seems to have the right sorts of experiences to handle a young ballclub and help the organization sort out its homegrown talent.

- What He's Got: All sorts of goodies, but more on the hitting side of the ledger than on the pitching. He does still have to move beyond the decision to limit his choices for an outfield job between Damon Hollins and Joey Gathright.
- Who Might Catch a Break: It depends on what you think about Aubrey Huff, but moving him to third certainly exploits his positional flexibility while making space for the organization's up-and-coming outfielders. It also improves Huff's value on the trade market, and you can be sure that's an active consideration as well. Josh Paul, if only because Maddon seemed to want to forgive him his October postseason boner and give him another opportunity when most people would have left him in a gutter to be named later. Edwin Jackson, because Maddon's being patient with him so far and might not share Piniella's fascination with Mark Hendrickson. Perhaps a minor-league veteran reliever like Jason Childers or Ruddy Lugo will stick, in part because of how badly the guys who were expected to stick have pitched.
- What to Watch For: Whether or not he'll stick with the decision to push Huff back to third, and at what point Delmon Young, B.J. Upton, and Wes Bankston will be given opportunities to push past Gathright, Hollins, and Travis Lee. How he'll cope with the pitching staff, which will probably be ulceriffic all summer.

Jim Tracy, Pittsburgh Pirates

- The Past: A brilliant four-year run with the Dodgers, capped by a division title in 2004, followed by the enormous disappointment of 2005. Over his career, he established a reputation for flexibility with lineups and roles and finding ways to put his bench to work. He broke in a few solid journeyman regulars, guys like Paul Lo Duca, Dave Roberts, and Cesar Izturis. He's been able to handle good but not great starters effectively, getting valuable work out of guys like Jeff Weaver and Odalis Perez and surprising mileage out of Jose Lima in 2004. However, with the arguable exception of Eric Gagne, he's never really had to break in and develop a star player, hitter or pitcher. Instead, Tracy made his reputation by handling veteran players well and making the most out of the back end of his roster.
- What He's Got: A few unfortunate veteran pickups in the lineup, some serious minor-league pitching talent, and tough choices in the outfield and behind the plate. In center, will he pick Chris Duffy, the speed and defense candidate? Or will he go for Nate McLouth, the gamer trying to break away from the 'tweener' label? And is either of them worth really getting worked up over?
- Who Might Catch a Break: McLouth really seems to have struck Tracy's fancy, and Duffy's not a star in the making, so don't be surprised if McLouth wins the job and turns in a Lo Duca-like career: workmanlike, admirable, and short of greatness. Jose Hernandez and

Mike Edwards, because it pays to have played for the old man in his previous place of employ, but this is a matter of having players around to help explain how the new manager does things. Brandon Duckworth, of all people, seems to have nabbed the Giovanni Carrara pity-pickup award, but then Carrara himself is here and might also make it. Carrara was already past 30 when Tracy put him to good use in 2001, so there's no reason to believe that he might be similarly successful with Duckworth, despite his Carrara-like early career struggles.

- <u>What to Watch For</u>: Will the first choice in center field be the last one? Will Ryan Doumit start claiming a larger share of the catching job away from Humberto Cota? Will the spiteful streak that came out during 2005's organization-wide meltdown in L.A. show up in Pittsburgh? How will he handle young starters like Zach Duke and Paul Maholm, given his limited experience with young pitchers? Will he be able to get Kip Wells back on track, or was the magic worked with Weaver a Chavez Ravine thing?

You probably didn't need more reasons to look forward to Opening Day, but these five will certainly bear watching as the season kicks off.

JULY 7, 2009 — http://bbp.cx/a/7774

TRANSACTION OF THE DAY
Harden-ed
Christina Kahrl

The A's traded the oft-injured Rich Harden and Chad Gaudin for a passel of prospects, but Christina Kahrl contended that they didn't receive sufficient talent in return.

OAKLAND ATHLETICS
Acquired RHP Sean Gallagher, 2B/OF-L Eric Patterson, OF-R Matt Murton, and C-R Josh Donaldson from the Cubs for RHPs Rich Harden and Chad Gaudin. [7/8]

> We knew all the answers
> And we shouted them like anthems
> Anxious and suspicious
> That God knew how much we cheated
> —Scissor Sisters

I'm as big a Billy Beane fan as any person who prefers to stop short of going all fanboy or fangirl over the man—that's for real genius, not canny baseball executives—but it's really, really hard to see what it is that the A's got that would compel them to accept this offer, as opposed to treat it as a conversational cul-de-sac to head back out of and see whether a real deal might be struck. Why make a deal with the Cubs, who just don't have all that much to offer? As Kevin Goldstein noted in January, theirs isn't a great farm system, and even if you're landing three of their eight best pre-season prospects, that's relative. Put it this way—who is the best player that the A's received in the deal? We'll try and answer that in a second, but there's a second question that has to be asked in conjunction with the first: How likely is the best player received in the deal to have a significant role with the club in 2010 (when Harden would have been a free agent signed by somebody else) or 2011 (when Gaudin would have expended his salary arbitration seasons and potentially also left for a team and contract of his choosing)?

Let's start with the guy I'm willing to label the best in the deal, Gallagher. Perhaps he's an undervalued commodity in the same way that Dana Eveland was, because in a uniform he doesn't fulfill any Greek ideals of the human form any better than Eveland does. So, a Sir Mix-a-Lot acquisition strategy might mean you're not competing with nearly as many other people, while still finding just as much joy. That's swell. The problem is that there isn't a whole lot of projectability here—he's a guy who throws strikes and has solid command of low-90s heat and good breaking and off-speed stuff. Good, but not great, those pitches. If you really want to depress yourself, A's fans, sign up for the suggestion that the Cubs are cheating in their home park and look at Gallager's road performance, where opposing hitters have pasted him at a .271/.341/.472 clip. Sure, it's not a lot of work (35 2/3 IP), and sure, that involves bad days in Houston and Bridgeport, parks where fly balls find seats instead of leather that much more easily. Maybe this is an overly elaborate concern, since he'll be pitching in Al Davis' Mausoleum, but it's going to be in the DH league, and it just doesn't seem like he's a lock to be a good one-for-one replacement of Gaudin on the staff, let alone Harden in the rotation. Since nobody mentions Gallagher and projectability in the same sentence, as WYSIWYG propositions go, we're in danger of getting into Gertrude Stein territory, where there's just not much there there.

Sounds great, right? Well, maybe the best player is Matt Murton. Lots of my fellow statheads love Matt Murton. He's a redhead, so that's a good start, but I would think A's fans would be better off taking that visual cue and remembering Bobby Kielty, whom we also got all worked up about and who presented many of the same benefits and hazards. We're not talking about a young player here—Murton is already 26 and has a thousand plate appearances in the majors, so we know quite a bit about what he's good for. Like Kielty was, Murton is pretty dangerous against lefties, having hit .316/.389/.494 against them, and he's pretty patient, having walked in 8.5 percent of his PAs. Like Kielty, he may not be good for a lot of power against right-handed pitchers, having hit only .282/.346/.422 against them; that's better than more than 6.7 billion people on the planet and pretty weak for a major-league left fielder. Unlike Kielty, he can't really play anywhere but left, and not all that well there. Again, at 26, he's ready now and as good as he's going to get. I've left off mentioning how poorly he's hit in Iowa this year (.298/.397/.382), hoping it's a case of the mopes over spending too much time in the cornfields. If it isn't, I guess the River Cats can always use another hitter. Right now, this looks like an upgrade—on Emil Brown, and on whomever you're platooning Jack Cust with. Gee, that's swell.

OK, so maybe Eric Patterson is the best player. He's already 25 and in his second full season at Triple-A (or higher), so he's also a relatively finished product. As an offensive contributor, there aren't any real questions—he has fine plate coverage, good enough patience, solid power, and he contributes a useful dose of speed on the bases. This year, he's hitting .320/.358/.517 in Iowa, which boils down into an unimpressive .269 EqA. Past concerns over how well he'll hit lefties seem to have been addressed a bit, in that he's slugging over .600 against them, but that's in 49 PA, which doesn't mean you can't still be concerned. The real problem with Patterson is the question of his position. Call him a second baseman, and he's one of the best prospects at the position, and that would be swell for the A's, because Mark Ellis is a free agent after the season. The trouble is that he's not really a good second baseman—scouts feel he lacks the reactions and instincts to be an asset at the position, and performance metrics like Clay Davenport's and Dan Fox's Fielding Runs both see him as pretty lousy at the keystone. Hence the Cubs' interest in moving him to the outfield, where he's not one of the best prospects, just a guy who runs well and hits right-handers, and maybe his athleticism makes him into a good center fielder someday, and maybe it doesn't and you've got... another underpowered left fielder. Maybe he platoons with Murton for a year or two, maybe that puts Cust at DH, and maybe that sounds like a formula for a pretty mediocre offense. Fundamentally, the problem with Patterson is that his perceived value is higher than his actual utility. If the A's decide to damn the spreadsheets and the scouts and plow Patterson into the second-base slot, that's sort of admirably brazen in its indifference to defense, certainly the best way to make his offensive contributions valuable (position-relative), and not something the pitching staff will thank management for later.

If there's a player I wouldn't call the best player in the deal, it's the guy Kevin rated as the best prospect before the season, the catcher, Josh Donaldson. Hitting only .217/.276/.349 for Peoria in the Low-A Midwest League, the nicest things you can say are that he's 21, and you can never have too much catching. Did I mention that he's 21? The bad news is that as a product of Auburn and as someone who was expected to be an offense-oriented catcher, he's supposed to be hitting, and he isn't. Maybe that gets turned around at Kane County; maybe a coach or scout has seen something they can fix. Maybe he's just not all that.

On some level, I segregate this deal into two segments, because I'm merely human and I create patterns where none might exist. First, I put Gaudin-for-Gallagher to one side as something of a push, where the benefits are pretty straightforward: Gaudin is getting expensive through arbitration, where Gallagher is five years removed from free agency and three years younger. Consider it an exchange of an established fourth starter for a potential fourth starter, with the attendant cost savings. The problem is that this leaves you with Patterson, Murton, and Donaldson for Harden. Somebody would bite on that? Billy Beane would bite on that? Where's Felix Pie? Where's Rich Hill? Where's... well, something or somebody with real upside? This is it?

Naturally, people are already scrambling to credit Beane with the sort of inside information that led him to dump Jeremy Giambi for John Mabry. No doubt they'll genuflect should Harden hurt himself (again) and assure themselves that Billy must have known—he's all-knowing and wise, donchaknow. It is not Beane's fault that people are ready to home-brew their Kool-Aid so quickly, but no special brand of genius is required to recognize that Harden is a property whose value could go to nil in the next month, the next start, perhaps even the next pitch. But there is also the concern that this team, having already surprised people so very nicely three months into the season, had done all it needed to do where Beane's legend is concerned, and that converting Harden and Gaudin for new commodities comes across as especially cold-blooded.

Again, I doubt he cares, nor should he. Pushing past the atmospherics that must have some people muttering into their coffee this morning, the real problem is with what he got for Harden and Gaudin. In terms of the talent acquired, it looks and feels more like a salary dump than a deal that should be ranked with the winter deals made with the D-Backs or the White Sox that refurbished the farm system. Except even then, Harden's deal wasn't guaranteed for next year, so if he's about to explode, the A's were really only out the rest of this year's salary, plus Gaudin's arbitrations to come. What does that add up to, $10-12 million above baseline expenditures over three years? That's not a whole lot of money, not in baseball. If you can nevertheless accept it on that level, that's probably eminently sensible of you, and better that than getting overly worked up over Murton or Patterson. Gallagher fills out a rotation at a pretty low cost, but the pitching staff on the next A's contender becomes that much more dependent on being all about the Ynoas or the Cahills or winding up wherever a Gio (Gonzalez) quiz takes them.

This year's hot start was nice. It was also gratuitously unnecessary, because the focus remains not on this year, or next, but on the big picture: finding a path to Fremont, and the more distant future. This deal doesn't get them any closer to it because it expended the potential value of two major-league starting pitchers and converted them into a group of cheap players whose value in a few pre-season rankings or in some subsets of fandom have been more than a little exaggerated. If you wanted to call that a setback, you'd be right.

CHICAGO CUBS

Acquired RHPs Rich Harden and Chad Gaudin from the Athletics for RHP Sean Gallagher, 2B/OF-L Eric Patterson, OF-R Matt Murton, and C-R Josh Donaldson. [7/8]

Perhaps like Dallas Green or Jim Frey or Gene Michael, Jim Hendry is never going to be accused of any particular genius, but that's not especially fair or unfair—at the end of the day, he's made his share of sensible baseball moves, a few bad ones (perils of the job), and sometimes he puts together something that just works. This isn't a deal without risks, but at the price that he's paying, there's no reason for him not to take them, and in light of the Brewers' move to add CC Sabathia, making a trade to forestall any Milwaukee move towards second-half glory without hurting the Cubs' bid for a division title now (or next year, or ever) was nothing less than inspired.

Take a look at what this means for the rotation on paper:

Before	SNLVAR	After	SNLVAR
Carlos Zambrano	3.5	Zambrano	3.5
Ryan Dempster	2.9	Harden	3.2
Ted Lilly	2.1	Dempster	2.9
Jason Marquis	1.1	Lilly	2.1
Sean Gallagher	1.0	Marquis	1.1
Sean Marshall	0.7	Marshall	0.7
(Jon Lieber)		Gaudin	0.5

That looks and feels a lot more like a playoff rotation—the workhorse and the fragile ace up top, and the more workmanlike third and fourth starters you pick your spots with, with Lilly avoiding teams that kill lefties, and Dempster perhaps sticking to starting home games. Keep in mind that Gaudin's value is cheapened by this exercise—he finished the 2007 season with a SNLVAR of 3.8, which would have been ranked fourth on last year's Cubs, ahead of Marquis. If you plug Gaudin into the Cubs' rotation as well as Harden, you're talking about adding two good starting pitchers to your front five without giving up anybody who was contributing that significantly this year. However, it sounds like the Cubs will initially reserve Gaudin to plug in once somebody struggles or should anybody get hurt.

I'm struck by the similarity between Marquis and Gaudin, in that both seem to live dangerously with more baserunners aboard than is good for their managers' digestion, but Gaudin is only 25, and brief bits of greatness like the run he enjoyed last year in the first half at least give you cause for hope that he'll outgrow this level. In getting Gaudin to plug into their rotation as their best bet for their fifth starter, whether or not you want to draw up images involving handcuffs and Harden, having the cookin' Cajun as an add-on is nothing short of inspired, perhaps even downright tasty. (Could a guest chef appearance in Andersonville be in the offing for Gaudin? Inquiring minds want to know.)

Now, to turn to the main course as far as what's been added to the menu, there's what Harden has been good for so far this season: eight quality starts in 13 (although only one in his last four), and a month-long trip to the DL with a shoulder problem. Sadly, that's the kind of scorecard you're always going to have to keep where Harden is concerned; as great as a pitcher who is striking out almost 30 percent of the batters he's seen this season can be, we're talking about a guy who's pitched something close to one full season in the majors only once in the last five years. It's easy to kid around over how the team that squandered Mark Prior's career and perhaps a good bit of Kerry Wood's might be less inclined to take another bite of this particular apple and take a chance on a commodity as notoriously fragile as Harden. It's also important to recognize that caution has played a significant part in Harden's workload; in another era, Harden might have blazed as briefly as Mark Fidrych and already be done as an effective starting pitcher. While people both inside the A's organization and out could get frustrated with Harden and perhaps inevitably question whether he was too high-maintenance in more than one sense of the word, he's been brilliant this season.

It's also easy to anticipate that the same Chicago sports market that played to Dusty Baker's worst instincts and routinely castigated Prior for lacking the fortitude to just get out there and pitch when he was trying to pitch through pain and injury didn't learn a thing from the experience, and will jump all over Harden when there's that first missed start, or that perhaps-inevitable trip to the DL. I admit, the prospect makes me a bit squeamish, because when it happpens, it's going to be unfair, it's going to be fed by understandably frustrated people (those always-admirable "anonymous sources") within the organization, and it'll get feral, and fast. However, it appears that the Cubs have reviewed the necessary medical reports, and that they're comfortable that Harden's as good to go as he needs to be.

That's fine, but it also shouldn't be taken as a guarantee that Harden has suddenly been recast in Chobham armor and is ready for anything. Even so, if there's an extra-perishable commodity in a major-league rotation that you should be willing to risk employing, it's Harden, and it isn't as if the Cubs weren't already dealing with a large amount of assumed risk. Remember, we're talking about a rotation that was already counting on Dempster and Marquis, meaning that before this deal it was a real possibility that in a seven-game postseason series, you were looking at three of seven getting started by that pair. Whatever their value over the season's long slog, or Dempster's fine work so far, does that really sound like a good idea to anybody? Which Dempster would the team get, the guy who's given them three quality starts in eight on the road, or eight of ten at home? Would the playoff schedule cooperate? (And is this another brickbat in the burgeoning conspiracy theory that the Cubs are enjoying something extra in their home-field advantage?)

Now, consider the cost to the organization—you get a potential ace starter, albeit one who, like John Tudor in the '80s, you can't be too sure how long you have him for. Happily, Harden comes with a club option for 2009, so if he's healthy enough to want to keep for $7 million next year, that's the opportunity to retain a fragile ace at a level of compensation significantly below market pricing. Gaudin is Cubs property for at least two seasons, although he'll be arbitration-eligible the next two winters, but that's still a matter of adding a quality pitcher for two and a half years, one who would cost more than that on the open market, and one of a caliber that there were no guarantees that Gallagher was going to be able match. As for the talent surrendered, on a practical level it boils down to Gallagher—whom you just replaced with two better starters—two position players you didn't like and probably couldn't use, and a Low-A catcher who wasn't doing anything to convince people he's the next Jeff Goldbach, let alone that he might become a prospect.

If there's an interesting development, it's how this effectively buries Rich Hill. We can argue over whether or not he'd already dug himself a hole he can't get out of, but with his bout of Blassitis down on the farm—two baserunners per inning, and more than a walk per? Yikes—it isn't like he's making a case for his ability to contribute this year.

TRANSACTION OF THE DAY
Teixeira Two-Step
Christina Kahrl

The Rangers got quite a haul from the Braves in return for Mark Teixeira in 2008, but Christina Kahrl noted that they didn't get anything like the same value when they dealt him themselves the following year.

ANAHEIM ANGELS

Acquired 1B-S Mark Teixeira from the Braves for 1B-L Casey Kotchman and RHP Stephen Marek. [7/29]

One of the tropes I tend to hammer on is gunning for a team that's built to win in October, not simply get there. It's always lovely to run up a tri-pennant or say you were a wild-card heartthrob, but at the end of the day, it's actually winning a few post-season series that really makes all the difference in terms of winning hearts and minds, opening check books for subsequent season ticket sales, and getting better ad revenue. Winning is the gift that keeps on giving, good for attendance spikes, better local market media and ad revenue, and permanent satisfaction that you've done more than somebody like the Yankees or Braves lately. Who knows, it might even make you an acceptably Angeleno franchise, instead of a suburban wannabe.

This isn't going to be a paean to current GM Tony Reagins versus former GM Bill Stoneman; neither man is Branch Rickey, but Stoneman already has a ring, Reagins has the ambition and the brains to add a second, and neither man is Bill Bavasi in terms of an unfortunate capacity to be smacked around by the reality stick. In terms of acquiring a premium first baseman to help make the difference between a merely good team and a squad good enough to take its best shot at the cream of the better league and then stomp the senior circuit, this does that.

In practical terms, Tex is the kind of slugger you love to have. Against top fireballers, he'll fight off being overpowered, get in a few rips, and take a base, that last representing something the Angels don't see much of; he simply murders off-speed pitchers. He's a true switch-hitter, in that he's not losing much to opposing pitchers because of their handedness. The Angels make a bit of a fetish of their mastery of situational hitting, and on that score, you would think that Tex should fit in, having already delivered on 16.3 percent of his baserunners; ranking 96th among the 378 hitters with 100 or more PA is more good than bad, and it's definitely not like they brought in someone decisively anathematic, like Jack Cust (298th). Consider the team-level rankings for non-pitchers:

Rank	Team	OBI%
1	Twins	16.5
2	Pirates	15.7
3	Rangers	15.6
4	Orioles	15.3
5	Angels	15.0
6	Phillies	14.9
7	Astros	14.9
8	White Sox	14.9
9	Royals	14.6
10	Brewers	14.6
11	Indians	14.5
12	Tigers	14.5
13	Rockies	14.5
14	Marlins	14.4
15	Mets	14.4
16	D'backs	14.4
17	Cubs	14.4
18	Yankees	14.3
	MLB Average	14.2
19	Dodgers	14.2
20	Giants	14.2
21	Braves	13.9
22	Red Sox	13.7
23	Reds	13.6
24	Rays	13.5
25	Cardinals	13.5
26	A's	13.4
27	Blue Jays	12.9
28	Mariners	12.7
29	Padres	12.3
30	Nationals	12.2

All very interesting, and all very validating for the Angels' way of doing things, but the semi-amusing thing about this is that Kotchman wasn't a problem, at least not through this way of seeing things, because he was plating 18.3 percent of his baserunners, 40th in the majors. It's instructive to put those percentages in the context of the lineups that created those opportunities; the Angels rank 11th in the league in Equivalent Average and 12th in the league in unintentional walks drawn. Playing in that low-OBP offense, Kotchman was getting significantly fewer opportunities than Teixeira was with the Braves, with only 174 PA with runners on base while spending most of the season hitting sixth, behind the heart of the order, while Teixeira had 247 batting fourth in the DH-less league, a slot where the pitcher's hitting (and rarely reaching base) affected his total opportunities.

So talk about Teixeira as an RBI guy in the middle of the order is relatively unimportant, not on an Angels team that's just not going to give him that many baserunners to plate in the first place. Instead, what's really going to matter are the things he can control—the power he'll deliver and the OBP that he'll add from the middle of the order. In terms of what he adds to the lineup, he spares the Angels the indignity of Maicer Izturis batting third, putting some lefty-hitting power between Vlad Guerrero and Torii Hunter in the cleanup slot against right-handed pitching. Maybe that pushes Izturis to the second slot, where his past-but-not-yet-present OBP skills might help maximize the value of the damage Tex can do. If not Izturis, maybe they push Howie Kendrick into the two-hole and go for some short-sequence violence up front.*

In terms of the expense, giving up a bullpen arm and a still not-yet-something first baseman who's going to be arbitration-eligible and is only under control for three years is definitely a price worth paying, and against that you're getting two months with a premium first baseman in a lineup that needed a difference-making hitter of Teixeira's caliber. Beyond that, the Angels will also then get first shot at re-signing said premium first baseman (perhaps an attractive proposition, since the Angels are regular winners) and a pair of Type-A-free-agent-generated compensatory draft picks if said premium first baseman decides that he doesn't like the color of your money, or that California taxes just aren't what he wants to pay. In the abstract, the picks themselves might have been worth it as a matter of repurposing Kotchman and Marek after both have come up short relative to the hopes invested in them as prospects, so from that point of view adding the two months with Tex at first base to take their best shot at winning the whole shebang just makes this that much tastier. Add in that they'll be up a spot on the 40-man over the winter, and it's a move that creates all sorts of little benefits beyond the big obviousness of adding Teixeira's bat.

If there's really something to credit Tony Reagins for, it's some combination of the following factors:

- The recognition that no matter how much Kotchman was an organizational favorite son—literally, since his dad is in his third decade as a scout and manager in the organization—he wasn't blossoming into the kind of premium bat you need at first base;
- Accepting the math that tells you that three years of an adequate first baseman is something you give up to get two months of one of the best at the position to maximize this team's shot at another World Series win, because an adequate Kotchman is something you can replace without any effort (with Kendry Morales, perhaps);

- You didn't have to give up a blue-chip prospect to address your lineup's shortcomings. An arm to flavor the deal in an exchange of first basemen can be written off as the cost of doing business.
- You didn't settle. The Angels are playing to win, not just against their divisional rivals, but with an eye towards playing deep into October. This last might seem obvious, but Terry Ryan never figured it out in Minnesota, and nobody's suggesting that Ryan was a bad GM, just that this is an element of organizational management and opportunity management that not everybody gets.

*: I know, sabermetric orthodoxy insists that lineup order doesn't matter; I guess I keep forgetting to drink all of my Kool-Aid, especially when lineup-related research depends on so many lazy assumptions and/or involves redoing some of the same Markov Chain analysis that's been done for decades, all of which ends up suggesting that... well, that Joe McCarthy or Earl Weaver or Casey Stengel or Bobby Cox are smarter than the models (or the modelers). Consider me a firm believer in the proposition that much of sabermetrics is about the documentation of already-observed phenomenon, and that the best-placed observers did not and do not need sabermetric re-educations, they need to be learned from to create historically-informed sabermetrics.

ATLANTA BRAVES
Acquired 1B-L Casey Kotchman and RHP Stephen Marek from the Angels for 1B-S Mark Teixeira. [7/29]

Yesterday, Joe explored the reason why Frank Wren wasn't going to get anything like the package that John Schuerholz surrendered to bring in Teixeira, which is pretty straightforward: Schuerholz was getting an impact player who could help his team win two division titles as well as an element of certainty as far as the makeup of his lineup over the winter of 2007-08, while Wren is giving up just one shot at Tex's helping you win something, plus the attendant draft picks. Even so, this isn't a package that really helps the Braves all that much, not in any meaningful way beyond controlling costs, and given that they can look forward to three years in arbitration with Kotchman, perhaps not even that.

As a result, since Kotchman's going to be a seven-figure player for the rest of his pre-free-agency career with the Braves after his two-month introduction, the real question is whether he's worth it, or if he isn't the sort of player you go out of your way to avoid this kind of commitment to. The answer isn't really a very happy one for Braves fans. Kotchman is usually evaluated in terms of power potential (mostly unrealized) and fielding acumen. Granting him the fielding, that leaves us with the first baseman's primary responsibility, hitting prowess. Kotchman's career has had its share of hiccups, between too much time spent cooling his heels waiting for the organization's man crush on Darin Erstad to subside in 2005, to a 2006 season wiped out by a bad case of mono, but last year, aged only 24, it finally appeared that he was breaking out, delivering a .294

Equivalent Average, and he also reached that stathead's joyspot by walking at least once every 10 plate appearances. The power was all against right-handers and not really masked by any park effect; he had an ISO of .189 against right-handers and .082 against lefties, so decent work, but not game-breakingly great.

This year, he hasn't improved any in the power department while getting dramatically worse as hitting coach Mickey Hatcher's latest hacktastic hero, as his walk rate has dropped to less than four percent, with no commensurate payoff at the plate. Slick-fielding, moderate-powered first basemen who hit .269/.307/.414 against right-handed pitching don't get compared to John Olerud or Wally Joyner, they get "maybe he'll grow up to be Vic Power or even Pete O'Brien if things start going right for him." If that doesn't sound like a championship ballplayer, you're beginning to get the idea. Obviously, his inconsistency is both his bane and his best defense against criticism; as he moves deeper into his expected peak period through his age-25 through age-29 seasons, if he can lean more towards that 2007 campaign, he's a worthwhile placeholder. If he keeps up the Mickey Vernon-like see-saw between millstone and asset, however, he'll be an exasperating player who will be hard to trade high when his value's up and hard to stomach low if he continues hitting the way he has this year.

The second player in the deal, Marek, has value, but it's not really enough to say this is an exchange that's going to do the franchise that much good. He's a max-effort hurler who has been moved to the pen in his first season in Double-A this year and has consistently good velocity and a usable curve to keep people honest. With 57 strikeouts in 46 2/3 IP, he's punched out slightly more than 28 percent of the hitters he's faced, but he's also walked 21 hitters. He's not overly fly ball-prone, which bodes well for his future in any environment. You can always hope that some Braves scout might think he can work with him to perhaps move him back to the rotation and maximize the value he might have; he did manage to strike out more than seven per nine over 25 starts in Rancho Cucamonga in the high-offense Cal League last year. However, it initially looks like he's slotted to stay in the pen, where maybe he becomes a useful guy, and maybe he knocks around for a while as something less than a premium reliever; the margin between the two is very slim, and so broad that it seems unlikely he'll do all that much to recoup the value expended—both Teixeira and the draft picks that left with him—in the deal.

To give Wren credit, he was in a tough spot, and he also wound up having to make a pretty quick call. The Angels gave him an erratically valuable first baseman who will be under team control for the next three years, and a live-armed minor league reliever. It isn't inconceivable that Wren will look good in a year or two, especially if Kotchman finally finds himself and settles in, but even if he just recaptures the walks, a low-powered first baseman is the kind of player whom you have to compensate for in your lineup, not build around.

MARCH 4, 2008
http://bbp.cx/a/7202

PROSPECTUS TOOLBOX
Is Moneyball Dead?
Derek Jacques

That the A's began to struggle on the field while their front office distanced itself from the philosophy found in Michael Lewis' bestseller didn't mean that Moneyball was dead, as Derek Jacques explained.

The news that Jeremy Brown was hanging up his spikes due to "personal issues" made more of a stir last week than you'd expect from the retirement of a 28-year-old catcher who's spent the last two years in Triple-A. Our prospects expert, Kevin Goldstein, gave Brown an extremely evenhanded send-off over on Unfiltered; others have been less charitable, invoking imaginary choruses of scouts cheering the end of Brown's career. At least, I hope the cheering is imaginary: it'd take a Grinch-sized heart to rejoice in the end of someone's big-league dreams, unless his name is, say, Ben Christensen. The reason that Brown is the focus of such attention and schadenfreude is that the A's drafted him in the first round of the 2002 draft—an overdraft which by itself wouldn't be that noteworthy—and because Michael Lewis wrote a best-selling book that hailed Brown's selection as the bellwether of a new way of doing business, which the author dubbed "Moneyball" in the book of the same name. Apparently, those celebrating Brown's retirement are marking the occasion as the death of Moneyball acumen—a festive wake, with dancing and ironic toasts.

Now, Brown never asked to be the Luke Skywalker of a sabermetric revolution. He was a guy who was already going to face a fair amount of hazing in the minors because his body was not quite one that Calvin Klein would put on a billboard. After *Moneyball* was published, not only was he much more famous than the average 35th overall pick, the negative aspects of his physique were cataloged in the book for ease of heckling. Saddling him with the additional burden of representing the A's organizational philosophy—as interpreted by Lewis—was never particularly fair. However, five years removed from the book's initial release, it is a reasonable time to look back at the 2002 draft and at the A's organization in general, and ask: is Moneyball really dead?

History hasn't been particularly kind to the book. The organization's failure to reach the World Series, and the substantial fall-off suffered after back-to-back 100-win seasons in 2001 and 2002 have certainly diminished Oakland's mystique. Also, some of the players and executives derided in

Moneyball have flourished, while many of the players Lewis touted have faltered. While Billy Beane's Athletics only won one Division Series over a seven-year stretch of contention, one of his purportedly clueless foils in the book, Kenny Williams, got a World Series ring in 2005. While plus-sized A's draftees like Brown were mired in the minors in 2007, Prince Fielder, whom Lewis claimed was "too fat even for the Oakland A's" was hitting 50 homers for the Brewers, and other high-school players whom Lewis scoffed it was a "not-so-bright" decision to draft, like Scott Kazmir, have become established major-league pitchers. These days, it's a little hard to laugh along with Lewis about the absurdity of Steve Phillips selecting Kazmir, seeing that Kazmir led the AL in strikeouts last season.

However, when criticizing the 2002 draft, it's important to remember that what the A's thought of Fielder or Kazmir is largely irrelevant. You can't fault the A's for not taking them—or B.J. Upton, or Zack Greinke, or Jeff Francis, or Jeremy Hermida, or Khalil Greene—because none of those players was available when they made their first selection with the 16th overall pick. Whether the Oakland front office thought those grapes were sour—and it's unclear whether the insulting comments about these guys are Beane's opinions or Lewis'—doesn't matter, because they couldn't reach them. Taking things a step further, I think everyone can agree that the A's first two picks of the draft, Nick Swisher at 16 and Joe Blanton at 24, were good picks who proved to be major-league regulars within three years of being drafted. It's hard, then, to take Oakland to task for not drafting Cole Hamels, James Loney, Jeff Francoeur, or Matt Cain, since those guys would have come at the expense of Swisher or Blanton.

Claiming, as some have, that the A's went four-for-seven on their first-round picks, while the rest of the league was 20-for-32 (this "critique" excludes the last two picks of the round, ending it right after the A's got Mark Teahen) is also a bit ridiculous. First of all, it ignores the fact that high draft picks (particularly the top 10 overall) are much more likely to make it to the majors than the players picked later in the first round. Most of the A's selections were in the bottom third of the round's 41 picks. Second, it puts all prospects who've reached the majors for any amount of time on equal footing—counting Brown's 10 career at-bats, Drew Meyer's 14, and Dan Meyer's and Bryan Bullington's respective 18 1/3 innings as successes. Impose some minimums on the total major-league playing time needed to consider a prospect successful (I've arbitrarily chosen about a half-season's worth of regular playing time, 300 PA or 100 IP) and count all the picks, and the A's went three-for-seven with their first-rounders, while the field was 15-for-34, which is pretty close to even.

That aside, any serious critique of "the Moneyball draft" would have to start with the 26th pick, John McCurdy. Hailed as a Jeff Kent type, McCurdy wasn't what you'd expect in an Oakland draftee—his plate discipline wasn't terribly good, and his on-base percentage was based largely on hit by pitches rather than walks (42 walks and 22 HBP against 460 at-bats in college). He didn't get on base enough in the minors, and his power never developed, either, so he was released before the 2007 season. Right-hander Ben Fritz, selected at 30, was sidelined by injuries, including Tommy John surgery, and has since been taken by the Tigers in the minor-league portion of the Rule 5 draft. Those two were full-price flops, signed for roughly what you'd expect at those slots. The next three selections were signed for a savings. Brown (35th overall) got a bonus of $350,000, about a third of what the players selected with the picks before and after him cost. The next two, pitcher Steve Obenchain (37) and Mark Teahen (39), signed for $750,000 and $725,000 respectively, about $150-200K less than what the other players around them at the bottom of the first round could expect.

Teahen is the only one of the three—indeed, the only player in the last 16 picks of the first round—to get significant major-league playing time. Obenchain hit the ceiling at Double-A; he split last year between the independent Northern and Frontier leagues. As Kevin mentioned in his Unfiltered piece, Brown showed evidence of a decent bat (posting a .263 EqA in Sacramento last year) but not the defensive acumen to start behind the plate or even join the Fraternal Order of Backup Catchers. It's possible that, if not for the personal problems that drove him to quit, Brown might have found a place in The Show, but it likely wasn't going to be as anything more than a spare part.

The evaluation of the 2002 draft doesn't end with the first round, however. The book presented a list of eight college hitters the team was targeting. Aside from Brown and McCurdy, the list included John Baker, Brant Colamarino, Mark Kiger, Shaun Larkin, Steve Stanley, and Brian Stavisky. The team was able to draft seven of the eight players, missing out only on Larkin, who was picked up by the Cleveland Indians. None of these guys has made it to the majors, and since the youngest of them is entering his age-27 season, we can safely say that they're no longer prospects. Colamarino, whom Paul DePodesta claimed in *Moneyball* was "the best hitter in the draft," spent 2007 in the Texas League, posting a .215 EqA. Aside from the first-rounders we've already discussed, only three of the A's other 2002 draftees have made it to the majors. Put together, pitchers Jared Burton, Shane Komine, and Bill Murphy have fewer than 70 career innings, and Burton and Murphy are no longer with Oakland.

Six players reach the majors, three of them become regulars—those aren't the worst results a team has received from a major-league draft. Unlike other professional sports, baseball's draft is a low-yield proposition. However, it is disappointing, mainly because of the breathless way in which Lewis described the draft and the A's preparations for it. It'd be easy to chalk this up to Lewis getting carried away in the moment, but the A's seemed to get just about all of the ballplayers they wanted from the 2002 draft, which made the expectations of a superior haul reasonable.

Since it started to become evident that the 2002 draft wouldn't be the bonanza the book made it out to be, many commentators have pointed to signs that the Athletics have turned away from the "Moneyball philosophy" and become a more orthodox organization again. These critics point to the organization's recent drafting of high-school pitchers—described as a major draft-day no-no in the book—as an indication that *Moneyball* is dead as Dillinger. Adding to that impression is the fact that the team has seemed eager to put some distance between itself and the book. If the A's won't stand up for the philosophy, why should anyone else?

Whether or not one views the Moneyball acumen as being in good or poor health typically depends on what definition of Moneyball one subscribes to. Many people have defined Moneyball based upon specific rules or strategies outlined in the book: "Don't draft high-school pitchers," "College players are better than high-school players," or, "Get fat guys that walk a lot and hit for power." By each of those rules, Moneyball may not be doing so well. The team's home run power has declined since the book's publication. Where the Moneyball A's seemed indifferent to defense, the acquisition of players like Mark Kotsay showed a renewed interest in glove work.

However, this focus on the specifics seems to put Moneyball's tools ahead of its overall methodology. The idea of the book was that the A's were using performance-based valuation techniques to look for bargains in the baseball talent market. Fat guys who walk weren't just a good source of on-base percentage, but a cheap source, as well. High-school pitchers weren't bad so much as being too risky for the price you'd pay them in draft bonuses. And while those were likely the conditions in 2002, if you want to look at baseball as if it was the stock market, you have to keep in mind that markets aren't static. Yesterday's bargain could be bid through the roof tomorrow and no longer be a good buy. This is particularly likely to happen if someone writes a bestselling book popularizing your methods so that others imitate them. In any case, new bargains would replace the old ones—maybe it's defensive wizards with injury problems this time out.

The fact that the Oakland front office doesn't like the "Moneyball" tag doesn't mean that the philosophy's dead, either. While Lewis had incredible access to the A's operation, his book was hardly a team-sanctioned public relations brochure. No sooner did *Moneyball* hit bookstores than the A's front office started to distance itself from it. There was fallout from Beane's trading partners, like Williams, many of whom had been characterized by Lewis as stupid, gullible, and/or ignorant. The book's portrait of Paul DePodesta—who was already a top GM candidate prior to *Moneyball*'s publication—as a man/laptop hybrid did him no favors, as DePodesta went to work for the Dodgers with a *Moneyball*-branded bullseye on his back. You can't blame the Oakland front office for wanting to define itself rather than being defined by Lewis' book, particularly in light of all the bile that was directed at poor Jeremy Brown.

PROSPECTUS TOOLBOX
Cardinals' Special Era Reaches a Crossroads
Bradford Doolittle

As the long, successful pairing of Tony La Russa and Albert Pujols approached its end, Bradford Doolittle ruminated on the pair's significance while waiting for an elusive Pujols to return to his locker in the visiting clubhouse at Wrigley Field.

It's the last day of the season at Wrigley Field, and I'm determined to wait out Albert Pujols. I've been assigned to cover the Cardinals for the weekend series, the last three games at the antique ballpark in the 2010 season. Before each game, I spend about three hours hanging around the Cardinals in the visiting team clubhouse at Wrigley—a dank, cramped space that isn't as big as the locker room at the high school I attended in small-town Iowa. It's an awkward setup, leaving you hovering around 30-35 big-league personnel with no place to stand. On the flip side, there really is no place for them to hide. If you need to interview someone, this is the place to do it. Only the most resolute can avoid the press in there.

Unfortunately, that is a perfect description of Pujols. After five trips to the clubhouse over three days, I've barely caught a glimpse of him. On Saturday, he's sitting at the table in the middle of the room eating breakfast when I walk in, the first media member to invade the team's privacy. He finishes his food and disappears. My entrance is his signal to leave. I don't see him again until the dugout, when he breezes by on his way to the field to stretch. He hasn't been rude. He hasn't refused to talk. He just adeptly avoids putting himself in position where I could ask my annoying questions.

Pregame is one thing, but Pujols proves to be just as scarce after the first two games of the series. The only places to hide in that closet of a dressing room are the showers and the trainer's room, and I assume he hangs out in one or the other, invisible till the coast is clear. I can't really blame him. I don't like strangers asking me questions either. Pujols had some hits in the first two games of the series but wasn't really the story in either contest. The game stories and notebook pieces I put together really didn't call for his comments, and there was no reason to blow my deadline by holding vigil by Pujols' locker. It's disappointing, though. This is the first time I've covered the Cardinals. How could I go three days without speaking to Albert Pujols?

The series finale, a Sunday afternoon game, is Fan Appreciation Day at Wrigley Field. It feels like a last game. The air is crisp. It's autumn. Everyone you encounter is cause for another goodbye. Faces that have become familiar over the months—the guy who checks your credential when you come through the gate, the guy who cracks one-liners as he guards the visiting clubhouse entrance, his more stalwart counterpart on the Cubs side, the cook that puts out the food in the press room, the woman who serves beverages in the press box. You thank them all and wish them a pleasant winter. Before the game, the Cubs run onto the field and throw a few dozen baseballs to their adoring fans.

Upstairs, unbeknownst to us all, Ron Santo is calling his last game. It's the end of an era in Chicago, but this is about an era in St. Louis, one that is both unique and durable, and one that may be ending pretty soon. We'll get back to that.

The Cardinals aren't yet eliminated from the playoff race, but they are on the brink. With eight days to go in the season, they've got to win them all and hope the Reds go into the tank. No one believes it can happen, but you have to proceed as if it might. There is a first time for everything, right? Still, Tony La Russa is asked about the possibility of an expanded playoff field before Saturday's game, which offers a window into his state of mind.

"I haven't time to think about it too much," he says. "I've been too busy trying to get us into October."

He pauses and looks down at his desk.

"It doesn't look like that's going to happen, barring a miracle."

The Cubs have Jeff Samardzija on the mound, which seems appropriate on a day better suited for football. As is his wont, Samardzija is wild early, walking Skip Schumaker to start the game and allowing a hard base hit to Allen Craig. Two on, none out, Pujols up to the plate. It's a recipe for disaster. After taking a ball, Pujols uncoils on a Samardzija fastball. The blast rockets over bleachers in left-center field, clears the outer wall, and bounces out onto Waveland Avenue. It's Pujols' 42nd and, ultimately, last home run of the season. It turns out to be enough to lead the National League for the second straight season. He also winds up leading the league in runs scored and RBI. He finishes .0003 behind Matt Holliday in batting average, the first time in his career he hasn't led the Cardinals in that category. Pujols' WARP1 total of 8.2 is the most of any position player in the league. It's the second-worst total of his career.

The question about whether or not to wait out Pujols is now moot. His three-run shot was the key blow in the game, though the Cubs eventually rallied from an 8-0 deficit to make the late innings interesting. Deadline or not, I'm determined to stand near Pujols' locker until he comes out. I conduct my other interviews first, then take my position. It's getaway day for St. Louis—the bus is waiting outside and a flight awaits at O'Hare. He can't hide from me forever.

###

In his own way, La Russa is almost as elusive as Pujols. Most teams have a set time and place in which the manager speaks before a game. Typically, they speak in the dugout when the players go out to stretch. Jim Leyland likes to get it over with, so you better be ready to talk as soon as the clubhouse opens. Ron Gardenhire likes to talk in his office, so he can watch golf while he takes questions. La Russa just sort of mills around like an old, bow-legged bear. There is no set time to speak to him, and he has a way of always looking like he's in the middle of something. You have to just pick a time that looks good, pop in, and hope for the best. The first day, he never talks, and I practically have to tackle him on the field before batting practice just to get a couple of injury updates.

La Russa has managed the Cardinals longer than any man before him. He has 429 games on Red Schoendienst and nearly 1,000 on Whitey Herzog, and he darn near has tripled up Billy Southworth and Branch Rickey. Only two managers in big-league history have won more games. With Bobby Cox, Joe Torre, and Lou Piniella all calling it quits during and after the 2010 season, La Russa now has 1,645 more wins than Leyland, who is second on the active list. If a manager is fortunate enough to win, say, 53 percent of his games, it'd take him over 19 seasons to win 1,645 games. In many respects, La Russa is the last man standing from a great, or at least durable, generation of skippers.

La Russa was already entrenched in St. Louis when Pujols broke into the big leagues, fully formed it seemed, back in 2001. It's been one of the most productive player-manager partnerships in bigleague history. Here's an unofficial rundown of the most wins by a manager-player combination during the Retrosheet era, which now happily extends back to 1920.

Most Wins By A Player-Manager Combination since 1920

Team	Player	Manager	Wins
Braves	Chipper Jones	Bobby Cox	1317
Tigers	Lou Whitaker	Sparky Anderson	1162
Yankees	Derek Jeter	Joe Torre	1099
Orioles	Mark Belanger	Earl Weaver	1092
Dodgers	Willie Davis	Walter Alston	1089
Tigers	Alan Trammell	Sparky Anderson	1083
Braves	Andruw Jones	Bobby Cox	1034
Yankees	Frankie Crosetti	Joe McCarthy	1020
Dodgers	Jim Gilliam	Walter Alston	1014
Yankees	Yogi Berra	Casey Stengel	1001
Yankees	Bill Dickey	Joe McCarthy	956
Cardinals	Lou Brock	Red Schoendienst	956
Yankees	Bernie Williams	Joe Torre	928
Dodgers	Maury Wills	Walter Alston	904
Athletics / Cardinals	Mark McGwire	Tony LaRussa	901
Yankees	Hank Bauer	Casey Stengel	874
Cardinals	Albert Pujols	Tony LaRussa	871
Reds	Pete Rose	Sparky Anderson	858
Yankees	Babe Ruth	Miller Huggins	858
Yankees	Mickey Mantle	Casey Stengel	856
Athletics	Jimmy Dykes	Connie Mack	853
Yankees	Jorge Posada	Joe Torre	834
Yankees	Gil McDougald	Casey Stengel	823

data courtesy baseball-reference.com

The La Russa-Pujols combination is the only one still going, now that Cox has retired. At 86 wins per season, they could reach the top spot in about five years, but La Russa is 66 years old, and Pujols can become a free agent after next season. They've already won more regular-season games than any other pairing in the Cardinals' storied history except for Lou Brock and Schoendienst, whom they could pass in 2011. They've won more than Herzog and Ozzie Smith (705 wins), Marty Marion and Southworth (520), Joe Medwick and Frankie Frisch (501), and Rickey and Rogers Hornsby (426).

This has been a golden era for one of baseball's flagship teams, but do the fans in St. Louis appreciate it? Pujols' popularity in the Gateway City is unchallenged, but La Russa has lost supporters with each passing season. Fans don't like La Russa's micromanagement of late-inning matchups, his affinity for stopgap veterans, his increasingly cantankerous demeanor. Most of the complaints echo those that fans of every team have about their manager, but 15 years is a long time for a skipper to spend in one city.

Last season, the happy La Russa-Pujols marriage showed some signs of strain. On May 21, Pujols was at the plate in the eighth inning against the Angels with Ryan Ludwick on first and two outs. La Russa called for a steal on the first pitch of Pujols' at-bat, and Ludwick was thrown out at second. According to the *St. Louis Post-Dispatch*, Pujols threw a bit of a tantrum in the dugout after the inning and the two exchanged words, culminating with La Russa saying, "I know how to (expletive) manage." Later in the season, La Russa and Pujols received a lot of negative attention when they attended Glenn Beck's August rally in Washington, D.C.

In September, Pujols said, "I hope he can continue to be my manager for the rest of my career, but that's not my job, and I don't make those decisions. I think this city should be appreciative of the things he has accomplished in his 15 years as manager in this organization. Hopefully, he'll be here next year and for the rest of my career."

It's doubtful that La Russa is going to manage when he's well into his 70s, so Pujols probably won't get his wish. Given La Russa's age, fatigue from the fans, and maybe even Pujols' contract status, you have to wonder if this marriage is going to break up sooner than later. If the Cardinals miss the postseason again in 2011, will next year be the end?

###

Most of the Cardinals are already dressed, and some of them have left the clubhouse. Many of the reporters have already circulated and returned to the press box to punch out their post-game tales. Still, no Pujols. I'm not giving up. A colleague has graciously agreed to type up quotes from the interviews we teamed up on, buying me some time. In return, I offer to pass along some Pujols quotes, if I get some.

While the crowd is thinning, it's still cramped in the little clubhouse. Because it's the last day and a getaway day, clubhouse attendants and equipment managers are starting to cart off equipment, further pinching the space to stand. I move over to a little beverage refrigerator near Pujols' stall and lean on the side of it, growing ever more puzzled at just where the slugger could be hiding. There are only so many places to go. Suddenly I feel a big hand on my arm, as Mark McGwire, the Cardinals' hitting coach, maneuvers me out of the way so he can grab a bottle of water. McGwire nods at me, which I take as an invitation to say, "Can you take a couple of questions about Albert?"

I put extra emphasis on Albert just so he understands I'm not going to ask him questions about something that he'd rather not talk about.

McGwire looks at me with a blank expression on his face. Then he brushes past me, actually bumping me out of the way, brusquely saying over his shoulder, "He's the best."

I'm a little stunned. More than a little, in fact. For a millisecond, I even think to myself, "Dude, I'm going to have a Hall of Fame vote in a few years."

But McGwire is only kidding. He turns and comes back and says, "I'm just messing with you."

You might have noticed from the chart above that the La Russa-Pujols pairing isn't even the most prolific of La Russa's career, though that will change before next season's All-Star break. McGwire played in 901 winning games with La Russa as his manager, the majority of those coming in Oakland. His last year with the Cardinals' was Pujols' first. I ask him if Pujols is the most consistent player he's ever seen. (Bob Costas I am not.)

"I saw him in his first year, and I've seen him in his 10th year, and I watched him from afar in the years in between," said McGwire. "He was just born with it. His swing hasn't changed since I saw him on day one. He's got the best plate coverage in the game."

McGwire is returning to the Cardinals in the same capacity next year. Since St. Louis struggled offensively at times, some fans aren't too happy about that. Pujols told reporters, "I believe that McGwire does not get the credit he deserves as the great batting coach that he is." It's a nice vote of confidence for McGwire, but Pujols is probably the pupil with which he had to expend the least amount of time.

"He just keeps pounding every day," said McGwire. "Every day he comes to the ballpark, wanting to get hits, wanting to win the ballgame. He never gives in to anything."

The Cardinals were eliminated the day after they left Chicago. A few weeks later, Pujols was beaten out by Cincinnati's Joey Votto in the voting for the National League's MVP award. There are arguments for either player, but no matter how you slice it, the gap between them wasn't that big. However, there is one indisputable fact: the Reds made the postseason, and the Cardinals didn't. As much as anything, that likely turned the vote in Votto's favor. For Pujols, it probably wasn't a big deal. He's won MVP awards before, and he'll probably win them again. But while the Reds were playing in the playoffs, the Cardinals' attention turned to an important offseason.

First up was La Russa, who mulled over retirement before deciding to return for a 16th season in St. Louis and his 33rd as a big-league manager. Only Connie Mack has managed more. This is astounding. When La Russa managed his first game for the White Sox on Aug. 3, 1979, Danny Ainge was the opposing starting second baseman. The top song in the country was "Bad Girls" by Donna Summer. There are a lot of ways to try to put it in perspective, but you get the idea. (Neither Larry Bird nor Magic Johnson had debuted in the NBA. Roger Staubach was the quarterback of the Dallas Cowboys. OK, I'll stop.) He's been around for a long time.

With La Russa remaining in place, Cardinals general manager John Mozeliak then went about setting up next season's roster knowing that any major forays were unlikely, largely because of Pujols' uncertain future. It's a work in progress for Mozeliak, who surprised many by signing aging slugger Lance Berkman to a one-year, $8 million deal over the weekend. After the Winter Meetings, Mozeliak will turn his attention to Pujols.

"Timing is important," Mozeliak told reporters at last month's general managers meeting. "We don't want it to drag out this winter. I wouldn't say it's at a critical juncture right now, but I'd like to think between now and the Christmas holiday we'd start addressing it."

For his part, Pujols has said all along that he wants to be a Cardinal for life, and it's really difficult to imagine him playing with another team. Those covering the team seem to feel that if a deal isn't reached over the next three months, then Pujols is likely headed for free agency. What sort of deal will Pujols demand? One would think he'd be looking for the game's biggest contract, and he deserves it. His MORP projections for the next few years suggest he could justify upward of $40 million per season. He won't be asking for that, but the Cardinals won't like the numbers if Pujols hits the open market. It's a crucial three months in Cardinals history.

There are similarities to the Derek Jeter situation that was just resolved in New York, but the differences are key. Pujols is younger, first of all, and shows no indication of skill erosion. However, there is another thing that sets Pujols apart: certainty.

Albert Pujols owns the Mona Lisa of career statistical records. The numbers he put up at 30 aren't significantly different than the ones he put up at 21. And every season in between has been more of the same. Every single one. The only real change in Pujols' game since his early years in the majors is that the opposition pitches to him less often, seemingly more so with each passing season. Yet he still manages to produce more runs and wins than any other player in baseball.

Part of the package that Jeter offered the Yankees was the allure of having him reach and surpass 3,000 hits in a few years. Imagine the milestones that Pujols could reach as a Cardinal a decade from now. Going by Pujols' 10-year PECOTA projections, he'll reach 3,000 hits in 2018. He'll get to 600 homers in 2017. But that's given a realistic projection for a decline in availability. Players get old, hurt, and are rested more often. Those projections suggest that Pujols will play in 65 percent of possible games over the next decade.

If you raise that level to even 75 percent, the numbers become even more Ruthian. Or Cobbesque.

Or a combination of the two, which is probably more like Hank Aaron. At 75 percent, Pujols would be looking at more than 3,300 hits a decade from now, and over 700 homers. He'd be closing in on Aaron's career RBI mark. At 90 percent (or 146 games per season), if Pujols' rate stats meet projected marks, he'll be considered the consensus best player of all-time 10 years from now.

That's whom the Cardinals will be negotiating with, and how they determine the value of Pujols' singular career path will determine how a significant chapter in baseball's long history is going to be written. One person who seems to recognize this is McGwire, a person with a couple of historical footnotes in his own ledger.

"If you (have his work ethic) and you have the talent that he has, the determination to be the best, god knows what's going to happen for him in the next 10 years," McGwire told me. "I've said many times, I hope people understand what's happening before their eyes as far as what this guy has been. I don't know if the people are taking for granted how good he is, but they're not really accepting that, 'Wow, he's the best ever, in the history of the game.' He's just unbelievable."

###

When I left Wrigley Field that day, it was with a notable feeling of melancholy. The ivy was already turning brown in spots. The sun was going down and was shining through the west side of the ballpark. Stadium workers were sweeping the trash from the aisles so that the power washers could be deployed. Fork trucks were buzzing around, carting off the leftover hot dog buns. The 'L' was flying on the flagpole in center field for the final time till the spring.

I was mostly thinking about La Russa as I exited the ballpark. I wondered what it must have been like to cover John McGraw in his latter days, a man who traversed eras. I thought about Pujols and how long the two have been together, wondering if it was historically unique (resulting in the research reflected in my initial table). At any given time, there are only a handful of players or managers who achieve icon status, and to have them paired together for more than a decade is special.

I don't know whether Pujols is going to sign a $200 million extension or whether La Russa will manage beyond next season. It could be their last season together. They could be together for another half-decade. Hopefully, baseball fans—not just the ones in St. Louis—appreciate that which may be drawing to a close.

Pujols finally did return to his locker that last day at Wrigley. He was dressed and fully groomed—the clothes in his stall must have been a decoy. When I stepped forward to speak to him, he turned and the straggling reporters moved in for the kill. I had about two minutes, and there were about 100 questions I wanted to ask, but decorum insists that you stick to the matters at hand.

Pujols' homer was his 47th career long ball against the Cubs, more than he's hit against any other opponent. I wondered if he had a particular affinity for hitting at Wrigley Field.

"Just another park, man," Pujols said. "It's part of the game. It doesn't matter which park you're in, you still have to go out there and execute. This is not the only park in the league that I've had success in."

Another reporter wondered why the Cubs were pitching him away. Pujols said that they weren't. "They were aggressive," he said. "I was aggressive too."

Maybe it's all that simple to him. Work hard. Be aggressive. Maybe it's that simple for all the great ones, leaving the rest of us to marvel over the results.

Bonus Baseball
CAUGHT IN THE CAMERA EYE
The Story of Max Bishop
by Geoff Young

Our patience will achieve more than our force.
—Edmund Burke

Those of us born without an abundance of athletic ability may not be able to imagine what it is like to hit a baseball 500 feet or sprint from home plate to first base in 3.7 seconds. We may struggle to understand how Michael Jordan worked his magic on a basketball court or how Walter Payton did the same on a gridiron. Their actions were marvelous enough without considering that they did what they did against the best in the world.

We can appreciate a Jordan, a Payton, a Wayne Gretzky, a Roger Federer. But few of us can relate in any meaningful way to their accomplishments. We might as well try to imagine what it would be like for J.S. Bach to compose the Brandenburg Concertos or for Neil Armstrong to set foot on the moon. These are superhuman feats and, in Armstrong's case, literally otherworldly.

On the other hand, we can relate to a guy standing at home plate and taking pitches. As it happens, this is a skill—assuming the player takes the right pitches, i.e., ones that do not cross into the strike zone—that has significant value in baseball.

There is a certain erudition that accompanies stellar plate discipline. It requires a discerning eye—the ability to immediately and accurately assess the location of a hurled baseball—and patience. Even those of us with limited skills grew up learning to swing at pitches in the knowledge that if we did not swing, we had no chance of making contact. (Some of us had no chance of making contact anyway, but that is beyond the scope of our current discussion.)

As one who couldn't hit the ball far or run fast, I did understand the ability to take pitches. Even if I wasn't particularly adept at choosing which pitches to take, I could relate to watching a guy stand at home plate and seemingly not do anything. Of course, he is making a decision not to do anything, but that is a subtlety I didn't come to appreciate until later, when I started reading Bill James and realized the value of the base on balls.

Venturing deep into the annals of baseball history, we find a man from Waynesboro, Pennsylvania, who excelled at drawing walks as few others have. His name was Max Bishop, and he played second base in the 1920s and 1930s, mostly for the Philadelphia A's. The left-handed hitting Bishop stood at 5'8" and weighed 165 pounds, and his ability to discern balls from strikes was sufficiently advanced that he became known as "Camera Eye."

Just how good was Bishop's plate discipline? In the history of Major League Baseball dating back to 1871, 915 players have accumulated 5,000 or more plate appearances. Of those, three have drawn walks in at least 20 percent of their trips to the plate:

- Ted Williams (20.6%)—Last man to hit .400 or better in a season, 521 career home runs; fourth in career walks
- Barry Bonds (20.3%)—Single-season (73) and career (762) home run leader; first in career walks
- Max Bishop (20.0%)—Uh, well he once (1929) led the American League in walks (65th in career walks, if you must know)

Williams is in the Hall of Fame, and Bonds, politics permitting, will be one day as well. Bishop is just a guy most folks don't know ever played the game, which is a shame.

* * *

Bishop began his professional career starring for the International League's Baltimore Orioles. He joined the Orioles out of high school at age 18 and played for them from 1918 to 1923, winning four straight IL championships from 1919 to 1922 (these were dominant teams with records of 100-49, 110-43, 119-47, and 115-52). His best seasons came in 1921, when he hit .319 with 14 homers, and in 1923, when he hit .333 with 22 homers.

The latter almost didn't happen. According to an item in the February 13, 1923, *New York Times*, Baltimore owner/manager Jack Dunn had made a "promise to sell at least three of his star Orioles before the beginning of the [1923] season" because his teams were too good for the league. Although Bishop was reportedly close to being sold to the Boston Red Sox in 1923, he remained with the Orioles, leading them to a 111-53 record.

Bishop finally reached the big leagues in 1924 as a member of Connie Mack's A's. After sharing second base duties with Jimmy Dykes that year and the next, Bishop took over full time in 1926. From then until 1933, he drew 100 or more walks every year. During that time, he walked more than every other player in baseball except for one: Babe Ruth. The top 10 contains some impressive names:

Most walks, 1926 – 1933

Rnk	Player	BB	PA	BB%
1	Babe Ruth	998	5117	.195
2	Max Bishop	905	4452	.203
3	Lou Gehrig	849	5618	.151
4	Lu Blue	664	4075	.163
5	Mickey Cochrane	568	4382	.130
6	Hack Wilson	566	4671	.121
7	Jimmie Foxx	556	3929	.142
8	Willie Kamm	546	4568	.120
9	Paul Waner	538	5429	.099
10	Mel Ott	537	3974	.135

All but Bishop, Blue, and Kamm are in the Hall of Fame. None—not even the Babe himself, who was pitched to a tad more carefully—walked in a greater percentage of plate appearances than did Bishop.

With a career slash line of .271/.423/.366, Bishop owns the 15th-highest on-base percentage in MLB history (minimum 3,000 plate appearances)—ahead of Mickey Mantle, Frank Thomas, Edgar Martinez, Stan Musial, Wade Boggs, and the overwhelming majority of men who have played the game.

Bishop is one of eight men since at least 1919 (as far back as readily available records go) to have two games in which he drew five or more walks. Only Bonds (three) and Mel Ott (four) have more. Bishop also drew four or more walks 15 times. Only four men did that more often, and all played a great deal more than Bishop:

Four or more walks in a game

Player	G	PA	4+ BB	Per 1,000 G
Barry Bonds	2986	12606	25	8.4
Ted Williams	2292	9791	18	7.9
Babe Ruth	2503	10617	17	6.8
Eddie Yost	2109	9175	16	7.6
Max Bishop	1338	5789	15	11.2

Bishop's best season came in 1928, with the A's, when he hit .316/.438/.432. He tore a nail off a finger on his left hand during spring training, but it didn't affect his regular-season performance. The March 10 *New York Times* account of Bishop's injury identifies him as a shortstop, a position he never played in the minors and played just twice (but not until 1935) at the big-league level.

Bishop caught fire in the season's second half, hitting .349/.474/.467. He hit .400/.519/.543 in August, which featured one of his best-ever individual performances. On August 25, in the second game of a doubleheader at home against the Chicago White Sox, Bishop went 4-for-5 with two doubles and a triple, leading his A's to a 13-4 romp over the visitors.

However, Bishop wasn't done yet. His most memorable game of 1928 came at Yankee Stadium on September 12, while Bishop's A's were chasing Ruth's Yankees in pursuit of the AL pennant. The headline in the following morning's *New York Times* read, "Bishop's Home Run in 9th Beats Yanks":

> With the score tied and two out in the final inning of the final game of the series, Max Bishop knocked the ball into the right-field bleachers to turn the tide toward Philadelphia, 4-3... It came without a warning. [Waite] Hoyt had retired [Joe] Boley and [Ossie] Orwoll with ease and grace. He had two strikes on Bishop, and then suddenly the ball sped off the swinging bat and flew into the right-field bleachers. Ruth didn't even turn. He knew where it was going.

The A's left New York down 1 ½ games and finished the season in second place, 2 ½ back of the Yankees, who went on to sweep the Cardinals in the World Series.

Bishop's A's would take home the championship in each of the following two seasons. He didn't distinguish himself in those series (or in 1931, when Philadelphia lost to the Cardinals), hitting .182/.316/.182 in 18 career post-season games. However, he had his moments.

In Game 5 of the 1929 World Series, Bishop singled—the AP's Alan J. Gould called it "a zipping drive" along the left field line—with one out in the bottom of the ninth and his team trailing, 2-0. George Haas followed with "a smashing home run over the right field wall" to tie the game, with Bing Miller doubling home Al Simmons four batters later to win the contest.

Bishop also played a key role in the decisive sixth game of the 1930 World Series. And as John Kieran observed in the October 9 *New York Times*, Bishop did so in his own unique way:

> Max Bishop was up five times and didn't get a hit. But he got two bases on balls, was hit by the pitcher and scored two runs. This chap doesn't need a bat at all. He gets on in a variety of ways. The Cardinals think he does it by political influence.

In Game 1 of that series, with president Herbert Hoover among those in attendance at Shibe Park, Bishop went 0-for-3 but scored the eventual winning run when Jimmy Dykes doubled him home in the sixth after Bishop had walked against Cardinals starter Burleigh Grimes. Bishop also drew praise for his defense, with Associated Press reports singling out his leaping catch of a drive off the bat of Frankie Frisch that ended a seventh-inning threat, leaving two St. Louis runners stranded.

(Throughout his career, Bishop was regarded as a fine glove man, leading American League second basemen in fielding percentage—a flawed metric, to be sure, but the one by which players of his era were judged—in 1926, 1928, and 1932.)

The following year, Bishop's A's fell just short, losing in seven games. On October 10, 1931, representing the go-ahead run, Bishop made the final out of the series, flying out to Cardinals center fielder Pepper Martin.

In 1933, Bishop enjoyed the last of his great seasons. He hit .294/.446/.399 that year, including .357/.487/.473 in the second half. Among other accomplishments, Bishop drew at least one walk in 15 straight games, one of the longest such streaks in history. Since 1919, only seven men have had longer single-season consecutive walk streaks:

Walks in 15 or more straight games since 1919

Rnk	Player	G	Dates
1	Roy Cullenbine	22	Jul 2 – Jul 22, 1947
2	Ted Williams	19	Aug 24 – Sep 14, 1941
3	Barry Bonds	18*	Sep 9 – Sep 28, 2002
4	Babe Ruth	17	Jun 1 – Jun 18, 1921
4	Barry Bonds	17	May 4 – May 25, 2007
6	Toby Harrah	16	Apr 20 – May 11, 1985
6	Chipper Jones	16	Aug 19 – Sep 5, 1999
6	Nick Johnson	16	Apr 16 – May 3, 2003
9	Max Bishop	15	Apr 13 – Apr 30, 1933
9	Mel Ott	15	Jun 7 – Jun 22, 1944
9	Milt Byrnes	15	Aug 4 – Aug 15, 1945
9	Ted Williams	15	May 3 – May 19, 1946
9	Darrell Evans	15	Apr 9 – Apr 27, 1976
9	Willie Randolph	15*	Sep 18 – Oct 4, 1980
9	Lenny Dykstra	15	May 12 – May 28, 1994
9	Barry Bonds	15	Jun 20 – Jul 7, 2004

If we include streaks that continue across multiple seasons, Bonds' extends to 19 (with an end date of Apr 1, 2003) and Randolph's to 17 (with an end date of Apr 11, 1981).

After the 1933 season, "financial pressure [from] Philadelphia bankers" forced Connie Mack to sell off his best players (he sold Mickey Cochrane to Detroit and George Earnshaw to the White Sox). Bishop was traded with Lefty Grove and Rube Walberg to the Red Sox for Bob Kline, Rabbit Warstler, and $125,000.

According to Harry Grayson in the March 15, 1935, edition of the *Pittsburgh Press*, Bishop "reports himself cured" from a stomach ailment that limited the aging second baseman to 97 games in 1934. And although Bishop started strong in 1935–his ninth-inning homer in the second game of a doubleheader on April 17 beat the Yankees in their house–he could not sustain that level of play. Bishop hit .196/.338/.196 in May and lost his starting job to light-hitting Ossie "Ski" Melillo after going 0-for-3 against the St. Louis Browns on the 27th of that month.

Opportunities came few and far between for Bishop from that point forward. He started two games in June and two more in July, making his final big-league start on August 1 at Washington. Bishop went 2-for-4 with a walk in that game, but he was done. From May 30 to season's end, Bishop received a total of 40 plate appearances (typically, walking in 10 of them) and in October, the Red Sox released the man they had failed to acquire 12 years earlier.

Bishop then returned to his hometown Orioles, where he served as player-manager before retiring. From there, Bishop went on to become head baseball coach for the U.S. Naval Academy; he remained in that role from 1938 until his death in 1962. He led the Midshipmen to a 306-143 record, and their home ballpark in Annapolis is called Max Bishop Stadium in his honor.

Bishop died on February 24, 1962, in Waynesboro. In a particularly cruel twist of fate, he died mere days before he was set to retire, having returned to his place of birth to attend his mother's funeral.

###

Bill Nowlin, in his excellent SABR biography of Bishop, includes a quote from Lefty Gomez that sums up Bishop as a player. After walking Bishop four times on Opening Day 1932, Gomez said:

> This Bishop just stands there and takes 'em and the umpires call 'em balls. He doesn't look or act any tougher to pitch to than anybody else.

The New Bill James Historical Baseball Abstract ranks Bishop as the 43rd-best second baseman in history, nestled between Robby Thompson and Steve Sax. That same tome also recalls a common attitude of the era toward walks, which may help explain why Bishop's exploits aren't better remembered today. In his discussion of another high-OBP player of the era, Roy Cullenbine, James offers a quote (taken from William B. Mead's *Baseball Goes to War*) from former St. Louis Browns executive Bill DeWitt:

> Cullenbine wouldn't swing the bat... Sewell would give him the hit sign and he'd take it, trying to get the base on balls. Laziest human being you ever saw.

It is tempting to view Bishop's walks the way DeWitt would have. Bishop watched a lot of pitches go by without swinging at them. We think to ourselves, in a way that we wouldn't dare think of duplicating Albert Pujols' ability to swat baseballs with great force, that we could do what Bishop did.

We cannot, of course, and to pretend otherwise is to give short shrift to the man's achievements on the field. Bishop excelled at reaching base in ways that almost nobody in the history of the game has before or since. And if his skill set makes those achievements easier for us to relate to in some way, great. It isn't easy to exercise patience in baseball or in life. Those that succeed in so doing often aren't as revered as those who would dazzle us with their demonstrations of strength, speed, and action. This in no way diminishes their accomplishments.

Bishop didn't do the sorts of things that one witnesses and then passes down to future generations. People will marvel at Mark McGwire taking Randy Johnson deep in the Kingdome, or Bo Jackson hitting three routine ground balls to the left side and turning them all into singles, or Nolan Ryan blowing hitters away with his fastball. They will share these stories with their children and grandchildren.

But very few among us would have our imaginations captured by Bishop waiting out the opposing pitcher to work the walk. Telling those who follow us about such exploits, rooted in seeming inaction (there is plenty of action involved in exercising sound judgment and making good decisions, but this is a difficult narrative to sell in our world), may not be the highest priority.

Regardless of our possible delusions about the ease of drawing walks, Bishop did something special that is worth celebrating. Maybe the next time you are discussing great baseball players with your friends or family, you can find it in your heart to put in a good word for Max Bishop, man of great patience and great judgment.

Biographies

Tommy Bennett is a law student in New York. He has written various columns for Baseball Prospectus and was formerly editor of Beyond the Box Score. He believes the best way to judge a baseball city is by the number of people who keep score at the games. His interests include statutes, administrative law, and Mickey Morandini's unassisted triple play.

Will Carroll wrote for Baseball Prospectus for several years and left in 2010.

James Click is currently the Director of Baseball Research and Development for the Tampa Bay Rays.

Bradford Doolittle is freelance sports journalist who writes for Basketball Prospectus, Baseball Prospectus, MLB.com, and the Associated Press, and has written for Slate, ESPN, *Sports Illustrated*, *The Kansas City Star*, Deadspin, *The Hardball Times*, and numerous other outlets. He is a member of the Pro Basketball Writers Association, SABR, and the Baseball Writers' Association of America. Bradford is based in the Uptown/ Edgewater area of Chicago, where he lives with his wife, Amy. You can follow him on Twitter under the handle of @bbdoolittle.

Jeff Euston writes the "Contractual Matters" column at Baseball Prospectus and maintains BP's Compensation Pages, an extensive online database of contracts and salaries dating back to 2000. In 2005, he founded Cot's Baseball Contracts, a web site tracking players, agents, salaries, and payrolls for each of the 30 major-league clubs. He lives near Kansas City, where he practices commercial real estate law and fixes his own speeding tickets.

Mike Fast has been a Kansas City Royals fan since 1986 and was introduced to his love of baseball analysis by Bill James through the *Baseball Abstract* series. He is recognized as a leader in pitching analysis using PITCHf/x data. Mike lives in Austin, Texas, with his wife Lori and their four children.

Dan Fox serves as the Director of Baseball Systems Development for the Pittsburgh Pirates, a role he has enjoyed since the spring of 2008. Prior to joining the Pirates, he worked as a software architect, consultant, trainer, developer, and conference speaker in several organizations, including Compassion International in Colorado Springs. Dan caught the writing bug after starting the blog *Dan Agonistes* where he wrote about whatever came to mind, which turned out to be primarily baseball. From there he wrote for *The Hardball Times* and went on to pen 100 weekly columns for *Baseball Prospectus* under the moniker "Schrodinger's Bat." He lives with his very patient and supportive wife Beth and daughters Laura and Anna in Marshall Township, PA.

Steven Goldman is the Editor-in-Chief of Baseball Prospectus. In addition to writing numerous columns for BaseballProspectus.com, he has edited the BP-authored books *Mind Game*, *It Ain't Over 'Til It's Over*, and *Extra Innings: More Baseball Between the Numbers* and contributed to *Baseball Between the Numbers*. Steven is also the author of the biography *Forging Genius: The Making of Casey Stengel*. He has contributed to the BP annual since 2005 and was editor or co-editor of the 2006 through 2011 editions. He is the creator of the longrunning Pinstripedbible.com for the YES Network, cited by *Sports Illustrated* as "an essential online baseball destination," and has appeared on several of the network's television programs. He was a baseball columnist for the *New York Sun* from 2004 to 2008, and his work has appeared in *Yankees Magazine*, *The Village Voice*, *Commentary*, *American Heritage*, and other publications. Steven lives in New Jersey with his wife and two children.

After leaving Baseball Prospectus in 2006, **Thomas Gorman** worked for MLB's outside counsel on the Mitchell Investigation into performance-enhancing drug use in baseball. He then returned to school, getting his J.D. with high honors in 2010 from the University of Chicago Law School. From 2010-11, Tom clerked for Judge Richard A. Posner on the Federal Court of Appeals for the Seventh Circuit. He is now a practicing litigator in San Francisco. Many partners at Tom's firm have season tickets at AT&T Park, and he hopes they bring him to lots of games in the Spring.

Gary Huckabay is the Founder of Baseball Prospectus. He has served in a consulting capacity for several MLB clubs and player representation firms. His areas of focus are performance forecasting and valuation. Mr. Huckabay currently works in small business lending for a large financial services firm and serves on the Board of Directors of the Epilepsy Foundation of Northern California. He lives in the NorCal East Bay with his wife Kathryn and son Charlie. Gary is a frequent speaker at universities, charitable fundraisers, and corporate events.

Derek Jacques resides in New York City, where he works with his wife, Paula, running an editorial services firm, Kepos Media, and raising their twin sons, Gabriel and Leo. He writes about baseball on Twitter as @derekbaseball.

Jay Jaffe is the founder of the 11-year-old Futility Infielder website (www.futilityinfielder.com), one of the oldest baseball blogs. He's been a part of Baseball Prospectus since 2004, writing the "Prospectus Hit and Run" column, covering the annual Hall of Fame ballot, and contributing to seven BP annuals as well as *It Ain't Over 'Til it's Over* and *Mind Game*. Elsewhere, he has written regularly for Fantasy Baseball Index and the YES Network's Pinstriped Bible. He once came in third in the famous Milwaukee Brewers sausage race, and in December 2010, he became a member of the Baseball Writers' Association of America.

Rany Jazayerli was a first-year medical student when he co-founded Baseball Prospectus in 1996.

He's now a dermatologist in private practice in the western suburbs of Chicago, where he lives with his wife and three daughters. He writes regularly about the Kansas City Royals at ranyontheroyals.com and hosts a weekly radio show on the Royals in Kansas City. He also writes regular baseball columns for Grantland.com. He still contributes to Baseball Prospectus when time allows. As you can guess from the rest of this paragraph, that isn't very often.

Christina Kahrl is one of the five founders of Baseball Prospectus. Like many of her colleagues, that led to an unexpected career in sports, sparing her from a life spent studying 19th-century Europe and trying to come up with witty jokes about *junkers*. She has participated as a contributor to or editor of every edition of the annual, as well as *Mind Game* and *It Ain't Over 'Til it's Over*. She has contributed columns to *Playboy*, Salon, Slate, the *New York Sun*, SportsIllustrated.com, and ESPN.com and is also an associate editor of *The ESPN Pro Football Encyclopedia*. She's now a member of the BBWAA and an editor at ESPN.com and lives in Chicago with her partner, dog, cat, fish, and an everlasting sense of curiosity.

David Laurila grew up in Michigan's Upper Peninsula and now writes about baseball from his home in Cambridge, Massachusetts. Formerly with Baseball Prospectus, he now authors the Q&A series at FanGraphs.com and is a regular contributor to several other publications, including *Red Sox Magazine* and *New England Baseball Journal*. A co-chair of SABR-Boston, he is the author of the book "Interviews From Red Sox Naton" and has similar projects in the works.

Ben Lindbergh is an author and editor of BaseballProspectus.com. He has contributed to three BP annuals, ESPN Insider, and *Yankees Magazine*, and he served as assistant editor of *BP2011* and editor of the two-volume *Best of Baseball Prospectus* collection. He daylights as a baseball analyst for Bloomberg Sports, has interned for multiple MLB teams, and was inducted into the Baseball Writers' Association of America in December. A recent graduate of Georgetown University, Ben makes his home on the western shore of his native Manhattan, where he fancies himself the first line of defense against New Jersey.

Marc Normandin wrote the "Fantasy Beat" and "Player Profile" columns at Baseball Prospectus and spent over five years and many hundreds of thousands of words with the website. Presently, Marc writes about the Red Sox at OvertheMonster.com, fantasy baseball at RotoHardball.com, and likes to juggle serious baseball news and photoshops at Baseball Nation (mlb.sbnation.com). He is formerly the video game editor of BlastMagazine.com, as well as the founder of SB Nation's BeyondtheBoxScore.com. When not tearing through foes with a chainsaw bayonet or beam katana in his living room, you can find him talking about baseball, both the real and the fantasy varieties, with friends, family, and whoever chooses to read his work.

Dayn Perry is a regular contributor to FanGraphs, FOXSports.com, and ESPN Insider. He's the author of two books, *Winners: How Good Teams Become Great Ones* and *Reggie Jackson: The Life and Thunderous Career of Baseball's Mr. October*. He lives in Chicago with his wife, son, and dog.

Eric Seidman is an accountant and statistical analyst from Philadelphia. He currently writes for Fangraphs and runs the popular Phillies site Brotherly Glove. Eric previously wrote the "Checking the Numbers" column for Baseball Prospectus.

Joe Sheehan was a founding member of Baseball Prospectus in 1996. He now writes for *Sports Illustrated* and contributes regularly to the MLB Network.

Ryan Wilkins lives in San Francisco with his wife, Sandy, and their imaginary dog, Avon Barksdale. Ryan works as a Baseball Research Analyst for one of the industry's leading sports agencies. He loves (in no particular order): Blue Bottle coffee, sitting in the front row at the Castro Theatre, '70s-era Brian Eno, and his sister-in-law, Paula.

Michael Wolverton wrote and crunched numbers for Baseball Prospectus from 1996 to 2004. He has degrees from two college baseball powerhouses, Rice and Stanford (although admittedly Wayne Graham and Mark Marquess have a little more to do with the success of those programs than he does). He lives in the San Francisco Bay Area with his wife, Cindy, and sons Scott and Mark.

Keith Woolner joined the Cleveland Indians in 2007 and currently holds the position of Director of Baseball Analytics. He is the inventor of VORP, a well-known sabermetric statistic, and has published seminal research on many topics, including catcher defense, replacement level theory, pitcher workload management, bullpen strategies, and win expectation. He was a longtime analyst for Baseball Prospectus, contributing to several editions of the BP annual, as well as *Baseball Between the Numbers* and *Mind Game*. His Column "Aim for the Head" ran for many years on the BP website, where he answered statistical questions from readers. He also worked behind the scenes at BP developing much of the technical infrastructure and statistical databases that powered the website. He holds dual Bachelor's degrees from MIT in Mathematics with Computer Science and in Management Science and has a Master's degree from Stanford University in Decision Analysis.

Colin Wyers is the Director of Statistical Operations for Baseball Prospectus, which means he does a fair amount of math and logical thinking. He writes the "Manufactured Runs" column, which also entails a fair amount of math and logical thinking. When doing neither of these things, he can frequently be found rooting for the Cubs, which requires him to ignore most of the math and logical thinking from the previous two items.

Geoff Young is the founder of Ducksnorts, which covered the Padres from 1997 to 2011. He also wrote and published three books under that title. His work has appeared in many places on the web, including *The Hardball Times* (2006-2011) and ESPN.com. Geoff has been a regular contributor to Baseball Prospectus since 2009 and lives in San Diego with his patient wife, Sandra.

Made in the USA
Lexington, KY
14 February 2012